AQA A LEVEL
SOCIOLOGY
BOOK TWO

Rob Webb
Hal Westergaard
Keith Trobe
Annie Townend

NAPIER PRESS **Sociology**

Published by Napier Press Limited
Email: enquiries@napierpress.com
Website: www.napierpress.com

ISBN-10: 0954007921
ISBN-13: 978-0954007928

British Library Cataloguing in Publication Data
A catalogue record for this book is available from the British Library.

Design by HL Studios
Cover design by Promo Design
Printed and bound by Pureprint

Acknowledgements
Aldine, for extract from Polsky N, Hustlers, Beats and Others. Bantam, for Hawking S, A Brief History of Time. Barnes Perpetua, for Pollak O, The Criminality of Women. Blackwell, for Heelas P et al, The Spiritual Revolution, and Bruce S, God is Dead. Christian Research, for Brierley P, Pulling out of the Nosedive, and Religious Trends. Clarendon Press, for Garland D, The Culture of Control. Duckworth, for Humphreys L, The Tea Room Trade. Free Press, for Becker H, Outsiders, and Schwendinger J and H, Defenders of order or guardians of human rights? Oxford University Press, for Maguire M et al The Oxford Handbook of Criminology. Penguin, for Gouldner A, For Sociology, Cohen S, Images of Deviance, and Worsley P, Introducing Sociology. Pluto Press, for Burden T, Social Policy and Welfare. Polity, for Held D et al, Global Transformations. Prentice-Hall, for Lemert E, Human Deviance, Social Problems and Social Control. Prometheus Books, for Marx K, Theses on Feuerbach. Routledge and Kegan Paul, for Smart C, Feminism and the Power of Law and Walklate S, Criminology. Rutgers University Press, for Michalowski R et al State-Corporate Crime. Sage, for Muncie J et al, Criminological Perspectives and Cain M, Growing up Good. Simon and Schuster, for Bennett W et al, Body Count. Stanford University Press, for Schramm W et al, Television in the Lives of Our Children. The Atlantic Monthly, for Wilson J & Kelling G, 'Broken Windows'. University of California Press, for Bellah R, Habits of the Heart. University of Chicago Press, for Kuhn T, The Structure of Scientific Revolutions. Vintage, for Wilson J, Thinking about Crime. The British Social Attitudes Survey, The World Values Survey, UK National Statistics and adherents.com for statistical sources.

The publishers would like to thank the following for permission to reproduce pictures: Alamy Images; Corbis; Getty Images; Reuters; Press Association; Mirrorpix; Shutterstock; PA Photos; Wikipedia.

Every effort has been made to contact the holders of copyright material, but if any have been inadvertently overlooked the publishers will be pleased to make the necessary arrangements at the first opportunity.

Go to www.sociology.uk.net
Online support for Sociology teachers and students using this book.

CONTENTS

Chapter 1   Beliefs in society   2

Chapter 2   Crime and deviance   68

Chapter 3   Theory and methods   156

Chapter 4   Preparing for the exams   250

Key concepts   264

Bibliography   270

Index   277

CHAPTER 1

Beliefs in Society

Topic 1	Theories of religion	4
Topic 2	Religion and social change	12
Topic 3	Secularisation	20
Topic 4	Religion, renewal and choice	28
Topic 5	Religion in a global context	38
Topic 6	Organisations, movements and members	46
Topic 7	Ideology and science	58
Examining beliefs in society		66

Sikh pilgrims at the Golden Temple, Amritsar, Punjab. Its four entrance doors symbolise openness to all people and religions.

Introduction

Understanding beliefs is central to sociology because beliefs shape the way we see the world and influence how we live. In this chapter, our main focus is on religious beliefs, practices and organisations.

Topic 1 investigates the social role of religion and its functions for individuals, groups and society. Religion is often seen as maintaining the status quo, but as Topic 2 shows, it can also be a force for change.

Some sociologists argue that religion today is in long-term decline. However, others believe we are witnessing a move from traditional religion to a more personal spirituality. Topics 3 and 4 focus on debates about the future of religion.

In Topic 5, we examine religion in its global context to understand causes of religious fundamentalism and conflict, as well as the ways religion and development are related.

There are many kinds of religious organisations, from churches to cults. Topic 6 examines different religious organisations and movements, their beliefs and the groups they attract.

In Topic 7, we look at science as a belief system. How do scientific explanations differ from those of religion or witchcraft? We also examine the concept of ideology and the way ideas can serve the interests of particular groups.

The AQA Specification

The specification is the syllabus produced by the exam board telling you what to study. The AQA Specification for Beliefs in Society requires you to examine sociological explanations of the following:

- Ideology, science and religion, including both Christian and non-Christian religious traditions.
- The relationship between social change and social stability, and religious beliefs, practices and organisations.
- Religious organisations, including cults, sects, denominations, churches and New Age movements, and their relationship to religious and spiritual belief and practice.
- The relationship between different social groups and religious/spiritual organisations and movements, beliefs and practices.
- The significance of religion and religiosity in the contemporary world, including the nature and extent of secularisation in a global context, and globalisation and the spread of religions.

Pentecostal Church of God, Kentucky, 1946: the power of belief. The Bible says that true believers 'shall take up serpents; and it shall not harm them'.

GETTING STARTED

A Working in pairs, answer the following questions. Give reasons and/or examples for your answers.

1 How would you define 'religion'? Which of the following would you include as essential features of a religion:

(a) belief in a supreme being
(b) belief in heaven
(c) belief in life after death
(d) a holy book
(e) collective worship
(f) specific practices and rituals

(g) rules for everyday life (e.g. diet, marriage)
(h) priests/priestesses
(i) an initiation ceremony
(j) particular symbols?

2 What reasons do you think people have for believing in or belonging to a religion?

B Compare your answers with the rest of the class.

C As a whole class, can you agree on what are the key features of religion? If so, what are they? If not, why not?

Learning objectives

After studying this Topic, you should:

- Understand different sociological definitions of religion.

- Understand how different sociological theories explain the role and functions of religion, and how religion contributes to social stability.

- Be able to evaluate different sociological definitions and theories of religion.

What is 'religion'? Should we define it in terms of particular kinds of beliefs, or in terms of its social role?

What is the role of religion in society. What functions does it perform, and who benefits from them?

Sociologists are also interested in how religion may meet individual needs, for example by helping people to cope with misfortune.

In this Topic, we begin by examining how sociologists define religion. We then focus on the main theories of the role of religion.

What is religion?

There are three main ways in which sociologists define religion: substantive; functional and social constructionist.

Substantive definitions

These focus on the content or substance of religious belief, such as belief in God or the supernatural. For example, Max Weber (1905) defines religion as belief in a superior or supernatural power that is above nature and cannot be explained scientifically. Substantive definitions are *exclusive* – they draw a clear line between religious and non-religious beliefs. To be a religion, a set of beliefs must include belief in God or the supernatural.

Substantive definitions conform to a widespread view of religion as belief in God. However, defining religion in this way leaves no room for beliefs and practices that perform similar functions to religion but do not involve belief in God. These are examined below. Substantive definitions are also accused of Western bias because they exclude religions such as Buddhism, which do not have the Western idea of a god.

Functional definitions

Rather than defining religion in terms of specific kinds of belief, functional definitions define it in terms of the social or psychological functions it performs for individuals or society. For example, Emile Durkheim (1915) defines religion in terms of the contribution it makes to social integration, rather than any specific belief in God or the supernatural. Another functionalist, Milton Yinger (1970) identifies functions that religion performs for individuals, such as answering 'ultimate questions' about the meaning of life and what happens when we die.

An advantage of functional definitions is that they are *inclusive* – allowing us to include a wide range of beliefs and practices that perform functions such as integration. Also, since they do not specify belief in god or the supernatural, there is no bias against non-Western religions such as Buddhism. However, just because an institution helps integrate individuals into groups, this does not make it a religion. For example, collective chanting at football matches might give individuals a sense of integration, but this doesn't mean it is a religion.

Constructionist definitions

Social constructionists take an interpretivist approach that focuses on how members of society themselves define religion. They argue that it is not possible to produce a single universal definition of religion to cover all cases, since in reality different individuals and groups mean very different things by 'religion'.

Social constructionists are interested in how definitions of religion are constructed, challenged and fought over. For example, Alan Aldridge (2013) shows how, for its followers, Scientology is a religion, whereas several governments have denied it legal status as a religion and sought to ban it. This shows that definitions of religion can be contested and are influenced by who has power to define the situation.

Social constructionists do not assume that religion always involves a belief in God or the supernatural, or that it performs similar functions for everyone in all societies. Their approach allows them to get close to the meanings people themselves give to religion. However, this makes it impossible to generalise about the nature of religion, since people may have widely differing views about what counts as a religion.

Functionalist theories of religion

For functionalists, society is a system of interrelated parts or social institutions, such as religion, the family and the economy. Society is like an organism, with basic needs that it must meet in order to survive. These needs are met by the different institutions. Each institution performs certain functions – that is, each contributes to maintaining the social system by meeting a need.

Society's most basic need is the need for social order and solidarity so that its members can cooperate. For functionalists, what makes order possible is the existence of value consensus – a set of shared norms and values by which society's members live. Without this, individuals would pursue their own selfish desires and society would disintegrate.

Durkheim on religion

For functionalists, religious institutions play a central part in creating and maintaining value consensus, order and solidarity. The first functionalist to develop this idea was Emile Durkheim (1858-1917).

The sacred and the profane

For Durkheim (1915; 1962), the key feature of religion was not a belief in gods, spirits or the supernatural, but a fundamental distinction between the sacred and the profane found in all religions. The *sacred* are things set apart and forbidden, that inspire feelings of awe, fear and wonder, and are surrounded by taboos and prohibitions. By contrast, the *profane* are things that have no special significance – things that are ordinary and mundane. Furthermore, a religion is never simply a set of beliefs. It also involves definite rituals or *practices* in relation to the sacred, and these rituals are *collective* – performed by social groups.

The fact that sacred things evoke such powerful feelings in believers indicates to Durkheim that this is because they are symbols representing something of great power. In his view, this thing can only be society itself, since society is the only thing powerful enough to command such feelings. When they worship the sacred symbols, therefore, people are worshipping society itself. For Durkheim, although sacred symbols vary from religion to religion, they all perform the essential function of uniting believers into a single moral community.

Totemism

Durkheim believed that the essence of all religion could be found by studying its simplest form, in the simplest type of society – clan society. For this reason, he used studies of the Arunta, an Aboriginal Australian tribe with a clan system.

Arunta clans consist of bands of kin who come together periodically to perform rituals involving worship of a sacred totem. The totem is the clan's emblem, such as an animal or plant that symbolises the clan's origins and identity. The shared totemic rituals venerating it serve to reinforce the group's solidarity and sense of belonging.

For Durkheim, when clan members worship their totemic animal, they are in reality worshipping society – even

though they themselves are not aware of this fact. The totem inspires feelings of awe in the clan's members precisely because it represents the power of the group on which the individual is 'utterly dependent'.

The collective conscience

In Durkheim's view, the sacred symbols represent society's *collective conscience* or consciousness (the French word 'conscience' means both conscience and consciousness). The collective conscience is the shared norms, values, beliefs and knowledge that make social life and cooperation between individuals possible – without these, society would disintegrate.

For Durkheim, regular shared religious rituals reinforce the collective conscience and maintain social integration. Participating in shared rituals binds individuals together, reminding them that they are part of a single moral community to which they owe their loyalty. Such rituals also remind the individual of the power of society – without which they themselves are nothing, and to which they owe everything.

In this sense, religion also performs an important function for the *individual*. By making us feel part of something greater than ourselves, religion reinvigorates and strengthens us to face life's trials and motivates us to overcome obstacles that would otherwise defeat us.

Cognitive functions of religion

Durkheim sees religion not only as the source of social solidarity, but also of our intellectual or cognitive capacities – our ability to reason and think conceptually. For example, in order to think at all, we need categories such as time, space, cause, substance, number etc (try thinking of an event that had no cause and that occurred outside time and space, for example). And secondly, in order to share our thoughts, we need to use the same categories as others.

In Durkheim's view, religion is the origin of the concepts and categories we need for reasoning, understanding the world and communicating. In their book *Primitive Classification*, Durkheim and Marcel Mauss (1903; 2009) argue that religion provides basic categories such as time, space and causation – for example, with ideas about a creator bringing the world into being at the beginning of time. Similarly, the division of tribes into clans gives humans their first notion of classification. Thus for Durkheim, religion is the origin of human thought, reason and science.

Criticisms

The evidence on totemism is unsound. Worsley (1956) notes that there is no sharp division between the sacred and the profane, and that different clans share the same totems. And even if Durkheim is right about totemism, this does not prove that he has discovered the essence of all other religions.

Durkheim's theory may apply better to small-scale societies with a single religion. It is harder to apply it to large-scale societies, where two or more religious communities may be in conflict. His theory may explain social integration *within* communities, but not the conflicts *between* them.

Similarly, postmodernists such as Stjepan Mestrovic (2011) argue that Durkheim's ideas cannot be applied to contemporary society, because increasing diversity has fragmented the collective conscience, so there is no longer a single shared value system for religion to reinforce.

> **Application**
> Suggest two recent examples of societies where religion may have caused conflict between communities.

Psychological functions

The anthropologist Bronislaw Malinowski (1954) agrees with Durkheim that religion promotes solidarity. However, in his view, it does so by performing psychological functions for individuals, helping them cope with emotional stress that would undermine social solidarity. Malinowski identifies two types of situation in which religion performs this role:

1 Where the outcome is important but is uncontrollable and thus uncertain In his study of the Trobriand Islanders of the Western Pacific, Malinowski contrasts fishing in the lagoon and fishing in the ocean.

- **Lagoon fishing** is safe and uses the predictable and successful method of poisoning. When the islanders fish in the lagoon, there is no ritual.
- **Ocean fishing** is dangerous and uncertain, and is always accompanied by 'canoe magic' – rituals to ensure a safe and successful expedition. This gives people a sense of control, which eases tension, gives them confidence to undertake hazardous tasks and reinforces group solidarity. He sees ritual serving as a 'god of the gaps' – it fills the gaps in human beings' control over the world, such as being unable to control the outcome of a fishing trip.

2 At times of life crises Events such as birth, puberty, marriage and especially death mark major and disruptive changes in social groups. Religion helps to minimise disruption. For example, the funeral rituals reinforce a feeling of solidarity among the survivors, while the notion of immortality gives comfort to the bereaved by denying the fact of death. In fact, Malinowski argues that death is the main reason for the existence of religious belief.

> **Analysis and Evaluation**
> Why might death be the main reason for religious belief?

Parsons: values and meaning

Like Malinowski, Talcott Parsons (1967) sees religion helping individuals to cope with unforeseen events and uncontrollable outcomes. In addition, Parsons identifies two other essential functions that religion performs in modern society.

- **It creates and legitimates society's central values.**
- **It is the primary source of meaning.**

Religion creates and legitimates society's basic norms and values by sacralising them (making them sacred). Thus in the USA, Protestantism has sacralised the core American values of individualism, meritocracy and self-discipline. This serves to promote value consensus and thus social stability.

Religion also provides a source of meaning. In particular, it answers 'ultimate' questions about the human condition, such as why the good suffer and why some die young. Such events defy our sense of justice and make life appear meaningless, and this may undermine our commitment to society's values. Religion provides answers to such questions, for example by explaining suffering as a test of faith that will be rewarded in heaven. By doing so, religion enables people to adjust to adverse events or circumstances and helps maintain stability.

Civil religion

Like Parsons, Robert Bellah (1991; 2013) is interested in how religion unifies society, especially a multi-faith society like America. What unifies American society is an overarching *civil religion* – a belief system that attaches sacred qualities to society itself. In the American case, civil religion is a faith in Americanism or 'the American way of life'.

Bellah argues that civil religion integrates society in a way that America's many different churches and denominations cannot. While none of these can claim the loyalty of all Americans, civil religion can. American civil religion involves loyalty to the nation-state and a belief in God, both of which are equated with being a true American. It is expressed in various rituals, symbols and beliefs; such as the pledge of allegiance to the flag, singing the national anthem, the Lincoln Memorial, and phrases such as 'One nation under God'. However, this is not a specifically Catholic, Protestant or Jewish God, but rather an 'American' God. It sacralises the American way of life and binds together Americans from many different ethnic and religious backgrounds.

Functional alternatives

Functional alternatives or functional equivalents to religion are non-religious beliefs and practices that perform functions similar to those of organised religion, such as reinforcing shared values or maintaining social cohesion.

For example, although in America civil religion involves a belief in God, Bellah argues that this doesn't have to be the case. Some other belief system could perform the same functions. For example, Nazi Germany and the Soviet Union had secular (non-religious) political beliefs and rituals around which they sought to unite society.

However, the problem with the idea of functional alternatives is the same as with functional definitions of religion that we saw earlier. That is, it ignores what makes religion distinctive and different – namely, its belief in the supernatural.

Activity	Media
American civil religion	
...go to www.sociology.uk.net	

Evaluation of functionalism

Functionalism emphasises the social nature of religion and the positive functions it performs, but it neglects negative aspects, such as religion as a source of oppression of the poor or women.

It ignores religion as source of division and conflict, especially in complex modern societies where there is more than one religion – e.g. Northern Ireland. Where there is religious pluralism (many religions), it is hard to see how it can unite people and promote integration.

The idea of civil religion overcomes this problem to some extent, by arguing that societies may still have an overarching belief system shared by all, but is this really religion – especially if it is not based on belief in the supernatural?

Marxist theories of religion

Unlike functionalists, who see society as based on harmony and consensus, Marxists see all societies as divided into two classes, one of which exploits the labour of the other. In modern capitalist society, the capitalist class who own the means of production exploit the working class.

In such a society, there is always the potential for class conflict, and Marx predicted that the working class would ultimately become conscious of their exploitation and unite to overthrow capitalism. This would bring into being a classless society in which there would no longer be exploitation.

Marx's theory of religion needs to be seen in the context of this general view of society. Whereas functionalism sees religion as a unifying force that strengthens the value consensus and is a feature of all societies, Marxism sees religion as a feature only of class-divided society. As such, there will be no need for religion in classless society and it will disappear.

Religion as ideology

For Marx, ideology is a belief system that distorts people's perception of reality in ways that serve the interests of the ruling class. He argues that the class that controls economic production also controls the production and distribution of ideas in society, through institutions such as the church, the education system and the media.

In Marx's view, religion operates as an ideological weapon used by the ruling class to legitimate (justify) the suffering of the poor as something inevitable and god-given. Religion misleads the poor into believing that their suffering is virtuous and that they will be favoured in the afterlife. For example, according to Christianity, it is easier for a camel to pass through the eye of a needle

than it is for a rich man to enter the kingdom of heaven. Such ideas create a *false consciousness* – a distorted view of reality that prevents the poor from acting to change their situation.

Similarly, Lenin (1870-1924) describes religion as 'spiritual gin' – an intoxicant doled out to the masses by the ruling class to confuse them and keep them in their place. In Lenin's view, the ruling class use religion cynically to manipulate the masses and keep them from attempting to overthrow the ruling class by creating a 'mystical fog' that obscures reality.

Religion also legitimates the power and privilege of the dominant class by making their position appear to be divinely ordained. For example, the 16th century idea of the Divine Right of Kings was the belief that the king is God's representative on earth and is owed total obedience. Disobedience is not just illegal, but a sinful challenge to God's authority. For another example of religion and legitimation see Box 1.1.

Religion and alienation

Marx (1844) also sees religion as the product of alienation. Alienation involves becoming separated from or losing control over something that one has produced or created. Alienation exists in all class societies, but it is more extreme under capitalism. Under capitalism, workers are alienated because they do not own what they produce and have no control over the production process, and thus no freedom to express their true nature as creative beings. Alienation reaches a peak with the detailed division of labour in the capitalist factory, where the worker endlessly repeats the same minute task, devoid of all meaning or skill.

In these dehumanising conditions, the exploited turn to religion as a form of consolation. As Marx puts it, religion:

'is the opium of the people. It is the sigh of the oppressed creature, the heart of a heartless world, the soul of soulless conditions, the spirit of a spiritless situation.'

Religion acts as an opiate to dull the pain of exploitation. But just as opium masks pain rather than treating its cause, so religion masks the underlying problem of exploitation that creates the need for it. Because religion is a distorted view of the world, it can offer no solution to earthly misery. Instead, its promises of the afterlife create an illusory happiness that distracts attention from the true source of the suffering, namely capitalism.

Thus, Marx sees religion as the product of alienation. It arises out of suffering and acts as a consolation for it, but fails to deal with its cause, namely class exploitation. Religion also acts as an ideology that legitimates both the suffering of the poor and the privileges of the ruling class.

Evaluation

- Marx shows how religion may be a tool of oppression that masks exploitation and creates false consciousness. However, he ignores positive functions of religion, such as psychological adjustment to misfortune. Neo-Marxists see certain forms of religion as assisting not hindering the development of class consciousness (see Topic 2).
- Some Marxists, such as Althusser (1971), reject the concept of alienation as unscientific and based on a romantic idea that human beings have a 'true self'. This would make the concept an inadequate basis for a theory of religion.

Box 1.1	Caste and the legitimation of inequality

Another example of religion justifying social inequality is the Hindu caste system. Caste is a system of social stratification based on ascribed status. You are born into the same caste as your parents and marriage between castes is forbidden. The highest caste is that of the priests, followed by a warrior caste, a merchant caste and the lowest caste of servants and labourers. Beneath these four groups are the untouchables who are not considered to have a caste at all.

The doctrine of *karma* teaches that if you behave well in this world by accepting and observing the rules of caste, after death you will be reincarnated (re-born) into a higher caste. These rules include strict norms about purity and impurity, governing what food may be eaten and what social contact allowed between members of different castes. Higher castes must maintain higher levels of purity. For example, touching someone from a lower caste may be seen as pollution and must be followed by elaborate cleansing rituals.

The doctrines of reincarnation and *karma* serve to maintain inequality by assuring those at the bottom of the caste system that their obedience will be rewarded (or disobedience punished) by reincarnation into a higher (or lower) caste. Meanwhile, higher castes perceive their privileged positions as a reward for their virtue in a previous life.

- Religion does not necessarily function effectively as an ideology to control the population. For example, Abercrombie, Hill and Turner (2015) argue that in pre-capitalist society, while Christianity was a major element of ruling-class ideology, it had only limited impact on the peasantry.

Feminist theories of religion

Feminists see society as patriarchal – that is, based on male domination. Many feminists regard religion as a patriarchal institution that reflects and perpetuates this inequality. Religious beliefs function as a patriarchal ideology that legitimates female subordination.

Evidence of patriarchy

Although the formal teachings of religions often stress equality between the sexes, there is considerable evidence of patriarchy within many of them. For example:

- **Religious organisations** are mainly male-dominated despite the fact that women often participate more than men in these organisations. For example, Orthodox Judaism and Catholicism forbid women to become priests. Karen Armstrong (1993) sees exclusion from the priesthood as evidence of women's marginalisation.

- **Places of worship** often segregate the sexes and marginalise women, for example seating them behind screens while the men occupy the central and more sacred spaces. Women's participation may be restricted, for example not being allowed to preach or to read from sacred texts. Taboos that regard menstruation, pregnancy and childbirth as polluting may also prevent participation. For example, in Islam, menstruating women are not allowed to touch the Qur'an. Jean Holm (2001) describes this as the devaluation of women in religion.

- **Sacred texts** largely feature the doings of male gods, prophets etc, and are usually written and interpreted by men. Stories often reflect anti-female stereotypes, such as that of Eve who, in the Judaeo-Christian story of Genesis, caused humanity's fall from grace and expulsion from the Garden of Eden.

- **Religious laws and customs** may give women fewer rights than men, for example in access to divorce, how many spouses they may marry, decision making, dress codes etc. Religious influences on cultural norms may also lead to unequal treatment, such as genital mutilation or punishments for sexual transgressions. Many religions legitimate and regulate women's traditional domestic and reproductive role. For example, the Catholic Church bans abortion and artificial contraception. Woodhead (2002) argues that the exclusion of women from the Catholic priesthood is evidence of the Church's deep unease about the emancipation of women generally.

However, feminists argue that women have not always been subordinate to men within religion. Karen Armstrong (1993) argues that early religions often placed women at the centre. For example, earth mother goddesses, fertility cults and female priesthoods were found throughout the Middle East until about 6,000 years ago. However, from about 4,000 years ago, the rise of monotheistic religions saw the establishment of a single, all-powerful male God, such as the Hebrews' Jehovah, and male prophets such as Abraham/Ibrahim, the first prophet of Judaism, Christianity and Islam.

While religion may be used to oppress women, Nawal El Saadawi (1980) argues that it is not the direct cause of their subordination. Rather, this is the result of patriarchal forms of society coming into existence in the last few thousand years. However, once in existence, patriarchy began to influence and re-shape religion. For example, men reinterpreted religious beliefs in ways that favoured patriarchy. Thus religion now contributes to women's oppression. Like Armstrong, El Saadawi sees the rise of monotheism as legitimating the power of men over women.

Religious forms of feminism

Linda Woodhead (2009) criticises feminist explanations that simply equate religion with patriarchy and the oppression of women. While accepting that much traditional religion is patriarchal, she emphasises that this is not true of all religion. She argues that there are 'religious forms of feminism' – ways in which women use religion to gain greater freedom and respect.

Woodhead uses the example of the hijab or veil worn by many Muslim women. While Western feminists tend to see it as a symbol of oppression, to the wearer it may be a means of liberation. According to Sophie Gilliat-Ray (2010), some young British Muslim women choose to wear the hijab in order to gain parental approval to enter further education and especially employment, where Muslim women's presence has traditionally been problematic. For them, the hijab is a symbol of liberation that allows them to enter the public sphere without being condemned as immodest.

Women also use religion to gain status and respect for their roles within the private sphere of home and family. For example, as Elisabeth Brusco (1995; 2012) found in Colombia, belonging to a Pentecostal group can be empowering for some women. Despite the strong belief in traditional gender roles that such groups hold, women are able to use religion to increase their power and influence. For example, a strongly held belief among Pentecostals is that men should respect women. This gives women power to influence men's behaviour by insisting that they practise what they preach and refrain from 'macho' behaviour. Similarly, women make use of activities linked to the church, such as Bible study groups, to share experiences and find support. (For more about the 'Pentecostal gender paradox', see Topic 6.)

Piety movements Rachel Rinaldo (2010) sees this pattern as typical of 'piety movements'. These are conservative movements that support traditional teachings about women's role, modest dress, prayer and Bible study. They include Pentecostal and evangelical groups, and some forms of non-Christian religions.

Like Brusco and Woodhead, Rinaldo argues that even within conservative religions, women may sometimes find ways to further their own interests. However, she notes that it is middle-class urban women who are most likely to join piety movements. These women may already have other resources, such as education and income, with which to pursue their goals.

Liberal Protestant organisations, such as the Quakers and the Unitarians, are often committed to gender equality and women play leading roles. For example, a third of Unitarian ministers are female. The Church of England, the official state church in England, has had female priests since 1992 and female bishops since 2015. Over a fifth of its priests are female.

Topic summary

Sociologists **define** religion in substantive, functional and social constructionist terms.

Functionalism sees religion performing **positive functions** for society and individuals. These include solidarity and integration; provision of values and meanings, and psychological functions. Functionalists also identify functional alternatives such as civil religion.

Marxists see religion as dulling the pain of class **exploitation** and as fostering **false consciousness**. They see religion as a form of **ideology** and a response to **alienation**.

Feminists see religion as an instrument of **patriarchy** – a set of beliefs and practices responsible for women's subordination. Some feminists argue that religion is not always patriarchal.

EXAMINING THEORIES OF RELIGION

QuickCheck Questions

Check your answers at www.sociology.uk.net

1 True or False? Substantive definitions of religion are inclusive.
2 How does Durkheim distinguish between the sacred and the profane?
3 Explain how religion may perform a cognitive function.
4 Explain what is meant by 'civil religion'.
5 Identify two criticisms of the functionalist view of religion.

6 According to Marx, what is the main cause of alienation?
7 Identify one way in which Hinduism may legitimate inequality.
8 Identify three examples of ways in which religions may be patriarchal.
9 Give one example of how religion may be empowering for women.

Questions to try

Item A

Some sociologists argue that religion performs an ideological function and operates in the interests of powerful groups in society. For example, feminists see religion as helping to sustain male domination of society. They point to the patriarchal nature of sacred texts, such as the Biblical story of Eve causing humanity's expulsion from the Garden of Eden, and their role in legitimating the subordination of women. Marxists, too, see religion as an ideology that distorts people's perception of reality in capitalist society and helps prevent revolution.

However, religion may also perform positive functions for society, and subordinate groups may also use religion to serve their interests.

1 Outline and explain two functions of religion. (10 marks)
2 Applying material from Item A and your knowledge, evaluate the claim that religion performs an ideological function in the interests of powerful groups. (20 marks)

The Examiner's Advice

Q1 Spend about 15 minutes on this question. Divide your time fairly equally between the two functions. You don't need a separate introduction; just start on the first function. Possible functions include: creating a collective conscience, helping individuals to cope with stress, legitimating central values, cognitive functions, providing a central source of meaning, creating civil religion, legitimating inequality, dulling the pain of exploitation, and justifying patriarchy.

Describe each function in some detail. Explain how each function meets a particular social and/or individual need. Do this by creating a chain of reasoning (see Box 4.1 in chapter 4). For example, religion can offer support in times of emotional stress, helping individuals to cope with danger and uncertainty. This also functions for society because too much stress on individual members would undermine social solidarity, without which society's basic need for social order could not be met.

Use concepts and issues such as value consensus, the sacred and the profane, ritual, totemism, social order, social solidarity, collective conscience, canoe magic, life crises, civil religion, ideology, alienation, exploitation, legitimation of inequality, religious forms of feminism, and patriarchy. Use material from studies such as Durkheim, Malinowski, Parsons, Bellah, Marx and Woodhead.

Q2 Spend about 30 minutes on this. Start by briefly explaining what is meant by ideology. Then take your lead from the Item by focusing on the feminist and Marxist perspectives on religion, identifying men and capitalists as the groups whose interests religion might serve. Explain each perspective in detail.

Make use of concepts from the Item (e.g. patriarchy, subordination, legitimation, capitalism, revolution) as well as others such as alienation, division of labour, false class consciousness, 'spiritual gin', the opium of the people and exploitation. Use examples of religion's ideological role, such as Hinduism's legitimation of caste inequality or the Divine Right of Kings, as well as examples of women's exclusion from priesthoods, religious ideas about menstruation, pregnancy and childbirth, women's representation in sacred texts and how religion may underpin laws and customs (e.g. on contraception or divorce) that subordinate women.

You can evaluate by considering the functionalist view that religion may serve positive functions for all members of society. Also consider examples of where subordinate groups may use religion in their own interests, such as women in Pentecostal churches. You can also use material from Topic 2, for example on the civil rights movement, to evaluate.

Martin Luther King ends his famous 'I Have a Dream' speech with the words, 'Free at last! Free at last! Thank God Almighty, we are free at last!' August 28, 1963

GETTING STARTED

In groups of three or four:

1 Use the link below to access the text of Dr Martin Luther King's 'I have a dream' speech.

www.sociology.uk.net/speech

2 Print a copy of the speech and highlight all the examples of religious language used by Dr King in his speech. (You may also like to watch the full speech by searching on the internet).

3 Use the link below to see the biblical references in the speech. Check these against your examples.

www.sociology.uk.net/sources

4 Which biblical references highlight racial inequality and injustice in America?

5 Which biblical references did Dr King use to motivate people to change society?

6 Which of the references do you find most powerful?

Learning objectives

After studying this Topic, you should:

- Be able to describe a range of examples of religion and analyse their role in social change.

- Understand sociological explanations of the role of religion in promoting social change.

- Be able to evaluate different sociological explanations of the relationship between religion, social stability and social change.

RELIGION AND SOCIAL CHANGE

Religion as a conservative force

Religion can be seen as a conservative force in two senses:

1. It is often seen as conservative in the sense of being 'traditional', defending traditional customs, institutions, moral views, roles etc. In other words, *it upholds traditional beliefs* about how society should be organised.
2. It is conservative because *it functions to conserve or preserve things as they are.* It stabilises society and maintains the status quo.

Religion's beliefs

Most religions have traditional conservative beliefs about moral issues and many of them oppose changes that would allow individuals more freedom in personal and sexual matters. For example, the Catholic Church forbids divorce, abortion and artificial contraception. It opposes gay marriage and condemns homosexual behaviour.

Similarly, most religions uphold 'family values' and often favour a traditional patriarchal domestic division of labour. For example, the belief that the man should be the head of the family was embedded in the traditional marriage ceremony of the Church of England dating from 1602. The bride vows to 'love, honour and *obey*', but the groom is only required to 'love and honour'.

Traditional conservative values also predominate in non-Christian religions. For example, Hinduism endorses male domestic authority and the practice of arranged marriage.

Religion's functions

Religion is also a conservative force in that it functions to conserve or preserve things as they are and maintain the status quo. As we saw in Topic 1, this view of religion is held by functionalists, Marxists and feminists. Although each of these perspectives sees the role of religion differently, all of them argue that it contributes to social stability.

Religion and consensus Functionalists see religion as a conservative force because it functions to maintain social stability and prevent society from disintegrating. For example, it promotes social solidarity by creating value consensus, thus reducing the likelihood of society collapsing through individuals pursuing their own selfish interests at the expense of others. It also helps individuals to deal with stresses that would otherwise disrupt the life of society.

By contrast, Marxists and feminists see religion as an ideology that supports the existing social structure and acts as a means of social control, creating stability in the interests of the powerful. This helps to maintain the status quo by preventing the less powerful from changing things.

Religion and capitalism Marx sees religion as a conservative ideology that prevents social change. By legitimating or disguising exploitation and inequality, it creates false consciousness in the working class and prevents revolution, thereby maintaining the stability of capitalist society.

Religion and patriarchy Feminists see religion as a conservative force because it acts as an ideology that legitimates patriarchal power and maintains women's subordination in the family and wider society.

Weber: religion as a force for change

We have seen how religion can be a conservative force, but sociologists have also shown it to be a force for change. Perhaps the most famous example of this view is Max Weber's (1905) study of *The Protestant Ethic and the Spirit of Capitalism*. In it, Weber argues that the religious beliefs of Calvinism (a form of Protestantism founded by John Calvin during the Reformation) helped to bring about major social change – specifically, the emergence of modern capitalism in Northern Europe in the 16th and 17th centuries.

Weber notes that many past societies had capitalism in the sense of greed for wealth, which they often spent on luxury consumption. However, modern capitalism is unique, he argues, because it is based on the systematic, efficient, rational pursuit of profit for its own sake, rather than for consumption. Weber calls this *the spirit of capitalism*. According to Weber, this spirit had what he calls an *elective*

affinity or unconscious similarity to the Calvinists' beliefs and attitudes. Calvinism had several distinctive beliefs.

Calvinist beliefs

Predestination God had predetermined which souls would be saved – 'the elect' – and which would not, even before birth. Individuals could do nothing whatsoever to change this, whether through their deeds, as the Catholics believed (e.g. through pilgrimages, prayer or giving to the Church), or through faith, as the Lutheran Protestants believed. God's decision is already made and cannot be altered.

Divine transcendence God was so far above and beyond this world and so incomparably greater than any mortal, that no human being could possibly claim to know his will (other than what he had chosen to reveal through the

Bible). This included the Church and its priests – leaving the Calvinists to feel 'an unprecedented inner loneliness'. When combined with the doctrine of predestination, this created what Weber calls a *salvation panic* in the Calvinists. They could not know whether they had been chosen to be saved, and they could not do anything to earn their salvation.

Asceticism This refers to abstinence, self-discipline and self-denial. For example, monks lead an ascetic existence, refraining from luxury, wearing simple clothes and avoiding excess in order to devote themselves to God and a life of prayer.

The idea of a vocation or calling Before Calvinism, the idea of a religious vocation (a calling to serve God) meant renouncing everyday life to join a convent or monastery. Weber calls this *other-worldly asceticism*. By contrast, Calvinism introduces for the first time the idea of *this-worldly asceticism*. The only thing Calvinists knew of God's plan for humanity came from the Bible, which revealed to them that we were put on the earth to glorify God's name by our work. Thus for the Calvinists the idea of a calling or vocation meant constant, methodical work in an occupation, not in a monastery. However, work could not earn salvation – it was simply a religious duty.

For this reason, the Calvinists led an ascetic lifestyle shunning all luxury, worked long hours and practised rigorous self-discipline. Idleness is a sin; as the Calvinist Benjamin Franklin put it, 'Lose no time; be always employed in something useful'. The Calvinists' hard work and asceticism had two consequences.

Firstly, their wealth and success performed a psychological function for the Calvinists that allowed them to cope with their salvation panic. As they grew wealthier, they took this as a sign of God's favour and their salvation – for why else would we have prospered, they asked themselves. This of course was contrary to their original doctrine that God's will was unknowable.

Secondly, driven by their work ethic, they systematically and methodically accumulated wealth by the most efficient and rational means possible. But not permitting themselves to squander it on luxuries, they reinvested it in their businesses, which grew and prospered, producing further profit to reinvest and so on and on. In Weber's view, this is the very spirit of modern capitalism – where the object is simply the acquisition of more and more money as an end in itself. Calvinism thus brought capitalism as we now know it into the world.

Activity   Media

Weber and Calvinism

...go to www.sociology.uk.net

Hinduism and Confucianism

It is very important to note that Weber was not arguing that Calvinist beliefs were *the* cause of modern capitalism, but simply that they were *one* of its causes. The Protestant ethic of the Calvinists was not sufficient on its own to bring modern capitalism into being. On the contrary, a number of material or economic factors were necessary, such as natural resources, trade, a money economy, towns and cities, a system of law and so on.

On the other hand, Weber notes that there have been other societies that have had a higher level of economic development than Northern Europe had in the 16th and 17th centuries, but that still failed to develop modern capitalism. In particular, he argues that ancient China and India were materially more advanced than Europe, but capitalism did not take off there. He argues that the failure of capitalism to take off there was due to the lack of a religious belief system like that of Calvinism that would have spurred its development.

Thus in ancient India, Hinduism was an ascetic religion, like Calvinism, favouring renunciation of the material world. However, its orientation was *other-worldly* – it directed its followers' concerns away from the material world and towards the spiritual world. In ancient China, Confucianism also discouraged the growth of rational capitalism, but for different reasons. Like Calvinism, Confucianism was a *this-worldly* religion that directed its followers towards the material world but, unlike Calvinism, it was not ascetic. Both Hinduism and Confucianism thus lacked the drive to systematically accumulate wealth that is necessary for modern capitalism. Calvinism was unique in combining asceticism with a this-worldly orientation to enable the spirit of modern capitalism to emerge.

Evaluation

Weber's work is often described as a 'debate with Marx's ghost'. Marx saw economic or material factors as the driving force of change, whereas Weber argues that material factors alone are not enough to bring about capitalism. As we have just seen, in Weber's view, it also needed specific cultural factors – the beliefs and values of Calvinism – to bring it into being.

Marxists have responded with their own criticisms of Weber. For example, Karl Kautsky (1927) argues that Weber overestimates the role of ideas and underestimates economic factors in bringing capitalism into being. He argues that in fact capitalism preceded rather than followed Calvinism.

Similarly, R.H.Tawney (1926) argues that technological change, not religious ideas, caused the birth of capitalism. It was only after capitalism was established that the bourgeoisie adopted Calvinist beliefs to legitimate their pursuit of economic gain.

Weber has also been criticised because capitalism did not develop in every country where there were Calvinists. For example, Scotland had a large Calvinist population but was slow to develop capitalism. However, Weberians such as Gordon Marshall (1982) argue that this was because of a lack of investment capital and skilled labour – supporting Weber's point that both material and cultural factors need to be present for capitalism to emerge.

Others argue that although Calvinists were among the first capitalists, this was not because of their beliefs but simply because they had been excluded by law from

political office and many of the professions, like the Jews in Eastern Europe. They turned to business as one of the few alternatives open to them. However, Weberians reply that other religious minorities were also excluded in this way but did not become successful capitalists.

Analysis and Evaluation

How does Weber's view of social change differ from the Marxist view?

Religion and social protest

Like Weber, Steve Bruce (2003) is interested in the relationship between religion and social change. Using case studies, he compares two examples of the role of religiously inspired protest movements in America that have tried to change society: the civil rights movement and the New Christian Right.

The American civil rights movement

Bruce describes the struggle of the black civil rights movement of the 1950s and 1960s to end racial segregation as an example of religiously motivated social change. Although slavery had been abolished in 1865, blacks were denied legal and political rights in many Southern states where segregation was enforced, preventing them from using the same amenities (such as buses, shops and toilets) as whites. Schools were segregated and inter-racial marriages forbidden. Blacks were often excluded from voting by various legal restrictions and intimidation.

The civil rights movement began in 1955 when Rosa Parks, a black civil rights activist in Montgomery, Alabama, refused to sit at the back of a bus, as blacks were expected to do. Campaigning involved direct action by black people themselves, including protest marches, boycotts and demonstrations. Almost a decade later, in 1964, segregation was outlawed.

Bruce describes the black clergy as the backbone of the movement. Led by Dr Martin Luther King, they played a decisive role, giving support and moral legitimacy to civil rights activists. Their churches provided meeting places and sanctuary from the threat of white violence, and rituals such as prayer meetings and hymn singing were a source of unity in the face of oppression. Bruce argues that the black clergy were able to shame whites into changing the law by appealing to their shared Christian values of equality. Although the impact on white clergy in the South was

limited, their message reached a wide audience outside the Southern states and gained national support.

Bruce sees religion in this context as an *ideological resource* – it provided beliefs and practices that protesters could draw on for motivation and support. Using the civil rights movement as an example, he identifies several ways in which religious organisations are well equipped to support protests and contribute to social change:

- **Taking the moral high ground** Black clergy pointed out the hypocrisy of white clergy who preached 'love thy neighbour' but supported racial segregation.
- **Channelling dissent** Religion provides channels to express political dissent. For example, the funeral of Martin Luther King was a rallying point for the civil rights cause.
- **Acting as honest broker** Churches can provide a context for negotiating change because they are often respected by both sides in a conflict and seen as standing above 'mere politics'.
- **Mobilising public opinion** Black churches in the South successfully campaigned for support across the whole of America.

Bruce sees the civil rights movement as an example of religion becoming involved in secular struggle and helping to bring about change. In his view, the movement achieved its aims because it shared the same values as wider society and those in power. It brought about change by shaming those in power to put into practice the principle of equality embodied in the American Constitution that all men and women are born equal.

The New Christian Right

The New Christian Right is a politically and morally conservative, Protestant fundamentalist movement. It has gained prominence since the 1960s because of its opposition to the liberalising of American society.

The aims of the New Christian Right seek to take America 'back to God' and make abortion, homosexuality, gay marriage and divorce illegal, turning the clock back to a time before the liberalisation of American culture and society.

The New Christian Right believes strongly in the traditional family and traditional gender roles. It campaigns for the teaching of 'creationism' (the view that the Bible's account of creation is literally true) and to ban sex education in schools.

The New Christian Right has made effective use of the media and networking, notably televangelism, where church-owned television stations raise funds and broadcast programmes aimed at making converts and recruiting new members. Right-wing Christian pressure groups have also become the focus for political campaigning and for strengthening links with the Republican Party.

However, the New Christian Right has been largely unsuccessful in achieving its aims. Bruce suggests these reasons:

- Its campaigners find it very difficult to cooperate with people from other religious groups, even when campaigning on the same issue, such as abortion.

- It lacks widespread support and has met with strong opposition from groups who stand for freedom of choice.

Application
Why might the New Christian Right campaigners find it difficult to cooperate with people from other religions, even when they are campaigning on the same issues?

Bruce describes the New Christian Right as a failed movement for change. Despite enormous publicity and a high profile in the media, it has not achieved its aim of taking America 'back to God'. In his view, its attempt to impose Protestant fundamentalist morality on others has failed because of the basically liberal and democratic values of most of American society. These values include a belief in the separation of church and state – very few Americans support the idea of a theocracy (rule by religious leaders).

Numerous surveys show that most Americans are comfortable with legalising activities that they personally believe are immoral, such as abortion, homosexuality and pornography, and unwilling to accept other people's definition of how they should live their lives. This poses an enormous problem for the New Christian Right, which believes in the literal truth of the Bible and insists everyone should be made to conform to its teaching. As Bruce points out, this is an impossible demand to make in a mature democracy.

Comparisons with the civil rights movement are interesting. They suggest that to achieve success, the beliefs and demands of religiously motivated protest movements and pressure groups need to be consistent with those of wider society. Thus in the American case, they need to connect with mainstream beliefs about democracy, equality and religious freedom, which the civil rights movement did but the New Christian Right has failed to do.

Marxism, religion and change

Marxists are often thought of as seeing religion as an entirely conservative ideology – a set of ruling-class ideas that are shaped by and legitimate the class inequalities in society's economic base. However, this is not the case – Marxists recognise that ideas, including religious ideas, can have *relative autonomy*. That is, they can be partly independent of the economic base of society. As a result, religion can have a dual character and can sometimes be a force for change as well as stability.

For example, Marx himself does not see religion in entirely negative terms, describing it as 'the soul of soulless conditions' and the 'heart of a heartless world'. He sees religion as capable of humanising a world made inhuman by exploitation, even if the comfort it offers is illusory.

The idea that religion has a dual character is taken up by Friedrich Engels (1895), Marx's life-long collaborator. Engels argues that although religion inhibits change by disguising

inequality, it can also challenge the status quo and encourage social change. For example, religion sometimes preaches liberation from slavery and misery. Also, although senior clergy usually support the status quo, lower ranks within the church hierarchy have often supported or even inspired and organised popular protest.

Ernst Bloch: the principle of hope

Ernst Bloch (1959) also sees religion as having a dual character. He argues for a view of religion that recognises both its positive and negative influence on social change. As a Marxist, he accepts that religion often inhibits change, but he emphasises that it can also inspire protest and rebellion. For Bloch, religion is an expression of 'the principle of hope' – our dreams of a better life that contain images of utopia (the perfect world).

Images of utopia can sometimes deceive people with promises of rewards in heaven, as Marx himself describes. However, they may also help people see what needs to be changed in this world. Religious beliefs may therefore create a vision of a better world, which, if combined with effective political organisation and leadership, can bring about social change.

In the next section we examine what some Marxists see as religion's dual character; that is, how religion can either encourage or discourage protest and change.

Liberation theology

Liberation theology is a movement that emerged within the Catholic Church in Latin America at the end of the 1960s, with a strong commitment to the poor and opposition to military dictatorships. Liberation theology was a major change of direction for the Catholic Church in Latin America. For centuries, it had been an extremely conservative institution, encouraging a fatalistic acceptance of poverty and supporting wealthy elites and military dictatorships.

The factors that led to liberation theology were:

- Deepening rural poverty and the growth of urban slums throughout Latin America.
- Human rights abuses following military take-overs, such as torture and death squads murdering political opponents, for example in Argentina, Brazil and Chile.
- The growing commitment among Catholic priests to an ideology that supported the poor and opposed violations of human rights.

Unlike traditional Catholicism, which supported the status quo, liberation theology set out to change society. For example, priests helped the poor to establish support groups, called 'base communities', and helped workers and peasants to fight oppression under the protection of the church. Priests took the lead in developing literacy programmes, educating the poor about their situation, raising awareness and mobilising support.

During the 1970s, priests were often the only authority figures who took the side of the oppressed when dictatorships used murder squads and torture to hold on to power. However, during the 1980s the Church's official attitude changed. Pope John Paul II condemned liberation theology on the grounds that it resembled Marxism, and instructed priests to concentrate on pastoral activities, not political struggle.

Since then, the movement has lost influence. However, as Casanova (1994) emphasises, it played an important part in resisting state terror and bringing about democracy. Although Catholicism in Latin America has since become more conservative, it continues to defend the democracy and human rights that were achieved in part by liberation theology.

The success of liberation theology has led some neo-Marxists to question the view that religion is always a conservative force. For example, Otto Maduro (1982)

believes that religion can be a revolutionary force that brings about change. In the case of liberation theology, religious ideas radicalised the Catholic clergy in defence of peasants and workers, making them see that serving the poor was part of their Christian duty. Similarly, Löwy (2005) questions Marx's view that religion always legitimates social inequality.

Both Maduro and Löwy see liberation theology as an example of religiously inspired social change but other Marxists disagree. Much depends on how social change is defined. Liberation theology may have helped to bring about democracy but it did not threaten the stability of capitalism.

The Pentecostal challenge

In recent decades, liberation theology has faced competition from Pentecostal churches, which have made big inroads in Latin America among the poor. David Lehmann (1996) contrasts the two:

Liberation theology offers an 'option *for* the poor' of community consciousness-raising and campaigning for social change, led by 'revolutionary priests and nuns in their jeans and sandals'.

Pentecostalism offers an 'option *of* the poor' for individuals to pull themselves out of poverty through their own efforts, supported by the congregation and led by the church pastors, 'uniformly respectable in their suits, white shirts and black ties'.

Thus, liberation theology offers a radical solution to poverty: collective improvement through political action in the public sphere, while Pentecostalism's solution is conservative: individual self-improvement through the private sphere of family and church.

Activity Media

Liberation theology

...go to www.sociology.uk.net

Millenarian movements

Because religion raises the hope of a better world in the afterlife, it may also create a desire to change things here and now, for example to bring about the kingdom of God on earth. Millenarian movements are an important example of this desire.

Millenarian movements take their name from the word 'millennium', meaning a thousand years. In Christian theology, this refers to the idea that Christ would come into the world for a second time and rule for a thousand years before the Day of Judgment and the end of the world. According to Peter Worsley (1968), such movements expect the total and imminent transformation of this world by supernatural means. This will create a heaven on earth, a life free from pain, death, sin, corruption and imperfection. The transformation will be collective – the *group* will be saved, not just individuals.

The appeal of millenarian movements is largely to the poor because they promise immediate improvement, and they often arise in colonial situations. European colonialism led to economic exploitation and cultural and religious domination, for example through the Christian missionaries and their schools. At the same time, it shattered the traditional tribal social structures and cultures of the colonised peoples. Local leaders and local gods lose power and credibility when their people are forced to work for colonists who live in luxury.

Worsley studied the millenarian movements in Melanesia (Western Pacific) known as *cargo cults*. The islanders felt wrongfully deprived when 'cargo' (material goods) arrived in the islands for the colonists. A series of cargo cults sprang up during the 19ᵗʰ and 20ᵗʰ centuries asserting that the cargo had been meant for the natives but had been diverted by the whites for themselves, and that this unjust social order was about to be overturned. These movements often led to widespread unrest that threatened colonial rule.

Worsley notes that the movements combined elements of traditional beliefs with elements of Christianity – such as ideas about a heaven where the suffering of the righteous will be rewarded, Christ's imminent second coming to earth, the Day of Judgment and punishment of the wicked. He describes the movements as *pre-political* – they used religious ideas and images, but they united native populations in mass movements that spanned tribal divisions. Many of the secular nationalist leaders and parties that were to overthrow colonial rule in the 1950s and 1960s developed out of millenarian movements. Similarly, from a Marxist perspective, Engels argues that they represent the first awakening of 'proletarian self-consciousness'.

Gramsci: religion and hegemony

Antonio Gramsci (1971) is interested in how the ruling class maintain their control over society through the use of ideas. He uses the term *hegemony* to refer to the way that the ruling class use ideas such as religion to maintain control. By hegemony, Gramsci means ideological domination or leadership of society. When hegemony is established, the ruling class can rely on popular consent to their rule, so there is less need for coercion. For example, writing in Italy in the 1920s and 1930s, Gramsci notes the immense conservative ideological power of the Catholic Church in helping to win support for Mussolini's fascist regime.

However, hegemony is never guaranteed. It is always possible for the working class to develop an alternative vision of how society should be organised – that is, a counter-hegemony. Like Engels, Gramsci sees religion as having a dual character and he notes that in some circumstances, it can challenge as well as support the ruling class. He argues that popular forms of religion can help workers see through the ruling-class hegemony by offering a vision of a better, fairer world. Similarly, some clergy may act as *organic intellectuals* – that is, as educators, organisers and leaders. They can help workers see the situation they are in and support working-class organisations such as trade unions.

Religion and class conflict

Dwight Billings (1990) applies Gramsci's ideas in a case study comparing class struggle in two communities – one of coalminers, the other of textile workers – in Kentucky during the 1920s and 1930s. Both were working-class and evangelical Protestant, but the miners were much more militant, struggling for recognition of their union and better conditions, while the textile workers accepted the status quo.

Following Gramsci, Billings argues that the differences in levels of militancy can be understood in terms of hegemony and the role of religion. Billings identifies three ways in which religion either supported or challenged the employers' hegemony:

- **Leadership** The miners benefited from the leadership of organic intellectuals – many of them lay preachers who were themselves miners and trade union activists. These clergy helped to convert miners to the union cause. Textile workers lacked such leadership.
- **Organisation** The miners were able to use independent churches to hold meetings and organise, whereas the textile workers lacked such spaces.
- **Support** The churches kept miners' morale high with supportive sermons, prayer meetings and group singing. By contrast, textile workers who engaged in union activity met with opposition from local church leaders.

Billings concludes that religion can play 'a prominent oppositional role'. His study shows that the same religion can be called upon either to defend the status quo or justify the struggle to change it.

Topic summary

Some sociologists argue that religion does not always maintain the status quo. **Weber** argues the **Protestant ethic** contributed to the birth of capitalism. **Marxists** such as Maduro, who gives **liberation theology** as an example, argue that religion has potential to bring about change. Religious organisations have actively supported campaigns for change. Some such as the US **civil rights movement** have succeeded. Others such as the **New Christian Right** have failed to gain popular support. **Millenarian movements** have been forerunners of anti-colonial political parties.

EXAMINING RELIGION AND SOCIAL CHANGE

QuickCheck Questions

Check your answers at www.sociology.uk.net

1 What was the Calvinist doctrine of predestination?
2 Explain what Weber means by 'this-worldly asceticism'.
3 Why does Weber argue that the Calvinists experienced 'salvation panic'?
4 According to Weber, why did Hinduism discourage social change?
5 Explain what is meant by 'hegemony'.

6 Identify two ways in which the churches were able to support the black civil rights movement.
7 Suggest one similarity between liberation theology and Marxism.
8 Identify three characteristics of millenarian movements.
9 Why do Marxists see religion as having a dual character?

Questions to try

Item A

Religions typically hold strong beliefs and values about issues such as family life, gender roles and relationships, sexuality, and how society should be organised. Through its rituals, religion can make individuals feel part of something greater than themselves and bind them together, curbing their selfishness and enabling them to cooperate to achieve shared goals. However, religion has also often been closely allied to privileged groups in society and has been accused of upholding their interests.

Item B

Max Weber argued that religious beliefs can lead to important social changes. According to Weber, Calvinist Protestant beliefs in the 16th century were crucial in bringing about the emergence of modern capitalism in Western Europe. By contrast, the beliefs of some other major religions have acted as a barrier to such change.

Some sociologists argue that religion has a dual character: its beliefs can have both a negative impact on social change and a positive one, for example by inspiring protest against the status quo.

1 Applying material from Item A, analyse two arguments in support of the idea that religion is a conservative social force. (10 marks)
2 Applying material from Item B and your knowledge, evaluate the extent to which religious beliefs can be a force for social change. (20 marks)

The Examiner's Advice

Q1 Spend about 15 minutes on this. Divide your time fairly equally between the two arguments. You don't need a separate introduction; just start on your first argument. To answer this question, it's essential that you take two points from the Item and show through a chain of reasoning (see Box 4.1 in chapter 4) how each relates to religion as a conservative force. (It is a very good idea to quote from the Item when doing so).

You could use arguments such as that religion promotes conservative values about women's role etc, promotes social solidarity, or legitimates the position of privileged groups. For example, it legitimates inequality by claiming that the proletariat's suffering is God-given and will be rewarded in heaven. This promotes false consciousness and prevents revolution.

Use concepts and issues such as ideology, false consciousness, alienation, patriarchy, subordination, hegemony, social control, functions, collective conscience, and value consensus. You can offer some brief evaluation by pointing out that religion may sometimes promote change.

Q2 Spend about 30 minutes on this. Note that it is specifically about *beliefs*, so you need to consider examples of particular religious beliefs and how far they may produce change. Use the Item to begin a detailed account of Weber on Calvinist beliefs, including predestination, divine transcendence, this-worldly asceticism and the idea of a vocation, to explain what made Calvinism distinctive. Using concepts such as the work ethic, salvation panic, accumulation, and the spirit of capitalism, explain how Weber saw Calvinism generating change.

Evaluate by contrasting this with Weber's account of Hinduism and Confucianism and by referring to criticisms of Weber's Protestant ethic thesis. Consider evidence from the civil rights movement, liberation theology, millenarian movements and religious support for working-class struggles.

Use concepts such as material factors, the dual character of religion, the principle of hope, utopia, colonialism, cargo cults, pre-political movements, hegemony, class consciousness and organic intellectuals. Use material from studies such as Engels, Bloch, Maduro, Casanova, Bruce, Worsley, Gramsci and Billings.

Emergency touchdown in the Hudson River, New York City: a miracle – or a pilot who kept his nerve?

GETTING STARTED

Some sociologists argue that religion is losing influence in society, for example in areas such as marriage and divorce.

A Working in pairs, answer the following questions:

   1 In what other ways, if any, do you think religion has lost influence in society?

   2 Comparing yourself, your parents and your grandparents, for which generation is religion most important?

   3 What measures could you use to see if there has been a decline in religion's influence in society?

B As a whole class:

   1 Compare your answers to questions A1 to A3.

   2 Discuss whether you think religion is losing influence in society.

Learning objectives

After studying this Topic, you should:

- Know the main trends in patterns of religious belief and practice in the UK and USA.
- Understand and be able to analyse the possible causes of secularisation.
- Be able to evaluate arguments and evidence for the view that secularisation is occurring.

SECULARISATION

Having examined arguments about the role of religion and how far it encourages or inhibits social change, we now look at arguments and evidence about the extent to which religion has declined.

Secularisation refers to the decline in the importance of religion. There is much disagreement among sociologists about whether or how far religion has declined.

In this Topic we shall:

- Consider the arguments and evidence put forward by sociologists who support the theory of secularisation.
- Look at how secularisation theory has been applied to both the UK and the USA.

Secularisation in Britain

Based on evidence from the 1851 Census of Religious Worship, Crockett (1998) estimates that in that year, 40% or more of the adult population of Britain attended church on Sundays. This is a much higher figure than today and it is certainly the case that there have been some major changes in religion in the UK since then. For example:

- A decline in the proportion of the population going to church or belonging to one.
- An increase in the average age of churchgoers.
- Fewer baptisms and church weddings.
- A decline in the numbers holding traditional Christian beliefs.
- Greater diversity, including more non-Christian religions.

Sociologists have put forward different explanations of these trends and reached different conclusions about whether, and how far, religion is declining.

In 1966, Bryan Wilson argued that Western societies had been undergoing a long-term process of secularisation. He defined secularisation as 'the process whereby religious beliefs, practices and institutions lose social significance'. For example, church attendance in England and Wales had fallen from 40% of the population in the mid-19th century to 10-15% by the 1960s. Church weddings, baptisms and Sunday school attendance had also declined, leading Wilson to conclude that Britain had become a secular society.

Church attendance today

The trends Wilson identified have continued. By 2015, about 5% of the adult population attended church on Sundays. Churchgoing in Britain has therefore more than halved since Wilson's research in the 1960s. For example, Sunday attendance in the Church of England fell from 1.6 million in 1960, to under 0.8 million in 2013. Sunday school attendance has declined further and only a tiny proportion of children now attend.

The English Church Census (2006) shows that attendances at large organisations such as the Church of England and the Catholic Church have declined more than small organisations, some of which are remaining stable or have grown. However, the growth of these small organisations has not made up for the decline of large ones, so the overall trend is still one of decline.

Similarly, while church *weddings and baptisms* remain more popular than attendance at Sunday services, here too the trend is downwards. In 1971, 60% of weddings were in church, but by 2012 the proportion was only 30%. The number of weddings in Catholic churches fell by three quarters between 1965 and 2011.

Similarly, infant baptisms have fallen steadily. The number of Catholic baptisms today is under half those in 1964.

'Bogus baptisms' While infant baptisms have declined, those of older children have increased in recent years. Research indicates that this is because many faith schools, which tend to be higher-performing schools, will only take baptised children. Baptism thus becomes an entry ticket to a good school rather than a sign of Christian commitment.

Religious affiliation today

A person's religious affiliation refers to their membership of or identification with a religion. The evidence indicates a continuing decline in the number of people who are affiliated to a religion. For example, as Figure 1.1 shows, between 1983 and 2014 the percentage of adults with no religion rose from around a third to around a half (British Social Attitudes Survey, 2015).

In the same period, those identifying as Christian fell by a third. The fall was sharpest for Anglicans (Church of England members), whose numbers more than halved.

The number of Catholics increased slightly, due to East European immigration. Those belonging to a non-Christian religion (mainly Islam) also increased, partly due to immigration and higher birth rates.

'Other Christians' include denominations such as Methodists and Baptists. This category has remained static since 1983 at 17% of the population. But while over four fifths of them identified with a specific denomination in 1983, only a fifth are now attached to a group.

Religious belief today

Evidence about religious beliefs from 80 years of survey research shows that religious belief is declining along with the decline in church attendance and membership.

For example, surveys show a significant decline in belief in a personal god, in Jesus as the son of God and in Christian teachings about the afterlife and the Bible.

Religious institutions today

Not only have religious belief and practice declined; so too has the influence of religion as a social institution. Although the church has some influence on public life, (for example, 26 Church of England bishops sit in the House of Lords, where they have some influence on lawmaking), this has declined significantly since the 19th century. In particular, the state has taken over many of the functions that the church used to perform. Thus, whereas religion once pervaded every aspect of life, it has increasingly been confined to the private sphere of the individual and the family.

For example, until the mid-19th century, the churches provided education, but since then it has been provided mainly by the state. Although there are still 'faith schools', these are mainly state-funded and must conform to the state's regulations. Similarly, although there is a legal requirement for schools to provide a daily act of collective worship of a 'broadly Christian character', a BBC survey in 2005 found that over half the secondary schools in Wales failed to comply with this.

The clergy One measure of the institutional weakness of the churches is the number of clergy. During the 20th century, this fell from 45,000 to 34,000. Had it kept pace with population growth, the clergy would now number over 80,000. The number of Catholic priests fell by a third between 1965 and 2011.

The clergy are also an ageing workforce. Only 12% of Anglican clergy are under 40, while new ordinations of Catholic priests are now below one tenth of their 1965 figure. As a result, the churches have reached a tipping

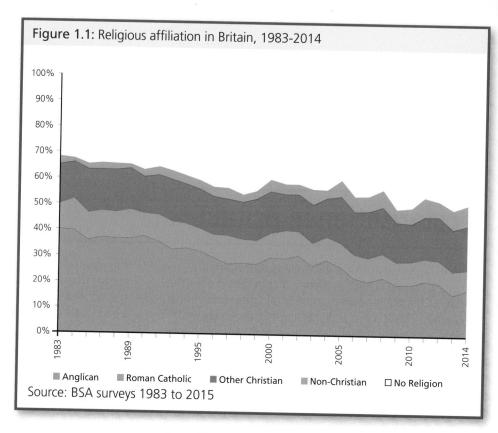

Figure 1.1: Religious affiliation in Britain, 1983-2014

Legend: ■ Anglican ■ Roman Catholic ■ Other Christian ■ Non-Christian □ No Religion

Source: BSA surveys 1983 to 2015

point, with a sharp decline in the number of clergy to be expected in the near future. As Linda Woodhead (2014) concludes:

> 'To put it bluntly, there are no longer enough troupers left to keep the show on the road.'

A lack of clergy on the ground in local communities means that the day-to-day influence of the churches is reduced.

Summing up the overall trend, Steve Bruce (2002) agrees with Wilson that all the evidence on secularisation has now been pointing in the same direction for many years. He concludes that:

> 'Whether we measure church membership, church attendance, the popularity of religious ceremonies to mark rites of passage (such as weddings and baptisms), or religious belief, we find that there is a steady and unremitting decline.'

Bruce predicts that if current trends continue, the Methodist Church will fold around 2030 and by then the Church of England will be merely a small voluntary organisation with a large amount of heritage property.

Evaluation

Suggest one fact or event that might contradict the conclusion that religion is declining in Britain today.

Explanations of secularisation

Sociologists have developed a variety of theories and concepts to explain the process of secularisation. A common theme is modernisation, involving the decline of tradition and its replacement with rational and scientific ways of thinking that tend to undermine religion. Secularisation theory also emphasises the effect of social change on religion. For example, industrialisation leads to the break up of small communities that were held together by common religious beliefs.

A major theme in explanations of secularisation is the growth of social and religious diversity. Not only are people increasingly diverse in terms of their occupational and cultural backgrounds but religious institutions are much more varied. Secularisation theorists argue that the growth of diversity has undermined both the authority of religious institutions and the credibility of religious beliefs. As a result of these changes religious practice, such as churchgoing, has also declined.

Max Weber: rationalisation

In relation to secularisation, rationalisation refers to the process by which rational ways of thinking and acting come to replace religious ones. Many sociologists have argued that Western society has undergone a process of rationalisation in the last few centuries. The most important of these is Max Weber (1905). He argued that the Protestant Reformation begun by Martin Luther in the 16th century started a process of rationalisation of life in the West. This process undermined the religious worldview of the Middle Ages and replaced it with the rational scientific outlook found in modern society.

For Weber, the medieval Catholic worldview that dominated Europe saw the world as an 'enchanted (or magical) garden'. God and other spiritual beings and forces, such as angels, the devil and so on, were believed to be present and active in this world, changing the course of events through their supernatural powers and miraculous interventions in it. Humans could try to influence these beings and forces by magical means such as prayers and spells, fasts and pilgrimages, the wearing of charms etc, in order to ensure a good harvest, protect against disease and so on.

Disenchantment

However, the Protestant Reformation brought a new worldview. Instead of the interventionist God of medieval Catholicism, Protestantism saw God as transcendent – as existing above and beyond, or outside, this world. Although God had created the world, he did not intervene in it, but instead left it to run according to its own laws of nature. Like a watchmaker, he had made the world and set it in motion, but thereafter it ran according to its own principles and its creator played no further part.

This meant that events were no longer to be explained as the work of unpredictable supernatural beings, but as the predictable workings of natural forces. All that was needed to understand them was rationality – the power of reason. Using reason and science, humans could discover the laws of nature, understand and predict how the world works and control it through technology. In other words, there was no longer a need for religious explanations of the world, since the world was no longer an enchanted garden.

In Weber's view, therefore, the Protestant Reformation begins the 'disenchantment' of the world – it squeezes out magical and religious ways of thinking and starts off the rationalisation process that leads to the dominance of the rational mode of thought. This enables science to thrive and provide the basis for technological advances that give humans more and more power to control nature. In turn, this further undermines the religious worldview.

A technological worldview

Following Weber, Bruce (2011) argues that the growth of a *technological worldview* has largely replaced religious or supernatural explanations of why things happen. For example, when a plane crashes with the loss of many lives, we are unlikely to regard it as the work of evil spirits or God's punishment of the wicked. Instead, we look for scientific and technological explanations.

A technological worldview thus leaves little room for religious explanations in everyday life, which only survive in areas where technology is least effective – for example, we may pray for help if we are suffering from an illness for which scientific medicine has no cure.

Bruce concludes that although scientific explanations do not challenge religion directly, they have greatly reduced the scope for religious explanations. Scientific knowledge does not in itself make people into atheists, but the worldview it encourages results in people taking religion less seriously.

Structural differentiation

Talcott Parsons (1951) defines structural differentiation as a process of specialisation that occurs with the development of industrial society. Separate, specialised institutions develop to carry out functions that were previously performed by a single institution. Parsons sees this as having happened to religion – it dominated pre-industrial society, but with industrialisation it has become a smaller and more specialised institution.

Disengagement According to Parsons, structural differentiation leads to the *disengagement* of religion. Its functions are transferred to other institutions such as the state and it becomes disconnected from wider society. For example, the church loses the influence it once had on education, social welfare and the law.

Privatisation Bruce agrees that religion has become separated from wider society and lost many of its former functions. It has become *privatised* – confined to the private sphere of the home and family. Religious beliefs are now largely a matter of personal choice and religious institutions have lost much of their influence on wider society. As a result, traditional rituals and symbols have lost meaning.

Even where religion continues to perform functions such as education or social welfare, it must conform to the requirements of the secular state. For example, teachers in faith schools must hold qualifications that are recognised by the state. At the same time, church and state tend to become separated in modern society. Modern states increasingly accept that religion is a personal choice and therefore that the state should not be identified with one particular faith.

Social and cultural diversity

Decline of community The move from pre-industrial to industrial society brings about the decline of community and this contributes to the decline of religion. Wilson argues that in pre-industrial communities, shared values were expressed through collective religious rituals that integrated individuals and regulated their behaviour. However, when religion lost its basis in stable local communities, it lost its vitality and its hold over individuals.

Industrialisation Similarly, Bruce sees industrialisation as undermining the consensus of religious beliefs that hold small rural communities together. Small close-knit rural communities give way to large loose-knit urban communities with diverse beliefs and values. Social and geographical mobility not only breaks up communities but brings people together from many different backgrounds, creating even more diversity.

Diversity of occupations, cultures and lifestyles undermines religion. Even where people continue to hold religious beliefs, they cannot avoid knowing that many of those around them hold very different views. Bruce argues that the plausibility (believability) of beliefs is undermined by alternatives. It is also undermined by individualism because the plausibility of religion depends on the existence of a practising community of believers. In the absence of a practising religious community that functions on a day-to-day basis, both religious belief and practice tend to decline.

Criticisms

The view that the decline of community causes the decline of religion has been criticised. Aldridge points out that a community does not have to be in a particular area:

- Religion can be a source of identity on a worldwide scale. This is true of Jewish, Hindu and Muslim communities, for example.
- Some religious communities are *imagined communities* that interact through the use of global media.
- Pentecostal and other religious groups often flourish in 'impersonal' urban areas.

Religious diversity

According to Berger (1969), another cause of secularisation is the trend towards religious diversity where instead of there being only one religious organisation and only one interpretation of the faith, there are many.

The sacred canopy In the Middle Ages, the Catholic Church held an absolute monopoly – it had no competition. As a result, everyone lived under a single *sacred canopy* or set of beliefs shared by all. This gave these beliefs greater plausibility because they had no challengers and the Church's version of the truth was unquestioned.

This all changed with the Protestant Reformation, when Protestant churches and sects broke away from the Catholic Church in the 16th century. Since the Reformation, the number and variety of religious organisations has continued to grow, each with a different version of the truth. With the arrival of this religious diversity, no church can now claim an unchallenged monopoly of the truth.

Society is thus no longer unified under the single sacred canopy provided by one church. Instead, religious diversity creates a *plurality of life worlds*, where people's perceptions of the world vary and where there are different interpretations of the truth.

Plausibility structure Berger argues that this creates a crisis of credibility for religion. Diversity undermines religion's 'plausibility structure' – the reasons why people find it believable. When there are alternative versions of religion to choose between, people are likely to question all of them and this erodes the absolute certainties of traditional religion. Religious beliefs become relative rather than absolute – what is true or false becomes simply a personal point of view, and this creates the possibility of opting out of religion altogether.

Bruce sees the trend towards religious diversity as the most important cause of secularisation. As he puts it:

'It is difficult to live in a world that treats as equally valid a large number of incompatible beliefs, without coming to suppose that there is no one truth.'

Activity	Media
Secularisation	
	...go to www.sociology.uk.net

Cultural defence and transition

Bruce identifies two counter-trends that seem to go against secularisation theory. Both are associated with higher than average levels of religious participation.

- **Cultural defence** is where religion provides a focal point for the defence of national, ethnic, local or group identity in a struggle against an external force such as a hostile foreign power. Examples include the popularity of Catholicism in Poland before the fall of communism and the resurgence of Islam before the revolution in Iran in 1979 (see Topic 5).
- **Cultural transition** is where religion provides support and a sense of community for ethnic groups such as migrants to a different country and culture. Herberg describes this in his study of religion and immigration to the USA. Religion has performed similar functions for Irish, African Caribbean, Muslim, Hindu and other migrants to the UK.

However, Bruce argues that religion survives in such situations only because it is a focus for group identity. Thus these examples do not disprove secularisation, but show that religion is most likely to survive where it performs functions other than relating individuals to the supernatural.

Evidence supports Bruce's conclusion. For example, churchgoing declined in Poland after the fall of communism and there is evidence that religion loses importance for migrants once they are integrated into society.

> **Application**
>
> Suggest three types of support that a religious community might be likely to give to recent immigrants.

Criticisms

Berger (1999) has changed his views and now argues that diversity and choice actually stimulate interest and participation in religion. For example, the growth of evangelicalism in Latin America and the New Christian Right in the USA point to the continuing vitality of religion, not its decline.

Beckford (2003) agrees with the idea that religious diversity will lead some to question or even abandon their religious beliefs, but this is not inevitable. Opposing views can have the effect of strengthening a religious group's commitment to its existing beliefs rather than undermining them.

Secularisation in America

In 1962, Wilson found that 45% of Americans attended church on Sundays. However, he argued that churchgoing in America was more an expression of the 'American way of life' than of deeply held religious beliefs. Wilson claimed that America was a secular society, not because people had abandoned the churches, but because religion there had become superficial.

Bruce (2002; 2011) shares Wilson's view. He uses three sources of evidence to support his claim that America is becoming increasingly secular: declining church attendance; 'secularisation from within' and a trend towards religious diversity and relativism.

Declining church attendance

Opinion poll research asking people about church attendance suggests that it has been stable at about 40% of the population since 1940. However, Kirk Hadaway (1993), working with a team of researchers employed by major churches, found that this figure did not match the churches' own attendance statistics. If 40% of Americans were going to church, the churches would be full – but they were not.

To investigate their suspicion that opinion polls exaggerate attendance rates, Hadaway et al (1993) studied church

attendance in Ashtabula County, Ohio. To estimate attendance, they carried out head counts at services. Then in interviews, they asked people if they attended church. They found that the level of attendance claimed by the interviewees was 83% higher than the researchers' estimates of church attendance in the county.

There is evidence that this tendency to exaggerate churchgoing is a recent development. Until the 1970s, the findings of opinion polls matched the churches' own estimates, but since then the 'attendance gap' has widened. For example, a study of attendance at Catholic mass in San Francisco found that in 1972, opinion polls exaggerated attendance by 47% but by 1996, the exaggeration had doubled to 101%.

Thus Bruce concludes that a stable rate of self-reported attendance of about 40% has masked a decline in actual attendance in the United States. The widening gap may be due to the fact that it is still seen as socially desirable or normative to go to church, so people who have stopped going will still say they attend if asked in a survey.

Secularisation from within

Bruce argues that the way American religion has adjusted to the modern world amounts to *secularisation from within*. The emphasis on traditional Christian beliefs and glorifying God has declined and religion in America has become 'psychologised' or turned into a form of therapy. This change has enabled it to fit in with a secular society. In short, American religion has remained popular by becoming less religious.

The purpose of religion has changed from seeking salvation in heaven to seeking personal improvement in this world. This decline in commitment to traditional beliefs can be seen in people's attitudes and lifestyles. Churchgoers are now much less strict than previously in their adherence to traditional religious morality, as Table 1A shows.

Table 1A	Moral attitudes of young American Evangelicals, 1951 and 1982	
% agreeing that the following are always morally wrong		
	1951	1982
Playing cards	77	0
Social dancing	91	0
Going to the movies	46	0
Smoking cigarettes	93	51
Drinking alcohol	98	17
Heavy petting	81*	45
Premarital sexual intercourse	94*	89

* 1961 figures

Adapted from Hunter (1987)

Religious diversity

The growth of religious diversity has also contributed to secularisation from within. Churchgoers are becoming less dogmatic in their views.

Bruce identifies a trend towards *practical relativism* among American Christians, involving acceptance of the view that others are entitled to hold beliefs that are different to one's own. This is shown in Lynd and Lynd's (1929) study which found in 1924 that 94% of churchgoing young people agreed with the statement, 'Christianity is the one true religion and all people should be converted to it'. However, by 1977 only 41% agreed.

The counterpart to practical relativism is *the erosion of absolutism* – that is, we now live in a society where many people hold views that are completely different to ours, which undermines our assumption that our own views are absolutely true.

Activity	Webquest
'U.S. public becoming less religious'	
	...go to www.sociology.uk.net

Criticisms of secularisation theory

Secularisation theorists put forward strong arguments and evidence to support their claim that religious beliefs, practices and institutions have declined both in Britain and America. However, secularisation theory has been criticised in several ways. Its opponents highlight the following points, which we shall examine in detail in the next Topic:

- Religion is not declining but simply changing its form.
- Secularisation theory is one-sided. It focuses on decline and ignores religious revivals and the growth of new religions.
- Evidence of falling church attendance ignores people who believe but don't go to church.
- Religion may have declined in Europe but not globally, so secularisation is not universal.
- The past was not a 'golden age' of faith from which we have declined, and the future will not be an age of atheism.
- Far from causing decline, religious diversity increases participation because it offers choice. There is no overall downward trend. Religious trends point in different directions and people make use of religion in all sorts of different ways.

Topic summary

Secularisation refers to the **decline in the social significance of religion**. Statistics show **church attendance** in the UK falling. The number of **baptisms** and church **weddings** has declined. Meanwhile opinion polls show that religious **belief is declining**.

Reasons include **rationalisation**, social and structural **differentiation**, social and religious **diversity**. Counter-trends are **cultural transition** and **defence**; for example where religion may be a focal point for preserving an ethnic minority's culture.

Secularisation theorists argue that religion is also **declining in America**. Although church attendance is comparatively high, nevertheless it is declining. American religion is also experiencing **secularisation from within**; becoming less strict and having to accept religious diversity.

EXAMINING SECULARISATION

QuickCheck Questions

Check your answers at www.sociology.uk.net

1 What percentage of the adult population of Britain attended church on Sundays in 1851?

2 What proportion of weddings now takes place in church: (a) 20%; (b) 30%; (c) 40%; (d) 50%?

3 Why did Weber think that the Protestant Reformation led to the 'disenchantment' of the world?

4 What term is used to describe a society containing a wide variety of religious groups?

5 What does Berger mean by the 'sacred canopy'?

6 Explain what is meant by 'disengagement'.

7 What is meant by the term 'cultural transition'?

8 Explain what is meant by 'secularisation from within'.

Questions to try

Item A

The United States is home to groups such as the New Christian Right that campaign to promote religious values in wider society, and opinion polls show that about 40% of Americans describe themselves as 'regular church attenders'. Although these figures may lack validity, church attendance in the USA is certainly higher than in European societies such as the United Kingdom. As such large numbers of people are churchgoers, it is likely that there are a wide variety of motives for church attendance.

1 Outline and explain two causes of the process of secularisation. (10 marks)

2 Applying material from Item A, analyse two reasons why apparently high church attendance figures may not mean that the United States is a religious society. (10 marks)

The Examiner's Advice

Q1 Spend about 15 minutes on this question. Divide your time fairly equally between the two causes. You don't need a separate introduction; just start on the first cause. Possible causes include rationalisation, structural differentiation, social and cultural diversity, and religious diversity.

Describe each cause in some detail. Explain how each may lead to a reduction in the social importance of religion. Do this by creating a chain of reasoning (see Box 4.1 in chapter 4). For example, industrialisation leads to structural differentiation, whereby institutions such as religion that previously performed many different functions, lose many of these to more specialised institutions such as the education and health care systems. Religion thus becomes separated or disengaged from society and confined to the private sphere of the family, losing much of its influence.

Use concepts and issues such as those above and the world as enchanted garden, disenchantment, scientific explanation, technological change, privatised religion, the state, diversity, decline of community, social and geographical mobility, individualism, secularisation from within, the sacred canopy, the Protestant Reformation, plausibility structure and plurality of life worlds.

Q2 Spend about 15 minutes on this. Divide your time fairly equally between the two reasons. You don't need a separate introduction; just start on your first reason. To answer this question, it's essential that you take two points from the Item and show through a chain of reasoning how each explains how high church attendance may not mean that the USA is a religious society. (It is a very good idea to quote from the Item when doing so).

You could use the idea that the New Christian Right have failed to persuade most Americans to share their views, that people attend church for non-religious motives (e.g. 'Americanness' or therapy) or that real attendance figures are lower than those in polls. For example, head counts at services indicate real attendance is under half that found by polls, showing that Americans today are less religious than they claim.

Use concepts and issues such as secularisation from within, religious diversity, practical relativism, erosion of absolutism, validity of statistics, mainstream values, fundamentalism and psychologised religion, and studies such as Hadaway and Bruce.

TOPIC 4

Sign of renewal? Evangelical churches are growing.

GETTING STARTED

A The following questions help you to consider how important religious and spiritual beliefs and practices are in your life.

1 Do you or your family attend a place of worship? If so, how often?

2 Is religion a purely private matter?

3 Can a person be a good Christian without going to church?

4 Do you believe in life after death; reincarnation; special healing powers; a soul; sin; the devil; angels; heaven; hell; the power of prayer; a spirit world?

5 Do you see yourself as a spiritual person?

6 Do you ever do any of the following: pray; meditate; read religious or spiritual literature?

7 Do you ever consult your horoscope? Do you believe that things like astrology can predict your future?

8 Which of these is most important to you: serving God; loving fellow humans; finding happiness; spiritual growth?

B Discuss your answers with the rest of the class. What do they tell you about the strength of people's religious and spiritual feelings? Do you think your class's answers are likely to be typical of British society generally?

Learning objectives

After studying this Topic, you should:

- Understand the reasons why some sociologists reject the idea of secularisation.

- Be able to analyse alternative interpretations of the nature and position of religion today.

- Understand and be able to evaluate debates about the nature and extent of secularisation.

Critics have challenged secularisation theory's claim that religion is declining:

- They question whether religion is in fact declining rather than simply changing.
- They reject the view that increased diversity and choice undermines religion's plausibility and claim that it encourages greater involvement in religion.
- They argue that religion is not declining on a global scale, but only in Europe.

In this Topic, we examine two main alternatives to secularisation theory:

- **Theories of late modernity and postmodernity** – these argue that religion is not declining but merely changing as society develops.
- **Religious market theory** – the view that secularisation is only one stage of a constant cycle of secularisation, revival and renewal.

New forms of religion

Some sociologists reject the secularisation thesis that religion is undergoing an inevitable decline in modern Western society. Instead they argue that, while some aspects of traditional religion are in decline, new forms are emerging, often as a result of changes in wider society such as greater individualism, choice and consumerism.

From obligation to consumption

Grace Davie (2013) argues that in today's late modern society, we are seeing a major change in religion, away from obligation and towards consumption or choice. In the past, churches such as the Church of England and the Catholic Church could 'oblige people to go to church, to believe certain things and to behave in certain ways.'

This is no longer the case: religion is no longer inherited or imposed, but a matter of personal choice. As Davie puts it,

> 'I go to church because I want to. I will continue my attachment so long as it provides what I want, but I have no obligation either to attend in the first place or to continue if I don't want to.'

For example, in England and France, infant baptism was once seen as an obligatory rite of passage, but now only a minority of babies are baptised. By contrast, there has been an increase in the number of adults making an individual choice to be baptised.

Believing without belonging

Davie argues that religion is not declining but simply taking a different, more *privatised* form. People are increasingly reluctant to belong to organisations, whether these are churches, political parties or trade unions. But despite this, people still hold religious beliefs – a situation that Davie calls *believing without belonging*.

Vicarious religion: the Spiritual Health Service

Davie also notes a trend towards 'vicarious religion'. By this, she means religion practised by an active minority (the professional clergy and regular churchgoers) on behalf of the great majority, who thus experience religion at second hand. This pattern is typical of Britain and Northern Europe where, despite low levels of attendance, many people still identify with the churches.

Davie argues that in Europe, the major national churches are seen as public utilities, or a sort of 'Spiritual Health Service' that, like the NHS, is there for everyone to use whenever they need to. This includes using the churches for rites of passage such as baptisms, weddings and funerals, as well as for major national occasions, like the public mourning over the death of Princess Diana in 1997 or tragedies such as the massacre of 93 people in Norway by the neo-Nazi Anders Breivik in 2011.

Davie compares vicarious religion to the tip of an iceberg and sees it as evidence of believing without belonging. Beneath the surface of what appears to be only a small commitment (very few attend church regularly) lies a much wider commitment. Most people may not normally go to church or pray, but they remain attached to the church as an institution that provides ritual and support when needed and they continue to share at some level its beliefs.

According to Davie, secularisation theory assumes that modernisation affects every society in the same way, causing the decline of religion. Davie questions this assumption. Instead of a single version of modern society, she argues there are *multiple modernities*. For example, Britain and America are both modern societies, but with very different patterns of religion, especially in relation to church attendance – high in America, low in Britain, but accompanied by believing without belonging.

Neither believing nor belonging

Voas and Crockett (2005) do not accept Davie's claim that there is more believing than belonging. Evidence from 5,750 respondents shows that both church attendance *and* belief in God are declining together. If Davie were right, we would expect to see higher levels of belief.

Bruce (2011) adds that if people are not willing to invest time in going to church, this just reflects the declining strength of their beliefs. When people no longer believe, they no longer wish to belong, and so their involvement in religion diminishes.

Census results show that 72% of people identified themselves as Christian, which supports the 'believing without belonging' view. However, Abby Day (2007) found that very few of the 'Christians' she interviewed mentioned God or Christianity. Their reason for describing themselves as Christian was not religious, but simply a way of saying they belonged to a 'White English' ethnic group. As Day puts it, they 'believe *in* belonging'. Describing themselves as 'Christian' was actually a *non-religious* marker of their ethnic or national identity.

Spiritual shopping

Danièle Hervieu-Léger (2000; 2006) continues the theme of personal choice and the decline of obligation. She agrees that there has been a dramatic decline in institutional religion in Europe, with fewer and fewer people attending church in most countries.

This is partly because of what she calls *cultural amnesia*, or a loss of collective memory. For centuries, children used to be taught religion in the extended family and parish church. Nowadays, however, we have largely lost the religion that used to be handed down from generation to generation, because few parents now teach their children about religion. Instead, parents today let children decide for themselves what to believe.

At the same time, the trend towards greater social equality has undermined the traditional power of the Church to impose religion on people from above. As a result, young people no longer have a fixed religious identity imposed on them through socialisation and they are ignorant of traditional religion.

However, while traditional institutional religion has declined, religion itself has not disappeared. Instead, individual consumerism has replaced collective tradition. People today now feel they have a choice as consumers of religion – they have become *spiritual shoppers*. Religion is now individualised – we now develop our own 'do-it-yourself' beliefs that give meaning to our lives and fit in with our interests and aspirations.

Religion has thus become a personal spiritual journey in which we choose the elements we want to explore and the groups we wish to join. As a result, Hervieu-Léger argues, two new religious types are emerging – *pilgrims* and *converts*:

- **Pilgrims** are like those in the holistic milieu in the Kendal Project (see below). They follow an individual path in a search for self-discovery, for example exploring New Age spirituality by joining groups, or through individual 'therapy'. The demand is created by today's emphasis on personal development.
- **Converts** join religious groups that offer a strong sense of belonging, usually based on a shared ethnic background or religious doctrine. Such groups re-create a sense of community in a society that has lost many of its religious traditions. As in the Kendal Project, these include evangelical movements and also the churches of ethnic minorities.

As a result of these trends, religion no longer acts as the source of collective identity that it once did. However, Hervieu-Léger notes that religion does continue to have some influence on society's values.

For example, the values of equality and human rights have their roots in religion, she argues. Such values can be a source of shared cultural identity and social solidarity, even for those who are not actively involved in religion.

> ### Application
> Suggest two other values, apart from equality and human rights, that are held by non-religious people but that could be said to have their roots in religion.

Hervieu-Léger's views can be related to the idea of *late modernity*. This is the notion that in recent decades some of the trends within modern society have begun to accelerate, such as the decline of tradition and increasing individualism. This explains the weakening of traditional institutions such as the church, as well as the growing importance of individual choice in matters of religion.

Postmodern religion

David Lyon (2000) agrees with Davie that believing without belonging is increasingly popular. He argues that traditional religion is giving way to a variety of new religious forms that demonstrate its continuing vigour.

As a postmodernist, he explains this in terms of a shift in recent decades from modern to postmodern society. In Lyon's view, postmodern society has a number of features that are changing the nature of religion. These include globalisation, the increased importance of the media and communications, and the growth of consumerism.

Globalisation, the media and religion

Globalisation refers to the growing interconnectedness of societies, which has led to greatly increased movements of ideas and beliefs across national boundaries.

This is due to the central role played in postmodern society by the media and information technology, which saturate us with images and messages from around the globe, compressing time and space to give us instantaneous access to the ideas and beliefs of previously remote places and religions.

Religious ideas have become 'disembedded' – the media lift them out of physical churches and move them to a different place and time.

For example, the 'electronic church' and televangelism disembed religion from real, local churches and relocate it on the Internet, allowing believers to express their faith without physically attending church – an example of how the boundaries between different areas of social life become blurred in postmodern society.

As a result, religion becomes de-institutionalised – detached from its place in religious institutions, floating in cyber-space. Removed from their original location in the church, religious ideas become a cultural resource that individuals can adapt for their own purposes.

Online religion and religion online

The internet thus creates a range of opportunities for religious organisations and individuals to exploit. Helland (2000) distinguishes between two kinds of internet activity, which he calls religion online and online religion.

Religion online is a form of top-down communication where a religious organisation uses the internet to address members and potential converts. There is no feedback or dialogue between the parties.

This is an electronic version of the traditional, hierarchical communication of churches to their members, communicating only the officially approved ideas.

Online religion is a form of 'cyber-religion' that may have no existence outside the internet. It is a 'many-to-many' form of communication that allows individuals to create non-hierarchical relationships and a sense of community where they can visit virtual worship or meditation spaces, explore shared spiritual interests and provide mutual support.

For example, the Pagans studied by Cowan (2005) gained a sense of self-worth from feeling that they belonged to a global network.

However, while postmodernists might see online religion as a radical new alternative that may be replacing religion, evidence from Hoover et al (2004) shows that for most users, it is just a supplement to their church-based activities rather than a substitute for them.

▲ Group meditation: a New Age route to self-discovery?

Religious consumerism

Postmodern society also involves the growth of consumerism, and especially the idea that we now construct our identities through what we choose to consume.

As Hervieu-Léger emphasises, this is also true of religion, where we act as 'spiritual shoppers', choosing religious beliefs and practices to meet our individual needs, from the vast range available in the religious marketplace.

We no longer have to sign up to any specific religious tradition; instead, we can pick and mix elements of different faiths to suit our tastes and make them part of our identity – until something more fashionable or attractive comes along. Box 1.2 has an example of an individualised religion.

Similarly, in Lyon's view, religion has relocated to the *sphere of consumption*. While people may have ceased to belong to religious organisations, they have not abandoned religion. Instead they have become 'religious consumers', making conscious choices about which elements of religion they find useful.

For example, the American Christian fundamentalists in Nancy Ammerman's (1987) study made use of a number of churches without giving strong loyalty to any of them. One family attended services at a Methodist church and bereavement counselling at a Baptist church, while taking their children to another church for day care.

One effect of having a great variety of religious products to choose from is a loss of faith in 'meta-narratives' – theories or worldviews that claim to have the absolute, authoritative truth. These include the traditional religions.

People now have access to a wide range of different and contradictory religious beliefs. As Berger notes, this weakens traditional religions that claim a monopoly of the truth and that try to oblige people to believe them. This is because exposure to many competing versions of the truth makes people sceptical that any of them is really or wholly true. Thus previously dominant religious institutions such as traditional mainstream churches lose their authority and decline.

However, postmodernists such as Lyon argue that the decline of traditional churches does not spell the end of religion. In their place, he argues, many new religious movements are now springing up that the religious consumer can 'sample' and from which he or she can construct their own personal belief system.

In this view, religion and spirituality are not disappearing; they are simply evolving, taking on new forms that fit the consumerist nature of postmodern society.

Self-religions and the New Age

Many of the new forms of religion or spirituality that Lyon refers to are New Age beliefs and practices. New Age spirituality rejects the idea of obligation and obedience to external authority found in traditional religions. Instead it emphasises the idea of life as a journey of discovery, personal development, autonomy and connecting with one's 'inner self'.

The key idea linking all these features is individualism: the notion that every individual is free to decide what is true for him or her, for example by engaging in spiritual shopping, picking and mixing ideas found online and so on. For this reason, New Age beliefs and practices have been called 'self-spirituality' or 'self-religion'. (For more about the growth of the New Age, see Topic 6.)

Re-enchantment of the world

Lyon criticises secularisation theory for assuming that religion is declining and being replaced by a rational, scientific worldview. Contrary to Weber's prediction of increasing rationalisation and disenchantment of the world, Lyon argues that we are now in a period of *re-enchantment*, with the growth of unconventional beliefs, practices and spirituality.

Although traditional forms of religion have declined, especially in Europe, Lyon points to the growing vitality of non-traditional religion in the West and its resurgence elsewhere in the world.

A spiritual revolution?

Some sociologists argue that a 'spiritual revolution' is taking place today, in which traditional Christianity is giving way to 'holistic spirituality' or New Age spiritual beliefs and practices that emphasise personal development and subjective experience.

Increased interest in spirituality can be seen in the growth of a 'spiritual market', with an explosion in the number of books about self-help and spirituality, and the many practitioners who offer consultations, courses and 'therapies', ranging from meditation to crystal healing. Table 1B identifies the key differences between religion and spirituality.

Table 1B	Contrasts between religion and spirituality	
Religion		**Spirituality**
Life as duty		Life as discovery
Self-sacrifice		Personal development
Deference		Autonomy
Conforming with external authority		Connecting with your inner self
Family life: traditional values and discipline		Family life: emotional bonds and self-expression
Employment: service to an organisation		Employment: professional growth
Future of religion: out of step and losing ground		Future of spirituality: growing and gaining ground

Adapted from Heelas and Woodhead (2005)

In their study of Kendal in Cumbria, Paul Heelas and Linda Woodhead (2005) investigate whether traditional religion has declined and, if so, how far the growth of spirituality is compensating for this. They distinguish between two groups:

- **The congregational domain** of traditional and evangelical Christianity.
- **The holistic milieu** of spirituality and the New Age.

They found that in 2000, in a typical week, 7.9% of the population attended church and 1.6% took part in the activities of the holistic milieu.

However, within the congregational domain, the traditional churches were losing support, while evangelical churches were holding their own and faring relatively well. Although fewer were involved in the holistic milieu, it was growing. Heelas and Woodhead offer an explanation for these trends:

1. New Age spirituality has grown because of a massive *subjective turn* in today's culture. This involves a shift away from the idea of doing your duty and obeying external authority, to exploring your inner self by following a spiritual path.

2. As a result traditional religions, which demand duty and obedience, are declining. As Heelas and Woodhead put it: *'Religion that tells you what to believe and how to behave is out of tune with a culture which believes it is up to us to seek out answers for ourselves.'*

3. Evangelical churches are more successful than the traditional churches. They both demand discipline and duty, but the evangelicals also emphasise the importance of spiritual healing and personal growth through the experience of being 'born again'.

In the spiritual marketplace, therefore, the winners are those who appeal to personal experience as the only genuine source of meaning and fulfilment, rather than the received teachings and commandments of traditional religion.

Activity | **Research**

Mind, body and spirit

...go to www.sociology.uk.net

The weakness of the New Age

Many of the sociologists we have considered so far in this Topic argue that there is no general trend towards secularisation. In their view, religion is not declining but rather changing its nature or form. However, critics challenge this claim. For example, Bruce makes the following points:

The problem of scale Even if New Age forms of individualised religion are springing up, this would have to be on a much larger scale if it is to fill the gap left by the decline of traditional institutionalised religions.

For example, in Kendal in 1851, about 38% of the population attended church every Sunday. To match that today, there would need to be 14,500 churchgoers, instead of the 3,000 who actually attend church. The 270 people involved in the holistic milieu in the town come nowhere near making up the shortfall.

Socialisation of the next generation For a belief system to survive, it must be passed down to the next generation.

However, in Kendal, only 32% of parents who were involved in the New Age said their children shared their spiritual interests. Yet to maintain the same number of believers in the next generation, a typical couple with two children would have to socialise both of them into New Age views.

Furthermore, women in the holistic milieu are more likely to be childless. And in at least three-quarters of marriages with a woman in the holistic milieu, the husband does not share his wife's beliefs – further reducing the likelihood of transmitting them to their children.

Weak commitment Glendinning and Bruce (2006) found that although many people dabbled in meditation, alternative medicine, astrology, horoscopes and so on, serious commitment to New Age beliefs and practices was very rare. Even among those who described themselves as 'spiritual', very few said that such practices were important in their lives. Bruce (2011) notes that 'most people in every demographic category show no interest in alternative spirituality'.

Structural weakness New Age spirituality is itself a cause of secularisation because of its subjective, individualistic nature – it is based on the idea that there is no higher authority than the self. This means that, unlike traditional religion, the New Age:

- lacks an external power (such as the church hierarchy) to extract commitment from New Age participants against their wishes.
- cannot achieve consensus about its beliefs because everyone is free to believe whatever they wish, so it lacks cohesion as a movement.
- cannot evangelise (persuade others of the truth) because it believes that enlightenment comes from within, not from someone else.

These characteristics make the New Age structurally weak and unlikely to fill the gap left by the decline of traditional institutional religion.

Box 1.2	**Sheilaism**

To illustrate the idea of self-religion, Bellah (1996) gives the example of 'Sheilaism'. This is the response from Sheila, a nurse interviewed for his study about personal beliefs:

'I believe in God. I'm not a religious fanatic. I can't remember the last time I went to Church. My faith carried me a long way. It's Sheilaism. Just my own little voice... It's just, try to love yourself and be gentle with yourself. You know, I guess, take care of each other. I think He would want us to take care of each other.'

Bellah comments that if everyone saw religion in the same way as Sheila, there would be 220 million religions in America: one for every individual. He adds that when individuals have their own interpretations, they may hold religious beliefs without ever practising their religion.

Application

What is meant by self-religion and how does it differ from the sort of religion Durkheim describes among Aboriginal clans (see Topic 1)?

Religious market theory

The main advocates of religious market theory (also called rational choice theory) are Stark and Bainbridge (1986). They are very critical of secularisation theory, which they see as *Eurocentric* – it focuses on the decline of religion in Europe and fails to explain its continuing vitality in America and elsewhere.

In their view, it also puts forward a distorted view of the past and future. Stark and Bainbridge argue that there was no 'golden age' of religion in the past, as they claim secularisation theory implies, nor is it realistic to predict a future end-point for religion when everyone will be an atheist.

Instead, Stark and Bainbridge propose religious market theory. This theory is based on two assumptions.

- **People are naturally religious and religion meets human needs**. Therefore the overall demand for religion remains constant, even though the demand for particular *types* of religion may vary.
- **It is human nature to seek rewards and avoid costs**. When people make choices, they weigh up the costs and benefits of the different options available.

Compensators

According to Stark and Bainbridge, religion is attractive because it provides us with *compensators*. When real rewards are scarce or unobtainable, religion compensates by promising supernatural ones. For example, immortality is unobtainable, but religion compensates by promising life after death. Only religion can provide such compensators. Non-religious ideologies such as humanism and communism do not provide credible compensators because they do not promise supernatural rewards.

The cycle of renewal As an alternative to secularisation theory, which sees a one-way process of continuous decline, Stark and Bainbridge put forward the concept of a *cycle* of religious decline, revival and renewal. They describe a perpetual cycle throughout history, with some religions declining and others growing and attracting new members.

For example, when established churches decline, they leave a gap in the market for sects and cults to attract new followers. From this point of view, secularisation theory is one-sided: it sees the decline, but ignores the growth of new religions and religious revivals.

Religious competition According to Stark and Bainbridge, churches operate like companies selling goods in a market. Where secularisation theory sees competition between different religious organisations as undermining religion, religious market theorists take the opposite view. They

argue that competition leads to improvements in the quality of the religious 'goods' on offer. The churches that make their product attractive will succeed in attracting more 'customers'. Meanwhile churches that are not responsive to the needs of their members will decline.

America vs. Europe

The demand for religion increases when there are different sorts to choose from, because consumers can find one that meets their needs. By contrast, where there is a religious monopoly – one church with no competition – it leads to decline. This is because without competition, a church has no incentive to provide people with what they want.

Stark and Bainbridge believe that religion thrives in the USA because there has never been a religious monopoly there. The Constitution guarantees freedom of religion and the separation of church and state, and there has always been a great variety of denominations to choose from. This has encouraged the growth of a healthy religious market where religions grow or decline according to consumer demand.

The situation in Europe is entirely different. Most European countries have been dominated by an official state church which had a religious monopoly, such as the Church of England. Competition has been held back and the lack of choice has led to decline.

Supply not demand Stark and Bainbridge conclude that the main factor influencing the level of religious participation is not the demand for religion, as secularisation theory suggests, but the supply. Participation increases when there is an ample supply of religious groups to choose from, but declines when supply is restricted. Also based on their comparison of America and Europe, Stark and Bainbridge argue that the decline of religion is not a universal trend happening in all societies, as some versions of secularisation theory suggest.

Supply-led religion

A range of studies support Stark and Bainbridge's view that demand for religion is greatly influenced by the quality and variety of religion on offer and the extent to which it responds to people's needs.

For example, Hadden and Shupe (1988) argue that the growth of 'televangelism' in America shows that the level of religious participation is supply-led. When commercial funding of religious broadcasts began in the 1960s, it opened up competition in which evangelical churches thrived. As a commercial enterprise, televangelism responded to consumer demand by preaching a 'prosperity gospel'.

Finke (1997) argues that the lifting of restrictions on Asian immigration into America in the 1960s allowed Asian religions such as Hare Krishna and Transcendental Meditation to set up permanently in the USA, and Asian faiths became another option that proved popular with consumers in the religious marketplace.

Another example is the growth of evangelical megachurches (churches with congregations of 2,000 or more). Most are in the United States but they are also found in South Korea and elsewhere. With such large congregations, they have lavish resources and are able to offer a vast range of activities to meet the diverse needs of their members. Miller (1997) compares them with hypermarkets.

According to Stark (1990), Japan is another society where a free market in religion has stimulated participation. Until 1945, Shintoism was the state religion and other religions were suppressed. However, after World War Two, religion was de-regulated, creating a market in which new religions such as Soka Gakkai (a type of Buddhism) have thrived. Japan's experience contrasts with that of post-war Germany, where religion was closely regulated by the state and as a result declined.

Activity Media

Supply-led religion

...go to www.sociology.uk.net

Criticisms

Religious market theory is the approach adopted by most American sociologists of religion. It highlights the supply side of religion and consumer choice, and can be useful for understanding the growth of new religions. However, there are several criticisms.

1 Bruce (2011) rejects the view that diversity and competition increase the demand for religion. Statistics show that diversity has been accompanied by religious decline in both Europe *and* America.

2 Bruce argues that Stark and Bainbridge misrepresent secularisation theory. The theory does not claim there was a past 'golden age' of religion, or that everyone will become atheists. It simply claims that religion is in long-term decline. Nor does it claim secularisation is universal – just that it applies to Europe and America.

3 Norris and Inglehart (2011) show that high levels of religious participation exist in Catholic countries where the Church has a near monopoly, such as Ireland and Venezuela. By contrast, countries with religious pluralism, such as Holland and Australia, often have low levels of participation. This contradicts Stark and Bainbridge's theory.

4 Beckford criticises religious market theory as unsociological, because it assumes people are 'naturally' religious and fails to explain why they make the choices they do.

An alternative view: secularisation and security

Norris and Inglehart (2011) reject religious market theory on the grounds that it only applies to America and fails to explain the variations in religiosity between different societies. For example, international studies of religion have found no evidence of the link between religious choice and religious participation that Stark and Bainbridge claim exists.

Existential security theory

Norris and Inglehart argue that the reason for variations in religiosity between societies is not different degrees of religious choice, but different degrees of *existential security*. By this, they mean 'the feeling that survival is secure enough that it can be taken for granted'. Religion meets a need for security, and therefore societies where people already feel secure have a low level of demand for religion:

- **Poor societies**, where people face life-threatening risks such as famine, disease and environmental disasters, have high levels of insecurity and thus high levels of religiosity. Poor people who live in rich societies also face greater insecurity and are therefore more religious than rich people in those societies.

- **Rich societies**, where people have a high standard of living and are at less risk, have a greater sense of security and thus lower levels of religiosity.

Thus the demand for religion is not constant, as Stark and Bainbridge claim, but varies both within and between societies. Demand is greatest from low-income groups and societies, because they are less secure. This explains why poor developing countries remain religious, while prosperous Western countries have become more secular.

However, Norris and Inglehart note that global population growth undermines the trend towards secularisation. Rich, secure, secular Western countries have low levels of population growth, whereas poor, insecure, religious countries have high rates. As a result, while rich countries are becoming more secular, the majority of the world is becoming more religious.

Europe vs. America

In Western Europe, the trend is towards increasing secularisation. Norris and Inglehart argue that this is not surprising, because these societies are among the most equal and secure in the world, with well developed welfare states offering comprehensive health care, social services and pensions. This reduces poverty and protects those at the bottom from insecurity.

By comparison with Europe, the United States remains much more religious. Norris and Inglehart argue that this is because America is also the most unequal of the rich societies, with an inadequate welfare safety-net and individualistic 'dog eat dog' values. This creates high levels of poverty and insecurity, which creates a greater need for religion.

Thus, although America is more religious than Europe, this is explained by Norris and Inglehart's general theory of religiosity as the result of insecurity. For example, they point out that although America is religious by the standards of other rich nations, it is less religious than poor ones.

State welfare and religiosity

Norris and Inglehart's argument is supported by Gill and Lundegaarde (2004), who found that the more a country spends on welfare, the lower the level of religious participation. Thus European countries, which spend more than the USA, are also more secular than the USA.

Gill and Lundegaarde note that in the past religion used to provide welfare for the poor, and still does so in poorer countries. However, from the 20th century, the state in the West began to provide welfare and this contributed to religion's decline.

Nevertheless, Gill and Lundegaarde do not expect religion to disappear completely, because although welfare provision meets the need for security, it does not answer 'ultimate' questions about the meaning of life, unlike religion. Thus although the availability of welfare reduces the need for religion, it does not eliminate that need completely.

Box 1.3	The case of Uruguay

Gill and Lundegaarde identify the interesting case of Uruguay, a small Latin American country which has religious diversity but low levels of religious participation. This goes against Stark and Bainbridge's claim that a free market in religion stimulates participation.

Uruguay is culturally very similar to neighbouring countries that have substantially higher rates of religious participation, but the difference is that Uruguay has more generous welfare provision. This supports existential security theory.

Evaluation

Vásquez (2007) accepts that Norris and Inglehart offer a valuable explanation of different levels of religious participation not only in Europe and the USA, but globally. However, he makes two criticisms:

They use only quantitative data about income levels; they don't examine people's own definitions of 'existential security'. Vásquez argues that qualitative research is also needed.

Norris and Inglehart only see religion as a negative response to deprivation. They ignore the positive reasons people have for religious participation and the appeal that some types of religion have for the wealthy.

Topic summary

Some sociologists see religion changing rather than declining, linked to a shift from obligation to consumption.

New forms of religion and spirituality include believing without belonging, vicarious religion, spiritual shopping, online religion and the New Age holistic milieu. Critics argue that these changes are **not enough to offset the decline** in traditional religion.

Religious market theory argues that demand for religion is constant because it meets human needs by providing supernatural **compensators**. Religion thrives where there is **diversity and choice** (USA), but declines where one church has had a **monopoly** (Europe). Rather than secularisation, there is a **perpetual cycle** of decline, renewal and revival.

Existential security theory disagrees, arguing that **religion declines in richer societies** that are more equal with good welfare provision because people are more secure, but is growing in poorer countries where there is greater insecurity.

EXAMINING RELIGION, RENEWAL AND CHOICE

QuickCheck Questions

Check your answers at www.sociology.uk.net

1 Explain what is meant by 'believing without belonging'.
2 Explain what is meant by 'vicarious religion'.
3 According to Hervieu-Léger, how do 'pilgrims' differ from 'converts'?
4 What do Stark and Bainbridge mean by 'compensators'?

5 Suggest two reasons why patterns of religiosity in America and Europe are different.
6 Why do some sociologists criticise secularisation theory as 'Eurocentric'?
7 Identify two criticisms of religious market theory.
8 What is meant by 'existential security'?

Questions to try

Item A

Some sociologists claim that society has entered a new era, that of postmodernity, in which religion and spirituality take on new forms. In postmodern society, tradition loses its influence over people. Consumption and choice become more important, and people are free to choose their identity and their beliefs. Postmodern society is increasingly globalised, and the media and information technology become much more important, for example moving religious ideas and images out of their traditional physical home in churches and making them available around the globe.

However, other sociologists argue that these trends merely promote secularisation.

1 Outline and explain two reasons why figures on attendance at mainstream churches may overstate the degree of secularisation in Britain today.
(10 marks)

2 Applying material from Item A and your knowledge, evaluate the impact of postmodernity on religious and spiritual beliefs and practices.
(20 marks)

The Examiner's Advice

Q1 Spend about 15 minutes on this question. Divide your time fairly equally between the two reasons. You don't need a separate introduction; just start on the first reason. Possible reasons include the existence of believing without belonging, the growth of non-church beliefs and practices such as the New Age, the growth of evangelicalism, or the growth of non-Christian religions as a result of immigration.

Describe each reason in some detail, explaining how each may mean that the degree of secularisation has been overstated. Do this by creating a chain of reasoning (see Box 4.1 in chapter 4).

For example, while attendance rates have fallen, most people still identify themselves as Christians but are content to let religious professionals act on their behalf most of the time, only using them as a 'spiritual health service' at times of need. These include personal rites of passage and national occasions such as Princess Diana's funeral.

Use concepts and issues such as those above and vicarious religion, privatised religion, individualism, cultural defence, cultural assimilation, consumption versus obligation, churches as public utilities, converts and pilgrims, the holistic milieu and the congregational domain.

Q2 Spend about 30 minutes on this. Use the Item to identify some of the key features of postmodernity, such as consumption, choice, identity, globalisation, the media and information technology. You need to link these to particular features of religion and spirituality in today's society. For example, you can examine the shift from obligation to consumption in relation to ideas such as vicarious religion and believing without belonging, the decline of traditional religion and religious socialisation and its replacement by cultural amnesia and individual spiritual shopping, and the disembedding of religion via televangelism. Also consider the rise of New Age pick and mix 'self-spiritualities' in relation to features of postmodern society such as individualism.

Use concepts and issues such as those referred to above plus online religion/religion online, 'neither believing nor belonging', obligation, converts and pilgrims, multiple modernities, institutional religion, meta-narratives, re-enchantment of the world, secularisation and de-secularisation. Use studies such as Davie, Hervieu-Léger, Lyon, Heelas and Woodhead, Bruce, Day, and Voas and Crockett. You can evaluate by considering whether these developments mean religion and spirituality are thriving, or whether they are forms of 'weak religion' and symptoms of secularisation.

A clash of cultures?

GETTING STARTED

For thousands of years, religions have spread around the world from place to place, and they continue to do so today. For example, Christianity began in the Middle East and spread through the Roman Empire, eventually becoming its official religion. Today, Pentecostalism, which began in modern Western societies such as Britain and the USA, has spread to developing countries around the globe.

What might the effects be of the following?

1 Increased contact between religions that have originated in different parts of the world.

2 Increased exposure of members of society to these different religious traditions and ideas.

Give some examples in your answers. These could be from events in the news, from history and/or from your personal knowledge or experience.

Learning objectives

After studying this Topic, you should:

- Understand some of the different ways in which religion interacts with its global context.
- Understand the role of religion in economic development in a globalising world.
- Understand and be able to evaluate explanations of the nature of religious fundamentalism.
- Understand and be able to evaluate explanations of the role of religion in international conflict.

Religious fundamentalism

In a global context, the issue of religious fundamentalism has emerged as a major area of media and political concern in recent decades, notably in relation to international Islamist terrorism. However, the term 'fundamentalist' has also been applied to followers of other religions, including Protestant Christians. In this section, we examine explanations of fundamentalism and its relationship to globalisation and modernity.

The characteristics of fundamentalism

Fundamentalists appeal to tradition and often look back to a supposed golden age in the past. They seek a return to the basics or fundamentals of their faith. But religious fundamentalism is quite different from traditional religion. It arises only where traditional beliefs and values are threatened or challenged by modern society and especially by the impact of an increasingly globalised economy.

The threat to traditional beliefs can come from outside, for example through capitalist globalisation, the penetration of Western culture, or military invasion. Or it can come from within, for example when sections of society adopt new secular ideas, such as liberal attitudes to sexuality and gender.

Sociologists have identified a number of key features of fundamentalism:

An authoritative sacred text For Christian fundamentalists every word of the Bible is literally true, its truths are valid for all eternity, and it contains the answers to all life's important questions, from politics to family life. The text is inerrant (without error) and not open to questioning.

Thus for example, Christian fundamentalism requires belief in the Virgin Birth of Christ, his divinity, his bodily resurrection from the dead and his imminent Second Coming, all of which are described in the Bible. Only those who accept these as historical facts are true Christians. Fundamentalists are intolerant of all other views and refuse to engage in rational argument with them.

However, as Aldridge (2013) notes, no text speaks for itself; it has to be interpreted, so in reality what fundamentalists hold to be true is not the text itself, but their interpretation of its meaning. They interpret the Bible solely as a set of historical facts and prophecies about the future, ignoring other interpretations of it as poetry, symbolism or metaphor.

An 'us and them' mentality Fundamentalists separate themselves from the rest of the world and refuse to compromise with it. As Davie (2013) puts it, they seek to establish islands of certainty against what they see as social and cultural chaos.

Aggressive reaction Fundamentalist movements aim to draw attention to the threat to their beliefs and values, and their reactions are therefore aggressive and intended to shock, intimidate or cause harm. Authoritative leaders such as clergy or elders who interpret the sacred text are important in giving direction to the reactions.

Use of modern technology Although fundamentalists oppose modern culture, which they see as corrupted by secularism, liberalism, materialism, permissiveness and promiscuity, they are keen to use modern technology to achieve their aims – from computers and the internet to televangelism and military weaponry.

Patriarchy Hawley (1994) notes that fundamentalists favour a world in which control over women's sexuality, reproductive powers, and their social and economic roles, is fixed for all time by divine decree.

Prophecy Christian fundamentalists proclaim the relevance of biblical prophecies to contemporary events. They believe that the 'last days' will soon be upon us, when the faithful dead will be resurrected and transported to heaven with the faithful living, before the seven-year rule of the Antichrist and ultimately the final defeat of Satan in the War of Armageddon.

Conspiracy theories Fundamentalists are often attracted to conspiracy theories: the idea that powerful, hidden, evil forces and organisations are in control of human destiny. Many Christian and Islamic fundamentalists hold anti-Semitic conspiracy theories that believe Jews are conspiring to secure world domination.

Fundamentalism and modernity

As Davie (2013) argues, fundamentalism occurs where those who hold traditional orthodox beliefs and values are threatened by modernity and feel the need to defend themselves against it. In this sense, 'fundamentalists are themselves products of modernity, in so far as they are born out of the clash between modernity and traditional cultures'.

Similarly, Giddens (1999) argues that 'fundamentalism' is a product of and reaction to globalisation, which undermines traditional social norms concerning the nuclear family, gender and sexuality (such as the prohibition of abortion, homosexuality and sex outside marriage). In today's 'late modern' society, individuals are constantly faced with choice, uncertainty and risk. The attraction of fundamentalism and its rigid, dogmatic beliefs is the certainty that it promises in an uncertain world. It is a retreat into faith-based answers and away from the risks and uncertainties of a globalising world. Giddens identifies fundamentalist versions of several major religions, including Islam, Christianity and Hinduism.

Cosmopolitanism

Giddens contrasts fundamentalism with cosmopolitanism – a way of thinking that embraces modernity and is in keeping with today's globalising world. Cosmopolitanism is tolerant of the views of others and open to new ideas, constantly reflecting on and modifying beliefs in the light of new information (which Giddens calls 'reflexive' thinking). It requires people to justify their views by the use of rational arguments and evidence rather than by appealing to sacred texts. One's lifestyle is seen as a personal choice rather than something prescribed by an external religious or other authority. Cosmopolitan religion and spirituality emphasises the pursuit of personal meaning and self-improvement rather than submission to authority. This is very similar to Hervieu-Léger's 'pilgrims' who explore New Age spirituality.

Responses to postmodernity

In a similar argument to that of Giddens, Zygmunt Bauman (1992) sees fundamentalism as a response to living in postmodernity. Postmodern society brings freedom of choice, uncertainty and a heightened awareness of risk, undermining the old certainties about how to live that were grounded in tradition. In this situation, while some embrace the new freedom, others are attracted to fundamentalism by its claims of absolute truth and certainty.

Similarly, Manuel Castells (2010) distinguishes between two responses to postmodernity:

- **Resistance identity** – a defensive reaction of those who feel threatened and retreat into fundamentalist communities.
- **Project identity** – the response of those who are forward-looking and engage with social movements such as feminism and environmentalism.

Criticisms

Beckford (2011) criticises Giddens, Bauman and Castells on several grounds:

- They distinguish too sharply between cosmopolitanism and fundamentalism, ignoring 'hybrid' movements.
- They are 'fixated on fundamentalism', ignoring other important developments – including how globalisation is also affecting non-fundamentalist religions such as Catholicism.
- Giddens lumps all types of fundamentalism together, ignoring important differences between them.

- Giddens' description of fundamentalism as a defensive reaction to modernity ignores the fact that reinventing tradition is also a modern, 'reflexive' activity.

Jeff Haynes (1998) argues that we should not focus narrowly on the idea that Islamic fundamentalism is a reaction against globalisation. For example, in the Middle East, conflicts caused by the failure of local elites to deliver on their promises to improve the standard of living are often the fuel that drives fundamentalism.

Monotheism and fundamentalism

Like Giddens, Steve Bruce (2008) sees the main cause of fundamentalism as the perception of religious traditionalists that today's globalising world threatens their beliefs.

However, Bruce regards fundamentalism as being confined to monotheistic religions – that is, those believing in a single almighty God – such as Judaism, Islam and Christianity. Polytheistic religions that believe in the existence of many gods, such as Hinduism, are unlikely to produce fundamentalism.

In Bruce's view, this is because monotheistic religions are based on a notion of God's will as revealed through a single, authoritative sacred text such as the Qur'an or the Bible. This is believed to contain the actual word of God and it lays down specific rules for believers to follow. By contrast, polytheistic religions lack a single all-powerful deity and a single authoritative text, so there is much more scope for different interpretations and none has an over-riding claim to legitimacy or absolute truth. For example, Hinduism has been described as being more like a collection of religions than just one.

Two fundamentalisms

In Bruce's view, while all fundamentalists share the same characteristics such as belief in the literal truth of a sacred text and detestation of modernity, different fundamentalist movements may have different origins. In particular, some are triggered by changes within their own society, while others are a response to changes being thrust upon a society from the outside. Bruce illustrates this distinction with the examples of Christian and Islamic fundamentalisms:

- **In the West**, fundamentalism is most often a reaction to change taking place within a society, especially the trends towards diversity and choice typical of secular late modern society. For example, the New Christian Right in America has developed in opposition to family diversity, sexual 'permissiveness', gender equality and abortion rights, secular education and the privatisation of religion (its removal from public life). Its aim is to reassert 'true' religion and restore it to a public role where it can shape the laws and morals of wider society.
- **In the Third World**, fundamentalism is usually a reaction to changes being thrust upon a society from outside, as

in the case of the Islamic revolution in Iran (see below). It is triggered by modernisation and globalisation, in which 'Western' values are imposed by foreign capitalism or by local elites supported by the West. Here, fundamentalism involves resistance to the state's attempts to sideline it and confine it to the private sphere.

Secular fundamentalism

So far, we have considered fundamentalism to be a particular *religious* response to modernity and globalisation. However, Davie (2013) argues that recent decades have seen the emergence of *secular* forms of fundamentalism. She links this to changes in the nature of modern society. She distinguishes between two phases of modernity.

The first phase gave rise to religious fundamentalism. This phase stretched from the time of the philosophical movement known as the Enlightenment in the late 18th century, to about the 1960s. Enlightenment philosophy held an optimistic secular belief in the certainty of progress based on the power of science and human reason to improve the world. This 'Enlightenment project' dominated European thought and helped to secularise all areas of social life, attacking and undermining religious certainties. Religious fundamentalism is one reaction to this secularisation process.

The second phase is giving rise to secular fundamentalism. Since the 1970s, the optimism of the Enlightenment project has itself come under attack. This is the result of a growing mood of pessimism and uncertainty. This mood is the product of the insecurity caused by changes such as globalisation, concerns about the environment and the collapse of communism in 1989. This has led to a loss of faith in the major secular Enlightenment ideologies such as liberalism and rationalism (in Western Europe) and Marxism (in Eastern Europe) whose claims to truth and belief in progress have been undermined.

As a result, these secular ideologies are themselves struggling for survival, just like traditional religion. As Davie puts it, they are 'past their sell-by date'. And as with religion when it came under attack, some supporters of secular ideologies such as nationalism have also been attracted to fundamentalism. For example, the disintegration of communist Yugoslavia in the early 1990s led to a secular nationalist fundamentalism that justified the ethnic cleansing of territory to create a clear-cut separation between ethnic groups – between 'us and them'.

In Western Europe, perceived religious challenges to liberal secular values have provoked a secular fundamentalist reaction. For example, in 2004 France banned pupils from wearing religious symbols in school, and in 2010 made it illegal for women to wear the veil in public. In 2015, some French local councils controlled by right-wing political parties stopped serving alternatives to pork in their school meals, on the grounds that all pupils must be treated equally and that

religion must be kept out of the secular public sphere. This discriminates against Muslims and Jews who do not eat pork.

Ansell (2000) sees such trends as a form of cultural racism that uses the apparently liberal language of universal equality and social integration, while denying racist aims. In reality, however, it is about preserving cultural identity and 'our' way of life, and it legitimates the exclusion of religious and cultural minorities.

In conclusion, Davie argues that both religious and secular movements can become fundamentalist as a result of the greater uncertainties of life in the late modern or postmodern world, in which reasserting truth and certainty is increasingly attractive. As a result, competing fundamentalisms have become a normal feature of today's society.

Similarly, Hervieu-Léger (2000) sees fundamentalism as a form of 'recreated memories' in late modern societies that have suffered 'cultural amnesia' (see Topic 4) and forgotten their historic religious traditions.

The 'clash of civilisations'

In recent years, religion has been at the centre of a number of global conflicts. These include the 9/11 terrorist attacks by fundamentalist Islamists in the US on 11 September 2001. In the view of American neo-conservative Samuel Huntington (2002; 2004), such conflicts have intensified since the collapse of communism in 1989 and are symptoms of a 'clash of civilisations'. However, for Huntington, the problem is not Islamic fundamentalism, it is Islam itself.

Huntington identifies seven civilisations: Western, Islamic, Latin American, Confucian (China), Japanese, Hindu, and Slavic-Orthodox (Russia and Eastern Europe). Most civilisations are larger than a single nation. Each has a common cultural background and history, and is closely identified with one of the world's great religions.

In today's world, religious differences between civilisations are a major source of conflict. This is because globalisation has made nation-states less significant as a source of identity, creating a gap that religion has filled. At the same time, globalisation increases the contacts between civilisations, increasing the likelihood of conflict.

In Huntington's view, religious differences are creating a set of hostile 'us and them' relationships, with increased competition between civilisations for economic and military power, for example in the Middle East. He sees religious differences as harder to resolve than political ones because they are deeply rooted in culture and history.

Huntington sees history as a struggle of 'progress against barbarism'. He believes the West is under threat, especially from Islam, and urges the West to reassert its identity as a liberal-democratic Christian civilisation.

Criticisms

Jackson (2006) sees Huntington's work as an example of *orientalism* – a western ideology that stereotypes Eastern nations and people (especially Muslims) as untrustworthy, inferior or fanatical 'Others' and serves to justify exploitation and human rights abuses by the West.

Casanova (2005) argues that Huntington ignores important religious divisions within the 'civilisations' he identifies – e.g. between Sunni and Shi'a Islam.

Horrie and Chippindale (2007) see 'the clash of civilisations' as a grossly misleading neo-conservative ideology that portrays the whole of Islam as an enemy. In reality, only a tiny minority of the world's 1.5 billion Muslims are remotely interested in a 'holy war' against the West.

Similarly, Karen Armstrong (2001; 2015) argues that hostility towards the West does not stem from fundamentalist Islam, but is a reaction to Western foreign policy in the Middle East. The West has propped up oppressive regimes and continues to support Israel despite its aggressive treatment of Palestinians.

The real clash of civilisations?

Huntington's work suggests that the Muslim world holds fundamentally different, anti-democratic values from those of the West. However, evidence indicates that this is not the case.

Using data from the *World Values Survey*, Inglehart and Norris (2011) conclude that the issue that divides the West from the Muslim world is not democracy but gender and sexuality. They find that support for democracy is similarly high in both the West and the Muslim world, but there are great differences when it comes to attitudes to divorce, abortion, gender equality and gay rights. While Western attitudes have become more liberal, in the Muslim world they remain traditional. Inglehart and Norris comment that in the last decade, democracy has become the political ideology to gain global appeal, but there is no global agreement about *self-expression values*, such as tolerance of diversity, gender equality and freedom of speech. In their view, 'these divergent values constitute the real clash of civilisations between Muslim societies and the West'.

Cultural defence

As we saw in Topic 3, Bruce (2002) sees one function of religion in today's world as cultural defence. This is where religion serves to unite a community against an external threat. In such situations, religion has special significance for its followers because it symbolises the group or society's collective identity. Defending the community against a threat often gives religion a prominent role in politics.

Two examples of religion as cultural defence from the late 20th century are Poland and Iran. They illustrate how religion can be used in defence of national identity in the face of political domination by an external power. In Poland, the external power was Soviet communism, while in Iran it was Western culture and capitalism. In both cases, therefore, the role of religion has to be understood in a *transnational* context.

Poland

From 1945 to 1989, Poland was under communist rule, imposed from outside by the Soviet Union. During this time, the Catholic Church was suppressed, but for many Poles it continued to embody Polish national identity. The Church served as a popular rallying point for opposition to the Soviet Union and the Polish communist party. In particular, it lent its active support to the Solidarity free trade union movement in the 1980s that did much to bring about the fall of communism. Thereafter, the Church regained

a public role and has had significant influence on Polish politics since.

Iran

Western capitalist powers and oil companies had long had influence in Iran, including involvement in the illegal overthrow of a democratic government in the 1950s to install a pro-Western regime headed by the Shah of Iran. During the 1960s and 70s, his successor embarked on a policy of modernisation and Westernisation. This included banning the veil and replacing the Muslim calendar. Meanwhile, modernisation was widening the gap between rich and poor, while protest was ruthlessly suppressed.

Change was imposed rapidly and from above, causing great suffering. Under these conditions, Islam became the focus for resistance to the Shah's regime, led by clerics such as the Ayatollah Khomeini. The revolution of 1979 brought the creation of the Islamic Republic, in which clerics held state power and were able to impose Islamic Sharia law.

However, Haynes argues that the Iranian revolution was not typical of the Middle East, in that it was led by the religious leaders. In countries such as Saudi Arabia, the religious leadership is closely tied to the local elite, who in turn are tied to Western imperialism. As such, local religious leaders are opposed by local fundamentalists, who regard them as enemies of Islam.

Religion and development

For secularisation theory, modernisation undermines religion. The importance of science and technology in economic development, and the rational worldview on which they depend, are seen as destroying belief in the supernatural. On the other hand, religion may contribute to development, as Weber argued in the case of the Protestant ethic. More recently, sociologists have examined what role religion may play in development in today's globalising world.

God and globalisation in India

Globalisation has brought rapid economic growth and has seen India become a more important player on the world political stage. It has also brought rising prosperity to some – notably India's new middle class. Meera Nanda's (2008) book, *God and Globalization*, examines the role of Hinduism, the religion of 85% of the population, in legitimating both the rise of a new Hindu 'ultra-nationalism' and the prosperity of the Indian middle class.

Hinduism and consumerism

Globalisation has created a huge and prosperous, scientifically educated, urban middle class in India, working in IT, pharmaceuticals and biotechnology sectors closely tied into the global economy. These are precisely the people whom secularisation theory predicts will be the first to abandon religion in favour of a secular worldview.

Yet, as Nanda observes, a vast majority of this class continue to believe in the supernatural. A survey by the Centre for the Study of Developing Societies (2007) found that Indians are becoming more religious. Only 5% said their religiosity had declined in the last five years, while 30% said they had become more religious. The survey also found that 'urban educated Indians are more religious than their rural and illiterate counterparts'. Increased interest in religion has also been reflected in a dramatic growth of religious tourism, such as visits to shrines and temples. Nanda notes that it is becoming fashionable to be religious and to be seen to be so.

Another feature of this middle-class religiosity is that they are attracted to what were once low-status village gods and goddesses worshipped by the poor. This is because these deities are seen as being more responsive to people's needs than the traditional Hindu 'great gods'.

Nanda examines what motivates the sophisticated, urban middle classes to continue to believe in miracles and supernatural beings. She rejects poverty and existential insecurity as an explanation, because they are not poor.

She also rejects the idea that their religiosity is a defensive reaction to modernisation and Westernisation. On the contrary, the Indian middle classes are optimistic about the opportunities that globalisation brings them. Instead, Nanda argues, their increasing religiosity is the result of their ambivalence about their newfound wealth.

This ambivalence stems from a tension between the traditional Hindu belief in renunciation of materialism and worldly desires, and the new prosperity of the middle classes. This is resolved for them by the modern holy men and tele-gurus to whom they turn, who preach the message that desire is not bad, but rather a manifestation of divinity that motivates people to do things. Similarly, they dispense business-friendly versions of Hinduism and take the edge off guilt by teaching that middle-class consumerism can be 'spiritually balanced' by paying for the performance of appropriate and often extravagant rituals – which also serve as a way of displaying one's wealth. Modern versions of Hinduism therefore legitimate the position of the middle class and allow them to adjust to globalised consumer capitalism.

Hindu ultra-nationalism

Nanda (2003) also examines the role of Hinduism in legitimating a triumphalist version of Indian nationalism. For example, the Pew Global Attitude Survey found that 93% of Indians – more than any other country – agreed with the statement that, 'Our people are not perfect, but our culture is superior to others'. Nanda notes that India's success in the global market is increasingly attributed to the superiority of 'Hindu values', a view constantly promoted by the media and politicians, along with the idea that Hinduism is the essence of Indian culture and identity.

In this Hindu ultra-nationalism, the worship of Hindu gods has become the same as worshipping the nation of India, and Hinduism has become a *civil religion* (see Topic 1). However, as Nanda points out, this is creating a widening gulf between Hindus and non-Hindu minorities.

Hinduism has also penetrated public life, so that the supposedly secular state is increasingly influenced by religion. For example, 'Hindu sciences' such as astrology are being taught as an academic subject in universities and being used supposedly to predict natural disasters. Meanwhile, the Ministry of Defence is sponsoring development of weapons with magical powers mentioned in the ancient Hindu texts, and the Health Ministry is investing in development and sale of cow urine (cows being sacred animals) as a cure for ailments from AIDS to TB.

Capitalism in East Asia

In recent decades, 'East Asian tiger economies' such as South Korea, Singapore and Taiwan, have industrialised and become significant players in the global economy. China is now a major global industrial power.

The success of capitalism in East Asia has led some sociologists to argue that religion has played a role similar to the one Calvinism played in the development of capitalism in 16th and 17th century Europe.

For example, Gordon Redding (1990) describes the spirit of capitalism among Chinese entrepreneurs in the tiger economies. He sees their 'post-Confucian' values encouraging hard work, self-discipline, frugality and a commitment to education and self-improvement. (Confucianism is a traditional Chinese belief system.) The effect of this value system is similar to that of the Protestant ethic, in that it leads to economic productivity and the accumulation of capital.

Pentecostalism in Latin America

Similarly, Peter Berger (2003) argues that Pentecostalism in Latin America acts as a 'functional equivalent' to Weber's Protestant ethic. That is, it encourages the development of capitalism today in the same way as Calvinism did in 16th and 17th century Europe. Latin American Pentecostalists embrace a work ethic and lifestyle similar to that of the Calvinists. Like Calvinism, Pentecostalism demands an ascetic (self-denying) way of life that emphasises personal discipline, hard work and abstinence from alcohol. In this way, it encourages its members to prosper and become upwardly mobile. Berger concludes that Pentecostalism has a strong affinity with modern capitalism.

Berger agrees with Weber that an ethic like Protestantism is necessary to promote economic development and raise a society out of poverty. This process can be led by an active minority with an ethic of this-worldly asceticism, such as the Pentecostalists. Thus in Chile and southern Brazil, there is now a growing and prosperous Pentecostalist middle class leading capitalist development.

However, Berger underlines Weber's point that religious ideas alone are not enough to produce economic development – natural resources are also needed. For example, while Pentecostalism has grown in northern Brazil, the region lacks resources and remains backward. By contrast, the south, which is developing rapidly, has both a work ethic and the necessary resources.

Pentecostalism: global and local

In the last five centuries, Christianity has globalised itself by expanding out of Europe, first into South America and then Africa. David Lehmann (2002) distinguishes between two phases in this expansion:

- In the first phase, Christianity accompanied colonisation and was imposed on the indigenous populations by conquest, often forcibly suppressing local religions.
- In the second phase, over the last century or so, it has spread because it gained a popular following from below. For example, by 2015 there were 25 million Pentecostalists in Brazil alone.

Lehmann attributes the success of Pentecostalism as a global religion in part to its ability to incorporate local beliefs. Although it preaches a similar message worldwide, it uses imagery and symbolism drawn from local cultures and beliefs, especially spirit possession cults. Pentecostalists attack such cults as the work of the devil, but their ministers conduct exorcisms to rid people of evil spirits. By doing so, Pentecostalism validates local traditional beliefs, while at the same time claiming to give believers access to a greater power, that of the Christian Holy Spirit.

In this way, Pentecostalism creates new local religious forms, rather than simply replacing existing local beliefs with an imported one, as the first phase of Christianisation had done. In Africa, this has led to the 'Africanisation' of Christianity rather than the total disappearance of indigenous religions. As a result of this ability to adapt to local customs and establish a local identity for itself, Pentecostalism shows considerable local diversity in different parts of the world.

Pentecostalism has also been successful in developing countries because it is able to appeal to the poor who make up the majority of the population, and because it uses global media to spread its message.

Activity	Media
Pentecostalism	

...go to www.sociology.uk.net

Topic summary

Fundamentalism is a quest for certainty in response to **modernity**. It may be a response to changes from within or from outside. Similarly, one function of religion today is **cultural defence**. Huntington argues that globalisation is leading to a **'clash of civilisations'**. Religion may contribute to **development**. **Hinduism** legitimates middle-class prosperity, while **post-Confucian** and Pentecostalist ideas perform a similar role to the Protestant ethic. **Pentecostalism** has achieved global success by incorporating local beliefs.

EXAMINING RELIGION IN A GLOBAL CONTEXT

QuickCheck Questions

Check your answers at www.sociology.uk.net

1 Identify two characteristics of religious fundamentalism.
2 According to Castells, what is the difference between a resistance identity and a project identity?
3 Identify two policies to which the New Christian Right are opposed.
4 Give one example of secular fundamentalism.
5 According to Huntington, why is a 'clash of civilisations' increasingly likely?

6 Suggest two criticisms of the view that there is a 'clash of civilisations'.
7 Over what type of values are Western and Muslim societies most likely to disagree?
8 According to Lehmann, what were the two main stages in the globalisation of religion?
9 What is meant by the term 'Hindu ultra-nationalism'?

Questions to try

Item A

Religious fundamentalists seek to return to what they regard as the basics of their faith. Fundamentalists believe unquestioningly in the literal truth of their faith's sacred text. They are intolerant of the views of others, believing that their view of the world is the only true one. The growth of fundamentalism is often seen as a response to the threat posed by modern society, which challenges and undermines the values and certainties offered by traditional religion.

1 Outline and explain two ways in which religion and development may be related in the world today. (10 marks)

2 Applying material from Item A and your knowledge, evaluate the view that fundamentalism is a response to modern society. (20 marks)

The Examiner's Advice

Q1 Spend about 15 minutes on this question. Divide your time fairly equally between the two ways. You don't need a separate introduction; just start on the first way. Possible ways include the role of Hinduism in legitimating the prosperity of the new middle class in India, post-Confucian values among Chinese entrepreneurs in the East Asian 'tiger economies', the economic role of Pentecostalism in Latin America, and fundamentalism as a response to modernisation and Westernisation in Iran.

Describe each way in some detail. Explain how each way indicates a relationship between religion and economic development in the world today. Do this by creating a chain of reasoning (see Box 4.1 in chapter 4).

For example, Pentecostalism in Chile and southern Brazil encourages a similar work ethic and this-worldly asceticism to that of Calvinism, enabling Pentecostals to become upwardly mobile. This means that Pentecostalism functions as a modern 'Protestant ethic' to create a prosperous middle class who are leading economic development.

Use concepts and issues such as those above plus globalisation, colonialism, Westernisation, cultural defence, civil religion, consumerism, tele-gurus, Hindu ultra-nationalism, the role of the Protestant ethic, risk, cosmopolitanism and resistance identity.

Q2 Spend about 30 minutes on this. Begin by describing the characteristics of fundamentalism, including those referred to in the Item plus others such as an 'us and them' mentality, use of technology, patriarchy and prophecy. Explain why fundamentalism is not the same thing as traditional religion. You should identify the features of modern society that may lead to fundamentalist responses, such as globalisation, Westernisation, economic modernisation, information technology, choice, risk and uncertainty, consumerism, spread of liberal values relating to the family, gender and sexuality, secularisation and the privatisation of religion. Explain how these may be creating fundamentalist responses.

Use concepts such as cosmopolitanism, project identity, resistance identity, monotheistic religions, cultural defence, the Enlightenment project, late modernity and recreated memories. Use examples such as the Iranian revolution, the New Christian Right and the banning of religious symbols in public, and studies such as Bruce, Davie, Hervieu-Léger, Giddens, Bauman, Beckford, Haynes and Huntington.

Evaluate by discussing secular fundamentalism and late modernity, by considering other causes of fundamentalism such as the failure of elites to deliver prosperity, and by asking whether polytheistic religions can be fundamentalist.

TOPIC 6

The Goddess Conference, Glastonbury. Does the New Age have a special appeal for women?

1 In groups of three or four, research and compile a list of as many New Age practices and practitioners as you can find in your town or neighbourhood.

   Use the internet and local directories, library noticeboards or advertisements in newsagents' windows as sources.

2 Give a brief description of some of the practices that you find interesting.

3 Are there any common themes that link some of these practices, for example in the benefits they claim to provide, whether the participant has to pay, what the participant has to do etc?

Learning objectives

After studying this Topic, you should:

- Know the main types of religious organisation and their characteristics.
- Understand and be able to evaluate explanations of different types of religious/spiritual organisations and movements.
- Understand and be able to evaluate explanations of the reasons for the growth and development of different religious/spiritual organisations and movements.
- Know the main patterns of participation by class, ethnicity, gender and age and the reasons for these patterns.

At various points so far in the chapter, we have touched on different religious groups and organisations while we were examining other issues such as the role of religion or the secularisation debate.

In this Topic, we make these organisations and movements the focus of our attention. We examine the main types of religious organisation, such as churches, sects, denominations and cults, and how they develop.

In recent years, there has been a growth in the number of different religious organisations and spiritual movements such as the New Age, and we examine the reasons for this.

Membership and participation in different religious organisations and movements varies by social class, ethnicity, gender and age. In this Topic, we examine some of the explanations for these patterns.

Types of religious organisation

While some people hold religious beliefs without belonging to any organised group, many others express their faith through membership of a religious organisation such as a church. Sociologists are interested in the different types of religious organisation, how they develop and who joins them.

Church and sect

The first attempt to identify the features of different types of religious organisation was by Ernst Troeltsch (1912; 1980). He distinguished between two main types – the church and the sect. *Churches* are large organisations, often with millions of members such as the Catholic Church, run by a bureaucratic hierarchy of professional priests, and they claim a monopoly of the truth. They are universalistic, aiming to include the whole of society, although they tend to be more attractive to the higher classes because they are ideologically conservative and often closely linked to the state. For example, the British sovereign is head of both the state and the Church of England. They place few demands on their members.

By contrast, Troeltsch sees *sects* as small, exclusive groups. Unlike churches, sects are hostile to wider society and they expect a high level of commitment. They draw their members from the poor and oppressed. Many are led by a charismatic leader rather than a bureaucratic hierarchy. The only similarity with churches is that sects too believe they have a monopoly of religious truth.

Denomination and cult

In addition to the church and sect, sociologists have identified other types of religious organisation. Richard Niebuhr (1929) describes *denominations* such as Methodism as lying midway between churches and sects. Membership is less exclusive than a sect, but they don't appeal to the whole of society like a church. Like churches, they broadly accept society's values, but are not linked to the state. They impose some minor restrictions on members, such as forbidding alcohol, but are not as demanding as sects. Unlike both church and sect, they are tolerant of other religious organisations and do not claim a monopoly of the truth.

A fourth type of religious organisation – and the least organised of all – is the *cult*. This is a highly individualistic, loose-knit and usually small grouping around some shared themes and interests, but usually without a sharply defined and exclusive belief system. Cults are usually led by 'practitioners' or 'therapists' who claim special knowledge. Like denominations, cults are usually tolerant of other organisations and their beliefs. Cults do not demand strong commitment from followers, who are often more like customers or trainees than members. They may have little further involvement with the cult once they have acquired the beliefs or techniques it offers. Many cults are world-affirming, claiming to improve life in this world.

Similarities and differences

In summing up the similarities and differences between religious organisations, Roy Wallis (1984) highlights two characteristics:

- **How they see themselves** *Churches and sects* claim that their interpretation of the faith is the only legitimate or correct one. *Denominations and cults* accept that there can be many valid interpretations.
- **How they are seen by wider society** *Churches and denominations* are seen as respectable and legitimate, whereas *sects and cults* are seen as deviant.

From cathedrals to cults

Sociologists argue that some of the above descriptions of religious organisations do not fit today's reality. For example, Bruce (1996) argues that Troeltsch's idea of a church as having a religious monopoly only applies to the Catholic Church before the 16th century Protestant Reformation, when it had a religious monopoly over society, symbolised by its massive and imposing cathedrals. Since then, sects and cults have flourished and religious diversity has become the norm. In today's society, churches are no longer truly churches in Troeltsch's sense because they have lost their monopoly and been reduced to the status of denominations competing with all the rest.

> **Application**
>
> What type of religious organisation is each of the following: the Jehovah's Witnesses; Roman Catholicism; Scientology; Methodism; Anglicanism; Baptists; Transcendental Meditation; the Mormons?

New religious movements

Since the 1960s, there has been an explosion in the number of new religions and organisations, such as the Unification Church or 'Moonies', the Children of God, Transcendental Meditation (TM), Krishna Consciousness and many more. This has led to new attempts to classify them. Roy Wallis (1984) categorises these new religious movements (NRMs) into three groups based on their relationship to the outside world – whether they reject the world, accommodate to it, or affirm it.

World-rejecting NRMs

These are similar to Troeltsch's sects. Examples include the Moonies, Krishna Consciousness, Children of God, the Manson Family, the Branch Davidian and the People's Temple. They vary greatly in size, from a handful of members to hundreds of thousands. They have several characteristics:

- They are clearly religious organisations with a clear notion of God.
- They are highly critical of the outside world and they expect or seek radical change.
- To achieve salvation, members must make a sharp break with their former life.
- Members live communally, with restricted contact with the outside world. The movement controls all aspects of their lives and is often accused of 'brainwashing' them.
- They often have conservative moral codes, for example about sex.

World-accommodating NRMs

These are often breakaways from existing mainstream churches or denominations, such as neo-Pentecostalists who split from Catholicism, or Subud, an offshoot of Islam. They neither accept nor reject the world, and they focus on religious rather than worldly matters, seeking to restore the spiritual purity of religion. For example, neo-Pentecostalists believe that other Christian religions have lost the Holy Spirit. Members tend to lead conventional lives.

World-affirming NRMs

These groups differ from all other religious groups and may lack some of the conventional features of religion, such as collective worship, and some are not highly organised. However, like religions, they offer their followers access to spiritual or supernatural powers. Examples include Scientology, Soka Gakkai, TM and Human Potential.

- They accept the world as it is. They are optimistic and promise followers success in terms of mainstream goals and values, such as careers and personal relationships.
- They are non-exclusive and tolerant of other religions, but claim to offer additional special knowledge or techniques that enable followers to unlock their own spiritual powers and achieve success or overcome problems such as unhappiness or illness. They have been described as *psychologising* religions offering this-worldly gratification.
- Most are cults, whose followers are often customers rather than members, and entry is through training. The movement places few demands on them and they carry on normal lives.

In general, world-affirming NRMs have been the most successful of the movements Wallis studied. For example, Scientology had about 165,000 members in the UK in 2005, as compared with only 1,200 Moonies.

Evaluation

Wallis offers a useful way of classifying the new religious movements that have developed in recent decades. However, some argue that it is not clear whether he is categorising them according to the movement's teachings, or individual members' beliefs. He also ignores the diversity of beliefs that may exist *within* an NRM.

Wallis himself recognises that real NRMs will rarely fit neatly into his typology (list of types) and some, such as 3HO (the Healthy Happy Holy Organisation), may have features of all three types. Nevertheless, many sociologists find such typologies useful as a way of analysing and comparing the significant features of NRMs.

However, Stark and Bainbridge (1986) reject the idea of constructing such typologies altogether. Instead, they argue that we should distinguish between religious organisations using just one criterion – the degree of conflict or tension between the religious group and wider society.

Sects and cults

Stark and Bainbridge identify two kinds of organisation that are in conflict with wider society – sects and cults:

- **Sects** result from *schisms* – splits in existing organisations. They break away from churches usually because of disagreements about doctrine.

- **Cults** are new religions, such as Scientology and Christian Science, or ones new to that particular society that have been imported, such as TM.

In general, Stark and Bainbridge see sects as promising *other-worldly* benefits (e.g. a place in heaven) to those suffering economic deprivation or ethical deprivation (where their values conflict with wider society). By contrast, cults tend to offer *this-worldly benefits* (e.g. good health) to more prosperous individuals who are suffering psychic deprivation (normlessness) and organismic deprivation (health problems).

> **Analysis and Evaluation**
>
> What similarities are there between Stark and Bainbridge's explanation of the attraction of sects for the deprived and the Marxist view of the role of religion in society?

Stark and Bainbridge subdivide cults according to how organised they are.

- **Audience cults** are the least organised and do not involve formal membership or much commitment. There is little interaction between members. Participation may be through the media. Examples include astrology and UFO cults.
- **Client cults** are based on the relationship between a consultant and a client, and provide services to their followers. In the past, they were often purveyors of medical miracles, contact with the dead etc, but the emphasis has shifted to 'therapies' promising personal fulfilment and self-discovery.
- **Cultic movements** are the most organised and demand a higher level of commitment than other cults. The movement aims to meet all its members' religious needs and unlike followers of audience and client cults, they are rarely allowed to belong to other religious groups at the same time. An example of a cultic movement is the Moonies. Some client cults become cultic movements for their most enthusiastic followers, such as Scientology, which developed out of the client cult Dianetics. Some well publicised Doomsday cults that predict the end of the world and practise mass suicide may be best seen as cultic movements.

Stark and Bainbridge make some useful distinctions between organisations. For example, their idea of using the degree of conflict with wider society to distinguish between them is similar to Troeltsch's distinction between church (which accepts society) and sect (which rejects society). However, some of the examples they use do not fit neatly into any one of their categories.

Activity | **Discussion**

Types of religious organisations

...go to www.sociology.uk.net

Explaining the growth of religious movements

Since the 1960s, there has been a rapid growth in the number of sects and cults, and in the number of people belonging to them. For example, there are estimated to be over 800 NRMs and over half a million individuals belonging to these and other non-mainstream Christian churches in the UK. Sociologists have offered three main explanations for this trend: marginality, relative deprivation, and social change.

Marginality

As Troeltsch noted, sects tend to draw their members from the poor and oppressed. Similarly, according to Max Weber (1922; 1993), sects tend to arise in groups who are marginal to society. Such groups may feel that they are disprivileged – that is, that they are not receiving their just economic rewards or social status.

In Weber's view, sects offer a solution to this problem by offering their members a *theodicy of disprivilege* – that is, a religious explanation and justification for their suffering and disadvantage. This may explain their misfortune as a test of faith, for example, while holding out the promise of rewards in the future for keeping the faith.

Historically, many sects, as well as millenarian movements, have recruited from the marginalised poor. For example, in the 20th century the Nation of Islam (the Black Muslims) recruited successfully among disadvantaged blacks in the USA. However, since the 1960s, the sect-like world-rejecting NRMs such as the Moonies have recruited mainly from more affluent groups of often well-educated young, middle-class whites. However, Wallis argues that this does not contradict Weber's view, because many of these individuals had become marginal to society. Despite their middle-class origins, most were hippies, dropouts and drug users.

Relative deprivation

Relative deprivation refers to the subjective sense of being deprived. This means that it is perfectly possible for someone who is in reality quite privileged nevertheless to *feel* that they are deprived or disadvantaged in some way compared with others. Thus, although middle-class people are materially well off, they may feel they are spiritually deprived, especially in today's materialistic, consumerist world, which they may perceive as impersonal and lacking in moral value, emotional warmth or authenticity. As a result, Wallis argues, they may turn to sects for a sense of community.

Similarly, Stark and Bainbridge argue that it is the relatively deprived who break away from churches to form sects. When middle-class members of a church seek to compromise its beliefs in order to fit into society, deprived members are likely to break away to form sects that safeguard the original message of the organisation.

For example, the deprived may stress Christ's claim that it is harder for a rich man to enter the Kingdom of Heaven than for a camel to pass through the eye of a needle – a message that the better off might want to play down. By contrast, the deprived may want to emphasise Christ's message that 'the meek shall inherit the earth'. Stark and Bainbridge argue that *world-rejecting sects* offer to the deprived the *compensators* that they need for the rewards they are denied in this world. By contrast, the privileged need no compensators or world-rejecting religion. They are attracted to *world-accepting churches* that express their status and bring them further success in achieving earthly rewards. This distinction is very similar to Wallis' two main types of NRMs. (For more on compensators, see Topic 4.)

Social change

A third explanation for the recent growth of religious movements is social change. Thus Wilson (1970) argues that periods of rapid change disrupt and undermine established norms and values, producing *anomie* or normlessness. In response to the uncertainty and insecurity that this creates, those who are most affected by the disruption may turn to sects as a solution. For example, the dislocation created by the industrial revolution in Britain in the late 18th and early 19th century led to the birth of Methodism, which offered a sense of community, warmth and fellowship, clear norms and values and the promise of salvation. Methodism succeeded in recruiting large numbers of the new industrial working class.

Similarly, Bruce (1995; 1996; 2011) sees the growth of sects and cults today as a response to the social changes involved in modernisation and secularisation. In Bruce's view, society is now secularised and therefore people are less attracted to the traditional churches and strict sects, because these demand too much commitment. Instead, people now prefer cults because they are less demanding and require fewer sacrifices.

The growth of NRMs

Explanations have been put forward for the growth of both world-rejecting and world-affirming NRMs.

World-rejecting NRMs Wallis points to social changes from the 1960s impacting on young people, including the increased time spent in education. This gave them freedom from adult responsibilities and enabled a counter-culture to develop. Also, the growth of radical political movements offered alternative ideas about the future. World-rejecting NRMs were attractive in this context because they offered young people a more idealistic way of life. Bruce (1995) argues that it was the failure of the counter-culture to change the world that led to disillusioned youth turning to religion instead.

World-affirming NRMs Bruce argues that their growth is a response to modernity, especially to the rationalisation of work. Work no longer provides meaning or a source of identity – unlike the past, when the Protestant ethic gave work a religious meaning for some people. Yet at the same time, we are expected to achieve – even though we may lack the opportunities to succeed. World-affirming NRMs provide both a sense of identity and techniques that promise success in this world.

Wallis also notes that some 'movements of the middle ground' such as the Jesus Freaks have grown since the mid-1970s. These have attracted disillusioned former members of world-rejecting NRMs (which have generally been less successful) because they provide a halfway house back to a more conventional lifestyle.

The dynamics of sects and NRMs

While churches such as the Catholic Church and the Church of England have a history stretching over many centuries, sects by contrast are often short-lived organisations, frequently lasting only a single generation or less. Sociologists have therefore been interested to understand the dynamics of sect development. There is also interest in how the NRMs described by Wallis will fare in the longer term.

Denomination or death

Niebuhr (1929) argues that sects are world-rejecting organisations that come into existence because of *schism* – splitting from an established church because of a disagreement over religious doctrine. Niebuhr argues that sects are short-lived and that within a generation, they either die out, or they compromise with the world, abandon their extreme ideas and become a denomination. There are several reasons for this:

- **The second generation**, who are born into the sect, lack the commitment and fervour of their parents, who had consciously rejected the world and joined voluntarily.

- **The 'Protestant ethic' effect** Sects that practise asceticism (hard work and saving) tend to become prosperous and upwardly mobile, as was the case with the Methodists in the 19th century. Such members will be tempted to compromise with the world, so they will either leave or it will abandon its world-rejecting beliefs.

- **Death of the leader** Sects with a charismatic leader either collapse on the leader's death, or a more formal bureaucratic leadership takes over, transforming it into a denomination.

The sectarian cycle

Similarly, Stark and Bainbridge (1986) see religious organisations moving through a cycle. In the first stage, *schism*, there is tension between the needs of deprived and privileged members of a church. Deprived members break away to found a world-rejecting sect. The second stage is one of *initial fervour*, with a charismatic leadership and great tension between the sect's beliefs and those of wider society. In the third stage, *denominationalism*, the 'Protestant ethic' effect and the coolness of the second generation mean the fervour disappears. The fourth stage, *establishment*, sees the sect become more world-accepting and tension with wider society reduces. In the final stage, *further schism* results when more zealous or less privileged members break away to found a new sect true to the original message.

Established sects

However, Wilson (1966; 2008) argues that not all sects follow the patterns outlined above. Whether or not they do so, depends on how the sect answers the question, 'What shall we do to be saved?'

- **Conversionist** sects such as evangelicals, whose aim is to convert large numbers of people, are likely to grow rapidly into larger, more formal denominations.
- **Adventist** sects such as the Seventh Day Adventists or Jehovah's Witnesses await the Second Coming of Christ. To be saved, they believe they must hold themselves separate from the corrupt world around them. This separatism prevents them from compromising and becoming a denomination.

Wilson goes on to argue that some sects have survived over many generations, such as Adventists, Pentecostalists, the Amish, Mormons and Quakers for example. Instead of becoming denominations, these groups become *established sects*. Contrary to Niebuhr's predictions, many of them have succeeded in socialising their children into a high level of commitment, largely by keeping them apart from the wider world.

However, Wilson argues that globalisation will make it harder in future for sects to keep themselves separate from the outside world. On the other hand, globalisation will make it easier to recruit in the Third World, where there are large numbers of deprived people for whom the message of sects is attractive, as the success of Pentecostalists has shown.

The growth of the New Age

The term 'New Age' covers a range of beliefs and activities that have been widespread since at least the 1980s – Heelas (2008) estimates that there are about 2,000 such activities and 146,000 practitioners in the UK. Many of them are very loosely organised audience or client cults. They are extremely diverse and eclectic (putting unconnected ideas together in new combinations). They include belief in UFOs and aliens, astrology, tarot, crystals, various forms of alternative medicine and psychotherapy, yoga, meditation, magic etc. However, according to Heelas (1996) there are two common themes that characterise the New Age:

- **Self-spirituality** New Agers seeking the spiritual have turned away from traditional 'external' religions such as the churches and instead look inside themselves to find it.
- **Detraditionalisation** The New Age rejects the spiritual authority of external traditional sources such as priests or sacred texts. Instead it values personal experience and believes that we can discover the truth for ourselves and within ourselves.

Beyond these common features, New Age beliefs vary. For example, they include world-affirming aspects that help people succeed in the everyday *outer world*, as well as world-rejecting elements that allow individuals to achieve enlightenment in their *inner world*. However, Heelas argues that most New Age beliefs and organisations offer both.

Postmodernity and the New Age

Several explanations for the popularity of the New Age have been offered. For example, John Drane (1999) argues that its appeal is part of a shift towards postmodern society. One of the features of postmodern society is a loss of faith in *meta-narratives* or claims to have 'the truth'. Science promised to bring progress to a better world but instead it has given us war, genocide, environmental destruction and global warming. As a result, people have lost faith in experts and professionals such as scientists and doctors, and they are disillusioned with the churches' failure to meet their spiritual needs. As a result, they are turning to the New Age idea that each of us can find the truth for ourselves by looking within.

The New Age and modernity

By contrast, Bruce (1995; 2011) argues that the growth of the New Age is a feature of the latest phase of *modern* society, and not postmodernity. Modern society values individualism, which is also a key principle of New Age beliefs (e.g. the idea that each individual has the truth within themselves). It is also a particularly important value among those in the 'expressive professions' concerned with human potential, such as community workers or artists – the group to whom the New Age appeals most.

Bruce notes that New Age beliefs are often softer versions of much more demanding and self-disciplined traditional Eastern religions such as Buddhism that have been 'watered down' to make them palatable to self-centred Westerners. This explains why New Age activities are often audience or client cults, since these make few demands on their followers. Bruce sees the New Age eclecticism or 'pick and mix spiritual shopping' as typical of religion in late modern society, reflecting the consumerist ethos of capitalist society.

Similarly, Heelas (1996) sees the New Age and modernity as linked in four ways:

- **A source of identity** In modern society, the individual has many different roles (at work, in the family, with friends etc) but there is little overlap between them, resulting in a fragmented identity. New Age beliefs offer a source of 'authentic' identity.
- **Consumer culture** creates dissatisfaction because it never delivers the perfection that it promises (e.g. in advertising). The New Age offers an alternative way to achieve perfection.
- **Rapid social change** in modern society disrupts established norms and values, resulting in anomie. The New Age provides a sense of certainty and truth in the same way as sects.
- **Decline of organised religion** Modernity leads to secularisation, thereby removing the traditional alternatives to New Age beliefs. For example, in the USA, the New Age is strongest where churchgoing is at its lowest, in California.

Religiosity and social groups

There are important differences between social groups in their religious participation and in the types of belief they hold. As we have seen, different social classes are likely to be attracted by different organisations and ideas – lower classes towards world-rejecting sects and higher classes towards world-accepting churches and cults. As this Topic so far has dealt mainly with class differences, we shall now focus on age, gender and ethnic differences in religiosity.

Gender and religiosity

As Table 1C shows, there are some clear gender differences in religiosity in the UK. These differences can be found among all age groups, and in both non-Christian religions and almost every Christian denomination. As Davie (2013) notes, there are gender differences in terms of religious practice, belief, self-identification, private prayer and many other aspects of religiosity. For example:

- Most churchgoers are female and they are more likely than men to attend church regularly. Female churchgoers outnumber males by almost half a million (Brierley, 2005).
- More women than men (55% versus 44%) say they have a religion (British Social Attitudes Survey 2012).
- More women than men (38% versus 26%) say religion is important to them and more women (40% versus 28%) describe themselves as 'spiritual' (British Social attitudes Survey, 2008).
- Many fewer women than men (34% as against 54%) are atheists or agnostics. Even among atheists, men are nearly twice as likely to say they definitely do not believe in life after death (Voas 2015).
- In all major faiths in the UK except for Sikhs, women are more likely than men to practise their religion (Ferguson and Hussey, 2010).
- Women express greater interest in religion and have a stronger personal commitment to it (Miller and Hoffman, 1995).

Table 1C	Religious beliefs, by gender				
	Percentage believing in:				
	God	Sin	Evil	The Devil	Life after death
Women	84	72	76	42	57
Men	75	66	58	32	39
Source: Davie (1994)					

Reasons for gender differences

Sociologists have put forward several explanations for gender differences in religious belief and practice. These tend to focus on the reasons for women's relatively higher levels of participation compared with men's.

Risk, socialisation and roles

According to Miller and Hoffman, there are three main reasons for women's higher levels of religiosity.

Firstly, they suggest that gender differences in risk-taking are a reason for differences in religiosity. By not being religious, people are risking that religion might be right and they will be condemned to hell. As men are less risk-averse than women, they are more likely to take the risk of not being religious. (Interestingly, as Davie notes, the virtual disappearance today of the dangers associated with childbirth that women had always faced throughout history, means that women in Western societies face fewer risks and may be becoming less religious as a result.)

Secondly, women are more religious because they are socialised to be more passive, obedient, and caring. These are qualities valued by most religions, so it follows that women are more likely than men to be attracted to religion. Interestingly, men who have these qualities are also more likely to be religious.

Thirdly, Miller and Hoffman note that women's gender roles mean they are more likely than men to work part-time or to be full-time carers, so they have more scope for organising their time to participate in religious activities. Women are also more likely to be attracted to the church as a source of gender identity, and Greeley (1992) argues that their role in taking care of other family members increases women's religiosity because it involves responsibility for their 'ultimate' welfare as well as their everyday needs.

Similarly, Davie (2013) argues that women are closer to birth and death (through child-bearing and caring for elderly, sick and dying relatives) and this brings them closer to 'ultimate' questions about the meaning of life that religion is concerned with. This also fits with differences in the way men and women see God: men are more likely to see a God of power and control, while women tend to see a God of love and forgiveness.

Paid work

Bruce (1996; 2011) argues that women's religiosity is a result of their lower levels of involvement in paid work. He links this to secularisation processes such as rationalisation. Over the past two centuries, this has gradually driven religion out of the male-dominated public sphere of work, confining it to the private sphere of family and personal life – the sphere that women are more concerned with. As religion has become privatised, so men's religiosity has declined more quickly than women's.

However, by the 1960s, many women had also taken on secular, masculinised roles in the public sphere of paid work, and this led to what Callum Brown (2009) calls 'the decline of female piety': women too were withdrawing from religion.

Yet, despite the decline, religion remains more attractive to women than to men for at least two reasons:

- Religion has a strong affinity with values such as caring for others. Women continue to have a primary role in caring for the young and old, both in the private sphere of the family and also in the kind of paid work they often do.
- Men's withdrawal from religion in the last two centuries meant that the churches gradually became feminised

spaces that emphasise women's concerns such as caring and relationships. Woodhead (2001) argues that this continues to make religion more attractive to women. The introduction of women priests in the Church of England in 1994 and women bishops in 2015 may have reinforced this.

To consider other reasons for the greater appeal of religion to women, we shall now focus on three specific examples: the New Age, sects, and Pentecostalism.

Women and the New Age

As women are more often associated with 'nature' (for example through childbirth) and a healing role, they may be more attracted than men to New Age movements and ideas. For example, Heelas and Woodhead found that 80% of the participants in the holistic milieu in Kendal were female.

This is because such movements often celebrate the 'natural' and involve cults of healing, which gives women a higher status and sense of self-worth. Bruce (2011) argues that women's experience of child-rearing make them less aggressive and goal-oriented, and are more cooperative and caring – where men wish to achieve, women wish to feel. In Bruce's view, this fits the expressive emphasis of the New Age.

Women may also be attracted to the New Age because it emphasises the importance of being 'authentic' rather than merely acting out roles – including gender roles. Women may be more attracted than men to this because they are more likely to perceive their roles as restrictive.

The individual sphere Similarly, women in paid work may experience a role conflict: between their masculinised, *instrumental* role in the public sphere of work, and their traditional *expressive* feminine role in the private sphere of the family. Woodhead (2001) suggests that for these women, New Age beliefs are attractive because they appeal to a third sphere, which she calls the individual sphere. This sphere is concerned with individual autonomy and personal growth rather than role performance. New Age beliefs bypass the role conflict by creating a new source of identity for women based on their 'inner self' rather than these contradictory social roles, giving them a sense of wholeness.

Similarly, Callum Brown (2009) argues that the New Age 'self' religions – those that emphasise subjective experience rather than external authority – attract women recruits because they appeal to women's wish for autonomy. On the other hand, some women may be attracted to fundamentalism because of the certainties of a traditional gender role that it prescribes for them.

Class differences Bruce (1996; 2011) points out that there are class differences in the types of religion that appeal to women. While New Age beliefs and practices emphasising personal autonomy, control and self-development appeal to some middle-class women, working-class women are more attracted to ideas that give them a passive role, such as belief in an all-powerful God or fatalistic ideas such as superstition, horoscopes and lucky charms.

These differences fit with other class differences in areas such as education, where the middle-class belief in the ability of individuals to control their own destiny contrasts with fatalistic working-class attitudes.

Women, compensators and sects

Bruce (1996) estimates that there are twice as many women as men involved in sects. One explanation for this comes from the religious market theorists, Stark and Bainbridge (1985). They argue that people may participate in sects because they offer compensators for organismic, ethical and social deprivation. These forms of deprivation are more common among women and this explains their higher level of sect membership:

- **Organismic deprivation** stems from physical and mental health problems. Women are more likely to suffer ill health and thus to seek the healing that sects offer.
- **Ethical deprivation** Women tend to be more morally conservative. They are thus more likely to regard the world as being in moral decline and be attracted to sects, which often share this view.
- **Social deprivation** Sects attract poorer groups and women are more likely to be poor.

The Pentecostal gender paradox

Since the 1970s, Pentecostalism has grown rapidly in many parts of the world, particularly among the poor. For example, in Latin America an estimated 13% of the continent's population are now members of Pentecostal churches.

Pentecostalism is generally regarded as a patriarchal form of religion: men are seen both as heads of the household and as heads of the church (all its clergy are male). Despite this, however, Pentecostalism has proved attractive to women. Bernice Martin (2000) describes this as the 'Pentecostal gender paradox': why should a conservative patriarchal religion be attractive to women?

According to Elizabeth Brusco's (1995; 2012) study of Pentecostals in Colombia, the answer lies in the fact that Pentecostalism demands that its followers adopt an ascetic (self-denying) lifestyle. As we saw in Topic 5, this resembles the personal discipline of the 16th century Calvinists. Pentecostalism also insists on a traditional gender division of labour that requires men to provide for their family.

Pentecostal women can use these ideas to combat a widespread culture of machismo in Latin America, where men often spend 20-40% of the household's income on alcohol, as well as further spending on tobacco, gambling and prostitutes. Pentecostal men are pressured by their

▲ York Minster, 2015: the Church of England's first female bishop is consecrated.

pastor and church community to change their ways, act responsibly and redirect their income back into the household, thereby raising the standard of living of women and children.

Pentecostalism is not offering Western-style women's liberation: men retain their headship role in the family and church. But as Brusco shows, Latin American women can and do use Pentecostalism as a means of improving their position. Thus, although Pentecostalism is patriarchal, its critique of the sexual irresponsibility and wastefulness of machismo culture makes it popular with women. Carol Ann Drogus (1994) also notes that although official Pentecostal doctrine is that men should have authority over women, church magazines and educational materials often encourage more equal relations within marriage.

Recent trends

Although women remain more likely to be religious than men, there has been a decline in their participation in religious activities in the UK. We have already encountered some possible reasons for these trends, notably the movement of women into paid work and, related to this, their rejection of traditional subordinate gender roles.

Because traditional religions have tended to be closely bound up with traditional gender roles, women's rejection of subordination has led them to reject traditional religion at the same time. Although some women are now attracted to New Age beliefs and practices, their numbers are relatively modest.

Ethnicity and religiosity

The UK today is a multi-ethnic, multi-religious society. Although the biggest religious group are those describing themselves as Christians (about 72% of the population), there are significant numbers of Muslims, Hindus and Sikhs, almost all of whom belong to ethnic minorities originating in the Indian subcontinent, while many Christians are of black African or Caribbean origin.

There are clear ethnic patterns in religious participation, with higher than average rates for most minority ethnic groups, as Table 1D shows. For example, in London, Brierley (2013) found that black people are twice as likely to attend church as whites. Muslims, Hindus and black Christians are also considerably more likely than white Christians to see their religion as important and to attend a place of worship every week. Among Christians, blacks are more likely than whites to be found in the Pentecostal churches, where they make up 40% of the membership. However, while minorities have higher participation rates, Modood et al (1994) found some decline in the importance of religion for all ethnic groups and that fewer were observant, especially among the second generation.

Table 1D	Ethnic differences in religious affiliation	
	% rating religion very important in their lives	% likely to attend weekly worship
White Anglicans	11	9
White Catholics	32	29
Hindus	43	43
African Caribbean Protestants	81	57
Muslims	74	62

Source: Davie (1994)

Reasons for ethnic differences

Several reasons have been suggested for ethnic differences in religiosity. One is the idea that most ethnic minorities originate from poorer countries with traditional cultures, both of which produce higher levels of religious belief and practice. On arrival in the UK, they and their children maintain the pattern they brought with them from their country of origin. However, this disregards the impact of their experiences as *immigrants* and as *minorities* in a new society, and how this may give religion a new role as cultural defence and cultural transition.

Cultural defence

As we saw in Topic 3, Bruce (2002) argues that religion in such situations offers support and a sense of cultural identity in an uncertain or hostile environment. As Bird (1999) notes, religion among minorities can be a basis for community solidarity, a means of preserving one's culture and language, and a way of coping with oppression in a racist society. In the case of black African and Caribbean Christians, many found that white churches in the UK did not actively welcome them and some turned to founding or joining black-led churches, especially Pentecostal churches. Similarly, evidence from Brierley (2013) shows a significant growth of new churches in London catering for specific languages and nationalities as a result of recent immigration.

Cultural transition

Religion can also be a means of easing the transition into a new culture by providing support and a sense of community for minority groups in their new environment. This is the explanation Will Herberg (1955) gives for high levels of religious participation among first-generation immigrants in the USA. Bruce sees a similar pattern in the history of immigration into the UK, where religion has provided a focal point for Irish, African Caribbean, Muslim, Hindu and other communities. However, once a group – such as Irish Catholics, for example – has made the transition into the wider society, religion may lose its role and decline in importance.

Ken Pryce's (1979) study of the African Caribbean community in Bristol shows both cultural defence and cultural transition have been important. He argues that Pentecostalism is a highly adaptive 'religion of the oppressed' that provided migrants with values appropriate to the new world in which they found themselves. Pentecostalism helped African Caribbeans to adapt to British society, playing a kind of 'Protestant ethic' role in helping its members succeed by encouraging self reliance and thrift. It gave people mutual support and hope of improving their situation. On the other hand, Rastafarianism represented a different response for some African Caribbeans radically rejecting the wider society as racist and exploitative.

Age and religious participation

The general pattern of religious participation is that the older a person is, the more likely they are to attend religious services. However, as Table 1E shows, there is one partial exception to this pattern: the under 15s are generally more likely to go to church than those in most of the age groups above them. This is because they may have less choice in the matter and are made to go by their parents.

However, the overall trend is clear from the Table: for any given age group apart from those aged 65 and over, there is an ongoing fall in church attendance, and the fall is sharpest among the young. For example, the number of 15-19 year olds is projected to fall by half between 2015 and 2025, from 126,000 to 63,000. As Brierley (2015) notes, by 2025 15-19 year olds will be a mere 2.5% of all churchgoers. Half of all English churches have no-one under 20 attending.

Table 1E	Usual Sunday church attendance, England: by age (thousands)		
Age	**1980**	**2015**	**2025***
Under 15	1,165	493	338
15-19	394	126	63
20-29	492	170	114
30-44	718	432	328
45-64	897	751	614
65 and over	810	957	1,070

*projected figure

Source: Brierley (2015)

Reasons for age differences

Voas and Crockett (2005) suggest three possible explanations for age differences in religiosity:

- **The ageing effect** This is the view that people turn to religion as they get older. For example, using evidence from the Kendal Project, Heelas (2005) argues that people become more interested in spirituality as they age. As we approach death, we 'naturally' become more concerned about spiritual matters and the afterlife, repentance of past misdeeds and so on. As a result, we are more likely to go to church.
- **The period or cohort effect** People born during a particular period may be more or less likely to be religious because of the particular events they lived through, such as war or rapid social changes.
- **Secularisation** As religion declines in importance, each generation becomes less religious than the one before it.

Voas and Crockett found little evidence for either of the first two explanations. Instead, they argue that secularisation is the main reason why younger people are less religious

than older people. They found that in each succeeding generation, only half as many people are religious compared with the generation before it.

This is because of what Arweck and Beckford (2013) describe as the 'virtual collapse of religious socialisation' after the 1960s. For example, traditional Sunday schools, which in the 1950s enrolled a third of all 14-year-olds, have all but disappeared. According to Voas (2003), even parents who share the same faith (for example, where both are Anglicans) have only a 50/50 chance of raising their child to be a churchgoer as an adult. When they are of different faiths (which are on the increase), the chances fall to one in four.

We are therefore likely to see a steadily ageing population of churchgoers. In 2015, one in three were aged 65 or over. By 2025, this will be over four in ten and without significant numbers of young people joining the congregations, within two or three generations practising Christians will have become a very small and very old minority of the UK population.

Topic summary

The main types of religious organisations are **churches, sects, denominations** and **cults**. The growth of sects can be seen as a response to **marginality, relative deprivation** and **social change**. Weber sees sects as providing a theodicy of disprivilege for the poor. Wallis identifies three types of new religious movement – **world rejecting, world affirming** and **world accommodating**. Niebuhr describes a **sectarian cycle** leading to denominationalism. Wilson identifies established sects as a separate type. Bruce sees sects and cults as resulting from **secularisation** where Stark and Bainbridge explain them as a response to different sorts of **deprivation**. **New Age cults** (audience and client cults) have grown since the 1970s, reflecting characteristics of modernity and postmodernity. **Religious participation** varies by **class, gender, age** and **ethnicity**. For example, it is higher among women and the old, as well as ethnic minorities for whom religion is a source of identity and community support.

EXAMINING ORGANISATIONS, MOVEMENTS AND MEMBERS

QuickCheck Questions

Check your answers at www.sociology.uk.net

1 Explain what is meant by a 'theodicy of disprivilege'.
2 Identify one similarity and one difference between churches and sects.
3 Suggest two examples of established sects.
4 Explain what is meant by an 'audience cult'.

5 Suggest two ways in which the New Age might be linked to modernity.
6 Suggest two reasons why women might be more religious than men.
7 How may religion be important for 'cultural transition'?

Questions to try

Item A

In today's secular Western societies such as Britain, traditional religion still remains an important source of identity and belonging for some people. For many, religious socialisation into the faith of their parents has formed an important part of their upbringing. Traditional religion may also appeal to some because it celebrates their role. For others, New Age spirituality may have particular appeal because it allows them to deal with the role conflicts that arise in modern societies and choose an 'authentic' identity for themselves.

Item B

There is a wide variety of different kinds of religious and spiritual organisations and movements in today's society. As well as the major churches, there are now also a large number of sects, cults and new religious movements that lie outside the traditional religious mainstream. These terms cover a diverse range of groups, some of which offer their followers worldly success, while others are resolutely hostile to wider society. Some have particular appeal to the poor and oppressed, but others draw support from more affluent groups.

1 Applying material from Item A, analyse two reasons for differences in religiosity between social groups. (10 marks)
2 Applying material from Item B and your knowledge, evaluate sociological explanations for the existence of sects, cults and new religious movements. (20 marks)

The Examiner's Advice

Q1 Spend about 15 minutes on this question. Divide your time fairly equally between the two reasons. You don't need a separate introduction; just start on your first reason. To answer this question, it's essential that you take two points from the Item and show through a chain of reasoning (see Box 4.1 in chapter 4) how each explains a difference in religiosity between social groups. (It is a very good idea to quote from the Item when doing so). You can deal with gender, ethnic, age and/or class differences in religiosity.

You could use reasons such as: secularisation means that younger generations no longer undergo religious socialisation; traditional religion enables immigrant minorities to cope with British society, or validates women's traditional role; New Age emphasis on 'naturalness' allows women to cope with conflicts between public and private sphere roles. For example, immigrant groups may use their 'home' religion as a means of cultural defence and transition in a hostile society, resulting in higher attendances at worship and a stronger attachment to the faith.

Use concepts such as those above, plus risk, paid work, rationalisation, the individual sphere, 'self' religions, compensators, ageing effect, cohort effect and racism.

Q2 Spend about 30 minutes on this. Consider the characteristics of the different groups. Start with Troeltsch on sects and add a definition of cults as loose-knit. Outline some of the different types (e.g. established sects; cultic movements, audience and client cults) and explain the difference between Wallis' three types of new religious movements (NRMs).

You should also examine different views of the origins, appeal and development of these movements. Include Wallis' explanation of why NRMs have grown and who they attract, Stark and Bainbridge's distinction between sects and cults, and the dynamics of sects (e.g. why some become denominations). You can evaluate by contrasting different views on some of these issues, and by using examples that support or challenge these views.

Use concepts such as the above plus typologies of organisations and movements, world-rejecting, world-accommodating and world-affirming NRMs, the cultic milieu, audience and client cults, cultic movements, marginality, relative deprivation, social change, the sectarian cycle, schism, denominationalisation, established sects (e.g. conversionist, Adventist), postmodernity/ late modernity, self-spirituality and detraditionalisation. Use studies such as Troeltsch, Bruce, Heelas, Wallis, Niebuhr, Wilson, Stark and Bainbridge. Use examples of different sects, cults and NRMs to illustrate your points.

Olympic Games closing ceremony. Do such sporting events reinforce nationalist ideology?

GETTING STARTED

Science and religion are both belief systems. Belief systems are sets of ideas that claim to have knowledge about reality.

In small groups, answer the following questions:

1 What kind of knowledge does religion claim to offer us?
2 What kind of knowledge does science claim to offer us?
3 How does (a) science and (b) religion claim to know that what it believes is true?
4 Can you think of any similarities between religion and science?

Learning objectives

After studying this Topic, you should:

- Know the difference between open and closed belief systems.
- Understand and be able to evaluate different views of science as a belief system.
- Understand and be able to evaluate different views of the nature of ideology.

Although religions make claims about what the world is or ought to be like, they are not the only belief systems to do this. For example, political ideologies make claims about how society ought to be organised. Similarly, science claims to tell us about how the world is. In other words, many different belief systems make *knowledge-claims* – they claim they are giving us the facts about how things are.

In this Topic, therefore, we focus on *science* as a belief system and in particular, whether and how it differs from other belief systems such as religion. We also examine the concept of *ideology* and how it has been used to understand belief systems.

Science as a belief system

Many sociologists see modern science as a product of the process of rationalisation that began with the Protestant Reformation of the 16th century. Some sociologists, such as secularisation theorists, argue that it has undermined religion by changing the way we think and how we see the world.

The impact of science

Science has had an enormous impact on society over the last few centuries. Its achievements in medicine have eradicated many once fatal diseases. Many basic features of daily life today – transport, communications, work and leisure – would be unrecognisable to our recent ancestors due to scientific and technological development. Perhaps most strikingly, science and technology have revolutionised economic productivity and raised our standard of living to previously undreamt of heights. This success has led to a widespread 'faith in science' – a belief that it can 'deliver the goods'.

More recently, this faith has been somewhat dimmed by a recognition that science may cause problems as well as solve them. Pollution, global warming and weapons of mass destruction are as much a product of science and technology as are space flight, 'wonder drugs' and the internet. While science may have helped to protect us from natural dangers such as disease and famine, it has created its own 'manufactured risks' that increasingly threaten the planet.

Yet in fact, both the 'good' and the 'bad' effects of science demonstrate the key feature distinguishing it from other belief systems or knowledge-claims – that is, its *cognitive power*. In other words, science enables us to explain, predict and control the world in a way that non-scientific or pre-scientific belief systems cannot do.

Open belief systems

Why has science been successful in explaining and controlling the world? According to Sir Karl Popper (1959), science is an 'open' belief system where every scientist's theories are open to scrutiny, criticism and testing by others. Science is governed by the principle of *falsificationism*. That is, scientists set out to try and falsify existing theories,

deliberately seeking evidence that would disprove them. If the evidence from an experiment or observation contradicts a theory and shows it to be false, the theory can be discarded and the search for a better explanation can begin. In science, knowledge-claims live or die by the evidence.

In Popper's view, discarding falsified knowledge-claims is what enables scientific understanding of the world to grow. Scientific knowledge is *cumulative* – it builds on the achievements of previous scientists to develop a greater and greater understanding of the world around us. As the discoverer of the law of gravity, Sir Isaac Newton, put it, 'If I have been able to see so far, it is because I have stood on the shoulders of giants' – that is, on the discoveries of his predecessors.

However, despite the achievements of great scientists such as Newton, no theory is ever to be taken as definitely true – there is always a possibility that someone will produce evidence to disprove it. For example, for centuries it was held to be true that the sun revolved around the earth, until Copernicus demonstrated that this knowledge-claim was false. In Popper's view, the key thing about scientific knowledge is that it is not sacred or absolute truth – it can always be questioned, criticised, tested and perhaps shown to be false. (For more on Popper, see Chapter 3, Topic 3.)

The CUDOS norms

If Popper is correct, this still leaves the question of why science has only grown so rapidly in the last few centuries. The functionalist Robert K. Merton (1973, 2007) argues that science can only thrive as a major social institution if it receives support from other institutions and values.

He argues that this first occurred in England as a result of the values and attitudes created by the Protestant Reformation, especially Puritanism (a form of Calvinism). The Puritans' this-worldly calling and industriousness, and their belief that the study of nature led to an appreciation of God's works, encouraged them to experiment. Puritanism also stressed social welfare and they were attracted by the fact that science could produce technological inventions to improve the conditions of life. The new institution of science also received support from economic and military institutions as the value of the practical applications of science became obvious in areas such as mining, navigation and weaponry.

Merton also argues, like Popper, that science as an institution or organised social activity needs an 'ethos' or set of norms that make scientists act in ways that serve the goal of increasing scientific knowledge. He identifies four such norms, known as 'CUDOS' for short from their initial letters:

Communism Scientific knowledge is not private property. Scientists must share it with the scientific community (by publishing their findings); otherwise, knowledge cannot grow.

Universalism The truth or falsity of scientific knowledge is judged by universal, objective criteria (such as testing), and not by the particular race, sex etc of the scientist who produces it.

Disinterestedness This means being committed to discovering knowledge for its own sake. Having to publish their findings makes it harder for scientists to practise fraud, since it enables others to check their claims.

Organised Scepticism No knowledge-claim is regarded as 'sacred'. Every idea is open to questioning, criticism and objective investigation.

Analysis and Evaluation

What similarities are there between Merton's CUDOS norms and Popper's view of science as an open belief system?

Closed belief systems

In this respect, science appears to differ fundamentally from traditional religious belief systems. While scientific knowledge is provisional, open to challenge and potentially disprovable, religion claims to have special, perfect knowledge of the absolute truth. Its knowledge is literally sacred and religious organisations claim to hold it on God's divine authority. This means that it cannot be challenged – and those who do so may be punished for their heresy. It also means that religious knowledge does not change – how could it, if it already has the absolute truth? Unlike scientific knowledge, therefore, it is fixed and does not grow.

Robin Horton (1973) puts forward a similar argument. He distinguishes between open and closed belief systems. Like Popper, he sees science as an open belief system – one where knowledge-claims are open to criticism and can be disproved by testing. By contrast, religion, magic and many other belief systems are closed. That is, they make knowledge-claims that cannot be successfully overturned. Whenever its fundamental beliefs are threatened, a closed belief system has a number of devices or 'get-out clauses' that reinforce the system and prevent it from being disproved – at least in the eyes of its believers. These devices vary from one belief system to another. One example is witchcraft beliefs. Edward

Evans-Pritchard's (1936) classic anthropological study of the Azande people of the Sudan illustrates Horton's idea of a self-reinforcing, closed belief system.

Witchcraft among the Azande

Like Westerners, the Azande believe that natural events have natural causes. For example, the snake bit me because I accidentally stepped on it as I was walking down the path. However, unlike most Westerners, the Azande do not believe in coincidence or chance. I have walked down the same path a thousand times and never been bitten before – so why me; why now? Thus, when misfortune befalls the Azande, they may explain it in terms of witchcraft. Someone – probably a jealous neighbour – is practising witchcraft against me.

In such cases, the injured party may make an accusation against the suspected witch and the matter may be resolved by consulting the prince's magic poison oracle. Here, the prince's diviner will administer a potion (called 'benge') to a chicken, at the same time asking the benge whether the accused is the source of the witchcraft and telling it to kill the chicken if the answer is 'Yes'. If the chicken dies, the sufferer can go and publicly demand the witchcraft to stop.

This is usually enough to end the problem, because the Azande regard witchcraft as a psychic power coming from a substance located in the witch's intestines, and it is believed possible that the witch is doing harm unintentionally and unconsciously. This allows the accused to proclaim their surprise and horror, to apologise and promise that there will be no further bewitching.

Evans-Pritchard argues that this belief system performs useful social functions. It not only clears the air and prevents grudges from festering; it encourages neighbours to behave considerately towards one another to reduce the risk of an accusation. Also, since the Azande believe witchcraft to be hereditary, children have a vested interest in keeping their parents in line, since a successful accusation against the parent also damages the child's reputation. As such, the belief system is an important social control mechanism ensuring conformity and cooperation.

As Evans-Pritchard points out, this belief system is highly resistant to challenges – that is, it is a closed system that cannot be overturned by the evidence. For example, non-believers might argue that if the benge killed the chicken *without* the diviner first addressing the potion, this would be a decisive test showing that the oracle did not work. However, for the Azande, such an outcome would just prove that it was not good benge. As Evans-Pritchard says, 'The very fact of the fowl dying proves to them its badness'. Thus, the 'test' doesn't disprove the belief system in the eyes of the believers; instead, it actually reinforces it. The believers are trapped within their own 'idiom of belief' or way of thinking. Because they accept the system's basic assumptions (such as the existence of witchcraft), they cannot challenge it.

Activity	Media
Witchcraft among the Azande	

...go to www.sociology.uk.net

Self-sustaining beliefs

Polanyi (1958) argues that all belief systems have three devices to sustain themselves in the face of apparently contradictory evidence:

- **Circularity** Each idea in the system is explained in terms of another idea within the system and so on, round and round.
- **Subsidiary explanations** For example, if the oracle fails, it may be explained away as due to the incorrect use of the benge.
- **Denial of legitimacy to rivals** Belief systems reject alternative worldviews by refusing to grant any legitimacy to their basic assumptions. For example, creationism rejects outright the evolutionists' knowledge-claim that the earth is billions of years old, and therefore that species have gradually evolved rather than all having been created.

Science as a closed system

Despite Popper's view of science as open and critical, some other writers argue that science itself can be seen as a self-sustaining or closed system of belief. For example, Polanyi argues that *all* belief systems reject fundamental challenges to their knowledge-claims – science is no different, as the case of Dr Velikovsky indicates (see Box 1.4).

Box 1.4	The case of Dr Velikovsky

In 1950, Immanuel Velikovsky published *Worlds in Collision*, in which he put forward a new theory on the origins of the earth. Velikovsky's theory challenged some of the most fundamental assumptions of geology, astronomy and evolutionary biology. The response from the scientific community was far from the 'open' one advocated by Popper. Instead of putting the new theory to the test to see if it explained the observed facts, scientists rushed to reject it out of hand – without even having read the book. A boycott of Velikovsky's publisher was organised. Scientists who called for a fair hearing and for the theory to be put to the test were victimised and some even lost their jobs.

One explanation for scientists' refusal even to consider such challenges comes from a historian of science, Thomas S. Kuhn (1970). Kuhn argues that a mature science such as geology, biology or physics is based on a set of shared assumptions that he calls a *paradigm*. The paradigm tells scientists what reality is like, what problems to study and what methods and equipment to use, what will count as evidence, and even what answers they should find when they conduct research. For most of the time, scientists are engaged in normal science, which Kuhn likens to *puzzle solving* – the paradigm lays down the broad outlines and the scientists' job is to carefully fill in the details. Those who do so successfully are rewarded with bigger research grants, professorships, Nobel Prizes and so on.

Scientific education and training is a process of being socialised into faith in the truth of the paradigm, and a successful career depends on working within the paradigm. For these reasons, any scientist who challenges the fundamental assumptions of the paradigm, as Velikovsky did, is likely to be ridiculed and hounded out of the profession. Indeed, others in the scientific community will no longer regard him or her as a scientist at all. The only exceptions to this are during one of the rare periods that Kuhn describes as a *scientific revolution*, when faith in the truth of the paradigm has already been undermined by an accumulation of anomalies – results that the paradigm cannot account for. Only then do scientists become open to radically new ideas. (For more on Kuhn, see Chapter 3, Topic 3.)

The sociology of scientific knowledge

Interpretivist sociologists have developed Kuhn's ideas further. They argue that all knowledge – including scientific knowledge – is socially constructed. That is, rather than being objective truth, it is created by social groups using the resources available to them. In the case of science, scientific 'facts' – those things that scientists take to be true and real – are the product of shared theories or paradigms that tell them what they should expect to see, and of the particular instruments they use.

Thus, Karin Knorr-Cetina (1981; 1999) argues that the invention of new instruments, such as telescopes or microscopes, permits scientists to make new observations and construct or 'fabricate' new facts. Similarly, she points out that what scientists study in the laboratory is highly 'constructed' and far removed from the natural world that they are supposedly studying. For example, water is specially purified, animals specially bred and so on.

Little green men

According to the ethnomethodologist Steve Woolgar (1992), scientists are engaged in the same process of 'making sense' or interpreting the world as everyone else. When confronted by 'evidence' from their observations and experiments, they have to decide what it means. They do so by devising and applying theories or explanations, but they then have to persuade others to accept their interpretation.

For example, in the case of the discovery of 'pulsars' (pulsating neutron stars) by researchers at the Cambridge astronomy laboratory in 1967, the scientists initially annotated the patterns shown on their printouts from the radio telescope as 'LGM1', 'LGM2' and so on – standing for 'Little Green Men'. Recognising that this was an unacceptable interpretation from the viewpoint of the scientific community (and one that would have finished their careers had they published it), they eventually settled on the notion that the patterns represented the signals from a type of star hitherto unknown to science. However, more than a decade later, there was still disagreement among astronomers as to what the signals really meant. As Woolgar notes, a scientific fact is simply a social construction or belief that scientists are able to persuade their colleagues to share – not necessarily a real thing 'out there'.

Marxism, feminism and postmodernism

Other critical perspectives such as Marxism and feminism see scientific knowledge as far from pure truth. Instead, they regard it as serving the interests of dominant groups – the ruling class in the case of Marxists, and men in the case of feminists. Thus, many advances in supposedly 'pure' science have been driven by the need of capitalism for certain types of knowledge. For example, theoretical work on ballistics (the study of the path followed by objects under the influence of gravity) was driven by the need to develop new weaponry.

Similarly, biological ideas have been used to justify both male domination and colonial expansion. In this respect, science can be seen as a form of *ideology* (see below).

> **Application**
>
> Suggest three ways in which science, technology or medicine can be seen as serving the interests of men rather than women.

Postmodernists also reject the knowledge-claims of science to have 'the truth'. In the view of Lyotard (1984), for example, science is one of a number of *meta-narratives* or 'big stories' that falsely claim to possess the truth. Other meta-narratives include religion, Marxism and psychoanalysis. In Lyotard's view, science falsely claims to find the truth about how the world works as a means of progress to a better society, whereas in reality, science is just one more 'discourse' or way of thinking that is used to dominate people. Similarly, rather like Marxists, some postmodernists argue that science has become *technoscience*, simply serving capitalist interests by producing commodities for profit.

Ideology

A basic definition of ideology is that it is a worldview or a set of ideas and values – in other words, a belief system. However, the term is very widely used in sociology and has taken on a number of related meanings. These often include negative aspects such as the following:

- Distorted, false or mistaken ideas about the world, or a partial, one-sided or biased view of reality.
- Ideas that conceal the interests of a particular group, or that legitimate (justify) their privileges.
- Ideas that prevent change by misleading people about the reality of the situation they are in or about their own true interests or position.
- A self-sustaining belief system that is irrational and closed to criticism.

Therefore, very often when someone uses the term ideology to describe a belief system, it means they regard it as factually and/or morally wrong.

> **Activity** Media
>
> What is ideology?
>
> ...go to www.sociology.uk.net

Marxism and ideology

Marxism sees society as divided into two opposed classes: a minority capitalist ruling class who own the means of production and control the state, and a majority working class who are propertyless and therefore forced to sell their labour to the capitalists. The capitalist class take advantage of this, exploiting the workers' labour to produce profit. It is therefore in the workers' interests to overthrow capitalism by means of a socialist revolution and replace it with a classless communist society in which the means of production are collectively, not privately, owned and used to benefit society as a whole.

For this revolution to occur, the working class must first become conscious of their true position as exploited 'wage slaves' – they must develop *class consciousness*. However, the ruling class control not only the means of material production (factories, land etc); they also control the means of production of ideas, through institutions such as education, the mass media and religion. These produce *ruling-class ideology* – ideas that legitimate or justify the status quo (the existing social set-up).

Ruling-class ideology includes ideas and beliefs such as:

- That equality will never work because it goes against 'human nature'.

- Victim blaming ideas about poverty, such as what Bowles and Gintis (1976) call 'the poor are dumb' theory of meritocracy: everyone has an equal chance in life, so the poor must be poor because they are stupid or lazy.
- Racist ideas about the inferiority of ethnic minorities, which divide black and white workers and make them easier to rule.

Thus the dominant ideas are the ideas of the ruling class and they function to prevent change by creating a *false consciousness* among the workers. However, despite these ideological barriers, Marx believes that ultimately the working class will develop a true class consciousness and unite to overthrow capitalism.

Hegemony and revolution

This idea is developed further by Antonio Gramsci (1971). Gramsci refers to the ruling class' ideological domination of society as hegemony. He argues that the working class can develop ideas that challenge ruling-class hegemony. This is because in capitalist society, workers have a *dual consciousness* – a mixture of ruling-class ideology and ideas they develop from their own direct experience of exploitation and their struggles against it. It is therefore possible for the working class to develop class consciousness and overthrow capitalism. In Gramsci's view, this requires a political party of 'organic intellectuals' – that is, workers who through their anti-capitalist struggles have developed a class consciousness.

However, some critics argue that it is not the existence of a dominant ideology that keeps the workers in line and prevents attempts to overthrow capitalism. For example, Abercrombie et al (2015) argue that it is economic factors such as the fear of unemployment that keep workers from rebelling.

The ideology of nationalism

Nationalism is an important political ideology that has had a major impact on the world over the last 200 years. Nationalism claims that:

- Nations are real, distinctive communities each with its own unique characteristics and a long, shared history.
- Every nation should be self-governing.
- National loyalty and identity should come before all others, such as tribe, class or religion.

However, Benedict Anderson (2006) argues that a nation is only an 'imagined community', not a real one. Although we identify with it, we will never know most of its other members. This imagined community can bind millions of strangers together and create a sense of common purpose.

Marxism: nationalism as false consciousness

Marx was an internationalist. His *Communist Manifesto* (1848) ends with the words, 'Workers of all countries, unite. You have nothing to lose but your chains. You have a world to win.' In the Marxist view, nationalism is a form of false class consciousness that helps to prevent the overthrow of capitalism by dividing the international working class.

This is because nationalism encourages workers to believe they have more in common with the capitalists of their own country than with workers of other countries. This has enabled the ruling class of each capitalist country to persuade the working class to fight wars on their behalf.

Functionalism: nationalism as civil religion

Functionalists see nationalism as a secular civil religion. Like religion, it integrates individuals into larger social and political units by making them feel part of something greater than themselves.

In modern secular societies, people may be unwilling to believe in supernatural beings but may be willing to see themselves as part of a nation. Modern societies also often contain many different faiths, so religion is likely to be a source of division. By contrast, nationalism functions as a civil religion that unites everyone into a single national community, regardless of differences such as religion or class.

For functionalists, education plays an important part in creating social solidarity, and this may include collective rituals involving nationalist symbols such as the flag and national anthem, as well as learning the nation's history (which may be more myth than fact).

Gellner: nationalism and modernity

Ernest Gellner (1994; 2006) also sees nationalism as false consciousness: its claim that nations have existed since time immemorial is untrue. On the contrary, in Gellner's view, nationalism is a very *modern* phenomenon. Pre-industrial societies were held together not by nationalism, but by face-to-face relationships in small-scale communities with a fixed hierarchy of ascribed statuses.

Modern society is very different. Industrialisation creates large-scale, impersonal societies with a complex division of labour, administered by vast bureaucracies, and where all citizens are of relatively equal status (for example, all are equal before the law).

Modern states therefore need some means of enabling communication between strangers to take place, especially in the economy. This is what nationalism makes possible, by using a mass state education system to impose a single, standard, national culture and language on every member of society. Similarly, nationalism regards all citizens as equal and this makes economic and social cooperation between them easier.

Gellner also notes that elites use nationalism as an ideology to motivate the population to endure the hardships and suffering that accompany the first phase of industrialisation, thereby enabling a state to modernise.

Karl Mannheim: ideology and utopia

Much of Karl Mannheim's work on ideology was done between the two World Wars (1918-39) – a time of intense political and social conflict – and this undoubtedly influenced his views.

Mannheim (1929; 2015) sees all belief systems as a partial or one-sided worldview. Their one-sidedness results from being the viewpoint of one particular group or class and its interests. This leads him to distinguish between two broad types of belief system or worldview:

- **Ideological thought** justifies keeping things as they are. It reflects the position and interests of privileged groups such as the capitalist class. These groups benefit from maintaining the status quo, so their belief system tends to be conservative and favours hierarchy.
- **Utopian thought** justifies social change. It reflects the position and interests of the underprivileged and offers a vision of how society could be organised differently. For example, the working class are disadvantaged by the status quo and may favour radical change to a classless society. Mannheim sees Marxism as an example of utopian thought.

Mannheim sees these worldviews as creations of groups of intellectuals who attach themselves to particular classes. For example, the role of Gramsci's organic intellectuals is to create a working-class or socialist worldview.

However, because these intellectuals represent the interests of particular groups, and not society as a whole, they only produce partial views of reality. The belief system of each class or group only gives us a partial truth about the world.

For Mannheim, this is a source of conflict in society. Different intellectuals, linked to different groups and classes, produce opposed and antagonistic ideas that justify the interests and claims of their group as against the others.

The free-floating intelligentsia

In Mannheim's view, the solution is therefore to 'detach' the intellectuals from the social groups they represent and create a non-aligned or *free-floating intelligentsia* standing above the conflict. Freed from representing the interests of this or that group, they would be able to synthesise elements of the different partial ideologies and utopias so as to arrive at a 'total' worldview that represented the interests of society as a whole.

However, many of the elements of different political ideologies are diametrically opposed to one another and it is hard to imagine how these could be synthesised. For example, how could Marxist ideas about the need to create a classless society be synthesised with the conservative idea that hierarchy is essential and beneficial?

Feminism and ideology

Feminists see gender inequality as the fundamental division in society and patriarchal ideology as playing a key role in legitimating it.

Because gender difference is a feature of all societies, there exist many different ideologies to justify it. For example, Pauline Marks (1979) describes how ideas from science have been used to justify excluding women from education. She quotes 19th century (male) doctors, scientists and educationalists expressing the view that educating females would lead to the creation of 'a new race of puny and unfeminine' females and 'disqualify women from their true vocation', namely the nurturing of the next generation.

In addition to patriarchal ideologies in science, those embodied in religious beliefs and practices have also been used to define women as inferior. There are numerous examples from a wide range of religions of the idea that women are ritually impure or unclean, particularly because of childbirth or menstruation. This has given rise to purification rituals such as 'churching' after a woman has given birth. In some Christian churches, a new mother may not receive communion until after she has been churched.

However, not all elements of religious belief systems subordinate women. For example, there is evidence that, before the emergence of the monotheistic patriarchal religions, matriarchal religions with female deities were widespread, with female priests and the celebration of fertility cults. Similarly, in Hinduism, goddesses have often been portrayed as creators of the universe.

Topic summary

Popper sees science as an **open belief system**, while religion and witchcraft are closed systems. Kuhn argues that normal science is a **closed** system that does not permit challenges to its paradigm. Interpretivists see scientific knowledge as **socially constructed**. Marxists and feminists see science as serving dominant interests.

Ideology is a one-sided worldview, legitimating a group's interests. **Marxists** see institutions such as religion producing ruling-class ideology. **Nationalism** is an ideology binding modern societies together. **Mannheim** distinguishes between ideological and utopian thought. **Feminists** see patriarchal ideology as legitimating gender inequality.

EXAMINING IDEOLOGY AND SCIENCE

QuickCheck Questions

Check your answers at www.sociology.uk.net

1   What does Popper mean by 'falsificationism'?
2   What are the four CUDOS norms?
3   In what sense is witchcraft among the Azande a closed belief system?
4   Why does the case of Dr Velikovsky suggest that science may be a closed belief system?

5   Explain Mannheim's distinction between 'ideological thought' and 'utopian thought'.
6   What is false consciousness?
7   According to Mannheim, why is there a need for a 'free-floating intelligentsia'?
8   What does Gramsci see as the two sides of workers' dual consciousness?

Questions to try

Item A

The term 'ideology' usually refers to a belief system that serves the interests of a particular social group or class. For example, Marxists argue that the ruling class use ideologies that portray inequality as inevitable and/or desirable. By doing so, they seek to persuade subordinate classes to accept the dominance of the ruling class over society. Institutions such as religion, the media and education play an important role in creating ideology.

From a functionalist perspective, civil religion and political beliefs such as nationalism may be seen as ideologies that can bind society together.

1   Outline and explain two criticisms of the view that science is an open system.   (10 marks)
2   Applying material from Item A and your knowledge, evaluate sociological explanations of the nature and role of ideology.   (20 marks)

The Examiner's Advice

Q1 Spend about 15 minutes on this question. Divide your time fairly equally between the two criticisms. You don't need a separate introduction; just start on the first criticism. Possible criticisms include the idea that science is based on a shared paradigm, that scientific knowledge is socially constructed, and that science is just one meta-narrative or discourse.

Describe each criticism in some detail. Explain how each criticism relates to science not being an open system. Do this by creating a chain of reasoning (see Box 4.1 in chapter 4).

For example, an open system means that theories are open to falsification through criticism and testing by other scientists. However, according to Kuhn, science takes place within a paradigm which sets the agenda for research, determining what questions are to be investigated, what methods are appropriate and what counts as acceptable evidence. Anyone who steps outside of the shared paradigm will be excluded from the scientific community. Hence science is not open but closed.

Use concepts and issues such as those above as well as objectivity, scientific revolutions, normal science, puzzle solving, ethnomethodology, ideology, capitalism, patriarchy, technoscience and discourse.

Q2 Spend about 30 minutes on this question. Note that it refers to both the nature and the role of ideology. 'Nature' refers to characteristics such as ideologies being partial, distorted and self-sustaining belief systems, so start your answer by using these ideas along with those in the Item to outline ideology's main features. 'Role' refers to the function of ideology in society, particularly including which social groups may benefit from it.

You should examine different views, including Marxism, feminism, Mannheim and functionalism. Explain how each one sees the nature and role of ideology. Use concepts and issues such as legitimation of inequality, false consciousness, hegemony, dual consciousness, organic intellectuals, ideological and utopian thought, the free-floating intelligentsia, patriarchy, as well as examples of nationalism, religion and science as ideologies.

Use studies such as Marx, Gramsci, Mannheim, Gellner, Anderson, Durkheim, Bellah and Marks. If you have studied education, you could also apply Bowles and Gintis' or Althusser's ideas. You can show evaluation by contrasting views such as Marxism and feminism on who benefits from ideology and by considering rival interpretations of particular ideologies such as nationalism (e.g. Gellner, Marx) or religion (Marxists, functionalists and feminists).

CHAPTER 1

EXAMINING BELIEFS IN SOCIETY

Item A   As a result of globalisation, the world today is increasingly interconnected. New information technology has created a global communication network and the media transmit images and ideas around the world, often spreading Western values to the developing world. Globalisation has produced economic growth and brought rising prosperity to some groups in developing countries, creating a new middle class, but it has also widened the gap between rich and poor. It has also led to greater flows of people across frontiers as people seek opportunities in the developed countries.

Item B   Marxist sociologists tend to take a negative view of the nature of religion and its role in society. For example, Marx regards religion as the product of the alienation that is found in all class societies. In his view, its role is to act as an ideology that keeps the proletariat subordinated. Religion acts like a drug to dull the pain of exploitation and oppression.

However, religion may also be a channel through which people protest against these conditions and make demands for change.

1   Outline and explain two reasons why some people join sects.   (10 marks)
2   Applying material from Item A, analyse two effects of globalisation on religion.   (10 marks)
3   Applying material from Item B and your knowledge, evaluate Marxist views of the nature and role of religion.   (20 marks)

The Examiner's Advice

Q1 Spend about 15 minutes on this question. Divide your time fairly equally between the two reasons. You don't need a separate introduction; just start on the first reason. Possible reasons include marginality and poverty, relative deprivation, social change and anomie, to obtain compensators (for organismic, moral or social deprivation), and as a response to modernity.

Describe each reason in some detail. Explain how each reason may explain why people join sects. Do this by creating a chain of reasoning (see Box 4.1 in chapter 4). For example, some people may feel relative or subjective deprivation. Although they may not be economically deprived, they feel spiritually deprived in a materialistic, consumer society, feeling that their lives are empty and inauthentic. They may be attracted to sects that reject the material world, finding the purer spiritual message of such sects more attractive.

Use concepts and issues such as world-rejecting, hostility to wider society, marginality, theodicy of disprivilege, deprivation, relative deprivation, social change, anomie, compensators, social class, gender, ethnicity and counter-culture. Make use of examples such as the Branch Davidian, the Moonies, TM, Krishna Consciousness, Seventh Day Adventists or Jehovah's Witnesses.

Q2 Spend about 15 minutes on this question. Divide your time fairly equally between the two effects. You don't need a separate introduction; just start on your first effect. To answer this question, it's essential that you take two points from the Item and show through a chain of reasoning how each has affected religion. (It is a very good idea to quote from the Item when doing so.)

You could use the impact of IT or the media, the impact of Western values on developing countries, the impact of prosperity for some and widening inequality, and increased migration to developed countries. For example, Western ideas have challenged existing traditional religious views, undermining their authority on issues such as gender roles, sexuality and authority structures. The response in some cases has been the rise of fundamentalism. This offers certainties that are based on traditional religious values and acts as a barrier to Western influence.

Use concepts and issues such as Westernisation, economic development, global religions, televangelism, disembedding, risk, fundamentalism, cosmopolitanism, modernity, postmodernity, resistance identity, cultural defence, cultural transition, consumerism and ultra-nationalism. Use examples such as Hindu nationalism, Pentecostalism and the Iranian revolution.

For question 3, see the student answer by Gabriella on the next page, along with the examiner's comments and marks.

Answer by Gabriella

Q3 Applying material from Item B and your knowledge, evaluate Marxist views of the nature and role of religion.

Sociologists have different views on the nature and role of religion and its functions for the individual and society. Marxists argue that the role of religion is to oppress the working class but other sociologists see religion as uniting individuals together. I will discuss these views in this essay.

> Touches on Marxism on role of religion, but not on its nature.

Marxists see religion acting as the opium of the masses. They believe that the ruling class use religion as a tool to keep themselves in power by preventing a working-class revolution to change society. Religion's function is to keep the workers passive and it does this for example by telling them they will receive their reward in the afterlife rather than on Earth. This is an important psychological function that diverts the workers from revolution.

> Deals with 'function of religion for capitalism'. Needs concept of false consciousness. Doesn't deal with nature of religion as alienation.

Functionalists take the view that religion performs positive functions for society and individuals, which means it acts as a conservative force. For example, according to Durkheim, religion creates social cohesion by integrating individuals into something greater than themselves through shared rituals. Without religion of some sort, existing society could disintegrate. This differs from Marxism, which sees religion in negative terms.

> Juxtaposing different views. A hint of evaluation but undeveloped.

Some other perspectives agree with Marxism that religion functions to preserve society by keeping people in their subordinate positions, though not necessarily the working class. For example, feminists take the view that religion is used as a means to control and dominate females. Some feminists argue that men have reinterpreted religion so that it benefits them and marginalises women.

> Some analysis of the similarities and differences. It could do with some examples of religion marginalising women.

However, Woodhead argues that religion does not necessarily always oppress women. She claims there can be religious forms of feminism. For example, some Muslim women choose to wear the hijab (veil) as it allows them to enter the public sphere of higher education and employment while maintaining their image as pious Muslims and retaining their cultural identity. Therefore religion can also help to liberate women to improve their social position. However, this is not always the case. In some countries women don't have a choice, because the law requires them to wear the veil. In these cases, religion is functioning as a conservative force in society.

> Good knowledge and some evaluation, but not explicitly applied to Marxist view.

However, religion does not always act to oppress people and prevent change. For example, Bruce argues that religion played an important part in the black civil rights movement for racial equality in the United States. The black churches provided meeting places and Bruce argues that their clergy were the backbone of the movement, providing it with its most important leaders, such as Dr Martin Luther King. The movement drew inspiration from parts of the Bible that talk about equality, and about freedom from slavery and oppression. Bruce argues that the movement succeeded because its values were the same as those of wider society (equality and justice), so it could appeal to the public at large.

> Good knowledge, used to evaluate religion's role. Link it to Marxist ideas, e.g. 'principle of hope'.

In conclusion, the Marxist view holds some truth, because religion can act to oppress people, but as we have seen, there are cases where it can have a positive effect.

> Relevant though very brief summing up.

> Overall, there is some reasonable knowledge of material on the role of religion, including different theories and evidence from studies. However, although there are some appropriate comparisons and contrasts with other theories, there needs to be more on Marxist views. For example, you could use material from Engels, Lenin, Bloch, Maduro, Gramsci or Billings. The question asks about both the nature and the role of religion, but apart from a brief mention of rewards in the afterlife in paragraph two, the answer is only about its role. To tackle its nature, use Marx's concepts of alienation and false consciousness, and explain how religion offers hope to the oppressed of a better world (Bloch's idea of the 'principle of hope'). Illustrate this with examples of religion acting as a force for change, such as liberation theology, millenarian movements or Billings' study.

CHAPTER 2

Crime and Deviance

Topic 1   Functionalist, strain and subcultural theories   70

Topic 2   Interactionism and labelling theory   78

Topic 3   Class, power and crime   86

Topic 4   Realist theories of crime   96

Topic 5   Gender, crime and justice   104

Topic 6   Ethnicity, crime and justice   114

Topic 7   Crime and the media   122

Topic 8   Globalisation, green crime, human rights and state crime   130

Topic 9   Control, punishment and victims   142

Examining crime and deviance   154

Police attending riot, Tottenham, north London

Introduction

The sociology of crime and deviance is about rules and rule breaking. For example, sociologists are interested in who breaks rules and why they do so, why some groups of people are more likely to be rule breakers – or more likely to be seen as rule breakers – and who makes and enforces the rules.

Some sociologists look for the causes of crime and deviance in the offender's social background, upbringing or social position. For example, inadequate socialisation or poverty might be responsible for some people being unable or unwilling to conform.

Other sociologists are more interested in the way society reacts to rule breaking, for example by labelling certain people as offenders and treating them differently. For example, members of less powerful groups are more likely to be labelled 'criminal'.

Still others are interested in how and why some acts – but not others – come to be defined as crimes in the first place. For example, those with power to make and enforce the law may criminalise threats to their interests. At the same time, the powerful may be able to avoid punishment for the crimes they commit. They may even be able to avoid defining the harm that they cause as 'crime' in the first place.

In this chapter, we shall examine some major sociological theories. We shall also look at a range of issues in relation to crime and deviance, such as class, gender and ethnicity; the media; globalisation, the environment and human rights; crime prevention, surveillance, control and victims.

The AQA Specification

The specification is the syllabus produced by the exam board, telling you what you have to study. The AQA specification for Crime and Deviance requires you to examine the following:

- Different theories of crime, deviance, social order and social control.
- The social distribution of crime and deviance by ethnicity, gender and social class, including recent patterns and trends in crime.
- Globalisation and crime in contemporary society; the media and crime; green crime; human rights and state crimes.
- Crime control, surveillance, prevention and punishment, victims, and the role of the criminal justice system and other agencies.

Outside the ring, this would be deviant. What functions does this 'licensed deviance' perform?

GETTING STARTED

Working in pairs, discuss and answer the following questions:

1 How would you distinguish between crime and deviance? (If you're not sure, you can look the terms up.)

2 In what ways, if any, might not owning a television set be seen as deviant?

3 'Killing is always deviant'. Do you agree with this statement? Give your reasons.

4 Apart from killing, can you think of any acts that would be seen as deviant at all times and in all places?

5 Can you think of any acts that used to be regarded as deviant until recently, but which are no longer seen as deviant today?

6 Can you think of any acts that were previously regarded as acceptable, but which have recently come to be seen as deviant?

7 Sociologists see deviance as relative. Based on your answers so far, explain what this means.

8 Can you think of any positive functions that crime or deviance might perform for individuals or society?

Learning objectives

After studying this Topic, you should:

- Understand the functionalist perspective on crime, including the functions of crime.

- Understand the concept of strain and its role in explaining deviance.

- Be able to explain the differences between different strain and subcultural theories.

- Be able to evaluate functionalist, strain and subcultural theories of crime and deviance.

FUNCTIONALIST, STRAIN AND SUBCULTURAL THEORIES

Although functionalists see deviance as disrupting social stability, they regard it as inevitable and even beneficial. They are interested in the causes of deviance, such as blocked opportunities to achieve. Functionalists also seek to explain deviant subcultures – groups whose values are opposed to those of wider society.

Durkheim's functionalist theory

Functionalism sees society as based on value consensus. That is, it sees members of society as sharing a common culture. A culture is a set of shared norms (rules), values, beliefs and goals. Sharing the same culture produces social solidarity – it binds individuals together, telling them what to strive for and how to conduct themselves.

Functionalists argue that in order to achieve this solidarity, society has two key mechanisms:

- **Socialisation** instils the shared culture into its members. This helps to ensure that individuals internalise the same norms and values, and that they feel it right to act in the ways that society requires.
- **Social control** mechanisms include rewards (or positive sanctions) for conformity, and punishments (negative sanctions) for deviance. These help to ensure that individuals behave in the way society expects.

The inevitability of crime

From the above account, we might expect that functionalists would regard crime and deviance as wholly negative – a threat to social order and even the very existence of society. For example, if each of us chose to 'do our own thing' – whether it be refusing to work or helping ourselves to others' possessions – it is hard to imagine how society could continue to exist.

However, while functionalists see too much crime as destabilising society, they also see crime as inevitable and universal. Every known society has some level of crime and deviance – a crime-free society is a contradiction in terms. For Durkheim (1893), 'crime is normal… an integral part of all healthy societies'.

There are at least two reasons why crime and deviance are found in all societies. Firstly, not everyone is equally effectively socialised into the shared norms and values, so some individuals will be prone to deviate. Secondly, particularly in complex modern societies, there is a diversity of lifestyles and values. Different groups develop their own subcultures with distinctive norms and values, and what the members of the subculture regard as normal, mainstream culture may see as deviant.

In Durkheim's view, modern societies tend towards anomie or normlessness – the rules governing behaviour become weaker and less clear-cut. This is because modern societies have a complex, specialised division of labour, which leads to individuals becoming increasingly different from one another. This weakens the shared culture or collective conscience and results in higher levels of deviance. For example, Durkheim sees anomie as a cause of suicide.

The positive functions of crime

For Durkheim, not only is crime inevitable; it also fulfils two important positive functions.

1 Boundary maintenance

Crime produces a reaction from society, uniting its members in condemnation of the wrongdoer and reinforcing their commitment to the shared norms and values.

For Durkheim, this explains the function of punishment. This is not to make the wrongdoer suffer or mend his ways, nor is it to remove crime from society. In Durkheim's view, the purpose of punishment is to reaffirm society's shared rules and reinforce social solidarity. (See also Topic 9.)

This may be done through the rituals of the courtroom, which dramatise wrongdoing and publicly shame and stigmatise the offender. This reaffirms the values of the law-abiding majority and discourages others from rule breaking. Similarly, Stanley Cohen (1972) has examined the important role played by the media in this 'dramatisation of evil'. In his view, media coverage of crime and deviance often creates 'folk devils' (see Topic 7).

2 Adaptation and change

For Durkheim, all change starts with an act of deviance. Individuals with new ideas, values and ways of living must not be completely stifled by the weight of social control. There must be some scope for them to challenge and change existing norms and values, and in the first instance this will inevitably appear as deviance. For example, the authorities often persecute religious visionaries who espouse a new 'message' or value-system. However, in the long run their values may give rise to a new culture and morality. If those with new ideas are suppressed, society will stagnate and be unable to make necessary adaptive changes.

Thus, for Durkheim, neither a very high nor a very low level of crime is desirable. Each of these signals some malfunctioning of the social system:

- Too much crime threatens to tear the bonds of society apart.
- Too little means that society is repressing and controlling its members too much, stifling individual freedom and preventing change.

Other functions of crime

Others have developed Durkheim's idea that deviance can have positive functions. For example, Kingsley Davis (1937; 1961) argues that prostitution acts as a *safety valve* for the release of men's sexual frustrations without threatening the monogamous nuclear family. Similarly, Ned Polsky (1967) argues that pornography safely 'channels' a variety of sexual desires away from alternatives such as adultery, which would pose a much greater threat to the family.

Albert Cohen identifies another function of deviance: a *warning* that an institution is not functioning properly. For example, high rates of truancy may tell us that there are problems with the education system and that policy-makers need to make appropriate changes to it.

Functionalists have also developed Durkheim's idea of the normality or inevitability of deviance. For example, Kai Erikson (1966) argues that if deviance performs positive social functions, then perhaps it means society is actually organised so as to *promote* deviance. He suggests that the true function of agencies of social control such as the police may actually be to sustain a certain level of crime rather than to rid society of it. The idea that agencies of social control actually produce rather than prevent crime has been developed further by labelling theory (see Topic 2).

Societies sometimes also manage and regulate deviance rather than seeking to eliminate it entirely. For example, demonstrations, carnivals, festivals, sport and student rag weeks all license misbehaviour that in other contexts might be punished. Similarly, the young may be given leeway to

'sow their wild oats'. From a functionalist perspective, this may be to offer them a way of coping with the strains of the transition from childhood to adulthood.

Functionalism is useful in showing the ways in which deviance is integral to society. It provides an important and interesting analysis that directs attention to the ways in which deviance can have hidden or latent functions for society – i.e. not everything that is bad, is bad for society!

...go to www.sociology.uk.net

Criticisms

For Durkheim, society requires a certain amount of deviance to function successfully, but he offers no way of knowing how much is the right amount.

Functionalists explain the existence of crime in terms of its supposed function – for example, to strengthen solidarity. But this doesn't mean society actually creates crime in *advance* with the *intention* of strengthening solidarity. In other words, just because crime does these things is not necessarily why it exists in the first place.

Functionalism looks at what functions crime serves for society as a whole and ignores how it might affect different groups or individuals within society. For example, seeing a murderer punished for his crime might be functional in reinforcing solidarity among the rest of society, but it obviously isn't 'functional' for the victim. Functionalism misses this because it fails to ask, 'functional *for whom*?'

Crime doesn't always promote solidarity. It may have the opposite effect, leading to people becoming more isolated, for example forcing women to stay indoors for fear of attack. On the other hand, some crimes do reinforce collective sentiments, for example uniting the community in condemnation of a brutal attack.

Merton's strain theory

Strain theories argue that people engage in deviant behaviour when they are unable to achieve socially approved goals by legitimate means. For example, they may become frustrated and resort to criminal means of getting what they want, or lash out at others in anger, or find comfort for their failure in drug use.

The first strain theory was that developed by the functionalist Robert K. Merton (1938), who adapted

Durkheim's concept of anomie to explain deviance. Merton's explanation combines two elements:

- **Structural factors** – society's unequal opportunity structure.
- **Cultural factors** – the strong emphasis on success goals and the weaker emphasis on using legitimate means to achieve them.

▲ The Wall Street Crash, New York 1929. The mismatch between aspiration and reality was central to the development of Merton's strain theory in depression-era America.

For Merton, deviance is the result of a strain between two things:

- The goals that a culture *encourages* individuals to achieve.
- What the institutional structure of society *allows* them to achieve legitimately.

For example, American culture values 'money success' – individual material wealth and the high status that goes with it.

The American Dream

Americans are expected to pursue this goal by legitimate means: self-discipline, study, educational qualifications, and hard work in a career. The ideology of the 'American Dream' tells Americans that their society is a meritocratic one where anyone who makes the effort can get ahead – there are opportunities for all.

However, the reality is different: many disadvantaged groups are denied opportunities to achieve legitimately. For example, poverty, inadequate schools and discrimination in the job market may block opportunities for many ethnic minorities and the lower classes.

The resulting strain between the cultural goal of money success and the lack of legitimate opportunities to achieve it produces frustration, and this in turn creates a pressure to resort to illegitimate means such as crime and deviance. Merton calls this pressure to deviate, *the strain to anomie*.

According to Merton, the pressure to deviate is further increased by the fact that American culture puts more emphasis on achieving success at any price than upon doing so by legitimate means. Winning the game becomes more important than playing by the rules.

To summarise, the goal creates a desire to succeed, and lack of opportunity creates a pressure to adopt illegitimate means, while the norms are not strong enough to prevent some from succumbing to this temptation.

Deviant adaptations to strain

Merton uses strain theory to explain some of the patterns of deviance found in society. He argues that an individual's position in the social structure affects the way they adapt or respond to the strain to anomie. Logically, there are five different types of adaptation, depending on whether an individual accepts, rejects or replaces approved cultural goals and the legitimate means of achieving them. These are summarised in Table 2A.

Table 2A	Types of adaptation to the strain to anomie	
Response	**Goal**	**Means**
Conformity	+	+
Innovation	+	−
Ritualism	−	+
Retreatism	−	−
Rebellion	−/+	−/+

Key: (+) acceptance (−) rejection (−/+) rejection of mainstream values and replacement with new ones

Conformity Individuals accept the culturally approved goals and strive to achieve them legitimately. This is most likely among middle-class individuals who have good opportunities to achieve, but Merton sees it as the typical response of most Americans.

Innovation Individuals accept the goal of money success but use 'new', illegitimate means such as theft or fraud to achieve it. As we have seen, those at the lower end of the class structure are under greatest pressure to innovate.

Ritualism Individuals give up on trying to achieve the goals, but have internalised the legitimate means and so they follow the rules for their own sake. This is typical of lower-middle class office workers in dead-end, routine jobs.

Retreatism Individuals reject both the goals and the legitimate means and become dropouts. Merton includes 'psychotics, outcasts, vagrants, tramps, chronic drunkards and drug addicts' as examples.

Rebellion Individuals reject the existing society's goals and means, but they replace them with new ones in a desire to bring about revolutionary change and create a new kind of society. Rebels include political radicals and counter-cultures such as hippies.

Evaluation of Merton

Merton shows how both normal and deviant behaviour can arise from the same mainstream goals. Both conformists and innovators are pursuing money success – one legitimately, the other illegitimately.

He explains the patterns shown in official crime statistics:

- Most crime is property crime, because American society values material wealth so highly.
- Lower-class crime rates are higher, because they have least opportunity to obtain wealth legitimately.

However, the theory is criticised on several grounds:

- It takes official crime statistics at face value. These over-represent working-class crime, so Merton sees crime as a mainly working-class phenomenon. It is also too deterministic: the working class experience the most strain, yet they don't all deviate.
- Marxists argue that it ignores the power of the ruling class to make and enforce the laws in ways that criminalise the poor but not the rich.

- It assumes there is a value consensus – that everyone strives for 'money success' – and ignores the possibility that many may not share this goal.
- It only accounts for utilitarian crime for monetary gain, and not crimes of violence, vandalism etc. It is also hard to see how it could account for state crimes such as genocide or torture.
- It explains how deviance results from *individuals* adapting to the strain to anomie but ignores the role of *group* deviance, such as delinquent subcultures.

Activity	Media

Why do people commit crime?

...go to www.sociology.uk.net

Subcultural strain theories

Subcultural strain theories see deviance as the product of a delinquent subculture with different values from those of mainstream society. They see subcultures as providing an alternative opportunity structure for those who are denied the chance to achieve by legitimate means – mainly those in the working class. From this point of view, subcultures are a solution to a problem and therefore functional for their members, even if not for wider society. Subcultural strain theories both criticise Merton's theory and build on it.

A.K. Cohen: status frustration

Albert K. Cohen (1955) agrees with Merton that deviance is largely a lower-class phenomenon. It results from the inability of those in the lower classes to achieve mainstream success goals by legitimate means such as educational achievement. However, Cohen criticises Merton's explanation of deviance on two grounds:

1 Merton sees deviance as an *individual* response to strain, ignoring the fact that much deviance is committed in or by groups, especially among the young.

2 Merton focuses on *utilitarian* crime committed for material gain, such as theft or fraud. He largely ignores crimes such as assault and vandalism, which may have no economic motive.

Cohen focuses on deviance among working-class boys. He argues that they face anomie in the middle-class dominated school system. They suffer from cultural deprivation and lack the skills to achieve. Their inability to succeed in this middle-class world leaves them at the bottom of the official status hierarchy.

As a result of being unable to achieve status by legitimate means (education), the boys suffer *status frustration*. They face a problem of adjustment to the low status they are given by mainstream society. In Cohen's view, they resolve their frustration by rejecting mainstream middle-class values and they turn instead to other boys in the same situation, forming or joining a delinquent subculture.

Alternative status hierarchy

According to Cohen, the subculture's values are spite, malice, hostility and contempt for those outside it. The delinquent subculture *inverts* the values of mainstream society – turns them upside down. What society condemns, the subculture praises and vice versa. For example, society upholds regular school attendance and respect for property, whereas in the subculture, boys gain status from vandalising property and truanting.

For Cohen, the subculture's function is that it offers the boys an alternative status hierarchy in which they can achieve. Having failed in the legitimate opportunity structure, the boys create their own illegitimate opportunity structure in which they can win status from their peers through their delinquent actions.

One strength of Cohen's theory is that it offers an explanation of non-utilitarian deviance. Unlike Merton, whose concept of innovation only accounts for crime with a profit motive, Cohen's ideas of status frustration, value inversion and alternative status hierarchy help to explain non-economic delinquency such as vandalism and truancy.

However, like Merton, Cohen assumes that working-class boys start off sharing middle-class success goals, only to reject these when they fail. He ignores the possibility that they didn't share these goals in the first place and so never saw themselves as failures.

Cloward and Ohlin: three subcultures

Like Cohen, Richard Cloward and Lloyd Ohlin (1960) take Merton's ideas as their starting point. They agree that working-class youths are denied legitimate opportunities to achieve 'money success', and that their deviance stems from the way they respond to this situation.

Cloward and Ohlin note that not everyone in this situation adapts to it by turning to 'innovation' – utilitarian crimes such as theft. Different subcultures respond in different ways to the lack of legitimate opportunities. For example, the subculture described by Cohen resorts to violence and vandalism, not economic crime or illegal drug use.

Cloward and Ohlin attempt to explain why different subcultural responses occur. In their view, the key reason is not only unequal access to the *legitimate* opportunity structure, as Merton and Cohen recognise – but unequal access to *illegitimate* opportunity structures.

For example, not everyone who fails by legitimate means, such as schooling, then has an equal chance of becoming a successful safecracker. Just like the apprentice plumber, the would-be safecracker needs the opportunity to learn their trade and the chance to practise it.

Drawing on the ideas of the Chicago School (see Box 2.1), Cloward and Ohlin argue that different neighbourhoods provide different illegitimate opportunities for young people to learn criminal skills and develop criminal careers. They identify three types of deviant subcultures that result:

Criminal subcultures provide youths with an apprenticeship for a career in utilitarian crime. They arise only in neighbourhoods with a longstanding and stable criminal culture with an established hierarchy of professional adult crime. This allows the young to associate with adult criminals, who can select those with the right aptitudes and abilities and provide them with training and role models as well as opportunities for employment on the criminal career ladder.

Conflict subcultures arise in areas of high population turnover. This results in high levels of social disorganisation and prevents a stable professional criminal network developing. Its absence means that the only illegitimate opportunities available are within loosely organised gangs. In these, violence provides a release for young men's frustration at their blocked

opportunities, as well as an alternative source of status that they can earn by winning 'turf' (territory) from rival gangs. This subculture is closest to that described by Cohen.

Retreatist subcultures In any neighbourhood, not everyone who aspires to be a professional criminal or a gang leader actually succeeds – just as in the legitimate opportunity structure, where not everyone gets a well-paid job. What becomes of these 'double failures' – those who fail in both the legitimate and the illegitimate opportunity structures? According to Cloward and Ohlin, many turn to a retreatist subculture based on illegal drug use.

> **Analysis and Evaluation**
>
> What similarities and differences are there between retreatist subcultures and Merton's idea of a retreatist adaptation?

Box 2.1 | **The Chicago School**

The University of Chicago sociology department was the first of its kind to be established in the United States, in 1892, and it remained extremely influential, notably in the study of crime and deviance. Among its contributions were:

Cultural transmission theory (Clifford Shaw and Henry McKay, 1942). They noted how some neighbourhoods develop a criminal tradition or culture that is transmitted from generation to generation, while other neighbourhoods remain relatively crime-free over the same period.

Differential association theory (Edwin Sutherland, 1939). Sutherland was interested in the processes by which people become deviant. He argued that deviance was behaviour learned through social interaction with others who are deviant. This includes learning both criminal values and criminal skills.

Social disorganisation theory (Robert Park and Ernest Burgess, 1925). They argued that deviance is the product of social disorganisation. Changes such as rapid population turnover and migration create instability, disrupting family and community structures. These become unable to exercise social control over individuals, resulting in deviance.

Evaluation of Cloward and Ohlin

They agree with Merton and Cohen that most crime is working-class, thus ignoring crimes of the wealthy. Similarly, their theory over-predicts the amount of working-class crime. Like Merton and Cohen, they too ignore the wider power structure, including who makes and enforces the law.

While they agree with Cohen that delinquent subcultures are the source of much deviance, unlike Cohen they provide an explanation for different *types* of working-class deviance in terms of different subcultures.

However, they draw the boundaries too sharply between these. For example, South (2014) found that the drug trade is a mixture of both 'disorganised' crime, like the conflict subculture, and professional 'mafia' style criminal subcultures. Likewise, some supposedly 'retreatist' users are also professional dealers making a living from this utilitarian crime. In Cloward and Ohlin's theory, it would not be possible to belong to more than one of these subcultures.

Strain theories have been called *reactive* theories because they explain subcultures as forming in reaction to the failure to achieve mainstream goals. They have been criticised for assuming that everyone starts off sharing the same mainstream success goal.

By contrast, Walter B. Miller (1962) argues that the lower class has its own *independent* subculture separate from mainstream culture, with its own values. This subculture does not value success in the first place, so its members are not frustrated by failure.

Although Miller agrees deviance is widespread in the lower class, he argues that this arises out of an attempt to achieve their *own* goals, not mainstream ones.

David Matza (1964) claims that most delinquents are not strongly committed to their subculture, as strain theories suggest, but merely drift in and out of delinquency.

Strain theory has had a major influence both on later theories of crime and on government policy. For example, Merton's ideas play an important part in left realist explanations of crime (see Topic 4). Similarly, in the 1960s Ohlin was appointed to help develop crime policy in the USA under President Kennedy.

Recent strain theories

Recent strain theorists have argued that young people may pursue a variety of goals other than money success. These include popularity with peers, autonomy from adults, or the desire of some young males to be treated like 'real men'.

Like earlier strain theorists, they argue that failure to achieve these goals may result in delinquency. They also argue that middle-class juveniles too may have problems achieving such goals, thus offering an explanation for middle-class delinquency.

Institutional anomie theory

Like Merton's theory, Messner and Rosenfeld's (2001) institutional anomie theory focuses on the American Dream. They argue that its obsession with money success and its 'winner-takes-all' mentality, exert 'pressures towards

crime by encouraging an anomic cultural environment in which people are encouraged to adopt an 'anything goes' mentality in pursuit of wealth.

In America (and arguably the UK), economic goals are valued above all, and this undermines other institutions. For example, schools become geared to preparing pupils for the labour market at the expense of inculcating values such as respect for others. Messner and Rosenfeld conclude that in societies based on free-market capitalism and lacking adequate welfare provision, such as the USA, high crime rates are inevitable.

Downes and Hansen (2006) offer evidence for this view. In a survey of crime rates and welfare spending in 18 countries, they found societies that spent more on welfare had lower rates of imprisonment. This backs up Messner and Rosenfeld's claim that societies that protect the poor from the worst excesses of the free market have less crime.

Similarly, Savelsberg (1995) applies strain theory to post-communist societies in Eastern Europe, which saw a rapid rise in crime after the fall of communism in 1989. He attributes this rise to communism's collective values being replaced by new western capitalist goals of individual 'money success'.

Topic summary

For **functionalists**, society is based on **value consensus**, which deviance threatens, but it also performs **positive functions** such as reinforcing solidarity and adapting to change.

Strain theories argue that deviance occurs when people cannot achieve society's goals by legitimate means. **Merton** argues that this produces a 'strain to **anomie**' that may result in innovation, ritualism, retreatism or rebellion.

Subcultural theories see much deviance as a collective rather than individual response. **A.K. Cohen** argues that subcultural deviance results from **status frustration** and takes a non-utilitarian form. **Cloward and Ohlin** see three **different deviant subcultures** (criminal, conflict and retreatist) arising from differences in access to illegitimate opportunity structures.

Recent strain theories argue that **capitalist economies** generate greater strain to crime.

EXAMINING FUNCTIONALIST, STRAIN AND SUBCULTURAL THEORIES

QuickCheck Questions

Check your answers at www.sociology.uk.net

1 Why does Durkheim regard crime as inevitable in all societies?
2 Identify two ways in which crime and deviance may have positive functions.
3 Explain the difference between goals and means.
4 Explain the difference between ritualism and retreatism.
5 In what sense is Merton's theory deterministic?

6 What is meant by non-utilitarian crime?
7 What is meant by 'status frustration'?
8 In Cloward and Ohlin's view, why are there different types of deviant subculture?
9 Identify two features of American society that Messner and Rosenfeld claim produce high crime rates.

Questions to try

Item A   Many people see deviance as being dysfunctional and negative for society because it represents the potential for social breakdown. However, some sociologists suggest that deviance might actually be functional for society and act as a warning.

For example, imprisonment, fines and so on are not simply there to punish offenders; they convey other messages as well. Society's values are also not fixed and new ideas sometimes emerge to challenge existing values.

Item B   Strain theories focus on the ways in which people may resort to crime or deviance when they are unable to achieve socially approved goals by legitimate means. For example, Merton argues that American culture emphasises achieving success, but an unequal structure limits some individuals' opportunity to do so legitimately. This may induce frustration in the individuals concerned.

Some strain theorists see the response to this situation as a group reaction, in which individuals create or join deviant subcultures.

1 Outline two reasons why functionalists see crime as inevitable.   (4 marks)
2 Applying material from Item A, analyse two functions of deviance.   (10 marks)
3 Applying material from Item B and your knowledge, evaluate the contribution of strain theories to our understanding of crime and deviance.   (30 marks)

The Examiner's Advice

Q2 Spend about 15 minutes on this question. Divide your time fairly equally between the two functions. You don't need a separate introduction; just start on your first function. To answer this question, it's essential that you take two points from the Item and show through a chain of reasoning (see Box 4.1 in chapter 4) how each can perform a function. (It is a very good idea to quote from the Item when doing so.)

You could use the idea that deviance may be a sign of new ideas that society must accommodate, that it is a warning that an institution is malfunctioning, or that punishment conveys a message to society. For example, public punishment of deviants highlights unacceptable behaviour and allows the public to condemn it. This reaffirms society's boundaries to everyone and reinforces the collective conscience.

Use concepts and issues such as socialisation, social control, value consensus, boundary maintenance, the dramatisation of evil, media coverage of deviance, adaptation, safety valve, social change and latent functions. You could offer some brief evaluation, for example by pointing out that it is unclear at what level deviance becomes dysfunctional rather than functional.

Q3 Spend about 45 minutes on this. Consider the different strain theories, focusing most of your attention on Merton's strain theory and the subcultural strain theories of A.K. Cohen and Cloward and Ohlin, but mention recent strain theories too. Locate these within a functionalist approach to deviance.

Examine Merton's idea of the 'strain to anomie' and his typology of adaptations to strain. Use his focus on individual and utilitarian adaptations to lead into subcultural strain theories, explaining how they criticise and build on his ideas. Evaluate by using South, Miller and Matza's criticisms, and issues such as determinism, neglect of power and who makes the law, and reliance on official statistics. Use Messner and Rosenfeld, Downes and Hansen, or Savelsberg for positive evaluation.

Use the concepts, issues and studies referred to above, plus structural and cultural factors, the American Dream, legitimate and illegitimate opportunity structures, conformity, innovation, ritualism, retreatism, rebellion, non-utilitarian crime, status frustration, inversion of values, alternative status hierarchy, different types of subculture, reactive versus independent subcultures, institutional anomie theory and capitalism.

Arizona, USA: female prisoners in a chain gang.

GETTING STARTED

In pairs, consider the following three scenarios in which an individual is caught apparently shoplifting:

a The shop takes the goods back and warns the individual not to do it again.

b The shop immediately calls the police. The individual is arrested, taken to the police station and given a caution.

c The shop immediately calls the police. The individual is arrested, charged, tried and convicted.

1 For each scenario, who would be aware of the crime?

2 For each scenario, what might be the impact on the individual?

3 What would be the impact of each scenario if the person was innocent?

Learning objectives

After studying this Topic, you should:

● Understand why interactionists regard crime and deviance, and official statistics on crime, suicide and mental illness, as socially constructed.

● Understand the labelling process and its consequences for those who are labelled.

● Be able to evaluate the strengths and limitations of labelling theory in explaining crime and deviance.

INTERACTIONISM AND LABELLING THEORY

The theories we have looked at so far have all been described as 'problem takers'. That is, they take the official definitions of crime and criminals for granted. Crime is activity that breaks the criminal law, and criminals are the people who behave in this way. They also take it for granted that the official crime statistics are a reasonably accurate picture of the real patterns of crime and who commits it. The main aim of these theories is to discover the causes of crime (for example as a reaction to blocked opportunities or other external forces) and to provide solutions to the 'problem of crime'.

Labelling theorists take a very different approach. Instead of seeking the causes of criminal behaviour, they ask how and why some people and actions come to be labelled as criminal or deviant, and what effects this has on those who are so labelled.

Similarly, instead of accepting official statistics as a valid picture of crime, they regard them not as hard facts, but as social constructs. This reflects the origins of labelling theory in symbolic interactionism, which takes the view that individuals construct the social world through their face-to-face interactions.

For labelling theorists, this constructionist view applies also to crime and deviance. Crime is the product of interactions between suspects and police, for example, rather than the result of wider external social forces such as blocked opportunity structures.

The social construction of crime

Rather than simply taking the definition of crime for granted, labelling theorists are interested in how and why certain acts come to be defined or labelled as criminal in the first place. They argue that no act is inherently criminal or deviant in itself, in all situations and at all times. Instead, it only comes to be so when others label it as such. In other words, it is not the nature of the act that makes it deviant, but the nature of society's *reaction* to the act.

In this view, therefore, deviance is in the eye of the beholder. As Howard Becker (1963) puts it:

> 'Social groups create deviance by creating the rules whose infraction [breaking] constitutes deviance, and by applying those rules to particular people and labelling them as outsiders.'

For Becker, therefore, a deviant is simply someone to whom the label has been successfully applied, and deviant behaviour is simply behaviour that people so label.

This leads labelling theorists to look at how and why rules and laws get made. They are particularly interested in the role of what Becker calls *moral entrepreneurs*. These are people who lead a moral 'crusade' to change the law. However, Becker argues that this new law invariably has two effects:

- The creation of a new group of 'outsiders' – outlaws or deviants who break the new rule.
- The creation or expansion of a social control agency (such as the police, courts, probation officers etc) to enforce the rule and impose labels on offenders.

For example, Platt (1969) argues that the idea of 'juvenile delinquency' was originally created as a result of a campaign by upper-class Victorian moral entrepreneurs, aimed at protecting young people at risk. This established 'juveniles'

as a separate category of offender with their own courts, and it enabled the state to extend its powers beyond criminal offences involving the young, into so-called 'status offences' (where their behaviour is only an offence because of their age) such as truancy and sexual promiscuity.

Becker notes that social control agencies themselves may also campaign for a change in the law to increase their own power. For example, the US Federal Bureau of Narcotics successfully campaigned for the passing of the Marijuana Tax Act in 1937 to outlaw marijuana use. Supposedly, this was on the grounds of its ill effects on young people, but Becker argues it was really to extend the Bureau's sphere of influence. Thus it is not the inherent harmfulness of a particular behaviour that leads to new laws being created, but rather the efforts of powerful individuals and groups to redefine that behaviour as unacceptable.

Who gets labelled?

Not everyone who commits an offence is punished for it. Whether a person is arrested, charged and convicted depends on factors such as:

- Their interactions with agencies of social control.
- Their appearance, background and personal biography.
- The situation and circumstances of the offence.

This leads labelling theorists to look at how the laws are applied and enforced. Their studies show that agencies of social control are more likely to label certain groups of people as deviant or criminal.

For example, Piliavin and Briar (1964) found that police decisions to arrest a youth were mainly based on physical cues (such as manner and dress), from which they made judgments about the youth's character. Officers' decisions were also influenced by the suspect's gender, class and ethnicity, as well as by time and place. For example, those stopped late at night in high crime areas ran a greater risk of arrest. Similarly, a study of anti-social behaviour orders found they were disproportionately used against ethnic minorities.

Cicourel: the negotiation of justice

Officers' decisions to arrest are influenced by their stereotypes about offenders. For example, Aaron Cicourel (1968) found that officers' *typifications* – their commonsense theories or stereotypes of what the typical delinquent is like – led them to concentrate on certain 'types'. This resulted in law enforcement showing a class bias, in that working-class areas and people fitted the police typifications most closely. In turn, this led police to patrol working-class areas more intensively, resulting in more arrests and confirming their stereotypes.

Cicourel also found that other agents of social control within the criminal justice system reinforced this bias. For example, probation officers held the commonsense theory that juvenile delinquency was caused by broken homes, poverty and lax parenting. They tended to see youths from such backgrounds as likely to offend in future and were less likely to support non-custodial sentences for them.

In Cicourel's view, justice is not fixed but negotiable. For example, when a middle-class youth was arrested, he was less likely to be charged. This was partly because his background did not fit the idea of the police's 'typical delinquent', and partly because his parents were more likely to be able to negotiate successfully on his behalf, convincing the control agencies that he was sorry, that they would monitor him and ensure he stayed out of trouble in future. As a result, typically, he was 'counselled, warned and released' rather than prosecuted.

Topic versus resource

Cicourel's study has implications for the use we make of official crime statistics recorded by the police. He argues that these statistics do not give us a valid picture of the patterns of crime and cannot be used as a *resource* – that is, as facts about crime.

Instead, we should treat them as a *topic* for sociologists to investigate. That is, we must not take crime statistics at face value; instead, we should investigate the processes that created them. This will shed light on the activities of the control agencies and how they process and label certain types of people as criminal.

Activity **Discussion**

The negotiation of justice

...go to www.sociology.uk.net

The social construction of crime statistics

Interactionists see the official crime statistics as socially constructed. At each stage of the criminal justice system, agents of social control (such as police officers or prosecutors) make decisions about whether or not to proceed to the next stage. The outcome depends on the label they attach to the individual suspect or defendant in the course of their interactions. This label is likely to be affected by the typifications or stereotypes they hold about him or her.

As a result, the statistics produced by the criminal justice system only tell us about the activities of the police and prosecutors, rather than about the amount of crime out there in society or who commits it. The statistics are really just counts of the decisions made by control agents at the different 'decision gates' or stages in the justice system. As Figure 2.1 shows, at each 'gate', a decision is made, steadily whittling down the number of people in the system.

The dark figure of crime The difference between the official statistics and the 'real' rate of crime is sometimes called the dark figure, because we do not know for certain how much crime goes undetected, unreported and unrecorded.

Alternative statistics Some sociologists use victim surveys (where people are asked what crimes they have been victims of) or self-report studies (where they are asked what crimes they have committed) to gain a more accurate view of the amount of crime. These can add to our picture of crime, but they have several limitations. For example, people may

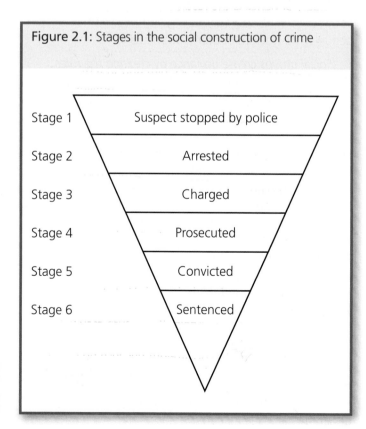

Figure 2.1: Stages in the social construction of crime

Stage 1	Suspect stopped by police
Stage 2	Arrested
Stage 3	Charged
Stage 4	Prosecuted
Stage 5	Convicted
Stage 6	Sentenced

forget, conceal or exaggerate when asked if they have committed a crime or been the victim of one. In addition, such surveys usually only include a selection of (generally less serious) offences.

The effects of labelling

Labelling theorists are interested in the effects of labelling upon those who are labelled. They claim that, by labelling certain people as criminal or deviant, society actually encourages them to become more so.

Primary and secondary deviance

Edwin Lemert (1951) distinguishes between primary and secondary deviance. Primary deviance refers to deviant acts that have not been publicly labelled. Lemert argues that it is pointless to seek the causes of primary deviance, since it is so widespread that it is unlikely to have a single cause, and in any case it is often trivial, e.g. fare dodging, and mostly goes uncaught.

These acts are not part of an organised deviant way of life, so offenders can easily rationalise them away, for example as a 'moment of madness'. They have little significance for the individual's status or self-concept. In short, primary deviants don't generally see themselves as deviant.

Master status However, some deviance *is* labelled. Secondary deviance is the result of societal reaction – that is, of labelling. Being caught and publicly labelled as a criminal can involve being stigmatised, shamed, humiliated, shunned or excluded from normal society. Once an individual is labelled, others may come to see him only in terms of the label. This becomes his *master status* or controlling identity, overriding all others. In the eyes of the world, he is no longer a colleague, father or neighbour; he is now a thief, junkie or paedophile – in short, an outsider.

This can provoke a crisis for the individual's *self-concept* or sense of identity. One way to resolve this crisis is for the individual to accept the deviant label and see themselves as the world sees them. In turn, this may lead to a *self-fulfilling prophecy*, in which the individual acts out or lives up to their deviant label, thereby becoming what the label says they are. Lemert refers to the further deviance that results from acting out the label as *secondary deviance*.

Deviant career Secondary deviance is likely to provoke further hostile reactions from society and reinforce the deviant's 'outsider' status. Again, this in turn may lead to more deviance and a *deviant career*. For example, the ex-convict finds it hard to go straight because no one will employ him, so he seeks out other outsiders for support. This may involve joining a *deviant subculture* that offers deviant career opportunities and role models, rewards deviant behaviour, and confirms his deviant identity.

Jock Young (1971) uses the concepts of secondary deviance and deviant career in his study of hippy marijuana users in Notting Hill. Initially, drugs were peripheral to the hippies' lifestyle – an example of primary deviance. However, persecution and labelling by the *control culture* (the police) led the hippies increasingly to see themselves as outsiders. They retreated into closed groups where they began to develop a deviant subculture, wearing longer hair and more 'way out' clothes. Drug use became a central activity, attracting further attention from the police and creating a self-fulfilling prophecy.

The work of Lemert and Young illustrates the idea that it is not the act itself, but the hostile societal reaction to it, that creates serious deviance. Ironically, therefore, the social control processes that are meant to produce law-abiding behaviour may in fact produce the very opposite.

However, although a deviant career is a common outcome of labelling, labelling theorists are quick to point out that it is not inevitable. As Downes and Rock (2003) note, we cannot predict whether someone who has been labelled will follow a deviant career, because they are always free to choose not to deviate further.

> **Application**
>
> Suggest two ways in which a person might try to resist a label.

Deviance amplification spiral

The deviance amplification spiral is a term labelling theorists use to describe a process in which the attempt to control deviance leads to an increase in the level of deviance. This leads to greater attempts to control it and, in turn, this produces yet higher levels of deviance. More and more control produces more and more deviance, in an escalating spiral, as in the case of the hippies described by Young.

Labelling theorists have applied the concept of the deviance amplification spiral to various forms of group behaviour. An example of this is Stanley Cohen's (1972) *Folk Devils and Moral Panics*, a study of the societal reaction to the 'mods and rockers' disturbances involving groups of youths at English seaside resorts.

Press exaggeration and distorted reporting of the events began a moral panic, with growing public concern and with moral entrepreneurs calling for a 'crackdown'. The police responded by arresting more youths, while the courts imposed harsher penalties. This seemed to confirm the truth of the original media reaction and provoked more public concern, in an upward spiral of deviance amplification. At the same time, the demonising of the mods and rockers as 'folk devils' caused their further marginalisation as 'outsiders', resulting in more deviant behaviour on their part. (See Topic 7 for more about the media's role in moral panics.)

We can see the deviance amplification spiral as similar to Lemert's idea of secondary deviance. In both cases, the societal reaction to an initial deviant act leads not to successful control of the deviance, but to further deviance, which in turn leads to a greater reaction and so on. It also illustrates an important difference between labelling theory and functionalist theories of deviance. As Lemert (1967) puts it, these theories:

> 'rest heavily on the idea that deviance leads to social control. I have come to believe the reverse idea, i.e. social control leads to deviance.'

Folk devils vs. the dark figure Folk devils are in a sense the opposites of the dark figure of crime. While the dark figure is about unlabelled, unrecorded crime that is ignored by the public and the police, folk devils and their actions are 'over-labelled' and over-exposed to public view and the attentions of the authorities. In terms of law enforcement and the justice system, the pursuit of folk devils draws resources away from detecting and punishing the crimes that make up the dark figure, such as the crimes of the powerful.

Labelling and criminal justice policy

Studies have shown how increases in the attempt to control and punish young offenders can have the opposite effect. For example, in the USA, Triplett (2000) notes an increasing tendency to see young offenders as evil and to be less tolerant of minor deviance. The criminal justice system has re-labelled status offences such as truancy as more serious offences, resulting in much harsher sentences. As predicted by Lemert's theory of secondary deviance, this has resulted in an increase rather than a decrease in offending. De Haan (2000) notes a similar outcome in Holland as a result of the increasing stigmatisation of young offenders.

These findings indicate that labelling theory has important policy implications. They add weight to the argument that negative labelling pushes offenders towards a deviant career. Therefore logically, to reduce deviance, we should make and enforce fewer rules for people to break.

For example, by decriminalising soft drugs, we might reduce the number of people with criminal convictions and hence the risk of secondary deviance. Similarly, labelling theory implies that we should avoid publicly 'naming and shaming' offenders, since this is likely to create a perception of them as evil outsiders and, by excluding them from mainstream society, push them into further deviance.

▲ Disintegrative shaming - convicted of burglary in Dougherty, Georgia, USA, this woman was sentenced to stand outside the courthouse wearing the sign.

Reintegrative shaming

Most labelling theorists see labelling as having negative effects. However, John Braithwaite (1989) identifies a more positive role for the labelling process. He distinguishes between two types of shaming (negative labelling):

- **Disintegrative shaming**, where not only the crime, but also the criminal, is labelled as bad and the offender is excluded from society.
- **Reintegrative shaming**, by contrast, labels the act but not the actor – as if to say, 'he has done a bad thing', rather than 'he is a bad person'.

The policy of reintegrative shaming avoids stigmatising the offender as evil while at the same time making them aware of the negative impact of their actions upon others, and then encourages others to forgive them. This makes it easier for both offender and community to separate the offender from the offence and re-admit the wrongdoer back into mainstream society. At the same time, this avoids pushing them into secondary deviance. Braithwaite argues that crime rates tend to be lower in societies where reintegrative rather than disintegrative shaming is the dominant way of dealing with offenders.

Activity	Webquest
Reintegrative shaming	

...go to www.sociology.uk.net

Mental illness and suicide: the sociology of deviance

Interactionists are interested not just in crime but in deviant behaviour more widely. Here we focus on two important areas generally regarded as deviant: mental illness and suicide.

Suicide

Suicide has been an important topic in the development of sociology. Durkheim (1897) studied it with the aim of showing that sociology is a science. Using official statistics, he claimed to have discovered the causes of suicide in how effectively society integrated individuals and regulated their behaviour.

However, interactionists reject Durkheim's positivist approach and his reliance on official statistics. They argue that to understand suicide, we must study its meanings for those who choose to kill themselves.

Douglas: the meaning of suicide

Jack Douglas (1967) takes an interactionist approach to suicide. He is critical of the use of official suicide statistics for the same reasons as interactionists distrust official crime statistics. Both are socially constructed and they tell us about the activities of the people who construct them, such as police (in the case of crime) and coroners (in the case of suicide), rather than the real rate of crime or suicide in society.

For example, whether a death comes to be officially labelled as suicide rather than, say, an accident or homicide, depends on the interactions and negotiations between social actors such as the coroner, relatives, friends, doctors and so on.

For instance, relatives may feel guilty about failing to prevent the death and press for a verdict of misadventure rather than suicide. Similarly, a coroner with strong religious beliefs that suicide is a sin may be reluctant to bring in a suicide verdict.

The statistics therefore tell us nothing about the meanings behind an individual's decision to commit suicide. If we want to understand their meanings, Douglas argues, we must use qualitative methods instead, such as the analysis of suicide notes, or unstructured interviews with the deceased's friends and relatives, or with people who have survived a suicide attempt. This would allow us to 'get behind' the labels coroners attach to deaths and discover their true meaning.

Atkinson: coroners' commonsense knowledge

Max Atkinson (1978) agrees that official statistics are merely a record of the labels coroners attach to deaths. He argues that it is impossible to know for sure what meanings the dead gave to their deaths.

Atkinson therefore focuses instead on the taken-for-granted assumptions that coroners make when reaching their verdicts. He found that their ideas about a 'typical suicide' were important; certain modes of death (e.g. hanging), location and circumstances of the death, and life history (e.g. a recent bereavement) were seen as typical of suicides. One coroner said that if the deceased had taken more than ten sleeping pills, 'I can be almost sure it was a suicide'.

However, Atkinson's approach can be used against him. If he is correct that all we can do is have interpretations of the social world, rather than real facts about it (such as how many deaths are really suicides), then his account is no more than an interpretation and there is no good reason to accept it.

Mental illness

As with crime and suicide, interactionists reject official statistics on mental illness because they regard these as social constructs. That is, they are simply a record of the activities of those such as psychiatrists with the power to attach labels such as 'schizophrenic' or 'paranoid' to others. Crime, suicide and mental illness statistics are artefacts (things made by human beings), not objective social facts.

Paranoia as a self-fulfilling prophecy

As with crime, interactionists are interested in how a person comes to be labelled as mentally ill, and in the effects of this labelling. An example of this is Lemert's (1962) study of paranoia. Lemert notes that some individuals don't fit easily into groups. As a result of this primary deviance, others label the person as odd and begin to exclude him.

His negative response to this is the beginning of his secondary deviance, and it gives others further reason to exclude him. They may begin discussing the best way of dealing with this difficult person. This seems to confirm his suspicions that people are conspiring against him. His reaction justifies their fears for his mental health, and this may lead to a psychiatric intervention, resulting in being officially labelled and perhaps placed in hospital against his will.

As a result, the label 'mental patient' becomes his *master status*. Henceforth, everything he says or does will be interpreted in this light.

An example of this comes from Rosenhan's (1973) 'pseudo-patient' experiment, in which researchers had themselves admitted to a number of hospitals claiming to have been 'hearing voices'. They were diagnosed as schizophrenic and this became their master status. Thus, despite acting normally, they were treated by staff as mentally ill. For example, the pseudo-patients kept notes of their experiences, but staff interpreted this as a symptom of illness.

Institutionalisation

Goffman's (1961) classic study *Asylums* shows some of the possible effects of being admitted to a 'total institution' such as a psychiatric hospital.

On admission, the inmate undergoes a 'mortification of the self' in which their old identity is symbolically 'killed off' and replaced by a new one: 'inmate'. This is achieved by various 'degradation rituals', such as confiscation of personal effects. Goffman notes the similarities with other total institutions such as prisons, armies, monasteries and boarding schools.

Goffman also shows that while some inmates become institutionalised, internalising their new identity and unable to re-adjust to the outside world, others adopt various forms of resistance or accommodation to their new situation.

An example of this comes from Braginski et al's (1969) study of long-term psychiatric patients. They found that inmates manipulated their symptoms so as to appear 'not well enough' to be discharged but 'not sick enough' to be confined to the ward. As a result, they were able to achieve their aim of free movement around the hospital.

Evaluation of labelling theory

Labelling theory shows that the law is not a fixed set of rules to be taken for granted, but something whose construction we need to explain. It shows that the law is often enforced in discriminatory ways, and that crime statistics are more a record of the activities of control agents than of criminals. It also shows that society's attempts to control deviance can backfire and create more deviance, not less.

However, it is criticised on several grounds:

- It tends to be deterministic, implying that once someone is labelled, a deviant career is inevitable.
- Its emphasis on the negative effects of labelling gives the offender a kind of victim status. Realist sociologists argue that this ignores the real victims of crime.
- It tends to focus on less serious crimes such as drug-taking.
- By assuming that offenders are passive victims of labelling, it ignores the fact that individuals may actively choose deviance.
- It fails to explain why people commit primary deviance in the first place, before they are labelled.
- It implies that without labelling, deviance would not exist. This leads to the strange conclusion that someone who commits a crime but is not labelled has not deviated. It also implies that deviants are unaware that they are deviant until labelled. Yet most are well aware that they are going against social norms.
- It recognises the role of power in creating deviance, but it fails to analyse the source of this power. As a result, it focuses on 'middle range officials' such as policemen who apply the labels, rather than on the capitalist class who (in the view of Marxists) make the rules in the first place. It also fails to explain the origin of the labels, or why they are applied to certain groups, such as the working class.

Topic summary

For labelling theory, an act only becomes deviant when **labelled** as such, through **societal reaction**. Not every offender is labelled, and labelling theory is interested in how the laws are **selectively enforced** against some groups. This means **official statistics are invalid**: they only tell us about the types of people the control agencies have labelled, not the real patterns of crime.

Labelling may cause the label to become the individual's **master status**. A deviance **amplification spiral** may result, in which increased control leads to increased deviance. Interactionists have applied labelling theory to the study of **suicide** and **mental illness**.

Labelling theory has implications for criminal **justice policies**, suggesting we should avoid labelling individuals unnecessarily. Labelling theory is **criticised** for determinism and failing to explain primary deviance and the origin of labels.

EXAMINING INTERACTIONISM AND LABELLING THEORY

QuickCheck Questions

Check your answers at www.sociology.uk.net

1 Explain what is meant by the phrase, 'deviance is in the eye of the beholder'.
2 True or false? Secondary deviance refers to less important acts of deviance.
3 Identify three agencies of social control.
4 What is meant by the 'dark figure' of crime?
5 What is meant by a 'total institution'?

6 Lemert argues that 'social control leads to deviance'. What does he mean?
7 What is a self-fulfilling prophecy?
8 According to Marxists, what does labelling theory fail to tell us about power?
9 What is determinism? Why do critics accuse labelling theory of being deterministic?

Questions to try

Item A   Labelling theorists argue that an act is not inherently criminal; it only becomes so when it is labelled as such. They are interested in the ways that labelling affects the actions of those with the power to label acts as criminal, such as the police and courts. Being labelled can also have important effects on individuals to whom the label is attached, and labelling a group as criminal can even lead to higher rates of crime being recorded.

Item B   Rather than look for the initial causes of the deviant act, as functionalists do, labelling theorists ask how and why some groups and acts come to be labelled as criminal or deviant while others do not. Coming from an interactionist perspective, they argue that what we mean by crime or deviance is the outcome of the same processes of social interaction – between police officer and suspect, for example – as any other social behaviour. Therefore to understand crime and deviance, we must grasp the meanings involved in the interaction.

1 Outline two criticisms of labelling theory.   (4 marks)
2 Applying material from Item A, analyse two effects of the labelling process on individuals and groups.   (10 marks)
3 Applying material from Item B and your knowledge, evaluate the contribution of labelling theory to our understanding of crime and deviance.   (30 marks)

The Examiner's Advice

Q2 Spend about 15 minutes on this question. Divide your time fairly equally between the two effects. You don't need a separate introduction; just start on your first effect. To answer this question, it's essential that you take two points from the Item and show through a chain of reasoning (see Box 4.1 in chapter 4) how each is an effect of the labelling process. (It is a very good idea to quote from the Item when doing so.)

You could use the idea of effects on those with power to label, effects on individuals who are labelled, or effects on recorded crime rates. For example, labelling may create a deviancy amplification spiral, where attempts to control a crime lead to further cases being uncovered and recorded, in turn producing a further reaction from the authorities and yet more cases being recorded. You can offer some brief evaluation, e.g. that labelling is deterministic.

Use concepts and issues such as those above plus moral entrepreneurs, primary and secondary deviance, self-concept, self-fulfilling prophecy, marginalisation, folk devils, moral panic, societal reaction, stigmatisation and shaming. Use studies such as Cicourel, Lemert, Young, Cohen, Triplett, De Haan and Braithwaite.

Q3 Spend about 45 minutes on this. Start with the key idea that an act or person is only deviant when labelled as such and link this to the concepts of social interaction and construction.

Examine the role of moral entrepreneurs and control agents' typifications in law-making and law enforcement, including the negotiation of justice. Consider what this means for the validity of crime statistics. Explain the role of societal reaction in creating secondary deviance and its impact on the individual. Examine the creation of deviance amplification spirals, including the role of the media. Use examples such as mental illness, drug users and suicide to illustrate key ideas. Evaluate labelling theory in terms of issues such as determinism, neglect of initial causes of deviance, and failure to explain the source of the power to label.

Use concepts and issues such as the above plus class, ethnicity, age, juvenile delinquency, topic versus resource, self-concept, self-fulfilling prophecy, deviant career, deviant subculture, moral panics, folk devils and social policy implications. Use studies such as Becker, Platt, Piliavin and Briar, Cicourel, Lemert, Goffman, Rosenhan, Braginski et al, Douglas, Atkinson, Young, Downes and Rock, Cohen, Triplett and De Haan.

TOPIC 3

24 April 2013, Dhaka, Bangladesh: a garment factory collapsed with a death toll of 1,129. Cracks appeared the day before, but the workers were ordered to work. Over two years later, only eight out of 3,425 factories inspected had remedied building violations adequately.

GETTING STARTED

Working in pairs, answer the following:

1. Using your knowledge of Marxism from other topics you have already studied in your course, write a summary of the Marxist view of society. Use as many of the following concepts as you can: capitalism, bourgeoisie, proletariat, consumerism, means of production, alienation, ideology, private property, the state, exploitation, repressive state apparatus.

2. What kinds of crime might the proletariat commit?

3. What kinds of crime might the bourgeoisie commit?

4. Of the two social classes, which one do you think would be more likely to get away with their crimes? Give reasons for your answer.

Learning objectives

After studying this Topic, you should:

- Understand why Marxists see crime as inevitable in capitalist society.

- Understand Marxist and neo-Marxist approaches to crime and deviance, and the similarities and differences between them.

- Be able to evaluate the strengths and limitations of Marxist and neo-Marxist approaches to crime and deviance.

- Understand the nature and extent of white collar and corporate crime, and be able to evaluate sociological explanations of it.

Explaining class differences in crime

Official statistics from a number of countries around the world consistently show social class differences in rates of offending, with the working class more likely to commit offences than higher social classes. The theories we examined in Topics 1 and 2 offer different explanations for this pattern and we re-cap them here before focusing on Marxist views.

Functionalism

Functionalism sees the law as a reflection of society's shared values, and crime as the product of inadequate or inappropriate socialisation into these values. Not everyone is equally well socialised into society's shared culture. In modern societies with their complex division of labour, different groups and classes may develop their own separate subcultures.

For example, Walter B. Miller argues that the lower class has developed an independent subculture with its own distinctive norms and values that clash with those of the mainstream culture, and this explains why the lower class have a higher crime rate. Conforming to subcultural norms such as toughness and the pursuit of excitement can lead to conflict with the law.

Strain theory

Strain theory argues that people engage in deviant behaviour when their opportunities to achieve in legitimate ways are blocked. For example, Merton argues that American society's class structure denies working-class people the opportunity to achieve the 'money success' that American culture values so highly.

As the working class are more likely to be denied legitimate opportunities to achieve success (for example, through educational achievement and a good job), so they are more likely to seek illegitimate means of achieving it. Merton calls this 'innovation': the use of 'new', deviant means such as theft, fraud or other property crime to gain wealth. In Merton's view, this explains why the working class has a higher rate of utilitarian crime (crime for material gain) than the middle class.

Subcultural theories

Subcultural theories start from Merton's idea that the working class suffer from blocked opportunities to achieve success by legitimate means. For example, A.K. Cohen sees working-class youths as culturally deprived – they have not been socialised into the mainstream, middle-class culture. As a result, they lack the means to achieve in education and find themselves at the bottom of the official status hierarchy. Their failure to achieve gives rise to status frustration.

The delinquent subculture that they form or join is a solution to the problem of status frustration. By inverting mainstream values such as respect for property, working-class youths can gain status from their peers, for example by vandalising property. Cohen's theory thus helps to explain why the working class are more likely to commit non-utilitarian crime.

Cloward and Ohlin build on Merton and Cohen. They use the concept of illegitimate opportunity structures to explain why a range of different crimes are more prevalent within the working class. They identify a criminal subculture in stable working-class neighbourhoods that offers professional criminal career opportunities, a conflict subculture of gang violence and 'turf wars' in poor areas with a high population turnover, and a retreatist, 'dropout' drug subculture made up of those who fail in both legitimate and illegitimate opportunity structures.

Labelling theory

The functionalist, strain and subcultural theories just described have been called 'problem takers'. That is, they take for granted that the official statistics are broadly accurate and that working-class crime is the problem that needs to be explained. They focus their efforts on discovering the cause of the problem, for example inappropriate socialisation or blocked opportunities.

As we saw in Topic 2, labelling theorists take a very different approach:

- They reject the view that official statistics are a useful resource for sociologists that give a valid picture of which class commits most crime.
- Instead of seeking the supposed causes of working-class criminality, they focus on how and why working-class people come to be *labelled* as criminal. They emphasise the stereotypes held by law enforcement agencies that see the working class as 'typical criminals', and the power of these agencies to successfully label powerless groups such as the working class.

For this reason, labelling theorists have been described as 'problem makers'. They do not see official crime statistics as valid social facts or a useful *resource*. Rather, crime statistics are a *topic* whose construction we must investigate by studying the power of control agents to label working-class people as criminal.

Marxism, class and crime

Marxists agree with labelling theorists that the law is enforced disproportionately against the working class and that therefore the official crime statistics cannot be taken at face value. However, they criticise labelling theory for failing to examine the wider structure of capitalism within which law making, law enforcement and offending take place. Marxist explanations of crime and deviance flow from their view of the nature of capitalist society.

Marxists see capitalist society as divided into two classes: the ruling capitalist class (or bourgeoisie) who own the means of production, and the working class (or proletariat), whose alienated labour the bourgeoisie exploit to produce profit.

Marxism is a structural theory. It sees society as a structure in which the economic base (the capitalist economy) determines the shape of the superstructure, which is made up of all the other social institutions, including the state, the law and the criminal justice system. Their function is to serve ruling-class interests and maintain the capitalist economy.

For Marxists, the structure of capitalist society explains crime. Their view of crime has three main elements:

- Criminogenic capitalism
- The state and law making
- Ideological functions of crime and law

Criminogenic capitalism

For Marxists, crime is inevitable in capitalism because capitalism is *criminogenic* – by its very nature it causes crime.

Capitalism is based on the exploitation of the working class – that is, on using them as a means to an end (profit), whatever the human cost of doing so. It is therefore particularly damaging to the working class and this may give rise to crime:

- Poverty may mean that crime is the only way the working class can survive.
- Crime may be the only way they can obtain the consumer goods encouraged by capitalist advertising, resulting in utilitarian crimes such as theft.
- Alienation and lack of control over their lives may lead to frustration and aggression, resulting in non-utilitarian crimes such as violence and vandalism.

However, crime is not confined to the working class. Capitalism is a 'dog eat dog' system of ruthless competition among capitalists, while the profit motive encourages a mentality of greed and self-interest. The need to win at all costs or go out of business, along with the desire for self-enrichment, encourages capitalists to commit white collar and corporate crimes such as tax evasion and breaches of health and safety laws. We deal with these 'crimes of the powerful' later in this Topic.

Thus, as David Gordon (1976) argues, crime is a rational response to the capitalist system and hence it is found in all social classes – even though the official statistics make it appear to be a largely working-class phenomenon.

The state and law making

Unlike functionalists, who see the law as reflecting the value consensus and representing the interests of society as a whole, Marxists see law making and law enforcement as only serving the interests of the capitalist class. For example, William Chambliss (1975) argues that laws to protect private property are the cornerstone of the capitalist economy.

Chambliss illustrates this with the case of the introduction of English law into Britain's East African colonies. Britain's economic interests lay in the colonies' tea, coffee and other plantations, which needed a plentiful supply of local labour.

At the time, the local economy was not a money economy and so, to force the reluctant African population to work for them, the British introduced a tax payable in cash, non-payment of which was a punishable criminal offence. Since cash to pay the tax could only be earned by working on the plantations, the law served the economic interests of the capitalist plantation owners.

The ruling class also have the power to prevent the introduction of laws that would threaten their interests. Thus, for example, there are few laws that seriously challenge the unequal distribution of wealth. Similarly, Laureen Snider (1993) argues that the capitalist state is reluctant to pass laws that regulate the activities of businesses or threaten their profitability.

Selective enforcement

Marxists agree with labelling theorists that although all classes commit crime, when it comes to the application of the law by the criminal justice system, there is selective enforcement. While powerless groups such as the working class and ethnic minorities are criminalised, the police and courts tend to ignore the crimes of the powerful.

> **Application**
> Suggest two examples of 'dog eat dog' situations produced by capitalism.

Ideological functions of crime and law

The law, crime and criminals also perform an ideological function for capitalism. Laws are occasionally passed that appear to be for the benefit of the working class rather than capitalism, such as workplace health and safety laws.

However, Frank Pearce (1976) argues that such laws often benefit the ruling class too – for example, by keeping workers fit for work. By giving capitalism a 'caring' face, such laws also create false consciousness among the workers.

In any case, such laws are not rigorously enforced. For example, despite a new law against corporate homicide being passed in 2007, in its first eight years there was only one successful prosecution of a UK company – despite the large numbers of deaths at work estimated to be caused by employers' negligence (Jenabi, 2014).

Furthermore, because the state enforces the law selectively, crime appears to be largely a working-class phenomenon. This divides the working class by encouraging workers to blame the criminals in their midst for their problems, rather than capitalism.

The media and some criminologists also contribute by portraying criminals as disturbed individuals, thereby concealing the fact that it is the nature of capitalism that makes people criminals.

Activity Webquest

Corporate manslaughter

...go to www.sociology.uk.net

Evaluation of Marxism

Marxism offers a useful explanation of the relationship between crime and capitalist society. It shows the link between law making and enforcement and the interests of the capitalist class. By doing so, it puts into a wider structural context the insights of labelling theory regarding the selective enforcement of the law.

However, the Marxist approach is criticised on several grounds:

- It largely ignores the relationship between crime and non-class inequalities such as ethnicity and gender.
- It is too deterministic and over-predicts the amount of crime in the working class: not all poor people commit crime, despite the pressures of poverty.
- Not all capitalist societies have high crime rates; for example, the homicide rate in Japan and Switzerland is only about a fifth of that in the United States. (However, as Marxists point out, societies with little or no state welfare provision, such as the USA, tend to have higher crime rates.)
- The criminal justice system does sometimes act against the interests of the capitalist class. For example, prosecutions for corporate crime do occur. (However, Marxists argue that such occasional prosecutions perform an ideological function in making the system seem impartial.)
- Left realists argue that Marxism ignores intra-class crimes (where both the criminals and victims are working-class) such as burglary and 'mugging', which cause great harm to victims.

Neo-Marxism: critical criminology

Neo-Marxists are sociologists who have been influenced by many of the ideas put forward by Marxism, but they combine these with ideas from other approaches such as labelling theory.

The most important neo-Marxist contribution to our understanding of crime and deviance has been *The New Criminology*, by Ian Taylor, Paul Walton and Jock Young (1973).

Taylor et al agree with Marxists that:

- Capitalist society is based on exploitation and class conflict and characterised by extreme inequalities of wealth and power. Understanding this is the key to understanding crime.

- The state makes and enforces laws in the interests of the capitalist class and criminalises members of the working class.
- Capitalism should be replaced by a classless society. This would greatly reduce the extent of crime or even rid society of crime entirely.

However, the views of Taylor et al also differ significantly from those of Marxists. Much of their book is a critique of existing theories of crime and deviance, including both Marxist and non-Marxist approaches, and they describe their approach as *critical criminology*.

Anti-determinism

Taylor et al argue that Marxism is *deterministic*. For example, it sees workers as driven to commit crime out of economic necessity. They reject this explanation, along with theories that claim crime is caused by other external factors such as anomie, subcultures or labelling, or by biological and psychological factors.

Instead, Taylor et al take a more *voluntaristic* view (voluntarism is the idea that we have free will – the opposite of determinism). They see crime as meaningful action and a conscious choice by the actor. In particular, they argue that crime often has a political motive, for example to redistribute wealth from the rich to the poor. Criminals are not passive puppets whose behaviour is shaped by capitalism: they are deliberately striving to change society.

A fully social theory of deviance

Taylor et al aim to create a 'fully social theory of deviance' – a comprehensive understanding of crime and deviance that would help to change society for the better. This theory would have two main sources:

- Marxist ideas about the unequal distribution of wealth and who has the power to make and enforce the law.
- Ideas from interactionism and labelling theory about the meaning of the deviant act for the actor, societal reactions to it, and the effects of the deviant label on the individual.

In their view, a complete theory of deviance needs to unite six aspects:

1 **The wider origins of the deviant act** in the unequal distribution of wealth and power in capitalist society.

2 **The immediate origins of the deviant act** – the particular context in which the individual decides to commit the act.

3 **The act itself** and its meaning for the actor – e.g. was it a form of rebellion against capitalism?

4 **The immediate origins of social reaction** – the reactions of those around the deviant, such as police, family and community, to discovering the deviance.

5 **The wider origins of social reaction** in the structure of capitalist society – especially the issue of who has the power to define actions as deviant and to label others, and why some acts are treated more harshly than others.

6 **The effects of labelling** on the deviant's future actions – e.g. why does labelling lead to deviance amplification in some cases but not in others?

For Taylor et al, these six aspects are interrelated and need to be understood together as part of a single unified theory.

> **Application**
>
> Taylor et al's sixth point comes from labelling theory. Which of the other five points owe most to labelling theory and which to Marxism?

Evaluation of critical criminology

Taylor et al's approach is criticised on several grounds:

Feminists criticise it for being 'gender blind', focusing excessively on male criminality and at the expense of female criminality.

Left realists make two related criticisms.

- Critical criminology romanticises working-class criminals as 'Robin Hoods' who are fighting capitalism by re-distributing wealth from the rich to the poor. However, in reality these criminals mostly prey on the poor.
- Taylor et al do not take such crime seriously and they ignore its effects on working-class victims.

Roger Hopkins Burke (2005) argues that critical criminology is both too general to *explain* crime and too idealistic to be useful in *tackling* crime. However, Stuart Hall et al (1978) have applied Taylor et al's approach to explain the moral panic over mugging in the 1970s (see Topic 6).

Taylor, Walton and Young have all changed their views since *The New Criminology* was published. However, Walton (1998) and Young (1998) defend some aspects of the book's approach. They argue that:

- In calling for greater tolerance of diversity in behaviour, the book combated the 'correctionalist bias' in most existing theories – the assumption that sociology's role is simply to find ways of correcting deviant behaviour.
- The book laid some of the foundations for later radical approaches that seek to establish a more just society, such as left realist and feminist theories.

Crimes of the powerful

As we saw earlier, Marxists note that although all classes commit crime, the law is selectively enforced so that higher-class and corporate offenders are less likely to be prosecuted than working-class offenders.

For example, Reiman and Leighton's (2012) book, *The Rich Get Richer and the Poor Get Prison*, shows that the more likely a crime is to be committed by higher-class people, the less likely it is to be treated as an offence. There is a much higher rate of prosecutions for the typical 'street' crimes that poor people commit, such as burglary and assault. Yet with the crimes committed by the higher classes, such as serious tax evasion, the criminal justice system takes a more forgiving view.

In this section we examine evidence of the extent and impact of the crimes of the powerful, as well as the failure of the criminal justice system to respond adequately to their crimes.

White collar and corporate crime

The term 'white collar crime' was coined by Edwin Sutherland (1949), which he defined as:

'a crime committed by a person of respectability and high social status in the course of his occupation'.

Sutherland's aim was to challenge the stereotype that crime is purely a lower-class phenomenon. However, his definition fails to distinguish between two different types of crime:

- **Occupational crime** committed by employees simply for their own personal gain, often *against* the organisation for which they work, e.g. stealing from the company or its customers.
- **Corporate crime** committed by employees *for* their organisation in pursuit of its goals, e.g. deliberately mis-selling products to increase company profits.

A further problem comes from the fact that many of the harms caused by the powerful do not break the criminal law. For example, some may be administrative offences such as a company failing to comply with codes of practice laid down by government regulators.

To overcome this problem, Pearce and Tombs (2003) widen the definition. They define corporate crime as

any illegal act or omission that is the result of deliberate decisions or culpable negligence by a legitimate business organisation and that is intended to benefit the business.

This includes breaches of civil and administrative law, not just criminal law. Tombs (2013) argues that the difference between these types of offence is more about who has the power to define an act as a crime than about how harmful the act is: powerful corporations can influence the law so that their actions are not criminalised.

The scale and types of corporate crime

White collar and corporate crime do far more harm than 'ordinary' or 'street' crime such as theft and burglary. For example, one estimate puts the cost of white collar crimes in the USA at over ten times that of ordinary crimes.

Tombs (2013) notes that corporate crime has enormous costs: physical (deaths, injuries and illnesses), environmental (pollution) and economic (to consumers, workers, taxpayers and governments). He concludes that corporate crime is not just the work of a few 'bad apples', but rather it is 'widespread, routine and pervasive'.

Corporate crime covers a wide range of acts and omissions, including the following:

Financial crimes such as tax evasion, bribery, money laundering and illegal accounting. Victims include other companies, shareholders, taxpayers and governments.

Crimes against consumers, such as false labelling and selling unfit goods (including 'food crime'). In 2011, the French government recommended that women with breast implants from the manufacturer, Poly Implant Prothèse, have these removed because they were filled with dangerous industrial silicone rather than more expensive medical silicone. Some 300,000 implants had been sold in 65 countries.

Crimes against employees, such as sexual and racial discrimination, violations of wage laws, of rights to join a union or take industrial action, and of health and safety laws. Tombs (2013) calculates that up to 1,100 work-related deaths a year involve employers breaking the law. This is more than the annual total of homicides. Palmer (2008) estimates that occupational diseases cause 50,000 deaths a year in the UK.

Crimes against the environment include illegal pollution of air, water and land, such as toxic waste dumping. Following an investigation by US authorities in 2015, Volkswagen admitted installing software in 11 million of its diesel vehicles globally. The software could detect when the engines were being tested and disguised emissions levels that were 40 times above the US legal limit. (For more on such 'green crimes', see Topic 8.)

State-corporate crime refers to the harms committed when government institutions and businesses cooperate to pursue their goals (Kramer and Michalowski, 2006).

This is an increasingly important area, because private companies now work alongside government in many areas, for example in marketised or privatised public services such as education, winning armaments contracts with foreign governments, and the 'war on terror'.

For example, private companies contracted to the US military have been accused of involvement in the torture of detainees during the American occupation of Iraq. (For more on state-corporate crime, see Topic 8.)

The abuse of trust

High-status professionals occupy positions of trust and respectability. As Carrabine et al (2014) note, we entrust them with our finances, our health, our security and our personal information. However, their position and status give them the opportunity to abuse this trust.

For example, the multinational accountancy firm KPMG admitted in the USA to criminal wrongdoing and paid a $456m fine for its role in a tax fraud, while a UK tribunal found a tax avoidance scheme devised by accountants Ernst and Young for wealthy clients unacceptable. Described by a Treasury spokesperson as 'one of the most blatantly abusive scams of recent years', the scheme could have cost the taxpayer over £300m per year (Sikka 2008).

Similarly, accountants and lawyers can be employed by criminal organisations, for example to launder criminal funds into legitimate businesses. They can also act corruptly by inflating fees, committing forgery, illegally diverting clients' money etc.

The respected status, expertise and autonomy of health professionals also afford scope for criminal activity. The USA has seen huge numbers of fraudulent claims to insurance companies for treatments that have not actually been performed, while in the UK dentists have claimed payments from the NHS for treatments they have not carried out.

However, perhaps the most notorious case of abuse of trust is that of the GP Harold Shipman. In 2000, Shipman was convicted of the murder of 15 of his patients, but over the course of the previous 23 years, he is believed to have murdered at least another 200.

In 1976, Shipman had been convicted of obtaining the powerful opiate pethidine by forgery and deception, and in the same year obtained (in the name of a dying patient) enough morphine to kill 360 people. Yet for this he received only a warning from the General Medical Council and was allowed to continue practising as a GP.

Crime of this kind violates the trust that society places in professionals. In Sutherland's view, this makes white collar crime a greater threat to society than working-class 'street' crime because it promotes cynicism and distrust of basic social institutions and undermines the fabric of society.

The invisibility of corporate crime

Despite all this, when compared with street crime, the crimes of the powerful are relatively invisible; and even when visible, they are often not seen as 'real' crime at all. There are several reasons for this.

The media give very limited coverage to corporate crime, thus reinforcing the stereotype that crime is a working-class phenomenon. They describe corporate crime in sanitised language, as technical infringements rather than as real crime. For example, embezzlement becomes 'accounting irregularities'; defrauding customers is 'mis-selling'; deaths at work are 'accidents' rather than employers' negligence or cost-cutting.

Lack of political will to tackle corporate crime: politicians' rhetoric of being 'tough on crime' is focused instead on street crime. For example, while the Home Office uses crime surveys to discover the true extent of 'ordinary' crime, it does not do so for corporate crime.

The crimes are often complex and law enforcers are often understaffed, under-resourced and lacking technical expertise to investigate effectively.

De-labelling At the level of laws and legal regulation, corporate crime is consistently filtered out from the process of criminalisation. For example, offences are often defined as civil not criminal, and even in criminal cases, penalties are often fines rather than jail. Investigation and prosecution are also limited.

For example, in 2010, French authorities provided their British counterparts with a list of 3,600 UK citizens holding secret bank accounts with the Swiss subsidiary of the UK-based bank HSBC. The accounts were believed to be a means of evading tax. However, UK tax authorities secured only one prosecution, and no action was taken against HSBC.

Under-reporting Often the victim is society at large, or the environment, rather than an identifiable individual. Individuals may be unaware that they have been victimised (for example, you may not realise you have been illegally duped into buying the wrong mortgage). Even when victims are aware, they may not regard it as 'real crime'. Equally, they may feel powerless against a big organisation and so may never report the offence to the authorities.

Partial visibility?

All the above factors help to remove corporate crime from the dominant definitions of crime and the 'law and order' agenda, rendering it largely invisible.

However, since the financial crisis of 2008, the activities of a range of different people may have made corporate crime more visible. These include campaigns against corporate tax avoidance such as Occupy and UK Uncut, investigative journalists, whistle-blowers inside companies and the media (for example, through adverts for compensation claims over pensions mis-selling).

Similarly, neoliberal policies such as the marketisation and privatisation of public services mean that large corporations are much more involved in people's lives and thus more exposed to public scrutiny than in the past.

Explanations of corporate crime

Sociologists have put forward a variety of explanations of white collar and corporate crime. Often, these are general theories of crime that sociologists have applied to this particular type of crime. In some cases, sociologists have combined different theories in their explanations.

Strain theory

As we saw in Topic 1, Merton's anomie or 'strain' theory argues that deviance results from the inability of some people to achieve the goals that society's culture prescribes by using legitimate means. For example, where opportunities to achieve the goal of material wealth by legal means are blocked, individuals may 'innovate' – that is, use illegal methods such as theft to acquire it.

Merton applied his concept of innovation to explain working-class crime, but others have used it to explain corporate crime. For example, Box (1983) argues that if a company cannot achieve its goal of maximising profit by legal means, it may employ illegal ones instead. Thus, when business conditions become more difficult and profitability is squeezed, companies may be tempted to break the law.

For example, in the most wide-ranging documentary study of corporate crime to date, Clinard and Yeager (1980) found law violations by large companies increased as their financial performance deteriorated, suggesting a willingness to 'innovate' to achieve profit goals.

Differential association

Sutherland (1949) sees crime as behaviour learned from others in a social context. The less we associate with people who hold attitudes favourable to the law and the more we associate with people with criminal attitudes, the more likely we are to become deviant ourselves.

Thus, if a company's culture justifies committing crimes to achieve corporate goals, employees will be socialised into this criminality. For example, Geis (1967) found that individuals joining companies where illegal price-fixing was practised became involved in it as part of their socialisation.

We can link the idea of differential association to two other concepts:

Deviant subcultures are groups who share a set of norms and values at odds with those of wider society. They offer deviant solutions to their members' shared problems. Company employees face problems of achieving corporate goals and may adopt deviant means to do so, socialising new members into these.

The culture of business may also favour and promote competitive, aggressive personality types who are willing to commit crime to achieve success.

Techniques of neutralisation Sykes and Matza (1957) argue that individuals can deviate more easily if they can produce justifications to neutralise moral objections to their misbehaviour.

For example, white collar criminals may say they were carrying out orders from above, blame the victim ('they should have read the small print') or normalise their deviance by claiming that 'everyone's doing it'. Learning these techniques is an important part of socialisation into a deviant corporate culture.

Labelling theory

As we saw in Topic 2, whether an act counts as a crime depends on whether it has been successfully labelled as such. Typically, it is the working class who are more likely to have their actions defined as crimes. As Cicourel (1968) shows, the middle class are more able to negotiate non-criminal labels for their misbehaviour (e.g. as 'youthful high spirits' rather than 'vandalism').

De-labelling Sociologists have applied this to white collar and corporate crime, in an approach that Nelken (2012) calls 'de-labelling' or 'non-labelling'. Unlike the poor, businesses and professionals often have the power to avoid labelling. For example, they can afford expensive experts such as lawyers and accountants to help them avoid activities they are involved in, such as tax avoidance schemes, being labelled criminal, or to get the seriousness of any charges reduced.

Likewise, the reluctance or inability of law enforcement agencies to investigate and prosecute (for example, due to lack of resources) also reduces the number of offences officially recorded as such.

This means that sociologists who rely on official records and statistics will inevitably under-estimate the extent of these offences. For example, Clinard and Yeager (1980) are criticised for taking law enforcement agency records for granted as true measures of the extent of corporate crime.

Marxism

For Marxists, corporate crime is a result of the normal functioning of capitalism. In this view, because capitalism's goal is to maximise profits, it inevitably causes harm, such as deaths and injuries among employees and consumers.

At the same time, capitalism has successfully created what Box (1983) calls a 'mystification'. That is, it has spread the ideology that corporate crime is less widespread or harmful than working-class crime. Capitalism's control of the state means that it is able to avoid making or enforcing laws that conflict with its interests. While some corporate crime is prosecuted, this is only ever the tip of the iceberg. As Pearce (1976) argues, this sustains the illusion that it is the exception rather than the norm, and thus avoids causing a crisis of legitimacy for capitalism.

Some sociologists have combined Marxism with other approaches such as strain theory. For example, Box (1983) sees corporations as criminogenic because, if they find legitimate opportunities for profit are blocked, they will resort to illegal techniques aimed at competitors, consumers or the public.

Companies comply with the law only if they see it enforced strictly; where effective controls are lacking, for example in developing countries, capitalism shows its true face, selling unsafe products, paying low wages for work in dangerous conditions, polluting the environment and bribing officials.

Evaluation

Both strain theory and Marxism seem to over-predict the amount of business crime. As Nelken (2012) argues, it is unrealistic to assume that all businesses would offend were it not for the risk of punishment: for example, maintaining the goodwill of other companies that they must do business with may also prevent them resorting to crime.

Furthermore, even if capitalist pursuit of profit is a cause of corporate crime, this doesn't explain crime in non-profit making state agencies such as the police, army or civil service. For example, state agencies in the former communist regimes committed crimes against health and safety, the environment, and consumers. (For more on state crime, see Topic 8.)

Law abiding may also be more profitable than law breaking. Braithwaite (1984) found that US pharmaceutical companies that complied with Federal Drug Administration regulations to obtain licences for their products in America were then able to access lucrative markets in poorer countries. These countries couldn't afford their own drug-testing facilities and therefore relied on the FDA's licensing procedures as a guarantee of quality.

Activity Webquest

Corporate crime

...go to www.sociology.uk.net

Topic summary

Marxists see crime as **inevitable** in capitalist society because it breeds poverty, competition and greed. All classes commit crime, but because the **ruling class** control the state, they **make and enforce laws** in their own interests, criminalising the working class while escaping punishment for their own corporate crimes.

The law also performs an **ideological function** by giving capitalism a caring face. Marxism is criticised for ignoring **non-class inequalities** that affect crime and for **determinism** (over-predicting working-class crime).

Neo-Marxism or critical criminology sees crime as a conscious meaningful **choice** often with a political motive – a **rebellion** against capitalism. Critical criminology combines elements of Marxism and **labelling theory** in a 'fully social theory' of deviance. It has been **criticised** by left realists for ignoring the real harm crime does to working-class people.

White collar and corporate crimes are committed by high-status individuals and businesses. They are widespread and cause great **harm** yet remain largely **invisible** and are often not considered 'real' crime. **Differential association, strain theory, labelling theory** and **Marxism** have offered explanations of these crimes.

EXAMINING CLASS, POWER AND CRIME

QuickCheck Questions

Check your answers at www.sociology.uk.net

1 Why are functionalist, strain and subcultural theories called 'problem takers'?
2 Identify three ways in which capitalism can be said to be criminogenic.
3 How does the study of East Africa by Chambliss support the Marxist view of crime?
4 Identify two ways in which crime and the law perform an ideological function for capitalism.
5 Explain the difference between deterministic and voluntaristic views of behaviour.

6 Explain why critical criminology has been accused of being too idealistic to be useful in tackling crime.
7 What is meant by the 'correctionalist bias' in some theories of crime?
8 What is Sutherland's definition of white collar crime?
9 Explain the difference between occupational crime and corporate crime.
10 Name three types of corporate crime.
11 Identify three reasons for the invisibility of corporate crime.

Questions to try

Item A   Marxism sees capitalist society as divided along social class lines. The ruling class own the means of production and use their power to exploit the working class in the pursuit of profits, often resulting in workers living in poverty. This relationship then determines the shape of the superstructure – that is, all the other institutions that make up society, including the state, the law and the criminal justice system. Capitalism is also intensely competitive, with companies and individuals motivated to seek profits.

Item B   Some sociologists focus on the 'crimes of the powerful'. Crimes committed in the interests of businesses and other large institutions can be far more harmful and costly than the street crimes that we tend to think of as 'real crime'. Corporate crime can involve breaking criminal laws but may also include breaking other kinds of law. Some sociologists argue that corporate crime results from pressures to succeed, leading to employees pursuing business aims by illegitimate means. However, others claim that it is the product of capitalism.

1   Outline three reasons why white collar and corporate crime may have low rates of prosecution.   (6 marks)
2   Applying material from Item A, analyse two ways in which Marxists see class and crime as related.   (10 marks)
3   Applying material from Item B and your knowledge, evaluate sociological explanations of corporate crime.   (30 marks)

The Examiner's Advice

Q2 Spend about 15 minutes on this. Divide your time fairly equally between the two ways. You don't need a separate introduction; just start on your first way. To answer this question, it's essential that you take two points from the Item and show through a chain of reasoning how each is a way in which Marxists see crime and class as related. (It is a very good idea to quote from the Item when doing so.)

You could use the idea that capitalism shapes the law or justice system, that capitalism breeds a competitive, 'dog eat dog' mentality, or that exploitation causes poverty. For example, exploitation creates a situation in which the only way that some workers can survive is through turning to utilitarian crime. Capitalism is inherently criminogenic – its very nature creates criminal activity. You could briefly evaluate by noting that this is a very deterministic view.

Use concepts such as the above, plus the state, alienation, white collar and corporate crime, colonialism, ideology, and selective enforcement and law making. Use studies such as Gordon, Chambliss, Reiman, Pearce and Tombs, and examples of different types of crime.

Q3 Spend about 45 minutes on this. You need to examine a range of explanations. Begin by examining problems of defining corporate (including white collar) crime, including civil and administrative law-breaking. Examine its scale in terms of harms caused (e.g. compared with 'ordinary' crime) and the different types of corporate crime. Consider reasons for its relative invisibility and lack of criminalisation, such as complexity, role of the media and under-reporting.

Examine strain theory, differential association, labelling theory and Marxism as explanations of corporate crime, including ways in which some of these explanations have been combined. You can evaluate by questioning how far these theories over-predict the amount of corporate crime (e.g. why not all businesses commit crime), why it occurs in non-capitalist societies, or problems of relying on official statistics of corporate crime.

Use concepts and issues such as the above, plus criminogenic capitalism, innovation, crimes of the powerful, media representations, de-labelling, techniques of neutralisation, mystification and the state. Use studies such as Kramer and Michalowski, Carrabine, Box, Clinard and Yeager, Sykes and Matza, Nelken and Braithwaite. Use examples of corporate crime.

The reality of crime? Billboard, east London. In the background, the City of London, home to global financial institutions.

GETTING STARTED

Working in pairs, answer the following:

1 Imagine you are in a 'high crime' area. Describe your surroundings.
2 Why or how might the environment you describe encourage crime?
3 Based on your description of the area, what strategies would you introduce to reduce crime in this area?
4 From your own ideas and your knowledge of sociological explanations of the causes of crime, suggest reasons why people who live in this area might be involved in crime.
5 Based on the reasons you have suggested, what government policies could be introduced to tackle these causes?

Learning objectives

After studying this Topic, you should:

- Understand the difference between realist and other approaches to crime.

- Know the main features of right and left realist approaches to crime and understand their political context and the similarities and differences between them.

- Be able to evaluate the strengths and limitations of right and left realist approaches to crime.

REALIST THEORIES OF CRIME

Realist approaches to crime differ markedly from the theories examined in the last two Topics. Approaches such as labelling theory and critical criminology regard crime as socially constructed – the result of the way police and others label, stereotype and criminalise members of certain groups.

By contrast, realists see crime as a real problem to be tackled, and not just a social construction created by the control agencies. In addition, all realists:

- Argue that there has been a significant rise in the crime rate – especially in street crime, burglary and assault.
- Are concerned about the widespread fear of crime and about the impact of crime on its victims.
- Argue that other theories have failed to offer realistic solutions to the problem of crime and they propose what they regard as practical policies to reduce it.

Realist approaches emerged in the 1970s and 1980s in the political context of a shift to the right in politics. On both sides of the Atlantic, New Right conservative governments came to power, led by Margaret Thatcher in the UK and Ronald Reagan in the USA.

These governments favoured rolling back the welfare state together with a strong commitment to law and order. They favoured a 'get tough' stance on crime, with increased use of prison (and in the USA, the death penalty) and a 'short, sharp shock' approach to dealing with young offenders.

We can divide realist approaches along political lines:

- **Right realists** share the New Right or neo-conservative political outlook and support the policies described above.
- **Left realists** are socialists and favour quite different policies for reducing crime.

Right realism

Right realism sees crime, especially street crime, as a real and growing problem that destroys communities, undermines social cohesion and threatens society's work ethic. The right realist approach to crime has been very influential in the UK, the USA and elsewhere. For example, its main theorist, James Q. Wilson, was special adviser on crime to President Reagan, and it has provided the justification for widely adopted policies such as 'zero tolerance' of street crime and disorder.

Right realist views on crime correspond closely with those of neo-conservative governments during the 1970s and 1980s. For example, policy-makers argued that 'nothing works' – criminologists had produced many theories of crime, but no workable solutions to curb the rising crime rate.

This led to a shift in official thinking, away from the search for the causes of crime and towards a search for practical crime control measures. It also dovetailed with the US and UK governments' tough stance towards offenders and their view that the best way to reduce crime was through control and punishment, rather than rehabilitating offenders or tackling causes of crime such as poverty.

Right realism reflects this political climate. Right realists criticise other theories for failing to offer any practical solutions to the problem of rising crime. They also regard theories such as labelling and critical criminology as too sympathetic to the criminal and too hostile to the forces of law and order. Right realists are less concerned to understand the causes of crime and more concerned to provide what they see as realistic solutions. However, although their main emphasis is on crime reduction strategies, they do offer an explanation of the causes of crime.

The causes of crime

Right realists reject the idea put forward by Marxists and others that structural or economic factors such as poverty and inequality are the cause of crime. For example, against the Marxist view, they point out that the old tend to be poor yet they have a very low crime rate. For right realists, crime is the product of three factors: individual biological differences, inadequate socialisation and the individual's rational choice to offend.

Biological differences

Wilson and Herrnstein (1985) put forward a biosocial theory of criminal behaviour. In their view, crime is caused by a combination of biological and social factors.

Biological differences between individuals make some people innately more strongly predisposed to commit crime than others. For example, personality traits such as aggressiveness, extroversion, risk taking and low impulse control put some people at greater risk of offending. Similarly, Herrnstein and Murray (1994) argue that the main cause of crime is low intelligence, which they also see as biologically determined.

Socialisation and the underclass

However, while biology may increase the chance of an individual offending, effective socialisation decreases the risk, since it involves learning self-control and internalising moral values of right and wrong. For right realists, the best agency of socialisation is the nuclear family.

The right realist Charles Murray (1990) argues that the crime rate is increasing because of a growing underclass or 'new rabble' who are defined by their deviant behaviour and who fail to socialise their children properly. According to Murray, the underclass is growing in both the USA and the UK as a result of welfare dependency.

What Murray calls the welfare state's 'generous revolution' since the 1960s allows increasing numbers of people to become dependent on the state. It has led to the decline of marriage and the growth of lone parent families, because women and children can live off benefits. This also means that men no longer have to take responsibility for supporting their families, so they no longer need to work.

However, lone mothers are ineffective socialisation agents, especially for boys. Absent fathers mean that boys lack paternal discipline and appropriate male role models. As a result, young males turn to other, often delinquent, role models on the street and gain status through crime rather than supporting their families through a steady job. As Bennett et al (1996) argue, crime is the result of:

'growing up surrounded by deviant, delinquent, and criminal adults in a practically perfect criminogenic environment – that is, [one] that seems almost consciously designed to produce vicious, predatory unrepentant street criminals'.

Rational choice theory

An important element in the right realist view of crime comes from rational choice theory, which assumes that individuals have free will and the power of reason. Rational choice theorists such as Ron Clarke (1980) argue that the decision to commit crime is a *choice* based on a rational calculation of the likely consequences. If the perceived rewards of crime outweigh the perceived costs, or if the rewards of crime appear to be greater than those of non-criminal behaviour, then people will be likely to offend.

Right realists argue that the perceived costs of crime are low and this is why the crime rate has increased. In their view, there is often little risk of being caught and punishments are in any case lenient. As Wilson (1975) puts it:

'If the supply and value of legitimate opportunities (i.e. jobs) was declining at the very time that the cost of illegitimate opportunities (i.e. fines and jail terms) was also declining, a rational teenager might well conclude that it made more sense to steal cars than to wash them.'

A similar idea is contained in Felson's (2002) routine activity theory. Felson argues that for a crime to occur, there must be a motivated offender, a suitable target (a victim or property) and the absence of a 'capable guardian' (such as a policeman or neighbour). Offenders are assumed to act rationally, so that the presence of a guardian is likely to deter them.

Criticisms of the right realist explanation of the causes of crime include the following:

- It ignores wider structural causes such as poverty.
- It overstates offenders' rationality and how far they make cost-benefit calculations before committing a crime. While it may explain some utilitarian crime, it may not explain impulsive or violent crime.
- Its view of criminals as rational actors freely choosing crime conflicts with its claim that their behaviour is determined by their biology and socialisation. It also over-emphasises biological factors: according to Lilly et al (2002), IQ differences account for less than 3% of differences in offending.

Analysis and Evaluation
Why might right realism be better at explaining utilitarian crime than violent crime?

Tackling crime

Right realists do not believe it is fruitful to try to deal with the causes of crime (such as biological and socialisation differences) since these cannot easily be changed. Instead they seek practical measures to make crime less attractive. Their main focus is on control, containment and punishment of offenders rather than eliminating the underlying causes of offending or rehabilitating them.

Crime prevention policies should therefore reduce the rewards and increase the costs of crime to the offender, for example by 'target hardening', greater use of prison and ensuring punishments follow soon after the offence to maximise their deterrent effect.

Zero tolerance Wilson and Kelling's (1982) article *Broken Windows* argues that it is essential to maintain the orderly character of neighbourhoods to prevent crime taking hold. Any sign of deterioration, such as graffiti or vandalism, must be dealt with immediately.

They advocate a 'zero tolerance' policy towards undesirable behaviour such as prostitution, begging and drunkenness. The police should focus on controlling the streets so that law-abiding citizens feel safe. Supporters of zero tolerance policing claim that it achieved huge reductions in crime after it was introduced in New York. (For more on zero tolerance, see Topic 9.)

Zero tolerance: an urban myth?

Zero tolerance policing was first introduced in New York in 1994 and was widely applauded for reducing crime. However, Jock Young (2011) argues that its 'success' was a myth peddled by politicians and police keen to take the credit for falling crime.

In fact, the crime rate in New York had already been falling since 1985 – nine years *before* zero tolerance – and was also falling in other US (and foreign) cities that didn't have zero tolerance policies.

Young argues that police need arrests to justify their existence, and New York's shortage of serious crime led police there to 'define deviance up'. That is, they took to arresting people for minor deviant acts that had previously fallen outside their 'net', re-labelling them now as worthy of punishment.

After zero tolerance was introduced in 1994, police and politicians then wrongly claimed that cracking down on these minor crimes had been the *cause* of the decline. In fact, the 'success' of zero tolerance was just a product of the police's way of coping with a decline that had already occurred.

Other criticisms of zero tolerance include that:

- It is preoccupied with petty street crime and ignores corporate crime, which is more costly and harmful.
- It gives the police free rein to discriminate against minorities, youth, the homeless etc.
- It over-emphasises control of disorder, rather than tackling the causes of neighbourhood decline such as lack of investment.
- Zero tolerance and target hardening just lead to displacement of crime to other areas.

Left realism

Left realism developed during the 1980s and 1990s. Like Marxists, left realists see society as an unequal capitalist one. However, unlike Marxists, left realists are reformist rather than revolutionary socialists: they believe in gradual change rather than the violent overthrow of capitalism as the way to achieve greater equality. They believe we need explanations of crime that will lead to practical strategies for reducing it now, rather than waiting for a revolution and a classless society to abolish crime.

Taking crime seriously

The central idea behind left realism is that crime is a real problem, and one that particularly affects the disadvantaged groups who are its main victims. They accuse other sociologists of not taking crime seriously:

- **Marxists** have concentrated on crimes of the powerful, such as corporate crime. Left realists agree that this is important, but they argue that it neglects working-class crime and its effects.
- **Neo-Marxists** romanticise working-class criminals as latter-day Robin Hoods, stealing from the rich as an act of political resistance to capitalism. Left realists point out that in fact working-class criminals mostly victimise other working-class people, not the rich.
- **Labelling theorists** see working-class criminals as the victims of discriminatory labelling by social control agents. Left realists argue that this approach neglects the real victims – working-class people who suffer at the hands of criminals.

Aetiological crisis Part of the left realists' project of taking crime seriously is to recognise that, from the 1950s on, there was a real increase in crime, especially working-class crime. Young (2011) argues that this led to an *aetiological crisis* – a crisis in explanation – for theories of crime. For example, critical criminology and labelling theory tend to deny that the increase was real. Instead, they argue that it was just the result of increased reporting, or an increased tendency to label the poor. In other words, the increase in the statistics was just a social construction, not a reality.

However, left realists argue that the increase was too great to be explained in this way and was real: more people were reporting crime because more people were actually falling victim to crime. As evidence, they cite victim surveys such as the British Crime Survey and many local surveys.

Taking crime seriously also involves recognising who is most affected by crime. Local victim surveys show that the scale of the problem is even greater than that shown by official statistics. They also show that disadvantaged groups have a greater risk of becoming victims, especially of burglary, street crime and violence. For example, unskilled workers are twice as likely to be burgled as other people.

Understandably, therefore, disadvantaged groups have a greater fear of crime and it has a greater effect on their lives. For example, fear of attack may prevent women from going out at night. At the same time, these groups are less likely to report crimes against them and the police are often reluctant to deal with crimes such as domestic violence, rape or racist attacks.

The causes of crime

The second part of the left realist project to take crime seriously involves explaining the rise in crime from the 1950s on. Lea and Young (1984) identify three related causes of crime: relative deprivation, subculture and marginalisation.

Relative deprivation

For Lea and Young, crime has its roots in deprivation. However, deprivation in itself is not directly responsible for crime. For example, poverty was rife in the 1930s, yet crime rates were low. By contrast, since the 1950s living standards have risen, but so too has the crime rate.

Left realists draw on Runciman's (1966) concept of relative deprivation to explain crime. This refers to how deprived someone feels in relation to others, or compared with their own expectations. This can lead to crime when people resent others unfairly having more and resort to crime to obtain what they feel they are entitled to.

Lea and Young explain the paradox that today's society is both more prosperous and more crime-ridden. Although people are better off, they are now more aware of relative deprivation due to the media and advertising, which raise everyone's expectations for material possessions. Those who cannot afford them may resort to crime instead.

However, relative deprivation alone does not necessarily lead to crime. For Young (1999), 'the lethal combination is relative deprivation and individualism'. Individualism is a concern with the self and one's own individual rights, rather than those of the group. It causes crime by encouraging the pursuit of self-interest at the expense of others.

For left realists, increasing individualism is causing the disintegration of families and communities by undermining the values of mutual support and selflessness on which they are based. This weakens the informal controls that such groups exercise over individuals, creating a spiral of increasing anti-social behaviour, aggression and crime.

Subculture

The left realist view of criminal subcultures owes much to Merton, A.K. Cohen and Cloward and Ohlin discussed in Topic 1, especially their concepts of blocked opportunity and subcultures as a group's reaction to the failure to achieve mainstream goals. Thus for left realists, a subculture is a group's collective solution to the problem of relative deprivation.

However, different groups may produce different subcultural solutions to this problem. Some may turn to crime to close the 'deprivation gap', while others may find that religion offers them spiritual comfort and what Weber calls a 'theodicy of disprivilege' – an explanation for their disadvantage.

Religious subcultures may encourage conformity. Within the African Caribbean community in Bristol, Ken Pryce (1979) identified a variety of subcultures, including hustlers, Rastafarians, 'saints' (Pentecostal churchgoers) and working-class 'respectables'.

For left realists, criminal subcultures still subscribe to the values and goals of mainstream society, such as materialism and consumerism. For example, as Young (2002) notes, there are ghettos in the USA where there is 'full immersion in the American Dream: a culture hooked on Gucci, BMW, Nikes'. However, opportunities to achieve these goals legitimately are blocked, so they resort to street crime instead.

Marginalisation

Marginalised groups lack both clear goals and organisations to represent their interests. Groups such as workers have clear goals (such as better pay and conditions) and often have organisations (such as trade unions) to put pressure on employers and politicians. As such, they have no need to resort to violence to achieve their goals.

By contrast, unemployed youth are marginalised. They have no organisation to represent them and no clear goals, just a sense of resentment and frustration. Being powerless to use political means to improve their position, they express their frustration through criminal means such as violence and rioting.

Late modernity, exclusion and crime

Young (2002) argues that we are now living in the stage of late modern society, where instability, insecurity and exclusion make the problem of crime worse. He contrasts today's society (since the 1970s) with the period preceding it, arguing that the 1950s and 1960s represented the 'Golden Age' of modern capitalist society. This was a period of stability, security and social inclusion, with full employment, a fairly comprehensive welfare state, low divorce rates and relatively strong communities. There was general consensus about right and wrong, and lower crime rates.

Since the 1970s, insecurity and exclusion have increased. De-industrialisation and the loss of unskilled jobs have increased unemployment, especially for young people and ethnic minorities, while many jobs are now short term or low paid. These changes have destabilised family and community life, as have New Right government policies to hold back welfare spending. All this has contributed to increased exclusion of those at the bottom.

Meanwhile, greater inequality between rich and poor and the spread of free market values encouraging individualism have increased the sense of relative deprivation. Young also notes the growing contrast between *cultural inclusion* and *economic exclusion* as a source of relative deprivation:

- Media-saturated late modern society promotes cultural inclusion: even the poor have access to the media's materialistic, consumerist cultural messages.
- There is a greater emphasis on leisure, personal consumption and immediate gratification, leading to higher expectations for the 'good life'.
- At the same time, despite the ideology of meritocracy, the poor are denied opportunities to gain the 'glittering prizes of a wealthy society'.

Young's contrast between cultural inclusion and economic exclusion is similar to Merton's notion of anomie – that society creates crime by setting cultural goals (material wealth), while denying people the opportunity to achieve them by legitimate means (decent jobs).

A further trend in late modernity is for relative deprivation to become generalised throughout society rather than being confined to those at the bottom. There is widespread resentment at the undeservedly high rewards that some receive, whether top-flight footballers or 'fat-cat' bankers. There is also 'relative deprivation downwards', where the middle class, who have to be hardworking and disciplined to succeed in an increasingly competitive work environment, resent the stereotypical underclass as idle, irresponsible and hedonistic, living off undeserved state handouts.

The result of exclusion is that the amount and types of crime are changing in late modern society. Firstly, crime is found increasingly throughout the social structure, not just at the bottom. It is also nastier, with an increase in 'hate crimes' – often the result of relative deprivation downwards, as in the case of racist attacks against asylum seekers.

Reactions to crime are also changing. Late modern society is more diverse and there is less public consensus on right and wrong, so that the boundary between acceptable and unacceptable behaviour becomes blurred. At the same time, informal controls become less effective as families and communities disintegrate. This makes the public more intolerant and leads to demands for harsher penalties and increased criminalisation of unacceptable behaviour. Late modern society is a high-crime society with a low tolerance for crime.

The falling crime rate

In a later study, Young (2011) points to a 'second aetiological crisis', or crisis of explanation. As we saw, the first crisis was the failure of existing theories to explain the cause of increases in crime from the 1950s to 1990s.

However, since the mid-1990s the crime rate has *fallen* substantially. This is a problem for realist explanations, because it suggests that crime is no longer the major threat they had originally claimed.

However, as Young notes, because crime is a social construction, it may continue to be *seen* as a problem. For example, the Crime Survey for England and Wales (2014) found that 61% thought crime had risen, not fallen.

The rising 'anti-social behaviour rate'

Crime surveys also show a high level of public concern about anti-social behaviour. Young sees this as a result of 'defining deviance up'. Since the 1990s, governments have aimed to control a widening range of behaviour, introducing ASBOs (Anti-Social Behaviour Orders) in 1998 and IPNAs (Injunctions to Prevent Nuisance and Annoyance) in 2015. These measures have several key features:

- **Blurring the boundaries of crime**, so 'incivilities' become crimes. Breaching an ASBO is itself a crime, thus 'manufacturing' more crime.

- **Subjective definition** Anti-social behaviour has no objective definition; it is in the eye of the beholder.
- **Flexibility** ASBOs have been used against people wearing hoodies, making a noise, letting off fireworks, flyposting or begging, and others besides. The subjective definition means the net can be constantly widened to generate an almost endless number of infringements.

Thus, while the crime rate is going down, governments have created a new 'crime' wave – or anti-social behaviour wave – to replace it.

Activity **Research**

Causes of and solutions to crime

...go to www.sociology.uk.net

Tackling crime

The final part of the left realists' project is to devise solutions to the problem of crime. They argue that we must both improve policing and control, and deal with the deeper structural causes of crime.

Policing and control

Kinsey, Lea and Young (1986) argue that police clear-up rates are too low to act as a deterrent to crime and that police spend too little time actually investigating crime. They argue that the public must become more involved in determining the police's priorities and style of policing.

Military policing The police depend on the public to provide them with information about crimes (90% of crimes known to the police are reported to them by the public). However, the police are losing public support, especially in the inner cities and among ethnic minorities and the young. As a result, the flow of information dries up and police come to rely instead on *military policing*, such as 'swamping' an area and using random stop and search tactics. This alienates communities and results in a vicious circle: locals no longer trust the police and don't provide them with information, so the police resort to military policing, and so on.

Left realists argue that policing must be made accountable to local communities and deal with local concerns. Routine beat patrols are ineffective and stop and search tactics cause conflict. Police need to improve their relationship with local communities by spending more time investigating crime, changing their priorities (they over-police minor drug crime, but under-police racist attacks and domestic violence) and involving the public in making policing policy.

Left realists also argue that crime control cannot be left to the police alone – *a multi-agency approach* is needed. This would involve agencies such as local councils' social services, housing departments, schools and leisure services, as well as voluntary organisations and victim support, and the public.

> **Application**
>
> Suggest possible roles for agencies such as social services, housing and leisure departments, and schools in reducing crime.

Tackling the structural causes

However, left realists do not see improved policing and control as the main solution. In their view, the causes of crime lie in the unequal structure of society and major structural changes are needed if we want to reduce crime. We must deal with inequality of opportunity and the unfairness of rewards, tackle discrimination, provide decent jobs for everyone, and improve housing and community facilities. We must also become more tolerant of diversity and cease stereotyping whole groups as criminal.

Left realism and government policy

Left realists have had more influence on government policy than most theorists of crime. In particular, their views have strong similarities with the 1997-2010 New Labour government's stance of being 'tough on crime, tough on the causes of crime'.

For example, New Labour's firmer approach to policing hate crimes, sexual assaults and domestic violence, along with anti-social behaviour orders (ASBOs), echoed left realist concerns to protect vulnerable groups from crime and low-level disorder. Similarly, New Labour's New Deal for unemployed youth and their anti-truanting policies attempted to reverse the exclusion of young people at risk of offending.

However, Young regards many of these policies as doomed attempts to recreate the 'Golden Age' of the 1950s. For example, the New Deal did not lead to secure, permanent jobs, while ASBOs did not recreate a sense of community. Young also criticises the record of governments, including New Labour. He argues that they have largely just addressed the symptoms, such as anti-social behaviour – they have been tougher on crime than on its underlying causes, such as the insecurity, inequality and discrimination that produce relative deprivation and exclusion.

Evaluation of left realism

Left realism has succeeded in drawing attention to the reality of street crime and its effects, especially on victims from deprived groups. However, it is criticised on several grounds.

- Henry and Milovanovic (1996) argue that it accepts the authorities' definition of crime as being street crime committed by the poor, instead of defining the problem as being one of how powerful groups do harm to the poor. Marxists argue that it fails to explain corporate crime, which is much more harmful.
- Interactionists argue that, because left realists rely on quantitative data from victim surveys, they cannot explain offenders' motives.
- Their use of subcultural theory means left realists assume that value consensus exists and that crime only occurs when this breaks down.
- Relative deprivation cannot fully explain crime because not all those who experience it commit crime. The theory over-predicts the amount of crime.
- Its focus on high-crime inner-city areas gives an unrepresentative view and makes crime appear a greater problem than it is.

Comparing right and left realism

There are both similarities and differences between the two realisms. For example, both see crime as a real problem and fear of crime as rational. On the other hand, they come from different ends of the political spectrum: right realists are neo-conservatives, while left realists are reformist socialists. This is reflected in how they explain crime – right realists blame individual lack of self-control, while left realists blame structural inequalities. Political differences are also reflected in their aims and solutions: the right prioritise social order, achieved through a tough stance against offenders, while the left prioritise justice, achieved through democratic policing and reforms to create greater equality.

Activity | **Discussion**

Left versus right

...go to www.sociology.uk.net

Topic summary

Realists see crime as a **real problem**, especially for the poor. **Right realists** are **conservatives**. They see the cause of crime as partly **biological** and partly **social**. They see it as a **rational choice** based on calculating the risks and rewards. Because causes cannot easily be changed, they focus on **deterring** offenders.

Left realists are reformist **socialists**. They identify **relative deprivation**, **subculture** and **marginalisation** as causes of crime. Relative deprivation and exclusion are increasing in **late modern** society. Their solution lies in **accountable policing** and **reducing inequality**.

EXAMINING REALIST THEORIES OF CRIME

QuickCheck Questions

Check your answers at www.sociology.uk.net

1 What is the main focus of right realism in crime prevention?
2 Explain what is meant by 'zero tolerance policing'.
3 Identify two biological factors that right realists see as important in causing criminal behaviour.
4 Why might a prosperous society be more likely to have high crime rates?

5 Explain what is meant by 'marginalisation'.
6 Explain what is meant by 'relative deprivation'.
7 Identify three policy changes suggested by left realists to reduce crime.
8 Identify two similarities between left and right realism.

Questions to try

Item A   Right realist theories have had a significant influence on government policies, especially because they appear to offer practical answers to the problem of crime. Like many sociologists, they see childhood experiences as very important in determining behaviour in later life. They focus on the idea that some people are naturally more aggressive or less intelligent than others, and they stress the need to ensure that crime does not go unpunished.

Item B   Left realists see crime as a real problem, especially for the disadvantaged groups who are its victims. They see the causes of crime as located in the structure of late modern society, with its high levels of exclusion and insecurity. Their views on how to tackle the problem of crime have had some influence on official policy, particularly under New Labour governments.

However, critics claim that left realists focus too narrowly on inner-city crime and ignore the crimes of the powerful.

1 Outline two realist solutions to the problem of crime.   (4 marks)
2 Applying material from Item A, analyse two explanations of the causes of crime put forward by right realists.   (10 marks)
3 Applying material from Item B and your knowledge, evaluate the contribution of left realism to our understanding of crime and deviance.   (30 marks)

The Examiner's Advice

Q2 Spend about 15 minutes on this question. Divide your time fairly equally between two right realist explanations. You don't need a separate introduction; just start on your first explanation. To answer this question, it's essential that you take two points from the Item and show through a chain of reasoning (see Box 4.1 in chapter 4) how each one explains the cause of crime. (It is a very good idea to quote from the Item when doing so.)

You could use ideas such as the importance of childhood experiences, natural or innate characteristics, or the need to ensure that crime is punished. For example, absence of punishment causes crime because criminals make a rational choice based on a calculation of the likely rewards versus the costs or risks of being punished.

Use concepts and issues such as rational choice theory, biological predisposition, welfare dependency, lone parents, socialisation, routine activity theory, zero tolerance, social control and crime prevention policies. Offer some brief evaluation e.g. that right realists neglect to explain crimes of the powerful. Refer to studies such as Wilson, Murray, Bennett et al, Clarke, Felson, Wilson and Kelling, and Lilly et al.

Q3 Spend about 45 minutes on this. Start by explaining what left realists mean by 'taking crime seriously', including the rising rate of crime and evidence about the disadvantaged as victims. Explain how their approach differs from other explanations such as Marxism and labelling theory.

Examine the left realist explanation of crime in terms of relative deprivation, subculture and marginalisation, and the relationship between late modernity and high crime rates. Examine left realist solutions to the problem of crime, including tackling structural causes (inequality and discrimination), community involvement in policing and a multi-agency approach.

You can evaluate left realism by questioning its focus on inner-city crime, its acceptance of official statistics and definitions of the problem of crime, and its failure to address the crimes of the powerful. You can also contrast it with right realist alternatives.

Use concepts such as the above plus aetiological crisis, blocked opportunity, theodicy of disprivilege, insecurity, de-industrialisation, cultural inclusion and economic exclusion, individualism, anomie, breakdown of consensus, over- and under-policing, and military policing. Use studies such as Lea and Young; Kinsey, Lea and Young; Pryce; Young; Merton; and Henry and Milovanovic.

Is female crime on the increase?

GETTING STARTED

Working in pairs, answer the following:

1 Why do you think far fewer women than men are convicted of sexual offences and violence against the person?

2 Why do you think (a) fraud and forgery, and (b) theft and handling stolen goods, both have a relatively high proportion of female offenders?

3 Overall, as the chart shows, men are much more likely than women to be convicted of criminal offences. What reasons can you suggest for this?

Learning objectives

After studying this Topic, you should:

- Know the main gender differences in recorded patterns of offending.
- Understand and be able to evaluate the debates about the treatment of men and women in the criminal justice system.
- Be able to evaluate explanations of the relationship between women and crime, and between men and crime.

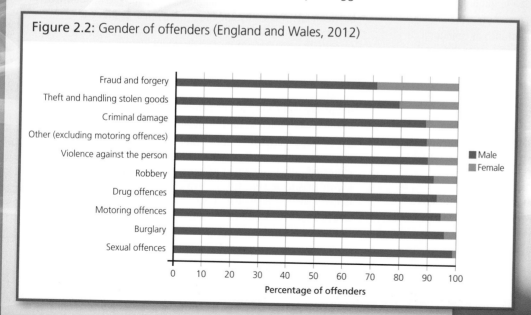

Figure 2.2: Gender of offenders (England and Wales, 2012)

Fraud and forgery
Theft and handling stolen goods
Criminal damage
Other (excluding motoring offences)
Violence against the person
Robbery
Drug offences
Motoring offences
Burglary
Sexual offences

■ Male
■ Female

0   10   20   30   40   50   60   70   80   90   100

Percentage of offenders

GENDER, CRIME AND JUSTICE

There are striking gender differences in the patterns of recorded crime. Girls and women appear to commit fewer crimes than boys and men and, when they do offend, females tend to commit different kinds of crimes from males.

Traditionally, male-dominated criminology neglected female criminality, both because females were seen as committing less crime, and because their behaviour was seen as less in need of controlling. However, more recently, feminists have focused attention on the patterns and causes of female criminality.

Sociologists have also turned their attention to the causes of *male* criminality. In particular, there has been considerable interest in the relationship between masculinity and crime, and some sociologists have argued that crime is a way for some males to achieve and express their masculinity.

Gender patterns in crime

Most crime appears to be committed by males. As Heidensohn and Silvestri (2012) observe, gender differences are the most significant feature of recorded crime. For example, official statistics show that:

- Four out of five convicted offenders in England and Wales are male.
- By the age of 40, 9% of females have a criminal conviction, as against 32% of males.

Among offenders, there are some significant gender differences. For example, official statistics show that:

- A higher proportion of female than male offenders are convicted of property offences (except burglary). A higher proportion of male than female offenders are convicted of violence or sexual offences.
- Males are more likely to be repeat offenders, to have longer criminal careers and to commit more serious crimes. For example, men are about 15 times more likely to be convicted of homicide.

Such statistics raise three important questions:

1 Do women really commit so few crimes, or are the figures an invalid picture of their offending?
2 How can we explain why those women who do offend commit crimes?
3 Why do males commit more crimes than females?

Analysis and Evaluation
One of the most common crimes committed by women is shoplifting. Suggest three reasons for this.

Do women commit more crime?

Do the official statistics on offending give us a true picture of the extent of gender differences in crime? Some sociologists and criminologists argue that the statistics underestimate the amount of female as against male offending. Two arguments have been put forward in support of this view.

- Typically 'female' crimes are less likely to be reported. For example, shoplifting is less likely to be noticed or reported than the violent or sexual crimes more often committed by men. Similarly, prostitution – which females are much more likely than males to engage in – is unlikely to be reported by either party.
- Even when women's crimes are detected or reported, they are less likely to be prosecuted or, if prosecuted, more likely to be let off relatively lightly.

The chivalry thesis

This second argument is known as the leniency or 'chivalry thesis'. The thesis argues that most criminal justice agents – such as police officers, magistrates and judges – are men, and men are socialised to act in a 'chivalrous' way towards women.

For example, Otto Pollak (1950) argues that men have a protective attitude towards women and that

> 'Men hate to accuse women and thus send them to their punishment, police officers dislike to arrest them, district attorneys to prosecute them, judges and juries to find them guilty, and so on.'

The criminal justice system is thus more lenient with women and so their crimes are less likely to end up in the official statistics. This in turn gives an invalid picture that exaggerates the extent of gender differences in rates of offending.

Self-report studies The chivalry thesis has been hotly debated. Evidence from some self-report studies – where individuals are asked about what crimes they have committed – does suggest that female offenders are treated more leniently.

For example, John Graham and Ben Bowling's (1995) research on a sample of 1,721 14-25-year-olds found that although males were more likely to offend, the difference was smaller than that recorded in the official statistics.

They found that males were 2.33 times more likely to admit to having committed an offence in the previous twelve months – whereas the official statistics show males as four times more likely to offend.

Similarly, Flood-Page et al (2000) found that, while only one in 11 female self-reported offenders had been cautioned or prosecuted, the figure for males was over one in seven self-reported offenders.

Official statistics At first sight, court statistics appear to give some support to the chivalry thesis. For example:

- Females are more likely than males to be released on bail rather than remanded in custody.
- Females are more likely than males to receive a fine or a community sentence, and less likely to be sent to prison. Women on average receive shorter prison sentences.
- Only one in nine female offenders receive a prison sentence for shoplifting, but one in five males.

Similarly, Roger Hood's (1992) study of over 3,000 defendants found that women were about one-third less likely to be jailed in similar cases.

Evidence against the chivalry thesis

There is considerable evidence against the chivalry thesis. For example, David Farrington and Alison Morris' (1983) study of sentencing of 408 offences of theft in a magistrates' court found that women were *not* sentenced more leniently for comparable offences. Steven Box's (1981) review of British and American self-report studies also concludes that women who commit serious offences are not treated more favourably than men.

Similarly, Abigail Buckle and David Farrington's (1984) observational study of shoplifting in a department store witnessed twice as many males shoplifting as females – despite the fact that the numbers of male and female offenders in the official statistics are more or less equal. This small-scale study thus suggests that women shoplifters may be *more* likely to be prosecuted than their male counterparts.

Self-report studies also provide evidence that males commit more offences. For example, young men are more likely than females to report binge drinking, taking illegal drugs or engaging in disorderly conduct. Hales et al (2009) found that they were significantly more likely to have been offenders in all major offence categories. Other studies suggest that the gender gap increases as the offences become more serious.

Under-reporting of male crimes against women The chivalry thesis also ignores the fact that many male crimes do not get reported. For example, in 2012, only 8% of females who had been victims of a serious sexual assault reported it to the police, while Yearnshire (1997) found that a woman typically suffers 35 assaults before reporting domestic violence.

Crimes of the powerful are also under-represented in self-report and victim surveys, and these are also more likely to be committed by men by virtue of their more privileged position in the job market.

If women appear to be treated more leniently, it may simply be because their offences are less serious. For example, the lower rate of prosecutions of females as compared with their self-reported offending may be because the crimes they admit to are less serious and less likely to go to trial. Women offenders also seem more likely to show remorse, and this may help to explain why they are more likely to receive a caution instead of going to court.

Bias against women

Many feminists argue that, far from the criminal justice system being biased in favour of women, as the chivalry thesis claims, it is biased *against* them. As Heidensohn (1996) argues, the courts treat females more harshly than males when they deviate from gender norms. For example:

- Double standards – courts punish girls but not boys for premature or promiscuous sexual activity. 'Wayward' girls can end up in care without ever having committed an offence. Sharpe (2009) found from her analysis of 55 youth worker records, that seven out of 11 girls were referred for support because they were sexually active, but none out of 44 boys.
- Women who do not conform to accepted standards of monogamous heterosexuality and motherhood are punished more harshly. As Stewart (2006) found, magistrates' perceptions of female defendants' characters were based on stereotypical gender roles.

Pat Carlen (1997) puts forward a similar view in relation to custodial sentences. She argues that when women are jailed, it is less for 'the seriousness of their crimes and more according to the court's assessment of them as wives, mothers and daughters'. Girls whose parents believe them to be beyond control are more likely to receive custodial sentences than girls who live more 'conventional' lives. Carlen found that Scottish judges were much more likely to jail women whose children were in care than women who they saw as good mothers.

Feminists argue that these double standards exist because the criminal justice system is patriarchal. Nowhere is this more evident than in the way the system deals with rape cases. There have been numerous cases of male judges making sexist, victim-blaming remarks. For example, Carol Smart (1989) quotes Judge Wild as saying that

> 'Women who say no do not always mean no. It is not just a question of how she says it, how she shows and makes it clear. If she doesn't want it she only has to keep her legs shut.'

Similarly, as Sandra Walklate (1998) argues, in rape cases it is not the defendant who is on trial but the victim, since she has to prove her respectability in order to have her evidence accepted. According to Adler (1987), women who are deemed to lack respectability, such as single parents, punks and peace protestors, find it difficult to have their testimony believed by the court.

Application

How might the concept of patriarchy be used to explain
(a) bias in *favour* of women (the chivalry thesis);
(b) bias *against* women?

Explaining female crime

Whether or not the criminal justice system is more lenient towards women, as the chivalry thesis claims, women in general do seem to have a lower rate of offending than men. How then can we explain the behaviour of those women who do commit crimes?

The first explanations of gender differences in crime were biological rather than sociological. For example, Lombroso and Ferrero (1893) argued that criminality is innate, but that there were very few 'born female criminals'. Some more recent psychological explanations have also argued that biological factors such as higher levels of testosterone in males can account for gender differences in violent offending.

However, sociologists take the view that social rather than biological factors are the cause of gender differences in offending. Sociologists have put forward three main explanations of gender differences in crime: sex role theory, control theory and the liberation thesis.

Functionalist sex role theory

Early sociological explanations of gender differences in crime focused on differences in the socialisation of males and females. For example, boys are encouraged to be tough, aggressive and risk taking, and this can mean they are more disposed to commit acts of violence or take advantage of criminal opportunities when they present themselves.

The functionalist Talcott Parsons (1955) traces differences in crime and deviance to the gender roles in the conventional nuclear family. While men take the instrumental, breadwinner role, performed largely outside the home, women perform the expressive role in the home, where they take the main responsibility for socialising the children.

While this gives girls access to an adult role model, it tends to mean that boys reject feminine models of behaviour that express tenderness, gentleness and emotion. Instead, boys seek to distance themselves from such models by engaging in 'compensatory compulsory masculinity' through aggression and anti-social behaviour, which can slip over into acts of delinquency.

Because men have much less of a socialising role than women in the conventional nuclear family, socialisation can be more difficult for boys than for girls. According to Albert K. Cohen (1955), this relative lack of an adult male role model means boys are more likely to turn to all-male street gangs as a source of masculine identity. As we saw in Topic 1, in these subcultural groups, status is earned by acts of toughness, risk-taking and delinquency.

Similarly, New Right theorists argue that the absence of a male role model in matrifocal lone parent families leads to boys turning to criminal street gangs as a source of status and identity.

Sandra Walklate (2003) criticises sex role theory for its biological assumptions. According to Walklate, Parsons assumes that because women have the biological capacity to bear children, they are best suited to the expressive role.

Thus, although the theory tries to explain gender differences in crime in terms of behaviour learned through socialisation, it is ultimately based on biological assumptions about sex differences.

More recently, feminists have put forward alternative explanations for women's patterns of crime and deviance. Feminists locate their explanations in the patriarchal (male-dominated) nature of society and women's subordinate position in it.

We can distinguish between two main feminist approaches:

- control theory
- the liberation thesis.

Heidensohn: patriarchal control

Frances Heidensohn (1996) argues that the most striking thing about women's behaviour is how *conformist* it is – they commit fewer and less serious crimes than men. In her view, this is because patriarchal society imposes greater control over women and this reduces their opportunities to offend. This patriarchal control operates at home, in public spaces and at work.

Control at home Women's domestic role, with its constant round of housework and childcare, imposes severe restrictions on their time and movement and confines them to the house for long periods, reducing their opportunities to offend. Women who try to reject their domestic role may find that their partners seek to impose it by force, through domestic violence.

As Dobash and Dobash (1979) show, many violent attacks result from men's dissatisfaction with their wives' performance of domestic duties. Men also exercise control through their financial power, for example by denying women sufficient funds for leisure activities, thereby restricting their time outside the home.

Daughters too are subject to patriarchal control. Girls are less likely to be allowed to come and go as they please or to stay out late. As a result, they develop a 'bedroom culture', socialising at home with friends rather than in public spaces. Girls are also required to do more housework than boys. As a result, they have less opportunity to engage in deviant behaviour on the streets.

Control in public Women are controlled in public places by the threat or fear of male violence against them, especially sexual violence. For example, the Islington Crime Survey found that 54% of women avoided going out after dark for fear of being victims of crime, as against only 14% of men.

Heidensohn notes that sensationalist media reporting of rapes adds to women's fear. Distorted media portrayals of the typical rapist as a stranger who carries out random attacks frightens women into staying indoors.

Females are also controlled in public by their fear of being defined as not respectable. Dress, make-up, demeanour and ways of speaking and acting that are defined as inappropriate can gain a girl or woman a 'reputation'. For example, women on their own may avoid going into pubs – which are sites of criminal behaviour – for fear of being regarded as sexually 'loose' or even as prostitutes.

Similarly, Sue Lees (1993) notes that in school, boys maintain control through sexualised verbal abuse, for example labelling girls as 'slags' if they fail to conform to gender role expectations.

Control at work Women's behaviour at work is controlled by male supervisors and managers. Sexual harassment is widespread and helps keep women 'in their place'. Furthermore, women's subordinate position reduces their opportunities to engage in major criminal activity at work. For example, the 'glass ceiling' prevents many women from rising to senior positions where there is greater opportunity to commit fraud. As a result, they are less likely to be involved in white collar crime.

In general, these patriarchal restrictions on women's lives mean they have fewer opportunities for crime. However, Heidensohn recognises that patriarchy can also push some women into crime. For example, women are more likely to be poor (for example, as a result of gender inequalities in the labour market) and may turn to theft or prostitution to gain a decent standard of living. We explore this issue – why some disadvantaged women become involved in crime – next.

Carlen: class and gender deals

Using unstructured tape-recorded interviews, Pat Carlen (1988) conducted a study of thirty-nine 15-46 year old working-class women who had been convicted of a range of crimes including theft, fraud, handling stolen goods, burglary, drugs, prostitution, violence and arson. Twenty were in prison or youth custody at the time of the interviews. Although Carlen recognises that there are some middle-class female offenders, she argues that most convicted serious female criminals are working-class.

Carlen uses a version of Travis Hirschi's (1969) control theory to explain female crime. Hirschi argues that humans act rationally and are controlled by being offered a 'deal', of rewards in return for conforming to social norms. People will turn to crime if they do not believe the rewards will be forthcoming, and if the rewards of crime appear greater than the risks.

Carlen argues that working-class women are generally led to conform through the promise of two types of rewards or 'deals':

- **The class deal:** women who work will be offered material rewards, with a decent standard of living and leisure opportunities.
- **The gender deal:** patriarchal ideology promises women material and emotional rewards from family life by conforming to the norms of a conventional domestic gender role.

If these rewards are not available or worth the effort, crime becomes more likely. Carlen argues that this was the case with the women in her study.

In terms of the *class deal*, the women had failed to find a legitimate way of earning a decent living and this left them feeling powerless, oppressed and the victims of injustice.

- Thirty-two of them had always been in poverty.
- Some found that qualifications gained in jail had been no help in gaining work upon release. Others had been on training courses but still could not get a job.
- Many had experienced problems and humiliations in trying to claim benefits.

As they had gained no rewards from the class deal, they felt they had nothing to lose by using crime to escape from poverty.

In terms of the *gender deal* for conforming to patriarchal family norms, most of the women had either not had the opportunity to make the deal, or saw few rewards and many disadvantages in family life.

- Some had been abused physically or sexually by their fathers, or subjected to domestic violence by partners.
- Over half had spent time in care, which broke the bonds with family and friends.
- Those leaving or running away from care often found themselves homeless, unemployed and poor.

Many of the women reached the conclusion that:

'crime was the only route to a decent standard of living. They had nothing to lose and everything to gain.'

Carlen concludes that, for these women, poverty and being brought up in care or an oppressive family life were the two main causes of their criminality. Drug and alcohol addiction, and the desire for excitement, were contributory factors, but these often stemmed from poverty or being brought up in care. Being criminalised and jailed made the class deal even less available to them and made crime even more attractive.

Evaluation

Heidensohn and Carlen's approaches to female crime are based on a combination of feminism and control theory:

- Heidensohn shows the many patriarchal controls that help prevent women from deviating.
- Carlen shows how the failure of patriarchal society to deliver the promised 'deals' to some women removes the controls that prevent them from offending.

However, both control theory and feminism can be accused of seeing women's behaviour as determined by external forces such as patriarchal controls or class and gender deals. Critics argue that this underplays the importance of free will and choice in offending.

Furthermore, Carlen's sample was small and may be unrepresentative, consisting as it did largely of working-class and serious offenders.

The liberation thesis

If patriarchal society exercises control over women to prevent them from deviating, then it would seem logical to assume that, if society becomes less patriarchal and more equal, women's crime rates will become similar to men's.

This is the 'liberation thesis' put forward by Freda Adler (1975). Adler argues that, as women become liberated from patriarchy, their crimes will become as frequent and as serious as men's. Women's liberation has led to a new type of female criminal and a rise in the female crime rate.

Adler argues that changes in the structure of society have led to changes in women's offending behaviour. As patriarchal controls and discrimination have lessened, and opportunities in education and work have become more equal, women have begun to adopt traditionally 'male' roles in both legitimate activity (work) and illegitimate activity (crime).

As a result, women no longer just commit traditional 'female' crimes such as shoplifting and prostitution. They now also commit typically 'male' offences such as crimes of violence and white-collar crimes.

This is because of women's greater self-confidence and assertiveness, and the fact that they now have greater opportunities in the legitimate structure. For example, there are more women in senior positions at work and this gives them the opportunity to commit serious white-collar crimes such as fraud.

There is some evidence to support this view. For example:

- Both the overall rate of female offending and the female share of offences rose during the second half of the 20th century. For example, between the 1950s and 1990s, the female share of offences rose from one in 7 to one in 6.

- Adler argues that the pattern of female crime has shifted. She cites studies showing rising levels of female participation in crimes previously regarded as 'male', such as embezzlement and armed robbery.
- More recently, there has been media talk of the growth of 'girl gangs', while a study by Martin Denscombe (2001) of Midlands teenagers' self-images found that females were as likely as males to engage in risk-taking behaviour and that girls were adopting more 'male' stances, such as the desire to be in control and look 'hard'.

Criticisms of the liberation thesis

Critics reject Adler's thesis on several grounds:

- The female crime rate began rising in the 1950s – long before the women's liberation movement, which emerged in the late 1960s.
- Most female criminals are working-class – the group least likely to be influenced by women's liberation, which has benefited middle-class women much more. According to Chesney-Lind (1997), in the USA poor and marginalised women are more likely than liberated women to be criminals.
- Chesney-Lind did find evidence of women branching out into more typically male offences such as drugs. However, this is usually because of their link with prostitution – a very 'unliberated' female offence.
- There is little evidence that the illegitimate opportunity structure of professional crime has opened up to women. Laidler and Hunt (2001) found that female gang members in the USA were expected to conform to conventional gender roles in the same way as non-deviant girls.

However, Adler's thesis does draw our attention to the importance of investigating the relationship between changes in women's position and changes in patterns of female offending.

However, it can be argued that she overestimates both the extent to which women have become liberated and the extent to which they are now able to engage in serious crime.

Activity Discussion

Female crime: explanations on trial

...go to www.sociology.uk.net

Females and violent crime

One trend in the official statistics that seems to support Adler's liberation thesis is the increase in the female arrest and conviction statistics for violent crime. For example, according to Hand and Dodd (2009), between 2000 and 2008, police statistics show the number of females arrested for violence rose by an average of 17% each year. Similar trends have been noted in other countries, including Canada, Australia and the USA.

If these police statistics are an accurate picture of offending, it suggests that females are increasingly committing typically 'male' crimes, since violent offending has traditionally been a male form of crime.

The criminalisation of females

However, evidence from other sources paints a different picture. For example, in the USA, Steffensmeier and Schwartz (2009) found that while the female share of arrests for violence grew from one-fifth to one-third between 1980 and 2003, this rise in the police statistics was not matched by the findings of victim surveys. That is, victims did not report any increase in attacks by females. Similarly, self-report studies showed no upward trend in females' criminality.

Net widening Steffensmeier and Schwartz conclude that in reality there has been no change in women's involvement in violent crime. They argue that the rise in arrests is due to the justice system 'widening the net' – arresting and prosecuting females for less serious forms of violence than previously.

Similarly, Chesney-Lind (2006) argues that a policy of mandatory arrests for domestic violence has led to a steep rise in the female violence statistics in the USA. Where a couple fight, both may be arrested, even though it is likely that the woman is the victim. Females previously ignored by the justice system now find themselves being labelled as violent offenders.

In the UK, too, Sharpe and Gelsthorpe (2009) note that net-widening policies are producing a rise in the official statistics for females' violent crimes. There is a growing trend towards prosecuting females for low-level physical altercations, even in some cases for playground fights. Most convictions are for minor offences not involving weapons.

This trend is an example of what Jock Young (2011) calls 'defining deviance up' to catch trivial offences in the net. Worrall (2004) argues that in the past, girls' misbehaviour was more likely to be seen as a 'welfare' issue, whereas now it has been re-labelled as criminality.

A moral panic about girls?

If female participation in violent crime is not in fact increasing, how do we account for the increase in criminalisation of females for this kind of crime? One view is that it is a social construction resulting from a moral

panic over young women's behaviour. For example, Burman and Batchelor (2009) point to media depictions of young women as 'drunk and disorderly, out of control and looking for fights'.

Reports featuring binge drinking, girl gangs and so on may be affecting the criminal justice system. For example, Sharpe (2009) found that professionals such as judges, probation officers and police were influenced by media stereotypes of violent 'ladettes' and many believed that girls' behaviour was rapidly getting worse. Similarly, in the USA, Steffensmeier et al (2005) found that media-driven moral panics about girls were affecting sentencing decisions.

The overall effect is a self-fulfilling prophecy and an amplification spiral: reports of girls' misbehaviour sensitise police and courts, who take a tougher stance, resulting in more convictions, which produces further negative media coverage and so on. As Burman and Batchelor put it,

'What we are witnessing is not an increase in violent offending, but the increased reporting, recording and prosecuting of young women accused of violent offences.'

Gender and victimisation

Large-scale national victim surveys such as the Crime Survey for England and Wales (CSEW 2012) show gender differences in the level and types of victimisation, and in the relationship between victims and offenders.

Homicide victims About 70% are male. Female victims are more likely to know their killer and in 60% of these cases, this was a partner or ex-partner. Males are most likely to be killed by a friend or acquaintance.

Victims of violence Fewer women than men are victims of violence (2% versus 4%). In addition:

- Women are most likely to be victimised by an acquaintance, men by a stranger.
- More women than men were victims of intimate violence (domestic abuse, sexual assault and stalking) during their adult lives (31% versus 18%).
- Ten times more women reported having been sexually assaulted than men.
- Only 8% of females who had experienced serious sexual assault reported it to the police. A third of those who didn't report it said they believed the police couldn't do much to help.

Mismatch between fear and risk? Research shows women have a greater fear of crime but the CSEW shows they are at less risk of victimisation. However, some local victim surveys such as by Lea and Young (1993) have found that women are in fact at greater risk than men. There is also some evidence from early studies (such as Sparks et al,

1977) that female victims of violence may be more likely to refuse to be interviewed.

Furthermore, victim surveys do not necessarily convey the frequency or severity of the victimisation. For example, in the case of domestic abuse, Walby and Allen (2004) have shown that women were much more likely to be victims of multiple incidents. Ansara and Hindin (2011) found that women victims experienced more severe violence and control.

Why do men commit crime?

Feminists argue that, although 'malestream', non-feminist theories of crime have in reality focused only on males, these theories have assumed that they were explaining *all* crime, rather than solely *male* crime. For example, as Maureen Cain (1989) puts it:

'Men as males have not been the subject of the criminological gaze. Yet the most consistent and dramatic finding [of criminology] is not that most criminals are working-class – a fact which has received continuous theoretical attention – but that most criminals are, and always have been, men.'

In other words, although criminologists have focused mainly on male criminality, until recently they have not generally asked what it is about *being male* that leads men to offend.

Masculinity and crime

However, influenced by recent feminist and postmodernist ideas, sociologists have begun to take an interest in why men are more likely to commit crime. Their attention has focused on the concept of masculinity as a way of explaining men's higher rate of offending.

For example, James Messerschmidt (1993) argues that masculinity is a social construct or 'accomplishment' and men have to constantly work at constructing and presenting it to others. In doing so, some men have more resources than others to draw upon.

Messerschmidt argues that different masculinities co-exist within society, but that one of these, *hegemonic masculinity*, is the dominant, prestigious form that most men wish to accomplish. Hegemonic masculinity is defined through:

'work in the paid-labour market, the subordination of women, heterosexism [i.e. difference from and desire for women] and the driven and uncontrollable sexuality of men'.

However, some men have *subordinated masculinities*. These include gay men, who have no desire to accomplish hegemonic masculinity, as well as lower-class and some ethnic minority men, who lack the resources to do so.

Messerschmidt sees crime and deviance as resources that different men may use for accomplishing masculinity. For example, class and ethnic differences among youths lead to different forms of rule breaking to demonstrate masculinity:

- **White middle-class youths** have to subordinate themselves to teachers in order to achieve middle-class status, leading to an *accommodating masculinity* in school. Outside school, their masculinity takes an oppositional form, for example through drinking, pranks and vandalism.
- **White working-class youths** have less chance of educational success, so their masculinity is oppositional both in and out of school. It is constructed around sexist attitudes, being tough and opposing teachers' authority. The 'lads' in Willis' (1977) study are a good example of this kind of masculinity.
- **Black lower working-class youths** may have few expectations of a reasonable job and may use gang membership and violence to express their masculinity, or turn to serious property crime to achieve material success.

Messerschmidt acknowledges that middle-class men too may use crime. The difference lies in the type of crime – while middle-class males commit white-collar and corporate crime to accomplish hegemonic masculinity, poorer groups may use street robbery to achieve a subordinated masculinity.

Criticisms of Messerschmidt

Several criticisms have been made of Messerschmidt:

- Is masculinity an *explanation* of male crime, or just a *description* of male offenders (e.g. tough, controlling etc)? Messerschmidt is in danger of a circular argument, that masculinity explains male crimes (e.g. violence) because they are crimes committed by males (who have violent characteristics).
- Messerschmidt doesn't explain why not all men use crime to accomplish masculinity.
- He over-works the concept of masculinity to explain virtually all male crimes, from joy riding to embezzlement.

Winlow: postmodernity, masculinity and crime

In recent decades, globalisation has led to a shift from a modern industrial society to a late modern or postmodern de-industrialised society. This has led to the loss of many of the traditional manual jobs through which working-class men were able to express their masculinity by hard physical labour and by providing for their families.

At the same time as job opportunities in industry have declined, there has been an expansion of the service sector, including the night-time leisure economy of clubs, pubs and bars. For some young working-class men, this has provided a combination of legal employment, lucrative criminal opportunities and a means of expressing their masculinity.

One example of this is Simon Winlow's (2001) study of bouncers in Sunderland in the north east of England, an area of de-industrialisation and unemployment. Working as bouncers in the pubs and clubs provided young men with both paid work and the opportunity for illegal business ventures in drugs, duty-free tobacco and alcohol and protection rackets, as well as the opportunity to demonstrate their masculinity through the use of violence.

Winlow draws on Cloward and Ohlin's distinction between conflict and criminal subcultures (see Topic 1). He notes that in *modern* society, there had always been a violent, conflict subculture in Sunderland, in which 'hard men' earned status through their ability to use violence. However, the absence of a professional criminal subculture meant there was little opportunity for a career in organised crime.

Bodily capital

Under *postmodern* conditions, by contrast, an organised professional criminal subculture has emerged as a result of the new illicit business opportunities to be found in the night-time economy. In this subculture, the ability to use violence becomes not just a way of displaying masculinity, but a commodity with which to earn a living.

To maintain their reputation and employability, the men must use their *bodily capital*. For example, many of the bouncers seek to develop their physical assets by bodybuilding.

Winlow notes that this is not just a matter of being able to use violence and win fights, but of maintaining the sign value of their bodies, 'looking the part' so as to discourage competitors from challenging them. In other words, the signs of masculinity become an important commodity in their own right. This reflects the idea that in postmodern society, *signs* take on a reality of their own independent of the thing they supposedly represent.

Winlow's study is important because it shows how the expression of masculinity changes with the move from a modern industrial society to a postmodern, de-industrialised one. At the same time, this change opens up new criminal opportunities for men who are able to use violence to express masculinity, by creating the conditions for the growth of an organised criminal subculture.

Activity | Media

Violence, media and masculinity

...go to www.sociology.uk.net

Topic summary

Official statistics show males commit more crime than females, but the **chivalry thesis** argues that they underestimate female offending because the criminal justice system treats women more leniently. However, this may be because their offences are **less serious**. Feminists argue that the system is **biased against women**, especially when they deviate from gender norms.

In explaining gender differences in offending, **sex role theory** focuses on socialisation. **Feminist theories** emphasise **patriarchal control** that reduces females' opportunity to offend. Carlen argues that when the **reward system** for female conformity fails, females are likely to offend.

The **liberationist thesis** argues that as women become more liberated, they adopt 'male' patterns of offending. Female **criminalisation rates** for violence have risen due to **net widening** and **moral panic**.

Messerschmidt argues that **crime is a resource** some subordinated men use to **accomplish masculinity**. Winlow argues that **globalisation** and **de-industrialisation** mean that some men now achieve masculinity through participation in a combination of paid work and crime in the night-time economy.

EXAMINING GENDER, CRIME AND JUSTICE

QuickCheck Questions

Check your answers at www.sociology.uk.net

1 What proportion of convicted offenders are male?
2 Suggest two ways in which 'chivalry' might operate in the treatment of females by the law.
3 Suggest two ways in which females may be treated more harshly than males by the criminal justice system.
4 How does sex role theory account for gender differences in offending?
5 According to Heidensohn, in what three areas are women controlled?

6 According to Carlen, in what ways may lower-class women miss out on both gender and class deals?
7 Suggest two criticisms of the liberation thesis.
8 Explain what is meant by 'net widening' in relation to female offending.
9 According to Messerschmidt, what type of masculinity do white middle-class youths typically adopt?
10 Messerschmidt is said to 'overwork the concept of masculinity'. Explain what this means.

Questions to try

Item A   Most criminals are men. The most consistent finding of research into crime in different societies and over many decades is that there is a clear link between crime and masculinity. However, the kind of crimes committed varies between different groups of men. So too does what counts as being a 'real man' and the resources to achieve it. Changes over time in the economy and the employment structure – such as de-industrialisation, for example – may also affect men's opportunities to express their masculinity.

Item B   Official crime statistics indicate that there are significant gender differences in the commission of crime. Only about 20% of convicted offenders are female, and they are far less likely to commit homicide, carry out violent crime or be repeat offenders.

However, some sociologists believe that these statistics underestimate the true extent and seriousness of female crime. They argue that the leniency of the criminal justice system may result in fewer girls and women ending up in the crime statistics than men.

1 Outline two differences between the recorded patterns of male and female offending.   (4 marks)
2 Applying material from Item A, analyse two reasons why men commit crime.   (10 marks)
3 Applying material from Item B and your knowledge, evaluate sociological explanations of female crime.   (30 marks)

The Examiner's Advice

Q2 Spend about 15 minutes on this. Divide your time fairly equally between the two reasons. You don't need a separate introduction; just start on your first reason. To answer this question, it's essential that you take two points from the Item and show through a chain of reasoning (see Box 4.1 in chapter 4) how each explains men's criminality. (It is a very good idea to quote from the Item when doing so.)

You could use the idea that different groups of men commit different kinds of crime, the role of economic changes, or that what counts as being a real man varies. For example, middle-class men have more resources (e.g. well-paid jobs) and may use white collar crime to achieve hegemonic masculinity, whereas poorer men may use violence to achieve a subordinated masculinity. You can briefly evaluate by noting that this doesn't explain why not all men use crime to achieve masculinity.

Use concepts and issues such as those above and masculinity as a construct or accomplishment, age, class and ethnic differences; globalisation; postmodernity; subcultures and bodily capital. Use studies such as Messerschmidt, Willis, Cloward and Ohlin, and Winlow.

Q3 Spend about 45 minutes on this. Consider the different explanations of patterns of female offending. Start with the issue of what the patterns of female offending actually are. Consider what official statistics tell us and whether this is supported by self-report or other studies. Include a range of types of offence, e.g. property crime, violence etc.

Examine functionalist and feminist explanations of why female crime rates are lower. Use Carlen's study to examine the 'exceptions' who do offend. Use the Item in debating whether the justice system is biased in favour of females (the chivalry thesis) or against them (feminism). Consider arguments about whether the system is becoming more punitive towards females e.g. increased criminalisation for violence. Lastly, examine the liberation thesis that women are adopting male patterns of criminality. Evaluate the above explanations using alternative views and relevant evidence on offending and enforcement.

Use concepts and issues such as the above, plus patriarchy, double standards, gender role socialisation, social control, class and gender deals, net widening, moral panics. Use studies such as Pollak, Flood-Page, Hood, Buckle and Farrington, Box, Heidensohn, Carlen, Walklate, Parsons, Adler, Chesney-Lind, Steffensmeier and Schwartz, Sharpe and Gelthorpe.

Brixton, south London: mural depicting black people who died in police custody or were shot by the police.

GETTING STARTED

Table 2B	Ethnic groups and court proceedings				
	White	Black	Asian	Other	Total
Percentage of UK population	87	3	7	3	100
Percentage of convictions	73	8	5	14	100
Average custodial sentence (months)	15.9	23.4	22.4	n/a	n/a

Population figures rounded to nearest whole number

Working in groups of three and referring to Table 2B, answer the following questions:

1 a For each ethnic group, how does their percentage of the population compare to their percentage of convictions?

   b Suggest two reasons for these patterns.

2 a What do the figures for average custodial sentences of the different ethnic groups show?

   b Suggest two reasons for these patterns.

Learning objectives

After studying this Topic, you should:

- Know the patterns of ethnicity and criminalisation as shown by different sources of data.

- Understand the relationship between the criminal justice process and ethnicity.

- Be able to evaluate sociological explanations of the relationship between ethnicity, offending and criminalisation.

- Understand the relationship between ethnicity, racism and victimisation.

ETHNICITY, CRIME AND JUSTICE

Official statistics on the criminal justice process show some striking differences between ethnic groups. For example, black people are more likely to be imprisoned than other groups.

How are we to explain these ethnic differences in criminalisation?

- Is it because some ethnic groups are more likely to offend in the first place – and if so, how do we explain such differences?

- Or is it because the criminal justice system is racist and discriminates against ethnic minorities (for example, by police targeting and harassment)?

Not only are there ethnic differences in criminalisation, but some ethnic groups are also more at risk of being victims of a crime. For example, there is considerable evidence of the scale of racially motivated offences against minority groups.

In this Topic, we examine these different aspects of the relationship between ethnicity, crime and justice.

Ethnicity and criminalisation

According to official statistics, there are some significant ethnic differences in the likelihood of being involved in the criminal justice system. Black people, and to a lesser extent Asians, are over-represented in the system. For example:

- Black people make up just 3% of the population, but 13.1% of the prison population.
- Asians make up 6.5% of the population, but 7.7% of the prison population.

By contrast, white people are under-represented at all stages of the criminal justice process. As the Ministry of Justice (2008) notes:

'Members of our Black communities are seven times more likely than their White counterparts to be stopped and searched, three and a half times more likely to be arrested, and five times more likely to be in prison.'

However, such statistics do not tell us whether members of one ethnic group are more likely than members of another group to commit an offence in the first place – they simply tell us about involvement with the criminal justice system. For example, differences in stop and search or arrest rates may simply be due to policing strategies or to discrimination by individual officers, while differences in rates of imprisonment may be the result of courts handing down harsher sentences to minorities.

Alternative sources of statistics

In addition to statistics on the ethnicity of those individuals who are involved with the criminal justice system, we can call on two other important sources of statistics that can throw a more direct light on ethnicity and offending. These are victim surveys and self-report studies.

Victim surveys

Victim surveys such as the Crime Survey for England and Wales (CSEW) ask individuals to say what crimes they have been victims of (usually during the past 12 months). We can gain information about ethnicity and offending from such surveys when they ask victims to identify the ethnicity of the person who committed the crime against them. For example, in the case of 'mugging' (a term that has no legal definition but is used to cover robberies and some thefts from the person), black people are significantly over-represented among those identified by victims as offenders.

Victim surveys also show that a great deal of crime is intra-ethnic – that is, it takes place *within* rather than between ethnic groups.

However, while victim surveys are useful in helping us to identify ethnic patterns of offending, they have several limitations:

- They rely on victims' memory of events. According to Coretta Phillips and Ben Bowling (2012), evidence suggests that white victims may 'over-identify' blacks – saying the offender was black even when they are not sure.
- They only cover personal crimes, which make up only about a fifth of all crimes.
- They exclude the under 10s: minority ethnic groups contain a higher proportion of young people.
- They exclude crimes by and against organisations (such as businesses), so they tell us nothing about the ethnicity of white collar and corporate criminals.

As a result, victim surveys can only tell us about the ethnicity of a small proportion of offenders, which may not be representative of offenders in general.

Self-report studies

Self-report studies ask individuals to disclose their own dishonest and violent behaviour. Based on a sample of 2,500 people, Graham and Bowling (1995) found that blacks (43%) and whites (44%) had very similar rates of offending, while Indians (30%), Pakistanis (28%) and Bangladeshis (13%) had much lower rates.

Similarly, Sharp and Budd (2005) note that the 2003 Offending, Crime and Justice survey of 12,000 people found that whites and those of 'mixed' ethnic origins were most likely to say they had committed an offence (around 40%), followed by blacks (28%) and Asians (21%).

The Home Office has conducted nine self-report studies on drug use since the early 1990s, all with remarkably similar findings. For example, Sharp and Budd (2005) found that 27% of males of 'mixed' ethnicity said they had used drugs (mostly cannabis) in the last year, compared with 16% of both black and white males and 5% of Asian males. Use of Class A drugs such as heroin and cocaine was much higher among whites (6%) than blacks (2%) or Asians (1%).

The findings of self-report studies challenge the stereotype of black people as being more likely than whites to offend, though they support the widely held view that Asians are less likely to offend. However, self-report studies have their limitations in relation to ethnicity and offending.

Overall, the evidence on ethnicity and offending is somewhat inconsistent. For example, while official statistics and victim surveys point to the likelihood of higher rates of offending by blacks, this is generally not borne out by the results of self-report studies.

Ethnicity, racism and the criminal justice system

There are ethnic differences at each stage of the criminal justice process. How can we explain them? How far are they the result of racism within the criminal justice system? We need to look at the main stages of the process that an individual may go through, possibly culminating in a custodial sentence.

Policing

As Phillips and Bowling (2012) note, since the 1970s there have been many allegations of oppressive policing of minority ethnic communities, including:

'mass stop and search operations, paramilitary tactics, excessive surveillance, armed raids, police violence and deaths in custody, and a failure to respond effectively to racist violence.'

Stop and search

Members of minority ethnic groups are more likely to be stopped and searched by the police. Police can use this power if they have 'reasonable suspicion' of wrongdoing. Compared with white people, black people are seven times more likely to be stopped and searched and Asian people over twice as likely. Data from the British Crime Survey and the CSEW indicate similar patterns. It should be noted that only a small proportion of stop and searches result in arrest.

In addition, under the Terrorism Act 2000, police can stop and search persons or vehicles whether or not they have reasonable suspicion. Statistics show that Asians are more likely to be stopped and searched than other people under the Terrorism Act.

It is therefore unsurprising that members of minority ethnic communities are less likely to think the police acted politely when stopping them, or to think they were stopped fairly. As Phillips and Bowling (2007) note, members of these communities are more likely to think they are 'over-policed and under-protected' and to have limited faith in the police.

Tasers The chance of being involved in a Taser incident varies with ethnicity. During 2010-14, police deployed Tasers over 38,000 times. For Asians, the chance of involvement was three in 10,000 and for whites six, but for blacks it was 18 in 10,000 (Hoyle 2015).

Explaining stop and search patterns

There are three possible reasons for the disproportionate use of stop and search against members of minority ethnic groups:

Police racism The Macpherson Report (1999) on the police investigation of the racist murder of the black teenager Stephen Lawrence concluded that there was institutional racism within the Metropolitan Police. Others have found deeply ingrained racist attitudes among individual officers.

For example, Phillips and Bowling (2012) point out that many officers hold negative stereotypes about ethnic minorities as criminals, leading to deliberate targeting for stop and search. Such stereotypes are endorsed and upheld by the 'canteen culture' of rank and file officers.

Ethnic differences in offending An alternative explanation is that disproportionality in stop and searches simply reflects ethnic differences in levels of offending. However, it is useful to distinguish between low discretion and high discretion stops.

- In low discretion stops, police act on relevant information about a specific offence, for example a victim's description of the offender.
- In high discretion stops, police act without specific intelligence. It is in these stops, where officers can use their stereotypes, that disproportionality and discrimination are most likely.

Demographic factors Ethnic minorities are over-represented in the population groups who are most likely to be stopped, such as the young, the unemployed, manual workers and urban dwellers. These groups are all more likely to be stopped, regardless of their ethnicity, but they are also groups who have a higher proportion of ethnic minorities in them, and so minorities get stopped more.

Arrests and cautions

Figures for England and Wales show that in 2014/15 the arrest rate for blacks was three times the rate for whites. By contrast, once arrested, blacks and Asians were less likely than whites to receive a caution.

One reason for this may be that members of minority ethnic groups are more likely to deny the offence and to exercise their right to legal advice (possibly out of mistrust of the police). However, not admitting the offence means they cannot be let off with a caution and are more likely to be charged instead.

Prosecution and trial

The Crown Prosecution Service (CPS) is the body responsible for deciding whether a case brought by the police should be prosecuted in court. In doing so, the CPS must decide whether there is a realistic prospect of conviction and whether prosecution is in the public interest.

Studies suggest that the CPS is more likely to drop cases against ethnic minorities. Bowling and Phillips (2002) argue that this may be because the evidence presented to the CPS by the police is often weaker and based on stereotyping of ethnic minorities as criminals.

When cases do go ahead, members of minority ethnic groups are more likely to elect for trial before a jury in the Crown Court, rather than in a magistrates' court, perhaps due to mistrust of magistrates' impartiality. However, Crown Courts can impose more severe sentences if convicted.

Convictions and sentencing

It is therefore interesting to note that black and Asian defendants are *less* likely to be found guilty.

This suggests discrimination, in that the police and CPS may be bringing weaker or less serious cases against ethnic minorities that are thrown out by the courts.

Black offenders have imprisonment rates three percentage points higher, and Asian offenders five point higher, than white offenders. This may be due to differences in the seriousness of the offences, or in defendants' previous convictions.

However, a study of five Crown Courts by Roger Hood (1992) found that, even when such factors were taken into account, black men were 5% more likely to receive a custodial sentence, and were given sentences on average three months (and Asian men nine months) longer than white men.

Pre-sentence reports

One possible reason for harsher sentences is the pre-sentence reports (PSRs) written by probation officers. A PSR is intended as a risk assessment to assist magistrates in deciding on the appropriate sentence for a given offender.

However, Hudson and Bramhall (2005) argue that PSRs allow for unwitting discrimination. They found that reports on Asian offenders were less comprehensive and suggested that they were less remorseful than white offenders. They place this bias in the context of the 'demonising' of Muslims in the wake of the events of 11 September 2001.

Prison

In 2014, just over a quarter of the prison population were from minority ethnic groups. Among British nationals, 5.5 per 1,000 black people were in jail compared with 1.6 per 1,000 Asians and 1.4 per 1,000 white people.

As such, blacks were four times more likely to be in prison than whites. Black and Asian offenders are more likely than whites to be serving longer sentences (of four years or more).

Within the total prison population, all minority groups have a higher than average proportion of prisoners on remand (awaiting trial rather than actually convicted and serving a sentence). This is because ethnic minorities are less likely to be granted bail while awaiting trial.

Finally, we can note the existence of similar patterns in other countries. For example, in the United States, two out of five prisoners held in local jails (both convicted and those awaiting trial) are black, while one in five is Hispanic.

Activity	Media
Ethnicity and criminal justice in America	
	...go to www.sociology.uk.net

Explaining the differences in offending

Large-scale migration from the Caribbean and the Indian subcontinent began in the 1950s. Until the 1970s, there was general agreement that the minority ethnic communities had a lower rate of offending than the white population.

However, from the mid-1970s, increased conflict between the police and the African Caribbean community and higher arrest rates for street crime meant that 'black criminality' increasingly came to be seen as a problem.

By contrast, it was not until the 1990s that crime by Asians also began to be viewed as a problem, with media concerns about the growth of 'Asian gangs'. The events of 2001 – widespread clashes between police and Asian youths in towns in northern England and 9/11 (the Islamist terrorist attacks in the United States on 11 September) – helped to crystallise the idea that Asians, and especially Muslims, were an 'enemy within' that threatened public order and safety.

As we have seen, official statistics on the criminal justice process show differences between ethnic groups. The question is therefore how we explain these patterns. There are two main explanations for ethnic differences in the statistics:

- **Left realism:** the statistics represent real differences in rates of offending.
- **Neo-Marxism:** the statistics are a social construct resulting from racist labelling and discrimination in the criminal justice system.

Left realism

Left realists such as Lea and Young (1993) argue that ethnic differences in the statistics reflect real differences in the levels of offending by different ethnic groups. As we saw in Topic 4, left realists see crime as the product of relative deprivation, subculture and marginalisation. They argue that racism has led to the marginalisation and economic exclusion of ethnic minorities, who face higher levels of unemployment, poverty and poor housing. At the same time, the media's emphasis on consumerism promotes a sense of relative deprivation by setting materialistic goals that many members of minority groups are unable to reach by legitimate means.

One response is the formation of delinquent subcultures, especially by young unemployed black males. This produces higher levels of *utilitarian* crime, such as theft and robbery, as a means of coping with relative deprivation. Furthermore, because these groups are marginalised and have no organisations to represent their interests, their frustration is liable to produce *non-utilitarian* crime such as violence and rioting.

Application

How could you use Merton's concept of anomie and A.K. Cohen's concept of status frustration to explain these patterns of utilitarian and non-utilitarian crime?

Lea and Young acknowledge that the police often act in racist ways and that this results in the unjustified criminalisation of some members of minority groups. However, they do not believe that discriminatory policing fully explains the differences in the statistics. For example,

they note that over 90% of crimes known to the police are reported by members of the public rather than discovered by the police themselves. Under these circumstances, even if the police do act in discriminatory ways, it is unlikely that this can adequately account for the ethnic differences in the statistics.

Similarly, Lea and Young argue that we cannot explain the differences between minorities in terms of police racism. For example, blacks have a considerably higher rate of criminalisation than Asians. The police would have to be very selective in their racism – against blacks but not against Asians – for it to be the cause of these differences.

Lea and Young thus conclude that the statistics represent real differences in levels of offending between ethnic groups, and that these are caused by real differences in levels of relative deprivation and marginalisation.

However, Lea and Young can be criticised for their views on the role of police racism. For example, arrest rates for Asians may be lower than for blacks not because they are less likely to offend, but because police stereotype the two groups differently, seeing blacks as dangerous, Asians as passive. Furthermore, these stereotypes may have changed since 9/11, because police now regard Asians too as dangerous – thus explaining the rising criminalisation rates for this group.

Neo-Marxism

While left realists see the official statistics as reflecting real differences in offending between ethnic groups, albeit in a somewhat distorted way, other sociologists argue that the differences in the statistics do not reflect reality. On the contrary, these differences are the outcome of a process of social construction that stereotypes ethnic minorities as inherently more criminal than the majority population. The work of the neo-Marxists Paul Gilroy (1982) and Stuart Hall et al (1979) illustrates this view.

Gilroy: the myth of black criminality

Gilroy argues that the idea of black criminality is a myth created by racist stereotypes of African Caribbeans and Asians. In reality, these groups are no more criminal than any other. However, as a result of the police and criminal justice system acting on these racist stereotypes, ethnic minorities come to be criminalised and therefore to appear in greater numbers in the official statistics.

In Gilroy's view, ethnic minority crime can be seen as a form of political resistance against a racist society, and this resistance has its roots in earlier struggles against British imperialism. Gilroy holds a similar view to that of critical criminology, which argues that working-class crime is a political act of resistance to capitalism.

Most blacks and Asians in the UK originated in the former British colonies, where their anti-imperialist struggles taught them how to resist oppression, for example through riots and demonstrations. When they found themselves facing racism in Britain, they adopted the same forms of struggle to defend themselves, but their political struggle was criminalised by the British state.

However, Lea and Young criticise Gilroy on several grounds:

- First-generation immigrants in the 1950s and 60s were very law-abiding, so it is unlikely that they passed down a tradition of anti-colonial struggle to their children.
- Most crime is intra-ethnic (criminals and their victims usually have the same ethnic background), so it can't be seen as an anti-colonial struggle against racism. Lea and Young argue that, like the critical criminologists, Gilroy romanticises street crime as somehow revolutionary, when it is nothing of the sort.
- Asian crime rates are similar to or lower than whites. If Gilroy were right, then the police are only racist towards blacks and not Asians, which seems unlikely.

Hall et al: policing the crisis

Stuart Hall et al adopt a neo-Marxist perspective. They argue that the 1970s saw a moral panic over black 'muggers' that served the interests of capitalism.

Hall et al argue that the ruling class are normally able to rule the subordinate classes through consent. However, in times of crisis, this becomes more difficult. In the early 1970s, British capitalism faced a crisis. High inflation and rising unemployment were provoking widespread industrial unrest and strikes, conflict in Northern Ireland was intensifying and student protests were spreading. At such times, when opposition to capitalism begins to grow, the ruling class may need to use force to maintain control. However, the use of force needs to be seen as legitimate or it may provoke even more widespread resistance.

Moral panic The 1970s also saw the emergence of a media-driven moral panic about the supposed growth of a 'new' crime – mugging. In reality, mugging was just a new name for the old crime of street robbery with violence, and Hall et al note that there was no evidence of a significant increase in this crime at the time. Mugging was soon to be associated by the media, police and politicians with black youth.

Hall et al argue that the emergence of the moral panic about mugging as a specifically 'black' crime at the same time as the crisis of capitalism was no coincidence – in their view, the moral panic and the crisis were linked. The myth of the black mugger served as a scapegoat to distract attention from the true cause of problems such as unemployment – namely the capitalist crisis.

The black mugger came to symbolise the disintegration of the social order – the feeling that the British way of life was 'coming apart at the seams'. By presenting black youth as a threat to the fabric of society, the moral panic served to divide the working class on racial grounds and weaken opposition to capitalism, as well as winning popular consent for more authoritarian forms of rule that could be used to suppress opposition.

However, Hall et al do not argue that black crime was solely a product of media and police labelling. The crisis of capitalism was increasingly marginalising black youth through unemployment, and this drove some into a lifestyle of hustling and petty crime as a means of survival.

Hall et al have been criticised on several grounds:

- Downes and Rock (2011) argue that Hall et al are inconsistent in claiming that black street crime was not rising, but also that it *was* rising because of unemployment.
- They do not show *how* the capitalist crisis led to a moral panic, nor do they provide evidence that the public were in fact panicking or blaming crime on blacks.
- Left realists argue that inner-city residents' fears about mugging are not panicky, but realistic.

More recent approaches

More recently, sociologists have offered other explanations for ethnic differences in crime rates, including the following.

Neighbourhood FitzGerald et al (2003) examine the role of neighbourhood factors in explaining the greater involvement of black youths in street robbery. They found that rates were highest in very poor areas and where very deprived young people came into contact with more affluent groups. Young blacks were more likely to live in these areas and to be poor. However, whites affected by these factors were also more likely to commit street crime. Thus, ethnicity as such was not a cause. However, black people may be more likely to live in poor areas because of racial discrimination in the housing and job markets.

Getting caught Some groups run a greater risk of being caught. Sharp and Budd (2005) found that black offenders were more likely than white offenders to have been arrested. Reasons included that they were more likely to commit crimes such as robbery, where victims can identify them, and to have been excluded from school or to associate with known criminals – factors that raised their 'visibility' to the authorities.

Activity	Media
Urban riots and 'race'	

...go to www.sociology.uk.net

Ethnicity and victimisation

Until recently, the focus of the 'ethnicity and crime' debate has been largely on the over-representation of black people in the criminal justice system. However, more recently, sociologists have taken an interest in other issues such as the racist victimisation of ethnic minorities.

Racist victimisation occurs when an individual is selected as a target because of their race, ethnicity or religion. Racist victimisation is nothing new, but was brought into greater public focus with the racist murder of the black teenager Stephen Lawrence in 1993 and the subsequent inquiry into the handling of the police investigation (Macpherson 1999).

Our information on racist victimisation comes from two main sources: victim surveys such as the CSEW, and police-recorded statistics. These generally cover:

- **Racist incidents** Any incident that is perceived to be racist by the victim or another person.
- **Racially or religiously aggravated offences** (assault, wounding, criminal damage and harassment) where the offender is motivated by hostility towards members of a racial or religious group.

Extent and risk of victimisation

- The police recorded 54,000 *racist incidents* in England and Wales in 2014/15 – mostly damage to property or verbal harassment.
- However, most incidents go unreported. The CSEW estimates there were around 89,000 racially motivated incidents in 2014/15.
- The police also recorded 38,000 *racially or religiously aggravated offences* in 2014/15, mostly harassment. 8,600 people were prosecuted or cautioned for racially aggravated offences in 2014.

The risk of being a victim of any sort of crime – not just racist crime – varies by ethnic group. The 2014/15 CSEW shows that people from mixed ethnic backgrounds had a higher risk (27.9%) of becoming a victim of crime than did blacks (18%), Asians (15.8%) or whites (15.7%).

The differences may be partly the result of factors other than ethnicity. For example for violent crime, factors such as being young, male and unemployed are strongly linked with victimisation. Ethnic groups with a high proportion of young males are thus likely to have higher rates of victimisation. However, some of these factors (such as unemployment) are themselves partly the result of discrimination.

While the statistics record the instances of victimisation, they do not necessarily capture the victims' experience of it. As Sampson and Phillips (1992) note, racist victimisation

tends to be ongoing over time, with repeated 'minor' instances of abuse and harassment interwoven with periodic incidents of physical violence.

The resulting long-term psychological impact needs to be added to the physical injury and damage to property caused by the offenders.

Responses to victimisation

Members of minority ethnic communities have often been active in responding to victimisation. Responses have ranged from situational crime prevention measures such as fireproof doors and letterboxes, to organised self-defence campaigns aimed at physically defending neighbourhoods from racist attacks.

Such responses need to be understood in the context of accusations of under-protection by the police, who have often ignored the racist dimensions of victimisation and failed to record or investigate reported incidents properly.

For example, the Macpherson Enquiry (1999) concluded that the police investigation into the death of the black teenager Stephen Lawrence was 'marred by a combination of professional incompetence, institutional racism and a failure of leadership by senior officers'. Others have found deeply ingrained racist attitudes and beliefs among individual officers.

Topic summary

Official statistics show that blacks and other ethnic minorities are more likely to be **stopped**, **arrested** and **imprisoned**. This may be because they are more **likely to offend**, or because of **racism** in the criminal justice system, or because they are more likely to fall into the **demographic groups** who are stopped. **Self-report studies** show lower offending rates among minorities than among whites. Black defendants are more likely to be acquitted but if convicted are more likely to be jailed.

Left realists argue that blacks do have a higher crime rate because of their greater **relative deprivation** and **social exclusion**, whereas **Neo-Marxists** argue that black criminality is a **social construction** serving to distract attention from the **crisis of capitalism**.

Minorities are more likely to be **victims** of crime, while being both over-policed and under-protected.

EXAMINING ETHNICITY, CRIME AND JUSTICE

QuickCheck Questions

Check your answers at www.sociology.uk.net

1 How much more likely are black people to be stopped and searched than whites: (a) 5 (b) 7 (c) 10 times?

2 Identify two problems in using self-report studies to study ethnic differences in offending.

3 How do Lea and Young account for (a) utilitarian and (b) non-utilitarian crime among blacks?

4 In what way does Gilroy see ethnic minority crime as political?

5 Suggest two criticisms of Gilroy's views.

6 According to Hall et al, how did the moral panic over mugging help capitalism?

7 What is meant by the term 'institutional racism'?

8 Identify two social characteristics of ethnic minority groups that make them more likely to be victims.

Questions to try

Item A   The risk of being a victim of crime appears to vary by ethnic group, both in terms of 'ordinary' crimes and racially motivated crimes. This is shown in victim surveys. Surveys are based on the assumption that people are aware of what is happening to them.

All suspected crimes have to go through a process of being reported and investigated before they are officially categorised as a crime. The role of the police is crucial to this process.

Item B   Official statistics suggest that there is a clear relationship between ethnicity and offending. These show black people and to a lesser extent Asians as being over-represented in the criminal justice system. In the view of some sociologists, this is because at each stage in the system, from policing through to sentencing, institutional racism distorts the picture of ethnic patterns of offending.

However, left realists argue that there are real differences in offending rates and that these differences can be explained in terms of factors such as relative deprivation and marginalisation.

1 Outline two reasons why members of some ethnic groups are more likely than others to receive custodial sentences.   (4 marks)

2 Applying material from Item A, analyse two explanations of the apparent differences in the rates of victimisation of ethnic groups.   (10 marks)

3 Applying material from Item B and your knowledge, evaluate sociological explanations of the relationship between ethnicity and offending.   (30 marks)

The Examiner's Advice

Q2 Spend about 15 minutes on this. Divide your time fairly equally between the two explanations. You don't need a separate introduction; just start on your first explanation. To answer this question, it's essential that you take two points from the Item and show through a chain of reasoning (see Box 4.1 in chapter 4) how each explains the apparent differences in the rates of victimisation between ethnic groups. (It is a very good idea to quote from the Item when doing so.)

You could use ideas such as patterns of victimisation in relation to 'ordinary' and racially motivated crime; reporting, investigating and categorising of crimes; the role of the police; and people's awareness of crimes.

For example, ethnic minorities may be unaware of being victimised or that the crime was racially motivated. Thus they may not report the crime, or not report it as a racist crime, leading to an under-estimate of victimisation.

Use concepts such as police-recorded statistics, over-policing, under-reporting and factors affecting risk of victimisation (e.g. age, employment status, area of residence). Offer some brief evaluation by noting that victimisation statistics are constructs produced by social processes.

Q3 Spend about 45 minutes on this. Consider different explanations of the relationship between ethnicity and offending. Organise your answer around a debate about whether the statistics represent reality or not. Start by examining the left realists' view that the statistics are a reasonably accurate representation of offending patterns and present their explanation.

Evaluate by contrasting the official statistics with the results of self-report studies. Use this to argue that offending rates may be socially constructed rather than real. Examine the social processes involved at different stages of the criminal justice system, e.g. stops and searches, arrests and sentencing, to show how the statistics are socially constructed. Examine in detail neo-Marxist explanations (Gilroy; Hall et al) that black criminality is a myth or the product of moral panic. Use Lea and Young, and Downes and Rock to evaluate these views.

Use the above concepts, issues and studies, plus relative deprivation, subculture, marginalisation, neighbourhood factors, hegemony, high and low discretion stops, institutional racism, demographic factors, police racism, over-policing, colonialism, resistance, capitalist crisis, criminalisation. Use studies such as Bowling and Phillips, Sharp and Budd, Hood and FitzGerald.

Do these images convey the reality of crime?

GETTING STARTED

Working in small groups, search the internet for a TV listings guide and use it to complete the following tasks:

1 Make a list of how many hours and minutes of crime fiction (not reality TV) programmes there are in a 24-hour period for BBC and ITV channels.

2 Categorise the programmes. For example, you could use amateur detective, 'cop' show, police procedural, criminal lives, and/or others that you think are appropriate. If you are not sure about how to classify a programme, look it up on the internet to obtain more information about it.

From what you have found and from your own knowledge of the programmes, answer the following questions:

3 What types of crime are covered in the programmes? What types are missing?

4 What are the criminals like? Consider their age, gender, ethnicity and social class.

5 How are the police and the justice system (e.g. prisons, courts and judges) portrayed?

6 How are victims portrayed?

7 In what ways would you say these programmes are unrealistic in their portrayals of crime, criminals, the police and the justice system? For example, are the cases always solved and the offender caught?

Learning objectives

After studying this Topic, you should:

- Know the patterns of media representations of crime and how these differ from the picture of crime in official statistics.

- Understand and be able to evaluate different views about the media as a cause of crime and fear of crime.

- Know and be able to evaluate views of the media's role in the creation of moral panics.

- Understand the relationships between the new information media and crime and social control.

CRIME AND THE MEDIA

We live today in a media-saturated society. The media are all around us – and the media are obsessed with crime. Crime is the central theme of media output, both fiction and non-fiction. In a world where we often have very little contact with people whose lifestyles and values differ from our own, the media have become our main source of knowledge about crime. What we know – or *think* we know – about crime is heavily influenced by the media's representation of it.

Sociologists are interested in several aspects of the media in relation to crime and deviance. In this Topic, we shall examine:

- How the media represent crime, both in fiction and in non-fiction such as news broadcasts – how far does this portray an accurate picture of crime?
- Do the media cause crime and fear of crime – for example, do the young imitate the deviance they see in the media? Do the media make us more afraid of becoming victims of crime?
- Moral panics – what role do the media play in defining some groups as 'folk devils' and in amplifying deviance?
- Cybercrime – how far do the Internet and other information and communication technology create new opportunities for crime, and for the surveillance and control of the population?

Media representations of crime

MIS understendly false picture

Crime and deviance make up a large proportion of news coverage. For example, Richard Ericson et al's (1991) study of Toronto found that 45-71% of quality press and radio news was about various forms of deviance and its control, while Williams and Dickinson (1993) found British newspapers devote up to 30% of their news space to crime.

However, while the news media show a keen interest in crime, they give a distorted image of crime, criminals and policing. For example, as compared with the picture of crime we gain from official statistics:

- The media over-represent violent and sexual crime. For example, Ditton and Duffy (1983) found that 46% of media reports were about violent or sexual crimes, yet these made up only 3% of all crimes recorded by the police. One review by Marsh (1991) of studies of news reporting in America found that a violent crime was 36 times more likely to be reported than a property crime.
- The media portray criminals and victims as older and more middle-class than those typically found in the criminal justice system. Felson (1998) calls this the 'age fallacy'. ?
- Media coverage exaggerates police success in clearing up cases. This is partly because the police are a major source of crime stories and want to present themselves in a good light, and partly because the media over-represents violent crime, which has a higher clear-up rate than property crime.
- The media exaggerate the risk of victimisation, especially to women, white people and higher status individuals.
- Crime is reported as a series of separate events without structure and without examining underlying causes.
- The media overplay extraordinary crimes and underplay ordinary crimes – Felson calls this the 'dramatic fallacy'. Similarly, media images lead us to believe that

to commit crime (and to solve it) one needs to be daring and clever – the 'ingenuity fallacy'.

There is some evidence of changes in the type of coverage of crime by the news media. For example, Schlesinger and Tumber (1994) found that in the 1960s the focus had been on murders and petty crime, but by the 1990s murder and petty crime were of less interest to the media. The change came about partly because of the abolition of the death penalty for murder and partly because rising crime rates meant that a crime had to be 'special' to attract coverage. By the 1990s, reporting had also widened to include drugs, child abuse, terrorism, football hooliganism and mugging.

There is also evidence of increasing preoccupation with sex crimes. For example, Keith Soothill and Sylvia Walby (1991) found that newspaper reporting of rape cases increased from under a quarter of all cases in 1951 to over a third in 1985. They also note that coverage consistently focuses on identifying a 'sex fiend' or 'beast', often by use of labels (such as 'the balaclava rapist'). The resulting distorted picture of rape is one of serial attacks carried out by psychopathic strangers. While these do occur, they are the exception rather than the rule – in most cases the perpetrator is known to the victim.

News values and crime coverage

The distorted picture of crime painted by the news media reflects the fact that news is a social construction. That is, news does not simply exist 'out there' waiting to be gathered in and written up by the journalist. Rather, it is the outcome of a social process in which some potential stories are selected while others are rejected. As Stan Cohen and Jock Young (1973) note, news is not discovered but *manufactured*.

*True Crime
dramatised crime*

A central aspect of the manufacture of news is the notion of 'news values'. News values are the criteria by which journalists and editors decide whether a story is newsworthy enough to make it into the newspaper or news bulletin. If a crime story can be told in terms of some of these criteria, it has a better chance of making the news. Key news values influencing the selection of crime stories include:

- **Immediacy** – 'breaking news'
- **Dramatisation** – action and excitement
- **Personalisation** – human interest stories about individuals
- **Higher-status** persons and 'celebrities'
- **Simplification** – eliminating shades of grey
- **Novelty or unexpectedness** – a new angle
- **Risk** – victim-centred stories about vulnerability and fear
- **Violence** – especially visible and spectacular acts.

One reason why the news media give so much coverage to crime is that news focuses on the unusual and extraordinary, and this makes deviance newsworthy almost by definition, since it is abnormal behaviour.

Fictional representations of crime

We don't just get our images of crime from the news media. Fictional representations from TV, cinema and novels are also important sources of our knowledge of crime, because so much of their output is crime-related. For example, Ernest Mandel (1984) estimates that from 1945 to 1984, over 10 billion crime thrillers were sold worldwide, while about 25% of prime time TV and 20% of films are crime shows or movies.

Fictional representations of crime, criminals and victims follow what Surette (1998) calls 'the law of opposites': they are the opposite of the official statistics – and strikingly similar to news coverage.

- Property crime is under-represented, while violence, drugs and sex crimes are over-represented.
- While real-life homicides mainly result from brawls and domestic disputes, fictional ones are the product of greed and calculation.
- Fictional sex crimes are committed by psychopathic strangers, not acquaintances. Fictional villains tend to be higher status, middle-aged white males.
- Fictional cops usually get their man.

However, three recent trends are worth noting. Firstly, the new genre of 'reality' infotainment shows tends to feature young, non-white 'underclass' offenders. Secondly, there is an increasing tendency to show police as corrupt and brutal (and as less successful). Thirdly, victims have become more central, with law enforcers portrayed as their avengers and audiences invited to identify with their suffering.

The media as a cause of crime

There has long been concern that the media have a negative effect on attitudes, values and behaviour – especially of those groups thought to be most susceptible to influence, such as the young, the lower classes and the uneducated. In the 1920s and '30s, cinema was blamed for corrupting youth; in the 1950s, horror comics were held responsible for moral decline, while in the 1980s it was 'video nasties'. More recently, rap lyrics and computer games such as Grand Theft Auto have been criticised for encouraging violence and criminality.

There are numerous ways in which the media might possibly cause crime and deviance. These include:

- Imitation – by providing deviant role models, resulting in 'copycat' behaviour.
- Arousal, e.g. through viewing violent or sexual imagery.
- Desensitisation, e.g. through repeated viewing of violence.
- By transmitting knowledge of criminal techniques.
- As a target for crime, e.g. theft of TVs.
- By stimulating desires for unaffordable goods, e.g. through advertising.
- By portraying the police as incompetent.
- By glamourising offending.

As a result of fears about the possible negative effects of the media on their audiences, literally thousands of studies have been conducted. Overall, however, most studies have tended to find that exposure to media violence has at most a small and limited negative effect on audiences. As Schramm et al (1961) say in relation to the effects of TV viewing on children:

'For some children, under some conditions, some television is harmful. For some children under the same conditions, it may be beneficial. For most children, under most conditions, most television is probably neither particularly harmful nor particularly beneficial.'

However, as Sonia Livingstone (1996) notes, despite such conclusions, people continue to be preoccupied with the effects of the media on children because of our desire as a society to regard childhood as a time of uncontaminated innocence in the private sphere.

Casual.

Fear of crime

As we have seen, the media exaggerate the amount of violent and unusual crime, and they exaggerate the risks of certain groups of people becoming its victims, such as young women and old people. There is therefore concern that the media may be distorting the public's impression of crime and causing an unrealistic fear of crime.

Research evidence to some extent supports the view that there is a link between media use and fear of crime. For example, in the USA, Gerbner et al found that heavy users of television (over four hours a day) had higher levels of fear of crime. Similarly, Schlesinger and Tumber (1992) found a correlation between media consumption and fear of crime, with tabloid readers and heavy users of TV expressing greater fear of becoming a victim, especially of physical attack and mugging.

However, the existence of such correlations doesn't prove that media viewing causes fear. For example, it may be that those who are already afraid of going out at night watch more TV just because they stay in more.

Finally, as Greer and Reiner (2012) note, much 'effects' research on the media as a cause of crime or fear of crime ignores the meanings that viewers give to media violence. For example, they may give very different meanings to violence in cartoons, horror films and news bulletins. This criticism reflects the interpretivist view that if we want to understand the possible effects of the media, we must look at the meanings people give to what they see and read.

The media, relative deprivation and crime

Laboratory based research has focused on whether media portrayals of crime and deviant lifestyles lead viewers to commit crime themselves. An alternative approach is to consider how far media portrayals of 'normal' rather than criminal lifestyles might also encourage people to commit crime.

For example, left realists argue that the mass media help to increase the sense of relative deprivation – the feeling of being deprived relative to others – among poor and marginalised social groups. As Lea and Young (1996) put it:

'The mass media have disseminated a standardized image of lifestyle, particularly in the areas of popular culture and recreation, which, for those unemployed and surviving through the dole queue or only able to obtain employment at very low wages, has accentuated the sense of relative deprivation.'

In today's society, where even the poorest groups have media access, the media present everyone with images of a materialistic 'good life' of leisure, fun and consumer goods as the norm to which they should conform. The result is to stimulate the sense of relative deprivation and social

exclusion felt by marginalised groups who cannot afford these goods. As Merton argues, pressure to conform to the norm can cause deviant behaviour when the opportunity to achieve by legitimate means is blocked. In this instance, the media are instrumental in setting the norm and thus in promoting crime.

Cultural criminology, the media and crime

Relative deprivation explains how the media *produce* or cause crime. By showing people lifestyles they desire but cannot afford, the media create a sense of relative deprivation that causes people to resort to crime to get the commodities they cannot obtain legitimately.

By contrast, cultural criminology argues that the media turn crime itself into the commodity that people desire. Rather than simply producing crime in their audiences, the media encourage them to *consume* crime, in the form of images of crime.

Cultural criminologists such as Mike Hayward and Jock Young (2012) see late modern society as a media-saturated society, where we are immersed in the 'mediascape' – an ever-expanding tangle of fluid digital images, including images of crime. In this world, there is a blurring between the image and the reality of crime, so that the two are no longer clearly distinct or separable. The way the media represent crime and crime control now actually constitutes or creates the thing itself.

For example, gang assaults are not just caught on camera, but staged *for* the camera and later packaged together in 'underground fight videos'. Similarly, police car cameras don't just *record* police activity; they actually alter the way in which the police work, with US police forces for example using reality TV shows like *Cops* as promo videos.

Media and the commodification of crime

A further feature of late modernity is the emphasis on consumption, excitement and immediacy. In this context, crime and its thrills become commodified. Corporations and advertisers use media images of crime to sell products, especially in the youth market. For example, 'gangster' rap and hip hop combine images of street hustler criminality with images of consumerist success. Similarly, leading hip hop stars parade designer chic clothing, jewellery, champagne, luxury cars and so on.

Crime and deviance thus become a style to be consumed. As Fenwick and Hayward (2000) put it, 'crime is packaged and marketed to young people as a romantic, exciting, cool, and fashionable cultural symbol.'

This is also true of mainstream products. For example, Hayward and Young cite examples of car ads featuring street riots, joyriding, suicide bombing, graffiti and pyromania. Likewise, the fashion industry and its advertisers trade on images of the forbidden (with brands such as *Opium*, *Poison* and *Obsession*), 'heroin chic', sadomasochism and violence against women, and the retailer FCUK 'brands' transgression into its name. Designer clothing *Section 60* is named after the section of the Act giving police the power to stop and search.

Even counter-cultures are packaged and sold. Graffiti is the marker of deviant urban cool, but corporations now use it in a 'guerrilla marketing' technique called 'brandalism' to sell everything from theme parks to cars and video games. Companies use moral panics, controversy and scandal to market their products.

Ironically, the designer labels valued by young people as badges of identity now function as symbols of deviance. For example, some pubs and clubs now refuse entry to individuals wearing certain brands, while Bluewater shopping centre has banned the wearing of hoodies (though they can still be purchased there). In some towns, local bars and police compile lists of branded clothing that they see as problematic. Brands become tools of classification for constructing profiles of potential criminals.

Activity	Media

Counter-culture and commodification

...go to www.sociology.uk.net

Moral panics

One further way in which the media may cause crime and deviance is through labelling. As we saw in Topic 2, moral entrepreneurs who disapprove of some particular behaviour – drug taking, for instance – may use the media to put pressure on the authorities to 'do something' about the alleged problem. If successful, their campaigning will result in the negative labelling of the behaviour and perhaps a change in the law, such as the introduction of the Marijuana Tax Act in the USA. By helping to label marijuana smoking, which previously had been legal, as criminal, the media helped to cause crime.

An important element in this process is the creation of a moral panic. A moral panic is an exaggerated over-reaction by society to a perceived problem – usually driven or inspired by the media – where the reaction enlarges the problem out of all proportion to its real seriousness. In a moral panic:

- The media identify a group as a *folk devil* or threat to societal values.
- The media present the group in a negative, stereotypical fashion and exaggerate the scale of the problem.
- Moral entrepreneurs, editors, politicians, police chiefs, bishops and other 'respectable' people condemn the group and its behaviour.

This usually leads to calls for a 'crackdown' on the group. However, this may create a self-fulfilling prophecy that amplifies the very problem that caused the panic in the first place. For example, in the case of drugs, setting up special drug squads led the police to discover more drug taking. As the crackdown identifies more deviants, there are calls for even tougher action, creating a deviance amplification spiral.

Mods and rockers

The most influential study of moral panics and the role of the media is Stanley Cohen's (1972) book, *Folk Devils and Moral Panics*. Cohen examines the media's response to disturbances between two groups of largely working-class teenagers, the mods and the rockers, at English seaside resorts from 1964 to 1966, and the way in which this created a moral panic.

Mods wore smart dress and rode scooters; rockers wore leather jackets and rode motorbikes – though in the early stages, distinctions were not so clear-cut, and not many young people identified themselves as belonging to either 'group'. The initial confrontations started on a cold, wet Easter weekend in 1964 at Clacton, with a few scuffles, some stone throwing, some windows being broken and some beach huts wrecked.

However, although the disorder was relatively minor, the media over-reacted. In his analysis, Cohen uses the analogy of a disaster, where the media produce an inventory or stocktaking of what happened. Cohen says this inventory contained three elements:

Exaggeration and distortion The media exaggerated the numbers involved and the extent of the violence and damage, and distorted the picture through dramatic reporting and sensational headlines such as 'Day of Terror by Scooter Gangs' and 'Youngsters Beat Up Town – 97 Leather Jacket Arrests'. Even non-events were news – towns 'held their breath' for invasions that didn't materialise.

Prediction The media regularly assumed and predicted further conflict and violence would result.

Symbolisation The symbols of the mods and rockers – their clothes, bikes and scooters, hairstyles, music etc –

were all negatively labelled and associated with deviance. The media's use of these symbols allowed them to link unconnected events. For example, bikers in different parts of the country who misbehaved could be seen as part of a more general underlying problem of disorderly youth.

deviance amplification spiral

Cohen argues that the media's portrayal of events produced a deviance amplification spiral by making it seem as if the problem was spreading and getting out of hand. This led to calls for an increased control response from the police and courts. This produced further marginalisation and stigmatisation of the mods and rockers as deviants, and less and less tolerance of them, and so on in an upward spiral.

The media further amplified the deviance by defining the two groups and their subcultural styles. This led to more youths adopting these styles and drew in more participants for future clashes. By emphasising their supposed differences, the media crystallised two distinct identities and transformed loose-knit groupings into two tight-knit gangs. This encouraged polarisation and helped to create a self-fulfilling prophecy of escalating conflict as youths acted out the roles the media had assigned to them.

Cohen notes that media definitions of the situation are crucial in creating a moral panic, because in large-scale modern societies, most people have no direct experience of the events themselves and thus have to rely on the media for information about them. In the case of the mods and rockers, this allowed the media to portray them as folk devils – major threats to public order and social values.

The wider context

Cohen puts the moral panic about the mods and rockers into the wider context of change in post-war British society. This was a period in which the newfound affluence, consumerism and hedonism of the young appeared to challenge the values of an older generation who had lived through the hardships of the 1930s and 1940s.

Cohen argues that moral panics often occur at times of social change, reflecting the anxieties many people feel when accepted values seem to be undermined. He argues that the moral panic was a result of a *boundary crisis*, where there was uncertainty about the where the boundary lay between acceptable and unacceptable behaviour in a time of change. The folk devil created by the media symbolises and gives a focus to popular anxieties about social disorder.

From a functionalist perspective, moral panics can be seen as ways of responding to the sense of anomie or normlessness created by change. By dramatising the threat to society in the form of a folk devil, the media raises the collective consciousness and reasserts social controls when central values are threatened.

▲ Mods arriving in Hastings, 1964.

Other sociologists have also used the concept of moral panics. For example, Stuart Hall et al (1979) adopt a neo-Marxist approach that locates the role of moral panics in the context of capitalism. They argue that the moral panic over 'mugging' in the British media in the 1970s served to distract attention from the crisis of capitalism, divide the working class on racial grounds and legitimate a more authoritarian style of rule.

In addition to concerns about mods and rockers and about mugging, commentators have claimed to identify numerous other examples of folk devils and moral panics in recent decades. These include dangerous dogs, New Age travellers, bogus asylum seekers, child sexual abuse, Aids, binge drinking, 'mad cow' disease and single parents.

Criticisms of the idea of moral panics

There are several criticisms of the concept of moral panics:

It assumes that the societal reaction is a disproportionate over-reaction – but who is to decide what is a proportionate reaction, and what is a panicky one? This relates to the left realist view that people's fear of crime is in fact rational.

What turns the 'amplifier' on and off: why are the media able to amplify some problems into a panic, but not others? Why do panics not go on increasing indefinitely once they have started?

Late modernity Do today's media audiences, who are accustomed to 'shock, horror' stories, really react with panic to media exaggerations? McRobbie and Thornton (1995) argue that moral panics are now routine and have less impact. Also, in late modern society, there is little consensus about what is deviant. Lifestyle choices that were condemned forty years ago, such as single motherhood, are no longer universally regarded as deviant and so it is harder for the media to create panics about them.

Activity | Media

Moral panic

...go to www.sociology.uk.net

Cyber-crime

The arrival of new types of media is often met with a moral panic. For example, horror comics, cinema, television, videos and computer games have all been accused of undermining public morality and corrupting the young. The same is true of the Internet – both because of the speed with which it has developed and its scale: over half the world's population are now online. The arrival of the Internet has led to fears of cyber-crime, which Douglas Thomas and Brian Loader (2000) define as computer-mediated activities that are either illegal or considered illicit by some, and that are conducted through global electronic networks.

As Yvonne Jewkes (2003) notes, the Internet creates opportunities to commit both 'conventional crimes', such as fraud, and 'new crimes using new tools', such as software piracy. Wall (2001) identifies four categories of cybercrime:

Cyber-trespass – crossing boundaries into others' cyber-property. It includes hacking and sabotage, such as spreading viruses.

Cyber-deception and theft – including identity theft, 'phishing' (obtaining identity or bank account details by deception) and violation of intellectual property rights (e.g. software piracy, illegal downloading and file-sharing).

Cyber-pornography – including porn involving minors, and opportunities for children to access porn on the Net.

Cyber-violence – doing psychological harm or inciting physical harm. Cyber-violence includes cyber-stalking (e.g. sending unwanted, threatening or offensive emails) and hate crimes against minority groups, as well as bullying by text.

Global cyber-crime Policing cyber-crime is difficult partly because of the sheer scale of the Internet and the limited resources of the police, and also because of its globalised nature, which poses problems of jurisdiction (e.g. in which country should someone be prosecuted for an Internet offence?). Police culture also gives cyber-crime a low priority because it is seen as lacking the excitement of more conventional policing.

▲ Cyber-crime, USA: hackers interfere with electronic road sign

However, the new information and communication technology (ICT) also provides the police and state with greater opportunities for surveillance and control of the population. As Jewkes (2003) argues, ICT permits routine surveillance through the use of CCTV cameras, electronic databases, digital fingerprinting and 'smart' identity cards, as well as the installation of listening devices called 'carnivores' at Internet service providers to monitor email traffic.

Topic summary

The media give a distorted image of crime. For example, they **over-represent violent crime** and exaggerate the risk of **victimisation**. The fact that news is a **social construction** based on **news values** such as dramatisation and violence helps to explain the media's interest in crime.

Some see the media as **causing crime**, for example through imitation. However, studies generally show only small and **limited effects**. **Left realists** argue that the media increase **relative deprivation** among the poor, who then turn to crime to achieve the lifestyle portrayed by the media. **Cultural criminologists** argue that in late modern society, the media **commodify crime**.

The media also cause **moral panics**, identifying a group as **folk devils** and exaggerating the threat they pose, leading to a crackdown and creating a **deviance amplification spiral**. New media such as the Internet have created new opportunities both for **cyber-crime** and for **surveillance** and control of the population.

EXAMINING CRIME AND THE MEDIA

QuickCheck Questions

Check your answers at www.sociology.uk.net

1 Identify three news values that the media use to select crime stories.
2 Identify three ways in which the media's fictional portrayal of crime and policing differs from that of the official statistics.
3 In what way may the media and fear of crime be linked?
4 Suggest three ways in which the media may encourage or cause crime and deviance.
5 How do left realists explain the role of the media in causing crime?
6 Explain what is meant by 'the commodification of crime'.
7 Explain what is meant by the term 'deviance amplification'.
8 Identify three ways in which the media amplified the deviance of the mods and rockers.
9 Identify two criticisms of the concept of moral panic.
10 Suggest three examples of cyber-crimes.

Questions to try

Item A   Some sociologists claim that the media do not just report criminal and deviant behaviour, but may actually be a cause of crime and deviance. Some media portrayals of crime may appear to be very realistic. The media also present a number of different lifestyles in a wide range of types of programmes, such as 'reality' TV, advertising, documentary and fiction, which some audiences may see as attractive. The same or similar crime storylines and images may be constantly repeated.

Item B   A media-generated moral panic occurs when the media present an exaggerated over-reaction to an issue which as a result makes the issue seem a much greater problem than it actually is. Usually, a group is represented as a 'folk devil' – a threat to society. This media amplification initiates a spiral of distortion, stereotypical representation and condemnation by powerful groups in society.

However, this approach has been criticised for failing to explain why particular moral panics develop in the first place.

1 Outline three media news values.   (6 marks)
2 Applying material from Item A, analyse two ways in which the media may cause crime.   (10 marks)
3 Applying material from Item B and your knowledge, evaluate sociological explanations of media-generated moral panics.
                                                                                       (30 marks)

The Examiner's Advice

Q2 Spend about 15 minutes on this. Divide your time fairly equally between the two ways. You don't need a separate introduction; just start on your first way. To answer this question, it's essential that you take two points from the Item and show through a chain of reasoning (see Box 4.1 in chapter 4) how each is a way in which the media may cause crime. (It is a very good idea to quote from the Item when doing so.)

You could use the idea that the media may portray crime realistically, that the same or similar crime storylines and images may be constantly repeated, or that the media portray attractive lifestyles. The media offer images of a desirable lifestyle of consumption and leisure. Advertising presents consumerism as something to be valued. For the poor, this accentuates feelings of relative deprivation, so they turn to crime to obtain desired goods. You can briefly evaluate by noting that relative deprivation does not always lead to crime.

Use concepts and issues such as those above, plus values, imitation, arousal, desensitisation, transmission, standardised images, marginalisation, subculture, exclusion. Use studies such as Schramm, Livingstone, Merton, and Lea and Young.

Q3 Spend about 45 minutes on this. Use the Item to define moral panics and folk devils. Use the concept of a deviance amplification spiral to help you describe the stages of a moral panic. Highlight the role of the different actors in the process, including the media.

It is important to explain moral panics, not just describe them. Do this by using a theoretical framework such as interactionism. For example, explain how it is a form of labelling and self-fulfilling prophecy that results from societal reaction and creates deviant identities and careers. Consider alternative explanations such as boundary crisis (Cohen), response to anomie (functionalism), and capitalist crisis (neo-Marxism). Evaluate for example by asking why not all problems are amplified, why amplification ceases and whether moral panics become routinised and have less impact in late modernity.

Use concepts and issues such as those above, plus exaggeration and distortion, sensitisation, prediction, moral entrepreneurs, stereotypes, polarisation, public order, normlessness, hegemony and capitalism. Use studies such as Cohen, Young, Hall et al, and McRobbie and Thornton, and examples such as Mods and Rockers, muggers and drug takers. You may find it useful to refer to Topic 2 and Topic 6.

28 January 1986. The space shuttle *Challenger* explodes 73 seconds after launch, killing all seven crew. A state-corporate crime?

GETTING STARTED

Working in groups, read the passage below and then answer the questions that follow it.

The Convention on International Trade in Endangered Species (CITES) is an inter-governmental agreement whose aim is to ensure that international trade in wild animals and plants does not threaten their survival.

Despite this agreement, the illegal trade in plants, animals and animal body parts continues. This includes trade in ivory, rhino horn and tiger bones, as well as live animals. The value of this trade is in the region of $10 billion a year and involves almost 100 million transactions.

The supply for the trade comes from developing countries lacking employment opportunities. There may also be problems enforcing laws in certain countries. Demand comes from more affluent Western and Far Eastern countries.

There may be difficulties identifying and tracing the origin of products once they have left a country. For example, this may require sophisticated scientific analysis, as in the case of ivory.

1 Why does the trade exist?

2 What conditions in the countries of origin might facilitate the trade?

3 Why might it be easy to move products out of the countries of origin?

4 Why might the fact that the trade is international make it more difficult to supress?

5 What difficulties might there be in identifying illegal animal or plant products?

6 Why do people buy these products?

You might be interested to find out more about the illegal trade in endangered species by visiting internet sites such as those of Interpol, WWF, CITES or the Born Free Foundation.

Learning objectives

After studying this Topic, you should:

- Understand the ways in which globalisation and crime are related and be able to evaluate explanations of this relationship.

- Understand the different types of green crime and be able to evaluate sociological explanations of environmental harm.

- Understand the relationship between state crimes and human rights and be able to evaluate definitions and explanations of such crimes.

In this Topic, we widen our horizons to look at crime on a global scale. As the world becomes more interconnected, so the opportunities for crime that crosses borders increase.

At the same time, we are becoming increasingly aware of the risks posed by the harms we do to the global environment, such as global warming. In this Topic, we examine sociologists' ideas about 'green crime'.

Our awareness of human rights abuses around the world has also grown. Very often, the perpetrators of these abuses are the same states that claim to protect their citizens' rights. Lastly, therefore, we look at state crimes.

Crime and globalisation

Globalisation refers to the increasing interconnectedness of societies, so that what happens in one locality is shaped by distant events and vice versa. For example, David Held et al (1999) define globalisation as:

'the widening, deepening and speeding up of world wide interconnectedness in all aspects of life, from the cultural to the criminal, the financial to the spiritual'.

Globalisation has many causes. These include the spread of new information and communication technologies (ICT) and the influence of global mass media, cheap air travel, the deregulation of financial and other markets and their opening up to competition, and easier movement so that businesses can easily relocate to countries where profits will be greater.

The global criminal economy

As Held et al suggest, there has also been a *globalisation of crime* – an increasing interconnectedness of crime across national borders. The same processes that have brought about the globalisation of legitimate activities have also brought about the spread of *transnational organised crime*. Globalisation creates new opportunities for crime, new means of committing crime and new offences, such as various cyber-crimes.

As a result of globalisation, Manuel Castells (1998) argues, there is now a global criminal economy worth over £1 trillion per annum. This takes a number of forms:

- **Arms trafficking** to illegal regimes, guerrilla groups and terrorists.
- **Trafficking in nuclear materials**, especially from the former communist countries.
- **Smuggling of illegal immigrants**, for example, the Chinese Triads make an estimated $2.5 billion annually.
- **Trafficking in women and children**, often linked to prostitution or slavery. Up to half a million people are trafficked to Western Europe annually.
- **Sex tourism**, where Westerners travel to Third World countries for sex, sometimes involving minors.
- **Trafficking in body parts** for organ transplants in rich countries. An estimated 2,000 organs annually are taken from condemned or executed criminals in China.
- **Cyber-crimes** such as identity theft and child pornography.
- **Green crimes** that damage the environment, such as illegal dumping of toxic waste in Third World countries.
- **International terrorism** Much terrorism is now based on ideological links made via the Internet and other ICT, rather than on local territorial links as in the past.
- **Smuggling of legal goods**, such as alcohol and tobacco, to evade taxes, and of stolen goods, such as cars, to sell in foreign markets.
- **Trafficking in cultural artefacts** and works of art, sometimes having first been stolen to order.
- **Trafficking in endangered species** or their body parts, for example to produce traditional remedies.
- **The drugs trade** worth an estimated $300-400 billion annually at street prices.
- **Money laundering** of the profits from organised crime, estimated at up to $1.5 trillion per year.

The global criminal economy has both a demand side and a supply side. Part of the reason for the scale of transnational organised crime is the demand for its products and services in the rich West. However, the global criminal economy could not function without a supply side that provides the source of the drugs, sex workers and other goods and services demanded in the West.

This supply is linked to the globalisation process. For example, Third World drugs-producing countries such as Colombia, Peru and Afghanistan have large populations of impoverished peasants. For these groups, drug cultivation is an attractive option that requires little investment in technology and commands high prices compared with traditional crops. In Colombia, for instance, an estimated 20% of the population depends on cocaine production for their livelihood, and cocaine outsells all Colombia's other exports combined. To understand drug crime, we cannot confine our attention merely to the countries where the drugs are consumed.

Global risk consciousness

Globalisation creates new insecurities and produces a new mentality of 'risk consciousness' in which risk is seen as global rather than tied to particular places. For example, the increased movement of people, as economic migrants seeking work or as asylum seekers fleeing persecution, has given rise to anxieties among populations in Western countries about the risks of crime and disorder and the need to protect their borders.

Whether such fears are rational or not is a different matter. Much of our knowledge about risks comes from the media, which often give an exaggerated view of the dangers we face. In the case of immigration, the media create moral panics about the supposed 'threat', often fuelled by politicians. Negative coverage of immigrants – portrayed as terrorists or as scroungers 'flooding' the country – has led to hate crimes against minorities in several European countries including the UK.

One result is the intensification of social control at the national level. The UK has toughened its border control regulations, for example fining airlines if they bring in undocumented passengers. Similarly, the UK now has no legal limits on how long a person may be held in immigration detention. Other European states with land borders have introduced fences, CCTV and thermal imaging devices to prevent illegal crossings. Another result of globalised risk is the increased attempts at international cooperation and control in the various 'wars' on terror, drugs and crime – particularly since the terrorist attacks of 11 September 2001.

Globalisation, capitalism and crime

Writing from a socialist perspective, Ian Taylor (1997) argues that globalisation has led to changes in the pattern and extent of crime. By giving free rein to market forces, globalisation has created greater inequality and rising crime.

Globalisation has created crime at both ends of the social spectrum. It has allowed transnational corporations to switch manufacturing to low-wage countries, producing job insecurity, unemployment and poverty. Deregulation means that governments have little control over their own economies, for example to create jobs or raise taxes, while state spending on welfare has declined. Marketisation has encouraged people to see themselves as individual consumers, calculating the personal costs and benefits of each action, undermining social cohesion. As left realists note, the increasingly materialistic culture promoted by the global media portrays success in terms of a lifestyle of consumption.

All these factors create insecurity and widening inequalities that encourage people, especially the poor, to turn to crime. The lack of legitimate job opportunities destroys self-respect and drives the unemployed to look for illegitimate ones, for instance in the lucrative drugs trade. For example, in Los Angeles, de-industrialisation has led to the growth of drugs gangs numbering 10,000 members.

At the same time, globalisation also creates criminal opportunities on a grand scale for elite groups. For example, the deregulation of financial markets has created opportunities for insider trading and the movement of funds around the globe to avoid taxation. Similarly, the creation of transnational bodies such as the European Union has offered opportunities for fraudulent claims for subsidies, estimated at over $7 billion per annum in the EU.

Globalisation has also led to new patterns of employment, which have created new opportunities for crime. It has led to the increased use of subcontracting to recruit 'flexible' workers, often working illegally or employed for less than the minimum wage or working in breach of health and safety or other labour laws.

Taylor's theory is useful in linking global trends in the capitalist economy to changes in the pattern of crime. However, it does not adequately explain how the changes make people behave in criminal ways. For example, not all poor people turn to crime.

Analysis and Evaluation
What advantages might there be for large companies in switching their production to a less developed country?

Crimes of globalisation

Rothe and Friedrichs (2015) examine the role of international financial organisations such as the International Monetary Fund (IMF) and the World Bank in what they call 'crimes of globalisation'.

These organisations are dominated by the major capitalist states. For example, the World Bank has 188 member countries, yet just five – the USA, Japan, Germany, Britain and France – hold over a third of the voting rights.

Rothe and Friedrichs argue that these bodies impose pro-capitalist, neoliberal economic 'structural adjustment programmes' on poor countries as a condition for the loans they provide. These programmes often require governments to cut spending on health and education, and to privatise publicly-owned services (such as water supply), industries and natural resources.

While this allows Western corporations to expand into these countries, it creates the conditions for crime. For example, Rothe et al (2008) show how the programme imposed on Rwanda in the 1980s caused mass unemployment and created the economic basis for the 1994 genocide (see below). Maureen Cain (2010) suggests that in some ways, the IMF and World Bank act as a 'global state' and, while they may not break any laws, their actions can cause widespread social harms both directly, through cutting welfare spending, and indirectly, as in the Rwandan case.

Patterns of criminal organisation

As we saw in Topic 5 with Winlow's study of bouncers in Sunderland, globalisation and de-industrialisation have created new criminal opportunities and patterns at a local level. Another local study of a post-industrial town, by Dick Hobbs and Colin Dunningham, shows similar results.

Hobbs and Dunningham found that the way crime is organised is linked to the economic changes brought by globalisation. Increasingly, it involves individuals with contacts acting as a 'hub' around which a loose-knit network forms, composed of other individuals seeking opportunities, and often linking legitimate and illegitimate activities. Hobbs and Dunningham argue that this contrasts with the large-scale, hierarchical 'Mafia'-style criminal organisations of the past, such as that headed by the Kray brothers in the East End of London.

'Glocal' organisation

These new forms of organisation sometimes have international links, especially with the drugs trade, but crime is still rooted in its local context. For example, individuals still need local contacts and networks to find opportunities and to sell their drugs. Hobbs and Dunningham therefore conclude that crime works as a 'glocal' system. That is, it is still locally based, but with global connections. This means that the form it takes will vary from place to place, according to local conditions, even if it is influenced by global factors such as the availability of drugs from abroad.

Hobbs and Dunningham argue that changes associated with globalisation have led to changes in patterns of crime – for example, the shift from the old rigidly hierarchical gang structure to loose networks of flexible, opportunistic, entrepreneurial criminals. However, it is not clear that such patterns are new, nor that the older structures have disappeared. It may be that the two have always co-existed. Equally, their conclusions may not be generalisable to other criminal activities elsewhere.

McMafia

Another example of the relationship between criminal organisation and globalisation is what Misha Glenny (2008) calls 'McMafia'. This refers to the organisations that emerged in Russia and Eastern Europe following the fall of communism – itself a major factor in the process of globalisation.

Glenny traces the origins of transnational organised crime to the break-up of the Soviet Union after 1989, which coincided with the deregulation of global markets.

Under communism, the Soviet state had regulated the prices of everything. However, following the fall of communism, the Russian government deregulated most sectors of the economy except for natural resources such as oil. These commodities remained at their old Soviet prices – often only a fortieth of the world market price. Thus anyone with access to funds – such as former communist officials and KGB (secret service) generals – could buy up oil, gas, diamonds or metals for next to nothing. Selling them abroad at an astronomical profit, these individuals became Russia's new capitalist class – often popularly referred to as 'oligarchs'.

Meanwhile, the collapse of the communist state heralded a period of increasing disorder. To protect their wealth capitalists therefore turned to the 'mafias' that had begun to spring up. These were often alliances between former KGB men and ex-convicts. Among the most ruthless were the Chechen mafia.

However, these mafias were unlike the old Italian and American mafias, which were based on ethnic and family ties, with a clear-cut hierarchy. The new Russian mafias were purely economic organisations formed to pursue self-interest. For example, the Chechen mafia originated in Chechnya, but soon began to 'franchise' its operations to non-Chechen groups. 'Chechen mafia' became a brand name that they sold to protection rackets in other towns, so long as they always carried out their word – otherwise the brand would be damaged.

With the assistance of these fluid and violent organisations, the billionaires were able to find protection for their wealth and a means of moving it out of the country. Criminal organisations were vital to the entry of the new Russian capitalist class in the world economy. At the same time, the Russian mafias were able to build links with criminal organisations in other parts of the world.

Activity   Webquest

Global crime networks

...go to www.sociology.uk.net

Green crime

Green or environmental crime can be defined as crime against the environment. Much green crime can be linked to globalisation and the increasing interconnectedness of societies. Regardless of the division of the world into separate nation-states, the planet is a single eco-system, and threats to the eco-system are increasingly global rather than merely local in nature. For example, atmospheric pollution from industry in one country can turn into acid rain that falls in another, poisoning its watercourses and destroying its forests. Similarly, an accident in the nuclear industry – such as the one at Chernobyl in Ukraine in 1986 – can spread radioactive material over thousands of miles, showing how a problem caused in one locality can have worldwide effects.

'Global risk society' and the environment

The above examples also show that most of the threats to human well being and the eco-system are now human-made rather than natural. Unlike the natural dangers of the past, such as drought and famine, the major risks we face today are of our own making.

Ulrich Beck (1992) argues that in today's late modern society we can now provide adequate resources for all (at least in the developed countries). However, the massive increase in productivity and the technology that sustains it have created new, 'manufactured risks' – dangers that we have never faced before. Many of these risks involve harm to the environment and its consequences for humanity, such as global warming caused by greenhouse gas emissions from industry. Like climate change, many of these risks are global rather than local in nature, leading Beck to describe late modern society as 'global risk society'.

A striking example of how the global nature of human-made risk can produce crime and disorder comes from Mozambique

| Box 2.2 | The Bhopal disaster |

On the night of 2 December 1984, the US majority-owned Union Carbide pesticide plant at Bhopal, India, started leaking cyanide gas. The plant was no longer in active production and had fallen into disrepair. All six safety-systems failed to operate and 30 tons of gas spread through the city. Half a million people were exposed and some estimate that over 20,000 died. (Union Carbide acknowledges only 3,800 deaths and claims the explosion was caused by sabotage.) 120,000 continue to suffer effects such as cancers, blindness, breathing difficulties, gynaecological disorders and birth defects. As one survivor has said, 'the lucky ones are the ones who died on that night'. Heavy metals have been found in the breast milk of women living nearby. Fifteen years after the accident, local groundwater was found to contain up to 6 million times more mercury than normal. Campaigners say the site has never been cleaned up. No one has ever faced a criminal court.

The approach of traditional criminology to Bhopal focuses on the breaches of safety legislation and failure to follow proper maintenance procedures. The approach of green criminology takes a wider view, noting the advantages for the company in locating their plant in a country with weak health and safety and environmental protection legislation.

in 2010. The story starts thousands of miles away, in Russia, where global warming triggered the hottest heatwave in a century, causing wildfires that destroyed parts of the country's grain belt. The resulting shortage led Russia to introduce export bans and pushed up the world price of grain.

The knock-on effect in Mozambique, which is heavily dependent on food imports, was a 30% rise in the price of bread. This sparked extensive rioting and looting of food stores that left at least a dozen dead. Mozambique's own harvest had been hit by drought, possibly also the result of global warming. At the same time, international speculators were engaging in what the World Development Movement called 'gambling on hunger in financial markets' (Patel, 2010).

Green criminology

But what if the pollution that causes global warming or acid rain is perfectly legal and no crime has been committed – is this a matter for criminologists? We can identify two opposed answers to this question.

Traditional criminology has not been concerned with such behaviour, since its subject matter is defined by the criminal law, and no law has been broken. The starting point for this approach is the national and international laws and regulations concerning the environment. For example, Situ and Emmons (2000) define environmental crime as 'an unauthorised act or omission that violates the law'. Like other traditional approaches in criminology, it investigates the patterns and causes of law breaking.

The advantage of this approach is that it has a clearly defined subject matter. However, it is criticised for accepting official definitions of environmental problems and crimes, which are often shaped by powerful groups such as big business to serve their own interests.

Green criminology takes a more radical approach. It starts from the notion of *harm* rather than criminal law. For example, Rob White (2008) argues that the proper subject of criminology is any action that harms the physical environment and/or the human and non-human animals within it, even if no law has been broken.

In fact, many of the worst environmental harms are not illegal, and so the subject matter of green criminology is much wider than that of traditional criminology. For this reason, green criminology is a form of *transgressive criminology* – it oversteps (transgresses) the boundaries of traditional criminology to include new issues. This approach is also known as 'zemiology' – literally, the study of harms.

Furthermore, different countries have different laws, so that the same harmful action may be a crime in one country but not in another. Thus, legal definitions cannot provide a consistent standard of harm, since they are the product of individual nation-states and their political processes.

By moving away from a legal definition, therefore, green criminology can develop a *global* perspective on environmental harm.

This approach is like the Marxist view of 'crimes of the powerful'. Marxists argue that the capitalist class are able to shape the law and define crime so that their own exploitative activities are not criminalised or, where they are, to ensure that enforcement is weak. Similarly, green criminologists argue that powerful interests, especially nation-states and transnational corporations, are able to define in their own interests what counts as unacceptable environmental harm.

Two views of harm

In general, nation-states and transnational corporations adopt what White (2008) calls an *anthropocentric* or human-centred view of environmental harm. This view assumes that humans have a right to dominate nature for their own ends, and puts economic growth before the environment.

White contrasts this with an *ecocentric* view that sees humans and their environment as interdependent, so that environmental harm hurts humans also. This view sees both humans and the environment as liable to exploitation, particularly by global capitalism. In general, green criminology adopts the ecocentric view as the basis for judging environmental harm.

> **Application**
>
> What rights if any do (a) animals and (b) the physical environment have? Do humans have more rights than animals and the environment? If so, what are they?

Types of green crimes

From a green criminology perspective, Nigel South (2014) classifies green crimes into two types: primary and secondary.

Primary green crimes

Primary green crimes are 'crimes that result directly from the destruction and degradation of the earth's resources'. South identifies four main types of primary crime:

Crimes of air pollution Burning fossil fuels from industry and transport adds 6 billion tons of carbon to the atmosphere every year and carbon emissions are growing at around 2% per annum, contributing to global warming. The potential criminals are governments, business and consumers. According to Walters (2013), twice as many people now die from air pollution-induced breathing problems as 20 years ago.

Crimes of deforestation Between 1960 and 1990, one-fifth of the world's tropical rainforest was destroyed, for example through illegal logging. In the Amazon, forest has been cleared to rear beef cattle for export. In the Andes, the 'war on drugs' has led to pesticide spraying to kill coca and marijuana plants, but this has created a new green crime, destroying food crops, contaminating drinking water and causing illness. The criminals include the state and those who profit from forest destruction, such as logging companies and cattle ranchers.

Crimes of species decline and animal abuse 50 species a day are becoming extinct, and 46% of mammal and 11% of bird species are at risk. 70-95% of earth's species live in the rainforests, which are under severe threat. There is trafficking in animals and animal parts. Meanwhile, old crimes such as dog-fights and badger-baiting are on the increase.

Crimes of water pollution Half a billion people lack access to clean drinking water and 25 million die annually from drinking contaminated water. Marine pollution threatens 58% of the world's ocean reefs and 34% of its fish. The Deepwater Horizon oil spill caused massive harm to marine life and coasts. Criminals include businesses that dump toxic waste and governments that discharge untreated sewage into rivers and seas.

Secondary green crimes

Secondary green crime is crime that grows out of the flouting of rules aimed at preventing or regulating environmental disasters. For example, governments often break their own regulations and cause environmental harms. South suggests two examples of secondary crimes.

State violence against oppositional groups States condemn terrorism, but they have been prepared to resort to similar illegal methods themselves. For example, in 1985 the French secret service blew up the Greenpeace ship *Rainbow Warrior* in Auckland harbour, New Zealand, killing one crew member. The vessel was there in an attempt to prevent a green crime, namely French nuclear weapons testing in the south Pacific. As Day (1991) says, 'in every case where a government has committed itself to nuclear weapons or nuclear power, all those who oppose this policy are treated in some degree as enemies of the state'.

Hazardous waste and organised crime Disposal of toxic waste from the chemical, nuclear and other industries is highly profitable. Because of the high costs of safe and legal disposal, businesses may seek to dispose of such waste illegally. For example, in Italy, *eco-mafias* profit from illegal dumping, much of it at sea. As Reece Walters (2007) notes, 'the ocean floor has been a radioactive rubbish dump for decades'. For example, 28,500 rusting barrels of radioactive waste lie on the seabed off the Channel Islands, reportedly dumped by UK authorities and corporations in the 1950s.

Illegal dumping often has a *globalised* character. For example, Fred Bridgland (2006) describes how, after the tsunami of 2004, hundreds of barrels of radioactive waste, illegally dumped by European companies, washed up on the shores of Somalia.

In other cases, Western businesses ship their waste to be processed in Third World countries where costs are lower and safety standards often non-existent. For example, as Rosoff et al (1998) note, the cost of legitimately disposing of toxic waste in the USA is about $2,500 a ton, but some Third World countries will dispose of it for $3 a ton. Similarly, transnational corporations may offload products (such as pharmaceuticals) onto Third World markets after they have been banned on safety grounds in the West.

Illegal waste disposal illustrates the problems of law enforcement in a globalised world. The very existence of laws to regulate waste disposal in developed countries pushes up the costs to business and creates an incentive to dump illegally in Third World countries. In some cases, it is not even illegal, since less developed countries may lack the necessary legislation outlawing it.

Environmental discrimination is how South (2014) describes the fact that poorer groups are worse affected by pollution. For example, black communities in the USA often find their housing situated next to garbage dumps or polluting industries.

Evaluation of green criminology

Both the strengths and the weaknesses of green criminology arise from its focus on global environmental concerns. It recognises the growing importance of environmental issues and the need to address the harms and risks of environmental damage, both to humans and non-human animals.

However, by focusing on the much broader concept of harms rather than simply on legally defined crimes, it is hard to define the boundaries of its field of study clearly. Defining these boundaries involves making moral or political statements about which actions ought to be regarded as wrong. Critics argue that this is a matter of values and cannot be established objectively.

State crimes

As we saw in Topic 3, Marxists and critical criminologists argue that traditional criminology focused on the 'crimes of the streets' and ignored the 'crimes of the suites' committed by big business. Like corporate crime, state crime is another example of the crimes of the powerful, and Marxists argue that we should investigate state crimes as well as those of capitalism.

Penny Green and Tony Ward (2012) define state crime as 'illegal or deviant activities perpetrated by, or with the complicity of, state agencies.' It includes all forms of crime committed by or on behalf of states and governments in order to further their policies. State crimes do not include acts that merely benefit individuals who work for the state, such as a police officer who accepts a bribe.

State crime is perhaps the most serious form of crime for two reasons.

1 The scale of state crime

The state's enormous power gives it the potential to inflict harm on a huge scale. For example, Green and Ward (2012) cite a figure of 262 million people murdered by governments during the 20th century. As Michalowski and Kramer (2006) note:

'Great power and great crimes are inseparable. Economic and political elites can bring death, disease, and loss to tens of thousands with a single decision.'

2 The state is the source of law

It is the state's role to define what is criminal, uphold the law and prosecute offenders. However, its power means that it can conceal its crimes, evade punishment for them, and even avoid defining its own actions as criminal in the first place. State crime undermines the system of justice and public faith in it.

States of all kinds, including democracies such as Britain and the USA, have been guilty of crimes, but the principle of national sovereignty – that states are the supreme authority within their own borders – makes it difficult for external authorities such as the United Nations to intervene.

Case studies of state crime

Eugene McLaughlin (2012) identifies four categories of state crime:

1 **Political crimes**, for example corruption and censorship.

2 **Crimes by security and police forces**, such as genocide, torture and disappearances of dissidents.

3 **Economic crimes**, for example official violations of health and safety laws.

4 **Social and cultural crimes**, such as institutional racism.

In this section, we consider a number of case studies that illustrate different types of state crime.

Genocide in Rwanda

The UN defines genocide as 'acts committed with intent to destroy, in whole or in part, a national, ethnic, racial or religious group'. In 1994, Rwanda was the scene of 'the 20th century's fastest genocide' (Straus 2015, 2016).

Rwanda became a Belgian colony in 1922 and the Belgians used the minority Tutsi to mediate their rule over the Hutu majority. But Hutus and Tutsis were not separate ethnic groups – they spoke the same language and often intermarried. Rather, they were more like social classes: Tutsis owned livestock and Hutus did not; Hutus could become Tutsis if they could afford to buy cattle. However, the Belgians 'ethnicised' the two groups, issuing them with racial identity cards, and educated the two groups separately.

Rwanda gained independence in 1962 and elections brought the majority Hutus to power. By the 1990s, an escalating economic and political crisis led to civil war, with Hutu hardliners in the government attempting to cling on to power by fuelling race hate propaganda against the Tutsis. The shooting down of the Hutu president's plane in 1994 triggered the genocide. In a hundred days, 800,000 Tutsis (along with moderate Hutus) were slaughtered, legitimated with dehumanising labels describing Tutsis as 'cockroaches' and 'rats'. Initially, the killing was done by marauding groups of Hutu militia. Later, many Hutu civilians were forced to either join in the killing or be killed themselves, and a third of the Hutu population are estimated to have actively participated in the genocide.

State-corporate crime

State crimes are often committed in conjunction with corporate crimes. Kramer and Michalowski (1993) distinguish between 'state-initiated' and 'state-facilitated' corporate crime.

The *Challenger* space shuttle disaster in 1986 is an example of *state-initiated* corporate crime. This occurs when states initiate, direct or approve corporate crimes. In the case of *Challenger*, risky, negligent and cost-cutting decisions by the state agency NASA and the corporation Morton Thiokol led to the explosion that killed seven astronauts 73 seconds after blast-off (Kramer 1992).

The *Deepwater Horizon* oil rig disaster in the Gulf of Mexico in 2010 is an example of *state-facilitated* corporate crime. This occurs when states fail to regulate and control corporate behaviour, making crime easier. The rig, leased by BP, exploded and sank, killing eleven workers and causing the largest accidental oil spill in history, with major health, environmental and economic impacts. The official enquiry found that while the disaster resulted from decisions by the companies involved (BP, Halliburton and Transocean), government regulators had failed to oversee the industry adequately or to notice the companies' cost-cutting decisions.

War crimes

We can distinguish between two kinds of war-related crime:

Illegal wars Under international law, in all cases other than self-defence, war can only be declared by the UN Security Council. On this basis, many see the US-led wars in Afghanistan and Iraq in the name of the 'war on terror' as illegal. For example, Kramer and Michalowksi (2005) argue that to justify their invasion of Iraq in 2003 as self-defence, the USA and UK knowingly made the false claim that the Iraqis possessed weapons of mass destruction.

Crimes committed during war or its aftermath For example, Whyte (2014) describes the USA's 'neo-liberal colonisation' of Iraq, in which the constitution was illegally changed so that the economy could be privatised. Iraqi oil revenues were seized to pay for 'reconstruction'. In 2004 alone, over $48 billion went to US firms. But poor oversight by the occupying powers meant it is unclear where much of this went, and 'cost-plus' contracts (where all the contractor's costs are met automatically by the government, regardless of what they are for) led to enormous waste. This case is also an example of state-corporate crime.

Kramer and Michalowski identify other crimes committed during the Iraq War, including torture of prisoners. A US military inquiry into Abu Ghraib prison found numerous instances of 'sadistic, blatant and wanton criminal abuses' of prisoners. Nine soldiers were convicted, the highest-ranking being a staff sergeant. No commanding officers were prosecuted. Personnel from private companies were also implicated but none were prosecuted.

Kramer (2014) also notes how the terror bombing of civilians has become 'normalised'. This began in the 1930s and continued through the Second World War with the American fire-bombing of 67 Japanese cities and atomic bombing of Hiroshima and Nagasaki. No trials for war crimes took place. Indiscriminate and often deliberate bombing of civilians has continued in recent conflicts in Iraq and Syria.

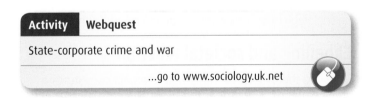

Activity Webquest

State-corporate crime and war

...go to www.sociology.uk.net

Defining state crime

As we have already seen with green crime and corporate crime, defining crime of any kind is not straightforward, and this is particularly true of state crime. In this section, we look at some of the definitions sociologists have put forward.

Domestic law

Chambliss (1989) defines state crime as 'acts defined by law as criminal and committed by state officials in pursuit of their jobs as representatives of the state'.

However, using a state's own domestic law to define state crime is inadequate. It ignores the fact that states have the power to make laws and so they can avoid criminalising their own actions. Furthermore, they can make laws allowing them to carry out harmful acts. For example, the German Nazi state passed a law permitting it to compulsorily sterilise the disabled. This definition also leads to inconsistencies. For example, the same act may be illegal on one side of a border but legal on the other.

Social harms and zemiology

This recognises that much of the harm done by states is not against the law. Michalowski (1985) therefore defines state crime as including not just illegal acts, but also 'legally permissible acts whose consequences are similar to those of illegal acts' in the harm they cause.

Similarly, Hillyard et al (2004) argue that we should take a much wider view of state wrongdoing. We should replace the study of crimes with 'zemiology' – the study of harms, whether or not they are against the law. For example, these harms would include state-facilitated poverty.

This definition prevents states from ruling themselves 'out of court' by making laws that allow them to misbehave. It also creates a single standard that can be applied to different states to identify which ones are most harmful to human or environmental wellbeing.

However, critics argue that a 'harms' definition is potentially very vague:

- What level of harm must occur before an act is defined as a crime? There is a danger that it makes the field of study too wide.
- Who decides what counts as a harm? This just replaces the state's arbitrary definition of crime with the sociologist's equally arbitrary definition of harm.

Labelling and societal reaction

Labelling theory argues that whether an act constitutes a crime depends on whether the social audience for that act defines it as a crime. The audience may witness the act either directly or indirectly, for example through media reports.

This definition recognises that state crime is socially constructed, and so what people regard as a state crime can vary over time and between cultures or groups. This prevents the sociologist imposing their own definition of state crime when this may not be how the participants (perpetrators, victims and audiences) define the situation.

However, this definition is even vaguer than 'social harms'. For example, Kauzlarich's (2007) study of anti-Iraq War protestors found that while they saw the war as harmful and illegitimate, they were unwilling to label it criminal. By contrast, from a 'harms' or an international law perspective, the war can be seen as illegal.

It is also unclear who is supposed to be the relevant audience that decides whether a state crime has been committed, or what to do if different audiences reach different verdicts about an act.

It also ignores the fact that audiences' definitions may be manipulated by ruling-class ideology. For example, the media may persuade the public to see a war as legitimate rather than criminal.

International law

Some sociologists base their definition of state crime on international law – that is, law created through treaties and agreements between states, such as the Geneva and Hague Conventions on war crimes. For example, Rothe and Mullins (2008) define a state crime as any action by or on behalf of a state that violates international law and/or a state's own domestic law.

The advantage of this is that it does not depend on the sociologist's own personal definitions of harm or who the relevant social audience is. Instead it uses globally agreed definitions of state crime. International law also has the advantage of being intentionally designed to deal with state crime, unlike most domestic law.

However, like the laws made by individual states, international law is a social construction involving the use of power. For example, Strand and Tuman (2012) found that Japan has sought to overturn the international ban on whaling by concentrating its foreign aid on impoverished 'microstates', including six small Caribbean island nations, to bribe them to vote against the ban.

Another limitation is that international law focuses largely on war crimes and crimes against humanity, rather than other state crimes such as corruption.

Human rights

Some sociologists use human rights as a way of defining state crime. Human rights include:

- **Natural rights** that people have simply by virtue of existing, such as the right to life, liberty and free speech.
- **Civil rights**, such as the right to vote, to privacy, to a fair trial, or to education.

Herman and Julia Schwendinger (1975) argue that we should define state crime as the violation of people's basic human rights by the state or its agents. States that practise imperialism, racism, sexism or economic exploitation are committing crimes because they are denying people their basic rights.

Risse et al (1999) argue that one advantage of this definition is that virtually all states care about their human rights image, because these rights are now global social norms. This makes them susceptible to 'shaming' and this can provide leverage to make them respect their citizens' rights.

For the Schwendingers, the definition of crime is inevitably political. If we accept a legal definition (that crimes are simply whatever the state says they are), we become subservient to the state's interests. The Schwendingers argue that the sociologist's role should be to defend human rights, if necessary against the state's laws. Like the 'harms' approach, their view is an example of *transgressive criminology*, since it goes beyond the traditional boundaries of criminology, which are defined by the criminal law.

However, Stanley Cohen (1996; 2001) criticises the Schwendingers' view. While gross violations of human rights, such as torture, are clearly crimes, other acts, such as economic exploitation, are not self-evidently criminal, even if we find them morally unacceptable.

There are also disagreements about what counts as a human right. While most would include life and liberty, some would not include freedom from hunger. However, Green and Ward (2012) counter this with the view that liberty is not much use if people are too malnourished to exercise it. Therefore if the state knowingly permits the export of food from a famine area, for example – like the British government did during the Irish famine of the 1840s – then this is a denial of human rights and a state crime.

Explaining state crime

While genocides may be ordered and organised by leaders of states, they cannot happen without the cooperation of ordinary soldiers, police and civilians. For example, in both Rwanda and Nazi Germany, genocide needed the involvement of a large proportion of the population.

Why and how do large numbers of normally law-abiding citizens become involved in atrocities? We now examine some possible explanations.

The authoritarian personality

Adorno et al (1950) identify an 'authoritarian personality' that includes a willingness to obey the orders of superiors without question. They argue that at the time of the Second World War, many Germans had authoritarian personality types due to the punitive, disciplinarian socialisation patterns that were common at the time.

Similarly, it is often thought that people who carry out torture and genocide must be psychopaths. However, research suggests that there is little psychological difference between

them and 'normal' people. For example, Arendt's (2006) study of the Nazi war criminal Adolf Eichmann showed him to be relatively normal and not even particularly anti-Semitic.

Crimes of obedience

Crime is usually defined as deviance from social norms. However, state crimes are crimes of conformity, since they require obedience to a higher authority – the state or its representative. For example, in a corrupt police unit, the officer who accepts bribes is conforming to the unit's norms, while at the same time breaking the law. Conforming to one norm means deviating from the other.

Research suggests that many people are willing to obey authority even when this involves harming others. Sociologists argue that such actions are part of a role into which individuals are socialised. They focus on the social conditions in which atrocities become acceptable or even required.

For example, according to Green and Ward (2102), in order to overcome norms against the use of cruelty, individuals who become torturers often need to be re-socialised, trained and exposed to propaganda about 'the enemy'. States also frequently create 'enclaves of barbarism' where torture is practised, such as military bases, segregated from outside society. This allows the torturer to regard it as a '9 to 5' job from which he can return to normal everyday life.

From a study of the My Lai massacre in Vietnam, where a platoon of American soldiers killed 400 civilians, Kelman and Hamilton (1989) identify three general features that produce crimes of obedience:

- **Authorisation** When acts are ordered or approved by those in authority, normal moral principles are replaced by the duty to obey.
- **Routinisation** Once the crime has been committed, there is strong pressure to turn the act into a routine that individuals can perform in a detached manner.
- **Dehumanisation** When the enemy is portrayed as sub-human, normal principles of morality do not apply.

Modernity

Some commentators argue that the Nazi Holocaust represented a breakdown of modern civilisation and a reversion to pre-modern barbarism. However, Zygmunt Bauman (1989) takes the opposite view: it was certain key features of modern society that made the Holocaust possible:

- **A division of labour** Each person was responsible for just one small task, so no-one felt personally responsible for the atrocity.
- **Bureaucratisation** normalised the killing by making it a repetitive, rule-governed and routine 'job'. It also meant that the victims could be dehumanised as mere 'units'.
- **Instrumental rationality**, where rational, efficient methods are used to achieve a goal, regardless of what

the goal is. In modern business, the goal is profit; in the Holocaust, it was murder.

- **Science and technology**, from the railways transporting victims to the death camps, to the industrially produced gas used to kill them.

The Holocaust was a modern, industrialised mass production 'factory' system, where the product was mass murder. For Bauman, the Holocaust was the result not of a breakdown of civilisation, but of the very existence of modern rational-bureaucratic civilisation.

evaluation

Not all genocides occur through a highly organised division of labour that allows participants to distance themselves from the killing. For example, the Rwandan genocide was carried out directly by large marauding groups.

Ideological factors are also important. Nazi ideology stressed a single, monolithic German racial identity that excluded minorities such as Jews, Gypsies and Slavs, who were defined as inferior or even sub-human. This meant they did not need to be treated according to normal standards of morality.

Thus, while the modern, rational division of labour may have supplied the means for the Holocaust, it was racist ideology that supplied the motivation to carry it out. A decade of anti-Semitic propaganda preceded the mass murder of the Jews and helped to create many willing participants and many more sympathetic bystanders.

The culture of denial

According to Alvarez (2010), recent years have seen the growing impact of the international human rights movement, for example through the work of organisations such as Amnesty International, and this is bringing pressure to bear on states.

As a result, Cohen (2006) argues, states now have to make a greater effort to conceal or justify their human rights crimes, or to re-label them as not crimes. Cohen is interested in the ways states do this. While dictatorships generally just flatly deny any human rights abuses, democratic states have to legitimate their actions in more complex ways. In doing so, their justifications follow a three-stage 'spiral of state denial':

Stage 1 'It didn't happen'; e.g. the state claims there was no massacre. But then human rights organisations, victims and the media show it did happen: 'here are the graves; we have the photos'.

Stage 2 'If it did happen, "it" is something else'; e.g. the state says it was self-defence, not murder.

Stage 3 'Even if it is what you say it is, it's justified', e.g. to fight the 'war on terror'.

Techniques of neutralisation Cohen examines the ways in which states deny or justify their crimes. He draws on the work of Sykes and Matza (1957), who identify five neutralisation techniques that delinquents use to justify their deviant behaviour. Cohen shows how states use the same techniques to justify human rights violations:

Denial of victim 'They exaggerate; they are terrorists; they are used to violence; look what they do to each other.'

Denial of injury 'We are the real victims, not them.'

Denial of responsibility 'I was only obeying orders, doing my duty.' This justification is often used by individual policemen, death camp guards etc.

Condemning the condemners 'They are condemning us only because of their anti-Semitism (Israeli version), their hostility to Islam (Arab version), their racism.'

Appeal to higher loyalty Self-righteous justifications that claim to be serving a higher cause, whether the nation, Zionism, Islam, the defence of the 'free world', national security etc.

These techniques do not deny that the event has occurred. Rather, 'they seek to impose a different construction of the event from what might appear to be the case'. For example, Cohen (2006) argues that in its 'war on terror', the USA had to publicly justify its coercive interrogation practices, which Cohen describes as 'torture lite'.

These included hooding, shaking, sleep deprivation, the use of stress positions and 'water boarding' (simulated drowning). The US claimed that these techniques were not torture because they merely induced stress and were not physically or psychologically damaging. Cohen sees this as a neutralisation technique aimed at normalising torture.

Topic summary

Globalisation brings **transnational organised crime**, e.g. trafficking drugs and people, as well as **de-industrialisation** and insecurity, leading to increased crime, and **'glocal'** criminal organisation with fluid networks and 'franchises' rather than mafia-style fixed hierarchies.

We now live in **global risk society**, where human-made threats include massive environmental damage. **Green criminology** adopts an **ecocentric** view based on **harm** rather than the law. It identifies both primary and secondary green crimes.

The state has the power to commit massive abuses. **Definitions** of state crime may be based on domestic or international **law**, **social harms** or **human rights**. **Explanations** include **authoritarian personalities**, **re-socialisation**, **modernity** and the **culture of denial**.

EXAMINING GLOBALISATION, GREEN CRIME, HUMAN RIGHTS AND STATE CRIME

QuickCheck Questions

Check your answers at www.sociology.uk.net

1 Name four types of globalised crime.
2 What is meant by 'global risk society'?
3 Explain what is meant by 'glocal' criminal organisation.
4 What advantage is there in defining green crime as breaking of the criminal law?
5 What disadvantage is there in defining green crime simply as breaking of the criminal law?
6 Suggest two examples of transgressive criminology.
7 Explain the difference between an anthropocentric and an ecocentric view of environmental harm.

8 Explain the difference between primary and secondary green crimes.
9 Explain the meaning of the term 'state-corporate crime'.
10 Explain one argument for a 'social harms' definition of state crime.
11 Explain one argument for a 'human rights' definition of state crime.
12 Name two features of modernity that Bauman sees as making the Holocaust possible.
13 Explain what is meant by 'neutralisation techniques' and give one example.

Questions to try

Item A   In common with other 'crimes of the powerful', state crime is not easy to define and sociologists have looked beyond conventional definitions of crime. Some sociologists have defined state crime in an international rather than national context, while others have seen it in relation to a higher moral context. Other sociologists have gone beyond the usual definition of crime as law-breaking by seeing state crime in terms of the damage states can cause.

Item B   The process of globalisation has made the world more interconnected and increased the scope for crime. Some forms of globalised crime are based on trafficking one commodity or another, while others involve green crimes against the environment. Green crime has been given a lot of attention because of the extent of damage to the environment caused, often by large transnational corporations.

Some sociologists have analysed the relationship between globalisation and crime using traditional criminological approaches. However, others see the relationship as being the inevitable product of capitalism.

1 Outline two types of green crime.   (4 marks)
2 Applying material from Item A, analyse two ways in which state crime can be defined.   (10 marks)
3 Applying material from Item B and your knowledge, evaluate sociological explanations of the relationship between globalisation and crime.   (30 marks)

The Examiner's Advice

Q2 Spend about 15 minutes on this. Divide your time fairly equally between the two ways. You don't need a separate introduction; just start on your first way. To answer this question, it's essential that you take two points from the Item and show through a chain of reasoning how each is a way in which state crime can be defined. (It is a very good idea to quote from the Item when doing so.)

You could use the idea that we can define state crime in terms of international law, or in moral terms (such as human rights), or in terms of the damage states cause. For example, states can cause massive harms to people and the environment, even when these harms do not break any laws, and they have the power to 'legalise' their actions. You can evaluate by noting that 'harm' is open to different definitions depending on a person's standpoint.

Use concepts and issues such as those above and zemiology, crimes of the powerful, social construction, labelling, legitimacy and human rights. Use studies such as Michalowski, Hillyard, Chambliss, Kauzlarich, Rothe and Mullins, the Schwendingers, and Green and Ward and examples of state crime.

Q3 Spend about 45 minutes on this. Start by defining globalisation and refer to different ways in which it is related to crime, such as transnational organised crime, new forms of crime and new means of committing crime.

You should consider a range of issues and explanations, such as the relationship between globalisation and green crime, including the idea of manufactured risks and global risk consciousness. Consider the Marxist view that globalisation has led to deregulation and created increased opportunities for crime. Examine the development of 'glocal' forms of criminal organisation, and the impact of the fall of communism.

Evaluate explanations, e.g. by showing the limitations of traditional criminology's definition of crime as law-breaking.

Use concepts and issues such as those above plus cyber-crime, trafficking, de-industrialisation, poverty, green crimes, human rights, and modernity. Use studies such as Castells, Taylor, Hobbs and Dunningham, Glenny, Beck, White and Walters. Use examples of globalised crime.

TOPIC 9

Main infirmary
475 places

Men's prison
1 194 places

EAST RIVER

Other cells
1 647 places

Men's prison
2 978 places

Women's prison
1 139 places

BRONX

Harlem

MANHATTAN   QUEENS

NEW Y...

BROOKLYN

West Facility
140 one-
person cells

Men's prison
1 130 places

Addiction treatment centre

Short sentence prison
2 351 places

Rikers Island Bridge

Key statistics

Area: **1.6 km²**
Capacity: **17,000 inmates**
It houses 10 of New York City's
15 detention centres
Staff: **7,000 guards and 1,500 civilians**

Youth prison
16-18 years

La Gua
Airport

Rikers Island Prison costs $860m a year to run.
75% of its inmates will return within a year of release.

GETTING STARTED

Working in pairs, answer the following:

1 Give at least five words that you would use to describe victims of crime.

2 From those words, which social groups are likely to fit the description you have given?

3 Suggest three situations where a victim of crime might be seen to have brought their victimisation upon themselves.

4. From what you have studied in previous topics, suggest situations where people who have been harmed may nevertheless not be officially defined as victims of crime.

Learning objectives

After studying this Topic, you should:

- Understand and be able to evaluate a range of crime prevention and control strategies.

- Understand and be able to evaluate different perspectives on punishment and surveillance.

- Know the main trends in sentencing and understand their significance.

- Know the main patterns of victimisation and be able to evaluate sociological perspectives on victimisation.

Most of this chapter has focused on criminals and criminalisation. By contrast, in this Topic, we turn our attention first to what can be done to prevent crime, ranging from changing the immediate situation where crime occurs, to community programmes designed to tackle the root causes of offending, as well as various forms of surveillance.

One view popular with politicians is that tougher punishments are the best way to prevent crime. In this Topic, we look at the nature and functions of punishment from a number of perspectives, and we consider reasons for the rapid growth in the prison population.

In previous Topics, we have seen how certain groups are likely to be victims of crime. We conclude this Topic with a closer look at victims and 'victimology', including which groups are at greatest risk of victimisation.

Crime prevention and control

What makes people conform? And when they are tempted not to do so, what can be done to prevent them deviating? These questions raise the issue of social control – the capacity of societies to regulate their members' behaviour – and crime prevention. This section examines different approaches to these questions.

Situational crime prevention

Ron Clarke (1992) describes situational crime prevention as 'a pre-emptive approach that relies, not on improving society or its institutions, but simply on reducing opportunities for crime'. He identifies three features of measures aimed at situational crime prevention:

- They are directed at specific crimes.
- They involve managing or altering the immediate environment of the crime.
- They aim at increasing the effort and risks of committing crime and reducing the rewards.

For example, 'target hardening' measures such as locking doors and windows increase the effort a burglar needs to make, while increased surveillance in shops via CCTV or security guards increase the likelihood of shoplifters being caught. Similarly, replacing coin-operated gas meters with pre-payment cards reduces the burglar's rewards.

Underlying situational crime prevention approaches is an 'opportunity' or rational choice theory of crime. This is the view that criminals act rationally, weighing up the costs and benefits of a crime opportunity before deciding whether to commit it. (For more on rational choice theory, see Topic 4.)

This contrasts with theories of crime that stress 'root causes' such as the criminal's early socialisation or capitalist exploitation. In the view of these theories, to deal with crime, we would have to transform the socialisation of large numbers of children or carry out a revolution. Clarke argues that most theories offer no realistic solutions to crime. The most obvious thing to do, he argues, is to focus on the immediate crime situation, since this is where scope for prevention is greatest. Most crime is opportunistic, so we need to reduce the opportunities.

Marcus Felson (2002) gives an example of a situational crime prevention strategy. The Port Authority Bus Terminal in New York City was poorly designed and provided opportunities for deviant conduct. For example, the toilets were a setting for luggage thefts, rough sleeping, drug dealing and homosexual liaisons. Re-shaping the physical environment to 'design crime out' greatly reduced such activity. For example, large sinks, in which homeless people were bathing, were replaced by small hand basins.

Application

What prevention measures (i) do you take personally to avoid being a victim of crime in different situations; (ii) are taken in the family home; (iii) have you seen elsewhere (e.g. school/college, shops, transport) in the last few days?

Displacement

One criticism of situational crime prevention measures is that they do not reduce crime; they simply displace it. After all, if criminals are acting rationally, presumably they will respond to target hardening simply by moving to where targets are softer. For example, Chaiken et al (1974) found that a crackdown on subway robberies in New York merely displaced them to the streets above.

Displacement can take several forms:

- **Spatial** – moving elsewhere to commit the crime.
- **Temporal** – committing it at a different time.
- **Target** – choosing a different victim.
- **Tactical** – using a different method.
- **Functional** – committing a different type of crime.

Perhaps the most striking example of the success of situational measures is not about crime, but about suicide. In the early 1960s, half of all suicides in Britain were the result of gassing. At that time, Britain's gas supply came from highly toxic coal gas. From the 1960s, coal gas was gradually replaced by less toxic natural gas, and by 1997 suicides from gassing had fallen to near zero. What is striking, however, is that the *overall* suicide rate declined, not just deaths from gassing. Those who might otherwise have killed themselves by gassing seem not to have switched to another method. In other words, there was no displacement.

Evaluation

- Situational crime prevention works to some extent in reducing certain kinds of crime. However, with most measures there is likely to be some displacement.
- It tends to focus on opportunistic petty street crime. It ignores white collar, corporate and state crime, which are more costly and harmful.
- It assumes criminals make rational calculations. This seems unlikely in many crimes of violence, and crimes committed under the influence of drugs or alcohol.
- It ignores the root causes of crime, such as poverty or poor socialisation. This makes it difficult to develop long-term strategies for crime reduction.

Activity | **Webquest**

Situational crime prevention

...go to www.sociology.uk.net

Environmental crime prevention

This approach is based on James Q. Wilson and George Kelling's (1982) article, *Broken Windows*, which has been described as 'perhaps the most influential single article on crime prevention ever written' (Downes 1999).

Wilson and Kelling use the phrase 'broken windows' to stand for all the various signs of disorder and lack of concern for others that are found in some neighbourhoods. This includes undue noise, graffiti, begging, dog fouling, littering, vandalism and so on. They argue that leaving broken windows unrepaired, tolerating aggressive begging etc, sends out a signal that no one cares.

In such neighbourhoods, there is an absence of both formal social control (the police) and informal control (the community). The police are only concerned with serious crime and turn a blind eye to petty nuisance behaviour, while respectable members of the community feel intimidated and powerless. Without remedial action, the situation deteriorates, tipping the neighbourhood into a spiral of decline. Respectable people move out (if they can) and the area becomes a magnet for deviants.

Zero tolerance policing

Wilson and Kelling's key idea is that disorder and the absence of controls leads to crime. Their solution is to crack down on any disorder, using a twofold strategy. First, an *environmental improvement strategy*: any broken window must be repaired immediately, abandoned cars towed without delay etc, otherwise more will follow and the neighbourhood will be on the slide.

Secondly, the police must adopt a *zero tolerance policing strategy*. Instead of merely reacting to crime, they must proactively tackle even the slightest sign of disorder, even if it is not criminal. This will halt neighbourhood decline and prevent serious crime taking root.

The evidence

Great successes have been claimed for zero tolerance policing, especially in New York (where Kelling was an adviser to the police). For example, a 'Clean Car Program' was instituted on the subway, in which cars were taken out of service immediately if they had any graffiti on them, only returning once clean. As a result, graffiti was largely removed from the subway. Other successful programs to tackle fare dodging, drug dealing and begging followed.

Later, the same approach was extended to the city's police precincts. For example, a crackdown on 'squeegee merchants' discovered that many had outstanding warrants for violent and property crimes. Between 1993 and 1996, there was a significant fall in crime in the city, including a 50% drop in the homicide rate – from 1,927 to 986.

However, it is not clear how far zero tolerance was the cause of the improvements.

- The NYPD benefited from 7,000 extra officers.
- There was a general decline in the crime rate in major US cities at the time – including ones where police did *not* adopt a zero tolerance policy.
- The early 1990s had seen a major recession and high unemployment, but from 1994 many new jobs were being created.
- There was a decline in the availability of crack cocaine.
- While deaths from homicides fell sharply, attempted homicides remained high. It has been suggested that the fall in the murder rate owed more to improved medical emergency services than policing.

Nonetheless, zero tolerance has been very influential globally, including the UK, where it has influenced anti-social behaviour policies. (For more on criticisms of zero tolerance, see Topic 4.)

Analysis and Evaluation

What problems might arise if a zero tolerance policy is introduced into a neighbourhood?

Social and community crime prevention

While Wilson and Kelling show some recognition of the role of the community and informal controls in preventing crime, the main emphasis of policies based on their ideas has been in terms of policing.

By contrast, social and community prevention strategies place the emphasis firmly on the potential offender and their social context. The aim of these strategies is to remove the conditions that predispose individuals to crime in the first place. These are longer-term strategies, since they attempt to tackle the root causes of offending, rather than simply removing opportunities for crime.

Because the causes of crime are often rooted in social conditions such as poverty, unemployment and poor housing, more general social reform programmes addressing these issues may have a crime prevention role, even if this is not their main focus. For example, policies to promote full employment are likely to reduce crime as a 'side effect'.

The Perry pre-school project

One of the best-known community programmes aimed at reducing criminality is the experimental Perry pre-school project for disadvantaged black children in Ypsilanti, Michigan. An experimental group of 3-4 year olds was offered a two-year intellectual enrichment programme, during which time the children also received weekly home visits.

A longitudinal study followed the children's subsequent progress. It showed striking differences with a control group who had not undergone the programme. By age 40, they had significantly fewer lifetime arrests for violent crime, property crime and drugs, while more had graduated from high school and were in employment. It was calculated that for every dollar spent on the programme, $17 were saved on welfare, prison and other costs.

What is missing?

The approaches that we have discussed above take for granted the nature and definition of crime. They generally focus on fairly low-level crimes and/or interpersonal crimes of violence. This disregards the crimes of the powerful and environmental crimes.

This definition of the 'crime problem' reflects the priorities of politicians and agencies tasked with crime prevention. For example, Whyte conducted a survey of 26 crime and disorder area partnerships in the North West of England to discover what crimes their strategies were targeting. The results are in Table 2C.

Table 2C	Targets of crime reduction strategies in the North West of England	
Vehicle crime		26
Burglary		24
Drug related crime		15
Violent crime		15
Anti social behaviour		12
Youth offending/causing a nuisance		12
Road safety/speeding		11
Domestic violence		8
Robbery		8
Fear of crime		7

Source: Walklate (2005)

Yet, at the same time, the Environment Agency instituted 98 prosecutions in 2001-02 in the North West, including 62 for waste offences, 32 for water quality offences, and two for radioactive substance offences. The North West also has one of the most heavily concentrated sites of chemical production in Europe, where just two plants between them release into the air about 40% of all the factory-produced cancer-causing chemicals in the UK every year.

Whyte points out that there is no logical reason why such activities should not be included in the crime and disorder partnership agendas – yet despite their potential and actual effect on the health of local communities, they are not.

Surveillance

Another important way of attempting to control people's behaviour and prevent crime is by means of surveillance. Surveillance can be defined as:

the monitoring of public behaviour for the purposes of population or crime control. It therefore involves observing people's behaviour to gather data about it, and typically, using the data to regulate, manage or 'correct' their behaviour.

Surveillance has a long history and takes many forms. During the 14th century plague, communities had to nominate an individual to monitor and record the spread of the plague, the information being used to stop people moving to uninfected areas. However, in today's late modern society, surveillance often involves the use of sophisticated technology, including CCTV cameras, biometric scanning, automated number plate recognition (ANPR), electronic tagging, and databases that collate information from different sources to produce profiles of groups and individuals. In turn, this data may be used for crime and disorder control, and to control the behaviour of workers and consumers.

Foucault: birth of the prison

Michel Foucault's (1979) *Discipline and Punish: The Birth of the Prison* opens with a striking contrast between two different forms of punishment, which he sees as examples of *sovereign power* and *disciplinary power* (see Box 2.3).

Sovereign power was typical of the period before the 19th century, when the monarch had absolute power over people and their bodies. Control was asserted by inflicting disfiguring, visible punishment on the body (such as branding or limb amputations). Punishment was a brutal, emotional spectacle, such as public execution.

Disciplinary power becomes dominant from the 19th century. In this form of control, a new system of discipline seeks to govern not just the body, but the mind or 'soul'. It does so through *surveillance*.

One view is that brutal bodily punishment disappeared from Western societies because they became more civilised or humane. Foucault rejects this liberal view. Instead, he claims

Box 2.3	Sovereign power and disciplinary power

Foucault illustrates the difference between the two types of power as follows:

Sovereign power: from a description of an execution in 1757

On a scaffold that will be erected, the flesh will be torn from his breasts, arms, thighs and calves with red hot pincers, his right hand burnt with sulphur, and, on those places where the flesh will be torn away, poured molten lead, boiling oil, burning resin, wax and sulphur melted together and then his body drawn and quartered by four horses and his limbs and body consumed by fire, reduced to ashes and thrown to the winds.

Disciplinary power: from a prison timetable in the 1830s

Article 17 The prisoners' day will begin at six in the morning and they will work for nine hours a day.

Article 18 Rising. At the first drum-roll, the prisoners must rise and dress in silence. At the second drum-roll, they must be dressed and make their beds. At the third, they must line up and proceed to the chapel for morning prayers.

Article 19 The prayers are conducted by the chaplain and followed by a moral or religious reading. This exercise must not last more than half an hour.

that disciplinary power replaced sovereign power simply because surveillance is a more efficient 'technology of power' – that is, a more effective way of controlling people.

The Panopticon Foucault illustrates disciplinary power with the *Panopticon*. This was a design for a prison in which each prisoner in his own cell is visible to the guards from a central watchtower, but the guards are not visible to the prisoners. Thus the prisoners don't know if they are being watched, but they do know that they *might* be being watched. As a result, they have to behave at all times as if they were being watched, and so the surveillance turns into *self*-surveillance and discipline becomes *self*-discipline. Instead of being a public spectacle that marks the outside of the body, control takes place 'inside' the prisoner.

Unlike sovereign power, which seeks simply to crush or violently repress offenders, disciplinary power involves intensively monitoring the individual with a view to *rehabilitating* them. For this reason, Foucault sees experts as having an important role to play in applying their specialised knowledge to correcting the individual's deviant behaviour. In fact, Foucault argues that the social sciences, and professions such as psychologists, were born at the same time as the modern prison.

The 'dispersal of discipline'

Foucault argues that the prison is just one of a range of institutions that, from the 19th century, increasingly began to subject individuals to disciplinary power to induce conformity through self-surveillance. These include mental asylums, barracks, factories, workhouses and schools.

Furthermore, non-prison-based social control practices, such as community service orders, form part of a 'carceral archipelago'. That is, a series of 'prison islands' spreading into other institutions and wider society, where professionals such as teachers, social workers and psychiatrists exercise surveillance over the population.

In Foucault's view, disciplinary power has now dispersed throughout society, penetrating every social institution to reach every individual. Thus the form of surveillance in the Panopticon is now a model of how power operates in society as a whole.

Criticisms of Foucault

Foucault's work has stimulated considerable research into surveillance and disciplinary power – especially into the idea of an 'electronic Panopticon' that uses modern technologies to monitor us.

However, Foucault has been criticised on several grounds. For example, the shift from sovereign power and corporal punishment to disciplinary power and imprisonment is less clear than he suggests. He is also accused of wrongly assuming that the expressive (emotional) aspects of punishment disappear in modern society.

Foucault also exaggerates the extent of control. For example, Goffman (1982) shows how some inmates of prisons and mental hospitals are able to resist controls. Foucault also overestimates the power of surveillance to change behaviour. As we have seen, in the Panopticon, people become self-disciplining because they cannot be sure they are not being monitored.

CCTV cameras are a form of panopticism – we are aware of their presence but unsure whether they are recording us. However, they are not necessarily effective in preventing crime. Norris's (2012) review of dozens of studies worldwide found that while CCTV reduced crimes in car parks, it had little or no effect on other crime, and may even cause displacement.

The case for CCTV assumes that criminals know they are being watched and care enough to be deterred by this. However, Gill and Loveday (2003) found that few robbers, burglars, shoplifters or fraudsters were put off by CCTV. Its real function may be ideological, falsely reassuring the public about their security, even though it makes little difference to their risk of victimisation.

Feminists such as Koskela (2012) also criticise CCTV as an extension of the 'male gaze'. While it renders women more visible to the voyeurism of the male camera operator, it does not make them more secure.

Surveillance theories since Foucault

Foucault's ideas have stimulated others to develop a theory of surveillance in today's late modern society. Some of these both build on and criticise his theory of panopticism.

Synoptic surveillance

Thomas Mathiesen (1997) argues that Foucault's account of surveillance only tells half the story when applied to today's society. In Mathiesen's view, while the Panopticon allows the few to monitor the many, today the media also enable the many to see the few. In late modernity, he argues, there is an increase in the top-down, centralised surveillance that Foucault discusses, but also in surveillance from below. Mathiesen calls this the 'Synopticon' – where everybody watches everybody.

For example, Thompson (2000) argues that powerful groups such as politicians fear the media's surveillance of them may uncover damaging information about them, and this acts as a form of social control over their activities.

Another example of synoptic surveillance is where the public monitor each other, as with video cameras mounted on cycle helmets or dashboards to collect evidence in the event of accidents. This may warn other road users that their behaviour is being monitored and result in them exercising self-discipline.

Similarly, widespread camera ownership means that ordinary citizens may now be able to 'control the controllers', for

example by filming police wrongdoing. Mann et al (2003) call this 'sousveillance' (from the French *sous* meaning 'under'). Foucault's panopticism cannot account for this surveillance from below.

However, as McCahill (2012) argues, occasional bottom-up scrutiny may be unable to reverse established 'hierarchies of surveillance'. For example, under anti-terrorism laws, police have powers to confiscate the cameras and mobile phones of 'citizen journalists'.

Surveillant assemblages

Foucault's panoptic approach is based on the idea that surveillance involves the manipulation of physical bodies in confined spaces such as prison. However, as Haggerty and Ericson (2000) argue, surveillance technologies now involve the manipulation of virtual objects (digital data) in cyberspace rather than physical bodies in physical space.

Until recently, surveillance technologies tended to be stand-alone and unable to 'talk' to one another. However, there is now an important trend towards combining different technologies. For example, CCTV footage can be analysed using facial recognition software. Haggerty and Ericson call these combinations 'surveillant assemblages'. They suggest that we are moving towards a world in which data from different technologies can be combined to create a sort of 'data double' of the individual.

Actuarial justice and risk management

Feeley and Simon (1994) argue that a new 'technology of power' is emerging throughout the justice system. It differs from Foucault's disciplinary power in three main ways:

- It focuses on groups rather than individuals.
- It is not interested in rehabilitating offenders, but simply in preventing them from offending.
- It uses calculations of risk, or 'actuarial analysis'. This concept derives from the insurance industry, which calculates the statistical risk of particular events happening to particular groups; for example, young drivers' risk of having an accident.

Feeley and Simon apply this idea to surveillance and crime control. For example, airport security screening checks are based on known offender 'risk factors'. Using information gathered about passengers (e.g. their age, sex, religion, ethnicity etc), they can be profiled and given a risk score (e.g. young males may be scored higher than old females). Anyone scoring above a given level is then stopped, questioned, searched etc.

Unlike disciplinary power, the aim of this surveillance is not to correct, treat or rehabilitate. Instead, it just seeks to predict and prevent future offending. According to Feeley and Simon, it does so by applying surveillance techniques 'to identify, classify and manage groups sorted by levels of dangerousness'. As Jock Young (1999) notes, actuarial justice is basically a damage limitation strategy to reduce crime by using statistical information to pick out likely offenders.

Social sorting and categorical suspicion According to David Lyon (2012), the purpose of this 'social sorting' is to be able to categorise people so they can be treated differently according to the level of risk they pose. One effect of this is to place entire social groups under what Gary T. Marx (1988) calls 'categorical suspicion' – where people are placed under suspicion of wrongdoing simply because they belong to a particular category or group. For example, in 2010 West Midlands police sought to introduce a counter-terrorism scheme to surround two mainly Muslim suburbs of Birmingham with about 150 ANPR cameras, some of them covert, thereby placing whole communities under suspicion (Lewis, 2010).

One problem with actuarial justice is the danger of a self-fulfilling prophecy. For example, profiles of typical offenders are often compiled using official crime statistics. If these show for example that young black inner-city males are the group most likely to carry a weapon, then police using this data will be more likely to stop them than members of other groups. Consequently, even if in reality all social groups have exactly the same likelihood of carrying a weapon, young black male offenders will still be more likely than others to be caught, convicted and end up in the crime statistics, thereby seeming to confirm the validity of the profiling.

Labelling and surveillance

According to Ditton et al (1999), in one major city centre CCTV system, the cameras were capable of zooming in on vehicle tax discs from hundreds of metres away to see whether the tax had expired. However, the system's managers did not think this was a suitable use of the technology and so the offences of the motorists were left unchecked.

By contrast, research shows that CCTV operators make discriminatory judgments about who among the thousands of potential 'suspects' appearing on their screens they should focus on. For example, Norris and Armstrong (1999) found that there is 'a massively disproportionate targeting' of young black males for no other reason than their membership of that particular social group.

Such judgments are based on the 'typifications' or stereotypical beliefs held by those operating surveillance systems about who are likely offenders. One result of these beliefs is a self-fulfilling prophecy in which the criminalisation of some groups (such as young black males) is increased as they are targeted and their offences are revealed, while the criminalisation of others (such as motorists) is lessened because their offences are ignored.

Activity | Media
Surveillance
...go to www.sociology.uk.net

Punishment

One measure that many believe to be effective in crime prevention is of course punishment. Given that punishment involves deliberately inflicting harm, two main justifications have been offered for it: reduction and retribution. These justifications link to different penal policies.

Reduction

One justification for punishing offenders is that it prevents future crime. This can be done through:

- **Deterrence** Punishing the individual discourages them from future offending. 'Making an example' of them may also serve as a deterrent to the public at large. Deterrence policies include Mrs Thatcher's Conservative government's 'short, sharp shock' regime in young offenders' institutions in the 1980s.
- **Rehabilitation** is the idea that punishment can be used to reform or change offenders so they no longer offend. Rehabilitation policies include providing education and

training for prisoners so that they are able to 'earn an honest living' on release, and anger management courses for violent offenders.
- **Incapacitation** is the use of punishment to remove the offender's capacity to offend again. Policies in different societies have included imprisonment, execution, the cutting off of hands, and chemical castration. Incapacitation has proved increasingly popular with politicians, with the American 'three strikes and you're out' policy (where committing even a minor third offence can lead to lengthy prison time) and the view that 'prison works' because it removes offenders from society.

This justification is an *instrumental* one – punishment is a means to an end, namely crime reduction.

Retribution

Retribution means 'paying back'. It is a justification for punishing crimes that have already been committed, rather than preventing future crimes. It is based on the idea that offenders deserve to be punished, and that society is entitled to take its revenge on the offender for having breached its moral code. This is an *expressive* rather than instrumental view of punishment – it expresses society's outrage.

Sociological perspectives on punishment

Sociologists are interested in the relationship between punishment and society. They ask questions about its function, why its form varies over time, and how it relates to the society in which it is found.

Durkheim: a functionalist perspective

Functionalists such as Durkheim (1893) argue that the function of punishment is to uphold social solidarity and reinforce shared values. Punishment is primarily expressive – it expresses society's emotions of moral outrage at the offence. Through rituals of order, such as public trial and punishment, society's shared values are reaffirmed and its members come to feel a sense of moral unity.

Two types of justice

While punishment functions to uphold social solidarity, it does so differently in different types of society. Durkheim identifies two types of justice, corresponding to two types of society.

Retributive justice In traditional society, there is little specialisation, and solidarity between individuals is based on their similarity to one another. This produces a strong collective conscience, which, when offended, responds with vengeful passion to repress the wrongdoer. Punishment is severe and cruel, and its motivation is purely expressive.

Restitutive justice In modern society, there is extensive specialisation, and solidarity is based on the resulting interdependence between individuals. Crime damages this interdependence, so it is necessary to repair the damage, for example through compensation. Durkheim calls this restitutive justice, because it aims to make restitution – to restore things to how they were before the offence. Its motivation is instrumental, to restore society's equilibrium. Nevertheless, even in modern society, punishment still has an expressive element, because it still expresses collective emotions.

In reality, however, traditional societies often have restitutive rather than retributive justice as Durkheim thought. For example, blood feuds (where a member of one clan is killed by a member of another) are often settled by payment of compensation rather than execution.

Marxism: capitalism and punishment

Marxists see society as divided into two classes, in which the ruling class exploits the labour of the subordinate class. They are interested in how punishment is related to the nature of class society and how it serves ruling-class interests.

For Marxists, the *function of punishment* is to maintain the existing social order. As part of the 'repressive state apparatus', it is a means of defending ruling-class property against the lower classes. For example, E.P. Thompson (1977) describes how in the 18th century punishments such as hanging and transportation to the colonies for theft and poaching were part of a 'rule of terror' by the landed aristocracy over the poor.

The *form of punishment* reflects the economic base of society. As Georg Rusche and Otto Kirchheimer (1939) argue, each type of economy has its own corresponding penal system. For example, money fines are impossible without a money economy. They argue that under capitalism, imprisonment becomes the dominant form of punishment.

Similarly, Melossi and Pavarini (1981) see imprisonment as reflecting capitalist relations of production. For example:

- Capitalism puts a price on the worker's time; so too prisoners 'do time' to 'pay' for their crime (or 'repay a debt to society').
- The prison and the capitalist factory both have a similar strict disciplinary style, involving subordination and loss of liberty.

The changing role of prisons

Pre-industrial Europe had a wide range of punishments, including warnings, banishment, transportation, corporal punishment and execution. Until the 18th century, prison was used mainly for holding offenders *prior* to their punishment (such as flogging). It was only following the Enlightenment that imprisonment began to be seen as a form of punishment in itself, where offenders would be 'reformed' through hard labour, religious instruction and surveillance.

Imprisonment today

In liberal democracies that do not have the death penalty, imprisonment is regarded as the most severe form of punishment. However, it has not proved an effective method of rehabilitation – about two-thirds of prisoners commit further crimes on release. Many critics regard prisons as simply an expensive way of making bad people worse.

Nevertheless, since the 1980s there has been a move towards 'populist punitiveness', where politicians have sought electoral popularity by calling for tougher sentences. For example, New Labour governments after 1997 took the view that prison should be used not just for serious offenders, but also as a deterrent for persistent petty offenders.

As a result, the prison population has swollen to record size: between 1993 and 2016, the number of prisoners in England and Wales almost doubled to reach a total of 85,000. One consequence has been overcrowding, added to existing problems of poor sanitation, barely edible food, clothing shortages, lack of educational and work opportunities, and inadequate family visits (Carrabine et al 2014).

This country imprisons a higher proportion of people than almost any other in Western Europe. For example, in England and Wales, 147 out of every 100,000 people are in prison. Corresponding figures for some other countries are France 100, Germany 76, Ireland 80, Sweden 55 and Iceland 45. However, the world leaders are Russia (447) and the USA (698).

The prison population is largely male (only about 5% are female), young and poorly educated. Black and ethnic minorities are over-represented.

The era of mass incarceration?

According to David Garland (2001), the USA, and to a lesser extent the UK, is moving into an era of mass incarceration. For most of the last century, the American prison population was stable, at around 100-120 per 100,000. In 1972, there were about 200,000 inmates in state and federal prisons.

However, from the 1970s, the numbers began to rise rapidly, and there are now 1.5 million state and federal prisoners in prisons like Rikers Island, plus 700,000 in local jails. A further 5 million are under the supervision of the criminal justice system (on parole, probation etc) – in total, over 3% of the adult population. This is over three times the European rate of imprisonment, despite the fact that rates of victimisation in the USA are about the same as those in Europe.

Once figures reach these proportions, Garland argues,

'It ceases to be the incarceration of individual offenders and becomes the systematic imprisonment of whole groups of the population. In the case of the USA, the group concerned is, of course, young black males'.

For example, while black Americans are only 13% of the US population, they make up 37% of the prison population. Compared with white males, black males are six times more likely to be in prison, and Hispanic and Native American males are twice as likely.

This may have an ideological function. As David Downes (2001) argues, the US prison system soaks up about 30-40% of the unemployed, thereby making capitalism look more successful.

Garland argues that the reason for mass incarceration is the growing politicisation of crime control. For most of the last century there was a consensus, which Garland calls 'penal welfarism' – the idea that punishment should reintegrate offenders into society.

However, since the 1970s, there has been a move towards a new consensus based on more punitive and exclusionary 'tough on crime' policies, and this has led to rising numbers in prison. As we saw in Topic 5, this has led for example to a rise in the number of females convicted of violent crime, despite a lack of evidence that they are actually committing more offences.

Another reason is the use of prison to wage America's 'war on drugs'. As Simon (2001) argues, because drug use is so widespread, this has produced 'an almost limitless supply of arrestable and imprisonable offenders'.

Transcarceration

As well as mass incarceration, there is a trend towards transcarceration – the idea that individuals become locked into a cycle of control, shifting between different carceral agencies during their lives.

For example, someone might be brought up in care, then sent to a young offenders' institution, then adult prison, with bouts in mental hospital in between.

Some sociologists see transcarceration as a product of the blurring of boundaries between criminal justice and welfare agencies. For example, health, housing and social services are increasingly being given a crime control role, and they often engage in multi-agency working with the police, sharing data on the same individuals.

Alternatives to prison

In the past, a major goal in dealing with young offenders was 'diversion' – diverting them away from contact with the criminal justice system to avoid the risk of a self-fulfilling prophecy turning them into serious criminals. The focus was on welfare and treatment, using non-custodial, community-based controls such as probation.

In recent years there has been a growth in the range of community-based controls, such as curfews, community service orders, treatment orders and electronic tagging. However, at the same time, the numbers in custody have been rising steadily, especially among the young.

This has led Stanley Cohen to argue that the growth of community controls has simply cast the *net of control* over more people. Following Foucault's ideas, Cohen argues that the increased range of sanctions available simply enables control to penetrate ever deeper into society.

Far from diverting young people from the criminal justice system, community controls may divert them into it. For example, some argue that the police have used ASBOs as a way of fast-tracking young offenders into custodial sentences.

The victims of crime

The United Nations defines victims as those who have suffered harm (including mental, physical or emotional suffering, economic loss and impairment of their basic rights) through acts or omissions that violate the laws of the state.

Nils Christie (1986) takes a different approach, highlighting the notion that 'victim' is socially constructed. The stereotype of the 'ideal victim' favoured by the media, public and criminal justice system is a weak, innocent and blameless individual – such as a small child or old woman – who is the target of a stranger's attack.

It is important to study victims not least because they play an essential role in the criminal justice process. For example, they provide much of the evidence used in the detection of offenders and they act as witnesses at trials. The study of victims is sometimes known as 'victimology'. We can identify two broad perspectives: positivist victimology, and critical victimology.

Positivist victimology

Miers (1989) defines positivist victimology as having three features:

- It aims to identify the factors that produce *patterns in victimisation* – especially those that make some individuals or groups more likely to be victims.
- It focuses on *interpersonal crimes of violence*.
- It aims to identify victims who have *contributed to their own victimisation*.

The earliest positivist studies focused on the idea of *victim proneness*. They sought to identify the social and psychological characteristics of victims that make them different from, and more vulnerable than, non-victims. For example, Hans Von Hentig (1948) identified 13 characteristics of victims, such as that they are likely to be females, elderly or 'mentally subnormal'. The implication is that the victims in some sense 'invite' victimisation by being the kind of person that they are. This can also include lifestyle factors such as victims who ostentatiously display their wealth.

An example of positivist victimology is Marvin Wolfgang's (1958) study of 588 homicides in Philadelphia. Wolfgang found that 26% involved *victim precipitation* – the victim triggered the events leading to the homicide, for instance by being the first to use violence. For example, this was often the case where the victim was male and the perpetrator female.

Evaluation

- As Fiona Brookman (2005) notes, Wolfgang shows the importance of the victim-offender relationship and the fact that in many homicides, it is a matter of chance which party becomes the victim.
- This approach identifies certain patterns of interpersonal victimisation, but ignores wider structural factors influencing victimisation, such as poverty and patriarchy.
- It can easily tip over into victim blaming. For example, Amir's (1971) claim that one in five rapes are victim precipitated is not very different from saying that the victims 'asked for it'.
- It ignores situations where victims are unaware of their victimisation, as with some crimes against the environment, and where harm is done but no law broken.

Critical victimology

Critical victimology is based on conflict theories such as Marxism and feminism, and shares the same approach as critical criminology. It focuses on two elements:

- **Structural factors**, such as patriarchy and poverty, which place powerless groups such as women and the poor at greater risk of victimisation. As Mawby and Walklate (1994) argue, victimisation is a form of *structural powerlessness*.
- **The state's power to apply or deny the label of victim** 'Victim' is a social construct in the same way as 'crime' and 'criminal'. Through the criminal justice process, the state applies the label of victim to some but withholds it from others – for example when police decide not to press charges against a man for assaulting his wife, thereby denying her victim status.

Similarly, Tombs and Whyte (2007) show that 'safety crimes', where employers' violations of the law lead to death or injury to workers, are often explained away as the fault of 'accident prone' workers. As with many rape cases, this both denies the victim official 'victim status' and blames them for their fate.

Tombs and Whyte note the ideological function of this 'failure to label' or 'de-labelling'. By concealing the true extent of victimisation and its real causes, it hides the crimes of the powerful and denies the powerless victims any redress. In the *hierarchy of victimisation*, therefore, the powerless are most likely to be victimised, yet least likely to have this acknowledged by the state.

Evaluation

- Critical victimology disregards the role victims may play in bringing victimisation on themselves through their own choices (e.g. not making their home secure) or their own offending.

- It is valuable in drawing attention to the way that 'victim' status is constructed by power and how this benefits the powerful at the expense of the powerless.

Patterns of victimisation

The risk of being the victim of a crime is very unevenly distributed between social groups.

Class The poorest groups are more likely to be victimised. For example, crime rates are typically highest in areas of high unemployment and deprivation.

The fact that marginalised groups are most likely to become victims is borne out by a survey of 300 homeless people (Newburn and Rock 2006). This found that they were 12 times more likely to have experienced violence than the general population. One in ten had been urinated on while sleeping rough.

Application
Suggest three reasons why the poorest social groups are most likely to be victims of crime.

Age Younger people are at more risk of victimisation. Those most at risk of being murdered are infants under one, while teenagers are more vulnerable than adults to offences including assault, sexual harassment, theft, and abuse at home. The old are also at risk of abuse, for example in nursing homes, where victimisation is less visible, but in general, the risk of victimisation declines with age.

Ethnicity Minority ethnic groups are at greater risk than whites of being victims of crime in general, as well as of racially motivated crimes. In relation to the police, ethnic minorities, the young and the homeless are more likely to report feeling under-protected yet over-controlled. (For more about ethnicity and victimisation, see Topic 6.)

Gender Males are at greater risk than females of becoming victims of violent attacks, especially by strangers. About 70% of homicide victims are male. However, women are more likely to be victims of domestic violence, sexual violence, stalking and harassment, people trafficking and – in times of armed conflict – mass rape as a weapon of war.

Repeat victimisation refers to the fact that, if you have been a victim once, you are very likely to be one again. According to the British Crime Survey, about 60% of the population have not been victims of any kind of crime in a given year, whereas a mere 4% of the population are victims of 44% of all crimes in that period.

The impact of victimisation

Crime may have serious physical and emotional impacts on its victims. For example, research has found a variety of effects (depending on the crime), including disrupted sleep,

feelings of helplessness, increased security-consciousness, and difficulties in social functioning.

Crime may also create 'indirect' victims, such as friends, relatives and witnesses to the crime. For example, Pynoos et al (1987) found that child witnesses of a sniper attack continued to have grief-related dreams and altered behaviour a year after the event.

Similarly, hate crimes against minorities may create 'waves of harm' that radiate out to affect others. These are 'message' crimes aimed at intimidating whole communities, not just the primary victim. Even more widely, such crimes also challenge the value system of the whole society.

Secondary victimisation is the idea that in addition to the impact of the crime itself, individuals may suffer further victimisation at the hands of the criminal justice system. Feminists argue that rape victims are often so poorly treated by the police and the courts, it amounts to a double violation.

Fear of victimisation Crime may create fear of becoming a victim. Some sociologists argue that surveys show this fear to be often irrational. For example, women are more afraid of going out for fear of attack, yet it is young men who are the main victims of violence from strangers. However, feminists have attacked the emphasis on 'fear of crime'. They argue that it focuses on women's passivity and their psychological state, when we should be focusing on their *safety* – i.e. on the structural threat of patriarchal violence that they face.

Topic summary

Situational crime prevention focuses on reducing opportunities for crime, e.g. through target hardening. **Environmental crime prevention** focuses on mending 'broken windows' and zero tolerance policing. **Social and community prevention** strategies attempt to tackle the root causes of offending.

Foucault argues that **disciplinary power** now governs individuals through **surveillance** and self-surveillance. Other views include synoptic surveillance, surveillant assemblages, actuarial justice, social sorting and labelling.

For **functionalists**, punishment functions to promote solidarity. For **Marxists**, it preserves the status quo and is shaped by the economic base. Prisons have become the key institution of punishment and there is a trend towards **mass incarceration**. Community punishments may simply cast the **net of control** more widely.

Positivist victimology focuses on victim proneness or precipitation. **Critical victimology** emphasises structural factors such as poverty, and the state's power to apply or deny the label of victim. The poor, the young and ethnic minorities are at greater risk of victimisation.

EXAMINING CONTROL, PUNISHMENT AND VICTIMS

QuickCheck Questions

Check your answers at www.sociology.uk.net

1 Explain the difference between target hardening and displacement.
2 Suggest two criticisms of situational crime prevention strategies apart from displacement.
3 What is meant by 'zero tolerance policing'?
4 Give one example of synoptic surveillance.
5 Explain what is meant by 'surveillant assemblages'.
6 Explain what is meant by 'actuarial justice'.
7 Explain the difference between retributive and restitutive justice.
8 According to Marxists, why has imprisonment become the dominant form of punishment?
9 Explain what Foucault means by 'disciplinary power'.
10 What is meant by 'transcarceration'?
11 Suggest two criticisms of positivist victimology.

Questions to try

Item A   All societies have systems of punishment for dealing with deviance, and sociologists have explained their role in a variety of different ways. Some sociologists emphasise the importance of society having shared values. Others argue that punishment may take the form that it does because it reflects the nature of an unequal society. Some writers have pointed to the way in which punishment varies according to the type of society in which it is found.

Item B   There are several strategies for preventing or reducing crime and these reflect different views of the nature and causes of crimes. Crime depends on there being the opportunity to commit it. Some crimes may result from the degeneration of a particular locality, which suggests that crime is tolerated there by the community or the police. Of course, it may be that poor living conditions are themselves the cause of crime.

1 Outline two features of critical victimology.   (4 marks)
2 Applying material from Item A, analyse two functions of punishment.   (10 marks)
3 Applying material from Item B, analyse the effectiveness of two crime prevention strategies.   (10 marks)

The Examiner's Advice

Q2 Spend about 15 minutes on this. Divide your time fairly equally between the two functions. You don't need a separate introduction; just start on your first function. To answer this question, it's essential that you take two points from the Item and show through a chain of reasoning (see Box 4.1 in chapter 4) how each is a function of punishment. (It is a very good idea to quote from the Item when doing so.)

You could use the idea that punishment reflects societal inequality, the importance of shared values, or that punishment varies with the type of society. For example, functionalists argue that punishment functions to reinforce solidarity and reaffirm shared values by expressing society's outrage. Thus in traditional society, where the collective conscience is strong, deviance arouses strong passions and society seeks harsh retribution. You can briefly evaluate by pointing out that in fact traditional societies often have restitutive not retributive justice.

Use concepts and issues such as those above and deterrence, rehabilitation, incapacitation, social order, class society, sovereign power, disciplinary power, ideological function and mass incarceration. Use studies such as Durkheim, Rusche and Kirchheimer, Melossi and Pavarini, Foucault and Garland.

Q3 Spend about 15 minutes on this. Divide your time fairly equally between the two strategies. You don't need a separate introduction; just start on your first strategy. To answer this question, it's essential that you take two points from the Item and show through a chain of reasoning how each generates a different crime reduction strategy. (It is a very good idea to quote from the Item when doing so.)

You could use the idea of poor living conditions, neighbourhood degeneration and tolerance of crime, or opportunity to commit crime. For example, situational crime prevention strategies may involve reducing the opportunity for crime by altering the environment to make committing crime more difficult. For example by 'target hardening' via increased CCTV surveillance or fitting stronger locks, opportunities for crime are reduced and risks or difficulty are increased.

You can briefly evaluate by noting that situational crime prevention may result in displacement. Use concepts and issues such as those above and rational choice theory, environmental crime prevention, broken windows, zero tolerance policing, social control, social and community crime prevention and poverty. Use studies such as Clarke, Felson, Chaiken, and Wilson and Kelling.

EXAMINING CRIME AND DEVIANCE

> **Item A** According to official crime statistics, there is a clear relationship between ethnicity and offending. Some sociologists argue that these statistical patterns broadly reflect the reality of offending, but others reject this. It may be that the patterns are due to demographic factors, or to the way in which some groups respond to discrimination. Alternatively, it may be that processes involving the criminal justice system are responsible for ethnic differences in recorded rates of offending.
>
> **Item B** Functionalists see society as based on value consensus. Crime and deviance are a threat to this consensus and yet at the same time, they can be functional for society under some circumstances. Functionalists also see the value consensus itself as a cause of crime and deviance, for example when some individuals try to achieve approved goals by illegal means. However, some functionalists see deviance as a collective rather than purely individual phenomenon.

1 Outline two neutralisation techniques that offenders may use.   (4 marks)
2 Outline three reasons why Marxists see capitalism as criminogenic.   (6 marks)
3 Applying material from Item A, analyse two reasons why some ethnic groups have higher recorded rates of offending than others.   (10 marks)
4 Applying material from Item B and your knowledge, evaluate the usefulness of functionalist contributions to our understanding of crime and deviance.   (30 marks)

The Examiner's Advice

Q3 Spend about 15 minutes on this. Divide your time fairly equally between the two reasons. You don't need a separate introduction; just start on your first reason. To answer this question, it's essential that you take two points from the Item and show through a chain of reasoning (see Box 4.1 in chapter 4) how each explains ethnic differences in recorded rates of offending. (It is a very good idea to quote from the Item when doing so.)

You could use demographic factors, crime as a response to discrimination, or processes involving the criminal justice system. For example, there is evidence of institutional racism producing higher conviction rates for minority ethnic groups, such as racist stereotypes held by officers, higher rates of stops and searches, higher arrest rates and lower rates of caution for ethnic minorities.

Use concepts and issues such as the above and relative deprivation, marginalisation, high and low discretion stops, canteen culture, the Crown Prosecution Service, courts, sentencing, pre-sentence reports, myth of black criminality, resistance, folk devils and moral panics. Use studies such as victim surveys, Phillips and Bowling, Lea and Young, Gilroy, Hall et al and FitzGerald.

> For question 4, see the student answer by Michelle on the next page, along with the examiner's comments and marks.

Answer by Michelle

Q4 Applying material from Item B and your knowledge, evaluate the usefulness of functionalist contributions to our understanding of crime and deviance.

The functionalist approach to crime and deviance was founded by Emile Durkheim. As Item B says, functionalists argue that society is based on a value consensus or set of shared norms and values that enable everyone to cooperate. Deviance occurs when someone goes against these norms and values, which can threaten social stability. However, Durkheim argues that deviance is inevitable in society as not everyone is adequately socialised or may join different subcultures with their own norms and values.

As Item B notes, deviance can also be functional for society by reinforcing shared norms. For example, if people see that crime is punished, it makes it clear where the boundary lies between acceptable and unacceptable behaviour. In this way, deviance brings about a reaction and reaffirms the value consensus. On the other hand, Durkheim points out that too much deviance is dysfunctional because it can lead to social disintegration. However, this fails to specify exactly how much deviance is functional and at what point it becomes dysfunctional instead.

Another important function of crime and deviance is that it can create necessary change by introducing new values into society. It can be said that today's deviance is tomorrow's new moral code.

Another functionalist approach comes from Merton. He starts from the idea of shared values such as the American Dream of material wealth. Using Durkheim's idea of anomie, he argues that when the value consensus tells us to strive for a goal but blocks our opportunity to achieve it, we are likely to deviate. For example, the working class may turn to crime to achieve material wealth because they have little chance of gaining it legitimately. He argues that this is why property crime is mainly a working-class crime. Merton calls this 'innovation' because people are creating 'new' means of achieving shared goals.

But Merton has been criticised. He takes official crime statistics for granted, so he assumes most property crime is working-class, and he ignores crimes of the powerful. However, in support of Merton, Box has applied the concept of innovation to corporate crime. Box says that companies break the law if they can't achieve their success goal by legal means, e.g. by breaking health and safety laws for workers to cut costs.

Another functionalist approach is subcultural theory. A.K. Cohen argues that working-class boys deviate because they have failed at school. This means they cannot achieve by legitimate means (e.g. without qualifications, they will be unable to get a good job). This gives them a low status because they have failed in terms of society's goals, so to deal with their status frustration they form deviant subcultures with other failures. In the subculture they gain status by breaking society's rules instead of conforming to them.

Another functionalist approach is from Cloward and Ohlin, who found three different working-class subcultures – criminal, conflict and retreatist. All of these are the result of blocked opportunities.

> Good opening putting functionalist view of deviance into wider perspective. Good final point, but it needs developing

> Good account of 'boundary maintenance' function, plus good evaluation at the end.

> Relevant knowledge briefly applied but needs evaluation.

> Good analysis of Merton's basic idea – but could bring in his other types of deviance, plus the concept of 'strain'.

> Good evaluation point, plus a relevant counter-argument from Box – but should consider other criticisms of Merton too.

> Good understanding of Cohen, but apply concepts, e.g. alternative status hierarchy, inversion of values.

> A little knowledge, but needs a conclusion.

Overall, this is a good answer. It shows good knowledge of functionalist approaches, although it's stronger on Durkheim and Merton than on the subcultural theorists. This is especially so for Cloward and Ohlin, where an explanation of the three types and the idea of blocked opportunities is needed. Similarities and differences between Merton and the subcultural theorists should be analysed, for example in terms of the concept of 'strain', individual versus collective deviance and utilitarian versus non-utilitarian crime, or the idea of retreatism used both by Merton and by Cloward and Ohlin.

There is some relevant explicit evaluation of Durkheim and Merton, but criticisms from other perspectives such as Marxism and labelling theory should be included. They raise issues that functionalists ignore, such as who makes the law and who enforces it. The answer tails off at the end; it needs a separate conclusion.

CHAPTER 3

Theory and Methods

Topic 1	Quantitative research methods	158
Topic 2	Qualitative research methods	174
Topic 3	Sociology and science	186
Topic 4	Objectivity and values in sociology	196
Topic 5	Functionalism	202
Topic 6	Marxism	208
Topic 7	Feminist theories	216
Topic 8	Action theories	224
Topic 9	Globalisation, modernity and postmodernity	234
Topic 10	Sociology and social policy	242
Examining theory and methods		248

Sociologists aim to develop theories about all aspects of social life.

Introduction

Sociologists seek to answer questions and develop theories about the social world. Their theories usually take the form of explanations of how or why social life follows the patterns that it does.

The test of a theory is whether it stands up to the evidence. Sociologists engage in research to obtain evidence about the real world using a variety of methods and use their findings to test sociological theories.

Topics 1 and 2 of this chapter focus on the different research methods that sociologists use.

Topics 3 and 4 go on to examine whether sociology can be considered a scientific subject that produces unbiased, objective knowledge.

Topics 5 to 8 discuss four different 'modernist' theories of society. These theories have their roots in the 18th century Enlightenment, an extremely influential philosophical movement that believed in the power of reason and science to explain how the world works, and in the possibility of using this knowledge to create a better society. This belief, sometimes called the 'Enlightenment project', is shared by modernist sociologists.

Topic 9 looks at the major changes in today's society linked to globalisation and examines the attempts made by sociologists to understand and explain them.

Topic 10 examines the relationships between sociology and social policy. It picks up the theme of the Enlightenment project, asking the question: does sociological knowledge help to shape policies to improve society?

The AQA Specification

The specification is the syllabus produced by the exam board, telling you what you have to study. The AQA specification for Theory and Methods requires you to examine the following:

- Quantitative and qualitative research methods; research design.

- Sources of data, including questionnaires, interviews, participant and non-participant observation, experiments, documents and official statistics.

- The distinction between primary and secondary data, and between quantitative and qualitative data.

- The relationship between positivism, interpretivism and sociological methods; the nature of 'social facts'.

- The theoretical, practical and ethical considerations influencing choice of topic, choice of method(s) and the conduct of research.

- Consensus, conflict, structural and social action theories.

- The concepts of modernity and post-modernity in relation to sociological theory.

- The nature of science and the extent to which sociology can be regarded as scientific.

- The relationship between theory and methods.

- Debates about subjectivity, objectivity and value freedom.

- The relationship between sociology and social policy.

TOPIC 1

Quantitative research methods can often study large numbers of people quickly and cheaply

GETTING STARTED

In the first year of your course, you will probably have studied research methods. This activity will help you to recall some of the issues associated with quantitative research methods.

Working in pairs, explain why quantitative methods would be an appropriate way to study each of the topics below. For each topic, say which particular quantitative method would you use and why.

1 Differences in educational achievement between social classes.
2 The likelihood of members of different ethnic groups being practising Christians.
3 Differences in patterns of domestic labour between men and women.
4 Whether living in urban areas causes a person to be more likely to be a victim of crime.

Learning objectives

After studying this Topic, you should:

- Know the main features and types of the following quantitative research methods and sources of data: experiments, questionnaires, structured interviews and official statistics.

- Be able to evaluate the practical, ethical and theoretical strengths and limitations of each of these methods and sources.

- Understand the usefulness of each of these methods and sources in relation to wider issues of methodological and theoretical perspective, science, values and objectivity.

QUANTITATIVE RESEARCH METHODS

As you will know from your study of sociological research methods in the first year of your course, sociologists' choice of methods is influenced by practical, ethical and theoretical issues. We can summarise these as follows.

Practical issues

- Time and money
- The requirements of funding bodies
- The personal skills and characteristics of researchers
- The subject matter of the study
- Research opportunity

Ethical issues

- Informed consent
- Confidentiality and privacy
- Harmful effects
- Vulnerable groups
- Covert methods

Theoretical issues

- Reliability
- Validity
- Representativeness

Positivism and interpretivism

The theoretical issues that affect a sociologist's choice of research method also include their methodological perspective. Those who take an interpretivist perspective prefer research methods that produce qualitative data – that is, information that gives us a 'feel' for what something is like. These methods include unstructured interviews, participant observation and the analysis of personal documents.

By contrast, sociologists who adopt a positivist perspective prefer research methods that produce quantitative data – that is, information in numerical or statistical form.

In this Topic, we focus on the different quantitative research methods favoured by positivists. Topic 2 deals with the qualitative methods that interpretivist sociologists prefer.

Positivism and quantitative methods

Positivists believe that sociology can and should model its research methods on those of the natural sciences such as physics and chemistry. In their view, this will produce objective, true, scientific knowledge of society.

Positivists see society as an objective reality made up social facts that exist 'out there', just like the physical world that natural scientists study. Like physical reality, social reality is not random; rather, it follows patterns that can be observed and measured. For example, there are clear social patterns of educational achievement and underachievement.

In the view of positivists, these patterns exist because society exerts an influence over its members, systematically shaping their behaviour in various ways. Positivists believe that through careful observation and measurement, they can discover laws of cause and effect that explain these social patterns, just as physicists and chemists have discovered laws that determine the patterns we find in nature, such as the law of gravity.

To uncover and explain these patterns of behaviour and their causes, positivists use quantitative data. For example, quantitative data on exam results may show class differences in achievement. By correlating this with other quantitative data on class differences in income, we may be able to show that low income is a cause of underachievement.

Positivists thus prefer research methods that produce quantitative data, such as experiments, questionnaires, structured interviews and the analysis of official statistics.

We shall now examine the features of each of these quantitative methods and their strengths and limitations.

Laboratory experiments

In many of the natural sciences, such as physics and chemistry, the laboratory experiment is the main means by which scientists gather data, test theories and discover scientific laws of cause and effect.

Similarly, positivist sociologists, who model their approach to research on the logic and methods of the natural sciences, may also occasionally use laboratory experiments. However, sociologists often also use two other kinds of experiment in their research: field experiments, and the comparative

method or 'thought experiment'. We shall examine these two types of experiment shortly, but first we shall focus on the classic laboratory experiment as used in the natural sciences.

Key features of laboratory experiments

Control A laboratory experiment is a *controlled* experiment. The laboratory is an artificial environment in which the scientist can control different variables in order to discover what effect they have. In this way, the scientist can test hypotheses about the cause of a phenomenon, with the aim of discovering a causal law.

In a laboratory experiment, the researcher first takes a set of subjects (things or people on whom the experiment will be conducted). These must be identical in all relevant respects. They are then divided at random into two groups – an experimental group and a control group. The researcher then treats the two groups differently:

- **The experimental group** are exposed to a variable (called the independent variable) that the researcher believes may have a particular effect.
- **The control group** are not exposed to the independent variable – their conditions are kept constant.

Cause and effect The condition of both groups is measured before the experiment starts and again at the end. If we discover a change in the experimental group but none in the control group, we may conclude that this was caused by the different treatments the two groups received. In other words, by following the logic of the experimental method, we can discover cause-and-effect relationships. This allows us to predict what will happen under the same conditions in the future.

However, while laboratory experiments are the basic research method in most natural sciences, they are rarely used in sociology. There are a number of practical, ethical and theoretical reasons for this.

Practical issues

Open systems Sociologists such as Keat and Urry (1982) argue that laboratory experiments are only suitable for studying *closed systems* where the researcher can control and measure all the relevant variables and make precise predictions, as in physics or chemistry. However, society is an *open system* where countless factors are at work in any given situation, interacting with each other in complex ways. This makes it impossible for the researcher even to identify, let alone control, all the relevant variables. This makes laboratory experiments unsuitable for studying social phenomena.

Individuals are complex and therefore it is not really possible to 'match' the members of the control and experimental groups exactly. While we can find identical samples of chemicals, no two human beings are exactly alike.

Studying the past Laboratory experiments cannot be used to study an event in the past, since we cannot control variables that were acting in the past rather than the present. Nor can we keep people in laboratory conditions for long time periods so we can study them.

Small samples Laboratory experiments can usually only study small samples. This makes it very difficult to investigate large-scale social phenomena. For example, we cannot study all or even a large sample of the members of a major religion. Small samples also bring the risk that a result that appears to show one variable causing another, may in fact just be a chance correlation between the two.

The Hawthorne effect A laboratory experiment is an artificial environment and any behaviour that occurs in it may also be artificial. In particular, if the subjects know they are being experimented on, this may make them act differently. For example, they may feel self-important, anxious or resentful about being in the experiment and act differently as a result.

This is known as the *experimental effect* or *Hawthorne effect,* after the experiments in the 1920s at the Hawthorne factory in the United States where it was first observed. This 'subject reactivity' will of course ruin the experiment, since it depends on the subjects responding to the variables that the researcher introduces into the situation, and not reacting to the fact that they are being studied.

The expectancy effect is a form of experimenter bias. It refers to the fact that what a researcher expects to happen in the experiment can affect its actual outcome. This can occur by the experimenter consciously or unconsciously treating the subjects in such a way that it influences how they respond and produces the result the experimenter expected.

Analysis and Evaluation

Outline three reasons why the findings from laboratory experiments may not apply to the real world.

Ethical issues

The main ethical issues in relation to conducting experiments on human beings are informed consent and harmful effects on subjects.

Informed consent The researcher needs the informed consent of the subjects of the experiment. This means gaining their agreement to take part, having first explained to them in terms they can understand, the nature and purpose of the experiment, what risks and effects there may be, and the uses to which the findings will be put.

However, sometimes explaining the aim of the experiment beforehand will be self-defeating. In these cases, for the experiment to work, the subjects must be deceived because, if they know its true purpose, they may very well act differently.

Harm to subjects Research should not normally harm the participants. However, some argue that minor or temporary harm may be justified ethically if the results yield significant social benefits.

Research should also seek to do good. Where an experiment is seen to be benefiting the experimental group (who gain from the treatment to which they are subjected), there is an ethical case for halting the experiment and making the same treatment available to the control group. This is often done in medical experiments. It can also be done in sociological experiments, for example where two groups of pupils are subjected to different teaching methods: if one method is shown to be more effective, it can be offered to both groups.

Theoretical issues

For positivists, laboratory experiments have a major theoretical strength – their reliability. However, in other respects they suffer from important limitations even from a positivist perspective. Interpretivists go even further, criticising laboratory experiments as lacking validity and as unsuitable for studying actors' meanings.

Reliability and hypothesis testing

A reliable method is one that can be replicated – repeated exactly in every detail by other researchers to obtain the same results. Positivists see reliability as important because it enables us to check the work of other researchers by repeating it. If we can repeat the research and arrive at the same results, we can have more confidence that the original findings are true.

Positivists regard the laboratory experiment as highly reliable for three reasons:

- The original experimenter can control the conditions and specify the precise steps that were followed in the original experiment, so others can easily repeat these steps to re-run it.
- It produces quantitative data, so the results of the re-run experiments can be easily compared to the original.
- It is a very detached and objective method: the researcher merely manipulates the variables and records the results. Their subjective feelings and values have no effect on the conduct or outcome of the experiment.

Because laboratory experiments can isolate and control any variable that is of interest to the researcher, they are also an effective way to test hypotheses and predictions. If we believe a particular variable is the cause of a phenomenon, we simply set up an experiment where an experimental group is exposed to that variable and a control group is not, and then compare the outcomes.

Representativeness

For positivists, representativeness is important because they aim to make generalisations about how the wider social structure shapes individuals' behaviour. However, with laboratory experiments there is a danger that their findings lack *external validity*. That is, we cannot be confident they are true for the wider population. There are two reasons for this.

Firstly, because experiments can only study small samples, there is a greater risk that they are not a representative cross-section of the population the researcher is interested in. If so, the findings cannot be generalised beyond the experiment itself.

Secondly, lack of external validity arises out of the high level of control the experimenter has. Control over the conditions in the experiment is valuable, because it enables us to establish that a particular variable causes a particular effect. On the other hand, however, the higher the level of control we have over the experiment, the more unnatural the circumstances this creates – which may not be at all true of the world outside the laboratory.

Internal validity

Laboratory experiments may also lack *internal* validity. That is, their findings may not even be true for the subjects of the experiment itself, let alone the wider world.

One reason for this is the artificiality of the laboratory environment. As we saw earlier, this may encourage the Hawthorne effect, where the subjects react simply to being studied, and do so in ways that produce invalid results.

Interpretivism and free will

Interpretivists argue that human beings are fundamentally different from the plants, rocks and other natural phenomena that natural scientists study. Unlike these objects, we have free will and choice. Our behaviour is not 'caused' by external forces, so it cannot be explained in terms of cause-and-effect statements, as positivists believe.

Instead, our actions can only be understood in terms of the choices we freely make on the basis of the meanings we give to events. For interpretivists, therefore, the laboratory experiment, with its search for causes, is a fundamentally inappropriate method for studying human beings.

Field experiments

Given the limitations of laboratory experiments, sociologists have developed two alternative methods. These follow the same logic in seeking to identify causes, but they aim to overcome the unnaturalness and lack of validity of laboratory experiments. These methods are field experiments and the comparative method.

A field experiment differs from a laboratory experiment in two ways:

- **It takes place in the subject's natural surroundings** rather than in an artificial laboratory environment.
- **Those involved do not know they are the subjects** of an experiment, thereby avoiding the Hawthorne effect.

The researcher isolates and manipulates one or more of the variables in the situation to see what effect it has on the unwitting subjects of the experiment. For example, Rosenthal and Jacobson (1968) manipulated teachers' expectations about pupils by giving them misleading information about the pupils' abilities in order to discover what effects this had on the children's achievement.

Actor tests and correspondence tests are also types of field experiment. For example, to test the hypothesis that there is racial discrimination in employment, Colin Brown and Pat Gay (1985) sent a white actor and a black actor for interviews for the same posts, to see which one would be offered the job. The actors were of different ethnicity, but matched for age, gender, qualifications, etc. Similarly, in a correspondence test, Wood et al (2010) sent closely matched job applications for almost 1000 vacancies, apparently from three applicants of different ethnicity.

Such studies show the value of field experiments. They are more natural and valid for real life, and they avoid the artificiality of laboratory experiments. However, there is a trade-off between naturalism and control: the more natural and realistic we make the situation, the less control we have over the variables that might be operating. If so, we cannot be certain that we have identified the true cause. For example, while it may have been racism that resulted in the white actor getting more job offers, we cannot be certain, because Brown and Gay could not control (or even know about) all the other variables in the situation.

Critics also argue that field experiments are unethical, since they involve carrying out an experiment on subjects without their knowledge or consent. However, it can be argued that in the case of Brown and Gay's and Noon's experiments, although the researchers did deceive their subjects (the employers), no harm was done, and something of value to society was learnt as a result.

| Activity | Media |

Racial discrimination in everyday life

...go to www.sociology.uk.net

The comparative method

Unlike both field experiments and laboratory experiments, the comparative method is carried out only in the mind of the sociologist. It is a 'thought experiment' – sometimes called a 'natural experiment'. That is, it does not involve the researcher actually experimenting on real people at all. Instead, it usually relies on re-analysing secondary data that has already been collected. However, like the laboratory experiment, it too is designed to discover cause-and-effect relationships. It works as follows:

- Identify two groups that are alike in all major respects except for the one variable we are interested in.
- Then compare the two groups to see if this one difference between them has any effect.

The most famous example of the comparative method is Emile Durkheim's (1897) classic study of suicide, which relied on analysing official statistics. (See Topic 3.)

In seeking to discover cause-and-effect relationships, the comparative method has three advantages over laboratory experiments:

- It avoids artificiality.
- It can be used to study past events.
- It avoids the ethical problems of harming or deceiving subjects.

However, it gives the researcher even less control over variables than do field experiments, so we can be even less certain whether a thought experiment really has discovered the cause of something.

While laboratory experiments are rarely used in sociological research, even by positivists, written or self-completion questionnaires are a research method that is very widely used. Questionnaires can be given out by hand and completed on the spot, sent out and returned by post or email, or filled in online. We examine this method next.

Questionnaires

Questionnaires ask people to provide written answers to pre-set, written questions. These questions may be:

- **Closed-ended** (also called 'forced choice' questions) Respondents must choose from a limited range of possible answers that the researcher has selected in advance, such as yes/no/don't know. These answers are often pre-coded for ease of analysis.
- **Open-ended** Respondents are free to answer however they wish, in their own words, without any pre-selected choices being offered by the researcher.

In most questionnaires, closed-ended questions are more common, but open-ended ones may be used as well or instead.

We can evaluate the usefulness of questionnaires as a research method in terms of a number of practical, ethical and theoretical issues.

Practical issues in using questionnaires

Questionnaires are a very widely used research method in sociology, in part due to their practical strengths:

- They are a quick and cheap way to gather large amounts of quantitative data from large numbers of people, widely spread geographically.
- There is no need to recruit and train interviewers – respondents complete the questionnaires themselves.
- Data is usually easy to quantify, particularly where pre-coded questions are used, and can be computer-processed to reveal relationships between variables.

Limitations

However, questionnaires face certain practical limitations:

- Data is often limited and superficial. This is because questionnaires need to be fairly brief – most people are unlikely to complete a long, time-consuming questionnaire.
- It may be necessary to offer incentives (such as entry into a prize draw) to persuade respondents to complete the questionnaire. This adds to the cost.

- With *postal and emailed* questionnaires, we cannot be sure whether an unreturned questionnaire was ever actually received by the respondent. Also, we cannot be sure that the intended recipient completed the questionnaire and not someone else.
- Very low response rates are a major problem. A higher response rate can be obtained by sending follow-up questionnaires or by collecting them by hand, but this adds to the cost and time. Non-response may be caused by faulty questionnaire design. For example, a questionnaire that uses complex language may only be completed by the well educated.
- Questionnaires are *inflexible*. Once it is finalised, the researcher is stuck with the questions they have decided to ask and cannot explore any new areas of interest should they come up during the course of the research.
- Because the questionnaire is drawn up in advance, the researcher must already have some knowledge of the subject and a clear hypothesis to test. This makes it less suitable for investigating unfamiliar topics where the researcher has little idea as to the important issues.
- Questionnaires are only snapshots – pictures of reality at one moment in time, when the respondent answers the questions. They fail to capture the way people's attitudes and behaviour change.

Analysis and Evaluation

Suggest two advantages and two disadvantages of postal questionnaires as compared with those given out and collected in person.

Theoretical issues in using questionnaires

A major factor in the decision whether to use questionnaires is the sociologist's methodological perspective. While positivists favour questionnaires, interpretivists and others are more critical of their use.

Positivism

Positivists take a scientific approach and they believe questionnaire-based research achieves the main goals of scientific sociology. For positivists, questionnaires produce representative findings that can be generalised to the wider population. They are a reliable, objective and detached method for producing quantitative data, testing hypotheses and developing causal laws of social behaviour.

Hypothesis testing

Positivists model their approach on the natural sciences and seek to discover laws of cause and effect. Questionnaires are attractive to positivists because they enable them to test hypotheses and identify possible cause-and-effect relationships between different factors or variables.

For scientists to test the hypothesis that variable A causes variable B, they must first establish whether there is a correlation between the two. (A correlation is a pattern of relationship between variables – for example, between social class and educational achievement.)

Questionnaires can establish correlations because they yield quantitative data about the links between different variables. For example, by correlating respondents' answers to a question about their occupation and one about their level of education, we might be able to make the generalisation that working-class people are less likely to go to university.

Once the correlation has been established, we can construct a hypothesis about its possible cause – for example, working-class people are less likely to go to university, because of material deprivation. In turn, this can be tested with a further questionnaire. In this way, laws of cause and effect can be discovered, just as in the natural sciences.

Reliability

Reliability involves replicability: if another researcher repeats the research using the same method, they should gain the same results (a replica) as the first researcher. For positivists, reliability is important because it allows a scientist's findings to be checked and confirmed or falsified by others. If others can repeat the research and obtain the same results, we can have more confidence that its findings are true.

Questionnaires are regarded as a reliable method of collecting data. This is because, when we repeat someone's research, we can use a questionnaire identical to the original one, so new respondents are asked exactly the same questions as the original ones. In other words, the questionnaire is a *standardised measuring instrument* – a fixed yardstick that can be used by any researcher, just like a thermometer or pressure gauge in the natural sciences. This means one researcher's study can easily be replicated and checked by another.

It also means that, if we do find differences in the answers that respondents give, we can assume that these are the result of real differences between the respondents, and not simply the result of different questions – since the questions were the same for all respondents.

A related advantage is that questionnaires allow us to make comparisons. By asking the same questions in different times or societies, we can compare the results obtained. If the results differ, we can assume this is because there is a real difference between the societies or times we are comparing.

Representativeness

If a method produces representative data, then the findings can be generalised from the sample studied to the wider population from which the sample is drawn. Representativeness is important to positivists because they are macro or structural theorists – they aim to make generalisations about how the wider social structure shapes our behaviour. Positivists favour questionnaires because they are more likely to yield representative data. There are two main reasons for this:

- **They are large-scale** Because questionnaires can be distributed quickly and cheaply by post or email over wide geographical areas, they can collect information from a large sample of people. As a result, their findings stand a better chance of being truly representative of the wider population.

Box 3.1	Sampling

Sociologists often aim to produce generalisations that apply to all cases of a topic. However, we may not have the resources to study every case, so we must choose a *sample* or smaller sub-group drawn from the wider research population we are interested in.

The aim of sampling is usually to ensure that the people we have chosen to study are *representative* or typical of the research population. If they are, we can *generalise* our findings to the whole research population. This is particularly attractive to positivists, who wish to make law-like statements.

The sampling frame is a list of members of the research population. From this, we select a representative sample of the research population, using a technique such as:

- Random sampling, where the sample is selected purely by chance, e.g. names drawn out of a hat.
- Quasi-random sampling is similar, e.g. selecting every tenth name on a list.
- Stratified random sampling We subdivide ('stratify') the population into the relevant categories (e.g. working-class males, working-class females), and then randomly select a sample of each, ensuring that the proportions of the total sample in each category are the same as in the overall population.
- Quota sampling is similar, but instead of choosing the samples randomly, researchers go looking for the right number (quota) of each sort of person required in each category.

Non-representative sampling may be used where there is no sampling frame for the population, e.g. there is no complete list of all criminals. Techniques include:

- Snowball sampling collects a sample by contacting key individuals, who are asked to suggest others to be interviewed, and so on, adding to the sample 'snowball' fashion. This is a way to contact a sample who might otherwise be difficult to find, e.g. criminals.
- Opportunity (or convenience) sampling chooses from those individuals who are easiest to access, e.g. a captive audience such as prisoners.

Interpretivists have less need for representative samples. They believe it is more important to gain a valid understanding of actors' meanings than to discover laws of behaviour, so they are less concerned to make generalisations.

- **They use representative samples** Researchers who use questionnaires tend to use more sophisticated sampling techniques designed to obtain a representative sample.

However, representativeness can be undermined by low response rate, especially if those who do return their questionnaires are different in some way from those who don't (for example, better educated). If so, this will produce distorted and unrepresentative results, from which no accurate generalisations can be made.

Detachment and objectivity

For positivists, scientific research is objective (unbiased) and detached. The scientist's own subjective opinions and values must be kept separate from the research and not be allowed to 'contaminate' or affect the subject matter or the research findings in any way.

Positivists favour questionnaires because they see them as a detached and scientific form of research, where the sociologist's personal involvement with their respondents is kept to a minimum. For example, postal questionnaires are completed at a distance and involve little or no personal contact between researchers and respondents. Unlike in an interview, no researcher is present to influence the answers.

Interpretivism

Interpretivists seek to discover the meanings that underlie our actions and from which we construct social reality. Their main concern is with validity – obtaining an authentic or truthful picture of how actors construct and experience social reality.

For this reason, interpretivists tend to reject the use of questionnaires. They argue that questionnaires cannot yield valid data about the meanings of social actors. In their view, there are several reasons for this.

Detachment

Interpretivists reject the positivist preference for detachment and objectivity because they believe it fails to produce a valid picture of actors' meanings. To obtain valid data, they argue, we must use methods that involve us closely with the people we research, so that we can gain a subjective understanding of their meanings – ideally, by enabling us to see the world through their eyes.

For interpretivists, questionnaires fail to do this because they are the most detached of all primary methods. The lack of contact between researcher and respondent makes it almost impossible to clarify what the questions mean for the respondent or to check that the researcher has correctly understood the answers given. This can be a serious problem, especially where there are cultural or language differences between researcher and respondent. Interpretivists argue that the cost of this detachment

is invalid data that fails to give a true picture of the respondent's meanings.

Lying, forgetting and trying to impress

The validity of questionnaire data depends on the willingness and ability of respondents to provide full and accurate answers. Problems of validity are created when respondents lie, forget, do not know or do not understand (and do not admit that they don't understand). For example, in Michael Schofield's (1965) research on the sexual behaviour of teenagers, in reply to the question, 'Are you a virgin?' one girl answered, 'No, not yet'. Whether she did not understand, or was simply being mischievous, the resulting data lacked validity.

Similarly, respondents may try to please or second-guess the researcher, or impress them by giving 'respectable' answers they feel they ought to give, rather than tell the truth. For example, among groups where churchgoing is thought socially desirable, respondents to questionnaires on church attendance exaggerate how often they attend.

It is often impossible to confirm whether respondents are telling the truth or not. For this reason, interpretivists often favour observation instead of questionnaires, since this allows us to see for ourselves what people actually do, rather than what they say they do.

Box 3.2	Ethics and questionnaires

Questionnaires pose relatively few ethical problems. Questions are often about less sensitive, routine factual topics. Even where questions are about more sensitive or personal issues, respondents are not obliged to answer them. Nevertheless, researchers should still take care to avoid causing psychological harm through their questions.

Researchers should gain respondents' informed consent and make it clear that they have a right not to answer any of the questions that they do not wish to. Parental consent may be required before administering questionnaires to children. Guaranteeing confidentiality is generally straightforward, since most questionnaires are completed anonymously.

Imposing the researcher's meanings

For interpretivists, it is important that our research methods reveal the meanings of the social actors we are studying. In their view, however, questionnaires are more likely to impose the researcher's framework of ideas on the respondent than to reveal the respondent's meanings. For example, by choosing in advance which questions to ask, the researcher has already decided what is important and what isn't.

Furthermore, whatever type of questions we use, we risk distorting the reality and undermining validity:

- **Closed-ended questions** are a kind of straitjacket where respondents have to try and fit their views into the answers on offer. If they feel some other answer to be important, they have no opportunity to express it.
- **Open-ended questions** allow respondents to give whatever answer they wish, but when the researcher codes them to produce quantitative data, non-identical answers may get lumped together. As Marten Shipman (1997) says, when the researcher's categories are not the respondent's categories, 'pruning and bending' of the data is inevitable.

Feminism and questionnaires Some feminists are critical of the use of survey methods such as questionnaires and structured interviews. We deal with these criticisms, and with the use of unstructured interviews as an alternative feminist approach, in the next section and in Topic 2.

Structured interviews

While social surveys can be conducted by means of written questionnaires, a widely used alternative is interviews. These can be carried out either face to face or by telephone.

Sociologists use different types of interview. The main difference is in how free the interviewer is to vary the questions:

- **Structured** or formal interviews. Each interview is conducted in the same standardised way, with precisely the same questions, wording, order, tone of voice etc.
- **Unstructured**, informal or discovery interviews are like a guided conversation. The interviewer is free to vary the questions, wording, order etc, pursuing whatever line of questioning seems appropriate, asking follow-up questions etc. Group interviews are usually relatively unstructured. They include focus groups, where the researcher asks the group to discuss certain topics and records their views.
- **Semi-structured** interviews have the same set of questions in common, but the interviewer can also probe for more information and ask additional questions.

Structured interviews are like questionnaires: both involve asking people a fixed set of prepared questions. In both cases, the questions are usually closed-ended with pre-coded answers. Both produce mainly quantitative data.

The main difference is that in a structured interview, the questions are read out and the answers filled in by a trained interviewer, rather than by the interviewee. Interviews thus involve a social interaction between interviewer and interviewee, whereas with written questionnaires the respondent usually answers the questions without the researcher's involvement.

The basic similarity between the two methods means they share many of the same strengths and limitations. Where there are differences, these often come from the fact that structured interviews involve interaction between researcher and interviewee.

Practical issues

- Structured interviews can cover quite large numbers of people because they are quick and fairly cheap to administer. For example, Young and Willmott (1962) interviewed 933 people in this way in their research on families in east London.
- They are suitable for gathering straightforward factual information such as a person's age, job, religion, daily routine etc.
- Results are easily quantified because they use closed-ended questions with pre-coded answers. This makes them suitable for hypothesis testing.

Box 3.3	Ethics and interviewing

Most sociologists argue that there are relatively few ethical problems in using structured interviews. Questions are more likely to be of a routine factual nature about less sensitive topics. Even where questions are intrusive, interviewees are under no obligation to answer them.

Nevertheless, because the interview is a social interaction, the interviewee may feel under some pressure to answer questions. Some feminists also regard structured interviews as at least potentially oppressive to women interviewees.

Where unstructured interviews deal with sensitive or painful issues, care needs to be exercised to avoid causing psychological harm.

Researchers should gain interviewees' informed consent, make it clear they have a right not to answer any questions that they do not wish to, and guarantee anonymity and confidentiality.

However, there may sometimes be difficulties. For example, Fiona Brookman (1999) notes that it can be difficult to keep confidential the identity of murderers who have been interviewed. If their case has received much publicity, even minimal details may make them identifiable.

There are also special considerations in interviewing vulnerable people, such as children or those with mental health problems. For example, such interviews may need to be kept brief and special care needs to be taken not to put pressure on the interviewee. Parental consent may be required when interviewing children.

- Training interviewers is relatively straightforward and inexpensive, since all they are really required to do is follow a set of instructions. However, this is more costly than simply posting questionnaires to people.
- Response rates are usually higher than for questionnaires – perhaps because people find it harder to turn down a face-to-face request, and some may welcome the opportunity to talk. Young and Willmott had only 54 refusals out of 987 people they approached. Higher response rates can be obtained by making additional call backs, but this adds to the cost and time.
- Like questionnaires, structured interviews are inflexible, because the interview schedule is drawn up in advance and the interviewer must stick to it rigidly. This makes it impossible to pursue any interesting leads that may emerge in the course of the interview.
- Because the interview schedule is drawn up in advance, researchers must already have some knowledge of the subject and a clear hypothesis to test. This makes structured interviews unsuitable for investigating unfamiliar topics where the researcher has little idea what the important issues are.
- Structured interviews are only *snapshots* taken at one moment in time, so they fail to capture the dynamic nature of social life.

Theoretical issues and structured interviews

The sociologist's methodological perspective plays an important part in deciding whether to use structured interviews. While positivists favour structured interviews, interpretivists, feminists and others are more critical of them.

Positivism

Positivists adopt a scientific approach to the study of society. In their view, research using structured interviews can achieve the main goals of scientific sociology. For positivists, structured interviews produce representative and generalisable findings. They are a reliable, objective and detached method for producing quantitative data, testing hypotheses and developing causal laws of social behaviour.

Hypothesis testing

Positivists model their approach on the natural sciences and seek to discover laws of cause and effect. Structured interviews are attractive to positivists because they enable them to test hypotheses and identify possible cause-and-effect relationships.

Just like questionnaires, structured interviews can establish correlations between variables (between gender and crime, say) by analysing interviewees' answers. This allows us to make generalisations about behaviour patterns – for example, that women are less likely than men to commit crime.

Once a correlation has been established, we can construct a hypothesis about its possible cause – for example, women commit less crime because of their socialisation. In turn, this hypothesis can be tested with a further set of interviews. In this way, causal laws can be discovered, just as in the natural sciences.

Reliability

If a method is reliable, then any other sociologist can repeat the research and obtain the same results. Positivists see structured interviews, like questionnaires, as a fixed yardstick or *standardised measuring instrument* – they are reliable because they are easy to standardise and control.

For example, interviewers can be trained to conduct each interview in precisely the same way, with the same questions, wording, order, tone of voice and so on.

These procedures are easy for other researchers to replicate, since they do not depend on the interviewer's personal characteristics – all interviewers conduct each interview in identical fashion. Similarly, pre-coded answers to questions mean that a later researcher will categorise answers in the same way as the original researcher. The structured interview thus provides a 'recipe' for repeating the research: as in cookery, anyone who follows it should get the same result.

The fact that all interviewees are asked exactly the same questions also means we can compare their answers easily to identify similarities and differences.

Analysis and Evaluation
Is it possible for, say, twenty trained interviewers all to ask a set of questions in exactly the same way? Give your reasons.

Representativeness

Structured interviews are relatively quick and cheap to conduct, so large numbers can be surveyed. This increases the chances of obtaining a representative sample. Relatively high response rates and the sophisticated sampling techniques that are often used also help to improve representativeness.

These features make structured interviews attractive to positivists because they can use the representative data as a basis for making generalisations and cause-and-effect statements about the wider population.

On the other hand, as with questionnaires, those with the time or willingness to be interviewed may be untypical (for example, they may be lonely). This makes for unrepresentative findings and undermines the validity of any generalisations made.

Interpretivism

Interpretivists are concerned to uncover the meanings that actors use to construct social reality. They argue that to do this, we need a method high in validity – one that gives a true picture of the subject being researched. In their view, this can only be achieved through the use of qualitative methods. Quantitative methods such as structured interviews tend to produce a false picture. There are several reasons for this:

- Structured interviews usually use closed-ended questions. This forces interviewees to choose from a limited number of pre-set answers. If none of these fits what the interviewee really wishes to say, the data produced will be invalid.
- Structured interviews give interviewers little freedom to explain questions or clarify misunderstandings.
- People may lie or exaggerate and this will produce invalid data.
- The sociologist has to draw up the interview schedule in advance, perhaps with little prior knowledge of the

Box 3.4	Interviews as social interactions

All interviews involve social interaction between interviewer and interviewee, and this may undermine the validity of the data in several ways.

Status differences between interviewer and interviewee may affect the latter's honesty or willingness to cooperate. In general, the bigger the status difference, the less valid the data.

Cultural differences may lead to misunderstandings when different meanings are given to words. Interviewers may also not realise when they are being lied to.

Social desirability Interviewees may give answers that make them appear more interesting, normal etc. They may wish not to appear ignorant and so may offer any answer at all rather than admit they don't know.

Interviewer bias The interviewer may ask 'leading' questions, or influence answers by their tone of voice. Interviewer bias can also occur where the interviewer identifies too closely with the interviewees.

While all interviews risk distorting the data, structured interviews may be less susceptible because there are more controls over the interaction. For example, following a standard list of pre-set questions restricts the interviewer's ability to ask leading questions.

topic. In effect, the researcher has to decide in advance what is important – yet this may not coincide with what the *interviewee* thinks is important. Structured interviews thus risk imposing the researcher's framework of ideas on interviewees. Their findings may lack validity because they do not reflect the interviewee's concerns and priorities.

All interviews – whether structured or unstructured – are interaction situations. The interaction between interviewer and interviewee may undermine the validity of the interview, as Box 3.4 shows.

Feminism

Many feminists reject survey methods such as structured interviews and questionnaires. They argue that the relationship between researcher and researched reflects the exploitative nature of gender relationships in patriarchal society. Shulamit Reinharz (1983) goes so far as to call this approach to data collection 'research as rape':

'The researchers take, hit and run. They intrude into their subjects' privacy… manipulate the relationships, and give little or nothing in return. When the needs of the researchers are satisfied, they break off contact with the subjects.'

Ann Oakley (1981) argues that this positivistic 'masculine' approach to research places a high value on objectivity, detachment and hierarchy, and regards 'science' as more important than furthering the interests of the people it researches.

Thus, interviewers must remain detached and in control and avoid any personal involvement with interviewees. In structured interviews, there is a strict division of labour:

- **The researcher takes the active role** in asking the questions.
- **Interviewees have a passive role** as mere objects of study, to be milked for information by answering the questions. They have no role in deciding the subject or direction of the interview.

This mirrors the gender divisions and hierarchies of patriarchal society.

Hilary Graham (1983) takes a similar view. She claims that questionnaires and structured interviews give a distorted and invalid picture of women's experience. They impose the researcher's categories on women, making it difficult for them to express their experiences, and concealing the unequal power relationships between the sexes.

This 'masculine' approach to interviewing is very similar to the positivist view of how research should be conducted. Similarly, the feminist criticisms of structured interviews and questionnaires recall those made by interpretivists.

Like the interpretivists, Oakley and Graham argue that sociologists should use methods that allow the researcher to understand women's experiences and viewpoint. For example, Graham advocates the use of direct observation, while Oakley argues for unstructured interviews.

Activity Discussion

Which quantitative method?

...go to www.sociology.uk.net

Official statistics

The research methods we have examined so far – experiments, questionnaires and structured interviews – all produce primary data. This is data created and collected by sociologists themselves for their own sociological purposes, such as testing a particular hypothesis. However, sociologists often also make use of pre-existing or secondary data – that is, data collected by someone else for their own non-sociological purposes.

Official statistics produced by the government and similar official bodies are a major source of quantitative secondary data. For example, governments produce statistics on many areas of social life, including births, marriages and deaths, exam results, school exclusions, crime, suicide, unemployment and health. The ten-yearly Census of the entire UK population is a major source of statistics.

Governments collect such official statistics for their own purposes, such as policy-making. For example, statistics on births help the government plan future school provision.

There are several types of source for the information that is used to create official statistics:

- **Registration** – for example, the law requires parents to register births.
- **Official surveys**, such as the Census or the General Household Survey.
- **Administrative records** of state agencies such as hospitals, courts and schools. These include records of illnesses, convictions, truancy etc.

As well as official statistics produced by government, various non-state organisations also produce 'non-official' statistics. For example, churches produce membership and attendance statistics, while the charity Shelter produces statistics on homelessness.

Both the advantages and the disadvantages of official statistics stem largely from the fact that they are secondary data. That is, they are collected not by sociologists, but by official agencies for their own particular purposes – which may differ from those of the sociologist.

Practical advantages

They are a free source of huge amounts of quantitative data. Only the state has the resources to conduct large-scale surveys costing millions of pounds, such as the ten-yearly Census of every household in the UK. The results of these are usually published and can be accessed by sociologists to use in their research.

Similarly, only the state has the power to compel individuals to supply certain data. For example, parents are required by law to register births, while heads of household must complete the Census form. This reduces the problem of non-response – for example, in the last Census the refusal rate was only 5%.

Official statistics allow us to make comparisons between groups. For example, the Census covers the whole UK population at the same time and asks everyone the same core questions. This makes it easy to compare different social groups, regions and so on.

Because official statistics are collected at regular intervals, they show trends and patterns over time. This means sociologists can use them for 'before and after' studies to identify correlations between variables and suggest possible cause-and-effect relationships.

Practical disadvantages

The government creates statistics for its own purposes, and not for the benefit of sociologists, so there may be none available on the topic we are interested in. For example, the French state does not collect data on the race, religion or ethnicity of its citizens. This means it produces no official statistics on issues such as the religion of people who commit suicide or of prisoners in its jails.

There may be mismatches between sets of statistics. For example, if we want to compare statistics on ill health with statistics on unemployment for the people of a particular town, we may find that the two sets of data cover slightly different areas and therefore different populations. This makes it impossible to establish the degree of correlation between ill health and unemployment precisely.

The definitions that the state uses in collecting the data may be different from those that sociologists would use. For example, they may define 'homelessness' or 'truancy' differently. In turn, this may lead to different views of how large the problem is. It may be in the state's interests to make a problem appear smaller by redefining it.

The state may change the definitions it uses over time, and different states may define the same term differently. This makes comparisons over time or between countries difficult. Some statistics are collected infrequently, such as the ten-yearly Census, and therefore do not always give an up-to-date picture of social trends.

Theoretical issues and official statistics

A major factor in the decision whether to use official statistics is the sociologist's methodological and theoretical perspective. While positivists favour official statistics as objective facts about society, others are more critical. Interpretivists see them as social constructs, and Marxists and feminists regard them as performing an ideological function.

Positivism and statistics

Positivists take it for granted that official statistics are reliable, objective social facts. As such, they are a very important resource in the scientific study of society. They are a major source of representative, quantitative data that allows the sociologist to identify and measure behaviour patterns, test hypotheses and develop causal laws to explain the patterns of behaviour that the statistics reveal.

For example, by using official statistics to identify patterns in mental illness, positivists can establish correlations. Statistics might reveal, say, gender differences in rates of depression.

From this knowledge, a testable hypothesis can be put forward to explain a possible causal link between the variables. For instance, if the statistics show a correlation between being a full-time housewife and a high risk of depression, we might hypothesise that this is due to social isolation.

Representativeness

Representativeness is important to positivists because they wish to make general statements about society as a whole and how it shapes our behaviour. It is therefore important that the samples they study are typical or representative, so that the findings can be generalised to the wider population and used to test hypotheses.

Official statistics often provide a more representative sample than surveys conducted with the limited budget available to the sociologist. This is because they are very large-scale, often covering the entire population. For example, statistics gathered by compulsory registration, such as birth and death statistics, are likely to cover virtually all cases and therefore be extremely 'representative'.

Statistics from official surveys may be somewhat less representative because they are only based on a sample of the relevant population. Nonetheless, these surveys are still much bigger than most sociologists could afford to carry out. For example, the Crime Survey for England and Wales interviews about 38,000 people.

Furthermore, great care is taken with sampling procedures when conducting official surveys. For these reasons, official statistics may provide a sound basis for making generalisations and testing hypotheses.

Reliability

Positivists regard official statistics as a reliable source of data. In other words, if a different person collected the statistics, it is argued that they would produce the same set of figures. This is because they are compiled by trained staff who use standardised categories and collection techniques, and follow set procedures that can be easily replicated by others.

This is particularly true of statistics created from *official surveys* such as the Census. In these cases, the survey is carried out using a *standardised measuring instrument* such as a written questionnaire or an interview schedule, which is then administered in the same way to all respondents. The official statistics created from the survey results are therefore reliable, because any other researcher could repeat the survey and get the same results.

Similarly, when producing statistics from *registration data* such as births, marriages and deaths, government statisticians follow a standard procedure. For example, in compiling death rates for different social classes, they use the occupation recorded on each person's death certificate to identify their class. The statistics are therefore reliable because, in principle, any properly trained person will allocate a given case to the same category.

However, official statistics are not always wholly reliable. For example, Census coders may make errors or omit information when recording data from Census forms, or members of the public may fill in the form incorrectly.

Interpretivism and statistics

Interpretivists such as Cicourel (1968) reject the positivist claim that official statistics are real, objective social facts that exist out there in the world. In their view, statistics are merely social *constructs* that represent the labels officials attach to people. Therefore, rather than taking statistics at face value as a useful resource – as positivists do – we should treat them as a topic in themselves and investigate how they are socially constructed.

For example, official statistics on mental illness are largely a record of the number of people who consult a doctor about their problem, and whom the doctor then deems to be suffering from a mental illness. Thus to end up as a statistic, the individual has to go through a series of social interactions. These may include pressure from relatives to see a doctor, consultations with the GP and perhaps also a psychiatrist. At the end of this process, the individual may or may not have achieved the label 'officially mentally ill' and become a statistic.

Interpretivists therefore reject the positivist view that such statistics are a true and valid measure of the 'real rate' of mental illness. Instead, they are merely the total number of decisions made by doctors to label people as mentally ill. The statistics are therefore more a measure of the way doctors go about labelling patients than of the actual level of mental illness in society. For this reason, interpretivists are interested in studying the social processes, such as labelling and stereotyping, by which official statistics are constructed. The same can be said about suicide statistics, as we saw in Chapter 2, Topic 2.

Hard and soft statistics

For interpretivists, then, official statistics such as those for mental illness are invalid – they do not measure what they claim to measure. However, this doesn't mean that all official statistics are equally invalid. We can distinguish between 'hard' and 'soft' statistics.

Soft statistics tend to give a much less valid picture of reality. They are often compiled from the administrative records created by state agencies such as the health service, police, courts, schools and so on. What they represent is a record of the decisions made by these agencies, rather than a picture of the world 'out there'. For example, truancy statistics represent the number of pupils that schools have defined as truanting – not necessarily the same thing as the number who *actually* truanted.

Soft statistics also often neglect an unknown or 'dark figure' of unrecorded cases. For example, schools may keep a record of racist incidents, but pupils don't report every incident, and teachers don't record all those that are reported. The problem is that there may be no way of discovering what proportion of actual cases goes unrecorded.

Hard statistics by contrast provide a much more valid picture. For example, they include statistics on births, deaths, marriages and divorces. While a small number of births and deaths go unrecorded, we can place a high level of trust in the validity of hard statistics. This is because:

- There is little dispute as to how to define the categories used to collect the data (e.g. death, divorce).
- They are often created from registration data – for example, there is a legal requirement to register births and deaths.

Application
Suggest three other examples of (a) hard and (b) soft statistics. In each case, explain your answer.

Marxism and statistics

Like interpretivists, Marxists reject the positivist claim that official statistics are objective facts. However, unlike interpretivists, Marxists do not see them as merely the outcome of the labels applied by officials. Instead they regard official statistics as serving the interests of capitalism.

Marxists see capitalist society as composed of two social classes in conflict with each other: the capitalist ruling class and the working class. In this conflict, the state is not neutral, but serves the interests of the capitalist class. The statistics that the state creates are part of what Althusser terms the *ideological state apparatus* – a set of institutions that produce ruling-class ideology. As ideology, the function of official statistics is to conceal or distort reality and maintain the capitalist class in power.

Ideological functions

Marxists see official statistics as performing this function in several ways. For example, politically sensitive data that would reveal the unequal, exploitative nature of capitalism may not be published. For example, since the 1980s, data derived from analysis of Census returns no longer includes class differences in death rates.

The *definitions used* in creating official statistics also conceal the true reality of capitalism. For example, the state has frequently changed its definition of unemployment, and this has reduced the numbers officially defined as unemployed. Similarly, social class categories used in official statistics are based on occupation. This gives the impression of a gradual hierarchy of several classes, rather than a conflict between two opposed classes. It also conceals the existence of a ruling class whose position is based on ownership of vast wealth, not on occupation.

However, critics argue that not all official statistics reflect the interests of capitalism. For example, statistics on differences in illness and life expectancy show clear evidence of class inequality.

Activity	Discussion

Official statistics – a useful resource?

...go to www.sociology.uk.net

Feminism and statistics

Feminists criticise official statistics for several reasons. Firstly, feminists such as Oakley and Graham reject the use of quantitative survey methods such as structured interviews and questionnaires because they regard this as a 'masculine' or patriarchal model of research. Since official statistics are

Compared with primary sources, data from secondary sources tend to present fewer ethical problems. With official statistics, there are few problems of confidentiality and privacy. The data refers to whole groups (such as social classes) and it is rarely possible for the sociologist to identify actual individuals. Because of this, the issue of informed consent is largely irrelevant. Although individuals often have no choice about providing information (e.g. they are required by law to complete Census forms), it is the state that compels them to do so, and not the sociologist who subsequently makes use of the data.

However, the use of an organisation's unpublished statistics may raise ethical issues. For example, if a researcher made public a school's confidential statistics on bullying, this could harm its reputation and chances of recruiting pupils. In such cases, informed consent and concealing the organisation's identity may both be essential.

often created using these methods, this is also a criticism of the statistics they produce.

Secondly, official statistics are created by the state, which feminists regard as maintaining patriarchal oppression. In this view, official statistics are a form of patriarchal ideology – they conceal or legitimate gender inequality and maintain women's subordination. For example, while there is a wealth of official data on paid employment outside the home, few statistics are collected on women's unpaid domestic labour, thereby maintaining its invisibility and giving the impression that it is of little importance. In fact, full-time housewives are defined for statistical purposes as 'economically inactive'.

Thus official statistics underestimate women's economic contribution and they reflect the patriarchal nature of the state. However, not all official statistics can be seen as reflecting patriarchy. Some statistics, such as those on earnings from paid work, show clear evidence of gender inequality.

There have also been changes in the definitions used in official statistics that may reveal women's position more clearly. For example, a family's class used to be determined by the occupation of the male head of household. This changed in 2001 so that the person who owns or rents the home is now the 'household reference person' (HRP) and their occupation is used to define the family's class. Where the home is jointly owned, the person with the highest income becomes the HRP. These changes increase

the chance that a woman's occupation will determine her family's class.

However, as men are still more likely both to be the homeowner and to earn more, official statistics continue to give a distorted picture of gender and social class. For this reason, many feminists argue that official statistics should allocate women and men to a social class as individuals, not as households.

Topic summary

Natural scientists use **laboratory experiments** to discover causal laws. However, despite their reliability, they are rarely used in sociology. Instead, sociologists use **field experiments** and the **comparative method** as alternatives. However, although more naturalistic, these methods give the sociologist less control over variables.

Written questionnaires can gather easily analysable data cheaply, quickly and on a large scale, but they face practical problems such as non-response and inflexibility. However, they pose few ethical problems. **Positivists** see them as detached and objective, producing reliable, representative data for testing hypotheses and developing causal laws. However, **interpretivists** regard them as lacking validity. They produce superficial data that fails to give us an understanding of actors' meanings, imposing those of the researcher instead.

Structured interviews share many of the strengths and limitations of questionnaires. For example, they can gather basic information quickly and cheaply, but they are inflexible. **Positivists** favour them because they are standardised measuring instruments, offering reliability. Their large sample sizes mean findings can be generalised. However, **interpretivists** criticise their lack of validity and for imposing the researcher's meanings. **Feminists** criticise them for reflecting patriarchal attitudes to research.

Official statistics are secondary sources that save the sociologist time and money, providing data that sociologists may not be able to gather themselves. **Positivists** regard them as reliable and representative data from which cause-and-effect statements can be derived. However, 'soft' statistics in particular may lack validity. **Interpretivists** see official statistics as social constructs, and **Marxists and feminists** regard them as ideological.

EXAMINING QUANTITATIVE RESEARCH METHODS

QuickCheck Questions

Check your answers at www.sociology.uk.net

1 Suggest two ethical problems of conducting laboratory experiments.
2 Identify two reasons why experiments are seen as high in reliability.
3 What are the similarities and differences between a laboratory experiment and a field experiment?
4 Suggest one advantage and one disadvantage of using the comparative method.
5 Identify two advantages of pre-coded questions.
6 Suggest two reasons why questionnaires have few ethical problems.
7 Explain why questionnaires are high in reliability.

8 Explain why (a) positivists see 'detachment' as an advantage of questionnaires and (b) why interpretivists see it as a disadvantage.
9 Explain why structured interviews are described as standardised measuring instruments.
10 Suggest two advantages of structured interviews over postal questionnaires.
11 Suggest two reasons why structured interviews may lack validity.
12 Identify three advantages of official statistics.
13 What are the three main sources of information from which official statistics are collected?
14 What is the difference between 'soft' and 'hard' statistics?

Questions to try

Item A

Some sociologists favour using quantitative research methods such as structured interviews and questionnaires. These two methods are similar in many ways. Both use a fixed list of questions, often with pre-set, pre-coded answer categories, and both are relatively quick to complete. Their differences come mainly from how they deliver the questions – either face-to-face or in written form.

However, interpretivists argue that quantitative research methods impose the researcher's views on respondents and do not allow them to express themselves in the way they would like to.

1 Outline and explain two reasons why positivists prefer to use quantitative research methods. (10 marks)

2 Applying material from Item A and your knowledge, evaluate the claim that quantitative research methods may have many advantages, but they tell us little about what people really think and do. (20 marks)

The Examiner's Advice

Q1 Spend about 15 minutes on this question. Divide your time fairy equally between the two reasons. You don't need an introduction; just start on the first reason. Possible reasons include reliability, representativeness, establishing cause-and-effect relationships, objectivity, and investigating large-scale issues. Choose two reasons and describe each one in some detail. Explain how the reason applies specifically to positivism.

Do this by creating a chain of reasoning (see Box 4.1 in chapter 4). For example, positivists value representative data to allow them to make law-like generalisations. Quantitative methods such as mailed questionnaires enable them to sample a large number of respondents relatively cheaply and quickly. This large sample is more likely to produce representative data from which positivists can make generalisations about the target population.

Apply your knowledge of methods such as questionnaires, structured interviews, experiments and official statistics to illustrate your explanation of the reasons. Use concepts and issues such as objective reality, correlation, causal laws, patterns and trends, social facts, macro-level, detachment and science, as well as the ideas referred to above.

Q2 Spend about 30 minutes on this question. Be clear which methods are quantitative (questionnaires, structured interviews, experiments and official statistics), but avoid working through them one by one. It will be more effective to make a point about quantitative methods in general and then refer to a specific method to illustrate it.

Start by explaining why positivists prefer quantitative methods and then link the main advantages of such methods, such as reliability, representativeness, identifying trends and correlations, hypothesis testing and objectivity, to the positivist view. Include also the practical and ethical advantages of such methods. Create a chain of reasoning (see page 000). For example, positivists argue that scientific research involves identifying relationships between variables. This means we must be able to quantify how far each variable has changed so that we can establish cause-and-effect relationships between them.

Apply material from the Item, developing it by using your own knowledge. Your answer may focus on structured interviews and questionnaires, but it is legitimate to refer to experiments and/or official statistics as well. Evaluate from an interpretivist perspective, focusing on quantitative methods' lack of validity.

Can we understand just by observing?

GETTING STARTED

In the first year of your course, you will probably have studied research methods. This activity will help you to recall some of the issues associated with qualitative research methods.

Work in pairs to answer the following:

1 State whether qualitative methods are likely to give you:

  a reliable data

  b valid data

  c representative data

  Explain your answers and give examples of particular qualitative methods to illustrate your explanation.

2 List three topics that you might investigate using qualitative methods. Explain why these methods might be suitable for the topics you have chosen.

3 How do the reasons you gave in your answers to Question 2 compare with the ones you gave in your answers to the questions in the Getting Started activity for Topic 1 of this chapter?

Learning objectives

After studying this Topic, you should:

- Know the main features and types of the following qualitative research methods and sources of data: unstructured interviews, participant observation and documents.

- Be able to evaluate the practical, ethical and theoretical strengths and limitations of each of these methods and sources.

- Understand the usefulness of each of these methods and sources in relation to wider issues of methodological and theoretical perspective, science, values and objectivity.

QUALITATIVE RESEARCH METHODS

Interpretivism and qualitative methods

As we saw in Topic 1, positivists see sociology as a science, and they favour using methods that collect quantitative data in order to discover causal laws about society.

By contrast, interpretivists reject the idea that sociology should model itself on the natural sciences. In their view, this approach is inappropriate for the study of humans.

Interpretivists reject the positivist view of social reality as a set of objective facts 'out there'. Instead, they see it as the subjective meanings internal to people's consciousness. They argue that we can only understand society by interpreting the meanings people give to their actions.

This means we need to use qualitative research methods, since only these can give us a 'feel' for what the world is like from the actor's point of view. These methods include unstructured interviews, participant observation and the analysis of personal documents.

Unstructured interviews

Unstructured interviews differ from the structured interviews we examined in Topic 1. Rather than having to follow the fixed, standardised format of a structured interview, the interviewer is free to vary the questions, their wording or order as seems appropriate to the situation. They can pursue whatever line of questioning they wish, probing for further details, asking follow-up questions and so on.

Probably the main attraction of unstructured interviews is that they can produce rich, detailed qualitative data that give an insight into the meanings and life-world of the interviewee.

Practical issues

- Their informality allows the interviewer to develop a rapport (relationship of trust and understanding). This helps to put the interviewee at ease and encourage them to open up, and is particularly useful when researching sensitive topics. Empathy can enable interviewees to discuss difficult subjects such as abuse.
- Training needs to be more thorough than for structured interviews. Interviewers need to have a background in sociology so they can recognise when the interviewee has made a sociologically important point and can probe further with appropriate questioning. All this adds to the cost. Interviewers also need good interpersonal skills to establish rapport with interviewees.
- They take a long time – often several hours each. This limits the number that can be carried out and means the researcher will have a relatively small sample.
- They produce large amounts of data, which can take time to transcribe (e.g. from recordings of the interviews). There are no pre-coded answers, making analysis and categorisation of data time-consuming and difficult.
- Unstructured interviews make it much easier for interviewer and interviewee to check they have understood each other's meanings. If the interviewee doesn't understand a question, it can be explained. If the interviewer doesn't understand an answer, they can ask follow-up questions to clarify matters.
- They are very flexible. The interviewer is not restricted to a fixed set of questions, but can explore whatever seems interesting. The researcher can formulate new hypotheses and put them to the test as they arise during the interview.
- They are useful where the subject is one we know little about, because they are open-ended and exploratory – they allow us to learn as we go along. Some sociologists use unstructured interviews as a starting point to develop their initial ideas before using more structured methods.
- Because there are no pre-set questions, unstructured interviews allow the interviewee more opportunity to speak about those things they think are important.

Theoretical issues: interpretivism

A major factor in deciding whether to use unstructured interviews is the sociologist's methodological and theoretical perspective. While positivists reject their use, interpretivists favour unstructured interviews. The key criterion by which interpretivists judge the usefulness of a method is how far it produces valid (true and authentic) data.

Interpretivists are concerned with understanding actors' meanings. They prefer to use qualitative methods such as unstructured interviews, because they regard these as producing a more valid picture of how actors give meaning to their actions. They argue that there are several reasons for this, as follows.

Validity through involvement

For interpretivists, valid data can only be obtained by getting close to people's experiences and meanings – understanding only comes through involvement. They argue that unstructured interviews allow us to do this. By becoming involved and developing a rapport with the interviewee, we can see the world through their eyes and appreciate what is important to them and why they act as they do.

Grounded theory

Interpretivists such as Glaser and Strauss (1968) reject the positivist idea that research involves beginning with a fixed hypothesis that we then test by collecting data, for example through a set of predetermined questions. They argue that it is important to approach the research with an open mind; otherwise we are unlikely to discover the truth about the situation or the actors' meanings.

In their view, we should develop *grounded theory.* That is, we build up and modify our hypothesis during the actual course of the research itself, based on the facts we discover as we learn more about the subject.

In this view, unstructured interviews are an ideal research tool, particularly when investigating unfamiliar subjects. They allow us to ask whatever questions we like, and to pursue lines of enquiry that appear important as and when they arise – unlike a structured interview, with its fixed set of questions.

Unstructured interviews thus fit well with the interpretivist view of research as a flexible, open-ended and open-minded process of exploration.

The interviewee's view

The absence of a pre-set structure of fixed questions gives interviewees freedom to raise issues and discuss what is important to them. This may bring fresh insights that had not previously occurred to the sociologist. Conversely, the interviewer's probing and encouragement can help the interviewee to formulate their thoughts more clearly.

The open-ended questions used also permit interviewees to express themselves as they choose, in their own words, rather than having to select one from a limited range of forced choice answers, none of which may fully match their real opinions. Thus an unstructured interview is more likely to reveal the interviewee's true meanings.

Theoretical issues: positivism

Positivists reject the use of unstructured interviews as unscientific. In their view, this method lacks objectivity and reliability and fails to produce representative data that can be generalised to the wider population.

Reliability

Positivists argue that the unstructured interview is not reliable, because it is not a standardised measuring instrument. This is because each interview is unique. For example, interviewers are free to omit or add questions, ask different ones or change their wording each time if they feel it is relevant to do so.

As a result, it is virtually impossible for another researcher to replicate the interviews and check the findings or compare them with their own. For positivists, this is a major

shortcoming: if the original study cannot be checked by others by replicating its methods, we cannot be confident that its findings are in fact true.

Quantification

Because unstructured interviews use open-ended questions, answers cannot easily be categorised and quantified. In turn, this makes unstructured interviews less useful for correlating variables, testing hypotheses and establishing cause-and-effect relationships.

Representativeness

Positivists dislike unstructured interviews because they are less likely to produce representative data from which generalisations can be made and causal laws discovered.

Because they take longer, sample sizes are often much smaller than with structured interviews. This makes it less likely that the sample will be representative. Therefore it will be harder to make valid generalisations about the wider population based on the findings of the interviews.

However, interpretivists see this as less of a problem because they do not place as much emphasis on representativeness and generalisation. This is because they are not seeking to discover causal laws about the workings of the social structure, but to understand the meanings of actors in specific contexts.

Lack of validity

Interpretivists see unstructured interviews as producing valid data. However, positivists argue that the interaction between interviewer and interviewee inevitably undermines their validity. Because the success of unstructured interviews often relies on establishing rapport, there is a danger of this distorting the information obtained.

For example, interviewees may be more concerned to please their 'friend' the interviewer by providing what they believe are the expected answers.

However, not all unstructured interviews rely on rapport. For example, Becker (1971) used aggression, disbelief and 'playing dumb' to get teachers to reveal how they classified pupils in stereotypical ways.

Unstructured interviews yield qualitative data, and positivists argue that this too can undermine validity. Because the answers are not pre-coded, the sociologist has to analyse and categorise the data as they see fit. Positivists argue that this inevitably involves the researcher making value judgments about the meanings of answers.

Therefore, rather than giving us a valid picture of social life, unstructured interviews merely give us a picture as seen through the eyes of the sociologist.

Thus, positivists turn the standard interpretivist criticism of *structured* interviews – that they inevitably involve imposing the researcher's categories on the data – into a criticism of unstructured interviews.

Application

Suggest two reasons why the data from unstructured interviews 'merely gives us a picture as seen through the eyes of the sociologist'.

Feminism

As we saw above, many feminists reject the use of structured interviews, which they regard as 'masculine' and positivistic. Some feminists, such as Oakley, argue that there is a superior and distinctively feminist approach to research. This kind of research:

- Is *value-committed:* it takes women's side and aims to give a voice to their experience and to free them from patriarchal oppression.
- Requires the researcher's *involvement* with, rather than detachment from, the lives of the women she studies.
- Aims for *equality and collaboration* between the researcher and researched, rather than hierarchy and control by the researcher.

To illustrate this approach, Oakley draws on her own experience of conducting 178 unstructured interviews with women about becoming mothers. On average, she spent over nine hours interviewing each woman and even attended some of the births. Unlike in the 'masculine' approach, Oakley wished to involve the women as active collaborators and friends. She willingly answered their questions about herself and her research and met their requests for advice about childbirth. She also helped them with housework and childcare, and many of the women showed an interest in the research and assisted by phoning her up with more information.

Oakley argues that developing a more equal and intimate relationship improved the quality of her research by allowing her to get closer to the women's experiences and point of view. As a feminist, it was also important to her that the research helped to improve the women's lives. For example, many of them found that being interviewed helped reduce their anxieties about childbirth.

Evaluation of Oakley

However, Ray Pawson (1992) argues that there is nothing distinctively feminist or original about Oakley's approach. Her view of interviewing is basically the same as that of interpretivism, with its 'time-honoured tradition of positivism-bashing in general, and structured-interviewing bashing in particular'.

However, feminists argue that Oakley goes beyond the interpretivist approach. For example, she had direct involvement in the women's lives outside the interview situation, offering them help and advice. This reflects the value-committed nature of feminist research, which explicitly takes women's side and seeks to improve their lives.

Participant observation

One problem of using interviews or questionnaires is that what people say they do and what they actually do are often two quite different things. One way round this might be simply to see what people really do by observing them in their natural environment.

We can distinguish between participant and non-participant observation:

- **Non-participant observation** The researcher observes the group without taking part.
- **Participant observation** The researcher takes part in the life of the group while observing it.

Participant observation is used much more often than non-participant observation. Interpretivists in particular favour it as a way of gaining insight into actors' meanings.

However, positivists sometimes use *structured non-participant observation*. This involves using a structured observational schedule. This is a pre-determined list of the types of behaviour the sociologist is interested in. Each time the behaviour occurs, the observer records it on the schedule. The number of times each event occurs is added up to produce quantitative data, from which patterns and correlations can be established.

Whether participant or non-participant, observation can be either overt or covert:

- **Overt observation** The researcher reveals their true identity and purpose to those being studied and asks their permission to observe.
- **Covert observation** The researcher conceals their true identity and purpose, usually posing as a genuine member of the group.

In sociology, most observation is *unstructured participant observation*. The main reason for using this method is the insight it offers into a group's way of life. For this reason, it is often used by interpretivists.

Whether sociologists use overt or covert participant observation, they face problems of getting into, staying in and finally getting out of the group that they are studying.

Getting in

Some groups that we may wish to study are easier to enter than others. For example, joining a football crowd is likely to be easier than joining a criminal gang. Making initial contact with the group may depend on factors such as personal skills, having the right connections, or even pure chance.

Once contact is made, the researcher may have to overcome the group's suspicions and win their trust. In doing so, it may help to make friends with a key informant. However, the researcher's age, gender, class or ethnicity may prove an obstacle if it differs from the group's.

On entering the group, the researcher may need to adopt a particular role. If so, then ideally the role should offer a good vantage point from which to make observations.

At the same time, it should not disrupt the group's normal behaviour. Unfortunately, it is not always possible to take a role that is both non-disruptive and a good vantage point.

Some roles may also involve taking sides in conflicts, with the result that the researcher may become estranged from one faction or the other, making observation more difficult.

Staying in

Once accepted, the researcher is faced with a dilemma:

- They must be *involved* in the group and its activities to understand it fully.
- Yet they must also be *detached* from the group so as to remain objective and unbiased.

If they are too detached, they risk not understanding what they observe. Yet if they become too involved, they risk *going native* – over-identifying with the group. They have ceased to be an objective researcher and are simply a member of the group. Striking a balance between these two extremes can be very difficult.

A further problem is that the longer the researcher spends with the group, the less strange its ways will appear. The researcher gradually ceases to notice things that would earlier have struck them as noteworthy: the observer becomes less observant. As William F. Whyte (1955) put it, 'I started as a non-participating observer and ended as a non-observing participator.'

Getting out

Getting out of the group at the end of the research is generally less of a problem: if the worst comes to the worst, the researcher can usually just leave. Nevertheless, leaving a group with whom one has become close can be difficult – as can re-entering one's normal world. These problems can be worse if the research is conducted on and off over a period of time, with multiple 'crossings' between the two worlds. Researchers may also find that loyalty to the group prevents them from fully disclosing everything they have learnt, for fear that this might harm group members.

Practical issues in participant observation

In addition to getting in, staying in and getting out, there are other practical issues for the researcher who chooses to use participant observation.

Insight

For supporters of participant observation, the best way to truly understand what something is like is to experience it for oneself. The key strength of the method is that it gives us insight into other people's lives by allowing us to put ourselves in their place – a process known as verstehen, a German word meaning empathy or subjective understanding.

Participant observation allows the sociologist to gain verstehen through first hand experience. By living as a member of a group, in their natural environment, we can develop a rapport with its members and gain insight into their way of life, their meanings, values and problems. We can come to understand their life-world as they themselves

understand it. In the process, participant observation produces large amounts of rich, detailed qualitative data that give us a 'feel' for what it is like to be a member of the group.

Access

Sometimes participant observation may be the only suitable method for accessing and studying certain groups. For example:

- Groups who engage in deviant activities may be suspicious of outsiders who come asking questions, but more willing to cooperate with someone who seeks to share their way of life.
- Where members of a group are unaware of the unconscious stereotypes behind their actions, observation may be the only means of uncovering them – since it would be pointless asking questions about them.

Box 3.6	Overt versus covert observation – practical issues

Overt	Covert
The researcher can behave normally and does not have to put on an act.	The researcher must keep up an act. This can be stressful, especially if it involves staying in role for long periods.
Because the researcher is known to be an outsider, they do not need any special knowledge or personal characteristics to join.	The researcher may need detailed knowledge of the group's way of life before joining, and characteristics (e.g. gender) that allow them to fit in.
The group may refuse to let an outsider join them, or may prevent them witnessing certain activities.	It may be the only way to obtain information. The researcher may have more chance of being accepted and seeing things outsiders could not.
As an outsider, the researcher can ask naïve but important questions.	The researcher cannot ask naïve questions, as this could blow their cover.
The researcher can take notes openly and does not have to rely on memory.	The researcher usually has to rely on memory and write notes in secret.
The researcher can use interviews or other methods to check insights derived from observations.	The researcher cannot combine observation with any 'overt' methods such as interviews.
The researcher can opt out of any dangerous or illegal activities.	To maintain cover, the researcher may have to engage in dangerous activities.
It risks creating the Hawthorne effect, where those who know they are being observed behave differently as a result.	There is less risk of altering the group's behaviour, because they don't know they are being observed.

Flexibility

By comparison with survey methods (questionnaires and structured interviews), participant observation is very *flexible*. With survey methods, we have to begin with a fixed hypothesis and pre-set questions. One problem with this is that, if the questions we think are important turn out not to be important to the subjects of our research, we are still stuck with them.

With participant observation, this is not a problem. We can enter the research with a relatively open mind and formulate new hypotheses and research questions as and when we encounter new situations. This allows the researcher to discover things that other methods miss.

As Whyte noted, simply by observing, 'I learned answers to questions that I would not have had the sense to ask if I had been using interviews.' Similarly, Ned Polsky (1971) offers some sound, if blunt, advice: 'initially, keep your eyes and ears open but keep your mouth shut'.

Limitations

There are several practical disadvantages in using participant observation:

- The fieldwork is very time-consuming and may take years to complete. It also produces large amounts of qualitative data, which can be hard to analyse and categorise.
- The researcher needs to be sociologically trained so they recognise the aspects of a situation that are significant and worth investigating.
- It can be personally stressful and demanding, and sometimes dangerous.
- It requires observational and interpersonal skills that not everyone possesses.
- Powerful groups may be able to prevent sociologists participating in them. This is one reason why participant observation often focuses on relatively powerless groups – they are less able to resist being studied.

While these practical strengths and limitations are largely true of both overt and covert participant observation, others are more typical of one than of the other, as Box 3.6 shows.

Theoretical issues in participant observation

A major factor in the decision whether to use participant observation is the sociologist's methodological perspective. While interpretivists favour participant observation, positivists are critical of its use in research. When using observational methods, positivists are more likely to employ structured non-participant observation (see Box 3.7).

Interpretivism

The main concern of interpretivists is to understand actors' meanings. The key criterion by which they judge the usefulness of a method is how far it is able to produce valid data – that is, a true account of the phenomena it studies. Interpretivists thus prefer to use a qualitative method such as participant observation, because they regard it as producing a richly detailed and authentic picture of actors' meanings and life-worlds. Interpretivists argue that there are several reasons for this, as follows.

Validity through involvement

Participant observation requires the sociologist to have a higher level of involvement with the group being studied than any other method. Interpretivists argue that by experiencing the life of the group at first hand, the sociologist is able to get close to people's lived reality and gain a deep subjective understanding of their meanings. This produces uniquely valid, insightful, qualitative data.

This compares favourably with methods such as questionnaires and interviews. While people may lie when answering questions about themselves, direct observation can give us a truer picture of how they really live.

Flexibility and grounded theory

The flexibility of participant observation also helps to produce valid data and is particularly useful when studying unfamiliar situations, groups or cultures about which we know little before we start the research. As Glaser and Strauss (1968) argue, by being able to enter the research without a pre-formed hypothesis or questions, the researcher can develop and modify their ideas in the course of the research to produce *grounded theory*. That is, concepts, categories and hypotheses are grounded in the observed realities, rather than imposed on the data by the researcher.

Similarly, by spending lengthy periods of time with a group, we are able to see actors' meanings as they develop. For this reason, participant observation gives us a more valid picture than the 'snapshots' taken at a single moment in time by interviews or questionnaires.

Positivism

Positivists reject the use of participant observation as an unscientific method. In their view, it lacks objectivity and reliability and does not yield representative data that can be generalised to the wider population. They also reject the interpretivists' claim that it produces valid data.

Representativeness

Quantitative methods such as questionnaires usually study large, carefully selected representative samples that provide a sound basis for making generalisations. By contrast, with participant observation:

- The group studied is usually very small.
- The 'sample' is often selected haphazardly, for example through a chance encounter with someone who turns out to be a key informant.

This means that the group studied may be unrepresentative of the wider population and therefore not a suitable basis for making generalisations. As Downes and Rock (2003) note, although participant observation may provide valid insights into the particular group being studied, it is doubtful how far these 'internally valid' insights are 'externally valid' – that is, generalisable to the wider population.

Reliability

Reliability means that if another researcher repeats the method, they will obtain the same results. To achieve reliability, research procedures must be standardised so that other researchers can reproduce them. For example, in structured interviews all interviewers ask the same questions, so other sociologists can repeat the research.

Positivists criticise participant observation as unsystematic and lacking in reliability. Unlike structured methods, it is not a standardised, scientific measuring instrument. Instead, the success of the research depends heavily on the personal skills and characteristics of the lone researcher. For example, as Whyte recognised, his method was to some extent unique to him. This means it is impossible for any other investigator to check the original study by replicating it, so we cannot be as confident its findings are true.

The fact that participant observation usually produces qualitative data also makes comparisons with other studies difficult. This is a further reason why the method is unlikely to produce reliable data.

Bias and lack of objectivity

Positivists argue that the researcher's close involvement with the group results in a lack of objectivity.

- Involvement means the sociologist risks 'going native', over-identifying with the group and producing a biased or over-sympathetic view of them.
- Involvement breeds loyalty to the group and may lead the sociologist to conceal sensitive information. This denies those who read the published study a full and objective account of the research.
- Participant observation appeals to sociologists whose sympathies often lie with the underdog. Because it is seen as an effective method for 'telling it like it is' from the actor's point of view, those who use it may be biased in favour of their subjects' viewpoint.

Lack of validity

For interpretivists, participant observation's great strength lies in its validity. They claim that it avoids imposing the sociologist's own categories and ideas on the facts. Instead, as a form of verstehen, it gives an authentic account of the actor's world, from the actor's viewpoint.

Positivists reject this claim. They argue that findings of such studies are merely the biased subjective impressions of the observer. Rather than being the actor's view of their world, it is merely the observer's view. The observer selects only those facts they think are worth recording, and these are likely to fit in with their own values and prejudices.

In any case, participant observation studies generally collect masses of qualitative data, only a small portion of which is likely to be published. The sociologist therefore has to make judgments about what to omit from the final account, and this too will reflect their values.

Analysis and Evaluation

Can engaging in illegal or immoral actions in the course of a covert study ever be justifiable? If so, on what grounds?

The Hawthorne effect

The Hawthorne effect can also undermine the validity of participant observation studies, because the observer's presence may make the subjects act differently. This defeats a central aim of participant observation, namely to produce a 'naturalistic' account of behaviour. This is more of a problem in overt observation, but even in covert studies, the presence of an extra member (the researcher) may change the group's behaviour.

Box 3.7	Positivism and structured observation

When positivists use observational methods, they generally favour *structured non-participant observation*:

- It is quicker, so a larger, more representative sample can be studied, from which firmer generalisations can be made.
- The observer remains detached. By avoiding involvement, they do not influence the group's behaviour, and they do not 'go native' and lose objectivity.
- Like the standardised questions in a questionnaire, standardised observational categories produce reliable data because other researchers can replicate the observation.
- Pre-coded observational categories allow the sociologist to produce quantitative data, identify and measure behaviour patterns, and establish cause-and-effect relationships.

However, interpretivists reject structured observation because it imposes the researcher's view of reality and risks producing invalid data.

However, interpretivists argue that, over time, the group generally gets used to the observer's presence and behaves normally. The researcher can also try to adopt a less obtrusive role to minimise the threat to validity.

Structure versus action perspectives

Participant observation is normally associated with 'action' perspectives, especially interactionism. This is because interactionists see society as constructed from the 'bottom up', through the small-scale, face-to-face interactions of individual actors and their meanings. Participant observation is a valuable tool for examining these micro-level interactions and meanings at first hand because it allows us to see them through the actor's eyes.

Box 3.8	Ethics and observation

Covert participant observation (PO) raises serious ethical issues. These often conflict with the practical advantage it offers of avoiding the Hawthorne effect and enabling us to observe people's natural behaviour.

- It is unethical to deceive people in order to obtain information by pretending to be their friend or 'in the same boat' as them. Researchers should obtain their informed consent, revealing the purpose of the study and the use to which its findings will be put. With covert observation, this cannot normally be done. However, some argue that the ends may justify the means if the results of the research are of benefit to society.
- Covert observers may have to lie about why they are leaving the group at the end of their research. Others simply abandon the group without explanation. Critics argue that this is unethical.
- They may have to participate in immoral or illegal activities as part of their 'cover' role.

Overt PO avoids these problems, but is not free of other ethical problems. As witnesses to immoral or illegal activities, both overt and covert researchers may have a moral or legal duty to intervene or to report them to the police. Yet this could undermine their relationship with the group and, for covert PO, blow the researcher's cover.

Because PO is open-ended, researchers may not know where it will lead – so they cannot easily explain the research to subjects to obtain their informed consent. Also, as many people float in and out of view during the course of the research; it would be impractical to ask them all for their consent.

PO leads to close personal attachments with the group, so the researcher risks 'going native'. This may result in condoning ethically unacceptable behaviour, or withholding information from the police etc about the group's activities.

Non-participant observation (NPO) avoids most of these ethical problems, but covert NPO involves 'spying' on people without their knowledge and consent.

However, structural sociologists such as Marxists and functionalists see this as inadequate. They argue that, because participant observation focuses on the micro level of actors' meanings, it tends to ignore the macro (large-scale) structural forces that shape our behaviour, such as class inequality or the shared value system into which we are socialised.

In the structuralist view, therefore, seeing things only through the individual actors' eyes will never give us an adequate picture. For example, Marxists argue that the actors may suffer from false consciousness and misunderstand their true position or class interests.

If so, then their own account of their lives, revealed through participant observation, will give us only a distorted or partial view. Similarly, functionalists distinguish between an action's manifest function – what the actors think its

purpose is – and its latent or 'true' function for society, which may be very different.

However, theoretical perspective is not the only factor affecting the choice of method. For example, functionalists have employed participant observation as the only practical way of studying small-scale, non-literate societies and cultures. Similarly, neo-Marxists such as Willis (1977) have used qualitative data from participant observation.

Activity | **Research**

Different types of observation

...go to www.sociology.uk.net

Documents

As well as using primary methods such as participant observation and unstructured interviews to gather qualitative data, sociologists may also analyse existing documents as a secondary source of qualitative data.

Documents include the following kinds of information sources:

- **Written texts:** diaries, letters, e-mails, SMS texts, internet pages, novels, newspapers, school reports, government reports, medical records, parish registers, train timetables, shopping lists, financial records, graffiti etc.
- **Other texts:** paintings, drawings, photographs, maps, and recorded or broadcast sounds and images from film, TV, music, radio, home video etc.

Sociologists make use of the following types of documents:

- **Public documents** produced by organisations such as government departments, schools, welfare agencies, businesses and charities. Public documents include Ofsted reports, council meeting minutes, media output, records of parliamentary debates and the reports of public inquiries such as the Macpherson Inquiry into the death of the black teenager Stephen Lawrence.
- **Personal documents** include items such as Facebook pages, letters, diaries, photo albums and autobiographies. These are first-person accounts of social events and personal experiences and often include the writer's feelings and attitudes.
- **Historical documents** are simply personal or public documents created in the past.

Practical issues and documents

Documents have several advantages for the researcher:

- They may be the only available source of information, for example in studying the past.
- They are a free or cheap source of large amounts of data, because someone else has already gathered the information.
- For the same reason, using existing documents saves the sociologist time.

However, there may be practical difficulties in using documents. For example:

- It is not always possible to gain access to them.
- Individuals and organisations create documents for their own purposes, not the sociologist's. Therefore they may not contain answers to the kinds of questions the sociologist wishes to ask.

Theoretical issues and documents

The choice of whether and how to use documents in sociological research depends in part on the sociologist's methodological perspective. While interpretivists often favour the use of documents, positivists tend to reject them other than as material for content analysis (see below). Positivists regard them as unreliable and unrepresentative sources. However, they do sometimes carry out content analysis on documents as a way of producing quantitative data.

Validity

Interpretivists' preference for documents comes from the fact that they believe documents can give the researcher a valid picture of actors' meanings. For example, the rich qualitative data of diaries and letters give us an insight into the writer's worldview and meanings by enabling us to get close to their reality.

For example, *The Polish Peasant in Europe and America,* Thomas and Znaniecki's (1919) interactionist study of migration and social change, used a variety of documents. These included 764 letters bought after advertising in a Polish newspaper in Chicago, autobiographies, and public documents such as newspaper articles and court and social work records. They used the documents to reveal the meanings individuals gave to their experience of migration.

Also, because documents are not written with the sociologist in mind, they are more likely to be an authentic statement of their author's views – unlike interviews or questionnaires, where the respondent knows that their answers are to be used for research purposes.

However, documents may lack validity as a source of data. John Scott (1990) identifies three reasons for this. Firstly, a document can only yield valid data if it is *authentic* – if it is genuinely what it claims to be. Researchers may not be certain it really was written by its supposed author, or whether it is a forgery.

Secondly, there is the issue of *credibility*. Is what the document says believable? For example, politicians may write diaries or autobiographies intended for publication that produce a self-serving account of events, for example by glossing over their mistakes. A document may also lack credibility if it was written long after the events it describes, when key details might have been forgotten.

Thirdly, while interpretivists value documents because they give us access to their authors' meanings, there is a danger of us *misinterpreting* what the document meant to the writer and the audience, imposing instead our own meaning on the data. There may be added difficulties if the document is in a foreign language, or if words have changed their meaning since it was written. Different sociologists may also interpret the same document differently.

Reliability

Positivists regard documents as unreliable sources of data. Unlike official statistics on a topic, which are compiled in a standard format according to fixed criteria that allow us to compare them, documents are not standardised in this way. For example, every person's diary is unique, compiled in its own way according to the writer's own meanings and concerns. This is true even when each diarist is recording the same events, such as their experiences of a war. Their uniqueness also undermines their representativeness and makes it difficult to draw generalisations from them.

Representativeness

Documents may also be unrepresentative for other reasons. As Scott notes, some groups may not be represented in documents. For example, the illiterate and those with limited leisure time are unlikely to keep diaries.

Box 3.9	Ethics and documents

Compared with primary sources, data from secondary sources tend to present fewer ethical problems. However, the use of an organisation's unpublished documents may raise ethical issues. For example, if a researcher made public a school's confidential reports on bullying, this could harm its reputation and chances of recruiting pupils. In such cases, informed consent and concealing the organisation's identity may both be essential.

Where public documents have been 'leaked' to the researcher, informed consent will clearly not have been obtained. However, there may be an ethical defence of the use of such data if this can be justified as serving the public interest (e.g. if it revealed wrongdoing by officials).

Before using any document containing details about a living individual, the sociologist should obtain their informed consent and ensure that the data used does not allow them to be identified. In the case of letters and diaries, this may include both the author and anyone else referred to in the document. With historical documents, these issues do not arise if those concerned are dead. However, the sociologist should consider whether disclosure of identities might harm living relatives or others.

In addition, the evidence in the documents that we have access to may not be typical of the evidence in other documents that we don't have access to. For example:

- Not all documents survive: are the surviving ones typical of the ones that get destroyed or lost?
- Not all documents are available. The 30-year rule prevents access to many official documents for 30 years. If classified as official secrets, they will not be available at all. Private documents such as diaries may never become available.

If we cannot be sure that the data from the documents is representative, we cannot safely generalise from it.

Content analysis

Content analysis is a method for dealing with the contents of documents, especially those produced by the mass media. It has been used to analyse news broadcasts, advertisements, children's reading schemes, newspaper articles and so on. There are two main types of content analysis: formal content analysis and thematic analysis.

Formal content analysis

Although documents are normally regarded as a source of qualitative data, formal content analysis allows us to produce quantitative data from them. Ros Gill (1988) describes how formal content analysis works as follows. Imagine we want to measure particular aspects of a media message – for example, how many female characters are portrayed as being in paid employment in women's magazine stories.

- First we select a representative sample of women's magazine stories – for example, all the stories in the five most popular magazines during the last six months.
- Then we decide what categories we are going to use, such as employee, full-time housewife etc.
- Next, we study the stories and place the characters in them into the categories we have decided upon. This is called coding.
- We then quantify how women are characterised in the stories by counting up the number in each category.

Formal content analysis is attractive to positivists because they regard it as producing objective, representative, quantitative data from which generalisations can be made. It is also a reliable method because it is easy for others to repeat and check the findings. Repeating studies also allows us to identify trends over time, for example to see if media images of a group have changed.

Formal content analysis has also proved attractive to feminists in analysing media representations of gender. For example, Lesly Best (1993) analysed gender roles in children's reading schemes. She found that females were portrayed in a limited range of stereotyped roles.

However, interpretivists criticise formal content analysis for its lack of validity. They argue that simply counting up how many times something appears in a document tells us nothing about its meaning, either to its author or its audience.

The method is also not as objective as positivists claim. For example, the processes of drawing up the categories and deciding in which one to place each case are subjective processes involving value judgments by the sociologist.

Thematic analysis

This is a qualitative analysis of the content of media texts and has been used by interpretivists and feminists. It usually involves selecting a small number of cases for in-depth analysis. The aim is to reveal the underlying meanings that have been 'encoded' in the documents, as a way of uncovering the author's ideological bias. For example, working from a feminist perspective, Keith Soothill and Sylvia Walby (1991) made a thematic analysis of the ways newspapers reported rape cases.

However, thematic analysis can be criticised:

- It does not attempt to obtain a representative sample, so its findings cannot be safely generalised to a wider range of documents.
- There is often a tendency to select evidence that supports the sociologist's hypothesis rather than seeking to falsify it, which Karl Popper argues is unscientific.

- There is no proof that the meaning the sociologist gives to the document is the true one. For example, postmodernists would argue that there is no fixed or 'correct' meaning to a text and that the sociologist's reading of it is just one among many.

Content analysis, whether formal or thematic, has practical advantages: it is cheap, and it is easy to find sources of material in the form of newspapers, television broadcasts and so on. However, in both formal and thematic analysis, coding or analysing the data can be very time-consuming.

Activity	Research
Comparing research methods	
	...go to www.sociology.uk.net

Topic summary

Interpretivists favour **unstructured interviews** as a way of accessing actors' meanings, but they are more costly, time-consuming and difficult to analyse than structured interviews. **Positivists** criticise them for their lack of reliability and representativeness.

Participant observation (PO) gives first hand insight into a group's life but there can be problems both joining and leaving, as well as the risk of 'going native'. It can be time-consuming and stressful. **Covert** PO may produce valid data but poses ethical and practical problems. **Overt** PO avoids these difficulties but the group may act differently.

Interpretivists favour PO for its flexibility, validity and the opportunity to develop grounded theory, but **positivists** argue that it is unreliable and unrepresentative. Its micro-level focus means it cannot study structural factors. Positivists prefer structured non-participant observation.

Documents are secondary sources that save time and money, providing data that sociologists may not be able to gather themselves. Sociologists use personal and public documents. **Interpretivists** favour them for giving insight into actors' meanings, but they may not be authentic or representative. Sociologists may apply **content analysis** to documents.

EXAMINING QUALITATIVE RESEARCH METHODS

QuickCheck Questions

Check your answers at www.sociology.uk.net

1 Suggest two reasons why unstructured interviews may lack reliability.

2 Why are unstructured interviews particularly useful when investigating unfamiliar subjects?

3 What is 'rapport'? Why is it important?

4 Suggest two advantages and two disadvantages of using group interviews in research.

5 What is a structured observation schedule?

6 Suggest two reasons why participant observation might not produce (a) representative data and (b) reliable data.

7 Identify two ethical problems of using covert participant observation.

8 Explain why participant observation is attractive to 'action' approaches in sociology.

9 Identify three advantages of using overt rather than covert observation.

10 Why do secondary sources usually present fewer ethical problems to the sociologist than other methods of research?

11 Explain what is meant by content analysis.

12 What does Scott mean by the 'credibility' of a document?

Questions to try

Item A

Interpretivists argue that sociology is about investigating the meanings and motives of social actors, and so the aim of researchers should be to obtain an empathetic, subjective understanding of people's meanings. In the view of interpretivists, this can only be achieved by employing open-ended qualitative research methods such as participant observation and unstructured interviews. These methods allow people to act naturally or respond fully and freely to the sociologist's questions, producing data that is high in validity.

However, other sociologists argue that these methods produce biased data which is the result of the researcher's subjective interpretation of events and responses.

1 Outline and explain two ethical problems often associated with qualitative research methods.   (10 marks)

2 Applying material from Item A and your knowledge, evaluate the interpretivist claim that qualitative research methods are the most appropriate ones for the study of society.   (20 marks)

The Examiner's Advice

Q1 Spend about 15 minutes on this question. Divide your time fairly equally between the two problems. You don't need an introduction; just start on the first problem. Possible problems include informed consent, deception, confidentiality, privacy, harm to participants and studying illegal activities.

Choose two problems and describe each one in some detail. Explain how each problem applies specifically to qualitative research methods such as participant observation, unstructured interviews and documents, rather than to methods in general. Do this by creating a chain of reasoning (see Box 4.1 in chapter 4).

For example, qualitative methods involve enabling participants to express themselves freely and naturally in order to uncover the meanings they hold. For example, unstructured interviews allow researchers to ask probing questions to obtain detailed responses about sensitive issues such as domestic violence, which may cause psychological harm to the interviewee.

Use concepts and issues such as public interest, problems of covert research (e.g participation in illegal activities, deception), confidentiality, vulnerable groups and studying sensitive subjects.

Q2 Spend about 30 minutes on this question. Be clear what methods are qualitative (participant observation, unstructured interviews, analysis of documents), but avoid working through each method in turn. It will be more effective to make a point about qualitative methods in general and then refer to a specific method to illustrate it.

Start by outlining the interpretivist view of sociology as the study of meanings and why validity is therefore important. Then explain how qualitative methods deliver valid data. Do this by creating a chain of reasoning. For example, interpretivists prefer methods such as participant observation that allow them to experience reality in the same way as the actors and so see the world from their viewpoint. This means they can obtain valid insights into actors' lives and meanings.

Use concepts and issues such as verstehen, rapport, grounded theory, validity through involvement, the actor's perspective, and flexibility. Link these issues to the Item where appropriate. Evaluate by using positivist views about the nature of sociology as the study of causes, or by explaining why qualitative data is not necessarily always valid. Make reference to any relevant practical or ethical issues involved in using qualitative methods.

We can use scientific methods to study rocks, plants and animals – but can we use the same methods to study people?

GETTING STARTED

Working in groups of three or four, answer the following:

1 Suggest some reasons why science is a compulsory core subject in schools.
2 Suggest reasons why some sociologists want to model their work on natural sciences.
3 Do you think sociology should aim to be scientific? Give reasons for your answer.

Learning objectives

After studying this Topic, you should:

- Know the difference between positivist and interpretivist views of whether sociology can be a science and be able to apply this to the issue of suicide.

- Know a range of views on natural science and their implications for sociology as a science.

- Be able to evaluate the arguments for and against the view that sociology can or should be a science.

Science is a central feature of today's society. Science and technology have revolutionised practically every aspect of life, from living standards and healthcare to communications and warfare.

As we saw in the Introduction to this chapter, science was central to the 18th century Enlightenment project. Enlightenment thinkers were deeply impressed by the success of science in explaining and controlling nature.

They believed that the natural sciences would produce true, objective knowledge of the world around us, and that this would be used for progress and human betterment, for example by eradicating disease and hunger. Science would be the cornerstone of modern society.

The success of science also made a powerful impression on the 19th century modernist sociologists such as Comte, Durkheim and Marx. They sought to copy its success by producing a science of society. Just as the natural sciences enabled us to control nature, sociology would bring true knowledge of society that could be used to eradicate problems such as poverty, injustice and conflict. It seemed that sociologists simply needed to borrow the methods of the natural sciences, and success would be sure to follow.

Since then, however, others have argued that it is not possible or desirable for sociology to model itself on the natural sciences. In this Topic, we examine two related debates:

- Can and should sociology be a science?
- What is science, and what implications does this have for sociology?

Positivism

The 'founding fathers' of sociology in the 19th century were very impressed by the success of science in explaining the natural world and providing the knowledge with which humans could extend their control over nature. Many of these sociologists, such as Auguste Comte (1798-1857) who coined the term 'sociology', described themselves as 'positivists'.

Positivists believe that it is possible and desirable to apply the logic and methods of the natural sciences to the study of society. Doing so will bring us true, objective knowledge of the same type as that found in the natural sciences. This will provide the basis for solving social problems and achieving progress.

A key feature of the positivist approach is the belief that reality exists outside and independently of the human mind:

- Nature is made up of objective, observable, physical facts, such as rocks, cells, stars etc, which are external to our minds and which exist whether we like it or not.
- Similarly, society is an objective factual reality – it is a real 'thing' made up of social facts that exists 'out there', independently of individuals, just like the physical world.

Patterns, laws and inductive reasoning

For positivists, reality is not random or chaotic but patterned, and we can observe these empirical (factual) patterns or regularities – for example, that water boils at 100 degrees Celsius. It is the job of science to observe, identify, measure and record these patterns systematically – preferably through laboratory experiments – and then to explain them.

Positivists believe, in Durkheim's words, that 'real laws are discoverable' that will explain these patterns. Just as physicists have discovered laws that govern the workings of nature, such as the law of gravity, sociologists can discover laws that determine how society works. The method for doing so is known as *induction*, or inductive reasoning.

Induction involves accumulating data about the world through careful observation and measurement. As our knowledge grows, we begin to see general patterns. For example, we may observe that objects, when dropped, always fall towards the earth at the same rate of acceleration.

Verificationism

From this, we can develop a *theory* that explains all our observations so far. After many more observations have confirmed or verified the theory, we can claim to have discovered the truth in the form of a general *law*. In our example above, we can confirm the existence of a universal law of gravity. Because inductive reasoning claims to verify a theory – that is, prove it true – this approach is also known as *verificationism*.

For positivists, the patterns we observe, whether in nature or in society, can all be explained in the same way – by finding the facts that cause them. For example, physics explains an apple falling to the ground (one fact) in terms of gravity (another fact). Similarly, in sociology we might explain the social fact of educational failure in terms of another social fact such as material deprivation.

Positivist sociologists thus seek to discover the causes of the patterns they observe. Like natural scientists, they aim to produce general statements or scientific laws about how

▲ Japanese kamikaze suicide pilots, 1945. Their 'sacred mission' was to crash their planes into US warships.

Positivists believe that researchers should be detached and objective. They should not let their own subjective feelings, values or prejudices influence how they conduct their research or analyse their findings. In the natural sciences, it is claimed that the scientist's values and opinions make no difference to the outcome of their research. For example, water boils at 100 degrees Celsius whether the scientist likes that fact or not.

However, in sociology we are dealing with people, and there is a danger that the researcher may 'contaminate' the research – for example, by influencing interviewees to answer in ways that reflect the researcher's opinions rather than their own. Positivists therefore employ methods that allow for maximum objectivity and detachment, and so they use quantitative methods such as questionnaires, structured interviews and official statistics. These methods also produce reliable data that can be checked by others.

> **Analysis and Evaluation**
>
> 1 How might scientists test for the effect of light on plants? What variables (factors) would they need to control?
>
> 2 Compare this with the task of measuring the effect of material deprivation on educational achievement. What variables would be difficult to control?

society works. These can then be used to predict future events and to guide social policies. For example, if we know that material deprivation causes educational failure, we can use this knowledge to develop policies to tackle it.

Positivists favour 'macro' or structural explanations of social phenomena, such as functionalism and Marxism. This is because macro theories see society and its structures as social facts that exist outside of us and shape our behaviour patterns.

Objective quantitative research

Positivists believe that as far as possible sociology should take the experimental method used in the natural sciences as the model for research, since this allows the investigator to test a hypothesis in the most systematic and controlled way. (A hypothesis is a statement such as 'A causes B'.) Basically, experiments involve examining each possible causal factor to observe its effect, while simultaneously excluding all other factors.

Like natural scientists, positivists use quantitative data to uncover and measure patterns of behaviour. This allows them to produce mathematically precise statements about the relationship between the facts they are investigating. By analysing quantitative data, positivists seek to discover the laws of cause and effect that determine behaviour.

Positivism and suicide

Emile Durkheim (1897) chose to study suicide to show that sociology was a science with its own distinct subject matter. He believed that if he could prove that even such a highly individual act had social causes, this would establish sociology's status as a genuinely scientific discipline.

Using quantitative data from official statistics, Durkheim observed that there were patterns in the suicide rate. For example, rates for Protestants were higher than for Catholics. He concluded that these patterns could not be the product of the motives of individuals, but were social facts. As such, they must be caused by other social facts – forces acting upon members of society to determine their behaviour.

According to Durkheim, the social facts responsible for determining the suicide rate were the levels of integration and regulation. Thus, for example, Catholics were less likely than Protestants to commit suicide because Catholicism was more successful in integrating individuals.

Thus Durkheim claimed to have discovered a 'real law': that different levels of integration and regulation produce different rates of suicide. He claimed to have demonstrated that sociology had its own unique subject matter – social facts – and that these could be explained scientifically.

Interpretivism

Interpretivist sociologists do not believe that sociology should model itself on the natural sciences. Interpretivists criticise positivism's 'scientific' approach as inadequate or even as completely unsuited to the study of human beings.

The subject matter of sociology

Interpretivists argue that the subject matter of sociology is meaningful social action, and that we can only understand it by successfully interpreting the meanings and motives of the actors involved. Interpretivists say sociology is about unobservable internal meanings, not external causes. In their view, sociology is not a science, because science only deals with laws of cause and effect, and not human meanings.

Because of this, many interpretivists completely reject the use of natural science methods and explanations as a model for sociology. They argue that there is a fundamental difference between the subject matter of the natural sciences and that of sociology.

- **Natural science** studies matter, which has no consciousness. As such, its behaviour can be explained as a straightforward reaction to an external stimulus. For example, an apple falls to the ground because of the force of gravity. It has no consciousness, and no choice about its behaviour.
- **Sociology** studies people, who do have consciousness. People make sense of and construct their world by attaching meanings to it. Their actions can only be understood in terms of these meanings, and meanings are internal to people's consciousness, not external stimuli – they are ideas or constructs, not things.

Unlike matter, people have free will and can exercise choice. As G.H. Mead argued, rather than responding automatically to external stimuli, human beings interpret the meaning of a stimulus and then *choose* how to respond to it.

For example, on seeing a red light, a motorist must first interpret it as meaning 'stop'. Even then, this does not determine their behaviour, since they could still choose either to obey the signal or jump the light. How they act will depend on the meaning they give to the situation – for example, escaping a pursuing police car, avoiding a collision etc.

Thus, when motorists stop at a red light, it is not because there is some force outside them determining their behaviour. It is because they understand and interpret the rule concerning the meaning of red traffic lights, and because they then choose to act in accordance with it.

For interpretivists, then, individuals are not puppets on a string, manipulated by supposed external 'social facts', as positivists believe, but autonomous (independent) beings who construct their social world through the meanings they give to it. The job of the sociologist therefore is to uncover these meanings.

Verstehen and qualitative research

Interpretivists therefore reject the logic and methods of the natural sciences. They argue that to discover the meanings people give to their actions, we need to see the world from their viewpoint. For interpretivists, this involves abandoning the detachment and objectivity favoured by positivists. Instead, we must put ourselves in the place of the actor, using what Weber calls *verstehen* or empathetic understanding to grasp their meanings.

For this reason, interpretivists favour the use of qualitative methods and data such as participant observation, unstructured interviews and personal documents. These methods produce richer, more personal data high in validity and give the sociologist a subjective understanding of the actor's meanings and life-world.

Types of interpretivism

All interpretivists seek to understand actors' meanings. However, they are divided about whether or not we can combine this understanding with positivist-style causal explanation of human behaviour.

Interactionists believe that we can have causal explanations. However, they reject the positivist view that we should have a definite hypothesis before we start our research. For example, Glaser and Strauss (1968) argue that this risks imposing our own view of what is important, rather than taking the actors' viewpoint, so we end up distorting the reality we are seeking to capture.

Instead, Glaser and Strauss favour a 'bottom-up' approach, or *grounded theory*. Rather than entering the research with a fixed hypothesis from the start (when we know little about the topic we are researching), our ideas emerge gradually from the observations we make during the course of the research itself. These ideas can then be used later to produce testable hypotheses of the sort favoured by positivists.

Phenomenologists and ethnomethodologists such as Garfinkel completely reject the possibility of causal explanations of human behaviour. They take a radically anti-structuralist view, arguing that society is not a real thing 'out there' determining our actions. In this view, social reality is simply the shared meanings or knowledge of its members. As such, society is not an external force – it exists only in people's consciousness.

Therefore, in this view, the subject matter of sociology can only consist of the interpretive procedures that people use to make sense of the world. Because people's actions are not governed by external causes, there is no possibility of cause-and-effect explanations of the kind sought by positivists.

Interpretivism and suicide

The interactionist Jack Douglas (1967) rejects the positivist idea of external social facts determining our behaviour. Individuals have free will and they choose how to act on the basis of meanings. To understand suicide, therefore, we must uncover its meanings for those involved, instead of imposing our own meanings onto the situation.

Douglas also rejects Durkheim's use of quantitative data from official statistics. These are not objective facts, but simply social constructions resulting from the way coroners label certain deaths as suicides. Instead, Douglas proposes we use qualitative data from case studies of suicides, to reveal the actors' meanings and give us a better idea of the real rate of suicide than the official statistics.

Like Douglas, the ethnomethodologist J. Maxwell Atkinson (1978) rejects the idea that external social facts determine behaviour, and agrees that statistics are socially constructed.

Unlike Douglas, however, Atkinson argues that we can never know the 'real rate' of suicide, even using qualitative methods, since we can never know for sure what meanings the deceased held.

For Atkinson, the only thing we *can* study about suicide is the way that the living make sense of deaths – the interpretive procedures coroners use to classify deaths. For ethnomethodologists, members of society have a stock of taken-for-granted assumptions with which they make sense of situations – including deaths. The sociologist's role is to uncover what this knowledge is and how coroners use it to arrive at a verdict.

Postmodernism, feminism and scientific sociology

Postmodernists also argue against the idea of a scientific sociology. This is because they regard natural science as simply a *meta-narrative*. Despite its claim to have special access to the truth, science is just one more 'big story'; its account of the world is no more valid than any other. If this is so, there is no particular reason why we should adopt science as a model for sociology.

In fact, given the postmodernist view that there are as many different truths as there are points of view, a scientific approach is dangerous because it claims a monopoly of the truth and therefore excludes other points of view. Hence a scientific sociology not only makes false claims about having the truth; it is also a form of domination. For example, in the former Soviet Union, Marxism – a theory claiming to have discovered scientifically the truth about the ideal society – was used to justify coercion and oppression.

Poststructuralist feminists share this view of scientific sociology. They argue that the quest for a single, scientific feminist theory is a form of domination, since it covertly excludes many groups of women. Some other feminists argue that the quantitative scientific methods favoured by positivists are also oppressive and cannot capture the reality of women's experiences.

Some writers also argue that science is an undesirable model for sociology to follow because, in practice, science has not always led to the progress that positivists believed it would. For example, the emergence of 'risk society', with scientifically created dangers such as nuclear weapons and global warming, has undermined the idea that science inevitably brings benefits to humankind. If science produces such negative consequences, it is argued, it would be inappropriate for sociology to adopt it as a model.

What is science?

Although interpretivists reject the positivist view that sociology is a science, they tend to agree with the positivists' description of the natural sciences. As we have seen above, positivists see natural science as inductive reasoning or verificationism applied to the study of observable patterns.

However, not everyone accepts the positivists' portrayal of the natural sciences. A number of sociologists, philosophers and historians have put forward quite different pictures of science. We now examine three of these views, and we consider what implications each one has for whether sociology can or should be a science.

Karl Popper: how science grows

Sir Karl Popper (1902-94) was probably the most influential philosopher of science of the 20th century. His ideas about science have important implications for sociology.

Popper notes that many systems of thought claim to have true knowledge about the world, such as religions, political ideologies, tradition, intuition and common sense, as well as science. Given this, Popper sets out to answer two related questions about science:

1 What is it that distinguishes scientific knowledge from other forms of knowledge – what makes scientific knowledge unique?

2 Why has scientific knowledge been able to grow so spectacularly in just a few centuries?

The fallacy of induction

Popper differs from the positivists in that he rejects their view that the distinctive feature of science lies in inductive reasoning and verificationism. In Popper's view, the main reason why we should reject verificationism is what he calls 'the fallacy [error] of induction'. As we have seen, induction is the process of moving from the observation of particular instances of something to arrive at a general statement or law.

To illustrate the fallacy of induction, Popper uses the example of swans. Having observed a large number of swans, all of which were white, we might make the generalisation, 'All swans are white'. It will be relatively easy for us to make further observations that seem to verify this – there are plenty more white swans out there. But however many swans we observe, we cannot *prove* that all swans are white – a single observation of a black swan will destroy the theory. Thus, we can never prove a theory is true simply by producing more observations that support or 'verify' it.

Falsificationism

In Popper's view, what makes science a unique form of knowledge is the very opposite of verificationism – a principle he calls falsificationism. A scientific statement is one that in principle is capable of being falsified – proved wrong – by the evidence. That is, we must be able to say what evidence would count as falsifying the statement when we come to put it to the test. For example, a test would disprove the law of gravity if, when we let go of an object, it did not fall.

For Popper, a good theory has two features:

- It is in principle falsifiable but when tested, stands up to all attempts to disprove it.
- It is bold – that is, it claims to explain a great deal. It makes big generalisations that precisely predict a large number of cases or events, and so is at greater risk of being falsified than a more timid theory that only tries to explain a small number of events.

Analysis and Evaluation
1 Explain what Popper means by 'fallacy of induction'.
2 In Popper's view, what are the features of a good theory?

Truth

For Popper (1965), 'all knowledge is provisional, temporary, capable of refutation at any moment' – there can never be absolute proof that any knowledge is true. This is because, as the renowned physicist Stephen Hawking (1988) puts it:

> 'No matter how many times the results of experiments agree with some theory, you can never be sure that the next time the result will not contradict the theory.'

A good theory isn't necessarily a true theory, therefore – it is simply one that has withstood attempts to falsify it so far.

Criticism and the open society

For a theory to be falsifiable, it must be open to criticism from other scientists. In Popper's view, therefore, science is essentially a *public* activity. He sees the scientific community as a hothouse environment in which everything is open to criticism, so that the flaws in a theory can be readily exposed and better theories developed. Popper believes that this explains why scientific knowledge grows so rapidly.

Popper argues that science thrives in 'open' or liberal societies – ones that believe in free expression and the right to challenge accepted ideas. By contrast, 'closed' societies are dominated by an official belief system that claims to have the absolute truth – whether a religion, or a political ideology such as Marxism or Nazism. Such belief systems stifle the growth of science because they conflict with the provisional, falsifiable nature of scientific knowledge. For example, the 17th century astronomer Galileo was punished as a heretic by the church authorities in Rome for claiming that the earth revolved around the sun and not vice versa, as the church taught. We can see Rome at this time as a closed society, dominated by the church's doctrines.

Implications for sociology

Popper believes that much sociology is unscientific because it consists of theories that cannot be put to the test with the possibility that they might be falsified. For example, Marxism predicts that there will be a revolution leading to a classless society, but that it has not yet happened because of the false consciousness of the proletariat. Hence the prediction cannot be falsified. If there is a revolution, Marxism is correct – and if there isn't a revolution, Marxism is *still* correct.

However, Popper believes that sociology can be scientific, because it is capable of producing hypotheses that can in principle be falsified. For example, Julienne Ford (1969) hypothesised that comprehensive schooling would produce social mixing of pupils from different social classes. She was able to test and falsify this hypothesis through her empirical research.

Although Popper rejects Marxism as unscientific because it is untestable, he does not believe that untestable ideas are necessarily worthless. Such ideas may be of value, firstly because they may become testable at some later date, and secondly because we can still examine them for clarity and logical consistency. For example, debates between different sociological perspectives can clarify woolly thinking, question taken-for-granted assumptions and help to formulate testable hypotheses. While sociology may have a larger quantity of untestable ideas than the natural sciences,

this may simply be because it has not been in existence as long as they have.

Activity	Media

Karl Popper and falsificationism

...go to www.sociology.uk.net

Thomas Kuhn: scientific paradigms

Thomas S. Kuhn (1970) is a historian of science who presents a radically different view of what makes science unique. Like Popper's ideas, those of Kuhn also have important implications for sociology.

The paradigm

Kuhn's central idea is the paradigm. A paradigm is shared by members of a given scientific community (such as physicists) and defines what their science is. It provides a basic framework of assumptions, principles, methods and techniques within which members of that community work. It is a worldview that tells scientists what nature is like, which aspects of it are worth studying, what methods should be used, what kinds of questions they should ask and even the sort of answers they should expect to find.

The paradigm is thus a set of norms, or a kind of culture, because it tells scientists how they ought to think and behave. Scientists come to accept the paradigm uncritically as a result of their socialisation. For example, unlike sociology students, those in the natural sciences are not invited to consider rival perspectives. Scientists' conformity to the paradigm is rewarded with publication of their research and career success, while non-conformity may mean their work goes unpublished, or may even lead to dismissal (see Chapter 1, Topic 7 on the Velikovsky affair).

In Kuhn's view, a science cannot exist without a shared paradigm. Until there is general consensus on a single paradigm, there will only be rival schools of thought, not a science as such.

Normal science

For most of the time, the paradigm goes unquestioned and scientists do what Kuhn calls *normal* science. In normal science, scientists engage in puzzle solving. That is, the paradigm defines the questions and in broad terms, the answers. Scientists are left to fill in the detail or work out the 'neatest' solution.

This is rather like completing a jigsaw puzzle: we know from the picture on the box what the solution should be – our

job is simply to figure out how to put the pieces together to get the right result. We are not discovering or creating anything new. As Kuhn says:

'Everything but the detail is known in advance. The challenge is not to uncover the unknown, but to obtain the known.'

For Kuhn, the great advantage of the paradigm is that it allows scientists to agree on the basics of their subject and get on with productive 'puzzle-solving' work, steadily fleshing out the bare bones of the paradigm with more and more detail, thereby enlarging their picture of nature. This contrasts sharply with Popper's view of science. As John Watkins (1970) says, while Popper sees falsification as the unique feature of science, for Kuhn it is puzzle solving within a paradigm that makes science special.

Scientific revolutions

However, not all puzzle solving is successful. From time to time, scientists obtain findings contrary to those the paradigm led them to expect – pieces that don't fit the jigsaw puzzle. As these *anomalies* gradually mount up, confidence in the paradigm begins to decline, and this leads to arguments about basic assumptions and to efforts to reformulate the paradigm so as to account for the anomalies.

The science has now entered a period of *crisis*. Its previously taken-for-granted foundations are now in question; scientists become demoralised and begin to lose their sense of purpose. As Albert Einstein wrote about the crisis in physics in the early 20th century:

'It was as if the ground had been pulled out from under one, with no firm foundation to be seen anywhere upon which one could have built.'

Scientists begin to formulate rival paradigms and this marks the start of a *scientific revolution*. For Kuhn, rival paradigms are *incommensurable* – two competing paradigms cannot be judged or measured by the same set of standards to decide which one is 'best'.

Although they are looking at the same universe, they seem to be looking at totally different ones.

What supporters of one paradigm regard as a decisive refutation of the other, supporters of the rival paradigm will not even recognise as a valid test, because each paradigm is a totally different way of seeing the world. To move from one to the other requires a massive shift of mind-set. Many scientists find it impossible to switch from an old paradigm to a new one.

Application

1 What do you understand by the term 'revolution'?

2 What similarities can you see between a scientific revolution and a political revolution?

Eventually, one paradigm does win out and becomes accepted by the scientific community, allowing normal science to resume, but with a new set of basic assumptions, puzzles and so on. However, the process is not a rational one – in fact, Kuhn compares it with a religious conversion. Generally, the new paradigm gains support first of all from younger scientists, partly because they have less to lose than senior colleagues whose reputations have been built on the old one. In fact, as the physicist Max Planck said, the new theory triumphs 'because its opponents eventually die'.

Kuhn's view of the scientific community contrasts sharply with that of Popper. For Popper the scientific community is open, critical and rational, constantly seeking to falsify existing theories by producing evidence against them. Progress occurs by *challenging* accepted ideas.

For Kuhn, by contrast, the scientific community is not normally characterised by its openness, originality or critical spirit. For most of the time, during periods of normal science, scientists are conformists who unquestioningly

accept the key ideas of the paradigm as a basis for making progress. Only during a scientific revolution does this change. Even then, scientists have no *rational* means of choosing one paradigm rather than another.

Implications for sociology

Currently sociology is pre-paradigmatic and therefore pre-scientific, divided into competing perspectives or schools of thought. There is no shared paradigm – no agreement on the fundamentals of what to study, what method to use, what we should expect to find and so on. For example, functionalists disagree with Marxists about basic questions such as whether society is based on consensus or on conflict.

On Kuhn's definition, sociology could only become a science if such basic disagreements were resolved. Whether this is even *possible* is open to doubt. For example, so long as there are political differences between conservative and radical sociologists, rival perspectives will probably continue to exist in sociology. Even *within* perspectives, there are often disagreements about key concepts, issues and methods. It is hard to imagine such differences being overcome to create a unified paradigm.

Postmodernists might argue that a paradigm would also not be *desirable* in sociology. The paradigm sounds suspiciously like a meta-narrative – a dominant and dominating view of what reality is like. Postmodernists object to this both on the grounds that it silences minority views, and that it falsely claims to have special access to the truth.

Activity	Media

The case of Dr. Velikovsky

...go to www.sociology.uk.net

Realism, science and sociology

A third view of science comes from the approach known as realism. Realists such as Russell Keat and John Urry (1982) stress the similarities between sociology and certain kinds of natural science in terms of the degree of control the researcher has over the variables being researched. They distinguish between *open systems* and *closed systems*.

Closed systems are those where the researcher can control and measure all the relevant variables, and therefore can make precise predictions of the sort Popper advocates. The typical research method is the laboratory experiment, as used in sciences such as physics or chemistry.

Open systems are those where the researcher cannot control and measure all the relevant variables and so cannot make precise predictions. For example, a meteorologist cannot normally predict the weather with 100% accuracy. This is because the processes involved are too complex to measure or too large-scale to be studied in a laboratory.

Realists argue that sociologists study open systems where the processes are too complex to make exact predictions. For example, we cannot predict the crime rate precisely, because there are too many variables involved, most of which cannot be controlled, measured or identified.

Underlying structures

Realists reject the positivist view that science is only concerned with observable phenomena. Keat and Urry argue that science often assumes the existence of unobservable structures. For example, physicists cannot directly observe the interior of a black hole in space.

In the realist view, this also means that interpretivists are wrong in assuming that sociology cannot be scientific. Interpretivists believe that because actors' meanings are in their minds and not directly observable, they cannot be studied scientifically. However, if realists are correct and science can study unobservable phenomena, then this is no barrier to studying meanings scientifically.

For realists, then, both natural and social science attempt to explain the causes of events in terms of underlying structures and processes. Although these structures are often unobservable, we can work out that they exist by observing their effects. For example, we cannot directly see a thing called 'social class', but we can observe its effects on people's life chances.

In this view, much sociology is scientific. For example, unlike Popper, realists regard Marxism as scientific because it sees underlying structures such as capitalism producing effects such as poverty. Similarly, sociologists can also be scientific when they interpret behaviour in terms of actors' internal meanings – even though these are unobservable.

Unlike interpretivists, therefore, realists see little difference between natural science and sociology, except that some natural scientists are able to study closed systems under laboratory conditions.

Conclusion

Sociologists are divided as to whether sociology can be a science. While positivists favour adopting the natural sciences as a model, interpretivists reject the view that sociology can be scientific. This division derives largely from disagreement about the nature of sociology and its subject matter:

- **Positivists** see sociology as the study of causes: the social facts or structures external to individuals that cause them to behave as they do. In the positivists' view, this is the same approach as the natural sciences – to discover the cause of the patterns they observe, whether in nature or society.
- **Interpretivists** see sociology as the study of meaningful social action: the internal meanings that lead actors to choose their course of action. Human actions are not governed by external causes, unlike events in nature, so they cannot be studied in the same way as natural phenomena.

However, while positivists and interpretivists disagree about whether sociology can be a science, they both accept the positivist model of the natural sciences as described above. Basically, the positivist view sees natural science as inductive reasoning or verificationism applied to the study of observable patterns.

Yet as we have seen, since the positivist view of science was formulated in the 19th century, quite different pictures of science have emerged, and these have very different implications for the question of whether sociology can or should be scientific. For example:

- **Popper** rejects verificationism in favour of falsificationism as the defining feature of science and argues that on this definition much sociology is unscientific, but that a scientific sociology is possible in principle.
- **Kuhn** argues that sociology can only become a science once all sociologists adopt a single shared paradigm.
- **Realists** argue that science does not just study observable phenomena, as positivists argue, but underlying unobservable structures. On this basis, both Marxism and interpretivism may be seen as scientific.

Topic summary

Positivists argue that sociology can be a science by modelling itself on the natural sciences, using quantitative methods and induction or **verificationism** to establish observable patterns in behaviour and develop **causal laws**. **Interpretivists** argue that sociology cannot be scientific, because human conduct is not governed by external causes but by **internal meanings**. The task of sociology is to use qualitative methods to uncover these meanings through **verstehen**.

Others argue that natural science differs from what positivists and interpretivists imagine it to be. **Popper** argues that science is based on **falsificationism**, not verificationism. **Kuhn** argues that a shared **paradigm** is the hallmark of a science, while **realists** argue that science studies **unobservable structures** as well as observable facts. Each of these views has implications for whether or not we regard sociology as a science.

EXAMINING SOCIOLOGY AND SCIENCE

QuickCheck Questions

Check your answers at www.sociology.uk.net

1 What does Durkheim mean by 'social facts'?
2 Why do positivists favour 'macro' or structural explanations of behaviour?
3 According to interpretivists, what is the subject matter of sociology?
4 What is meant by verstehen and why do interpretivists favour its use?

5 Explain the difference between verificationism and falsificationism.
6 What does Kuhn mean by a 'paradigm'?
7 Explain what Kuhn means when he says that in normal science, scientists engage in puzzle solving.
8 According to realists, what is the difference between open and closed systems?

Questions to try

Item A

Positivists believe that sociology can be a science by following the logic and methods of the natural sciences. In the view of positivists, this involves gathering objective quantitative data to 'verify' or prove hypotheses and discover causal laws. While accepting the positivists' view of science, interpretivists reject the claim that we can study human beings in this way.

However, positivism is just one view of what constitutes science. For example, Popper argues that science involves seeking to falsify hypotheses, while Kuhn argues that a scientific subject is one that has a unified paradigm.

1 Outline and explain two reasons why some people argue that sociology cannot be a science. (10 marks)

2 Applying material from Item A and your knowledge, evaluate the claim that whether sociology can be a science depends on what we mean by science in the first place. (20 marks)

The Examiner's Advice

Q1 Spend about 15 minutes on this question. Divide your time fairly equally between the two reasons. You don't need a separate introduction; just start on your first reason. Possible reasons include lack of falsifiability; lack of a unified paradigm; free will; empathetic methods; the study of subjective meanings; the problems of using experimental methods.

Choose two reasons and describe each one in some detail, explaining how it concludes that sociology cannot be a science. Do this by creating a chain of reasoning (see Box 4.1 in chapter 4). For example, Kuhn argues that to be a science, a subject must have a unified paradigm. Sociology, with its rival theoretical and methodological perspectives, lacks a shared paradigm.

Apply your knowledge of one or two debates between perspectives, methods or theories to illustrate this. For example, positivists favour quantitative methods while interpretivists reject them, reflecting different views of sociology's subject matter. Use concepts and issues such as normal science, puzzle solving, free will, determinism, social constructs, social facts, testability, control of variables, verstehen/empathy, detachment, ethical problems of experiments.

Q2 Spend about 30 minutes on this question. It suggests that there are different views of science and that each has different implications for whether sociology is a science. Use the Item to start with the positivist view of science and the debate with interpretivism about whether on this view sociology is a science.

Then explain other views of science, applying each view in turn to sociology. Create a chain of reasoning to do this. For example, according to Popper, for a subject to be scientific, its theories must be open to falsification when tested. This means that many sociological theories (e.g. Marxism) cannot be considered a science. Use material from the Item, linking this to your own knowledge.

Use concepts and issues such as inductive reasoning, verificationism, verstehen, postmodernism, feminism, falsificationism (Popper), paradigms (Kuhn), normal science, scientific revolution, open and closed systems (realism), and underlying structures. Evaluate as you go along by drawing conclusions about whether, on each definition of science in turn, sociology can be seen as scientific. You can also offer a final evaluative overview at the end of your answer.

Afghanistan: US marine gathering intelligence. Should sociologists work with the military?

GETTING STARTED

On your own:

1 Note down what you understand by the term 'values'.

Working in pairs, answer the following questions:

2 Compare your answers to Question 1 with your partner. Do you agree with each other?

3 What values do you associate with the following sociologists?

   a feminists

   b Marxists

   c functionalists

   d the New Right

4 In what ways do the topics they choose to study reflect these values? Give an example for each perspective.

5 How might their values also affect what their research finds or the conclusions they draw from their research?

Learning objectives

After studying this Topic, you should:

- Understand the meaning of objectivity, subjectivity and value freedom.

- Know the main views put forward of the relationship between sociology and values.

- Be able to evaluate the strengths and limitations of different views as to whether sociology can and should be value-free.

OBJECTIVITY AND VALUES IN SOCIOLOGY

As we saw in Topic 3, one view of science is that it produces true knowledge. According to this view, scientists take a detached and objective approach to their research. They don't allow their own subjective values to get in the way of discovering the facts.

Everyone has values – beliefs, opinions and prejudices. Our values are influenced by many factors, including our class, gender, ethnicity, upbringing and experiences.

Given that sociologists are also members of society, can they study it objectively and without bias, unaffected by their own personal values? Can sociologists' research be 'value free' – free from contamination or distortion by their values?

- Some argue that it is both *possible and desirable* to keep subjective values out of research to produce true, scientific knowledge about society.
- Others argue that, because sociologists are humans (with values) studying other humans (with values), it is *impossible* to keep personal values out of one's research.
- Some go further, arguing that it is actually *desirable* for sociologists to use their values to improve society through their work. This is called 'committed sociology'.

In this Topic, we explore the answers different sociologists have given to the question of whether sociology can or should be objective and value-free.

The classical sociologists and values

The classical thinkers who shaped sociology in its early years, such as Comte, Durkheim, Marx and Weber, all had views on the question of objectivity and value freedom.

The early positivists

For the early positivists Auguste Comte (1798-1857) and Emile Durkheim (1858-1917), the creation of a better society was not a matter of subjective values or personal opinions about what was 'best'. They shared the Enlightenment or modernist view of the role of sociology. As the science of society, sociology's job was to discover the truth about how society works, uncovering the laws that govern its proper functioning. Equipped with this knowledge, social problems could be solved and human life improved.

In their view, scientific sociology would reveal the one correct society. This gave sociologists a crucial role. By discovering the truth about how society worked, sociologists would be able to say objectively and with scientific certainty what was really best for society – they would be able to prescribe how things ought to be. In fact, Comte regarded sociology as the 'queen of the sciences' and saw sociologists as latter-day priests of a new scientific religion of truth.

Karl Marx

There is debate about whether or not Karl Marx (1818-83) was a positivist. However, it is certainly true that he saw himself as a scientist and that he believed his method of historical analysis, historical materialism, could reveal the line of development of human society. This development involved an evolution through a series of different types of class-based society, leading ultimately to a future classless communist society, in which exploitation, alienation and poverty would be ended, and each individual would be free to achieve their true potential.

The role of Marx's sociology, therefore, was to reveal the truth of this development, especially to the proletariat, since they would be the class to overthrow capitalism and herald the birth of communist society. Marx thus takes for granted the value of the ideal communist society and argues that his scientific approach will show us how to reach it. In this he is similar to Comte and Durkheim, in that he sees science as helping to 'deliver' the good society.

Max Weber

Marx, Durkheim and Comte made no distinction between the facts as revealed by science and the values that we should hold – since they believed that science could tell us what these values should be. By contrast, Max Weber (1864-1920) makes a sharp distinction between value judgments and facts and he argues that we cannot derive the one from the other.

For example, research might show that divorcees are more likely to commit suicide. However, this fact does not demonstrate the truth of the value judgment that we should make divorce harder to obtain. There is nothing about the fact that logically compels us to accept the value. For example, we might argue that we should instead make it harder to get married (another value), or that people have every right to commit suicide if they wish (a third value). None of these value judgments are 'proven' by the established fact. Indeed, in Weber's view, a value can be neither proved nor disproved by the facts: they belong to different realms.

However, despite making a sharp distinction between facts and values, Weber still saw an essential role for values in sociological research. We can divide his views into four stages of the research process.

1 Values as a guide to research

Weber took the idea from phenomenology that social reality is made up of a 'meaningless infinity' of facts that make it impossible to study it in its totality. Therefore the best the researcher can do is to select certain facts and study these.

But how do we choose which facts to study? In Weber's view, we can only select them in terms of what we regard as important based on our own values – in other words, their *value relevance* to us.

Values are thus essential in enabling us to select which aspects of reality to study and in developing concepts with which to understand these aspects. For example, feminists value gender equality and this leads them to study women's oppression and to develop concepts such as patriarchy with which to understand it.

2 Data collection and hypothesis testing

While values are essential in selecting what to study, in Weber's view we must be as objective and unbiased as possible when we are actually collecting the facts, keeping our values and prejudices out of the process.

For example, we should not ask leading questions designed to give the answers that we *want* to hear: our questions should aim to get respondents to give us their view, not our own.

Once we have gathered the facts, we can use them to test a hypothesis. Again, we must keep our values out of the process – the hypothesis must stand or fall solely on whether or not it fits the observed facts.

3 Values in the interpretation of data

Values become important again when we come to interpret the data we have collected. The facts need to be set in a theoretical framework so that we can understand their significance and draw conclusions from them. In Weber's view, our choice of theoretical framework or perspective is influenced by our values. Therefore, we must be explicit about them, spelling out our values so that others can see if unconscious bias is present in our interpretation of our data.

4 Values and the sociologist as a citizen

Research findings often have very real effects on people's lives, but sociologists and scientists sometimes choose to ignore the uses to which their work is put. They argue that their job is merely to conduct objective research and discover the facts; it is for the politicians or public to decide what use to make of their findings.

Weber rejects this view. He argues that scientists and sociologists are also human beings and citizens and they must not dodge the moral and political issues their work raises by hiding behind words such as 'objectivity' or 'value freedom'. They must take moral responsibility for the harm their research may do. For example, Einstein's theories helped make the atomic bomb possible; yet subsequently he spoke out against nuclear weapons.

To summarise, Weber sees values as relevant to the sociologist in choosing what to research, in interpreting the data collected and in deciding the use to which the findings should be put. By contrast, the sociologist's values must be kept out of the actual process of fact gathering.

Value freedom and commitment

The issue of commitment that Weber raised has remained at the centre of debates about the place of the sociologist's values in research. For example, some modern positivists have shied away from any value commitments.

By contrast, Marxists, interactionists and feminists have argued for a 'committed sociology' in which the sociologist spells out the importance of their values to their research.

Modern positivists

Unlike Durkheim and Comte, who were openly committed to re-shaping society in certain ways, by the mid 20th century positivists tended to argue that their own values were irrelevant to their research. There were two reasons for this:

1 The desire to appear scientific

Science is concerned with matters of fact, not value – with 'is' questions, not 'ought' questions. Therefore, sociologists should remain morally neutral – their job is simply to establish the truth about people's behaviour, not to judge it.

Critics argue that this reflected a desire to make sociology respectable. Science has high prestige in modern society, so mimicking its ways would raise the subject's status and earn it respectability. This was particularly important in the early 20th century, when sociology was just becoming established as an academic discipline.

2 The social position of sociology

Alvin Gouldner (1975) argues that by the 1950s, American sociologists in particular had become mere 'spiritless technicians'. Earlier in the century, sociology had been a critical discipline, often challenging accepted authority. However, by the 1950s, sociologists were no longer 'problem makers' who defined their own research problems. Instead they had become 'problem takers' who hired themselves out to organisations such as business and the military, to take on and solve *their* problems for them.

Gouldner argues that, by leaving their own values behind them, sociologists were making a 'gentleman's promise' that they would not rock the boat by criticising their paymasters. Because they were simply hired hands, they saw their own values as irrelevant. This is exactly the attitude that Weber was criticising when he said that sociologists must take moral responsibility for the effects of their work.

Activity	Media

Social scientists and the military

...go to www.sociology.uk.net

Committed sociology

By contrast with the positivists, some sociologists argue for a committed sociology. For example, Gunnar Myrdal (1969) argues that sociologists should not only spell out their values – as Weber recommends – they should also openly 'take sides' by espousing the values and interests of particular individuals or groups.

Committed sociologists who advocate this approach, such as Myrdal and Gouldner, argue that it is neither possible nor desirable to keep values out of research. In Gouldner's view, value-free sociology is:

- **impossible**, because either the sociologist's own values, or those of their paymasters, are bound to be reflected in their work.
- **undesirable**, since without values to guide research, sociologists are merely selling their services to the highest bidder. For example, Gouldner argues that:

'From such a standpoint, there is no reason why one cannot sell his knowledge to spread a disease just as freely as he can to fight it. Indeed, some sociologists have had no hesitation about doing market research designed to sell more cigarettes, although well aware of the implications of recent cancer research.'

Whose side are we on?

If all sociology is influenced by values, this means the sociologist must inevitably take sides. By not choosing a side, the sociologist is in fact taking the side of the more powerful against the less powerful.

The interactionist Howard Becker (1970) asks, 'Whose side are we on?' He argues that values are always

present in sociology. Traditionally, however, positivists and functionalists have tended to take the viewpoint of powerful groups – police, psychiatrists and so on.

Becker argues that instead of seeing things from the perspective of these 'overdogs', sociologists should adopt a compassionate stance and take the side of the underdogs – the criminals, mental patients and other powerless groups. This is partly because less is known about these groups and their story needs to be told in order to redress the balance. By identifying with the underdog and giving them a voice, we can reveal a previously hidden side of social reality.

For example, by empathising with the mental patient, we can show the hidden rationality of behaviour that the psychiatrist thinks of as irrational. In fact, as the interactionist Erving Goffman (1968) argues, to describe the situation of the mental patient faithfully, we have to take their side. We have to be biased in favour of the patient and against the psychiatrist.

This emphasis on identifying and empathising with the powerless has clear links to the kinds of research methods favoured by interactionists. They have a strong preference for qualitative methods such as participant observation, which they see as revealing the meanings of these 'outsiders'.

However, Gouldner criticises Becker for taking a romantic and sentimental approach to disadvantaged groups. He accuses Becker of being concerned only with those who are 'on their backs' – the misunderstood, negatively labelled, exotic specimens of deviant behaviour.

Instead, Gouldner adopts a Marxist perspective. He argues that sociologists should take the side of those who are 'fighting back' – the political radicals struggling to change society. Sociology should not confine itself to describing the viewpoint of the underdog. It should be committed to ending their oppression by unmasking the ways in which the powerful maintain their position.

Funding and careers

Most sociological research is funded by someone other than sociologists themselves. Funding sources include government departments, businesses and voluntary organisations. Often, the body that pays for the research controls the direction it takes and the kinds of questions it asks – and fails to ask. Thus the sociologist's work is likely to embody the values and interests of their paymasters. Sometimes, funding bodies may block publication of the research if its findings prove unacceptable.

Sociologists may also wish to further their careers and reputations, and this may influence their choice of topic (for example, choosing something that is in fashion), their research questions and how they interpret their findings. Some may censor themselves for fear that being too outspoken will harm their career prospects or even cost them their job. Sociologists in university departments are also likely to be under pressure to publish research, perhaps regardless of its quality or usefulness.

For Gouldner, all research is inevitably influenced by values – whether it is the values of the sociologist, or those of the funding body that pays for the research.

Perspectives and methods

Different sociological perspectives can be seen as embodying different assumptions and values about how society is or should be. For example:

- **Feminism** sees society as based on gender inequality and promotes the rights of women.
- **Functionalism** sees society as harmonious and espouses conservative values that favour the status quo.
- **Marxism** sees society as conflict-ridden and strives for a classless society.

These assumptions and values influence the topics that sociologists of different perspectives choose to research, the concepts they develop and the conclusions they reach. For example, functionalists have concluded that inequality is beneficial for society, whereas Marxists conclude that it produces exploitation of the poor by the rich.

Similarly, there is a link between sociologists' methods and their value-stance. For example, interactionists' preference for qualitative methods fits with their desire to empathise with the underdog, since such methods give them access to the actor's meanings. Likewise, the functionalist and positivist tendency to take the side of the 'establishment' and the viewpoint of those in authority fits with their uncritical acceptance of official statistics produced by government. Thus both interactionists and functionalists can be accused of selecting methods that produce facts that reflect their values and outlook.

Objectivity and relativism

If all perspectives involve values, are their findings just a reflection of their values, rather than a true picture of society? If so, there would be no way of deciding which of these different versions of reality – if any – was true.

One version of this idea is known as relativism. Relativism argues that:

- Different groups, cultures and individuals – including sociologists – have different views as to what is true. Each sees the world in their own way, through their own perspectives, concepts, values and interests.
- There is no independent way of judging whether any view is truer than any other.

All sociologists would agree with the first statement. For example, as we saw in Chapter 1, different cultures hold often widely different religious beliefs that affect what they believe to be true.

However, relativism goes much further. It argues that there is no absolute or objective truth – just truths plural. What you believe is true, *is* true – for you. What I believe is true, *is* true – but only for me. So if you believe the earth is round, while I think it is flat, there is no way of saying who is right.

Relativism and postmodernism

In sociology, postmodernists take a relativist view of knowledge. They reject the idea that any one account of the social world is superior to any other – there are no 'privileged accounts' that have special access to the truth. Any perspective that claims to have the truth, such as Marxism, is just a meta-narrative or 'big story'. All knowledge, from whatever perspective, is based on values and assumptions and thus no perspective has any special claim to be true.

Of course, if this is correct, then it must apply to postmodernism too – which leads to the paradoxical conclusion that we shouldn't believe what postmodernism says either! In other words, relativism is self-defeating, since it claims to be telling us something true, while simultaneously telling us that no one can tell us what is true.

In practice, sociologists rarely go this far. After all, there is a real factual world 'out there', in which women generally do more housework than men, in which ethnic background may affect a person's life chances and so on. Regardless of our values, we can observe and record these facts. And once we have established the existence of such facts, they can be used to judge the worth of competing theories. In the end, it matters less whether a theory contains certain values, than whether it can explain the world we observe.

Topic summary

The early positivists and Marx believed we could discover objective scientific knowledge and use it to improve society. **Weber** argued that values are essential in deciding what to research, in interpreting findings and in determining how they should be used, but must be kept out of the data-collection process. However, **20th century positivists** claimed to be 'value-free', leading **Gouldner** to accuse them of being subservient to their paymasters. **Becker** argues that sociologists should take the side of the underdog. The values of those **funding** the research play a part in determining what gets researched. **Sociologists' own values** influence the kinds of research questions they ask, their methods and findings.

EXAMINING OBJECTIVITY AND VALUES IN SOCIOLOGY

QuickCheck Questions

Check your answers at www.sociology.uk.net

1 According to Weber, which is the stage of research into which values must not be allowed to enter?

2 True or false? Relativism argues that everyone's view of the world is equally valid.

3 What is Gouldner's main criticism of modern positivist sociologists?

4 Why do interactionists argue we should see things from the point of view of the underdog?

5 Explain what is meant by 'objectivity'.

6 Why do many sociologists wish to be seen as scientific?

Questions to try

Item A

Some sociologists argue that their research should take the side of the underdog. For example, Becker points out that traditionally, sociology has tended to take the side of powerful groups in society, often accepting their view of the world. As a result, the standpoints of less powerful groups have been largely hidden. Becker therefore argues that sociology should identify with the underdog, empathise with them and uncover their view of the world.

However, others have argued that there is no place for values in sociology and that sociologists should take an objective, 'value-neutral' approach to research.

1 Outline and explain two criticisms of the claim that sociologists can keep values out of their research. (10 marks)

2 Applying material from Item A and your knowledge, evaluate the view that sociologists should 'take the side of the underdog' and be committed to changing society. (20 marks)

The Examiner's Advice

Q1 Spend about 15 minutes on this question. Divide your time fairly equally between the two criticisms. You don't need a separate introduction; just start on your first criticism. Possible criticisms include the view that values are essential in choosing research topics or in interpreting research findings; that choice of research method involves values, and the influence of the values of those who fund the research.

Choose two criticisms and describe each of these in some detail, explaining how it criticises the claim that sociologists can keep values out of research. Do this by creating a 'chain of reasoning' (see Box 4.1 in chapter 4). For example, Weber argues that social reality is a meaningless infinity of facts and so it would be impossible for the sociologist to study it all. This means that sociologists have to use their values to select what is important to study.

You can apply examples of how different perspectives choose to study different topics based on their values. Use concepts and issues such as value relevance, data interpretation, choice of method, and influence of theoretical perspective.

Q2 Spend about 30 minutes on this question. Keep focused on whether it is *desirable* for values to enter into research, rather than on whether it is *possible* to keep them out. Explain the different views of this issue, including those of Weber, positivists, Becker, Gouldner and postmodernists.

Apply material from the Item where possible, linking this to your own knowledge. Use examples from other topic areas such as crime and deviance or from sociological perspectives, but make sure you apply them to the issue of values. Create a chain of reasoning. For example, Becker argues that functionalists and positivists have taken the side of the powerful, distorting our view of social reality. Sociologists should redress the balance by using empathetic methods to give voice to the underdogs.

Use concepts and issues such as value freedom, moral responsibility of sociologists as citizens, revealing underdogs' meanings, empathetic research, the influence of theoretical perspective, committed sociology, objectivity, science, funding, careers and relativism. Rather than leaving evaluation to a separate 'block' at the end, evaluate each view as you go.

Are we just puppets, pulled by the strings of society?

GETTING STARTED

A In pairs, choose two of the following topics. Make a list of the concepts, studies and issues that you already know in relation to functionalist views on your chosen topics.

1 Education
2 Families and households
3 Beliefs in society
4 Crime and deviance

B Combine your answers as a class.

1 What similarities are there between the functionalist views on these four topics?

2 What do their views on these specific topics tell you about their views on society as a whole?

Learning objectives

After studying this Topic, you should:

- Know the main features of the functionalist view of the social system.
- Understand Merton's contribution to the development of functionalism.
- Be able to evaluate the strengths and limitations of the functionalist perspective on society.

FUNCTIONALISM

The first major theoretical perspective we deal with in this chapter is functionalism. Many of the key ideas of functionalism can be traced back to Emile Durkheim in the 19th century.

However, it was Talcott Parsons (1902-79) who developed functionalism as a systematic theory of society in the mid 20th century. Parsons' theory became the basis of the dominant school of thought in sociology during the 1950s and 1960s, especially in the United States.

Functionalism is a macro, structural theory. It focuses on the needs of the social system as a whole and how these needs shape all the main features of society. It is also a consensus theory. It sees society as based on a consensus or agreement among its members about values, goals and rules.

Functionalism is a modernist theory that shares the goals of the Enlightenment project. Functionalists believe that we can obtain true knowledge of the functioning of society and that this knowledge can be used to improve society.

Society as a system

In describing society, functionalists often use an *organic analogy* – in other words, they say that society is like a biological organism. Parsons (1970) identifies three similarities between society and a biological organism.

1 **System** Organisms, such as the human body, and societies are both self-regulating systems of inter-related, interdependent parts that fit together in fixed ways. In the body, these parts are organs, cells etc. In society, the parts are institutions (the education system, the family), individual roles (such as teacher, mother) etc.

2 **System needs** Organisms have needs, such as nutrition for example. If these are not met, the organism will die. Functionalists see the social system as having basic needs that must be met if it is to survive. For example, its members must be socialised if society is to continue.

3 **Functions** For functionalists, the function of any part of a system is the contribution it makes to meeting the system's needs and thus ensuring its survival. For example, the circulatory system of the body carries nutrients and oxygen to the tissues. Similarly, the economy helps maintain the social system by meeting the need for food and shelter.

Analysis and Evaluation
What other characteristics do organisms have? Do societies have these characteristics too?

Value consensus and social order

For Parsons, the central question that sociology tries to answer is 'how is social order possible?' How are individuals able to cooperate harmoniously?

Parsons argues that social order is achieved through the existence of a shared culture or, in his words, a central value system. A culture is a set of norms, values, beliefs and goals shared by members of a society. It provides a framework that allows individuals to cooperate by laying down rules about how they should behave and what others may expect of them, defining the goals they should pursue, and so on. Social order is only possible so long as members of society agree on these norms and values. Parsons calls this agreement *value consensus*. Value consensus is the glue that holds society together.

Integration of individuals

The basic function of the value consensus is therefore to make social order possible. It does this by integrating individuals into the social system, thereby directing them towards meeting the system's needs. For example, the system has to ensure that people's material needs are met, and so the consensus may include a general value about the need for people to work. To achieve this goal, there also needs to be a set of specific rules of conduct or norms – for example about punctuality, how to obtain jobs etc.

For Parsons, the system has two mechanisms for ensuring that individuals conform to shared norms and meet the system's needs:

- **Socialisation** The social system can ensure that its needs are met by teaching individuals to want to do what it requires them to do. Through the socialisation process, individuals internalise the system's norms and values so that society becomes part of their personality structure. Different agencies of socialisation, such as the family, education system, media and religion, all contribute to this process.

- **Social control** Positive sanctions reward conformity, while negative ones punish deviance. For example, if the value system stresses individual achievement through educational success, those who conform may be rewarded with college diplomas, while those who deviate by dropping out may be stigmatised as layabouts.

Because individuals are integrated, through socialisation and social control, into a shared value system, their behaviour

Box 3.10   **Durkheim and functionalism**

Emile Durkheim (1858–1917) was the most important forerunner of functionalism. He was concerned by rapid social change and the transition to modern industrial society. He saw this as a change from a simple social structure to one with a complex, specialised division of labour.

Traditional society was based on 'mechanical solidarity' with little division of labour, where all its members were fairly alike. A strong *collective conscience* bound them so tightly together that individuals in the modern sense did not really exist. However, in modern society, the division of labour promotes differences between groups and weakens social solidarity. It brings greater freedom for the individual, but this must be regulated to prevent extreme egoism destroying all social bonds. Similarly, rapid change undermines old norms without creating clear new ones, throwing people into a state of anomie or normlessness that threatens social cohesion. These ideas are echoed in the functionalists' concern with social order and value consensus.

Another contribution of Durkheim's is the idea that society exists as a separate entity over and above its members – a system of external 'social facts' shaping their behaviour to serve society's needs. This is similar to Parsons' idea of a social system with its own needs. Similarly, Durkheim's belief that social facts can be explained in terms of their function is the basic principle of functionalist analysis.

is oriented towards pursuing society's shared goals and meeting its needs. The behaviour of each individual will be relatively predictable and stable, allowing cooperation between them. This integration into the shared normative order makes orderly social life possible. From these basic ideas, Parsons builds up a more detailed model of the social system.

The parts of the social system

We can take a 'building block' approach to describing Parsons' model of the social system. At the bottom, so to speak, we have individual *actions*. Each action we perform is governed by specific *norms* or rules. These norms come in 'clusters' called *status-roles*. Statuses are the positions that exist in a given social system; for example, 'teacher'. Roles are sets of norms that tell us how the occupant of a status must carry out their duties – for example, teachers must not show favouritism, must be knowledgeable and so on.

Status-roles also come in clusters, known as institutions. For example, the family is an institution made up of the related roles of father, mother, child, etc. In turn, related institutions are grouped together into *sub-systems*. For example, shops, farms, factories, banks and so on all form part of the economic sub-system, whose function is to meet society's material needs. Finally, these sub-systems together make up the *social system* as a whole.

The system's needs

As we have seen, for Parsons society is a system with its own needs. The shared value system coordinates the different parts of society to ensure that the system's needs are met. But what exactly are the system's needs?

Parsons identifies four basic needs, sometimes known as the 'AGIL schema' (from their initial letters). Each need is met by a separate sub-system of institutions:

1   **Adaptation** The social system meets its members' material needs through the economic sub-system.
2   **Goal attainment** Society needs to set goals and allocate resources to achieve them. This is the function of the political sub-system, through institutions such as parliament.
3   **Integration** The different parts of the system must be integrated together to pursue shared goals. This is the role of the sub-system of religion, education and the media.
4   **Latency** refers to processes that maintain society over time. The kinship sub-system provides *pattern maintenance* (socialising individuals to go on performing the roles society requires) and *tension management* (a place to 'let off steam' after the stresses of work).

Parsons describes adaptation and goal attainment as *instrumental* needs – instrumental refers to the means to an end, such as producing food to sustain the population. He describes integration and latency as *expressive* needs, since they involve the expression or channelling of emotions. By carrying out their respective functions, the four sub-systems ensure that all society's needs are met and social stability is maintained.

Activity   **Research**

The social system

...go to www.sociology.uk.net

Social change

Parsons identifies two types of society – traditional and modern. Each has its own set of norms. For example, in modern society we pursue our *individual* self-interest, *achieve* our status and are all judged by the same *universalistic* standards (such as equality before the law). By contrast, in traditional societies, individuals are expected to put *collective* interests first, status is *ascribed* and they are judged by *particularistic* standards (such as different laws for nobles and commoners).

If there are two types of society, how do societies change from one to the other? For Parsons, change is a gradual, evolutionary process of increasing complexity and structural differentiation. The organic analogy is relevant here. Organisms have evolved from simple structures like amoebas, where a single cell performs all the essential functions, to complex organisms like humans with many different organs, each performing a specialised function.

Similarly, societies move from simple to complex structures. For example, in traditional society, a single institution – the kinship system – performs many functions. It organises production and consumption (adaptation), often provides political leadership (goal attainment), socialises its members (latency) and performs religious functions (integration).

However, as societies develop, the kinship system loses these functions – to factories, political parties, schools, churches and so on. Parsons calls this *structural differentiation* – a gradual process in which separate, functionally specialised institutions develop, each meeting a different need.

In addition to the process of structural differentiation, Parsons also sees gradual change occurring through *moving (or dynamic) equilibrium*. As a change occurs in one part of the system, it produces compensatory changes in other parts. Thus, the rise of industry brings a change in the family from extended to nuclear. In this way society gradually changes from one type to another.

Merton's internal critique of functionalism

Criticisms of Parsons' systems theory have come from both outside and inside functionalism. Within functionalism, the most significant criticisms come from Robert K. Merton (1968). He criticises three key assumptions of Parsons.

1   **Indispensability** Parsons assumes that everything in society – the family, religion and so on – is functionally indispensable *in its existing form*. Merton argues that this is just an untested assumption and he points to the possibility of 'functional alternatives'. For example, Parsons assumes that primary socialisation is best performed by the nuclear family, but it may be that one-parent families or communes do it just as well or better.

2   **Functional unity** Parsons assumes that all parts of society are tightly integrated into a single whole or 'unity' and that each part is functional for all the rest. Similarly, he assumes that change in one part will have a 'knock-on' effect on all other parts. However, neither of these assumptions is necessarily true. Complex modern societies have many parts, some of which may be only distantly 'related' to one another. Instead of functional unity, some parts may have 'functional autonomy' (independence) from others. It is hard to see the connections between, say, the structure of banking and the rules of netball.

3   **Universal functionalism** Parsons assumes that everything in society performs a positive function for society as a whole. Yet some things may be functional for some groups and dysfunctional for others. The idea of dysfunction (negative function) introduces a neglected note into functionalism, by suggesting that there may be

conflicts of interest and that some groups may have the power to keep arrangements in place that benefit them at the expense of others. Critics writing from a conflict perspective have developed this idea further.

The central point behind Merton's criticisms is that we cannot simply assume, as Parsons does, that society is always and necessarily a smooth-running, well-integrated system.

Analysis and Evaluation

Does unemployment have a positive function for (a) society as a whole; (b) the unemployed; (c) other groups? If so, what is it?

Manifest and latent functions

Merton also contributes a useful distinction between 'manifest' and 'latent' functions. He cites the example of the Hopi Indians who, in times of drought, perform a rain-dance with the aim of magically producing rain. This is its *manifest* or intended function. From a scientific viewpoint, of course, this is unlikely to achieve its goal.

However, the ritual may also have an unintended or *latent* function – such as promoting a sense of solidarity in times of hardship, when individuals might be tempted to look after themselves at the expense of others. Merton's distinction is therefore useful in helping to reveal the hidden connections between social phenomena, which the actors themselves may not be aware of.

External critiques of functionalism

While Merton's criticisms came from within functionalism, many far less sympathetic writers have attacked functionalism from the outside. We can divide these criticisms into four kinds.

1 Logical criticisms

Critics argue that functionalism is teleological. Teleology is the idea that things exist because of their effect or function. For example, the functionalist claim that the family exists because children need to be socialised is teleological – it explains the existence of the family in terms of its effect.

However, critics argue that a real explanation of something is one that identifies its cause – and logically, a cause must come *before* its effect. By contrast, functionalism explains the existence of one thing (the family) in terms of something else that can only be its *effect* (socialisation), since socialisation can only come *after* we have families.

Functionalism is also criticised for being unscientific. For many, a theory is only scientific if in principle it is falsifiable by testing. Yet this is not true of functionalism. For example, functionalists see deviance as both dysfunctional (since society's needs can only be met if individuals conform) *and* functional (for example by reinforcing social solidarity). If deviance is both functional and dysfunctional, then the theory cannot be disproved and is unscientific.

2 Conflict perspective criticisms

Conflict theorists such as Marxists criticise functionalism for its inability to explain conflict and change. This inability arises partly out of the organic analogy: organisms are relatively stable and harmonious systems in which all the parts work together for the common good.

Marxists argue that society is not a harmonious whole. Rather, it is based on exploitation and divided into classes with conflicting interests and unequal power. Stability is simply the result of the dominant class being able to prevent change by using coercion (force) or ideological manipulation. In this view, 'shared' values are merely a cloak concealing the interests of the dominant class.

Conflict theorists see functionalism as a *conservative ideology* legitimating the status quo. Its focus on harmony and stability rather than conflict and change, along with its assumptions of 'universal functionalism' and 'indispensability', all help to justify the existing social order as inevitable and desirable. Critics argue that this approach legitimates the privileged position of powerful groups who would have most to lose from any fundamental changes in society. (See Topic 6 on Marxist approaches.)

3 Action perspective criticisms

From an action perspective, Dennis Wrong (1961) criticises functionalism's 'over-socialised' or *deterministic* view of the individual. He describes the functionalist view as follows: the social system uses socialisation to shape people's behaviour so that they will meet the system's needs by performing their prescribed roles. Individuals have no free will or choice – they are mere puppets whose strings are pulled by the social system. From an action perspective, this is fundamentally mistaken. While functionalism sees human beings as shaped by society, the action approach takes the opposite view – that individuals create society by their interactions.

A related criticism is that functionalism *reifies* society – that is, treats it as a distinct 'thing' over and above individuals, with its own needs. By contrast, action approaches argue that society is not a thing 'out there' with its own independent existence. For them, the only social reality is the one that individuals construct by giving meaning to their worlds. (See Topic 8 on action approaches.)

4 Postmodernist criticisms

Postmodernists argue that functionalism assumes that society is stable and orderly. As such, it cannot account for the diversity and instability in today's postmodern society.

In the postmodernist view, functionalism is an example of a meta-narrative or 'big story' that attempts to create a model of the workings of society as a whole. However, according to postmodernists, such an overall theory is no longer possible because today's society is increasingly fragmented. (See Topic 9 on postmodernism.)

Conclusion

Functionalism seeks to answer the fundamental question of how social order is possible – even if its answer neglects conflict and is too deterministic. It can also be said that Merton's notion of dysfunctions, and his distinction between manifest and latent functions, provide useful starting points for research. It is also true that many of functionalism's critics end up 'borrowing' its basic notion that society is a system of interdependent parts.

Finally as Ian Craib (1992) notes, Parsons' theory 'has its faults, but at least it is a theory of society as a whole'.

Topic summary

Functionalism is a **structural** perspective that sees social order as based on **value consensus**. Parsons sees society as a system of interdependent parts (the organic analogy). The function of each part is to help meet the needs of the system. Individuals are **integrated** into the system through socialisation and social control. **Merton** introduces ideas of dysfunction, and manifest and latent functions. Critics argue that functionalism is a **conservative** ideology that neglects conflict, exploitation and change, and has an **over-socialised view** of individuals.

EXAMINING FUNCTIONALISM

QuickCheck Questions

Check your answers at www.sociology.uk.net

1 What is the difference between a manifest and a latent function?
2 What does Wrong mean by 'over-socialised'?
3 Is functionalism a conservative or a radical ideology?
4 According to Parsons, how do societies change?

5 What is the organic analogy?
6 Identify Parsons' four system needs.
7 Identify two agencies of a) socialisation and b) social control.

Questions to try

Item A

Functionalism is a consensus theory. It sees society as based on a set of shared values and this value consensus is the basis for social order. It is also a systems theory. It emphasises the way the social system shapes social institutions and the behaviour patterns of individuals. Society is seen as a system with its own separate existence and needs.

However, some critics claim that functionalism understates the extent of conflict in society. Others argue that functionalism is too deterministic, portraying individuals as simply the puppets of the social system.

1 Outline and explain two functionalist concepts.   (10 marks)
2 Applying material from Item A and your knowledge, evaluate the claim that functionalism understates both the extent of conflict in society and the ability of social actors to create society through interaction.   (20 marks)

The Examiner's Advice

Q1 Spend about 15 minutes on this question. Divide your time fairly equally between the two concepts. You don't need a separate introduction; just start on your first concept. Possible functionalist concepts include value consensus, social order, system needs, functions, integration of individuals, society as a system, social stability and social change.

Choose two concepts and describe each one in some detail, explaining how it contributes to functionalist theory by linking it to other functionalist concepts; these can include concepts that appear in the list above outside of the two you have chosen to focus on.

Do this by creating a 'chain of reasoning' (see Box 4.1 in chapter 4). For example, social order is society's most basic need and it is made possible by value consensus, which enables individuals to cooperate to meet society's needs by defining shared goals and rules. Socialisation and social control ensure that individuals conform to the value consensus. Apply examples from one or two topics such as education, religion, the family or crime and deviance to illustrate your explanation.

Q2 Spend about 30 minutes on this question. There are two aspects to this question: a consensus-conflict dimension and a systems-action dimension. Explain the functionalist view of these issues using some of the concepts and issues listed below. Show how these relate to the notion of society as a consensus-based system shaping individual behaviour.

Apply material from the Item in your explanation, linking this to your own knowledge. You can use examples from other topics such as religion or crime and deviance, but make sure you apply them to the theoretical issues. Use concepts and issues such as the organic analogy, value consensus, social order, socialisation, social control, integration of individuals, system needs and the AGIL schema, social change, and manifest and latent functions.

Rather than leaving evaluation to a separate 'block' at the end, evaluate ideas and issues as you go along. Focus your evaluation on the two issues in the question. Use conflict or action theories such as Marxism, feminism and interactionism to challenge the functionalist view of these issues. You can also offer a final evaluative overview at the end of your answer.

Global capitalism – past and present.

TOPIC 6

GETTING STARTED

A In pairs, choose two of the four topics below. Make a list of the concepts, studies and issues you already know in relation to Marxist views on your chosen topics.

1 Education
2 Families and households
3 Beliefs in society
4 Crime and deviance

B Combine your answers as a class.

1 What similarities are there between the Marxist views on these four topics?

2 What do their views on these specific topics tell you about their views on society as a whole?

C Compare your answers to part B with your answers to part B of the Getting Started activity on functionalism (Topic 5). What similarities and differences are there between functionalist and Marxist views of society?

Learning objectives

After studying this Topic, you should:

- Know and understand Marx's main ideas and concepts.
- Understand the differences between humanistic and structural Marxism.
- Be able to evaluate the strengths and limitations of Marxist approaches to the study of society.

MARXISM

Marxism has at least one thing in common with functionalism. It tends to share the view that society is a structure or system that shapes individuals' behaviour and ideas. However, Marxism differs sharply from functionalism in two ways:

- **Conflict of interests** Marxists reject the functionalist view that the social structure is a harmonious one based on value consensus. Instead, they see it as based on a conflict of economic interests between social classes of unequal power and wealth.

- **Instability and change** Marxists also reject functionalism's view of society as stable, and stress the possibility of sudden, profound and revolutionary change. Stability is merely the result of the dominant class being able to impose their will on society.

Marx's ideas

Marxism is a perspective based on the ideas of Karl Marx (1818–83). Like Durkheim, Marx saw both the harm caused by the modern industrial society that was taking shape in 19th century Europe, and the promise of progress to a better world that it held. Also like Durkheim, Marx believed that it was possible to understand society scientifically and that this knowledge would point the way to a better society – indeed, he described his theory as 'scientific socialism'. In these ways, Marxism is a continuation of the Enlightenment project described earlier.

Unlike functionalists, however, Marx did not see progress as a smooth and gradual evolution. Instead, he saw historical change as a contradictory process in which capitalism would increase human misery before giving way to a classless communist society in which human beings would be free to fulfil their potential.

Marx was not just a theorist; he was also a revolutionary socialist. As he himself wrote, 'Philosophers have merely interpreted the world; the point, however, is to change it'. In other words, the classless society would need to be brought into being by conscious human action.

After his death, Marx's ideas came to form the basis of communism, a political movement that was enormously influential in shaping the modern world, and Marxism became the official doctrine of the former Soviet Union and other communist states. Here we shall examine his key ideas about human history, and about capitalism and its replacement by a future communist society.

1 Historical materialism

Materialism is the view that humans are beings with material needs, such as food, clothing and shelter, and must therefore work to meet them. In doing so, they use the *forces of production* (sometimes called means of production).

In the earliest stage of human history, these forces are just unaided human labour, but over time people develop tools, machines and so on to assist in production. In working to meet their needs, humans also cooperate with one another: they enter into *social relations of production* – ways of organising production.

Over time, as the forces of production grow and develop, so too the social relations of production also change. In particular, a division of labour develops, and this eventually gives rise to a division between *two classes*:

- A class that owns the means of production
- A class of labourers.

From then on, production is directed by the class of owners to meet their own needs.

Marx refers to the forces and relations of production together as the *mode of production*. For example, currently we live in a society with a capitalist mode of production. The mode of production forms the *economic base* of society. This economic base shapes or determines all other features of society – the *superstructure* of institutions, ideas, beliefs and behaviour that arise from this base. For example, it shapes the nature of religion, law, education, the state and so on.

2 Class society and exploitation

In the earliest stage of human history, there are no classes, no private ownership and no exploitation – everyone works, and everything is shared. Marx describes this early classless society as 'primitive communism'. But as the forces of production grow, different types of class society come and go.

In class societies, one class owns the means of production. This enables them to exploit the labour of others for their own benefit. In particular, they can control society's *surplus product*. This is the difference between what the labourers actually produce and what is needed simply to keep them alive and working.

Marx identifies three successive class societies, each with its own form of exploitation:

- **Ancient society**, based on the exploitation of slaves legally tied to their owners

- **Feudal society**, based on the exploitation of serfs legally tied to the land
- **Capitalist society**, based on the exploitation of free wage labourers.

3 Capitalism

Like previous class societies, capitalism is based on a division between a class of owners, the *bourgeoisie* or capitalist class, and a class of labourers, the *proletariat* or working class. However, capitalism has three distinctive features.

Firstly, unlike slaves or serfs, the proletariat are legally free and separated from the means of production. Because they do not own any means of production, they have to sell their labour power to the bourgeoisie in return for wages in order to survive.

However, this is not an equal exchange. The proletariat do not receive the value of the goods that their labour produces, but only the cost of subsistence – of keeping them alive. The difference between the two is the *surplus value* – the profit that the capitalist makes by selling the commodities that the proletariat have produced.

Secondly, through competition between capitalists, ownership of the means of production becomes *concentrated* in fewer and fewer hands (culminating in today's giant transnational corporations). This competition drives small independent producers into the ranks of the proletariat, until ultimately the vast majority are proletarianised. Competition also forces capitalists to pay the lowest wages possible, causing the *immiseration* (impoverishment) of the proletariat.

Thirdly, capitalism continually expands the forces of production in its pursuit of profit. Production becomes concentrated in ever-larger units. Meanwhile, technological advances de-skill the workforce.

Concentration of ownership and the deskilling of the proletariat together produce class *polarisation*. That is, society divides into a minority capitalist class and a majority working class that in Marx's words, 'face each other as two warring camps'.

4 Class consciousness

According to Marx, capitalism sows the seeds of its own destruction. For example, by polarising the classes, bringing the proletariat together in ever-larger numbers, and driving down their wages, capitalism creates the conditions under which the working class can develop a consciousness of its own economic and political interests in opposition to those of its exploiters.

As a result, the proletariat moves from being merely a *class in itself* (one whose members occupy the same economic position), to becoming a *class for itself*, whose members are class conscious – aware of the need to overthrow capitalism.

5 Ideology

For Marx, the class that owns the means of production also owns and controls the means of *mental* production – the production of ideas. The dominant ideas in society are therefore the ideas of the economically dominant class. The institutions that produce and spread ideas, such as religion, education and the media, all serve the dominant class by producing ideologies – sets of ideas and beliefs that legitimise (justify) the existing social order as desirable or inevitable.

Ideology fosters a *false consciousness* in the subordinate classes and helps to sustain class inequality. However, as capitalism impoverishes the workers, so they develop class consciousness. They see through capitalist ideology and become conscious of their true position as 'wage slaves'.

6 Alienation

Marx believes that our true nature is based on our capacity to create things to meet our needs. Alienation is the result of our loss of control over our labour and its products and therefore our separation from our true nature.

Alienation exists in all class societies, because the owners control the production process for their own needs. However, under capitalism alienation reaches its peak, for two reasons:

- Workers are completely separated from and have no control over the forces of production.
- The division of labour is at its most intense and detailed: the worker is reduced to an unskilled labourer mindlessly repeating a meaningless task.

Marx also sees religion as originating in the alienation of human labour (see Chapter 1, Topic 1).

7 The state, revolution and communism

Marx defines the state as 'armed bodies of men' – the army, police, prisons, courts and so on. The state exists to protect the interests of the class of owners who control it. As such, they form the *ruling class*. They use the state as a weapon in the class struggle, to protect their property, suppress opposition and prevent revolution. Any class that wishes to lead a revolution and become the economically dominant class must overthrow the existing ruling class.

Previous revolutions had always been one minority class overthrowing another, but in Marx's view, the proletarian revolution that overthrows capitalism will be the first revolution by the majority against the minority. It will:

- Abolish the state and create a classless communist society.
- Abolish exploitation, replace private ownership with social ownership, and replace production for profit with production to satisfy human needs.

- End alienation as humans regain control of their labour and its products.

Marx predicted the ultimate victory of the proletarian revolution and the establishment of communist society on a world scale. He expected the revolution to occur first of all in the most advanced capitalist societies. However, he wrote relatively little about exactly how the revolution would come about. This has led to debate among Marxists ever since.

Criticisms of Marx

Several criticisms have been made of Marx's theory of society.

Marx's view of class

- Marx has a simplistic, one-dimensional view of inequality – he sees class as the only important division. Weber argues that status and power differences can also be important sources of inequality, independently of class. For example, a 'power elite' can rule without actually owning the means of production, as it did in the former Soviet Union. Similarly, feminists argue that gender is a more fundamental source of inequality than class.
- Marx's two-class model is also simplistic. For example, Weber sub-divides the proletariat into skilled and unskilled classes, and includes a white-collar middle class of office workers and a petty bourgeoisie (small capitalists).
- Class polarisation has not occurred. Instead of the middle class being swallowed up by an expanding proletariat, it has grown, while the industrial working class has shrunk, at least in Western societies. On the other hand, the proletariat in countries such as China and India is growing as a result of globalisation.

Economic determinism

Marx's base-superstructure model is criticised for economic determinism – the view that economic factors are the sole cause of everything in society, including social change. Critics argue that this fails to recognise that humans have free will and can bring about change through their conscious actions.

Similarly, the base-superstructure model neglects the role of *ideas*. For example, Weber argues that it was the emergence of a new set of ideas, those of Calvinistic Protestantism, which helped to bring modern capitalism into being.

A related criticism is that Marx's predictions of revolution have not come true. Marx predicted that revolution would occur in the most advanced capitalist countries, such as Western Europe and North America. However, it is only economically backward countries such as Russia in 1917 that have seen Marxist-led revolutions.

However, in defence of Marx, while there are examples of economic determinism in his work, there are also instances where he argues that 'men make their own history' and that the working class would free themselves by their own conscious efforts – indicating that he gave a role to human action as well as economic forces.

Activity	Media
Karl Marx	

...go to www.sociology.uk.net

The 'two Marxisms'

Since Marx's death in 1883, the absence of revolutions in the West has led many Marxists to reject the economic determinism of the base-superstructure model. Instead, they have tried to explain why capitalism has persisted and how it might be overthrown. We can identify two broad approaches to these questions, which Alvin Gouldner (1973) describes as:

- **Humanistic or critical Marxism** This has some similarities with action theories and interpretive sociology.
- **Scientific or structuralist Marxism** As its name indicates, this is a structural approach and has similarities with positivist sociology.

Table 3A outlines the key differences between the two approaches.

Table 3A	The two Marxisms

Humanistic or critical Marxism	Scientific or structuralist Marxism
Example: Antonio Gramsci	Example: Louis Althusser
Draws on Marx's early writings, where he focuses on *alienation* and people's subjective experience of the world.	Draws on Marx's later work, where he writes about the *laws* of capitalist development working with 'iron necessity' towards inevitable results.
Marxism is a *political critique* of capitalism as alienating and inhuman, and a call to overthrow it.	Marxism is a *science*. It discovers the laws that govern the workings of capitalism.
Voluntarism: humans have free will. They are active agents who make their own history. Their consciousness and ideas are central in changing the world.	*Determinism*: structural factors determine the course of history. Individuals are passive puppets – victims of ideology manipulated by forces beyond their control.
Socialism will come about when people become *conscious* of the need to overthrow capitalism. *Encourages* political action, believing the time is always ripe for revolution.	Socialism will come about only when the *contradictions* of capitalism ultimately bring about the system's inevitable collapse. Tends to *discourage* political action.

Gramsci and hegemony

The most important example of humanistic Marxism is Antonio Gramsci (1891-1937). Gramsci introduces the concept of *hegemony*, or ideological and moral leadership of society, to explain how the ruling class maintains its position. He argues that the proletariat must develop its own 'counter-hegemony' to win the leadership of society from the bourgeoisie.

Gramsci was the first leader of the Italian Communist Party during the 1920s. He rejects economic determinism as an explanation of change: the transition from capitalism to communism will never come about simply as a result of economic forces. Even though factors such as mass unemployment and falling wages may create the preconditions for revolution, ideas play a central role in determining whether or not change will actually occur.

This can be seen in Gramsci's concept of hegemony. Gramsci sees the ruling class maintaining its dominance over society in two ways:

- **Coercion**: it uses the army, police, prisons and courts of the capitalist state to force other classes to accept its rule.
- **Consent (hegemony)**: it uses ideas and values to persuade the subordinate classes that its rule is legitimate.

Hegemony and revolution

In advanced capitalist societies, the ruling class rely heavily on consent to maintain their rule. Gramsci agrees with Marx that they are able to do so because they control the institutions that produce and spread ideas, such as the media, the education system and religion. So long as the rest of society accepts ruling-class hegemony, there will not be a revolution, even when the economic conditions might seem favourable.

However, the hegemony of the ruling class is never complete, for two reasons:

- **The ruling class are a minority**. To rule, they need to create a *power bloc* by making alliances with other groups, such as the middle classes. They must therefore make ideological compromises to take account of the interests of their allies.
- **The proletariat have a dual consciousness**. Their ideas are influenced not only by bourgeois ideology, but also by their material conditions of life – the poverty and exploitation they experience. This means they can 'see through' the dominant ideology to some degree.

Therefore there is always the possibility of ruling-class hegemony being undermined, particularly at times of economic crisis, when the worsening material conditions and increased poverty of the proletariat cause them to question the status quo.

However, this will only lead to revolution if the proletariat are able to construct a *counter-hegemonic bloc*. In other words, they must be able to offer moral and ideological leadership to society.

In Gramsci's view, the working class can only win this battle for ideas by producing their own 'organic intellectuals'. By this he means a body of class conscious workers, organised into a revolutionary political party, who are able to formulate an alternative vision of how society could be run in the future.

This counter-hegemony would win ideological leadership from the ruling class by offering a new vision of how society should be organised, based on socialist rather than capitalist values.

Evaluation of Gramsci

Gramsci is accused of over-emphasising the role of ideas and under-emphasising the role of both state coercion and economic factors.

For example, workers may see through ruling-class ideology and wish to overthrow capitalism, but be reluctant to try because they fear state repression or unemployment. They may tolerate capitalism simply because they feel they have no choice, not because they accept the moral leadership of the ruling class.

Sociologists working within a Marxist framework have adopted a similar approach to Gramsci. They stress the role of ideas and consciousness as the basis for resisting domination and changing society.

For example, Paul Willis (1977) describes the working-class lads he studied as 'partially penetrating' bourgeois ideology – seeing through the school's ideology to recognise that meritocracy is a myth.

These writers often draw on perspectives such as interactionism (Topic 8) that emphasise the role of ideas and meanings as the basis for action. Because they combine Marxism with other approaches, they are sometimes called neo-Marxists – 'new Marxists'.

Althusser's structuralist Marxism

While humanistic Marxists see humans as creative beings, able to make history through their conscious actions, for structuralist Marxists, it is not people's actions but social structures that really shape history and these are the proper subject of scientific enquiry. The task of the sociologist is to reveal how these structures work.

The most important structuralist Marxist thinker is Louis Althusser (1918-90), a leading intellectual of the French Communist Party. Althusser's version of Marxism rejects both economic determinism and humanism.

Criticisms of the base-superstructure model

In Marx's original base-superstructure model, society's economic base determines its superstructure of institutions, ideologies and actions. Contradictions in the base cause changes in the superstructure and ultimately bring about the downfall of capitalism.

Althusser rejects this model in favour of a more complex one, which Craib calls 'structural determinism'. In this model, capitalist society has three structures or levels:

- **The economic level**, comprising all those activities that involve producing something in order to satisfy a need.
- **The political level**, comprising all forms of organisation.
- **The ideological level**, involving the ways that people see themselves and their world.

In the base-superstructure model, there is a one-way causality: the economic level determines everything about the other two levels. By contrast, in Althusser's model, the political and ideological levels have *relative autonomy* or partial independence from the economic level. The political and ideological levels are not a mere reflection of the economic level, and they can even affect what happens to the economy. Instead of a one-way causality, we have *two-way causality* (see Box 3.11).

Ideological and repressive state apparatuses

Although the economic level dominates in capitalism, the political and ideological levels perform indispensable functions. For example, if capitalism is to continue, future workers must be socialised, workers who rebel must be punished, and so on.

In Althusser's model, the state performs political and ideological functions that ensure the reproduction of capitalism. He divides the *state* into two 'apparatuses':

- **The repressive state apparatuses (RSAs)** These are the 'armed bodies of men' – the army, police, prisons and so on – that coerce the working class into complying with the will of the bourgeoisie. This is how Marxists have traditionally seen the state.
- **The ideological state apparatuses (ISAs)** These include the media, the education system, the family, reformist political parties, trade unions and other institutions. ISAs ideologically manipulate the working class into accepting capitalism as legitimate. This is a much wider definition of the state than the traditional Marxist view.

This is similar to Gramsci's distinction between coercion (the RSAs) and consent (the ISAs) as different ways of securing the dominance of the bourgeoisie.

Althusser's criticisms of humanism

For structuralist Marxists, our sense of free will, choice and creativity is an illusion. The truth is that everything about us is the product of underlying social structures. As Ian Craib (1992) puts it, society is a puppet theatre, we are merely puppets, and these unseen structures are the hidden puppet master, determining all our thoughts and actions.

Althusser is therefore dismissive of humanism, including humanistic Marxists such as Gramsci. Humanists believe

---

Box 3.11	Althusser's structures: an analogy

Ian Craib (1992) uses an analogy to picture the ideas of relative autonomy and two-way causality. He compares the three levels in Althusser's model of society to a three-storey building housing a family business.

On the ground floor is a shop, while the first floor houses the office and the top floor is the family's living quarters. What goes on in the office is obviously partly affected by the nature of the activity in the shop, but there are different ways the office work might be organised, and some features of it might be the same whatever the kind of business. Similarly, the standard of living and lifestyle enjoyed by the owners on the top floor is affected by the business

they run (for example, they may be well off but cannot take long holidays away from it), but family life has its own dynamics and may be shaped by quite separate factors. And not only are the goings-on upstairs at least partly independent of what happens down below, they may also have an effect on it. For example, a divorce settlement may lead to the business being split up or sold off.

> Which parts of the analogy illustrate (a) relative autonomy; (b) two-way causality between structures?

that people can use their creativity, reason and free will to change society. For example, humanistic Marxists believe that a socialist revolution will come about as a result of the working class actively developing class consciousness and consciously choosing to overthrow capitalism.

Althusser argues that we are not the free agents that humanists think we are – our belief that we possess free will and choice is simply false consciousness produced by the ideological state apparatuses. For example, we may believe that education gives us the chance to achieve what we are capable of, but this is an illusion – the 'myth of meritocracy'.

In reality, we are merely products of social structures that determine everything about us, preparing us to fit into pre-existing positions in the structure of capitalism. This is similar to Parsons' idea of status-roles, where society socialises individuals to slot into pre-existing roles that will meet society's needs.

Therefore, in Althusser's view, socialism will not come about because of a change in consciousness – as humanistic Marxists argue – but will come about because of a crisis of capitalism resulting from what Althusser calls *over-determination*: the contradictions in the three structures that occur relatively independently of each other, resulting in the collapse of the system as a whole.

Evaluation of Althusser

Althusser claims to oppose both humanism and determinism, but he is harsher on humanism. Although he rejects *economic* determinism, he simply replaces it with a more complex 'structural determinism' in which everything is determined by the three structures and their interrelationships.

For humanistic Marxists such as Gouldner, this 'scientific' approach discourages political activism because it stresses the role of structural factors that individuals can do little to affect. Similarly, the Marxist historian, E.P. Thompson (1978), criticises Althusser for ignoring the fact that it is the active struggles of the working class that can change society. He

accuses Althusser of elitism – the belief that the Communist Party knows what is best for the workers, who should therefore blindly follow the Party's lead.

In Craib's view, Althusser 'offers the most sophisticated conception of social structure available in the social sciences'. Ironically, however, while Althusser believed he was developing a scientific analysis of society to help bring about progress to a better society, his structuralist Marxism has been a major influence on theories such as postmodernism that reject the very idea that scientific knowledge can be used to improve society.

Activity	Discuss

Can ideas bring about revolution?

...go to www.sociology.uk.net

Topic Summary

Marxism is a **structural** perspective that sees society as based on class conflict. In capitalism, the bourgeoisie **exploit** the labour of the proletariat. They maintain their position through control of the **repressive state apparatus** and through **ideology** or hegemony. However, Marx believed that ultimately, revolution leading to a classless, **communist society** was inevitable.

Critics argue that Marxism is too **deterministic**. However, there are differences between Marxists. For example, **Gramsci** takes a more voluntaristic view that sees a greater role for human consciousness and action in bringing about change, whereas **Althusser** sees change as the outcome of 'structural determinism'. Other critics argue that Marx's two-class model is simplistic, and that Marxism neglects **non-class** forms of inequality such as gender and ethnicity.

EXAMINING MARXISM

QuickCheck Questions

Check your answers at www.sociology.uk.net

1 What is the difference between a 'class in itself' and a 'class for itself'?
2 Suggest two similarities between Marxism and functionalism.
3 Which part of society did Marx see as dominating all other parts?
4 What is meant by 'alienation'?
5 Identify two aspects of Marxist theory that may no longer apply to modern society.

6 What is the difference between 'determinism' and 'voluntarism'?
7 According to Marxists, how may ruling-class hegemony be maintained?
8 What is meant by the term 'repressive state apparatus'?
9 Identify three classes of labourers from different historical periods.
10 According to Marx, what are the features of communist society?

Questions to try

Item A

Marxists see class as the fundamental division in society, in which the proletariat are exploited by the capitalist owners of the means of production. The capitalist class maintain their dominance partly by force and partly by ideological control through the media, the education system and so on. However, Marxists predict that ultimately, the proletariat will overthrow capitalism by means of a revolution. For Marxists, social change is not the gradual evolutionary process seen by consensus theories.

However, other sociologists argue that class is not the only basis for inequality and that revolutions have failed to occur in advanced capitalist societies.

1 Outline and explain two criticisms of Marxist views of society. (10 marks)

2 Applying material from Item A and your knowledge, evaluate the contribution of different Marxist theorists to an understanding of society. (20 marks)

The Examiner's Advice

Q1 Spend about 15 minutes on this question. Divide your time fairly equally between the two criticisms. You don't need a separate introduction; just start on your first criticism. Possible criticisms include that class is not the only important social division; economic determinism; the failure of revolution to occur or to lead to a classless society; and people are not simply the puppets of society.

Choose two criticisms and describe each one in some detail. Start by identifying the feature of a Marxist view you are going to criticise and then explain the criticism by creating a 'chain of reasoning' (see Box 4.1 in chapter 4). For example, Marxism has a one-dimensional view of inequality, where economic class is the only important division. But Weber argues that this neglects inequalities of power and status, while others argue that it ignores gender and ethnic inequalities.

Apply examples from other topics to illustrate your explanation. For example, radical feminists argue that gender inequality originating in the patriarchal family is more fundamental than class. Use concepts and issues such as those listed above and the base-superstructure model, false consciousness, polarisation, the role of ideas, and the state.

Q2 Spend about 30 minutes on this question. It refers to 'different' Marxist theorists, so you need to consider more than one, e.g. Gramsci and Althusser as well as Marx. Explain Marx's original views, applying key concepts such as historical materialism, class, capitalism, class consciousness, ideology, alienation, the state, revolution and classless society. Show how these fit together as an overall theory of society. Then explain humanistic and structuralist variants of Marxism.

Apply material from the Item where possible, linking this to your own knowledge. Apply examples from topic areas such as education (e.g. Bowles and Gintis, Willis) or religion, but make sure you link them to issues in Marxist theory (e.g. false consciousness, ideology). Use concepts and issues such as ideological and repressive state apparatuses, hegemony, structural determinism, over-determination, as well as those listed above.

Rather than leaving evaluation to a separate 'block' at the end, evaluate ideas and issues as you go along. You should consider debates between Marxists as well as using alternative theories such as functionalism, feminism and interactionism to challenge Marxist views.

London SlutWalk: women asserting their right to dress as they wish.

GETTING STARTED

1 In pairs, write down as many feminist ideas as you can recall from topics you have already studied. Include concepts, studies, names of sociologists and issues.

2 Pool your results as a class.

3 As a class, discuss your pooled results to identify any common themes linking the issues.

Learning objectives

After studying this Topic, you should:

- Know the main types of feminist theories.
- Understand the similarities and differences between feminist theories.
- Be able to evaluate the strengths and limitations of feminist theories.

FEMINIST THEORIES

Feminism sees society as male dominated and it seeks to describe, explain and change the position of women in society. It is therefore both a theory of women's subordination and a political movement.

The roots of feminism, like those of other modernist theories, can be traced back to the 18th century Enlightenment. This proclaimed universal principles of liberty and equality, along with the idea that human reason can liberate us from ignorance and create a better society.

Feminists argued that, since both sexes have the same power of reason, these principles should apply to women as much as to men and that women's emancipation must be included as part of the Enlightenment project.

A 'first wave' of feminism appeared in the late 19th century, with the suffragettes' campaign for the right to vote. The 1960s saw a 'second wave' emerge on a global scale.

Since then, feminism has had a major influence on sociology. Feminists criticise mainstream sociology for being 'malestream' – seeing society only from a male perspective. By contrast, feminists examine society from the viewpoint of women. Feminist sociologists see their work as part of the struggle against women's subordination.

However, although all feminists oppose women's subordination, there are disagreements among feminists about its causes and how to overcome it. In this Topic, we concentrate on those feminist theories that have had most impact on sociology.

Liberal or reformist feminism

Liberals are concerned with the human and civil rights and freedoms of the individual. In keeping with the Enlightenment tradition, they believe that all human beings should have equal rights. Since both men and women are human beings, so both should have the same inalienable rights and freedoms. Reformism is the idea that progress towards equal rights can be achieved by gradual reforms or piecemeal changes in society, without the need for revolution.

Laws and policies Liberal feminists (sometimes called reformist or 'equal rights' feminists) believe women can achieve gender equality in this way. For example, they argue that laws and policies against sex discrimination in employment and education can secure equal opportunities for women.

Cultural change Liberal feminists also call for cultural change. In their view, traditional prejudices and stereotypes about gender differences are a barrier to equality. For example, beliefs that women are less rational and more dominated by emotion and instinct are used to legitimate their exclusion from decision-making roles and their confinement to childrearing and housework. Liberal feminists reject the idea that biological differences make women less competent or rational than men, or that men are biologically less emotional or nurturing.

Sex and gender

Like Ann Oakley (1972), liberal feminists distinguish between sex and gender:

- **Sex** refers to biological differences between males and females, such as their reproductive role, hormonal and physical differences.

- **Gender** refers to culturally constructed differences between the 'masculine' and 'feminine' roles and identities assigned to males and females. It includes the ideas that cultures hold about the abilities of males and females, such as whether they are capable of rationality. These ideas are transmitted through socialisation.

While sex differences are seen as fixed, gender differences vary between cultures and over time. Thus, what is considered a proper role for women in one society or at one time may be disapproved of or forbidden in another. For example, until fairly recently it was rare to see women bus drivers in Britain, but this is now quite common, while in Saudi Arabia women are forbidden to drive any vehicle.

For liberal feminists, then, sexist attitudes and stereotypical beliefs about gender are culturally constructed and transmitted through socialisation. Therefore, to achieve gender equality, we must change society's socialisation patterns. Hence, liberal feminists seek to promote appropriate role models in education and the family – for example, female teachers in traditional male subjects, or fathers taking responsibility for domestic tasks. Similarly, they challenge gender stereotyping in the media. Over time, they believe, such actions will produce cultural change and gender equality will become the norm.

Liberal feminism is an optimistic theory, very much in keeping with the Enlightenment project and its faith in progress. Liberal feminists believe that:

- **Changes in socialisation and culture** are gradually leading to more rational attitudes to gender and overcoming ignorance and prejudice.

- **Political action to introduce anti-discriminatory laws and policies** is steadily bringing about progress to a fairer society in which a person's gender is no longer important.

Liberal feminism can be seen as a critique of the functionalist view of gender roles. Functionalists such as Parsons distinguish between instrumental and expressive roles:

- **Instrumental roles** are performed in the *public sphere* of paid work, politics, and decision-making. This sphere involves rationality, detachment and objectivity.
- **Expressive roles** are performed in the *private sphere* of unpaid domestic labour, childrearing and caring for family members. This sphere involves emotion, attachment and subjectivity.

In Parsons' view, instrumental roles are the domain of men, while expressive roles are the domain of women.

Liberal feminism challenges this division. It argues that men and women are equally capable of performing roles in both spheres, and that traditional gender roles prevent both men and women from leading fulfilling lives. Liberal feminism aims to break down the barrier between the two spheres.

However, despite its critique of the functionalist view of gender divisions, liberal feminism is the feminist theory closest to a consensus view of society. Although it recognises conflicts between men and women, these are not seen as inevitable but merely a product of outdated attitudes. Moreover, women's emancipation is a 'win-win' situation from which men too will gain. For example, ending the gender division of labour would allow men to express their 'feminine' nurturing side, which current gender stereotypes force them to suppress.

Evaluation of liberal feminism

In sociology, studies conducted by liberal feminists have produced evidence documenting the extent of gender inequality and discrimination, and legitimising the demand for reform in areas such as equal pay and employment practices, media representations of gender, and so on. Their work has also helped to demonstrate that gender differences are not inborn but the result of different treatment and socialisation patterns.

However, liberal feminists are criticised for over-optimism. They see the obstacles to emancipation as simply the prejudices of individuals or irrational laws that can be gradually reformed away by the onward 'march of progress'. They ignore the possibility that there are deep-seated structures causing women's oppression, such as capitalism or patriarchy. As Sylvia Walby (1997) argues, they offer no explanation for the overall structure of gender inequality.

Marxist feminists and radical feminists argue that liberal feminism fails to recognise the underlying causes of women's subordination and that it is naïve to believe that changes in the law or attitudes will be enough to bring equality. Instead, they believe that far-reaching, revolutionary changes are needed.

Radical feminism

Radical feminism emerged in the early 1970s. Its key concept is patriarchy. Literally, this means 'rule by fathers', but it has come to mean a society in which men dominate women. Radical feminists make the following claims:

- Patriarchy is universal: male domination of women exists in all known societies. According to Shulamith Firestone (1974), the origins of patriarchy lie in women's biological capacity to bear and care for infants, since performing this role means they become dependent on males.
- Patriarchy is the primary and most fundamental form of inequality and conflict. The key division is between men and women. Men are women's main enemy.
- All men oppress all women. All men benefit from patriarchy – especially from women's unpaid domestic labour and from their sexual services.

The personal is political

For radical feminists, patriarchal oppression is direct and personal. It occurs not only in the public sphere of work and politics, but also in the private sphere of the family, domestic labour and sexual relationships. Radical feminists see the personal as political. All relationships involve power and they are political when one person dominates another. Personal relationships are therefore political because men dominate women through them. Radical feminists refer to these power relationships as *sexual politics*.

Radical feminists therefore focus on the ways in which patriarchal power is exercised through personal relationships, often through sexual or physical violence or the threat of it. This has the effect of controlling all women, not just those against whom it is exercised. For example, as Susan Brownmiller (1976) notes, fear of rape is a powerful deterrent against women going out alone at night.

> **Application**
> Suggest three ways in which patriarchal power may be exercised within the family.

Sexuality Radical feminism also sheds new light on the nature of sexuality. In general, malestream sociology regards sexuality as a natural biological urge – and therefore outside the scope of sociology.

By contrast, radical feminists argue that patriarchy constructs sexuality so as to satisfy men's desires. For example, women are portrayed in pornography as passive sex objects and penetration as the main source of sexual pleasure. Similarly, Adrienne Rich (1981) argues that men continue to force women into a narrow and unsatisfying 'compulsory heterosexuality'.

Change

Given that patriarchy and women's oppression are reproduced through personal and sexual relationships, these must be transformed if women are to be free. Radical feminists have proposed a number of solutions or strategies to achieve this. These include:

Separatism Given that men's oppression of women is exercised through intimate domestic and sexual relationships, some radical feminists advocate separatism – that is, living apart from men and thereby creating a new culture of female independence, free from patriarchy.

For example, Germaine Greer (2000) argues for the creation of all-female or 'matrilocal' households as an alternative to the heterosexual family.

Consciousness-raising Through sharing their experiences in women-only consciousness-raising groups, women come to see that other women face the same problems. This may lead to collective action, such as 'SlutWalk' marches.

Political lesbianism Many radical feminists argue that heterosexual relationships are inevitably oppressive because they involve 'sleeping with the enemy' and that lesbianism is the only non-oppressive form of sexuality.

Evaluation of radical feminism

Radical feminists' idea that the personal is political reveals how intimate relationships can involve domination. They draw attention to the political dimension of areas such as marriage, domestic labour, domestic violence, rape and pornography. However, radical feminism is criticised on several grounds.

Marxists assert that class, not patriarchy, is the primary form of inequality. They also argue that capitalism is the main cause and beneficiary of women's oppression, and not men, as radical feminism claims.

Radical feminism offers no explanation of why female subordination takes different forms in different societies. Similarly, it assumes all women are in the same position and ignores class, ethnic etc differences between women. A middle-class woman may have more in common with a middle-class man than with a working-class woman.

Anna Pollert (1996) argues that the concept of patriarchy is of little value because it involves a circular argument. For example, male violence is explained as patriarchy, while patriarchy is seen as being maintained by male violence – so patriarchy is maintaining itself!

Radical feminism has an inadequate theory of how patriarchy will be abolished. Critics argue that vague utopian notions of separatism are unlikely to be achievable. Jenny Somerville (2000) argues that heterosexual attraction makes it unlikely that the nuclear family will be replaced by single-sex households.

Patriarchy may already be in decline. Liberal feminists argue that women's position has improved greatly in recent years as a result of social reforms and changing attitudes. Better education, job opportunities etc mean that gender equality is beginning to become a reality.

While drawing attention to male violence against women, radical feminism neglects women's violence against men and violence within lesbian relationships.

Marxist feminism

Marxist feminists dismiss the liberal feminist view that women's subordination is merely the product of stereotyping or outdated attitudes. They also reject the radical feminist view that it is the result of patriarchal oppression by men. Instead, as Marxists, they see women's subordination as rooted in capitalism. Although individual men may benefit from women's subordination, the main beneficiary is capitalism.

For Marxist feminists, women's subordination in capitalist society results from their primary role as unpaid homemaker, which places them in a dependent economic position in the family. Their subordination performs a number of important functions for capitalism:

- **Women are a source of cheap, exploitable labour** for employers. They can be paid less because it is assumed they will be partially dependent on their husbands' earnings.
- **Women are a reserve army of labour** that can be moved into the labour force during economic booms and out again at times of recession. They can be treated as marginal workers in this way because it is assumed their primary role is in the home.
- **Women reproduce the labour force** through their unpaid domestic labour, both by nurturing and socialising children to become the next generation of workers and by maintaining and servicing the current generation of workers – their husbands. They do this at no cost to capitalism.
- **Women absorb anger** that would otherwise be directed at capitalism. Fran Ansley (1972) describes wives as 'takers of shit' who soak up the frustration their husbands feel because of the alienation and exploitation they suffer at work. For Marxist feminists, this explains male domestic violence against women.

Because of these links between women's subordination and capitalism, Marxist feminists argue that women's interests lie in the overthrow of capitalism.

Application

1 What do (a) nurturing and socialising the next generation of workers and (b) maintaining and servicing the current generation actually involve?

2 How might women's domestic role enable capitalists to pay male workers less?

Barrett: the ideology of familism

All Marxist feminists agree that women's subordination within the family performs important *economic* functions for capitalism. However, some argue that non-economic factors must also be taken into account if we are to understand and change women's position. For example, Michèle Barrett (1980) argues that we must give more emphasis to women's consciousness and motivations, and to the role of *ideology* in maintaining their oppression.

For example, why do women marry and live in the conventional nuclear family when this is precisely what oppresses them? According to Barrett, the answer lies in the ideology of 'familism'. This ideology presents the nuclear family and its sexual division of labour (where women perform unpaid domestic work) as natural and normal. The family is portrayed as the only place where women can attain fulfilment, through motherhood, intimacy and sexual satisfaction. This ideology helps to keep women subordinated.

Therefore, while Barrett believes that the overthrow of capitalism is necessary to secure women's liberation, she argues that it is not sufficient. We must also overthrow the ideology of familism that underpins the conventional family and its unequal division of labour. This would free the sexes from restrictive stereotypes and ensure domestic labour was shared equally.

Some feminists take the analysis of ideology further to explain why women seem to freely accept oppressive family and marital relationships. These writers often draw on non-Marxist and even non-sociological ideas. For example, Juliet Mitchell (1975) uses Freud's psychoanalytic theory to argue that ideas about femininity are so deeply implanted in women's unconscious minds that they are very difficult to dislodge. The implication is that even after the overthrow of capitalism, it would still be hard to overcome patriarchal ideology because it is so deeply rooted.

Evaluation of Marxist feminism

Given the importance of economic production to most other areas of social life, Marxist feminists are correct to give weight to the relationship between capitalism and women's subordination. They show a greater understanding of the importance of structural factors than liberal feminism. However, Marxist feminism is criticised on several grounds.

It fails to explain women's subordination in non-capitalist societies. As women's subordination is also found in non-capitalist societies, it cannot be explained solely in terms of the needs of capitalism. However, in their defence, Marxist feminists are only seeking to explain the position of women in contemporary capitalist society.

Unpaid domestic labour may benefit capitalism, as Marxist feminists claim, but this doesn't explain why it is women and not men who perform it. Heidi Hartmann (1981) argues that this is because Marxism is 'sex-blind'.

Marxist feminism places insufficient emphasis on the ways in which men (including working-class men) – and not just capitalism – oppress women and benefit from their unpaid labour.

It is not proven that unpaid domestic labour is in fact the cheapest way of reproducing labour power. For example, it might be done more cheaply through the market or through state provision such as publicly funded nurseries.

Dual systems feminism

Dual systems feminists have sought to combine the key features of Marxist and radical feminism in a single theory. The two systems referred to are:

- An economic system: capitalism
- A sex-gender system: patriarchy

Patriarchal capitalism As we have seen, radical feminism regards patriarchy as the cause of women's oppression, while Marxist feminism sees capitalism as responsible. Dual systems theorists such as Heidi Hartmann (1979) see capitalism and patriarchy as two intertwined systems that form a single entity, 'patriarchal capitalism'. Like radical feminism, these theorists accept that patriarchy is universal, but they argue that patriarchy takes a specific form in capitalist societies.

From this viewpoint, to understand women's subordination, we must look at the relationship between their position both in the domestic division of labour (patriarchy) and in paid work (capitalism).

For example, domestic work limits women's availability for paid work – but the lack of work opportunities drives many women into marriage and economic dependence on a man. Thus, the two systems reinforce each other.

Similarly, Sylvia Walby (1988) argues that capitalism and patriarchy are inter-related. However, she argues that the interests of the two are not always the same. In particular, they collide over the exploitation of female labour. While capitalism demands cheap female labour for its workforce, patriarchy resists this, wanting to keep women subordinated to men within the private, domestic sphere.

However, in the long run, capitalism is usually more powerful and so patriarchy adopts a strategy of segregation instead: women are allowed into the capitalist sphere of paid work, but only in low status 'women's' jobs, subordinated to men.

Walby's approach is useful because it shows how the two systems interact and structure one another, without assuming that their interests always coincide.

However, Anna Pollert (1996) argues that patriarchy is not actually a system in the same sense as capitalism, which is driven by its own internal dynamic of profit making. By contrast, 'patriarchy' is merely a descriptive term for a range of practices such as male violence and control of women's labour.

Difference feminism and poststructuralism

All the feminist perspectives we have examined so far assume that all women share a similar situation and similar experience of oppression. By contrast, 'difference feminists' do not see women as a single homogeneous group. They argue that middle-class and working-class women, white and black women, lesbian and heterosexual women have very different experiences of patriarchy, capitalism, racism, homophobia and so on.

Difference feminism argues that feminist theory has claimed a 'false universality' for itself – it claimed to be about all women, but in reality was only about the experiences of white, Western, heterosexual, middle-class women.

For example, by seeing the family only as a source of oppression, white feminists have neglected black women's experience of racial oppression. By contrast, many black feminists view the black family positively as a source of resistance against racism.

This criticism raises two important issues – the problem of essentialism, and the relationship of feminism to the Enlightenment project.

The problem of essentialism

As applied to gender, essentialism is the idea that all women share the same fundamental 'essence' – all women are essentially the same and all share the same experiences of oppression.

Difference feminists argue that liberal, Marxist and radical feminists are essentialist – they see all women as the same. As a result, they fail to reflect the diversity of women's experiences and they exclude other women and their problems.

For example, some difference feminists argue that the preoccupation of Western feminism with sexuality is irrelevant to women in poorer countries, where access to clean water and primary healthcare are far more pressing problems.

Poststructuralist feminism

Poststructuralist feminists such as Judith Butler (Butler and Scott, 1992) offer an alternative approach. Poststructuralism is concerned with *discourses* and *power/knowledge*.

Discourses are ways of seeing, thinking or speaking about something. The world is made up of many, often competing, discourses – for example, religious, scientific, medical and artistic.

By enabling its users to define others in certain ways, a discourse gives power over those it defines. For example, by defining childbirth as a medical condition and healthy women as patients, medical discourse empowers doctors and disempowers women. Knowledge is power – the power to define or 'constitute' the identities of others. (For more on poststructuralism, see Topic 9.)

The Enlightenment project

Poststructuralists argue that the Enlightenment project, with its talk of reason, humanity and progress, is one such discourse – a form of power/knowledge. Butler uses this idea in her critique of existing feminist theories.

Butler argues that the Enlightenment ideals were simply a form of power/knowledge that legitimated domination by Western, white, middle-class males. These supposedly universal ideals that claimed to apply to all humanity in reality excluded women and other oppressed groups.

Similarly, Butler argues that the white, Western, middle-class women who dominate the feminist movement have falsely claimed to represent 'universal womanhood'. She concludes that feminists are wrong to believe they can adapt the Enlightenment project so that it somehow includes all women – because women are not a single entity who all share the same 'essence'.

For poststructuralism, there is no fixed essence of what it is to be a woman. Because our identities are constituted through discourses, and because there are many different discourses in different times and cultures, there can be no fixed entity called 'womanhood' that is the same everywhere.

For example, womanhood in Saudi Arabia is constituted partly by Islamic discourse. By contrast, womanhood in the West is constituted to a greater extent by the discourses of advertising and the media.

Butler argues that poststructuralism offers advantages for feminism. It enables feminists to 'de-construct' (analyse) different discourses to reveal how they subordinate women – as in the medicalisation of childbirth, for example. Thus, we can examine the discourses of medicine, sexuality, advertising, art, religion, science, pornography etc to uncover the power/knowledge by which they define and oppress women.

Different discourses give rise to different forms of oppression, and thus to different identities and experiences for women. Likewise, each discourse provokes its own distinct form of resistance and struggle, with its own aims and demands.

In Butler's view, therefore, by rejecting essentialism and by stressing the diversity of discourses, poststructuralism recognises and legitimates the diversity of women's lives and struggles, rather than prioritising some and excluding others.

Activity   Discussion

Which feminism?

...go to www.sociology.uk.net

Evaluation of poststructuralist feminism

While poststructuralist feminism seems to offer a theoretical basis for recognising the diversity of women's experiences and struggles, critics argue that it has weaknesses.

For example, Sylvia Walby (1992) agrees that there are differences among women, but she argues that there are also important similarities – they are all faced with patriarchy. For example, compared with men, women face a greater risk of low pay, domestic violence and sexual assault.

Similarly, celebrating difference may have the effect of dividing women into an infinite number of sub-groups, thereby weakening feminism as a movement for change.

Lynne Segal (1999) criticises poststructuralist feminism for abandoning any notion of real, objective social structures. Oppression is not just the result of discourses – it is about real inequality. Feminists should therefore continue to focus on the struggle for equality of wealth and income.

Topic Summary

Feminists study society from the viewpoint of women. They see women as subordinated by men, and seek to liberate women from oppression.

Liberal feminists seek legal reforms and changes in attitudes and socialisation to bring equality.

Radical feminists see patriarchy as the fundamental conflict in society – men are women's oppressors and separatism is the only solution.

Marxist feminists see capitalism rather than men as the main beneficiary of women's oppression.

Dual systems feminists regard patriarchy and capitalism as intertwined. **Difference and poststructuralist feminists** argue that other feminist theories are essentialist and disregard differences between women.

EXAMINING FEMINIST THEORIES

QuickCheck Questions

Check your answers at www.sociology.uk.net

1   What is meant by 'malestream' sociology?
2   Which type of feminist is most likely to believe equality can be gained through reforming legislation and changing attitudes?
3   Explain the difference between sex and gender.
4   Which feminist perspective argues that all men oppress all women?
5   True or false? Marxist feminists believe gender inequalities only benefit capitalism.

6   Suggest three ways women's subordination benefits capitalism.
7   How might capitalism and patriarchy reinforce each other?
8   Why do difference feminists criticise white Western feminists?
9   What is meant by 'essentialism'?
10 Suggest two criticisms of poststructuralist feminism.

Questions to try

Item A

All feminists argue that women occupy a subordinate position in society and all feminists wish to end this state of affairs. However, they differ about both the causes of the problem and its solution. For example, liberal feminists argue that traditional attitudes and cultural stereotypes about women's abilities have kept them subordinated, but that changes in laws, policies and socialisation patterns will gradually bring about gender equality.

However, both radical and Marxist feminists argue that women's oppression has deeper roots and requires more fundamental, revolutionary changes in order to end it.

1   Outline and explain two feminist views of the position of women in society.   (10 marks)
2   Applying material from Item A and your knowledge, evaluate the contribution of feminists to our understanding of society.   (20 marks)

The Examiner's Advice

Q1 Spend about 15 minutes on this question. Divide your time fairly equally between the two views. You don't need a separate introduction; just start on the first view. Possible feminist views include liberal, radical, Marxist, difference and poststructuralist feminism. Choose two of these views and describe each in some detail, showing how each one explains the position of women in society.

Do this by creating a 'chain of reasoning' (see Box 4.1 in chapter 4). For example, radical feminists argue that patriarchy is the fundamental form of inequality: gender is the key social division and all men oppress all women. Patriarchy thus explains why women are subordinated economically, physically, sexually and socially, and why their subordination is so universal and persistent.

Apply examples from one or two topics such as domestic violence to illustrate your explanation. Use concepts and issues such as patriarchy, socialisation, the reserve army of labour, the ideology of familism, class and ethnic differences among women etc, as appropriate to the two views you have chosen.

Q2 Spend about 30 minutes on this question. The question asks about feminists plural, so you need to consider more than one – for example, liberal, radical, Marxist and difference feminism. Start by identifying what feminists have in common and then examine the different branches, using the relevant key concepts and issues for each branch.

These concepts include sex versus gender, patriarchy, socialisation, anti-discrimination policies, public and private spheres, sexual politics, separatism, the reserve army of labour, reproduction of the labour force, familism, dual systems, essentialism, the Enlightenment project and the diversity of female experience. Use examples from other topic areas such as the family or education, but make sure you apply them to feminist theory. You could also refer briefly to feminist views about methodology.

Rather than leaving evaluation to a separate 'block' at the end, evaluate as you go along. Use debates between different branches of feminism about the causes of and solutions to women's oppression, as well as using alternative theories such as functionalism, Marxism etc to challenge feminist views.

For interactionists, we are all actors trying to carry off a convincing performance.

GETTING STARTED

Action theories look at society by examining the actions and interactions of individuals. This can be seen in the process of labelling.

Working in pairs, complete the following tasks:

A Review what you know about labelling in relation to other topics such as education and crime and deviance. What features does the labelling process have in these areas?

B Using the concepts below, plus any others you find useful, write a short account of labelling as a social process.

  1 self-fulfilling prophecy

  2 self-concept

  3 meaning

  4 interaction

  5 subculture

C How does the labelling process illustrate the importance of human interactions and meanings in understanding society as a social construct?

Learning objectives

After studying this Topic, you should:

- Understand the difference between structural and action theories.

- Know the main types of action theory and understand the differences between them.

- Be able to evaluate the strengths and limitations of action theories.

We can divide sociological theories into two broad types: structural theories and action theories.

Structural theories such as functionalism and Marxism are macro (large scale), top-down and deterministic: they see society as a real thing existing over and above us, shaping our ideas and behaviour – individuals are like puppets, manipulated by society. To understand people's behaviour, we must first understand the social structure that shapes it.

Action theories start from the opposite position. They are 'micro' level, bottom-up approaches that focus on the actions and interactions of individuals. Action theories are more voluntaristic – they see us as having free will and choice. Our actions are not determined by society. Rather, we are free agents, creating and shaping society through our choices, meanings and actions.

In this Topic we look at four action theories: Weber's social action theory, symbolic interactionism, phenomenology and ethnomethodology

Max Weber: social action theory

Max Weber (1864-1920) was one of the 'founding fathers' of sociology. Weber saw both structural and action approaches as necessary for a full understanding of human behaviour. He argued that an adequate sociological explanation involves two levels:

- **The level of cause** – explaining the objective structural factors that shape people's behaviour.
- **The level of meaning** – understanding the subjective meanings that individuals attach to their actions.

Unless we account for both of these levels, our explanation will be incomplete or false.

We can illustrate Weber's point by referring to his study *The Protestant Ethic and the Spirit of Capitalism*, originally published in 1905. At the level of structural *cause*, the Protestant Reformation introduced a new belief system, Calvinism. This changed people's worldview, which led to changes in their behaviour. For example, Calvinism promoted a work ethic that brought about the rise of capitalism.

At the level of subjective *meaning*, work took on a religious meaning for the Calvinists, as a calling by God to glorify his name through their labours. This motivated them to work systematically. As a result they accumulated wealth and became the first modern capitalists.

Analysis and Evaluation

1 How would you apply Weber's concepts of objective structural factors and subjective meanings to explain (a) hooliganism; (b) unemployment?
2 Suggest four possible meanings that unemployment might have for a person.

Types of action

However, there are an infinite number of subjective meanings that actors may give to their actions. Weber attempts to classify actions into four types, based on their meaning for the actor:

Instrumentally rational action is where the actor calculates the most efficient means of achieving a given goal. For example, a capitalist may calculate that the most efficient way of maximising profit is to pay low wages. This action is not about whether the goal itself is desirable – for example, the goal could be distributing charity or committing genocide. Rational action is simply about the most efficient way of reaching that goal, whatever it may be.

Value-rational action involves action towards a goal that the actor regards as desirable for its own sake – for example, a believer worshipping their god in order to get to heaven. Unlike instrumental rationality, there is no way of calculating whether the means of achieving the goal are effective. For example, the believer has no way of knowing whether performing a particular ritual will gain him salvation.

Traditional action involves customary, routine or habitual actions. Weber does not see this type of action as rational, because no conscious thought or choice has gone into it. Rather, the actor does it because 'we have always done it'.

Affectual action is action that expresses emotion – for example, weeping out of grief, or violence sparked by anger. Weber sees affectual action as important in religious and political movements with charismatic leaders who attract a following based on their emotional appeal.

Evaluation of Weber

Weber's ideas are a valuable corrective to the over-emphasis on structural factors that we see in functionalism and many forms of Marxism, and an affirmation that we must also understand actors' subjective meanings if we want to explain their actions adequately.

However, Weber has been criticised on several grounds.

- Alfred Schutz (1972) argues that Weber's view of action is too individualistic and cannot explain the *shared* nature of meanings. For example, when a person at an auction raises their arm, *they* mean that they are making a bid – but Weber doesn't explain how everyone else present also comes to give this gesture the same meaning.

- Weber's typology of action is difficult to apply. For example, among the Trobriand Islanders, individuals exchange ritual gifts called 'kula' with others on neighbouring islands. This could either be seen as traditional action (it has been practised in the same way for generations) – or it could be seen as instrumentally rational action (because it is a good way of cementing trading links between kula partners).

- Weber advocated the use of *verstehen* or empathetic understanding of the actor's subjective meaning – where we put ourselves in the actor's place to understand their motives and meanings. However, as we cannot actually *be* that other person, we can never be sure we have truly understood their motives.

Symbolic interactionism

Symbolic interactionism first developed at the University of Chicago in the first half of the 20th century. Like other action theories, it focuses on our ability to create the social world through our actions and interactions, and it sees these interactions as based on the *meanings* we give to situations. We convey these meanings through symbols, especially language.

G.H. Mead

The work of George Herbert Mead (1863-1931) forms the basis for that of many later interactionists.

Symbols versus instincts

Mead observed that, unlike animals, our behaviour is not shaped by fixed, pre-programmed instincts. Instead, we respond to the world by giving meanings to the things that are significant to us. In effect, we create and inhabit a world of meanings. We do this by attaching symbols to the world. A symbol is something that stands for or represents something else.

Unlike animals, therefore, we do not simply respond to a stimulus in an automatic, pre-determined way. Instead, an *interpretive phase* comes between the stimulus and our response to it – before we know how to respond to the stimulus, we have to interpret its meaning. Once we have done this, we can then choose an appropriate response.

Mead illustrates this with an example. When one dog snarls at another, the snarl acts as a direct stimulus, to which the second dog responds instinctively, automatically adopting a defensive posture. There is no conscious interpretation by the dog of the other's actions.

By contrast, if I shake my fist at you, I am using a *symbol* – one that has a variety of possible meanings. To understand what is going on, you must interpret the meaning of this symbol. For instance, am I angry, or just joking? You may decide I am angry with you. Only then will you be able to choose how to respond.

Taking the role of the other

But how do we manage to interpret other people's meanings? In Mead's view, we do so by *taking the role of the other* – putting ourselves in the place of the other person and seeing ourselves as they see us.

Our ability to take the role of the other develops through social interaction. We first do this as young children: through imitative play when we take on the role of *significant others* such as parents, and learn to see ourselves as they see us. Later, we come to see ourselves from the point of view of the wider community – the *generalised other*.

For Mead, to function as members of society, we need the ability to see ourselves as others see us. Through shared symbols, especially language, we become conscious of the ways of acting that others require of us.

Herbert Blumer

After Mead's death, Herbert Blumer (1900-87) did much to systematise his ideas. Blumer identified three key principles:

1 Our actions are based on the meanings we give to situations, events, people etc. Unlike animals, our actions are not based on automatic responses to stimuli.
2 These meanings arise from the interaction process. They are not fixed at the outset of the interaction, but are negotiable and changeable to some extent.
3 The meanings we give to situations are the result of the interpretive procedures we use – especially taking the role of the other.

Blumer's view of human conduct contrasts strongly with structural theories such as functionalism. Functionalists see the individual as a puppet, passively responding to the system's needs. Socialisation and social control ensure that individuals conform to society's norms and perform their roles in fixed and predictable ways.

By contrast, Blumer argues that although our action is *partly* predictable because we internalise the expectations of others, it is not completely fixed. There is always some room for negotiation and choice in how we perform our roles – even where very strict rules prevail, as in 'total institutions' such as prisons.

...go to www.sociology.uk.net

Labelling theory

The best-known application of interactionist ideas is that of labelling theory. Labelling theorists use interactionist concepts in the study of many areas, including education, health, and crime and deviance. Here, we examine three key interactionist concepts that underpin labelling theory – the definition of the situation, the looking glass self, and career.

The definition of the situation A definition of something is of course a *label* for that thing. W.I. Thomas (1966) argued that if people define a situation as real, then it will have real consequences. That is, if we believe something to be true, then this belief will affect how we act, and this in turn may have consequences for those involved. For example, if a teacher labels a boy as 'troublesome' (whether or not he really is), the teacher will be likely to act differently towards him – for example, punishing him more harshly.

The looking glass self Charles Cooley (1922) uses this idea to describe how we develop our *self-concept* – our idea of who we are. He argues that our self-concept arises out of our ability to take the role of the other. In interactions, by taking the role of the other, we come to see ourselves as they see us. In other words, others act as a looking glass to us – we see our self mirrored in the way they respond to us. Through this process, a *self-fulfilling prophecy* occurs – we become what others see us as.

Labelling theorists use the definition of the situation and the looking glass self to understand the effects of labelling. For example, an individual may find that relatives or psychiatrists define him as mentally ill and respond to him differently, reflecting their view of him as sick or abnormal.

Through the looking glass self, the label becomes part of the individual's self-concept. He takes on the role of 'mental patient' and a self-fulfilling prophecy is created when he acts it out. Even if the initial definition of him was false, it has become true and may have real consequences. For example, he may find himself detained in a psychiatric hospital.

Career In normal usage, a career is the stages through which an individual progresses in their occupation, each with its own status, job title, problems etc. However, labelling theorists such as Howard S. Becker (1961; 1963) and Edwin Lemert (1962) have extended the concept to

apply it to groups such as medical students, marijuana smokers and those suffering from paranoia.

For example, in relation to mental illness, we can see the individual as having a career running from 'pre-patient' with certain symptoms, through *labelling* by a psychiatrist, to hospital in-patient, to discharge. Each stage has its own status and problems. For example, on discharge the ex-patient may find it hard to reintegrate into society. And just as a 'normal' career may give us our status, so 'mental patient' may become our *master status* in the eyes of society.

Interactionism is generally regarded as a voluntaristic theory that emphasises free will and choice in how we act. However, labelling theory has been accused of determinism – of seeing our actions and identities as shaped by the way others label them.

Goffman's dramaturgical model

Labelling theory describes how the self is shaped through interaction. It often sees the individual as the passive victim of other people's labels. By contrast, the work of another interactionist, Erving Goffman (1963; 1967; 1968; 1969), describes how we actively construct our 'self' by manipulating other people's impressions of us.

Goffman's approach is often described as *dramaturgical* because he uses analogies with drama as a framework for analysing social interaction. We are all 'actors', acting out 'scripts', using 'props', resting 'backstage' between 'performances' we present to our 'audiences' and so on. Our aim is to carry off a convincing performance of the role we have adopted – just as the actor aims to persuade the audience that he is really Hamlet.

Impression management

Two key dramaturgical concepts are *the presentation of self and impression management*. For Goffman, we seek to present a particular image of ourselves to our audiences. To do so, we must control the impression our performance gives. This involves constantly studying our audience to see how they are responding, and monitoring and adjusting our performance to present a convincing image.

As social actors, we have many techniques for impression management. We may use language, tone of voice, gestures and facial expressions, as well as props and settings such as dress, make-up, equipment, furniture, décor and premises. By using these techniques skilfully, we can 'pass' for the kind of person we want our audience to believe we are.

Goffman uses the dramaturgical analogy to describe the different settings of interactions. As in the theatre, there is a 'front' or stage where we act out our roles, while backstage, we can step out of our role and 'be ourselves'. For example, the classroom is a front region where students must put on a convincing role-performance for the teacher, while the common room is a back region where they can 'drop the act'. However, the common room may become another front region where students may have to carry off a different performance in front of their friends.

> **Application**
> How might you behave differently at home or with intimate friends compared with when you are in the student common room?

Roles

Goffman's view of roles differs sharply from that of functionalism. Functionalists see roles as tightly 'scripted' by society and they see us as fully internalising our scripts through socialisation. As a result, they become part of our identity and society determines exactly how we will perform them.

Goffman rejects this view. Instead, he argues, there is a 'gap' or *role distance* between our real self and our roles. Like the stage actor who is not really Hamlet, we are not really the roles we play. In Goffman's view, roles are only loosely scripted by society and we have a good deal of freedom in how we play them – for example, some teachers are strict, others easy-going.

The idea of role distance also suggests that we do not always believe in the roles we play and that our role performance may be cynical or calculating. In Goffman's studies, the actor sometimes resembles a confidence trickster, manipulating his audience into accepting an impression that conceals his true self and real motives. In the dramaturgical model, appearances are everything and actors seek to present themselves to their best advantage.

Activity	Media
Goffman and the performed self	
	...go to www.sociology.uk.net

Evaluation of symbolic interactionism

Interactionism largely avoids the determinism of structural theories such as functionalism. It recognises that people create society through their choices and meanings. However, interactionism is criticised on several counts.

Some argue that it is more a loose collection of descriptive concepts (such as labelling, and Goffman's dramaturgical concepts) than an explanatory theory.

It focuses on face-to-face interactions and ignores wider social structures such as class inequality, and it fails to explain the origin of labels. Similarly, it cannot explain the consistent patterns we observe in people's behaviour. Functionalists argue that these patterns are the result of norms dictating behaviour.

Larry Reynolds (1975) offers some interesting evidence to show that interactionism lacks an idea of structure. Reynolds sent a questionnaire to 124 interactionists, of whom 84 responded. When asked to identify the concepts they felt were essential, the most popular were 'role' (chosen by 38), 'self' (37) and 'interaction' (37). Only two chose 'power' or 'class' – concepts that structural sociologists see as crucial.

Not all action is meaningful – like Weber's category of traditional action, much is performed unconsciously or routinely and may have little meaning for actors. If so, interactionism lacks the means to explain it.

Goffman's dramaturgical analogy is useful but has its limitations. For example, in interactions everyone plays the part of both actor and audience, and interactions are often improvised and unrehearsed.

Ethnomethodologists argue that interactionism is correct in focusing on actors' meanings, but that it fails to explain how actors create meanings (see below).

Phenomenology

In philosophy, the term 'phenomenon' is used to describe things as they appear to our senses. Some philosophers argue that we can never have definite knowledge of what the world outside our minds is really like 'in itself' – all we can know is what our senses tell us about it. This is the starting point for the philosophy known as phenomenology, developed by Edmund Husserl (1859-1938).

Husserl's philosophy

Husserl argues that the world only makes sense because we impose meaning and order on it by constructing mental categories that we use to classify and 'file' information coming from our senses. For example, a category such as 'four-legged furniture for eating off' enables us to identify a particular set of sensory data as 'table'.

In this view, we can only obtain knowledge about the world through our mental acts of categorising and giving meaning to our experiences. The world *as we know it* is, and can only be, a product of our mind.

Schutz's phenomenological sociology

Alfred Schutz (1899-1959) applies this idea to the social world. He argues that the categories and concepts we use are not unique to ourselves – rather, we share them with other members of society.

Typifications

Schutz calls these shared categories *typifications*. Typifications enable us to organise our experiences into a shared world of meaning.

In Schutz's view, the meaning of any given experience varies according to its social context. For example, raising your arm means one thing in class and quite another at an auction. The meaning is not given by the action in itself, but by its context. For this reason, meanings are potentially unclear and unstable – especially if others classify the action in a different way from oneself. Imagine what would happen if, at an auction, you behaved as if you were in class and raised your hand to ask a question.

Fortunately, however, typifications stabilise and clarify meanings by ensuring that we are all 'speaking the same language' – all agreeing on the meaning of things. This makes it possible for us to communicate and cooperate with one another and thus to achieve our goals. Without shared typifications, social order would become impossible. For example, if you see a certain object as a desk (for writing at), while I take it for an altar (for worshipping at), considerable problems might result.

However, in Schutz's view, members of society to a large extent do have a shared 'life world' – a stock of shared typifications or commonsense knowledge that we use to make sense of our experience. It includes shared assumptions about the way things are, what certain situations mean, what other people's motivations are and so on. Schutz calls this 'recipe knowledge': like a recipe, we can follow it without thinking too much, and still get the desired results in everyday life. For example, we all 'know' that a red light means stop or danger and this knowledge enables us to drive safely.

This commonsense knowledge is not simply knowledge about the world – it is the world. As we saw, for Husserl the world as we know it can only be a product of our mind. Similarly, for Schutz the social world is a shared, inter-subjective world that can only exist when we share the same meanings. For example, a red traffic light only 'means' stop because we all agree that it does.

The natural attitude

However, society *appears* to us as a real, objective thing existing outside of us. To illustrate this, Schutz gives the example of posting a letter to a bookshop to order a book. In doing so, he says, we assume that some unknown and unseen individuals (postal workers, a bookshop owner) will perform a whole series of operations in a particular sequence – and that all this will result in our receiving the book.

The fact that we *do* get the book encourages us to adopt what he calls 'the natural attitude' – that is, it leads us to assume that the social world is a solid, natural thing out there. However, for Schutz, it simply shows that all those involved (the book buyer and seller, the postal workers) share the same meanings, and this allows us to cooperate and achieve goals.

However, Peter Berger and Thomas Luckmann (1971) argue that while Schutz is right to focus on shared commonsense knowledge, they reject his view that society is merely an inter-subjective reality. Although reality is socially constructed, as Schutz believes, once it has been constructed, it takes on a life of its own and becomes an external reality that reacts back on us. For example, religious ideas may start off in our consciousness, but they become embodied in powerful structures such as churches, which then constrain us – for example, by influencing laws about our sexual relationships.

Ethnomethodology

Ethnomethodology (EM for short) emerged in America in the 1960s, mainly from the work of Harold Garfinkel (1967). Garfinkel's ideas stem from phenomenology. Like Schutz, Garfinkel rejects the very idea of society as a real objective structure 'out there'.

Like functionalists such as Parsons, Garfinkel is interested in how social order is achieved. However, he gives a very different answer from Parsons. Parsons argues that social order is made possible by a shared value system into which we are socialised. Parsons' explanation is in keeping with his top-down, structural approach: shared norms ensure that we perform our roles in an orderly, predictable way that meets the expectations of others.

Garfinkel takes the opposite view – social order is created from the bottom up. Order and meaning are not achieved because people are 'puppets' whose strings are pulled by the social system, as functionalists believe. Instead, social order is an *accomplishment* – something that members of society actively construct in everyday life using their commonsense knowledge. EM attempts to discover *how* we do this, by studying people's methods of making sense of the world.

This is also where EM differs from interactionism. While interactionists are interested in the *effects* of meanings (for example, the effects of labelling), EM is interested in the methods or rules that we use to produce the meanings in the first place.

Indexicality and reflexivity

Like Schutz, EM sees meanings as always potentially unclear – a characteristic Garfinkel calls *indexicality*. Nothing has a fixed meaning: everything depends on the context. For example as we saw earlier, raising one's arm means different things in different situations.

Now, indexicality is clearly a threat to social order because if meanings are inherently unclear or unstable, communication and cooperation become difficult and social relationships may begin to break down.

However, there is a paradox here. Indexicality suggests that we cannot take any meaning for granted as fixed or clear – yet in everyday life, this is exactly what we do most of the time. For Garfinkel, what enables us to behave *as if* meanings are clear and obvious is *reflexivity*. Reflexivity refers to the fact that we use commonsense knowledge in everyday interactions to construct a sense of meaning and order and stop indexicality from occurring. This is similar to Schutz's idea of typifications.

Language is of vital importance in achieving reflexivity. For EM, when we describe something, we are simultaneously *creating* it. Our description gives it reality, removing uncertainty about what is going on, and making it seem clear, solid and meaningful. But although language gives us a sense of reality existing 'out there', in fact all we have done is to construct a set of shared meanings.

Experiments in disrupting social order

Garfinkel and his students sought to demonstrate the nature of social order by a series of so-called 'breaching experiments'. For example, they acted as lodgers in their own families – being polite, avoiding getting personal etc. Similarly, they tried to haggle over the price of groceries at the supermarket checkout.

The aim was to disrupt people's sense of order and challenge their reflexivity by undermining their assumptions about the situation. For example, parents of students who behaved as lodgers became bewildered, anxious, embarrassed or angry. They accused the students of being nasty, or assumed they were ill.

Garfinkel concludes that by challenging people's taken-for-granted assumptions, the experiments show how the orderliness of everyday situations is not inevitable but is actually an *accomplishment* of those who take part in them. In his view, social order is 'participant produced' by members themselves.

Suicide and reflexivity

Garfinkel is interested in the methods we use to achieve reflexivity – to make sense of the world as orderly. In the case of suicide, coroners make sense of deaths by selecting particular features from the infinite number of possible 'facts' about the deceased – such as their mental health, employment status etc. They then treat these features as a real pattern. For example, they may use this information to conclude that 'typical suicides' are mentally ill, unemployed etc.

For Garfinkel, humans constantly strive to impose order by seeking patterns, even though these patterns are really just social constructs. For example, the seeming pattern that suicides are mentally ill becomes part of the coroner's taken-for-granted knowledge about what suicides are like.

Thus, when faced with future cases with similar features (mentally ill people who have died), the coroner interprets them as examples of the assumed pattern: 'the deceased was mentally ill, therefore he probably committed suicide'.

Finally, cases fitting the pattern will be classified as suicides and will seem to prove the existence of the pattern the coroner had originally constructed. The assumed pattern becomes self-reinforcing – but it tells us nothing about any external reality.

Garfinkel is critical of conventional sociology. He accuses it of merely using the same methods as ordinary members of society to create order and meaning. If so, then conventional sociology is little more than commonsense, rather than true and objective knowledge.

For example, positivists such as Durkheim take it for granted that official suicide statistics are social facts that tell us the real rate of suicide. In fact, they are merely the decisions made by coroners, using their commonsense understandings of what types of people kill themselves. Therefore the supposed 'laws' positivists produce are just an elaborate version of the coroners' commonsense. Sociologists' claims to know about suicide are thus no truer than those of other members of society, such as coroners.

Evaluation of ethnomethodology

EM draws attention to how we actively construct order and meaning, rather than seeing us as simply puppets of the social system, as functionalism does. However, it has come in for considerable criticism.

Craib argues that its findings are trivial. Ethnomethodologists seem to spend a lot of time 'uncovering' taken-for-granted rules that turn out to be no surprise to anyone. For example, one study found that in phone conversations, generally only one person speaks at a time!

EM argues that everyone creates order and meaning by identifying patterns and producing explanations that are essentially fictions. If so, this must also apply to EM itself, and so we have no particular reason to accept its views.

EM denies the existence of wider society, seeing it as merely a shared fiction. Yet, by analysing how members apply general rules or norms to specific contexts, it assumes that a structure of norms really exists beyond these contexts. From a functionalist perspective, such norms are social facts, not fictions.

EM ignores how wider structures of power and inequality affect the meanings that individuals construct. For example, Marxists argue that 'commonsense knowledge' is really just ruling-class ideology, and the order it creates serves to maintain capitalism.

Structure and action

So far in this chapter, we have examined a range of sociological theories and grouped them into 'structural' and 'action' theories.

As we have seen, structural theories such as functionalism and Marxism tend to be deterministic, seeing society as something objective, existing outside individuals and constraining them. By contrast, action theories tend to be voluntaristic, seeing society as the creation of its members through their subjective actions and meanings.

Both types of theory appear to hold some truth. It is easy to see society as a real, external structure constraining us. For example, society's laws regulate our behaviour.

Similarly, it is easy to feel that we freely choose our actions. For example, the existence of a law doesn't stop us from choosing to break it.

Given that there is much to be said for both types of approach, some sociologists have sought to combine them into a single unified theory of structure *and* action. The best known of these is Anthony Giddens' (1984) structuration theory.

Giddens' structuration theory

According to Giddens, there is a *duality of structure*. By this Giddens means that structure and action – or agency as he calls it – are two sides of the same coin; neither can exist without the other. Through our actions we produce and reproduce structures over time and space, while these structures are what make our actions possible in the first place. Giddens calls this relationship *structuration*.

Giddens illustrates this with language. A language is a structure – it is made up of a set of rules of grammar that govern how we can use it to express meanings. This structure seems to exist independently of any individual, and it constrains our behaviour, like one of Durkheim's 'social facts'.

For example, if we wish to use a language to communicate, we must obey its rules, otherwise, we will not be understood. This shows how our action (communication) depends on the existence of structure (language rules).

But structure also depends on action. For example, a language would not exist if no one used it. It is produced and reproduced over time through the actions of individuals speaking and writing it. Furthermore, these actions can also change the structure. People give words new meanings and create new rules.

Application
Suggest two examples, apart from language, that illustrate the duality of structure and action.

Reproduction of structures through agency

For Giddens, structure has two elements:

- **Rules** – the norms, customs and laws that govern action.
- **Resources** – both economic (raw materials, technology etc) and power over others.

Rules and resources can be either reproduced or changed through human action. For example, obeying the law reproduces the existing structure, while inventing new technology may change it.

However, in Giddens' view, although our action can change existing structures, it generally tends to reproduce them. He identifies two reasons for this.

First, society's *rules* contain a stock of knowledge about how to live our lives. Earning a living, shopping and so on largely involve applying this knowledge to everyday situations. Similarly, when shopping, for example, we use *resources* in the form of money. Thus as we go about our routine activities, we tend to reproduce the existing structure of society.

Second, we reproduce existing structures through our action because we have a deep-seated need for *ontological security* – a need to feel that the world, both physical and social, really is as it appears to be, and especially that it is orderly, stable and predictable. This need tends to encourage action that maintains existing structures, rather than changing them.

Change of structures through agency

However, despite this tendency to maintain the structure of society, action or agency can also change it. This can occur in two ways.

First, we 'reflexively monitor' our own action, constantly reflecting on our actions and their results, and we can deliberately choose a new course of action. This is more likely in late modern society, where tradition no longer dictates action, thus increasing the likelihood and pace of change.

Second, our actions may change the world, but not always as we intended. They may have unintended consequences. For example, according to Weber, the Calvinists who adopted the Protestant work ethic did so with the intention of glorifying God, but the actual consequence was the creation of modern capitalism.

Evaluation of Giddens

Although Giddens makes an important attempt to overcome the division between structure and action in sociological theory, his approach has been criticised.

Giddens implies that actors can change structures simply by deciding to do so. Margaret Archer (1995) argues that he underestimates the capacity of structures to resist change. For example, slaves may wish to abolish slavery but lack the power to do so.

According to Craib, structuration *theory* isn't really a theory at all, because it doesn't explain what actually happens in society. Instead, it just describes the kinds of things we will find when we study society, such as actions, rules, resources etc.

Craib argues that Giddens fails to unite structure and action. He regards Giddens' work as 'a thoroughgoing action theory' that reduces the idea of structure to the rules governing routine everyday actions. Giddens fails to explain how his theory applies to large-scale structures such as the economy and the state.

Topic Summary

Unlike structural theories, action theories are **micro-level** approaches that see society as constructed by members' interactions and meanings. **Weber's social action** theory identifies four main types of action.

Symbolic interactionists see us as creating meanings through interactions in which we take the role of the other. **Labelling theory** and Goffman's **dramaturgical analogy** are two major interactionist approaches.

Phenomenology and ethnomethodology see society as an inter-subjective reality created out of members' typifications or commonsense understandings.

Giddens' **structuration theory** attempts to unite structure and action. However, critics argue that Giddens fails to account for the ability of structures to resist change.

EXAMINING ACTION THEORIES

QuickCheck Questions

Check your answers at www.sociology.uk.net

1 What are the main differences between structural and action theories?
2 Identify the four types of action classified by Weber.
3 Why is Mead's interactionism 'symbolic'?
4 Explain what is meant by a 'dramaturgical model'.

5 Suggest two examples of techniques someone might use for impression management.
6 Explain the difference between indexicality and reflexivity.
7 According to Giddens, why does human 'agency' tend to reproduce rather than change existing structures?
8 Explain what is meant by 'ontological security'.

Questions to try

Item A

Action approaches reject the idea that we are simply 'puppets' whose behaviour is determined by tightly scripted roles imposed on us by society. Instead, they start from the assumption that we create and shape society through our choices and actions. For example, interactionists argue that we create the social world through our interactions with one another, based on the meanings we give to situations. Similarly, ethnomethodologists argue that we use commonsense knowledge to construct a set of shared meanings.

However, critics argue that action approaches ignore the influence of wider social structures.

1 Outline and explain two concepts that symbolic interactionists use to understand social life. (10 marks)

2 Applying material from Item A and your knowledge, evaluate the contribution of action approaches to our understanding of social behaviour. (20 marks)

The Examiner's Advice

Q1 Spend about 15 minutes on this question. Divide your time fairly equally between the two concepts. You don't need a separate introduction; just start on your first concept. Possible concepts include symbols, definition of the situation, self-concept, labelling, presentation of self, and roles.

Choose two concepts and describe them in some detail, explaining how each one helps interactionists to understand social life. Do this by creating a 'chain of reasoning' (see Box 4.1 in chapter 4) that links it to other interactionist ideas or studies.

For example, our self-concept comes from our ability to take the role of the other. This means we see ourselves 'mirrored' in the way they respond to us and this results in a self-fulfilling prophecy – we become what others see us as.

Apply examples from areas like deviance or education to illustrate your explanation, but make sure you link them to your chosen concepts.

Use concepts and issues such as taking the role of the other, the looking glass self, meanings, self-fulfilling prophecy, career, impression management and the dramaturgical analogy, as well as those referred to above.

Q2 Spend about 30 minutes on this. It refers to approaches plural, so you need to consider more than one action theory. Start by explaining how action theories differ from structural theories through being micro, 'bottom up', voluntaristic approaches that emphasise the actor's meanings. Then explain two or more of the following approaches: Weber, interactionism, phenomenology and EM.

Apply material from the Item where possible, linking this to your own knowledge. Use examples from other topic areas such as education or crime and deviance but make sure you apply them to the theoretical issues. Use concepts and issues such as Weber's typology of social action, the interactionist concepts referred to in the advice for Question 1, typifications, life world, recipe or commonsense knowledge, the natural attitude, indexicality, reflexivity, and duality of structure.

Rather than leaving evaluation to a separate 'block' at the end, evaluate ideas and issues as you go along. Use structural theories such as functionalism and Marxism to challenge action approaches, as well as differences between different action approaches, or Giddens' attempt to combine structure and action.

TOPIC 9

Global internet usage – a case of uneven development?

GETTING STARTED

Working in pairs, complete the following tasks:

1 From your work on other topics, make a list of all the concepts, studies and issues associated with globalisation that you can think of.

2 In pairs, look at the labels in your clothes and make a list of which countries they were made in.

3 Compare your answers with other pairs in the class.

    a How many different countries are there?

    b What does this tell you about the production of clothes?

4 Make a list of as many factors as you can that may encourage the global production of goods.

5 Using the factors from Question 4, explain how globalisation might affect people's lives.

6 What problems might the UK government face if it wanted to improve conditions for workers in the clothing industry in other countries? What measures could it take?

Learning objectives

After studying this Topic, you should:

- Know some of the reasons for the trend towards globalisation.
- Understand the difference between modernity, postmodernity and late modernity.
- Be able to evaluate the strengths and limitations of postmodernist and other theories of recent changes in society.

Modernity and globalisation

Most of the theories examined so far in this chapter can be placed under the heading of 'modernism'. Modernist theories are part of the Enlightenment project – the idea that society can progress through the use of human reason. Rationality and science will enable us to discover true knowledge about the world. With this knowledge, we can progress to a future of freedom and prosperity.

Modernist theories therefore set out to explain the workings of modern society and to identify the direction it should take if it is to progress.

Modern society

Modern society first emerged in Western Europe from about the late 18th century. It has a number of characteristics that distinguish it from previous traditional societies.

The nation-state is the key political unit in modern society – a bounded territory ruled by a powerful centralised state, whose population usually shares the same language and culture. We tend to think of the modern world as made up of a series of separate societies, each with its own state.

The state is the focal point of modern society, organising social life on a national basis. Modern states have created large administrative bureaucracies and educational, welfare and legal institutions to regulate their citizens' lives. The nation-state is also an important source of identity for citizens, who identify with its symbols such as the flag.

Capitalism The economy of modern societies is capitalist – based on private ownership of the means of production and the use of wage labourers. Capitalism brought about the industrialisation of modern society, with huge increases in wealth. However, wealth distribution is unequal, resulting in class conflict. The nation-state becomes important in regulating capitalism and maintaining the conditions under which it operates. Scott Lash and John Urry (1987; 1994) describe this as 'organised capitalism'.

In modern industry, production is organised on Fordist principles (after the Ford Motor Company's system): the mass production of standardised products in large factories, using low skilled labour. Cheap, mass produced consumer goods lead to a rising standard of living.

Rationality, science and technology Rational, secular, scientific ways of thinking dominate and the influence of magico-religious explanations of the world declines. Technically efficient forms of organisation, such as bureaucracies and factories, dominate social and economic life. Science becomes increasingly important in industry, medicine and communications.

Individualism Tradition, custom and ascribed status become less important as the basis for our actions. We experience greater personal freedom and can increasingly choose our own course in life and define our own identity. However, structural inequalities such as class remain important in shaping people's identity and restricting their choices.

Globalisation

Until recently, the nation-state provided the basic framework for most people's lives. However, many sociologists argue that we are now increasingly affected by *globalisation* – the increasing interconnectedness of people across national boundaries. We live in one interdependent 'global village' and our lives are shaped by a global framework. Four related changes have helped bring this about.

1 Technological changes

We can now cross entire continents in a matter of hours, or exchange information across the globe with the click of a mouse. Satellite communications, the internet and global television networks have helped to create *time-space compression*, closing the distances between people.

Technology also brings risks on a global scale. For example, greenhouse gases produced in one place contribute to global climate change that leads to a rise in sea levels and flooding in low-lying countries. Ulrich Beck (1992) argues that we are now living in 'risk society', where increasingly the threats to our well being come from human-made technology rather than natural disasters.

2 Economic changes

Economic factors play a huge part in globalisation. Economic activity now takes place within a set of global networks that are creating ever-greater interconnectedness.

The global economy is increasingly a 'weightless' or *electronic economy*. Instead of producing physical goods, much activity now involves the production of information, such as music, TV programmes and data processing. These commodities are produced, distributed and consumed through global electronic networks.

In the electronic economy, money never sleeps. Global 24-hour financial transactions permit the instantaneous transfer of funds around the world in pursuit of profit. This too contributes to the 'risk society'.

Another major economic force pushing globalisation forward is *trans-national companies* (TNCs). These companies operate across frontiers, organising production on a global scale.

Most TNCs are Western-based. Some, such as Coca-Cola, are colossal enterprises, and the largest 500 together account for half the total value of the commodities produced in the whole world. So powerful are the small elite who control these companies, that Leslie Sklair (2003) argues they now form a separate *global capitalist class*.

3 Political changes

Some sociologists claim that globalisation has undermined the power of the nation-state. For example, Kenichi Ohmae (1994) argues that we now live in a 'borderless world' in which TNCs and consumers have more economic power than national governments. States are now less able to regulate the activities of large capitalist enterprises, a situation Lash and Urry describe as 'disorganised capitalism'.

4 Changes in culture and identity

Globalisation makes it much harder for cultures to exist in isolation from one another. A major reason for this is the role of information and communications technology (ICT), especially the mass media.

Today we find ourselves living in a *global culture* in which Western-owned media companies spread Western culture to the rest of the world. Economic integration also encourages

a global culture. For example, TNCs such as Nike, selling the same consumer goods in many countries, help to promote similar tastes across national borders. In addition, the increased movement of people as tourists, economic migrants, refugees and asylum seekers helps to create globalised culture.

Globalisation also undermines traditional sources of *identity* such as class. For example, the shift of manufacturing from the West to developing countries has led to the fragmentation and decline of working-class communities that previously gave people their class identity.

Explaining the changes

The changes that we have just examined raise some important questions:

- Do they mean we are no longer living in modernity – are we now in a new, postmodern society?
- Do we need new theories to understand society as we now find it, or can we use our existing modernist theories to explain it?
- Is the Enlightenment project still viable – can we still hope to achieve objective knowledge and use it to improve society? Or have rapid changes made society too chaotic for us to understand and control?

We can identify three theories that offer answers to these questions: postmodernism, theories of late modernity and Marxist theories of postmodernity

Postmodernism

Postmodernism is a major intellectual movement that has emerged since the 1970s. It has been influential in many areas, including sociology. Postmodernists argue that we are now living in a new era of postmodernity. Postmodernity is an unstable, fragmented, media-saturated global village, where image and reality are indistinguishable. In postmodern society, we define ourselves by what we consume. It is not a continuation of modernity, but a fundamental break with it. For postmodernists, this new kind of society requires a new kind of theory – modernist theories no longer apply.

Knowledge

Drawing on the ideas of Michel Foucault (see Box 3.12), postmodernists argue that there are no sure foundations to knowledge – no objective criteria we can use to prove whether a theory is true or false. This view – known as anti-foundationalism – has two consequences:

1 The Enlightenment project of achieving progress through true, scientific knowledge is dead. If we cannot

guarantee our knowledge is correct, we cannot use it to improve society.

2 Any all-embracing theory that claims to have the truth about how to create a better society, such as Marxism, is a mere *meta-narrative* or 'big story' – just someone's *version* of reality, not the truth. Therefore there is no reason to accept the claims that the theory makes.

Postmodernists also reject meta-narratives such as Marxism on the grounds that they have helped to create oppressive totalitarian states that impose their version of the truth on people. For example, in the former Soviet Union, the state's attempt to re-mould society on Marxist principles led to political repression and slave labour camps.

Rejecting meta-narratives that claim absolute truth, postmodernists take a *relativist* position. That is, they argue that all views are true for those who hold them. No one has special access to the truth – including sociologists. All accounts of reality are equally valid. We should therefore celebrate the diversity of views rather than seek to impose one version of the truth on everyone.

But if knowledge is not about the truth, what is it about? According to Jean-Francois Lyotard (1992), in postmodern society, knowledge is just a series of different 'language games' or ways of seeing the world. However, in his view, postmodern society, with its many competing views of the truth, is preferable to modern society, where meta-narratives claimed a monopoly of truth and sometimes sought to impose it by force, as in the Soviet Union. Postmodernity allows groups who had been marginalised by modern society, such as ethnic minorities and women, to be heard.

Baudrillard: simulacra

Like Lyotard, Jean Baudrillard (1983) argues that knowledge is central to postmodern society. He argues that society is no longer based on the production of material goods, but rather on buying and selling knowledge in the form of images and signs. However, unlike signs in past societies, those today bear no relation to physical reality.

Instead, signs stand for nothing other than themselves – they are not symbols of some other real thing. Baudrillard calls such signs simulacra (singular: simulacrum). For example, tabloid newspaper articles about fictitious soap opera characters are 'signs about signs' rather than about an underlying reality.

Baudrillard describes this situation as *hyper-reality*: where the signs appear more real than reality itself and substitute themselves for reality. However, because the signs do not represent anything real, they are literally meaningless. In this respect, Baudrillard is particularly critical of television, which he sees as the main source of simulacra and of our inability to distinguish between image and reality.

Application
Suggest two other examples that would fit the category of 'simulacra'.

Culture, identity and politics

Postmodernists argue that culture and identity in postmodern society differ fundamentally from modern society, especially because of the role of the media in creating hyper-reality. The media are all pervading and they produce an endless stream of ever changing images, values and versions of the truth. As a result, culture becomes fragmented and unstable, so that there is no longer a coherent or fixed set of values shared by members of society.

This bewildering array of different messages and ideas also undermines people's faith in meta-narratives. Confronted by so many different versions of the truth, people cease to believe wholeheartedly in any one version. Furthermore,

given the failure of meta-narratives such as Marxism to deliver a better society, people lose faith in the possibility of rational progress.

In postmodernity, *identity* also becomes destabilised. For example, instead of a fixed identity ascribed by our class, we can now construct our own identity from the wide range of images and lifestyles on offer in the media. We can easily change our identity simply by changing our consumption patterns – picking and mixing cultural goods and media-produced images to define ourselves.

Baudrillard is pessimistic about the postmodern condition. Media-created hyper-reality leaves us unable to distinguish image from reality. This means that we have lost the power to improve society: if we cannot even grasp reality, then we have no power to change it. Political activity to improve the world is impossible, and so the central goal of the Enlightenment project is unachievable. It seems that, while we can change our identity by going shopping, we cannot change society.

Evaluation of postmodernism

Postmodernists make some important points about today's society, such as the significance of the media for culture and identity. Some also argue that its rejection of all-embracing meta-narratives is valuable. However, postmodernism is widely criticised.

From a Marxist perspective, Philo and Miller (2001) make several criticisms of postmodernism:

- It ignores power and inequality. For example, the idea that media images are unconnected with reality ignores the ruling class' use of the media as a tool of domination.
- Similarly, the claim that we freely construct our identities through consumption overlooks the effect of poverty in restricting such opportunities.
- Postmodernists are simply wrong to claim that people cannot distinguish between reality and media image.
- By assuming all views are equally true, it becomes just as valid to deny that the Nazis murdered millions as it does to affirm it. This is a morally indefensible position.

Postmodernism can be criticised on logical grounds. For example, Lyotard's theory is self-defeating: why should we believe a theory that claims that no theory has the truth? Moreover, Best and Kellner (1991) point out that postmodernism is a particularly weak theory: while it identifies some important features of today's society (such as the importance of the media and consumption), it fails to explain how they came about.

Postmodernists are criticised for their pessimism about the Enlightenment project – their view that objective knowledge is impossible and that nothing can be done to improve society. David Harvey (1989) rejects this pessimistic view.

Box 3.12 Poststructuralism: power, truth and discourse

Michel Foucault (1979) sees a discourse as a set of ideas that have become established as knowledge or a way of thinking and speaking about the world. When we use a discourse, it makes us see things in a particular way, and so it is not only a form of knowledge, but also a form of domination – Foucault describes discourse as *power/knowledge*.

For example, today our view of madness is formed by the discourse of psychiatry, which describes it using terms such as 'schizophrenia'. By contrast, in the past, when religious discourse was dominant, madness was seen as 'possession by spirits'. Accepting psychiatric discourse constrains us to think of madness as an absence of rationality, while in the past it was often seen as a divine 'gift'.

Although psychiatric discourse has now largely displaced religious discourse, this does not make it truer. Discourses are simply different and we cannot judge between them: truth is relative – each discourse is true for those who believe it and false for those who don't. There is no objective way of judging between opposed claims to knowledge.

This kills off the Enlightenment project, which depends on the idea that we can achieve progress by discovering true knowledge and using it to improve the world. For Foucault, there can be no progress, since our knowledge is no truer than anyone else's. New knowledge is not progress, just a new form of domination.

He argues that political decisions do make a real difference to people's lives and that knowledge *can* be used to solve human problems. Even if our theories cannot guarantee absolute truth, many sociologists argue that they are at least an approximation to it. As such, they are the best guide we have to improving the world.

While postmodernism has identified some important features of today's society, it is poorly equipped to explain them. By contrast, recent sociological theories have offered more satisfactory explanations of the changes society is undergoing. The remainder of this Topic looks at some of these sociological theories.

Analysis and Evaluation

Is Harvey correct in claiming that political decisions do make a real difference to people's lives? Identify three recent government decisions that could be said to have made a difference.

Theories of late modernity

Unlike postmodernism, theories of late modernity argue that the rapid changes we are witnessing are not the dawn of a new, postmodern era. On the contrary, these changes are actually a continuation of modernity itself.

However, theories of late modernity do recognise that something important is happening. In their view, key features of modernity that were always present have now become intensified. For example, social change has always been a feature of modern society, but now the pace of change has gone into overdrive. In other words, we are still within modernity, but we have entered its 'late' phase.

In this view, if we are still in the modern era, then the theories of modernist sociology are still useful. Unlike postmodernism, theories of late modernity do subscribe to the Enlightenment project – they still believe we can discover objective knowledge and use it to improve society.

Giddens: reflexivity

According to Giddens, we are now at the stage of late or high modernity. A defining characteristic of modern society is that it experiences rapid change – often on a global scale. This is because of two key features of modernity: disembedding and reflexivity.

Giddens defines disembedding as 'the lifting out of social relations from local contexts of interaction'. In other words, today we no longer need face-to-face contact in order to interact – disembedding breaks down geographical barriers and makes interaction more impersonal.

Giddens argues that in high modern society, tradition and custom become much less important and no longer serve as a guide to how we should act, and we become more individualistic. For example, sons are no longer expected to follow the same occupation as their fathers but are free to pursue their own individual goals instead.

Because tradition no longer tells us how to act, we are forced to become *reflexive*. That is, we have to constantly monitor, reflect on and modify our actions in the light of information about the possible risks and opportunities that they might involve.

Consequently, reflexivity means that we are all continually re-evaluating our ideas and theories – nothing is fixed or permanent, everything is up for challenge. Under these conditions, culture in late modern society becomes increasingly unstable and subject to change.

Together, disembedding and reflexivity account for the rapid and widespread nature of social change in high modernity.

In particular, by enabling social interaction to spread rapidly across the globe, they help to drive globalisation.

Modernity and risk

According to Giddens, in late modernity we face a number of *high consequence* risks – major threats to human society. These include military risks such as nuclear war, economic risks such as the instability of the capitalist economy, environmental risks such as global warming, and threats to our freedom from increased state surveillance. All of these are 'manufactured' or human-made rather than natural risks.

However, Giddens rejects the postmodernist view that we cannot intervene to improve things. He believes we can make rational plans to reduce these risks and achieve progress to a better society.

Beck: risk society

Like Giddens, Ulrich Beck (1992) is in the Enlightenment tradition. That is, he believes in the power of reason to create a better world. However, he believes that today's late modern society – which he calls 'risk society' – faces new kinds of dangers:

- In the past, society faced dangers as a result of its inability to control nature, such as drought, famine and disease.
- Today, the dangers we face are manufactured risks resulting from human activities, such as global warming.

Also like Giddens, Beck sees late modernity as a period of growing *individualisation*, in which we become increasingly reflexive. Tradition no longer governs how we act. As a result, we have to think for ourselves and reflect on the possible consequences of our choice of action. This means we must constantly take account of the risks attached to the different courses of action open to us. Beck calls this *reflexive modernisation*.

As a result, 'risk consciousness' becomes increasingly central to our culture – we become more aware of perceived risks and seek to avoid or minimise them. For example, we read of the dangers or benefits of this or that food and change our eating habits accordingly. However, a great deal of our knowledge about risks comes from the mass media, which often give a distorted view of the dangers we face.

Risk, politics and progress

Postmodernists such as Baudrillard reject the Enlightenment project, with its belief in the possibility of progress through action based on rational knowledge. Beck disagrees with this position. Although he is sceptical about scientific progress because of the risks it has brought, he still believes in our ability to use rationality to overcome them. Because we are capable of reflexivity, we can evaluate risks rationally and take political action to reduce them. For example, Beck looks to new political movements such as environmentalism to challenge the direction of technological development.

Activity Media

Risk society

...go to www.sociology.uk.net

Evaluation of theories of late modernity

The concept of reflexivity suggests that we reflect on our actions and then are free to re-shape our lives accordingly to reduce our exposure to risks. However, not everyone has this option. For example, the poor are generally exposed to more environmental risks because they are more likely to live in heavily polluted areas, but may be unable to afford to move to a healthier one.

Criticising Beck, Mike Rustin (1994) argues that it is capitalism, with its pursuit of profit at all costs, that is the source of risk, not technology as such.

Paul Hirst (1993) rejects Beck's view that movements such as environmentalism will bring about significant change, because they are too fragmented to challenge capitalism.

However, theories of late modernity do provide a sociological alternative to postmodernism. They show that rational analysis of society remains possible. They also recognise that, while our knowledge may never be perfect, we can still use it to improve society and reduce the risks we face.

Marxist theories of postmodernity

Like Beck and Giddens, Marxists believe in the Enlightenment project of achieving objective knowledge and using it to improve society. For example, Marx claimed that his theory showed how a working-class revolution could overthrow capitalism and bring an end to exploitation.

However, unlike Beck and Giddens, some Marxists such as Fredric Jameson (1984) and David Harvey (1989) believe that today's society has indeed moved from modernity to postmodernity. They agree with postmodernists that there have been major changes in society, and they describe postmodern culture in similar terms, emphasising the importance of media images, diversity and instability.

However, Marxists offer a very different analysis of postmodernity to Lyotard or Baudrillard. Rather than seeing postmodernity as a fundamental break with the past, Marxists regard it as merely the product of the most recent stage of capitalism. To understand postmodernity, therefore, we must examine its relationship to capitalism.

For Harvey, capitalism is a dynamic system, constantly developing new technologies and ways of organising production to make profits. However, capitalism is prone to periodic crises of profitability, and these produce major changes. Postmodernity arose out of the capitalist crisis of the 1970s, which saw the end of the long economic boom that had lasted since 1945.

Flexible accumulation

This crisis gave rise to a new *regime of accumulation* – a new way of achieving profitability, which Harvey describes as 'flexible accumulation' or post-Fordism. This replaced the more rigid pre-1970s Fordist mass production system.

Flexible accumulation involves the use of information technology, an expanded service and finance sector, job insecurity and the requirement for workers to be 'flexible' to fit their employers' needs. It permits the production of customised products for small, 'niche' markets instead of standardised products for mass markets, and easy switching from producing one product to producing another.

These changes brought many of the cultural characteristics of postmodernity, such as diversity, choice and instability. For example:

- Production of customised products for niche markets promotes cultural diversity.
- Easy switching of production from one product to another encourages constant shifts in fashion.

Flexible accumulation also brought changes in consumption. It turned leisure, culture and identity into commodities. Cultural products such as fashion, music, sports and computer games have become an important source of profit. As Jameson argues, postmodernity represents a more developed form of capitalism because it commodifies virtually all aspects of life, including our identities.

Harvey argues that this more developed form of capitalism also leads to another feature of postmodernity – the *compression of time and space*. The commodification of culture (for example, foreign holidays), the creation of worldwide financial markets, and new information and communications technologies, all serve to shrink the globe.

Politics and progress

Harvey and Jameson argue that flexible accumulation has also brought *political changes* characteristic of postmodernity. In particular, it has weakened the working-class and socialist movements. In their place, a variety of oppositional movements have emerged, such as environmentalism, women's liberation, anti-racism and so on. However, Harvey and Jameson are hopeful that these new social movements can form a 'rainbow alliance' to bring about change.

Thus, Marxist theorists of postmodernity agree with postmodernists that we have moved from modernity to postmodernity. However, as Best and Kellner note, they differ from postmodernists in two ways:

- They retain a faith in Marxist theory as a means of explaining these changes.
- They argue that the goal of the Enlightenment project – to change society for the better – can still be achieved.

Evaluation

Marx 's original view of the Enlightenment project was that it would be achieved by the working class leading a revolution to overthrow capitalism and create a better society. By contrast, by accepting that political opposition to capitalism has fragmented into many different social movements such as feminism and environmentalism, Marxist theories of postmodernity appear to abandon this possibility.

However, the strength of these theories is that by relating the recent changes in society to the nature of capitalism, they are able to offer a sociological explanation of them – something that postmodernists fail to do.

Topic Summary

The nation-state is the focal point of modern society, but with **globalisation** this is undermined. Technological, economic, political and cultural changes are creating a 'global village'. **Postmodernists** argue that these changes indicate the arrival of postmodern society. This society is unstable, fragmented and media-saturated. They reject the possibility of progress and meta-narratives such as Marxism that claim to have the truth about how to achieve it. By contrast, **Giddens and Beck** argue that rapid change is a characteristic of late modern rather than postmodern society. Although this is increasingly a 'risk society', they believe progress to a better society is still possible. **Marxist theories** of modernity argue that postmodernity is simply the latest phase of capitalism and a new means of achieving profits.

EXAMINING GLOBALISATION, MODERNITY AND POSTMODERNITY

QuickCheck Questions

Check your answers at www.sociology.uk.net

1 Identify three features of modern society.
2 Suggest two factors that may be giving rise to a global culture.
3 What does Foucault mean by the term 'discourse'?
4 What do postmodernists mean by the term 'meta-narrative'?
5 What criticisms do postmodernists make of meta-narratives?

6 What are 'simulacra'?
7 What does Giddens mean by 'reflexivity'?
8 What does Beck mean by 'risk society'?
9 Suggest two criticisms of postmodernism.
10 Suggest two ways in which Marxists see flexible accumulation as promoting a postmodern culture.

Questions to try

Item A

According to some sociologists, recent changes such as those associated with globalisation have resulted in a major change in the nature of today's society. For example, postmodernists argue that we no longer live in modern society but are now living in a media-saturated postmodern society in which it is impossible to distinguish image from reality or to change society for the better. As a result, postmodernists argue, we need new theories to explain this new kind of society.

However, some critics argue that although there have been major changes in society, these are a continuation of modernity rather than a completely new type of society.

1 Outline and explain two reasons for the growth of globalisation. (10 marks)

2 Applying material from Item A and your knowledge, evaluate the claim that we are now living in the postmodern age. (20 marks)

The Examiner's Advice

Q1 Spend about 15 minutes on this question. Divide your time fairly equally between the two reasons. You don't need a separate introduction; just start on your first reason. Possible reasons include technological changes, economic changes, political changes, and changes in culture and identity.

Start with a brief definition of globalisation. Then choose two reasons and describe each reason in some detail, explaining how it has led to the growth of globalisation. Do this by creating a 'chain of reasoning' (see Box 4.1 in chapter 4).

For example, technological change in developed and developing countries has led to industrial economies powered by fossil fuels. These produce greenhouse gases, causing global warming and extreme weather events that affect every country on the planet, not just the countries causing the problem.

Apply examples from other topics such as green crime or the global criminal economy to illustrate your explanation of reasons. Use concepts and issues such as the nation-state, trans-national companies, time-space compression, the electronic economy, the global capitalist class, migration, tourism, global culture, and global risk society.

Q2 Spend about 30 minutes on this. You need to consider a range of theories about the nature of today's society. Start by explaining Lyotard and Baudrillard's postmodernist views and then consider theories of late modernity such as those of Giddens and Beck, and Marxist theories of postmodernity such as Jameson and Harvey. Apply material from the Item where possible, linking this to your own knowledge.

Use concepts and issues such as anti-foundationalism, the Enlightenment project, meta-narratives, simulacra, hyper-reality, fragmentation, identity, power/knowledge, poststructuralism, reflexivity, disembedding, risk society, individualisation, reflexive modernisation, risk consciousness, post-Fordism and flexible accumulation.

Rather than leaving evaluation to a separate 'block' at the end, evaluate as you go along. Evaluation should focus on two issues: firstly, whether the changes amount to a new kind of society (postmodern), or simply a 'late modern' continuation of modern society, and secondly, how successful the different explanations of the changes are. Use theories of late modernity and Marxist theories of postmodernity to challenge the postmodernist view.

KEEP YOUR COINS
I WANT CHANGE

MEMBERS OF THE PUBLIC
DENIED ACCESS TO THE LIBRARY
BECAUSE THEY ARE HOMELESS

Campaigning against homelessness: who has more influence on policy – campaign groups or sociologists?

GETTING STARTED

Working in pairs, complete the following tasks:

1 Make a list of as many social problems as you can (for example, homelessness).

2 For three of the social problems you have identified, suggest a way in which government might intervene to overcome them (for example, providing shelters for the homeless).

3 Make a list of any pressure groups that might have an interest in influencing policy in this area (for example, charities such as Shelter).

4 What specific questions could sociologists try to answer through their research that might help governments to solve the social problems you have identified?

5 Governments often have a different view of social problems and their solution from the views of sociologists. For the problems you have chosen, suggest reasons why this might be the case.

Learning objectives

After studying this Topic, you should:

- Understand the difference between social problems and sociological problems.

- Know the factors that may affect the extent to which sociology can influence social policy.

- Know the main sociological perspectives on the relationship between sociology and social policy, and be able to evaluate their strengths and limitations.

SOCIOLOGY AND SOCIAL POLICY

Social policy is generally thought of as the plans and actions of governments to tackle 'social problems', especially the welfare of the population in areas such as education and health. Many sociologists are interested in solving social problems and much of their research produces policy proposals for government to act upon.

In this Topic, we examine the relationship between sociology and social policy. For example:

- Should it be the job of sociologists to influence social policies?
- What kinds of policies do different perspectives favour?
- How far does sociological research actually influence policies?

Social problems and sociological problems

In order to understand the role of sociology in relation to social policy, it is useful to distinguish first between social problems and sociological problems.

Social problems

According to Peter Worsley (1977), 'a social problem is some piece of social behaviour that causes public friction and/or private misery and calls for collective action to solve it'.

For example, poverty, educational underachievement, juvenile delinquency and divorce may all be seen as social problems by members of society, and governments may be called upon to produce policies to tackle them.

Sociological problems

According to Worsley, a sociological problem is 'any pattern of relationships that calls for explanation'. In other words, it is any piece of behaviour that we wish to make sense of.

This might be something that society regards as a social problem, for example why some people are poor or commit crime. But it can also include behaviour that society doesn't normally regard as a problem – for example, why people are prosperous or law-abiding. As Worsley puts it:

> 'From the point of view of the State or the neighbours, quiet families are not problem families. Sociologically speaking, they are.'

In other words, 'normal' behaviour is just as interesting to sociologists as behaviour that people see as a social problem. In fact, some sociologists show little or no interest in solving social problems. They see their goal as being to discover knowledge for its own sake.

On the other hand, many sociologists *are* interested in solving social problems through their research. For example, sociologists who feel strongly about poverty have conducted research aimed at discovering solutions. Similarly, many sociologists are employed directly by government departments such as the Home Office. These sociologists often have a direct input into making policies and evaluating their effectiveness, for example in reducing crime.

> **Application**
> Suggest three examples of behaviour that are usually regarded as normal rather than as problems. Why might sociologists be interested in them?

The influence of sociology on policy

However, even when sociologists do conduct research into social problems, there is no guarantee that policy-makers will study their findings, or that any solutions they propose will find their way into social policies. Many factors may affect whether or not sociological research succeeds in influencing policy:

- **Electoral popularity** Research findings and recommendations might point to a policy that would be unpopular with voters.
- **Ideological and policy preferences of governments** If the researcher's value-stance or perspective is similar to the political ideology of the government, they may stand more chance of influencing its policies.
- **Interest groups** These are pressure groups that seek to influence government policies in their own interests. For

example, business groups may succeed in persuading government not to raise the minimum wage, even though this might reduce poverty.

- **Globalisation** Social policy isn't just made by nation states in isolation. International organisations such as the European Union and the International Monetary Fund (IMF) may influence the social policies of individual governments. For example, the IMF's 'structural adjustment programmes' have required less developed countries to introduce fees for education and health care as a condition for aid, despite evidence from social scientists that this makes development less likely.
- **Critical sociology** Sociologists who are critical of the state and powerful groups, such as Marxists, may be

regarded as too extreme, hostile or impractical and therefore unlikely to influence policy.

- **Cost** Even if the government is sympathetic to the sociologist's findings, it may not have sufficient funds to implement an appropriate policy based on them, or it may have other spending priorities and commitments.

- **Funding sources** In some cases, sociologists may tone down their findings and policy recommendations so as to fit in with their paymasters' wishes – a case of 'he who pays the piper calls the tune'. Similarly, policymakers may recruit sociologists who share their assumptions and political values. The research findings may then be used to justify what the policymakers intended to do in the first place. Similarly, 'think tanks' or research institutes often have particular political sympathies – for example, some are seen as left leaning, while others have right-wing sympathies. Politicians seeking a particular result to justify their favoured policies can be selective in which think tanks they turn to for research.

In addition to any direct influence on policymakers, social scientists' ideas sometimes become part of mainstream culture and influence the way people see social problems.

This in turn can affect the policies that governments produce. For example, John Bowlby's (1965) idea that young children's relationships with their mother are crucial for normal development became widely accepted by many people. When this happens, it can influence the climate of opinion in favour of policies that reflect these social science-derived ideas. In the example above, it may have influenced policies on day care, young offenders and so on.

The power to define the problem

Sociological research is thus only one possible element in shaping social policy. Ultimately, any policy is the result of a political decision by those in power. As Tom Burden (1998) says, social policies:

> 'cannot be very well understood if they are simply treated as "neutral" attempts to deal with "problems". Indeed, what is to count as a problem is itself generally a matter of political debate.'

Often, those with power are the ones who are able to define what is and what is not a problem, and what if anything should be done about it.

Perspectives on social policy and sociology

Different sociological perspectives hold different views of the nature of the state and the social policy it produces. As a result, each perspective tends to take a different view of the role of sociology in relation to social policy. We shall now examine the major perspectives on policy and its relationship to sociology.

Positivism and functionalism

Early positivists such as Comte and Durkheim took the view that sociology was a science and would discover both the cause of social problems and scientifically based solutions to them. As such, their approach was part of the Enlightenment project to use science and reason to improve society. For example, Durkheim's analysis led him to propose a meritocratic education system and the abolition of inherited wealth as ways to foster a sense that society was fair, which would promote social cohesion.

Functionalists see society as based on value consensus and free from fundamental conflicts. Like the positivists, they see the state as serving the interests of society as a whole, producing and implementing rational social policies for the good of all. These policies help society run more smoothly and efficiently. For example, educational policies are seen as promoting equal opportunity and social integration, while health and housing policies assist the family in performing its functions more effectively.

For both functionalists and positivists, the sociologist's role is to provide the state with objective, scientific information. By investigating social problems and discovering their causes, sociologists provide the necessary information on which the state can base its policies.

In this view, the sociologist is rather like the medical researcher. Just as medical research discovers the causes of disease as a basis for prevention or cure, so the sociologist's role is to investigate social problems scientifically. This provides the state with objective information about their extent and explanations of their causes as well as possible 'cures' in the shape of policy recommendations.

Functionalists favour social policies that are sometimes referred to as 'piecemeal social engineering'. In other words, they favour a cautious approach, tackling one specific issue at a time.

However, the piecemeal approach has been criticised. For example, Marxists argue that educational policies aimed at equalising opportunity for children of different classes are often defeated by the influence of poverty in wider society. In other words, social problems such as underachievement are simply aspects of a wider structure of class inequality, and so we need to change the basic structure of society in order to solve these specific problems.

The social democratic perspective

The social democratic perspective on social policy shares this view. It favours a major redistribution of wealth and income from the rich to the poor. Sociologists adopting this perspective, such as Peter Townsend (1979), argue that they should be involved in researching social problems and making policy recommendations to eradicate them. For example, Townsend conducted research on poverty. On the basis of his findings, he made recommendations for policies such as higher benefit levels, and more public spending on health, education and welfare.

Similarly, the Black Report (1980) on class inequalities in health made 37 far-reaching policy recommendations for reducing these deep-rooted inequalities. These included free school meals for all children, improved working conditions and more spending to improve housing. The Labour government had originally commissioned the report in 1977 but it was only completed in 1980, the year after Mrs Thatcher's Conservative government came to power. Her government refused to implement the report's recommendations on grounds of cost, and tried to restrict its publication.

Criticisms

Marxists criticise the social democratic perspective. While they agree that social problems such as class inequalities in health are deep-rooted, they reject the idea that even policies as far-reaching as those proposed by the Black Report are enough to solve the problem. In their view, it is capitalism that is ultimately responsible for these inequalities and so the problem cannot be solved without abolishing capitalism. They also argue that in any event, as the government response to the Black Report showed, the capitalist state is unlikely to introduce costly public spending policies to benefit the working class. Thus, rational social policies proposed by sociologists such as Townsend will fall on deaf ears as far as policymakers are concerned.

From a different perspective, postmodernists criticise attempts by sociologists to influence policy. For postmodernists, it is impossible to discover objective truth. All knowledge produced by research is uncertain, and so sociological findings cannot provide a satisfactory basis for policy-making. In this view, sociologists can only take the role of 'interpreters', offering one view of reality among many, and not the role of 'legislators' (lawmakers), as modernist sociologists such as functionalists and social democrats have tried to do.

Marxism

Marxists see society as divided by a fundamental conflict of interest in which the ruling capitalist class exploit the labour of the working class. Unlike functionalists, they do not see the state and its policies as benefiting all members of society. In the Marxist view, the state represents the ruling class, and its social policies serve the interests of capitalism, not those of society as a whole:

- **Policies provide ideological legitimation** to mask capitalist exploitation. For example, the welfare state gives capitalism a 'human face', making it appear that the system cares about the poor, sick and old.
- **They maintain the labour force for further exploitation** For example, the NHS serves capitalism by keeping workers fit enough to work.
- **They are a means of preventing revolution** when class conflict intensifies and threatens the stability of capitalism. For example, Marxists see the policies that created the welfare state after the Second World War (1939-45) as a way of buying off working-class opposition to capitalism.

Marxists recognise that social policies do sometimes provide real, if limited, benefits to the working class. However, such gains are constantly threatened with reversal by capitalism's tendency to go into periodic crises of profitability, leading to cuts in state spending on welfare.

Therefore, research that reveals the unpleasant truth about the social problems capitalism creates will not be used to formulate policies to solve these problems – as the fate of the Black Report shows. In fact, for Marxists, such problems cannot be solved by the capitalist state in any case, since capitalism is based on putting profits before human needs. The only solution to social problems is a revolution to overthrow capitalism and create a classless society.

For Marxists, therefore, the sociologist's main role should be to criticise capitalist social policy, not to serve the capitalist state. The sociologist must reveal the exploitation that underpins capitalism, and the way in which the ruling class use social policies to mask this exploitation and buy off revolt with minor concessions.

However, critics argue that Marxist views on social policy and the role of sociologists are impractical and unrealistic. Social democrats criticise them for rejecting the idea that research can help bring about progressive policies within the capitalist system. For example, poverty researchers have at times had some positive impact on policy.

Feminism

Like Marxists, feminists see society as based on conflict, but in their view the fundamental conflict is between genders, not classes. Society is patriarchal (male dominated), benefiting men at women's expense, and the state perpetuates women's subordination through its social policies.

For example, family policies may assume that the 'normal' family is a conventional nuclear family with a heterosexual married couple. Thus, if the state assumes this and offers benefits to married couples but not to cohabiting ones, these policies may produce a self-fulfilling prophecy, encouraging the kind of family that the state assumed to be the norm in the first place and making it more difficult for people to live in other kinds of family.

Feminist research has had an impact in a number of policy areas. For example, in education, it has influenced policies such as learning materials that promote more positive images of females and training to sensitise teachers to the need to avoid gender bias.

Many of these policies reflect the liberal feminist view that anti-discrimination reforms will ultimately bring about gender equality.

On the other hand, radical feminist ideas have also had some influence on social policy. Radical feminists regard men as the direct oppressors of women, especially through the family. They therefore favour *separatism* – the idea that women need to separate themselves from men to be free from patriarchy. One policy that reflects this is refuges for women escaping domestic violence. For example, the Women's Aid Federation supports a national network of over 500 such services, often with funding from government.

Overall, it is clear that feminist sociological research has had some impact on social policies in areas that affect women, in part due to the success of the broader feminist movement in gaining greater political influence since the 1970s. However, many feminists reject the view that reformist social policies can liberate women. For example, both Marxist and radical feminists call for more far-reaching changes that the existing state cannot deliver.

The New Right

The New Right believe that the state should have only minimal involvement in society. In particular, they are opposed to using state provision of welfare to deal with social problems. In their view, state intervention in areas such as family life, income support, education and health care robs people of their freedom to make their own choices and undermines their sense of responsibility. This in turn leads to greater social problems, such as crime and delinquency.

For example, Charles Murray (1984) argues that generous welfare benefits act as 'perverse incentives' that weaken the family's self-reliance. They encourage the growth of a dependency culture and an underclass of lone mothers, undisciplined children, and irresponsible fathers who abandon their families. For this reason, Murray favours a reduction in state spending on welfare.

The New Right are therefore highly critical of many existing policies. However, they are not opposed to social policy as such, and they see the role of sociologists as being to propose alternative policies. These policies should aim to restore individuals' responsibility for their own welfare, rather than leaving it to the state.

For example, *Breakdown Britain*, a report by Conservative think tank, the Social Justice Policy Group (2007), proposes a range of new social policies aimed at the family. These include marriage preparation and parenting classes, and support from the tax and benefit system for mothers who stay at home. The report's main thrust is that governments have stripped citizens of responsibility for their own welfare and neglected the support networks that give people their quality of life. The role of social policy should be to enable people to help themselves, rather than the welfare state attempting, and failing, to do it for them.

Influence of New Right thinking

Because of its ideological opposition to the state having a major role in welfare, New Right thinking has tended to be particularly attractive to the Conservative Party. However, some Labour policies have shown the influence of New Right views. For example, New Labour regards a married couple as normally the best place to bring up children.

While not seeing a major role for the state in welfare, the New Right support a strong 'law and order' policy and research by right realists such as Wilson and Kelling has been influential in introducing zero tolerance policies.

However, the research used by the New Right has been questioned. For example, the validity of the data on which Murray bases his claims about a link between absent fathers and delinquency has been challenged. Similarly, New Right policy proposals often use the findings of politically sympathetic think tanks.

Activity	Discussion

Differing perspectives on policy

...go to www.sociology.uk.net

Topic Summary

Sociologists often research social problems, but many other factors influence policies. **Positivists and functionalists** see sociology as providing objective knowledge to guide policy for the good of society. **Social democrats** see sociology as proposing policies to make major structural changes, such as the abolition of poverty. **Marxists** argue that sociology must remain critical of the policies of the capitalist state. **Feminists** see policy as reflecting patriarchy and use research to influence policy in favour of women. The **New Right** propose policies to tackle the culture of dependency.

EXAMINING SOCIOLOGY AND SOCIAL POLICY

QuickCheck Questions

Check your answers at www.sociology.uk.net

1 Explain the difference between a social problem and a sociological problem.

2 Identify three factors affecting social policy apart from sociologists' research findings.

3 Which early sociologists argued that sociology should act as a guide to social policy?

4 Identify three ways in which Marxists see social policies as helping to maintain capitalism.

5 How might social research be affected by sources of funding?

6 Suggest three policies that feminist research may have influenced.

Questions to try

Item A

Early positivist sociologists believed that sociology was a 'science of society' that would enable us to discover the causes of social problems and offer solutions to them. Sociologists' research findings would then enable the state to implement appropriate social policies to deal with the problems. In the same way as medical research can discover cures for diseases, so sociological research would help solve society's problems.

However, Marxists claim that the main function of social policy is to maintain capitalism and that the role of sociologists should therefore be to criticise policy, not to serve the capitalist state.

1 Outline and explain two views of the role of social policy in society. (10 marks)

2 Applying material from Item A and your knowledge, evaluate different sociological perspectives' views of the relationship between sociology and social policy. (20 marks)

The Examiner's Advice

Q1 Spend about 15 minutes on this question. Divide your time fairly equally between the two views. You don't need a separate introduction; just start on your first view. Possible views of the role of social policy include positivist/functionalist, social democratic, Marxist, feminist and the New Right.

Choose two views and describe each view in some detail, explaining how it sees the role of social policy. Do this by creating a 'chain of reasoning' (see Box 4.1 in chapter 4). For example, New Right thinkers believe the state should have only a minimal role in society, leaving welfare to market forces instead. This means that they only advocate policies that give individuals responsibility for themselves or which control actions that threaten society.

Apply examples from topics such as the family, education or crime to illustrate your explanation. Use concepts and issues such as perverse incentives, dependency culture, right realism, zero tolerance, patriarchy, the self-fulfilling prophecy, capitalism, ideological legitimation, maintaining the labour force for capitalism, preventing revolution, reducing inequality, value consensus, piecemeal social engineering.

Q2 Spend about 30 minutes on this question. This question is about the relationship between sociology and social policy. It refers to perspectives plural, so you need to consider two or more from the following: positivism, functionalism, the social democratic perspective, Marxism, feminism and the New Right. Explain the different perspectives' views, using concepts and issues referred to in the advice for Question 1, plus others such as social problems and sociological problems, sociology as a science, objectivity, and the role of the state.

Apply material from the Item where possible, linking this to your own knowledge. Use examples of policies from other topic areas such as education, the family or crime, but make sure you apply them to the relevant sociological perspectives on policy.

Rather than leaving evaluation to a separate 'block' at the end, evaluate as you go along. Your evaluation should focus on how each perspective sees the relationship between sociology and social policy, including what kind of influence sociology does have or should have on policy. You can also offer a final evaluative overview at the end of your answer.

EXAMINING THEORY AND METHODS

Item A   Questionnaires are favoured by positivists as a method of research. By asking the same questions and with the same response categories, questionnaires are seen as producing reliable data because they can be repeated again and again. Questionnaires can be distributed often on a large scale, by hand, via the internet or through the mail. This can increase the representativeness of the resulting data.

Whichever way the questionnaire is distributed, the resulting data is easily quantifiable. This has limitations as well as benefits to the sociologist.

1   Outline and explain two criticisms of postmodernist theory.   (10 marks)
2   Outline and explain two problems of using documents in sociological research.   (10 marks)
3   Applying material from Item A and your knowledge, evaluate the usefulness of questionnaires in sociological research.   (20 marks)

The Examiner's Advice

Q1 Spend about 15 minutes on this question. Divide your time fairly equally between the two criticisms. You don't need a separate introduction; just start on your first criticism. Possible criticisms include its pessimism about progress, it ignores power and inequality, it ignores social constraints on our ability to freely choose identities, people can distinguish between reality and media imagery, logical criticisms, and it fails to explain features it describes.

Choose two criticisms and describe them in some detail, explaining how each connects to postmodernist ideas. Do this by creating a 'chain of reasoning'. For example, postmodernists argue that objective knowledge about society is impossible and so we cannot use it as the basis for changing society, but critics reject this pessimistic view. Sociological theories can approximate to the truth and can be used to make political decisions that improve society.

Apply examples from other topics such as the family. For example, postmodernists overstate people's freedom to choose what kinds of family relationships and structures they are involved in. Use concepts and issues such as those mentioned above plus relativism, the Enlightenment project, objective knowledge, simulacra.

Q2 Spend about 15 minutes on this question. Divide your time fairly equally between the two problems. You don't need a separate introduction; just start on your first problem. Possible problems include issues of access, representativeness, authenticity, credibility, reliability, interpretation, consent and selectivity. You can refer to specific types of documents such as public, private and historical documents.

Choose two problems and describe each problem in some detail. Do this by creating a 'chain of reasoning'. For example, not all social groups have the same literacy skills, leisure and resources to enable them to keep a diary. This means that using diaries as a source of data may give a distorted picture of events because they are more likely to reflect the experiences of more advantaged groups in society.

Apply examples from topics such as education, family or crime and deviance; for example, Hey's use of notes that girls had passed around in class. Use concepts and issues such as public interest, validity, interpretivism, positivism, formal and thematic content analysis, as well as those referred to above.

For question 3, see the student answer by Anna on the next page, along with the examiner's comments and marks.

Answer by Anna

Question 3: Applying material from Item A and your knowledge, evaluate the usefulness of mailed questionnaires in sociological research.

Sociologists disagree about the usefulness of mailed questionnaires. Positivists argue that they can produce reliable, representative, quantitative data which is easy to analyse, but interpretivists argue that they do not produce valid results.

One problem is that because the researcher is not present when the questionnaire is completed, they don't know if the right person filled it in (e.g. the wrong age group) or if they took it seriously. It also means the researcher is not there to explain the meaning of questions if the respondent doesn't understand them. If the respondent has learning difficulties, this can be a big problem. They are also less likely to return them, reducing representativeness. However, because the researcher isn't present, respondents don't feel pressurised to give socially desirable answers and may be more truthful, improving validity.

However, interpretivists argue that mailed questionnaires don't produce valid data. With pre-determined, usually closed-ended questions and limited choice of answers, respondents have no chance to raise issues that are not asked about in the questionnaire, or to express their thoughts in their own words. Instead they must force their views to fit the researcher's answer choices. Options like 'strongly disagree' may mean different things to different respondents.

However, positivists see fixed questions and answer categories as an advantage in terms of reliability, because it allows the questionnaire to be repeated with other samples – it is fully replicable. This also produces computer-analysable quantitative data that positivists can use to identify trends, patterns, and causal relationships between factors. This helps fulfil their aim to be scientific.

Positivists also like this method because the postal system allows them to reach a wide range of people over a large area, which increases representativeness. However, postal questionnaires may not always be representative because of low response rates, e.g. because they are seen as 'junk mail', or may go to the wrong address. Maybe only a certain type of person replies, such as those who are especially interested in the issue. This skews the data and reduces its representativeness.

Overall, mailed questionnaires have both strengths and weaknesses. Whether a sociologist chooses to use them or not will depend on their theoretical perspective (positivist or interpretivist) and which they value most – validity, reliability or representativeness.

> A good way to start – but could mention other issues, e.g. practical and ethical.

> Points made clearly about relevant problems, with example (learning difficulties) and evaluation (socially desirable answers/validity). Concept of detachment would be useful here.

> Good analysis of effects. 'Inflexibility' and 'imposing researcher's meanings' would be useful concepts here. Not very specific to mailed questionnaires.

> Quite good explanation of some theoretical advantages, though could give more context on positivism.

> Focuses on the mailed dimension, but more is needed.

> Correct to point out importance of perspective, but neglects other issues, e.g. preference of funding body, practical and ethical issues etc.

You should spend about 30 minutes on this question. Anna has covered a range of issues associated with mailed questionnaires, placed within the positivist-interpretivist debate. However, focus on the mailed dimension is fairly limited. You should look for ways to link this to issues of cost, time, inflexibility and detachment. Note that 'mailed' can include emailed as well as postal questionnaires, so you could consider whether the same strengths and limitations apply to both types.

Although Anna makes some reference to theory, you would need to give your answer more context on positivism, including reference to hypothesis testing, detachment and objectivity. You could also include broader issues such as the intrusion of the sociologist's values.

There is only limited consideration of practical and ethical factors in Anna's answer. Questionnaires have fewer ethical problems than most methods, but you should say that researchers still need to guarantee respondents anonymity and offer them the right to withdraw. Similarly, you could also mention factors such as the influence of funding bodies in determining research questions or the lack of need to train interviewers. Lastly, when you draw on material from the Item, it is always a good idea to point this out in your answer by using a phrase like 'As it says in Item A'.

CHAPTER 4

Preparing for the Exams

Preparing for the A level exams   252

Practice papers   257

The examiner's advice   260

GETTING STARTED

Here are some things to help you prepare for your exams.

1   Make a list of all the Topics in Chapters 2, 3 and 4 of Book One and Chapters 1, 2 and 3 of Book Two. This will give you a framework for your revision.

2   Organise your class notes, activities and homework assignments for each Topic. Use the subheadings in each Topic as a guide to how you can organise your notes etc. You might want to work with a partner or in a small group and share your work or fill in any gaps you may have together.

3   In preparing to tackle the exams, make a list of the main issues covered in each Topic and the debates about them. Using these issues and debates, go to your notes and textbook to find the material you need in order to understand them.

4   From your notes and textbook, make a list of the key concepts needed for each Topic. Link these to the debates and issues.

5   To familiarise yourself with some possible exam questions for each Topic, look at the questions at the end of each of the Topics and the practice papers in Book One and in this chapter.

For further revision help and advice, see our revision guides.

- Succeed at A level Sociology Book One, including AS level
- Succeed at A level Sociology Book Two

Go to www.sociology.uk.net

This chapter focuses on the examinations. It deals with:

- The knowledge and skills you have to show in your A level exams
- The format of the exam papers
- The different types of question and how to tackle them.

The assessment objectives

In the A level sociology exams, your answers are assessed in terms of three aims or 'assessment objectives' or AOs for short. These are:

AO1 Knowledge and Understanding

AO2 the skill of Application

AO3 the skills of Analysis and Evaluation.

Roughly 45% of the marks are for AO1 and the remaining 55% or so are for AO2 and AO3, so it's very important that you show evidence of all of the assessment objectives in your answers. Let's take a closer look at the kind of knowledge, understanding and skills you need to demonstrate in your answers.

Knowledge and Understanding

You need to know about and understand some of the main theories, research methods and concepts (ideas) that sociologists use in their work.

You also need to be familiar with some of the studies they have carried out and what these studies have found.

Application

The skill of application includes:

- Linking ideas, concepts, theories, studies and methods to each other and to the question.
- Showing how the material you have selected is relevant to the question. In questions on methods in context, connecting the strengths and limitations of a method to the characteristics of a particular research issue.
- Using material from an Item when the question tells you to, linking it to your own knowledge and to the question.
- Using relevant examples. These could be from studies, news and current events, personal experience, other topics you have studied in sociology etc.
- Linking ideas from one area in sociology to material in another area.

Analysis

The skill of analysis includes:

- Breaking down an argument or explanation into the ideas that make it up and showing how they fit together.
- Comparing and contrasting ideas to show their similarities and differences.
- Organising your essays with a well-focused introduction and a clear, logical line of reasoning both within and between paragraphs, leading to an appropriate conclusion.

Evaluation

Evaluation is about weighing things up, giving informed opinions or making balanced judgments about something. The 'something' could be different evidence, ideas, views, theories or methods.

The skill of evaluation includes:

- Looking at the arguments and evidence for and against a particular view.

- Examining a theory's assumptions or linking it to a particular perspective.
- Putting forward alternative views or perspectives to create a debate.
- Discussing the strengths (or advantages) and limitations (or disadvantages) of a research method.

In practice, the different assessment objectives are often interlinked. For example, in order to select and apply the right information (AO2), you first need to know and understand some sociology (AO1).

Preparing for the A level exams

For A level, you will take three written exam papers.

Each paper is two hours long and is worth 80 marks – so that's one and a half minutes per mark (the same as for AS).

Each paper is worth one third of the total marks for your A level.

If you took the AS exams in your first year, you will find that most of the A level questions have a very similar form to those at AS.

Next we look at the structure of the three papers and then we follow this with advice on how to answer the different types of question.

A level Paper 1

This paper covers Education, Methods in Context, and Theory and Methods. There are six questions and you must answer all of them. Questions 01 to 04 are on Education, worth a total of 50 marks.

Questions 01 and 02 are short questions on Education worth a total of 10 marks (four plus six).

Question 03 is on Education and is worth 10 marks. Note that this question type only appears at A level, not at AS. It comes with an Item containing material for you to apply in your answer. The question begins: 'Applying material from Item A, analyse two' things – such as two reasons, effects, factors, changes etc. Here is an example:

*Applying material from **Item A**, analyse **two** factors outside schools that contribute to working-class underachievement.*

Question 04 is a 30-mark essay question on Education. It is accompanied by Item B, which contains material for you to apply in your answer. Here is an example:

*Applying material from **Item B** and your knowledge, evaluate the view that although Marxist and functionalist approaches focus on similar issues,*

they reach very different conclusions about the role of education.

Question 05 is a Methods in Context (Education) question worth 20 marks. It is accompanied by Item C, which contains stimulus material for you to apply. This takes exactly the same form as the AS Methods in Context question. See below for details of how to tackle Methods in Context questions.

Question 06 is on Theory and Methods and is worth 10 marks. This takes the same form as the 10-mark questions you may be familiar with from the AS exams. Here is an example:

*Outline and explain **two** ethical problems sociologists may experience when conducting research.*

Before reading on, turn to page 257 and take a look at the practice paper for Paper 1. Focus on the overall structure of the paper rather than trying to figure out the answers to the questions, and check the paper against the points above.

A level Paper 2

This paper has two sections: A and B. Each section has four optional topics in it and you must choose one from each section. Each option is worth 40 marks.

Section A options are A1 Culture and Identity, A2 Families and Households, A3 Health, and A4 Work, Poverty and Welfare. (These are the same as the options on AS level Paper 2.)

Section B options are B1 Beliefs in Society, B2 Global Development, B3 The Media, and B4 Stratification and Differentiation.

If you used Book One in the first year of your course, you will have studied Families and Households as your Section A option. In Book Two, you will have studied Beliefs in Society as your Section B option.

Each of your two options has three compulsory questions:

A **10-mark question** asking you to 'Outline and explain two' things. Here is an example:

*Outline and explain **two** causes of increased diversity of family structures in the last 50 years.*

A **10-mark question** like Question 03 on Paper 1 (see above). This question is accompanied by an Item. Here is an example:

*Applying material from **Item A**, analyse **two** changes in the status of childhood since the 19th century.*

A **20-mark essay question** accompanied by an Item containing stimulus material for you to apply in your answer. Here is an example:

*Applying material from **Item B** and your knowledge, evaluate the contribution of feminist sociologists to our understanding of families and households today.*

Before reading on, take a look at the practice paper for Paper 2 on page 258. Focus on its overall structure and check it against the points above. You will see that we have only included the questions on Families and Households and Beliefs in Society, since these are the two topics you need to choose if you have been using this book and Book One.

You should also note that in the real exam paper, the subsection A2 Families and Households is the *second* subsection in the paper, not the first (it comes *after* A1 Culture and Identity). Don't make the mistake of diving in and starting to answer questions in the wrong subsection!

A level Paper 3

This paper covers Crime and Deviance, and Theory and Methods. There are six questions and you must answer all of them. Questions 01 to 04 are on Crime and Deviance, worth a total of 50 marks.

Questions 01 and 02 are short questions on Crime and Deviance worth a total of 10 marks (four plus six).

Question 03 is on Crime and Deviance. It is worth 10 marks. Note that this question type only appears at A level, not at AS. It comes with an Item containing material for you to apply in your answer. The question begins: 'Applying material from Item A, analyse two' things – such as two reasons, effects, factors, changes etc. Here is an example:

*Applying material from **Item A**, analyse **two** reasons why women appear less likely to commit crime than men.*

Question 04 is a 30-mark essay question on Crime and Deviance. It is accompanied by Item B, which contains material for you to apply in your answer. Here is an example:

*Applying material from **Item B** and your knowledge, evaluate the usefulness of right realist approaches to crime.*

Question 05 is on Theory and Methods and is worth 10 marks. This takes the same form as the 10-mark questions you may be familiar with from AS. Here is an example:

*Outline and explain **two** reasons why some sociologists choose to use official statistics in their research.*

Question 06 is a Theory and Methods essay question worth 20 marks. It is accompanied by Item C, which contains stimulus material for you to apply. This question takes exactly the same form as the 20-mark essay questions in A level Paper 2.

Before reading on, turn to page 259 and take a look at the practice paper for Paper 3. Focus on the overall structure of the paper rather than trying to figure out the answers to the questions, and check the paper against the points above.

How long to spend on each question

Now that you've got an idea of the overall structure of the A level papers, you need to be aware of how much time to spend on each question. Luckily, there's a simple rule you can apply to give you an idea of how much time to invest in each answer, which is this:

Take the number of marks the question is worth and multiply it by one and a half. This will give you the number of minutes you should spend on it.

For example, if the question is worth 10 marks, you should spend about 15 minutes answering it. If it's worth 20 marks, spend about 30 minutes on it.

However, in practice, you might be able to answer the short questions (ones worth less than 10 marks) a bit more quickly. This will give you a few extra minutes for the 10, 20 and 30 mark questions, where you need to do a little more thinking, studying the stimulus Item and planning your answer.

Answering the short questions

The short questions carry four or six marks. It's very important not to spend too much time writing long answers to them – you're not expected or required to do so. And as well as wasting time, long answers are often less clear and may end up scoring lower marks.

These questions ask you to outline two things (for 4 marks) or three things (for 6 marks). These could be things such as factors, features, reasons, causes, effects, functions, ways, problems, advantages, disadvantages, criticisms or other issues. For example:

*Outline **two** reasons why crime and deviance may be found in all societies.*

*Outline **three** ways in which the ethnocentric curriculum may operate in schools.*

There is a four-mark and a six-mark 'Outline' question on both Education (Paper 1), and Crime and Deviance (Paper 3).

points to remember

- Your answers should be quite short: for each advantage, way, reason etc that you are asked to provide, one or two sentences will be enough. For example, you could write, 'The ethnocentric curriculum operates through only teaching European languages and not offering languages spoken by pupils from minority ethnic backgrounds, such as Urdu or Bengali.'
- Start each point on a separate line.
- If you're not sure whether all your points are right but you can think of an extra one, you can put this one down too. But remember, the more points you give, the more time you use up.

Answering the longer questions

There are several types of longer question on the A level papers:

- 10-mark 'Outline and explain' questions on Theory and Methods, Families and Households, and Beliefs in Society.
- 10-mark 'Applying material from Item A, analyse' questions on Education and on Crime and Deviance.
- 20-mark essay questions on Families and Households, Beliefs in Society, and Theory and Methods.
- 30-mark essay questions on Education and on Crime and Deviance.
- 20-mark essay questions on Methods in Context (Education).

We shall now look at what each of these involves.

The 10-mark 'Outline and explain' questions

These require you to outline and explain two things, such as two factors, features, reasons, causes, effects, functions, ways, problems, advantages, disadvantages, criticisms or other issues in Families and Households, Beliefs in Society, and Theory and Methods. For example:

*Outline and explain **two** reasons for increases in family diversity.*

The instruction to explain rather than just outline (unlike in the short questions) means you need to show your knowledge and understanding by going into each reason, factor, effect etc, in some detail. You should do this by creating a chain of reasoning to link your ideas into a clear explanation. See Box 4.1 for more about chains of reasoning.

This question type has the same format as the 10-mark questions you will be familiar with if you have taken the AS exams.

The 10-mark 'Applying material from the Item, analyse' questions

These questions require you to analyse two factors, reasons etc, but you must find two points in the Item and use them in your answer by building them into chains of reasoning. See Box 4.1 for more about chains of reasoning.

The 20- and 30-mark essay questions

These are essay questions with stimulus Items. The questions require you to evaluate something.

Box 4.1	The chain of reasoning

A chain of reasoning is a series of steps in an explanation, where each idea is like a link that connects to the one before it, leading eventually to a reasoned conclusion. For example, in a question on gender differences in subject choice, you could take the idea that science is in the male gender domain, link it to how this idea is projected (through textbooks, examples, role models etc), then link this to its effect in putting girls off science.

Often, you can add further links, so your conclusion itself becomes part of a longer chain of reasoning and a more developed conclusion.

Building chains of reasoning is important because it shows the examiner you can put together sociological arguments to reach conclusions. This means chains of reasoning are essential to every question where you have to write more than a sentence or two. That is, any question worth 10, 20 or 30 marks.

When you answer these questions, write in full sentences organised into paragraphs. A basic chain of reasoning could be put in a single paragraph, while a more extended chain could run for two or more paragraphs, depending on the point you are developing and the time you have available to answer the question.

Your ideas for chains of reasoning will come from your own knowledge, but in questions with an Item, always study the Item for possible points to include in your chains of reasoning.

There is also a special case where you *must* use points from the Item. These are the questions that begin 'Applying material from the Item, analyse two...' For these, your chains of reasoning must draw directly from the Item. As you have to analyse two things, you need to create a separate chain for each. Each one should therefore incorporate a point from the Item. This point doesn't need to start your chain, but it must appear somewhere within it.

The **20-mark questions** on Families and Households, Beliefs in Society, and Theory and Methods ask you to evaluate something, such as an explanation or a view. For example:

*Applying material from **Item B** and your knowledge, evaluate the usefulness of structural approaches to our understanding of families and households.*

In these questions, as well as showing knowledge and understanding of relevant sociological theories, methods, concepts and studies, you need to show the AO2 skill of Application and the AO3 skills of Analysis and Evaluation. Look back at pages 251-2 to remind yourself of how you can show these skills. You will also find it very useful to study Box 4.2 *Using the Items,* because these questions require you to apply material from the Item.

The **30-mark questions** on Education and on Crime and Deviance follow the same pattern as the 20-mark essays above. For example:

*Applying material from **Item B** and your knowledge, evaluate the claim that education policies in the last 30 years have raised achievement for all through creating a market in the state education system.*

You should follow the same advice as for the 20-mark questions above, but note that for 30-mark questions you should write for about 15 minutes longer. Your answer should show more breadth and depth of knowledge and you should develop your evaluation points more fully.

See also 'points to remember for essay questions' below for further advice on answering 20- and 30-mark questions.

The Methods in Context question

The A level exam has a Methods in Context question. The context of the question is a particular issue in Education. The question is accompanied by an Item containing stimulus material which you must apply in your answer. The questions always have the same format as the following example:

*Applying material from **Item C** and your knowledge, evaluate the strengths and limitations of using questionnaires to investigate parental attitudes to education.*

The questions always ask you about **one** research method (such as questionnaires) and how it applies to **one** particular issue in education (such as parental attitudes).

The research method could be any one of those named in the specification: questionnaires, interviews, participant and non-participant observation, experiments, documents and official statistics. This includes any variants of these methods, such as structured, unstructured and group interviews, overt and covert observation, laboratory and field experiments, and postal questionnaires.

The particular issue could be any topic in education that sociologists might be interested in studying, such as labelling in schools or parental attitudes to education, for example.

If you took the AS exams at the end of your first year, you will have already answered a Methods in Context exam question. The A level question takes exactly the same form as the AS question, and you need to be able to do the same things for the A level as for the AS.

What you need to know

To answer Methods in Context questions, you need to know two main sorts of things.

Methods You need to know all the research methods that you will find in Chapter 3, Topics 1 and 2 of this book, and which are also covered in Book One, Chapter 4. For each method, make sure you know its key features, along with all its practical, ethical and theoretical strengths and limitations.

The research characteristics of the main groups and areas of education that sociologists study: that is, pupils, teachers, classrooms, schools and parents. By research characteristics, we mean the main features that a sociologist would have to take into account when choosing a method of studying them. For example, teachers are busy professionals who may not have time for long unstructured interviews. Similarly, some pupils may not have the literacy skills needed to fill in a questionnaire and so on. For a full account of research characteristics, see Book One, Chapter 3, Topic 2: *Education: the research context.*

You should also study the *Investigating* boxes found in every Topic in Book One, Chapter 2, because these contain many examples of the research characteristics of particular issues in education, such as racism in schools, gender and subject choice, teachers' expectations of pupils, and anti-school subcultures.

What you need to do

Although you need to know about research characteristics and about the different research methods, answering Methods in Context questions successfully is not just a matter of knowledge.

Above all, you must **apply** your knowledge of research methods to the study of the educational issue that the question asks you about. You will find it useful to study the examples of Methods in Context questions and examiner's advice at the end of Topics 2 to 7 in Chapter 3 of Book One. You should also look at the practice questions on pages 252 and 254 of Book One and on page 257 of this book.

In applying your knowledge of the method, be as specific as you can to the issue in the question. For example, in the question above about using questionnaires to study parental attitudes to education, you might say that this is a problematic method because parents are often too busy to fill in questionnaires. This shows some application, because the fact that parents are often busy is one of their obvious research characteristics. But your application of the method could be more specific to the issue in the question (parental attitudes) if you said for example that some parents have little interest in their children's education and so see no point in completing the questionnaire.

You should try to draw conclusions about the usefulness of the method for studying the particular educational issue in the question. Do so as you go along, rather than leaving it until the end of your answer.

You should make good use of the material in the Item. This will give you clues both on some of the method's strengths and limitations, and on some of the research characteristics of the issue.

Points to remember for essay questions

When answering A level questions worth 20 or 30 marks, you should follow this advice:

- Read the question carefully until you understand it; then make a brief plan.
- Write a short introduction linking to key aspects of the question.
- Stick to the question. Don't write 'Everything I know about crime and deviance (or education, or theory and methods)' answers.
- Discuss a range of concepts, explanations, theories/ perspectives and/or methods, depending on the question. Use evidence from sociological studies.
- Use the Items when instructed to do so, and use examples.
- Write a brief separate conclusion that follows logically from the main points in your essay.
- Focus on showing the skills of Application, Analysis and Evaluation, rather than just description.

Box 4.2	Using the Items

At A level, very many questions require you to apply material from an Item. Items are an important source of help, so read them through carefully at least twice, and keep checking back to the question. Highlight any words that seem important. Think how you can connect your own knowledge to points in the Item, such as:

- Criticisms of a view in the Item, or alternative views to those in the Item.
- Examples from studies, statistics, facts etc that support or contradict ideas in the Item.
- Any relevant concepts that link to points in the Item.
- Explanations or definitions of key ideas in the Item.

You will be rewarded for applying material from the Item, so draw the examiner's attention to the fact that you have done so by using a phrase like, 'as Item A says'.

You can quote from the Item or put it in your own words, but you must always build on it by linking it to the question and your own knowledge. Don't just copy it out or paraphrase it.

Here is an example of how you might use an Item for a 20- or 30-mark question. We have highlighted key words you could use in answering the question and suggested how you could link them to other material and the question. Always look for ways to link the Item to what you know and to the question.

Item A

There has been a significant increase in the number of divorces since 1970. One important factor behind the increase has been the changes in the law relating to divorce.

However, legal changes alone may not be enough to explain the trend and sociologists have suggested a number of possible causes of a higher divorce rate. One of these is a decline in the influence of traditional norms about marriage that used to stigmatise divorce.

Essay Applying material from Item A and your knowledge, evaluate sociological contributions to our understanding of the trends in divorce in the United Kingdom since 1970.

- Can you put a rough figure on the significant increase in the number of divorces?
- What changes in the law relating to divorce have there been? How have they contributed to the increase? (Remember to focus only on legal changes since 1970 – not the 19th century!)
- Why might these changes not be enough to explain the trend?
- There are lots of possible causes apart from legal changes. Examine several of them, evaluating them as you go.
- One of these is a decline in traditional norms... that used to stigmatise divorce. What is stigma? What concepts do sociologists such as Giddens and Beck use in explaining the decline in traditional norms?

A level practice papers

A Level Paper 1 Education with Theory and Methods

Answer all questions.
Time allowed: 2 hours

Item A   Some government education policies aim to introduce a market into the education system. This is done in part by creating competition among schools to attract pupils and their parents to apply for places. Supporters believe that this competition for 'customers' will drive up educational standards. Other education policies include selection of pupils for places in different types of school on the basis of their ability as measured through tests and examinations.

Item B   The role of the education system is central to most sociological theories of education. For example, for conflict theorists such as Marxists, education is a vital institution that both reproduces and legitimates social class inequality for capitalism. Not only is the education of working-class pupils structured so as to produce their underachievement, but the system justifies their failure by claiming to give everyone an equal opportunity to achieve.

However, functionalists argue that the education system performs positive functions for society as a whole, for example by generating social solidarity and preparing individuals for work that fits their abilities.

Item C

Investigating ethnic differences in educational achievement

There are pupils from many different ethnic groups in UK schools today. Pupils from some ethnic groups achieve very highly on average, while those from other groups are often less successful. Pupils' different experiences within school may play a part in this, as well as factors connected with their home background.

Sociologists may use unstructured interviews to investigate ethnic differences in educational achievement. These make it easy for interviewer and interviewee to check that they understand each other's meanings. Unstructured interviews also allow the interviewee the opportunity to speak about the things they think are important. However, interviewers require good interpersonal skills in order to conduct successful interviews with different pupils.

Education
1 Outline **two** processes within schools that may lead to working-class pupils underachieving.   (4 marks)
2 Outline **three** factors outside the education system that may affect gender differences in achievement.   (6 marks)
3 Applying material from **Item A**, analyse the effects of **two** government education policies on class differences in achievement.   (10 marks)
4 Applying material from **Item B** and your knowledge, evaluate sociological explanations of the role of the education system.   (30 marks)

Methods in Context
5 Applying material from **Item C** and your knowledge of research methods, evaluate the strengths and limitations of using unstructured interviews to study ethnic differences in achievement.   (20 marks)

Theory and Methods
6 Outline and explain **two** problems of using experiments in sociology.   (10 marks)

The examiner's advice can be found at the end of this chapter.

A Level Paper 2 Topics in Sociology

Answer all questions.
Time allowed: 2 hours

Families and Households

Item A   In the last 50 years or so, there have been major changes in the position of women in society. For example, girls now outperform boys in education and more females than males go to university. Major changes in the labour market and the economy, such as the expansion of the service sector, have benefited women. So too have equal rights laws and equal opportunities policies in many areas of society. These include sexuality, where there have been moves towards equality between heterosexual and lesbian women. Women now also have much greater access to reliable contraception.

Item B   Feminist sociologists take a critical view of the family, arguing that it perpetuates gender inequality and oppresses women. For example, women perform more domestic labour than men and are more likely to be victims of domestic violence.

However, different feminists hold different views as to the causes of this inequality and how it can be overcome. Some believe that gradual progress is being achieved, for example towards a more equal domestic division of labour, whereas others believe that there will be no real change in the family without the overthrow of capitalism.

---

1   Outline and explain **two** reasons why there is an ageing population in the United Kingdom today.   (10 marks)

2   Applying material from **Item A**, analyse **two** ways in which changes in women's position in society in the last 50 years have affected family patterns.   (10 marks)

3   Applying material from **Item B** and your knowledge, evaluate the contribution of feminist sociologists to our understanding of family life.   (20 marks)

Beliefs in Society

Item C   Religious organisations tend to be patriarchal. Many religions exclude women from leadership roles and segregate the sexes in worship. Often, religions legitimate and regulate women's domestic roles or require women to cover their bodies in particular ways, such as veiling.

However, despite this, women are generally more likely than men to hold religious beliefs and to participate in religious organisations. They are more likely to attend church and to be involved in its day to day functioning. For example, women are often heavily involved in running fundraising events and in carrying out pastoral work in the community as well as missionary work.

Item D   Many functionalist sociologists argue that religion is a universal feature of social life. In their view, this is because it performs indispensable functions without which society would disintegrate.

It symbolises the power of society and its shared rituals instil a sense of solidarity and loyalty to the community, and it legitimises society's central values. Religion also performs important psychological functions, answering 'ultimate' questions and enabling individuals to cope with emotional stress and thus to continue performing the roles society requires of them.

However, critics argue that functionalists ignore the negative aspects of religion and that functional definitions of religion disregard the particular nature of religious beliefs.

---

4   Outline and explain **two** reasons why secularisation may be occurring in Britain today.   (10 marks)

5   Applying material from **Item C,** analyse **two** reasons why women are generally more involved than men in religion, despite its apparently patriarchal nature.   (10 marks)

6   Applying material from **Item D** and your knowledge, evaluate functionalist explanations of the nature and role of religion.   (20 marks)

The examiner's advice can be found at the end of this chapter.

A Level Paper 3 Crime and Deviance with Theory and Methods

Answer all questions.
Time allowed: 2 hours

Crime and Deviance

> **Item A** In general women occupy a subordinate position in society. For many women, their primary role is a domestic one within the family, where they are the main carer and homemaker, socialising children. Many bear a double burden, combining domestic duties with paid work outside the home. Typically this involves employment in jobs with less power, status and pay than those performed by men. Some sociologists argue that in fact many women work a triple shift that includes emotional labour in addition to unpaid housework and low status employment.
>
> **Item B** Right realists see crime as the result of rational calculation on the part of individuals together with differences in biology and socialisation that predispose some individuals to offend. However, the main focus of right realism is on practical solutions that will prevent or reduce crime, such as target hardening, tougher policing and harsher punishments.
>
> However, critics argue that right realist strategies fail to tackle the real causes of crime, which they see as structural.

1 Outline **two** reasons why crime and deviance may be found in all societies. (4 marks)
2 Outline **three** ways in which blocked opportunity structures may lead to deviance. (6 marks)
3 Applying material from **Item A**, analyse **two** reasons why women appear less likely to commit crime than men. (10 marks)
4 Applying material from **Item B** and your knowledge, evaluate the usefulness of right realist approaches to crime. (30 marks)

Theory and Methods

> **Item C** Sociologists do not always collect their own data as part of their research but instead sometimes use existing secondary data such as official statistics. However, some critics argue that there are so many problems associated with secondary data that it has only a limited role to play in sociological research. Official statistics in particular have been criticised by interpretivists as lacking validity. For example, 'soft' official statistics such as those relating to crime and unemployment are open to manipulation.
>
> However, it has been argued that secondary data is often reliable and representative and in many cases is relatively cheap.

5 Outline and explain **two** ways in which values may affect sociologists' work. (10 marks)
6 Applying material from **Item C** and your knowledge, evaluate the claim that secondary data has only a limited role to play in sociological research. (20 marks)

> The examiner's advice can be found at the end of this chapter.

The Examiner's Advice

This section contains advice on how to tackle the 10, 20 and 30 mark questions in the A level practice papers in this chapter.

A level Practice Paper 1

Question 3

Spend about 15 minutes on this. Divide your time fairly equally between the two policies. Don't write a separate introduction; just start on your first policy. You must take two points from the Item and show through a chain of reasoning (see Box 4.1) the effect of each. Quote from the Item for each policy.

You could use different marketisation policies (such as free schools, competition, league tables, specialist schools, parental choice etc), or selection on ability such as the 11+ examination. For example, parental choice supposedly gives every pupil an equal chance of a place at a successful school. However, middle-class parents have more economic and cultural capital, and this enables them to make better informed choices. This means their children are more likely to get into 'better' schools.

Use concepts such as privileged-skilled and other choosers, parentocracy, cream-skimming and silt-shifting, selection by mortgage, economic and cultural capital, material and cultural deprivation, meritocracy, reproduction of inequality, and tripartite and comprehensive systems.

Include some brief evaluation, e.g. the Pupil Premium is not necessarily spent on the poorest pupils.

Question 4

Spend about 45 minutes on this. The question specifies explanations plural, so you need to discuss two or more. You could organise your answer around the key issues sociologists focus on in relation to the role of education. You can focus mainly on functionalist and Marxist views, but also make some reference to feminist and New Right/ neoliberal views.

Rather than list the theories one by one in sequence, take the key issues in turn and examine how each theory deals with it. For example, functionalists see education as transmitting society's shared values, whereas Marxists argue that these are merely ruling-class values, and feminists argue that they are patriarchal values.

Use concepts such as social solidarity, shared values, specialist skills, selection and role allocation, meritocracy, particularistic and universalistic standards, economic and

social functions, capitalism, ideological state apparatus, reproduction and legitimation, the myth of meritocracy, consensus versus conflict views, patriarchy. Use evidence from studies such as Durkheim, Parsons, Davis and Moore, Althusser, Bowles and Gintis, Willis, and Chubb and Moe, and develop the points in the Item.

Question 5

Spend about 30 minutes on this. You must apply your knowledge of unstructured interviews to the study of the particular issue of ethnic differences in achievement. It's not enough simply to discuss unstructured interviews in general.

Use the Item to help you. For example, it suggests that one research characteristic of ethnic differences in achievement is that there are a wide range of ethnic groups in UK schools today. However, unstructured interviews take a long time to complete and it may therefore be difficult to study a sample of all the different ethnic groups in schools.

Link other research characteristics of ethnic differences in achievement to the strengths and limitations of the method. For example, some pupils may not be fully fluent in English, which may make interviewing more difficult. However, because unstructured interviews are flexible, they may overcome this problem by rephrasing questions or asking for clarification of answers that are unclear.

Other characteristics include schools' possible reluctance to allow interviews on this issue, the influence of ethnic differences between interviewer and interviewee etc. Link these to particular strengths or limitations of the method.

Question 6

Spend about 15 minutes on this. Divide your time fairly equally between the two problems. Don't write a separate introduction; just start on your first problem. You could consider the problems of laboratory and/or field experiments. Possible problems include lack of informed consent, deception, harm to participants, studying the past or large-scale phenomena, the Hawthorne effect, representativeness, artificiality, difficulties identifying or controlling variables.

Choose two problems and describe each problem in some detail, explaining how it may arise in research. Do this by creating a chain of reasoning (see Box 4.1). For example, in laboratory experiments, participants should be told the true purpose of the research, so that they can give their informed consent. However, if this is done, they will know the researcher's aims and this may lead to the Hawthorne effect, where participants act in the way they believe the researcher wishes, rather than as they normally would. Use concepts and issues such as validity, free will, sample size, the expectancy effect, as well as those mentioned above. Use studies such as Rosenhan, Rosenthal and Jacobson, and Milgram.

A level Practice Paper 2

Question 1

Spend about 15 minutes on this. Divide your time fairly equally between the two reasons. Don't write a separate introduction; just start on your first reason. Possible reasons include lower birth and fertility rates, lower infant mortality rates, lower death rates and increased life expectancy.

Choose two reasons and describe each reason in some detail, explaining how it may lead to an ageing population. Do this by creating a chain of reasoning (see Box 4.1). For example, the United Kingdom birth rate has fallen over the last century because children are now an economic liability and because childhood is now constructed as uniquely important, so parents have fewer children but lavish more attention on them. This means that there are fewer babies and children in society, thereby raising the average age of the population.

Use concepts and issues such as total fertility rate, children as economic assets or liabilities, child centredness, contraception and abortion, dual earner couples, improved nutrition and medical care, changes in lifestyle, public health measures, decline of dangerous occupations, and higher living standards.

Question 2

Spend about 15 minutes on this. Divide your time fairly equally between the two ways. Don't write a separate introduction; just start on your first way. You must take two points from the Item and show through a chain of reasoning the effect on family patterns. Quote from the Item for each way you deal with.

You could use changes in women's position in relation to education, the labour market, equal rights or sexuality. For example, there is now a much higher proportion of married women in the labour market than 50 years ago, many of whom are working full-time. This means they make a more equal contribution to household income and some argue that this means they are able to demand that their partners do a greater share of the housework.

Use concepts such as the division of labour, patriarchy, dual burden, divorce, later childbearing, smaller families, individualisation, the pure relationship, negotiated family, risk society, same-sex relationships, lone parent families, family diversity and the neo-conventional family. Include some brief evaluation, e.g. that conjugal roles remain unequal despite women working.

Question 3

Spend about 30 minutes on this. You could begin by outlining the contribution of feminists to what we know about issues such as domestic violence and the division of labour in the family. You should also deal with a range of feminist views on the family, including liberal, Marxist and radical feminism. Cover both the explanation that each of these gives of the causes of inequality in the family, and the different solutions each one proposes.

Use concepts such as patriarchy, subordination, oppression, conjugal roles, socialisation, stereotyping, equality legislation, capitalism, reproduction of the labour force, reserve army of labour, ideology, domestic violence, housework, childcare, control of resources, political lesbianism, separatism, matrilocal households, triple shift etc. Use evidence from studies such as Ansley, Boulton, Braun et al, Walby and Allen, Crompton and Lyonette, Greer and Somerville, and develop the points noted in the Item.

Evaluate by considering the differences between liberal, Marxist and radical feminism. You can also use the views of difference feminists and those of functionalist and personal life perspectives.

Question 4

Spend about 15 minutes on this. Divide your time fairly equally between the two reasons. Don't write a separate introduction; just start on your first reason. Possible reasons include rationalisation, disenchantment, scientific and technological advances, structural differentiation, social and cultural diversity, religious diversity etc.

Choose two reasons and describe each reason in some detail, explaining how it may be leading to secularisation. Do this by creating a chain of reasoning. For example, the Protestant Reformation broke the Catholic Church's monopoly and brought religious diversity and many religious organisations, with competing and incompatible versions of the truth. This means people are likely to question all of them and see none as being true.

Use concepts and issues such as sacred canopy, crisis of credibility, plausibility structure, social change, mobility, individualism, specialisation, disengagement, disenchantment, scientific advance, technological worldview, privatisation of religion, and separation of church and state. Use studies such as Weber, Bruce, Wilson and Berger.

Question 5

Spend about 15 minutes on this. Divide your time fairly equally between the two reasons. Don't write a separate introduction; just start on your first reason. You must take two points from the Item and show through a chain of reasoning (see Box 4.1) the effect of each. Quote from the Item for each reason.

You could use legitimation and regulation of women's domestic roles, sex segregation of worshippers, veiling, women's religious beliefs, or women's involvement in Sunday schools, fundraising, community pastoral work or missionary work. For example, evangelical Christian churches legitimate the traditional domestic division of labour, and this is attractive to some women because it gives value and respect to their position in the family, as well as power over their men by insisting that they practise what they preach and act dutifully towards the family.

Use concepts such as patriarchy; religious feminism; division of labour; veiling and participation in the public sphere; monotheism and polytheism; organismic, ethical and social deprivation; the appeal of sects and the New Age; attractions of fundamentalism. You can include some brief evaluation, e.g. that not all religions are patriarchal.

Question 6

Spend about 30 minutes on this. Note that the question asks about both the nature of religion and its role; make sure you address both issues. Deal with the nature of religion by explaining what is meant by a functional definition of religion. On the role of religion, apply points from the Item to explain functionalist views, e.g. of how religion promotes solidarity, legitimises central values and performs psychological functions for individuals.

Use concepts such as social solidarity, stability and order, the sacred and the profane, totemism, collective conscience, ritual, cognitive functions, canoe magic, central value system, civil religion, class society, alienation, ideology, social change, religious conflict, religious pluralism, patriarchy, and different definitions of religion. Use evidence from studies such as Durkheim, Yinger, Malinowski, Parsons, Bellah, Marx, Weber and Bruce.

Evaluate by considering alternative views of the nature and role of religion. Contrast functional with substantive and social constructionist definitions of the nature of religion. Use Marxist and feminist views of what the functions of religion are and who benefits.

A level Practice Paper 3

Question 3

Spend about 15 minutes on this. Divide your time fairly equally between the two reasons. You don't need a separate introduction; just start on your first reason. To answer this question it's essential that you take two points from the Item and show through a chain of reasoning (see Box 4.1) how each relates to a reason why women appear to commit less crime. (It is a very good idea to quote from the Item when doing so).

You could use women's caring role, their subordinate role in paid work, their low pay in work or lack of pay for housework, or that they must perform a triple shift. For example, women's subordinate role in paid work means they are less likely to hold positions of power and authority that would give them the opportunity to commit white-collar crimes such as fraud and embezzlement.

Use concepts such as expressive and instrumental roles, patriarchy, gender role socialisation, social control, the glass ceiling, leisure opportunities, public sphere, private sphere etc. Include some brief evaluation, e.g. low pay may push some women into crime to obtain a better standard of living.

Question 4

Spend about 45 minutes on this. You need to deal with two major aspects of this question: the causes of crime, and the solutions to prevent or reduce crime. Use the Item to get you started on the right realist view of the causes, explaining the three different factors that it mentions. Use the Item also to start your explanation of the solutions right realists offer.

Use concepts such as underclass, lone parent families, delinquent role models, zero tolerance, rational choice theory, cost-benefit calculations, routine activity theory, situation crime prevention (SCP) strategies, target hardening, displacement, retributive and restitutive justice, capitalism, racism, relative deprivation, marginalisation, subculture, militaristic policing, and redistributive policies. Use evidence from studies such as Herrnstein and Murray, Bennett et al, Murray, Clarke, Felson, Wilson and Kelling, and Lea and Young.

Evaluate right realism by considering alternative perspectives on causes and solutions, including left realism, labelling theory and Marxism. Focus on issues such as right realism's neglect of underlying structural causes and corporate crime, criticisms of zero tolerance and SCP strategies, discriminatory policing etc.

Question 5

Spend about 15 minutes on this. Divide your time fairly equally between the two ways. Don't write a separate introduction; just start on your first way. Possible ways include the use of values in choosing a research topic, their role in formulating research questions and in collection of data, in interpreting results, the influence of the values of funding bodies etc.

Choose two ways and describe each way in some detail, explaining how it leads to values affecting sociologists' work. Do this by creating a chain of reasoning (see Box 4.1). For example, there is a potentially infinite number of 'facts' about society that could be studied and so the sociologist must make a selection of which facts to study. This means they must use their own values to decide which facts they think are important enough to be studied.

Use concepts and issues such as value relevance, value freedom, theoretical and methodological perspective, bias, objectivity, ideology, 'committed sociology', funding sources, career interests, political beliefs etc.

Question 6

Spend about 30 minutes on this. Be clear about what constitutes secondary data: the Item refers to official statistics, but you should consider personal and public documents as well. Frame these different kinds of secondary data in the positivist-interpretivist debate as a context for your answer. As well as evaluating the limitations of different specific types of documents and official statistics, you should compare the usefulness of secondary data as a whole with that of primary data as a whole.

As well as explaining the limitations of secondary data, you can evaluate the claim by considering its strengths. For example, you could note that although 'soft' official statistics can be manipulated, 'hard' official statistics cannot be. You should consider the usefulness of official statistics and documents from both a positivist and an interpretivist perspective. You could also look at statistics from Marxist and feminist viewpoints.

Use concepts and issues such as reliability, validity, representativeness, authenticity, credibility, meaning, content analysis, quantitative data, qualitative data, the 'dark figure', social construction, ideology, ethical issues, access, time and cost.

Key Concepts

The following is an alphabetical list of some of the key concepts you need to know. You can use the list as:

- a **handy reference** to find a quick definition of a term
- a **revision aid** to ensure you know and understand important sociological ideas.

When you look up a concept in the list, you may find that a lot of entries give you a 'see also' reference. Following these up will show you some of the links between concepts and broaden your understanding of them.

In addition to the list below, you will find more Key Concepts in *Book One*, pages 261-270.

action theories see individuals as having free will and choice, and the power to create society through their actions and interactions, rather than being shaped by society. Interactionism is the best-known theory of this type. Postmodernism also has certain features in common with action theories. See also structural theories.

alienation Where an individual or group feels socially isolated and estranged because they lack the power to control their lives and realise their true potential. Marx describes workers in capitalist society as alienated because they are exploited and lack control of the production process. See also Marxism.

anomie means normlessness. Durkheim argues that anomie arises when there is rapid social change, because existing norms become unclear or outdated. Merton's 'strain' theory argues that where individuals lack legitimate means of achieving culturally prescribed goals it results in a strain to anomie, which some resolve by adopting illegitimate means such as 'innovation'.

asceticism Abstinence, self-discipline and self-denial. Before Calvinism, Christian asceticism was 'other-worldly' and meant renouncing everyday life to join a convent or monastery. Calvinism introduced the idea of this-worldly asceticism. Calvinists believed that God had put them on earth to glorify his name by work in an occupation, not in a monastery. For this reason, the Calvinists led an ascetic lifestyle, working long hours, shunning luxury and practising rigorous self-discipline. See also disenchantment; rationalisation.

bourgeoisie The capitalist class, the owners of the means of production (factories, machinery, raw materials, land etc). Marx argues that ownership of the means of production also gives the bourgeoisie political and ideological power. See also exploitation; ideology; Marxism; proletariat.

capitalism See Marxism.

chivalry thesis, the This is the view that the criminal justice system is biased in favour of women, so that they are less likely than men to be charged, convicted or punished. It is argued that these gender differences result from male-dominated police, courts and prosecuting authorities basing their actions on a stereotype of females as incapable of serious criminality.

churches are large bureaucratic organisations, often with millions of members, run by a formal hierarchy of professional priests and claiming a monopoly of the truth. They aim to include the whole of society, but tend to attract the higher classes because they are conservative and often closely linked to the state. See also sects; denominations; cults.

civil religion A belief system that attaches sacred qualities to society itself and makes the nation-state the object of religious or quasi-religious worship. Civil religion is seen as promoting social solidarity, expressed through rituals and symbols such as pledging allegiance to the flag. In America, civil religion is a faith in 'the American way of life'.

collective conscience The shared norms, values, beliefs and knowledge that make cooperation between individuals possible. It integrates society by giving individuals a sense of belonging to something greater than themselves. See also social integration; value consensus.

compensators According to Stark and Bainbridge, when real rewards are scarce or unobtainable, religion compensates us by promising supernatural ones; e.g. immortality is unobtainable, but religion compensates by promising life after death. For Stark and Bainbridge, only religion provides such compensators. Non-religious ideologies such as humanism and communism do not provide credible compensators because they do not promise supernatural rewards. See also religious market theory.

critical criminology is a neo-Marxist approach that combines ideas from traditional Marxism and labelling theory to explain crime in capitalist society. It sees working-class crime as a conscious and often political act of resistance to the exploitation and oppression that they suffer under capitalism.

cults are loose-knit and usually small religious or spiritual groups of individuals with similar interests. Cults lack a sharply defined belief system and are tolerant of other beliefs. They are often led by 'practitioners' or 'therapists' who claim special knowledge. Many cults are world-affirming, claiming to improve life in this world. Those who take part are more like clients or customers than members of a church. See also churches; denominations; sects; new religious movements; New Age spirituality; spiritual shopping.

cultural defence Where religion provides a focal point for the defence of national, ethnic or other group identity in a struggle against an external force such as a hostile foreign power. Catholicism in Poland was a source of national identity for many people during the communist period, when the country was under the influence of the former Soviet Union.

cultural transition The process of moving from one culture to another. Bruce argues that religion plays an important role in cultural transition for minority ethnic groups who find themselves in a new culture, by providing support and a sense of community in a different country and culture.

culture All those things that are learnt and shared by a society or group and transmitted from generation to generation through socialisation, including shared norms, values, knowledge, beliefs and skills. See also subculture.

denominations are religious organisations that lie midway between churches and sects, e.g. Methodism. Like churches, they broadly accept society's values, but they are not linked to the state. They impose restrictions on their members (e.g. forbidding alcohol) but are not as demanding as sects. Unlike both churches and sects (but like cults), they are tolerant of other religious organisations and beliefs and do not claim a monopoly of the truth. See also churches; sects; cults.

determinism The idea that humans have no free will and that their thoughts and behaviour are shaped or caused by factors outside themselves, such as the social structure. Marxism is often accused of economic determinism – the view that the economic base shapes all other features of society's 'superstructure', such as social institutions and ideas. Determinism is the opposite of voluntarism. See also voluntarism.

deviance Behaviour that does not conform to the norms of a society or group. Deviance is a social construction – it is defined or created by social groups. Deviance is relative: what counts as deviant varies between groups and cultures and over time. Primary deviance refers to deviant acts that have not been publicly labelled and usually have little significance for the individual's status. Secondary deviance results from societal reaction (labelling) and may lead to the individual taking on a deviant master status and deviant career.

deviance amplification spiral is the process whereby attempts to control deviance actually produce an increase in deviance, leading to greater attempts at control and still higher levels of deviance. For example, in a moral panic a folk devil is identified as a threat to society's values, and the media and moral entrepreneurs call for a crackdown on the problem, but this results in an increase in the scale of the problem as more individuals are publicly labelled. See also labelling; self-fulfilling prophecy.

disciplinary power According to Foucault, disciplinary power is based on self-surveillance and self-discipline as a means of inducing conformity. Its model is the Panopticon, a design for a prison in which the inmates are visible to the guards but not vice versa, so the prisoners must always act as if they are being watched, thereby turning surveillance into self-surveillance.

discourse Foucault sees a discourse as a set of ideas that have become established as knowledge or a way of thinking and speaking about the world. A discourse makes us see things in a particular way, so it is also a form of domination or 'power/ knowledge'. A discourse is neither true nor false in any absolute sense, so there is no objective way of choosing between competing discourses. Knowledge cannot therefore be used to improve society or bring progress. See also relativism.

disenchantment The process whereby magical and religious ways of thinking are replaced by a rational mode of thought. Events cease to be explained as the work of unpredictable supernatural beings or forces. Instead, they are explained as being the result of natural forces governed by scientific laws. In a disenchanted world there is no longer any need for religious explanations. Weber sees the Protestant Reformation as beginning the process of disenchantment. See also rationalisation; secularisation.

dramaturgical model Developed by Goffman, this interactionist approach uses analogies with drama as a framework for analysing social interaction – 'actors' carry off convincing 'role-performances' using 'props' to act out their 'scripts' etc. The model sees us actively constructing the self through impression management to manipulate the 'audience's' perception of us.

Enlightenment project See modernism.

environmental crime prevention A crime reduction strategy associated with Wilson and Kelling's article, Broken Windows. It sees serious crime as arising out of disorder and advocates 'cracking down' on all forms of neighbourhood decline through a twofold strategy of environmental improvement and zero tolerance policing. See also right realism.

ethnomethodology An interpretivist approach developed by Garfinkel, it rejects the idea of an external social structure and sees society as a social construct. Although meanings are always potentially unclear (which Garfinkel calls indexicality), society's members use commonsense knowledge to achieve a sense of order (a process known as reflexivity). This is similar to the idea of typifications put forward by Schutz. See also phenomenology.

existential security theory Existential security is the feeling that survival is secure enough that it can be taken for granted. The theory is based on the view that religion arises where people lack economic security. It explains why religion has declined most in affluent societies where there is welfare provision, and why religion remains popular in poorer societies and among the poor in richer or more unequal societies. See also secularisation.

exploitation Paying workers less than the value of their labour. According to Marxists, it is the process whereby the bourgeoisie extract surplus value or profit from the labour of the proletariat. Feminists see men as exploiting the domestic labour of women. See also Marxism; feminism.

falsificationism According to Popper, falsificationism is the defining characteristic of scientific knowledge, which consists of statements that can in principle be falsified (disproved) by experiment or observation, unlike the knowledge-claims of religion, tradition or theories such as Marxism. Falsificationism is the opposite of verificationism – the idea that a theory can be proved true simply by gathering evidence that confirms or verifies it. See also open and closed belief systems.

feminism A sociological perspective and political movement that focuses on women's oppression and the struggle to end it. Feminists examine women's experiences and study society from a female perspective. There are different strands of feminism, including Marxist, radical, liberal and difference feminism. See also patriarchy.

folk devil See deviance amplification spiral.

Fordism A type of industrial production based on a detailed division of labour, using closely supervised, low-skilled workers and assembly-line technology to mass-produce standardised goods. Named after the manufacturing techniques first introduced by the Ford Motor Company. See also alienation; post-Fordism.

function The contribution that a part of society makes to the stability or well-being of society as a whole. Merton distinguishes between manifest and latent functions. The former are the intended consequences of an institution or practice, while the latter are its unintended or hidden consequences.

functional alternatives or functional equivalents are institutions that perform the same function as another institution. For example, some secular beliefs (such as political ideologies) may perform the same function as religious ones in maintaining social solidarity.

functionalism A consensus perspective that sees society as based on shared values into which members are socialised. It sees society as like an organism, each part performing functions to maintain the system as a whole; e.g. religion, the family and education system perform socialisation functions. See also function; value consensus.

fundamentalism Religion based on an unquestioning belief in the literal truth of a sacred text. Fundamentalists believe that there is only one true view of the world, which is revealed in a sacred text, not gained through scientific enquiry or rational argument.

globalisation The idea that the world is becoming increasingly interconnected and that barriers are disappearing, e.g. as a result of instantaneous communication systems, deregulation of trade, the creation of global markets and global media. Many see it as creating new risks, uncertainties and choices, and an increased rate of social change. See also postmodernity; risk society.

green crimes are crimes against the environment and the human and non-human animals within it. Primary green crimes involve the destruction and degradation of the earth's resources, species decline and animal abuse. Secondary green crime involves the breaking of laws aimed at preventing or regulating environmental disasters, such as illegal dumping of hazardous waste.

green criminology See zemiology.

hegemony A Marxist concept developed by Gramsci to explain how the ruling class holds the ideological and moral leadership of society, using ideas and values to prevent revolution by winning the consent of the subordinate classes to its rule. The ruling class is able to do this by controlling the institutions that produce ideas, such as the education system, religion and the media. See also ideology; Marxism.

identity The individual's sense of self, influenced by socialisation and interactions with others; a sense of belonging to a community. Postmodernists see identity as a choice that individuals make from among different identity sources such as gender, ethnic group, religion, sexuality, leisure interests, nationality etc.

ideology Originally a Marxist idea meaning a set of beliefs that serve the interests of a dominant group by justifying their privileged position. The term usually implies that the beliefs are false or only partially true. See also hegemony; legitimation; Marxism.

individualism The idea that the individual is more important than the group or community. In modern and postmodern society, individualism becomes more important than in traditional society and individuals' actions are influenced more by calculations of self-interest than by a sense of obligation to others. Secularisation theorists argue that individualism leads to the decline of religion but others argue that it has changed religion into a search for personal fulfilment. See also New Age spirituality; secularisation.

interactionism A perspective focusing on small-scale (micro-level) interactions between individuals and groups, rather than on the large-scale workings of society. Interactionists seek to understand the meanings that social actors give to actions and situations, usually by using qualitative research methods. See also interpretivism; labelling.

interpretivism A term covering a range of approaches including social action theory, symbolic interactionism, phenomenology and ethnomethodology. Interpretivists focus on how we construct our social worlds through the meanings we create and attach to events, actions and situations. They favour qualitative methods and see human beings as fundamentally different from the natural phenomena studied by scientists, in that we have free will, consciousness and choice. See also positivism; subjectivity.

knowledge claim A claim made by a belief system to know about the world, what it is like and, sometimes, how it ought to be and how we ought to act. For example, science, political ideologies and religions make knowledge claims. However, science does not make 'ought' claims, but merely claims to describe and explain the world. See also falsificationism; ideology; open and closed belief systems.

labelling is the process of attaching a definition or meaning to an individual or group. Often the label is a stereotype that sees

all members of a group as sharing the same attributes. Labelling theory uses concepts such as definition of the situation, the looking glass self and career to explain how individuals' actions and identities are shaped through the labels that are applied to them. See also deviance.

left realism regards crime as a real problem, particularly for disadvantaged groups, who are more likely to be its victims. Left realists are reformist socialists who see relative deprivation and the marginalisation of the poor as producing criminal subcultures whose members victimise other poor people. To tackle the problem of crime, they argue for structural reforms to reduce inequality and for democratic and accountable policing. See also right realism.

legitimation Justifying something by making it seem fair and natural. This is the main function of ideology. Marxists argue that institutions in capitalist society such as education, the media and religion are ideological state apparatuses whose function is to legitimate inequality.

macro-level Theories such as functionalism and Marxism that focus on the large scale, i.e. on the social structure as a whole or on the relationships between social institutions like the education system and the economy. These theories see the individual as shaped by society. See also micro-level; positivism.

Marxism A conflict perspective based on the ideas of Karl Marx (1818-83). It sees society as divided into two opposed classes, one of which exploits the labour of the other. In capitalist society, the bourgeoisie (capitalist class) owns the means of production and exploits the labour of the propertyless proletariat (working class). Marx predicted that the proletariat would unite to overthrow capitalism and create a classless society. See also alienation; exploitation; hegemony; ideology; modernism; polarisation.

micro-level Theories such as interactionism that focus on small-scale, face-to-face interaction, e.g. between teacher and pupils in a classroom. These theories see individuals constructing society through their interactions. See also interpretivism; macro-level.

modernism Modernist theories (e.g. functionalism, Marxism and positivism) believe that society has a fairly clear-cut, predictable structure and that it is possible to gain true and certain scientific knowledge of how society functions. This knowledge can be used to achieve progress to a better society. The modernist notion of progress through the application of rational knowledge to social problems is sometimes referred to as the Enlightenment project. See also modernity; postmodernism.

modernity, modern society is seen as beginning with the industrial revolution. It is characterised by rapid social change, scientific and technological development, secularisation, the decline of tradition, and the bureaucratic nation-state. Modernist perspectives seek to explain and predict its development. Beck, Giddens and others argue that in late or high modernity, many of these trends become accelerated. See also globalisation; modernism; postmodernism; postmodernity; risk society.

moral panic See deviance amplification spiral.

neutralisation techniques are used by delinquents to justify their deviant behaviour. Cohen argues that states also use such techniques to justify crimes that they commit. These include denial of victim, of injury and of responsibility, condemning the condemners and appeal to higher loyalty.

New Age spirituality includes a very diverse range of beliefs and practices that have grown rapidly since the 1980s, which reject external authority and traditional sources of religion such as churches, priests and sacred texts. Spirituality refers to personal and subjective aspects of religion and the supernatural. The New Age holds the view that we can discover the truth for ourselves through experience, by following a personal spiritual path and exploring one's inner self. See also new religious movements; cults; sects.

New Right A conservative political perspective whose supporters believe in self-reliance and individual choice, rather than dependence on the state. They believe in applying free market principles, e.g. the marketisation of education, and argue that generous welfare benefits encourage the growth of a criminal underclass. See also right realism.

new religious movements (NRMs) have grown since the 1960s. Wallis distinguishes between three types of NRM depending on whether their attitudes to wider society are world-rejecting, world-accepting or world-accommodating. They have grown because of the marginality of some groups and individuals, relative deprivation and rapid social change. See also cults; sects; New Age spirituality.

news values are the criteria by which journalists and editors decide whether a story is newsworthy enough to make it into the newspaper or news bulletin. News values include immediacy, dramatisation, personalisation, risk and violence. Crime often fits these criteria and is thus over-reported. Journalists' use of news values illustrates the idea that news is a social construction – something manufactured rather than discovered. See also social construction.

norms Social rules, expectations or standards that govern the behaviour expected in particular situations. Norms may be formal (e.g. written laws or rules) or informal (e.g. rules of politeness). See also values.

objectivity The absence of bias or preconceived ideas. It implies that we can look at things as they really are and get at the truth, without our opinions or values getting in the way. Positivists believe sociology can achieve objectivity by using methods that keep sociologists detached from their research subjects. See also positivism; subjectivity; value freedom.

open and closed belief systems Closed belief systems make knowledge claims that cannot be disproved. According to Popper, religion and Marxism are closed systems. Open belief systems make knowledge claims that are open to criticism and can in principle be falsified by testing. Popper describes science as an open belief system. See also falsificationism; knowledge claims.

paradigm According to Kuhn, a paradigm is shared by members of a scientific community. It defines for them what 'normal science' is, providing them with a shared framework of basic assumptions within which to work. It tells them what nature is like, which aspects to study, the methods to use and questions to ask, and even the sort of answers they should find. Kuhn likens science under the paradigm to puzzle solving. Eventually, the accumulation of anomalies produces a crisis, and a scientific revolution establishes a new paradigm.

patriarchy Literally, rule by the father. Feminists use the term to describe a society based on male domination; a system or ideology of male power over women. See also feminism.

phenomenology An interpretivist approach developed by Schutz. He argues that we make sense of the world through shared concepts or categories called 'typifications'. Meanings are potentially unstable and unclear, but typifications clarify and stabilise them, allowing us to communicate and cooperate. In doing so, they give the world the appearance of being natural, orderly and real, but in fact it is simply a construction produced by typifications. See also ethnomethodology; interpretivism.

pluralism A pluralistic society is one with many different cultures, religions or political parties. Berger sees religious pluralism undermining religion's plausibility structure or credibility because, where there are many competing versions of the truth being put forward by different religions, people become sceptical about all of them. See also postmodernism; secularisation.

polarisation A process that results in the creation of two opposite extremes. Marx describes how in capitalist society the class structure becomes polarised into a wealthy bourgeoisie and impoverished proletariat. See also Marxism.

positivism The belief that society is made up of 'social facts' that can be studied scientifically to discover laws of cause and effect. Durkheim took official statistics on suicide as social facts and tried to produce a law explaining why suicide rates vary between groups. With such knowledge, positivists believe we can find solutions to social problems. See also interpretivism; objectivity.

post-Fordism A type of industrial production. A highly skilled, adaptable workforce, combined with computerised technology, means that production takes the form of 'flexible specialisation', able to respond swiftly to changing consumer demands and to produce for a variety of small, customised 'niche' markets. See also Fordism.

postmodernism rejects modernism's belief in progress and its view that we can have certain, true knowledge of society that will enable us to improve it. Postmodern society is so unstable and diverse that it is now impossible to produce any absolute explanations. No one theory is truer than any other; theories such as Marxism and functionalism, as well as science, are merely 'meta-narratives' or viewpoints. See also modernism; postmodernity.

postmodernity Postmodernists argue that society has moved into a new era of postmodernity – a globalised, media-saturated society in which signs become 'hyper-real' simulacra with no reference to any external reality. Culture is fragmented, unstable and ever-changing, and individuals create and change their identities through consumption of signs and brands. Some Marxists see postmodernity as simply the latest phase of capitalism. See also modernity; post-Fordism; postmodernism.

privatisation The separation of an aspect of social life from the rest of society or the loss of its public role. For example, some sociologists argue that in modern society, religion has become privatised. Where previously religion played an important public role, influencing many areas of life such as education and the law, it is now merely a private matter of personal preference. See also structural differentiation; secularisation.

proletariat The working class in capitalist society. They own no means of production and are 'wage slaves', forced to sell their labour-power to the bourgeoisie in order to survive. See also exploitation; Marxism.

punishment Criminologists argue that punishment performs various functions. These include deterrence, rehabilitation, and incapacitation. Punishment may also be a form of retribution, in which society expresses its outrage and seeks vengeance against the criminal. Durkheim argues that punishment in modern society is largely restitutive, i.e. it seeks to restore the status quo.

rationalisation The process by which rational and scientific ways of thinking and acting gradually replace magico-religious ones.

Key Concepts

Weber argued that the Protestant Reformation started a process of rationalisation and played a key role in the emergence of modern capitalism. See also disenchantment; secularisation.

rational choice theory See right realism.

realism The view that science deals with unobservable underlying structures (such as class), in contrast to the positivist view that it only deals with observable phenomena. Realists distinguish between sciences dealing with closed systems that can be studied in the laboratory, and those studying open systems (such as society), which cannot. See also left realism; right realism.

reflexivity Used by Giddens to describe the situation in late or high modern society where tradition and custom no longer guide our actions. As a result, we are forced to become more reflexive – to constantly monitor, reflect on and modify our actions in the light of information about the possible risks and opportunities they might involve. Ethnomethodologists also use the term in a different sense to refer to constructing social order or making sense of reality. See also ethnomethodology; globalisation; modernity; risk society.

relativism The view that knowledge claims are not absolutely true or false, but merely true for those who believe them. Critics argue that relativism is self-defeating – if no knowledge claim is absolutely true, then why should we believe relativism's claims? See also fundamentalism; pluralism; postmodernism.

reliability Research is reliable if it produces exactly the same results (a replica) when repeated using identical methods and procedures. In general, quantitative methods are more reliable than qualitative methods because they use standardised procedures that are easier to replicate.

religious market theory Also called rational choice theory, this compares religious organisations with businesses competing for customers. Less popular religions decline, while others grow by offering people what they want. However, the overall demand for religion remains constant because, in this view, people are naturally religious; secularisation is only one stage in a perpetual cycle of religious decline and renewal. See also compensators; secularisation.

representative Typical; a cross-section. A researcher may choose to study a sample of a larger group. If the sample is representative, those in it will be typical of the larger group. This will allow the findings to be generalised, i.e. applied to all members of the group, not just those in the sample.

reserve army of labour A Marxist concept describing groups who can be brought into the workforce when there is a labour shortage as the capitalist economy expands during a boom, and discarded when it contracts. Women were used as a reserve army of labour during the two world wars. See also Marxism.

right realism sees crime as a real problem. Politically, right realists are conservatives who favour a tougher approach to crime. They reject as impractical, strategies that seek to tackle underlying causes of crime (such as poverty). They see crime as a rational choice, in which criminals weigh up the risks and rewards. Right realists therefore focus on situational and environmental crime prevention strategies as means of deterrence.

risk society According to Beck, in late modern society, the risks are increasingly human-made rather than the risks posed by nature such as famine, drought and plague to which humans were traditionally exposed. These risks are increasingly global leading Beck to describe late modern society as global risk society.

role How someone who occupies a particular status is expected to act; e.g. someone playing the role of bus driver is expected to drive safely, stop for passengers, charge the correct fare etc.

sects are small, exclusive religious groups that expect strong commitment from their members. They are often hostile to wider society and draw their members from the poor and oppressed. Others attract those seeking health, wealth and happiness in this world. Many are led by a charismatic leader. Like churches, sects claim a monopoly of religious truth. See also churches; denominations; cults.

secularisation The decline of religion; the process whereby religious beliefs, practices and institutions lose their importance or influence.

self-report studies ask individuals to disclose the crimes for which they have been responsible. They are often used as a corrective to official police statistics, since they can include crimes committed of which the police are unaware. However, they have their limitations; for example, they tend to focus on more trivial offences.

separatism A radical feminist idea that women should organise to live independently of men as the only way to free themselves from patriarchal oppression.

situational crime prevention is a strategy for reducing opportunities for crime. It aims to manage the immediate environment of specific crimes (e.g. burglary) so as to increase the effort and risks, and reduce the rewards, of committing the crime. It often involves 'target hardening' (e.g. installing CCTV) to deter criminals. Critics argue that this may lead to displacement. See also right realism.

social class Social groupings or hierarchy based on differences in wealth, income or occupation. Marx identified two classes in capitalist society: the bourgeoisie and proletariat. Many sociologists use occupation to distinguish between a manual working class and a non-manual middle class. See also Marxism.

social construction Where something is created by social processes, rather than simply occurring naturally. For example, interpretivists argue that official crime statistics are socially constructed through the interactions of police and suspects. When something is socially constructed, it is likely to vary historically and between cultures.

social control The means by which society tries to ensure that its members behave as others expect them to. Control can be formal (e.g. the law) or informal (e.g. peer pressure). Negative sanctions (punishments) and positive sanctions (rewards) may be used to encourage individuals to conform to society's norms.

social integration A socially integrated society or community is one where individuals are bound together by shared beliefs and practices. For example, shared religious rituals may remind individuals that they are part of a community to which they owe their loyalty. See also collective conscience; value consensus.

social policy The actions, plans and programmes of government bodies and agencies that aim to deal with a problem or achieve a goal, e.g. preventing crime or reducing poverty. Policies are often based on laws that provide the framework within which these agencies operate. Sociologists' findings may sometimes influence social policy, but many other factors also play a part, such as political ideologies and the availability of resources.

spiritual shopping is seen by some as a new pattern of religious participation found in late modern or postmodern society, where there is a spiritual market in which individual consumers 'pick and mix' from different religious and spiritual beliefs, practices and institutions. See also cults; New Age spirituality; postmodernity.

state apparatuses From a Marxist perspective, Althusser distinguishes between repressive and ideological state apparatuses (RSAs and ISAs). RSAs are 'armed bodies of men', such as police, prisons, the army etc, whose role is to coerce the working class into submission, while ISAs include institutions such as the media, religion and education, whose role is to persuade the working class to accept capitalist rule as legitimate. See also hegemony; ideology.

state crimes are crimes committed by, on behalf of, or with the complicity of governments or state agencies such as the police, armed forces or secret services. State crimes include genocide, war crimes, torture, imprisonment without trial and assassination of political opponents. State crimes are of concern because of the immense power of the state to do harm, and because the state can define its own harmful actions as legal because it makes the laws.

status A position in society. Ascribed status occurs where our social position is determined by fixed characteristics that we are born with and cannot normally change. Achieved status occurs where an individual's position is the result of their effort and ability.

stigma A negative label or mark of disapproval, discredit or shame attached to a person, group or characteristic. The stigma is used to justify the exclusion of the individual from normal social interaction; e.g. ex-offenders may be stigmatised and excluded from jobs. See also labelling.

strain theory See anomie.

stratification The division of society into a hierarchy of unequal groups. The inequalities may be of wealth, power and/or status. Stratification systems may be based on differences in social class, ethnic group, age, gender, religion etc. Members of different groups usually have different life chances.

structural differentiation A process of specialisation where separate institutions develop to carry out functions that were previously performed by a single institution. For example, according to Parsons, religion in pre-industrial society performed educational, legal and political functions, whereas in industrial society, it comes to specialise in providing meaning and values.

structural theories are deterministic theories that see individuals as entirely shaped by the way society is structured or organised; e.g. functionalism sees society as socialising individuals into shared norms and values that dictate how they will behave. Marxism and most types of feminism are also regarded as structural theories. See also action theories.

subculture A group of people within society who share norms, values, beliefs and attitudes that are in some ways different from the mainstream culture. Deviant subcultures are often seen as forming in reaction to a failure to achieve mainstream goals through the legitimate opportunity structure (e.g. education and work). In response, they substitute new, deviant goals or adopt illegitimate means of achieving legitimate goals. See also anomie.

subjectivity Bias or lack of objectivity, where the individual's own viewpoint or values influences their perception or judgement. Interpretivists believe sociology is inevitably subjective, since it involves understanding other humans by seeing the world through their eyes. See also interpretivism.

surveillance involves the monitoring of public behaviour to gather data for purposes such as crime control. The data gathered is generally used to regulate, manage or correct people's behaviour. For example, it may involve profiling people in order to sort them in terms of the risk they pose. Surveillance may involve the use of technology such as CCTV, facial recognition software and searchable databases. See also disciplinary power.

typifications See phenomenology.

validity The capacity of a research method to measure what it sets out to measure; a true or genuine picture of what something is really like. A valid method is thus one that gives a truthful picture. Methods that produce qualitative data are usually seen as high in validity. See also interpretivism.

value consensus Agreement among society's members about what values are important; a shared culture. See also functionalism.

value freedom The idea that values can and should be kept out of research. Modern positivists favour value freedom, but others argue that this is neither possible nor desirable, since values are necessary both to select a topic for research and to interpret findings. Radical sociologists reject value freedom in favour of a committed sociology in which the sociologist explicitly takes the side of the underdog.

values Ideas or beliefs about general principles or goals. They tell society's members what is good or important in life and what to aim for, and they underlie more detailed norms of conduct. See also functionalism; norms; value consensus.

verificationism See falsificationism.

victimology is the study of victims. Positivist victimology aims to explain patterns in victimisation. It focuses on interpersonal violent crime, especially on how victims contribute to their own victimisation. Critical victimology sees victimisation as a form of powerlessness. It focuses on the role of structural factors such as poverty that place powerless groups at greater risk of victimisation, and on the state's role in denying the label of victim to them.

victim surveys ask individuals to say what crimes they have been victims of. They are often used as a corrective to official police statistics, because they can reveal crimes that have not been reported to or recorded by the police. However, respondents may not report all crimes of which they have been a victim, while some crimes and some categories of victim (e.g. businesses, children) may not be covered.

voluntarism is the idea that humans have free will and can exercise choice in how they act, rather than their behaviour being determined or shaped by external forces such as the social structure. It is the opposite of determinism. See also determinism.

zemiology literally means 'the study of harms'. In criminology, it is concerned with why some harms come to be defined as crimes while others do not, even when they cause more damage than do many crimes; e.g. much environmental pollution is perfectly legal. Often such harms are committed by groups such as big business and the state, who have the power to define their actions as legal. Green criminology takes a zemiological approach and is an example of 'transgressive' criminology, i.e. it goes beyond the traditional boundaries of criminology (the study of law breaking) to study environmental harms even when they break no laws.

zero tolerance policing See environmental crime prevention.

Bibliography

Abercrombie N et al (1978; 1980) *The Dominant Ideology Thesis*, British Journal of Sociology

Adler F (1975) *Sisters in Crime*, McGraw Hill

Adler Z (1987) *Rape on Trial*, Routledge and Kegan Paul

Adorno T et al (1950) *The Authoritarian Personality*, Norton

Aldridge A (2013) *Religion in the Contemporary World*, Polity

Althusser L (1969) *For Marx*, Allen Lane

Althusser L (1971) *Lenin and Philosophy and Other Essays*, New Left Books

Alvarez A (2010) *Genocidal Crimes*, Routledge

Amir M (1971) *Patterns of Forcible Rape*, University of Chicago Press

Ammerman N (1987) *Bible Believers*, Rutgers University Press

Anderson B (2006) *Imagined Communities: Reflections on the Origin and Spread of Nationalism*, Verso

Ansara and Hindin M (2011) 'Psychosocial consequences of intimate partner violence' *Journal of Interpersonal Violence*

Ansell A E (2000) 'The new face of racism', in Kivisto P and Rundblad G, (eds) *Multiculturalism in the United States*, Pine Forge Press

Ansley F (1972) cited in Bernard J (1976) *The Future of Marriage*, Penguin

Archer M (1995) *Realist Social Theory*, Cambridge University Press

Arendt H (2006) *Eichmann in Jerusalem*, Penguin

Armstrong K (1993) *The End of Silence*, Fourth Estate

Armstrong K (2001) 'The War We Should Fight', *The Guardian*

Armstrong K (2015) *Fields of Blood*, Vintage

Arweck E and Beckford J (2013) 'Social perspectives' in Woodhead and Catto (eds) op cit

Atkinson J (1978) *Discovering Suicide*, Macmillan

Ball K et al (eds) (2012) *Routledge Handbook of Surveillance Studies*, Routledge

Barna G (2000) Church Attendance www.barna.org

Barrett M (1980) *Women's Oppression Today*, Verso

Baudrillard J (1983) *Simulations*, Semiotext

Bauman Z (1989) *Modernity and the Holocaust*, Polity

Bauman Z (1992) *Intimations of Postmodernity*, Routledge

Beck U (1992) *Risk Society*, Sage

Becker HS (1963) *Outsiders*, Free Press

Becker HS (1970), 'Whose side are we on?' in Becker HS (ed) *Sociological Work*, Transaction Books

Becker HS (1971) 'Social Class Variations in the Teacher-Pupil Relationship' in Cosin B et al (ed) *Education Structure and Society*, Penguin

Becker HS et al (1961) *Boys in White*, University of Chicago Press

Beckford J (2011) *Social Theory and Religion*, Cambridge University Press

Beechey V (1977) 'Some notes on female wage labour in the capitalist mode of production', *Capital and Class*

Bellah R (1991) *Beyond Belief*, University of California Press

Bellah R (1996) *Habits of the Heart*, University of California Press

Bellah R and Hammond P (2013) *Varieties of Civil Religion*, Wipf and Stock

Bennett W et al (1996) *Body Count*, Simon and Schuster

Berger P (1969) *The Social Reality of Religion*, Faber and Faber

Berger P (1999) *The Desecularisation of the World*, William B Eerdmans Publishing

Berger P (2003) Max Weber is Alive and Well and Living in Guatemala www.economyandsociety.com

Berger P and Luckmann T (1971) *The Social Construction of Reality*, Penguin

Best L (1993) 'Dragons, Dinner Ladies and Ferrets', *Sociology Review*

Best S and Kellner D (1991) *Postmodern Theory*, Macmillan

Beyer P (1994) *Religion in Globalisation*, Sage

Bibby R (1993) *Unknown Gods*, Stodart

Billings D (1990) 'Religion as Opposition', *American Journal of Sociology*

Bird J (1999) *Investigating Religion*, Collins

Birnbaum N (1971) *Towards a Critical Sociology*, Oxford University Press

Black Report, The (1980), published as Townsend P and Davidson N (1988) *Inequalities in Health,* Pelican

Bloch E (1959) *The Principle of Hope*, MIT Press

Blumer H (1969) *Symbolic Interactionism*, Prentice-Hall

Bowder B (2008) 'Sikh Girl Wins Bracelet Case', *Church Times*

Bowlby J (1965) *Child Care and the Growth of Love*, Penguin

Bowles S and Gintis H (1976) *Schooling in Capitalist America*, Routledge and Kegan Paul

Bowling B and Phillips C (2002) *Racism, Crime and Justice*, Longman

Box S (1981) *Deviancy, Reality and Society*, Holt, Rinehart & Winston

Box S (1983) *Power, Crime and Mystification*, Tavistock

Braginski B et al (1969) *Methods in Madness*, Holt Rinehart & Winston

Braithwaite J (1984) *Corporate Crime in the Pharmaceutical Industry*, Routledge and Kegan Paul

Breakdown Britain (2007) www.centreforsocialjustice.org.uk

Bridgland F (2006) 'Europe's new dumping ground', www.ban.org

Brierley P (2005) *Pulling Out of the Nosedive*, Christian Research

Brierley P (2005) *UK Christian Handbook: Religious Trends 5*, Christian Research

Brierley P (2013) *Capital Growth: What the 2012 London Church Census Reveals*, ADBC Publishers

Brierley P (2015) *Major UK Religious Trends: Revised Edition*, Brierley Consultancy

British Crime Survey, www.statistics.gov.uk

British Social Attitudes Survey (2008) www.natsen.ac.uk

British Social Attitudes Survey (2012) www.natsen.ac.uk

British Social Attitudes Survey (2014) www.natsen.ac.uk

Brookman F (1999) 'Assessing and analysing police murder files' in Brookman F et al (eds) *Qualitative Research in Criminology*, Ashgate

Brookman F (2005) *Understanding Homicide*, Sage

Brown C (2001) *The Death of Christian Britain*, Routledge

Brown C (2009) *The Death of Christian Britain*, Routledge

Brown C and Gay P (1985) *Racial Discrimination*, Policy Studies Institute

Brownmiller S (1976) *Against Our Will*, Penguin

Bruce S (1995) *Religion in Modern Britain*, Open University Press

Bruce S (1996) *Religion in the Modern World*, Oxford University Press

Bruce S (2002) *God is Dead*, Blackwell

Bruce S (2003) *Politics and Religion*, Polity

Bruce S (2008) *Fundamentalism*, Polity

Bruce S (2011) *Secularization*, Oxford University Press

Bruegel I (1979) 'Women as a reserve army of labour', *Feminist Review*

Brusco E (1995) *Reformation of Machismo: Evangelical Conversion and Gender in Columbia,* University of Texas Press, 2010

Brusco E (2012) 'Barred from the Pulpit, absent from the stage, and missing in the analysis', Boston University

Buckle A and Farrington D (1984) 'An observational study of shoplifting', *British Journal of Criminology*

Burden T (1998) *Social Policy and Welfare*, Pluto Press

Burman M and Batchelor S (2009) 'Between Two Stools: Responding to Young Women who Offend', Youth Justice 9(3)

Butler J (1992) 'Contingent Foundations' in Butler J and Scott J (eds) Feminists Theorize The Political, Routledge

Cain M (1989) Growing up Good, Sage

Carlen P (1988) Women, Crime and Poverty, Open University Press

Carlen P (1997) 'Women in the criminal justice system' in Haralambos M (ed) Developments in Sociology, Causeway Press

Carrabine E et al (2014) Criminology, Routledge

Carson W (1971) 'White-Collar Crime and the Enforcement of Factory Legislation' in Carson W and Wiles P (eds) Crime and Delinquency in Britain, Martin Robertson

Casanova J (1994) Public Religions in the Modern World, University of Chicago Press

Casanova J (2005) 'Catholic and Muslim Politics in Comparative Perspective', Taiwan Journal of Democracy

Castells M (2010) End of Millennium, Blackwell

Chaiken J et al (1974) The Impact of Police Activity on Crime, Rand Corporation

Chambliss W (1975) 'Toward a Political Economy of Crime', Theory and Society

Chambliss W (1989) 'State-Organized Crime', Criminology

Chaves M and Gorski P (2001) 'Religious Pluralism and Religious Participation', Annual Review of Sociology

Chesney-Lind M (1997) Female Offenders, Sage

Chesney-Lind M (2006) 'Patriarchy, Crime, and Justice', Feminist Criminology 1(1)

Christie N (1986) 'The Ideal Victim' in Fattah E A (ed) From Crime Policy to Victim Policy, Macmillan

Christie N (2004) A Suitable Amount of Crime, Routledge

Cicourel A (1968) The Social Organisation of Juvenile Justice, Wiley

Clancy A et al (2001) Crime, Policing and Justice, Home Office

Clarke R (1980) 'Situational Crime Prevention', British Journal of Criminology

Clarke R (1992) Situational Crime Prevention, Harrow and Heston

Clarke R and Mayhew P (1988) 'The British Gas Suicide Story' in Tonry M et al (eds) Crime and Justice, University of Chicago Press

Clinard M and Yeager P (1980) Corporate Crime, Free Press

Cloward R and Ohlin L (1960) Delinquency and Opportunity, The Free Press

Cohen A (1955) Delinquent Boys, Free Press

Cohen S (1972: 1973) Folk Devils and Moral Panics, Paladin

Cohen S (1996) 'Human rights and crimes of the state' in Muncie J et al (eds) Criminological Perspectives, Sage

Cohen S (2001) States of Denial, Polity

Cohen S (2006) 'Neither Honesty Nor Hypocrisy: The Legal Reconstruction of Torture' in Newburn T and Rock P (eds) The Politics of Crime Control, Oxford University Press

Cohen S and Young J (eds) (1973) The Manufacture of News, Constable

Connell R (1995) Masculinities, Polity Press

Cooley C (1922) Social Organization, Scribner

Cowan D E (2005) Cyberhenge: modern pagans on the internet, Routledge

Craib I (1992) Modern Social Theory, Harvester Wheatsheaf

Crockett A (2000) Variations in Churchgoing Rates, Oxford University Press

Daly M (1978) Gyn/Ecology, Beacon Press

Davie G (1994) Religion in Britain since 1945, Blackwell

Davie G (2007) The Sociology of Religion, Sage

Davie G (2013) The Sociology of Religion: A Critical Agenda, Sage

Davis K (1961) 'Prostitution' in Merton R and Nisbet R (eds) Contemporary Social Problems, Harcourt Brace and Company

Day A (2007) 'Believing in Belonging: Religion Returns to Sociology Mainstream', Network, BSA

Day D (1991) The Eco-wars, Paladin

de Beauvoir S (1953) The Second Sex, Jonathan Cape

De Haan W (2000) 'Explaining the Absence of Violence' in Karstedt S and Bussman K (eds) Social Dynamics of Crime and Control, Hart

Delphy C (1984) 'The Main Enemy' in Delphy C (ed) Close to Home, Hutchinson

Denscombe M (2001) 'Uncertain identities and health-risking behaviour', British Journal of Sociology

Ditton J (1977) Part-time Crime, Macmillan

Ditton J (2000) 'Crime Surveys and the Measurement Problem' in Jupp V et al (eds) Doing Criminological Research, Sage

Ditton J and Duffy J (1983) 'Bias in the Newspaper Reporting of Crime News', British Journal of Criminology

Ditton J et al (1999) 'The Effect of the Introduction of CCTV on Recorded Crime Rates', Scottish Office Central Research Unit

Ditton J and Farrall S (2000) The Fear of Crime, Ashgate

Dobash R and Dobash R (1979) Violence Against Wives, The Free Press

Douglas J (1967) The Social Meanings of Suicide, Princeton University Press

Downes D (1999) 'Crime and deviance' in Taylor S (ed) Sociology: Issues and Debates, Macmillan

Downes D (2001) 'The macho penal colony' in Garland D (ed) Mass Imprisonment, Sage

Downes D and Hansen K (2006) 'Welfare and punishment in comparative perspective' in Armstrong S et al (eds) Perspectives on Punishment, Oxford University Press

Downes D and Rock P (2011) Understanding Deviance, Oxford University Press

Drane J (1999) What is the New Age still saying to the Church? Marshal Pickering

Drogus C (1994) 'Religious change and women's status in Latin America', Helen Kellogg Institute for International Studies

Durkheim E (1893; 1964) The Division of Labour in Society, The Free Press

Durkheim E (1897; 1952) Suicide: A Study in Sociology, Routledge and Kegan Paul

Durkheim E (1915; 1961) The Elementary Forms of the Religious Life, Collier Books

Durkheim E and Mauss M (1903; 2009) Primitive Classification, Routledge Review

Dworkin A (1981) Pornography, The Women's Press

Eisenstadt S (1999) Fundamentalism, Sectarianism and Revolutions, Cambridge University Press

Eisenstadt S (2000) 'Multiple modernities', Daedalus 129

El Saadawi N (1980) The Hidden Face of Eve, Zed Books

Engels F (1895) 'On the History of Early Christianity' www.marxists.org

Ericson R et al (1991) Representing Order, Open University Press

Erikson K (1966) Wayward Puritans, Wiley

Evans-Pritchard E (1936) Witchcraft, Oracles and Magic among the Azande, Oxford University Press

Farrington D and Morris A (1983) 'Sex, sentencing and reconviction', British Journal of Criminology

Featherstone M (1991) Consumer Culture and Postmodernism, Sage

Bibliography

Feeley M and Simon J (1994) 'Actuarial Justice' in Nelken D *The Futures of Criminology*, Sage

Felson M (2012) *Crime and Everyday Life*, Pine Forge Press

Fenwick M and Hayward K (2000) 'Youth Crime, Excitement and Consumer Culture' in Pickford J (ed) *Youth Justice: Theory and Practice*, Cavendish

Ferguson C and Hussey D (2010) *Citizenship Survey: Race, Religion and Equalities Report*, ONS

Finke R (1997) 'The Consequences of Religious Choice' in Young L (ed) *Rational Choice Theory and Religion*, Routledge

Firestone S (1974) *The Dialectic of Sex*, Morrow

FitzGerald M et al (2003) *Young People and Street Crime*, Youth Justice Board

Flood-Page C et al (2000) *Youth Crime Findings from the 1998/99 Youth Lifestyles Survey*, Home Office

Ford J (1969) *Social Class and the Comprehensive School*, Routledge and Kegan Paul

Foucault M (1979) *Discipline and Punish*, Penguin

Garfinkel H (1967) *Studies in Ethnomethodology*, Prentice-Hall

Garland D (2001) *The Culture of Control*, Clarendon

Geis G (1967) 'White collar crime' in Clinard M and Quinney R (eds) *Criminal Behavior Systems*, Holt, Rinehart & Winston

Gellner E (1983; 2006) *Nations and Nationalism*, Blackwell

Gellner E (1992) *Postmodernism, Reason and Religion*, Routledge

Gellner E (1994) *Encounters with Nationalism*, Blackwell

Gelsthorpe (2010) 'Women, Crime & Control', *Criminology & Criminal Justice 10*

Giddens A (1984) *The Constitution of Society*, Polity

Giddens A (1990) *The Consequences of Modernity*, Polity

Giddens A (1991) *Modernity and Self Identity*, Polity

Giddens A (1999) Runaway World www.bbc.co.uk

Gill A and Lundegaarde E (2004) 'State welfare spending and religiosity', *Rationality and Society*

Gill M and Loveday M (2003) 'What do Offenders Think about CCTV?' in Gill M (ed) *CCTV*, Perpetuity Press

Gill R (1988) 'Altered Images', *Social Studies Review*

Gill R et al (1998) 'Is religious belief declining in Britain?' *Journal for the Scientific Study of Religion*

Gilliat-Ray S (2010) *Muslims in Britain*, Cambridge University Press

Gilroy P (1982) 'The Myth of Black Criminality', *Socialist Register*

Glaser B and Strauss A (1968) *The Discovery of Grounded Theory*, Weidenfeld & Nicholson

Glendinning T and Bruce S (2006) 'New Ways of Believing or Belonging', *British Journal of Sociology*

Glenny M (2008) *McMafia*, Bodley Head

Glock C and Stark R (1969) 'Dimensions of Religious Commitment' in Robertson R (ed) *Sociology of Religion*, Penguin

Goffman E (1961; 1968) *Asylums*, Penguin

Goffman E (1963) *Stigma*, Prentice-Hall

Goffman E (1967) *Interaction Ritual*, Doubleday

Goffman E (1969) *The Presentation of Self in Everyday Life*, Penguin

Goldacre B (2008) *Bad Science*, Fourth Estate

Gordon D (1976) 'Class and the Economics of Crime' in Chambliss W and Mankoff M (eds) *Whose Law? What Order?* John Wiley & Sons

Gottfredson M and Hirschi T (1990) *A General Theory of Crime*, Stanford University Press

Gouldner A (1970) *The Coming Crisis of Western Sociology*, Heinemann

Gouldner A (1973) *Sociology: renewal and critique in sociology today*, Penguin

Gouldner A (1975) *For Sociology*, Penguin

Graham H (1983) 'Do Her Answers Fit His Questions?' in Gamarnikow E et al (eds) *The Public and the Private*, Heinemann

Graham J and Bowling B (1995) *Young People and Crime*, HMSO

Gramsci A (1971) *Selections from the Prison Notebooks*, Lawrence and Wishart

Greeley A (1989) *Religious Change in America*, Harvard University Press

Greeley A (1992) *The Catholic Myth*, Prentice Hall

Green P and Ward T (2005) 'Special Issue on State Crime', *British Journal of Criminology*

Greer C and Reiner R (2012) 'Mediated Mayhem: Media, Crime, Criminal Justice' in Maguire M et al (eds) op cit

Greer G (2000) *The Whole Woman*, Anchor

Guest M et al (2013) 'Christianity: loss of monopoly' in Woodhead and Catto (eds) op cit

Gutierrez G (1971) *A Theology of Liberation*, SCM Press

Habermas J (1987) *The Theory of Communicative Action*, Beacon Press

Hadaway C et al (1993) 'What the Polls don't Show', *American Sociological Review*

Hadden J and Shupe A (1988) *Televangelism*, Henry Holt

Hagan J (2010) *Who are the Criminals?* Princeton University Press

Haggerty K and Ericson R (2000) 'The Surveillant Assemblage', *British Journal of Sociology 51*

Hales J et al (2009) 'Longitudinal Analysis of the Offending, Crime and Justice Survey 2003-06', *Home Office Research Report 19*

Hall S et al (1978: 1979) *Policing the Crisis*, Macmillan

Hamilton M (1995) *The Sociology of Religion*, Routledge

Hammond P and Machacek D (1999) *Soka Gakkai in America*, Oxford University Press

Hand T and Dodd L (2009) 'Arrests and Detentions' in Povey D and Smith K (eds) *Police Powers and Procedures*, Home Office

Hanegraaff W (2002) 'New Age Religion' in Woodhead (ed) *Religion in the Modern World*, Routledge

Hartmann H (1979; 1981) 'The Unhappy Marriage of Marxism and Feminism', *Capital and Class*; Pluto Press

Harvey D (1989) *The Condition of Postmodernity*, Blackwell

Hawking S (1988) *A Brief History of Time*, Bantam

Hawley J (ed) (1994) *Fundamentalism and Gender*, Oxford University Press

Haynes J (1998) *Religion in Global Politics*, Longman

Hayward K and Young J (2012) 'Cultural Criminology' in Maguire M et al (eds) op cit

Heelas P (1996) 'Detraditionalisation of religion and self' in Flanagan K et al (eds) *Postmodernity, Sociology and Religion*, Macmillan

Heelas P (2008) *Spiritualities of Life*, Blackwell

Heelas P and Woodhead L (2005) *The Spiritual Revolution*, Blackwell

Heidensohn F (1985; 1996) *Women and Crime*, Macmillan

Heidensohn F and Silvestri M (2012) 'Gender and Crime' in Maguire M et al (eds) op cit

Held D et al (1999) *Global Transformations*, Polity

Helland C (2000) 'Online-religion/religion-online and virtual communitas' in Hadden J and Cowan D (eds) *Religion on the Internet*, JAI

Henry S and Milovanovic D (1996) *Constitutive Criminology*, Sage

Herberg W (1955) *Protestant-Catholic-Jew*, Anchor Books

Herrnstein R and Murray C (1994) *The Bell Curve*, The Free Press

Hervieu-Léger D (2000) *Religion as a Chain of Memory*, Rutgers University Press

Hervieu-Léger D (2006) 'The role of religion in establishing social cohesion' www.eurozine.com/articles

Hill M (1983) *Understanding Social Policy*, Basil Blackwell and Martin Robertson

Hillyard P et al (2004) *Beyond Criminology: Taking Harm Seriously*, Pluto

Hindelang M et al (1981) *Measuring Delinquency*, Sage

Hindess B (1973) *The Use of Official Statistics in Sociology*, Macmillan

Hirschi T (1969) *Causes of Delinquency*, University of California Press

Hirst P (1993) *The Pluralist Theory of the State*, Routledge

Hobbs D (1988) *Doing the Business*, Oxford University Press

Holm J and Bowker J (2001) *Women in Religion*, Pinter

Hood R (1992) *Race and Sentencing*, Clarendon Press

Hoover S M et al (2004) *Faith Online*, www.pewInternet.org

Hopkins Burke R (2005) *An Introduction to Criminological Theory*, Willan Publishing

Horrie C and Chippindale P (2007) *What is Islam?* Virgin Books

Horton R (1973) 'African traditional thought and Western science' in Wilson B (ed) *Rationality*, Blackwell

Hough M and Tilley N (1998) *Auditing Crime and Disorder*, Home Office

Hudson B and Bramhall G (2005) 'Assessing the Other', *British Journal of Criminology*

Hunter J (1987) *Evangelicalism*, University of Chicago Press

Huntington S (2002) *The Clash of Civilizations and the Remaking of World Order*, Simon and Schuster

Huntington S (2004) *Who Are We? America's Great Debate*, Simon and Schuster

Inglehart R and Norris P (2003) *Rising Tide*, Cambridge University Press

Inglehart R and Norris P (2003) 'The True Clash of Civilizations', *Foreign Policy*

Jackson R (2006) 'Religion, Politics and Terror', *Working Paper*, University of Manchester

Jameson F (1984) 'Postmodernism, or the cultural logic of late capitalism', *New Left Review*

Jenabi F (2014) 'Is the Corporate Manslaughter and Corporate Homicide Act 2007 serving its purpose?' Durham University Pro Bono Society, 4 December

Jewkes Y (2003) 'Policing the Net' in Jewkes Y (ed) *Dot.cons*, Willan

Jones S (1998) *Criminology*, Butterworths

Kautsky K (1927; 1988) *The Materialist Conception of History*, Yale University Press

Kauzlarich D (2007) 'Seeing War as Criminal', *Contemporary Justice Review 10*

Keat R and Urry J (1982) *Social Theory as Science*, Routledge and Kegan Paul

Kelman H and Hamilton V (1989) *Crimes of Obedience*, Yale University Press

Kinsey R (1984) *Merseyside Crime* Survey, University of Edinburgh

Kinsey R et al (1986) *Losing the Fight Against Crime*, Blackwell

Knorr-Cetina K (1981) *The Manufacture of Knowledge*, Pergamon Press

Knorr-Cetina K (1999) *Epistemic Cultures*, Harvard University Press

Koskela H (2012) 'You shouldn't wear that body', in Ball K et al (eds) op cit

Kramer R (1992) 'The Space Shuttle *Challenger* Explosion', in Schlegel K and Weisburd D (eds) *White Collar Crime Reconsidered*, Northeastern UP

Kramer R (2014) 'From Guernica to Hiroshima to Baghdad', in Chambliss W et al (eds) *State Crime in the Global Age*, Routledge

Kuhn T (1970) *The Structure of Scientific Revolutions*, University of Chicago Press

Laidler K and Hunt G (2001) 'Accomplishing femininity among the girls in the gang', *British Journal of Criminology*

Lash S and Urry J (1987) *The End of Organised Capitalism*, Polity

Lash S and Urry J (1994) *Economies of Signs and Space*, University of Wisconsin Press

Lea J and Young J (1984; 1993) *What is to be Done About Law and Order?* Penguin

Lea J and Young J (1996) 'Relative Deprivation' in J Muncie et al (eds) *Criminological Perspectives*, Sage

Lees S (1993) *Sugar and Spice*, Penguin

Lehmann D (1996) *Struggle for the Spirit*, Polity Press

Lehmann D (2002) 'Religion and globalisation' in Woodhead L (ed) *Religions in the Modern World*, Routledge

Lemert E (1951) *Social Pathology*, McGraw-Hill

Lemert E (1962) 'Paranoia and the dynamics of exclusion', *Sociometry*

Lemert E (1967) *Human Deviance, Social Problems and Social Control*, Prentice-Hall

Lewis P (2010) 'CCTV aimed at Muslim areas in Birmingham to be dismantled' *The Guardian*, 25 October

Lilly J et al (2002) *Criminological Theory*, Sage

Livingstone S (1996) 'On the Continuing Problem of Media Effects' in Curran J and Gurevitch M (eds) *Mass Media and Society*, Arnold

Lombroso C and Ferrrero G (1893; 2004) *Criminal Woman, the Prostitute and the Normal Woman*, Duke University Press

Löwy M (2005) 'Marxism and Religion' www.internationalviewpoint.org

Lukes S (1975) *Emile Durkheim*, Allen Lane

Lukes S (1992) *Emile Durkheim: His Life and Work*, Penguin

Lynd R and Lynd H (1929) *Middletown*, Harcourt, Brace and Co

Lyon D (2000) *Jesus in Disneyland*, Polity

Lyon D et al (2012) 'Introducing surveillance studies' in Ball K et al (eds) op cit

Lyotard J (1984) *The Postmodern Condition*, Manchester University Press

Lyotard J (1992) *The Inhuman: reflections on time*, Polity

Macpherson W (1999) *The Stephen Lawrence Inquiry*, HMSO

Maduro O (1982) *Religion and Social Conflicts*, Orvis Books

Maguire M et al (eds) (1997; 2002; 2007; 2012) *The Oxford Handbook of Criminology*, Oxford University Press

Malinowski B (1954) *Magic, Science and Religion*, Anchor Books

Mandel E (1984) *Delightful Murder*, Pluto

Mann S et al (2003) 'Sousveillance', *Surveillance and Society 1*

Mannheim K (1929; 2015) *Ideology and Utopia*, Routledge

Mannheim K (1953) 'Conservative thought' in Kecskemeti P (ed) *Essays in Sociology and Social Psychology*, Routledge

Marks P (1979) 'Femininity in the Classroom' in Meighan R et al (eds) *Perspectives on Society*, Nelson

Marler P and Hadaway C (1997) 'Testing the attendance gap in a conservative church', *Sociology of Religion*

Marsh H (1991) 'A Comparative Analysis of Crime Coverage in the United States and Other Countries from 1960 to 1989', *Journal of Criminal Justice*

Marshall G (1982) *In Search of the Spirit of Capitalism*, Hutchinson

Marshall T (1975) *Social Welfare*, Hutchinson

Martin B (2000) 'The Pentecostal gender paradox' in R. Fenn (ed) *The Blackwell Companion to the Study of Religion*, Blackwell

Martin D (1967) *A Sociology of English Religion*, Heinemann

Bibliography

Martin D (1990) *Tongues of Fire*, Wiley Blackwell

Martin D (1994) 'Evangelical and Charismatic Christianity in Latin America' in Poewe K (ed) *Charismatic Christianity as a Global Culture*, University of South Carolina Press

Martin D (2002) *Pentecostalism*, Blackwell

Marx G T (1988) *Undercover: Police Surveillance in America*, University of California Press

Marx K (1844; 1998) *Theses on Feuerbach*, Prometheus Books

Marx K (1846; 1970) *The German Ideology*, International Publishers

Mathiesen T (1997) 'The Viewer Society: Foucault's Panopticon Revisited', *Theoretical Criminology 1*

Mawby R and Walklate S (1994) *Critical Victimology*, Sage

Maynard M (1987) 'Current Trends in Feminist Theory', *Social Studies Review*

McCahill M (2012) 'Crime, surveillance and media' in Ball K et al (eds) op cit

McLaughlin E (2012) 'State Crime' in McLaughlin E and Muncie J (eds) *The Sage Dictionary of Criminology*, Sage

McRobbie A and Thornton S (1995) 'Rethinking Moral Panics for Multi-mediated Social Worlds', *British Journal of Sociology*

Mead G (1918) 'The Psychology of Punitive Justice', *American Journal of Sociology*

Melossi D and Pavarini M (1981) *The Prison and the Factory*, Macmillan

Meltzer B et al (1975) *Symbolic Interactionism*, Routledge and Kegan Paul

Merton R (1938; 1949) 'Social Structure and Anomie' in Anshen R (ed) *The Family*, Harper Brothers

Merton R (1968) *Social Theory and Social Structure*, Free Press

Merton R (1973) *The Sociology of Science*, University of Chicago Press

Merton R (2007) *Science, Technology and Society in 17th century England*, www.jstor.org

Messerschmidt D (1993) *Masculinities and Crime*, Rowman and Littlefield

Messner S and Rosenfeld R (2001) *Crime and the American Dream*, Wadsworth

Mestrovic S (2011) *The Coming Fin-de-siècle*, Routledge

Michalowski R (1985) *Order, Law and Crime*, Random House

Michalowski R and Kramer R (2006) *State-Corporate Crime*, Rutgers University Press

Miers D (1989) 'Legislation and the Legislative Process', *Statute Law Review*

Miller A and Hoffman J (1995) 'Risk and Religion', *Journal for the Scientific Study of Religion*

Miller D (1997) *Reinventing American Protestantism*, University of California Press

Miller WB (1962) 'Lower class culture as a generating milieu of gang delinquency' in Wolfgang M et al (eds) *The Sociology of Crime and Delinquency*, Wiley

Mitchell J (1975) *Psychoanalysis and Feminism*, Penguin

Modood T et al (1994) *Changing Ethnic Identities*, Policy Studies Institute

Mulkay M (1969) 'Some aspects of cultural growth in the natural sciences', *Social Research*

Muncie J (2004) 'Youth justice' in Newburn T and Sparks R (eds) *Criminal Justice and Political Culture*, Willan

Murray C (1984) *Losing Ground*, Basic Books

Murray C (1990) *The Emerging British Underclass*, IEA

Myrdal G (1969) *An American Dilemma*, Harper & Row

Nanda M (2003) *Prophets Facing Backwards*, Rutgers University Press

Nanda M (2008) *God and Globalization in India*, Navayana Publishers

Nanda M (2008) 'Rush Hour of the Gods', *New Humanist*

Nelken D (1983) *The Limits of the Legal Process*, Academic Press

Nelken D (2002) 'Corruption in the European Union' in Bull M and Newell J (eds) *Corruption and Scandal in Contemporary Politics*, MacMillan

Nelken D (2012) 'White-collar and corporate crime' in Maguire M et al (eds) op cit

Nelken D and Levi M (1996) 'Introduction' to 'The Corruption of Politics and the Politics of Corruption', *Journal of Law and Society 23(1)*

Newburn T and Rock P (2006) *The Politics of Crime Control*, Clarendon Press

Nichols T (1996) 'Social class' in Levitas R and Guy M (eds) *Interpreting Official Statistics*, Routledge

Nicholson L (ed) *Feminism/Postmodernism*, Routledge

Niebuhr R (1929) *The Social Sources of Denominationalism*, Shoe String Press

Noon M (1993) 'Racial discrimination in speculative applications', *Human Resource Management Journal*

Norris C (2012) 'Accounting for the global growth of CCTV' in Ball K et al (eds) op cit

Norris C and Armstrong G (1999) *The Maximum Surveillance Society*, Berg

Norris P and Inglehart R (2004) *Sacred and Secular*, Cambridge University Press

Oakley A (1972) *Sex, Gender and Society*, Maurice Temple Smith

Oakley A (1981) *Subject Women*, Penguin

Ohmae K (1994) *The Borderless World*, HarperCollins

Palmer H (2008) 'The Whole Story', *Safety and Health Practitioner*, 10 December

Park R and Burgess E (1925) *The City*, University of Chicago Press

Parsons T (1951; 1970) *The Social System*, Routledge and Kegan Paul

Parsons T (1955) 'The American family' in Parsons T and Bales R (eds) *Family, Socialisation and Interaction Process*, The Free Press

Parsons T (1967) *Sociological Theory and Modern Society*, Free Press

Patel R (2010) 'Mozambique's Food Riots – The True Face of Global Warming' *The Observer*, 5 September

Patrick J (1973) *A Glasgow Gang Observed*, Methuen

Pawson R (1992) 'Feminist methodology' in Haralambos M (ed) *Developments in Sociology*, Causeway Press

Pearce F (1976) *Crimes of the Powerful*, Pluto

Pearce F and Tombs S (2003) *Toxic Capitalism: corporate crime and the chemical industry*, Dartmouth

Pearson G (1983) *Hooligan*, Palgrave Macmillan

Pease K (1997) 'Crime prevention' in Maguire M et al (eds) op cit

Pease K (2002) 'Crime reduction' in M. Maguire et al (eds) op cit

Phillips C and Bowling B (2007) 'Ethnicities, racism, crime, and criminal justice' in Maguire M et al (eds) op cit

Philo G and Miller D (eds) (2001) *Market Killing*, Longman

Piliavin I and Briar B (1964) 'Police Encounters with Juveniles', *American Journal of Sociology*

Platt A (1969) *The Child Savers*, University of Chicago Press

Plummer K (1979) 'Misunderstanding Labelling Perspectives' in Downes D and Rock P (eds) *Deviant Interpretations*, Martin Robertson

Polanyi M (1958) *Personal Knowledge*, University of Chicago Press

Polanyi M, cited in Ben-David J (1971) *The Scientist's Role in Society*, Prentice Hall

Pollak O (1950: 1961) *The Criminality of Women*, University of Philadelphia Press

Pollert A (1996) 'Gender and Class Revisited', *Sociology*

Polsky N (1971) *Hustlers, Beats and Others*, Aldine

Popper K (1959) *The Logic of Scientific Discovery*, Hutchinson

Popper K (1965) *The Open Society and Its Enemies, Volume II*, Routledge and Kegan Paul

Poyner B and Webb B (1997) 'Reducing thefts from shopping bags in city centre markets' in Clarke R (ed) *Situational Crime Prevention*, Harrow and Heston

Pryce K (1979) *Endless Pressure*, Penguin

Pynoos R et al (1987) 'Life threat and post-traumatic stress in school-age children', *Archives of General Psychiatry*

Ray L and Smith D (2001) 'Racist offenders and the politics of hate crime', *Law and Critique*

Redding G (2006) *The Spirit of Chinese Capitalism*, Walter de Gruyter

Reiman J and Leighton P (2012) *The Rich Get Richer and the Poor Get Prison*, Pearson

Reinharz S (1983) 'Experiential analysis' in Bowles G and Klein R (eds) *Theories of Women's Studies*, Routledge and Kegan Paul

Reynolds L (1975) cited in Meltzer B et al (1975) op cit

Rich A (1981) *Compulsory Heterosexuality and Lesbian Existence*, Onlywoman Press

Rinaldo R (2010) 'Women and piety movements' in Turner BS (ed) *The New Blackwell Companion to the Sociology of Religion*, Blackwell

Risse T et al (1999) *The Power of Human Rights*, Cambridge University Press

Robertson R (1992) *Globalisation*, Transaction

Rock P (1979) *The Making of Symbolic Interactionism*, Macmillan

Rosenhan D (1973) 'On Being Sane in Insane Places', *Science*

Rosenthal R and Jacobson L (1968), *Pygmalion in the Classroom*, Holt, Rinehart & Winston

Rosoff S et al (1998) *Profit Without Honour*, Prentice Hall

Rothe D and Friedrichs D (2015) *Crimes of Globalization*, Routledge

Rothe D and Mullins C (2008) 'State Crime', in Patillo V (ed) *Encyclopedia of Social Problems*, Sage

Runciman W (1966) *Relative Deprivation and Social Justice*, Routledge and Kegan Paul

Rusche G and Kirchheimer O (1939; 1968) *Punishment and Social Structure*, Russell and Russell

Rustin M (1994) 'Incomplete Modernity', *Radical Philosophy*

Said E (1978) *Orientalism*, Penguin

Sampson C and Phillips A (1992) *Reducing Repeat Racial Victimization*, Home Office

Savelsberg J (1995) 'Crime, inequality and Justice in Eastern Europe' in Hagen J and Peterson D (eds) *Crime and Inequality*, Stanford University Press

Schlesinger P and Tumber H (1992) 'Crime and Criminal Justice in the Media' in Downes D (ed) *Unravelling Criminal Justice*, Macmillan

Schlesinger P and Tumber H (1994) *Reporting Crime*, Oxford University Press

Schofield M (1965) *The Sexual Behaviour of Young People*, Longman

Schramm W et al (1961) *Television in the Lives of Our Children*, Stanford University Press

Schutz A (1972) *The Phenomenology of the Social World*, Heinemann

Schwendinger H and Schwendinger J (1975) 'Defenders of Order or Guardians of Human Rights?' in Taylor I et al (eds) op cit

Scott J (1990) *A Matter of Record*, Polity

Scott R (1972) 'A Proposed Framework for Analyzing Deviance' in Scott R and Douglas J (eds) *Theoretical Perspectives in Deviance*, Basic Books

Segal L (1999) *Why Feminism?* Polity Press

Sharp C and Budd T (2005) *Minority Ethnic Groups and Crime*, Home Office

Sharpe G (2009) 'The Trouble with Girls Today', *Youth Justice* 9(3)

Sharpe G and Gelsthorpe L (2009) 'Engendering the Agenda', *Youth Justice* 9(3)

Shaw D (2015) 'Black people "three times more likely" to be Tasered', *BBC*, 13 October

Shaw C and McKay H (1942) *Juvenile Delinquency and Urban Areas*, University of Chicago Press

Shipman M (1997) *Limitations of Social Research*, Longman

Sikka P (2008) 'Enterprise culture and accountancy firms', *Accounting, Auditing and Accountability Journal* 21(2)

Simmel G, cited in Wolff K (1950) *The Sociology of Georg Simmel*, Free Press

Simon J (2001) 'Fear and loathing in late-modernity' in Garland D (ed) *Mass Imprisonment*, Sage

Situ Y and Emmons D (2000) *Environmental Crime*, Sage

Skidmore W (1975) *Theoretical Thinking in Sociology*, Cambridge University Press

Sklair L (2003) 'Globalization, capitalism and power' in Holborn M (ed) *Developments in Sociology*, Causeway Press

Slapper G and Tombs S (1999) *Corporate Crime*, Longman

Smart C (1989) *Feminism and the Power of Law*, Routledge

Smeulers A and Hoex L (2010) 'Studying the Microdynamics of the Rwandan Genocide', *British Journal of Criminology 50*

Smith D (2002) 'Hinduism' in Woodhead L (ed) *Religion in the Modern World*, Routledge

Smith D et al (1983) *Police and People in London*, Policy Studies Institute

Snider L (1993) 'The politics of corporate crime control' in Pearce F and Woodiwiss M (ds) *Global Crime Connections*, Macmillan

Somerville J (2000) *Feminism and the Family*, Macmillan

Soothill K and Walby S (1991) *Sex Crime in the News*, Routledge

South N (2014) in Carrabine et al, op cit

Sparks R (1992) *Television and the Drama of Crime*, Open University Press

Sparks R et al (1977) *Surveying Victims*, Wiley

Stark R (1990) 'Modernisation, secularisation and Mormon success', in Robbins T et al (eds) *In God We Trust*, Transaction

Stark R and Bainbridge W (1986) *The Future of Religion*, University of California Press

Stark R and Iannaccone L (1997) 'Why the Jehovah's Witnesses Grow So Rapidly', *Journal of Contemporary Religion*

Statistics on Race and the Criminal Justice System, www.justice.gov.uk

Statistics on Women and the Criminal Justice System, www.justice.gov.uk

Steffensmeier D and Schwartz J (2009) 'Trends in Girls' Delinquency and the Gender Gap' in Zahn M (ed) *The Delinquent Girl*, Temple University Press

Stewart P (2008) 'Vatican City', *Reuters*

Strand J and Tuman J (2012) 'Foreign Aid and Voting Behavior in an International Organization', *Foreign Policy Analysis 8/4*

Surette R (1998) *Media, Crime and Criminal Justice*, Wadsworth

Sutherland E (1949) *White Collar Crime*, Holt, Rinehart and Winston

Swash R (2009) 'Online piracy', *The Guardian*, 17 January

Sykes, G and Matza D (1957) 'Techniques of Neutralization', *American Sociological Review*

Tawney R (1926) *Religion and the Rise of Capitalism*, J Murray

Taylor C (1991) *The Ethics of Authenticity*, Harvard University Press

Taylor I (1997) 'The political economy of crime' in Maguire M et al (eds) op cit

Taylor I et al (1973) *Critical Criminology*, Routledge and Kegan Paul

Thomas D and Loader B (2000) (eds) *Cybercrime*, Routledge

Bibliography

Thomas W and Znaniecki F (1919) *The Polish Peasant in Europe and America*, University of Illinois Press

Thomas W I (1966) 'On Social Organization and Social Personality' in Janowitz M (ed) *Selected Papers*, University of Chicago Press

Thompson EP (1977) *Whigs and Hunters*, Penguin

Thompson EP (1978) 'The Poverty of Theory' in Thompson EP *The Poverty of Theory and Other Essays*, Merlin

Thompson J (2000) *Political Scandal: Power and Visibility in the Media Age*, Polity

Tombs S (2013) 'Corporate crime' in Hale C et al (eds) *Criminology*, Oxford University Press

Tombs S and Whyte D (2007) *Safety Crimes*, Willan

Townsend P (1979) *Poverty in the United Kingdom*, Penguin

Triplett R (2000) 'The Dramatisation of Evil' in Simpson S (ed) *Of Crime and Criminality*, Pine Forge Press

Troeltsch E (1912; 1980) *The Social Teachings of the Christian Churches*, University of Chicago Press

Vásquez M (2007) '*Sacred and Secular*', Association for the Sociology of Religion

Velikovsky I (1950) *Worlds in Collision*, Macmillan

Voas D (2003) 'Intermarriage and the demography of secularization', *British Journal of Sociology*

Voas D (2015) 'Religious involvement over the life course', *Longitudinal and Life Course Studies*

Voas D and Crockett A (2005) 'Religion in Britain', *Sociology*

Voas D et al (2002) 'Religious pluralism and participation', *American Sociological Review*

von Hentig H (1948) *The Criminal and His Victim*, Yale University Press

von Hirsch A (1976) *Doing Justice*, Hill and Wang

Walby S (1988) 'The historical periodization of patriarchy', *BSA annual conference*

Walby S (1991) 'Post-post-modernism? Theorizing social complexity' in Barrett M and Phillips A (eds) *Destabilizing Theory*, Polity Press

Walby S (1997) *Gender Transformations*, Routledge

Walby S and Allen J (2004) *Domestic Violence, Sexual Assault and Stalking*, Home Office

Walklate S (1998; 2003) *Understanding Criminology*, Open University Press

Walklate S (2000) 'Researching victims' in King R and Wincup E (eds) *Doing Research on Crime and Justice*, Oxford University Press

Walklate S (2005) *Criminology*, Routledge

Wall D (2001) 'Cybercrimes on the Internet' in Wall D (ed) *Crime and the Internet*, Routledge

Wallis R (1984) *Elementary Forms of the New Religious Life*, Routledge

Walters R (2007) 'Crime, regulation and radioactive waste' in Beirne P and South N (eds) *Issues in Green Criminology*, Willan

Walton P (1998) 'Big Science' in Walton P and Young J (eds) *The New Criminology Revisited*, Palgrave Macmillan

Watkins J (1970) 'Against "Normal Science"' in Lakatos I and Musgrave A (eds) *Criticism and the Growth of Knowledge*, Cambridge University Press

Weber M (1905; 1958; 2002) *The Protestant Ethic and the Spirit of Capitalism*, Charles Scribner's Sons

Weber M (1915; 1984) *The Religion of China*, London School of Economics

Weber M (1922; 1993) *The Sociology of Religion*, Beacon Press

Weber M (1958) *The Religion of India*, Glencoe

White R (2008) *Crimes Against Nature*, Willan

Whyte D (2014) 'The neo-liberal state of exception in occupied Iraq' in Chambliss W et al (eds) *State Crime in the Global Age*, Routledge

Whyte W (1955) *Street Corner Society*, University of Chicago Press

Williams P and Dickinson J (1993) 'Fear of Crime', *British Journal of Criminology*

Willis P (1977) *Learning to Labour*, Saxon House

Wilson B (1966) *Religion in a Secular Society*, C A Watts

Wilson B (1970) *Religious Sects*, McGraw-Hill

Wilson B (2008) 'Salvation, Secularisation and De-moralisation' in Fenn R (ed) *The Blackwell Companion to the Sociology of Religion*, Blackwell

Wilson B and Dobbelaere K (1994) *A Time to Chant*, Oxford University Press.

Wilson J (1975) *Thinking about Crime*, Vintage

Wilson J and Herrnstein R (1985) *Crime and Human Nature*, Simon and Schuster

Wilson J and Kelling G (1982) 'Broken Windows', *Atlantic Monthly*

Winlow S (2001) *Badfellas*, Berg

Wolfgang M (1958) *Patterns in Criminal Homicide*, Patterson Smith

Woodhead L (2001) 'The impact of feminism on the sociology of religion' in R. Fenn (ed) *The Blackwell Companion to the Study of Religion*, Blackwell

Woodhead L (2014) 'Not enough boots on the ground', *Church Times*, 7 February

Woodhead L et al (eds) (2009) *Religions in the Modern World*, Routledge

Woodhead L and Catto R (eds) (2013) *Religion and Change in Modern Britain*, Routledge

Woolgar S (1992) *Science: the Very Idea*, Routledge

Worrall A (2004) 'Twisted Sisters, Ladettes, and the New Penology' in Alder C and Worrall A (eds) *Girls' Violence*, State University of New York Press

Worsley P (1956; 1968) *The Trumpet Shall Sound*, McGibon Kee

Worsley P (1977) *Introducing Sociology*, Penguin

Wrong D (1961; 1999) *The Oversocialized Conception of Man*, Transaction

Yearnshire S (1997) 'Analysis of Cohort' in Bewley et al (eds) *Violence Against Women*, RCOG Press

Yinger M (1970) *The Scientific Study of Religion*, Macmillan

Young J (1971) *The Drugtakers*, Paladin

Young J (1997) 'Left realist criminology' in Maguire M et al (eds) op cit

Young J (1998) 'Writing on the Cusp of Change' in Walton P and Young J (eds) *The New Criminology Revisited*, Palgrave Macmillan

Young J (1999) *The Exclusive Society*, Sage

Young J (2002) 'Crime and social exclusion' in Maguire M et al (eds) opcit

Young J (2011) *The Criminological Imagination*, Polity

Young M and Willmott P (1962) *Family and Kinship in East London*, Penguin

Young M and Willmott P (1975) *The Symmetrical Family*, Penguin

Youth Justice Board (2006) 'Anti-Social Behaviour Orders' www.direct.gov.uk

Index

Abercrombie N 9, 63
absolutism 26
achievement 74, 87
action theories 211, 224-232, 264
actuarial justice 147-148
adaptation 71-73, 204
Adler F 109
Adler Z 106
Adventist sects 51
aetiological crisis 99-101
Afghanistan 131, 137
African Caribbean 25, 55, 100, 117-118
ageing effect 56
agents of social control 80
AGIL schema 204
agnostics 52
AIDS 43, 116, 127
Aldridge A 5, 24, 39
alienation 8-10, 88, 197, 210-211, 220, 264
alternative status hierarchy 74-75
alternatives to prison 150
Althusser L 9, 171, 211, 213-214
Alvarez A 140
American Dream 76
Amir M 151
Amish 51
Ammerman N 31
Amnesty International 140
ancient society 209
Anderson B 63
anomie 50-52, 70-76, 90-93, 100, 118,
    127, 204
Ansara D and Hindin M 111
Ansley F 220
anthropocentric view 136
anti-determinism 90
anti-Semitism 140
antisocial behaviour 144
Arendt H 139
Armstrong K 9-10, 42, 148
arrests and cautions 117
Arweck E 56
ASBOs 101-102, 150
asceticism 14, 44, 50, 54, 264
ascribed status 9, 63, 235
astrology 33, 43, 49, 51
atheism, atheist 23, 36, 34-35, 52
Atkinson J 83, 190
audience cults 49

authoritarian personality 139
Azande 60

baptisms 21-22, 26, 29
Baptists 21
Barrett M 220
base superstructure model 211-213
Baudrillard J 237-240
Bauman Z 40, 139-140
Beck U 134, 235, 239-240
Becker H 79, 176, 199-200
Beckford J 25, 35, 40, 56
believe in belonging 30
believing without belonging 29-30, 36
Bellah R 7, 33-36
Bennett W 98
Berger P 24-25, 32, 44, 229
Best L 184
Best S and Kellner D 237, 240
Bhopal 134
Bible, the 10, 14, 16, 22, 39-40
Billings D 18
biological differences 97, 217
biosocial theory 97
Bird J 55
Black Report 245
Bloch E 16
Blumer H 226
bodily capital 112
boundary maintenance 71
bourgeoisie 14, 88, 210-214, 264
Bowlby J 244
Bowles S and Gintis H 63
Bowling B and Phillips C 115-117
Box S 93-94, 106,
Braginski B 84
Braithwaite J 82, 94
Branch Davidian 48
Bridgland F 135
Brierley P 52, 55-56
British Crime Survey 99, 116, 152
British Social Attitudes 21, 52
Broken Windows 98, 144, 152
Brookman F 151, 166
Brown C and Gay P 162
Brown, Callum 53
Brownmiller S 219
Bruce S 15-16, 22-26, 30, 33-35, 40-42,
    47, 50-56

Buckle A and Farrington D 106
Buddhism 5, 35, 52
Burden T 244
Butler J and Scott J 221-222

Cain M 111, 132
Calvinism 13-14, 44, 59, 225
canteen culture 116
capitalism and crime 88-90, 93-94, 118-
    120, 135-136, 149-150
capitalism and religion 8-9, 14-18, 41-44,
    62-63
capitalism and social theory 208-214, 218-
    222, 231-232, 235-236, 239-240
capitalist class 8, 62, 64, 84, 88, 89, 133-
    135, 171, 210, 236, 235
carceral agencies/archipelago 146, 150
career (deviant career) 81-84, 87, 105, 122,
    227
cargo cult 18
Carlen P 106, 108-109
Carrabine E 92, 150
Casanova J 17, 42
caste 9
Castells M 40, 131
categorical suspicion 148
Catholic 7, 9, 10, 13, 17-18, 21-25, 29, 35,
    40-42, 47-50, 55, 188
CCTV 128, 132, 143, 146-148
Census 21, 30, 169-172
Chaiken J 143
Challenger space shuttle 137
Chambliss W 88, 138
charismatic 47, 51, 225
Chernobyl 134
Chesney-Lind M 109-110
Children of God 48
chivalry thesis 105-107, 112, 264
Christianity 8-10, 18, 26, 30-32, 40, 44
Christie N 151
church attendance 21-22, 25-26, 29-30,
    55-56, 165
Church of England 10, 13, 21-22, 29, 34,
    47, 50, 53-54
churches 15-18, 21-25, 29-35, 47-56, 64,
    205, 264
Cicourel A 80, 93, 170
civil religion 7-8, 10, 43, 63, 264
civil rights 15-16, 18, 138, 217
Clarke R 98, 143

Index

clash of civilisations 41-42

class conflict 8, 18, 89, 206, 214, 235, 245

class consciousness 9, 62-63, 210

class deal 108

clergy 15-18, 22, 29, 39, 54

client cults 49-52, 56

climate change 134, 235

Clinard M and Yeager P 93

closed belief system 60

closed ended questions 166

Cloward R and Ohlin L 75-76, 87, 100, 112

cognitive functions of religion 6

Cohen A 74, 76, 87, 100

Cohen S 71, 123, 126-127, 139-140, 150

collective conscience 6-7, 71, 149, 204, 264

Colombia 10, 54, 131

committed sociology 197-199

commodification of crime 125-126

commonsense knowledge 83, 229-231

communism 25, 34, 41-42, 60-63, 76, 94, 131-133, 197, 209-214

comparative method 159-162, 172

compensators 34, 36, 50, 54, 264

Comte A 187, 197-198, 244

confidentiality 159, 165-166, 172

conflict subcultures 175

conflict theories 151

conformity 60, 71-73, 100, 112, 146, 192, 203

Confucianism 14, 44

congregational domain 32

Conservative 97, 148, 245-246

conspiracy theories 39

consumerism 29-31, 43, 86, 100, 118, 127

content analysis 182-184

control culture 81

control group 145, 160-161

control theory 107-109

convenience sampling 164

conversionist sects 51

converts 16, 30-31

convictions 82, 110, 114, 117, 169

Cooley C 227

coroners 83, 190, 230

corporate crime 86, 88-94, 99, 102, 111, 136-137

corporate homicide 89

cosmopolitanism 40

courts 79, 82, 88, 106, 110, 115-117, 152, 169-171, 210-212

covert participant observation 178-181

Cowan D 31

Craib I 206, 213-214, 231-232

creationism 16, 61

crime control 69, 97, 101, 125, 145-147, 150

crime prevention 69, 98, 120, 142-145, 148, 152

crime rates 74-76, 82, 89, 99-100, 109, 119, 123, 122

crime reduction 97, 144-145, 148

Crime Survey for England and Wales 101, 110, 115, 170

crime, fictional representations 124

crimes of globalisation 132

crimes of obedience 139

crimes of the powerful 82, 88, 91-92, 99, 106, 135-136, 145, 151

criminal culture 75

criminal justice 69, 82-84, 88-91, 104-107, 110-123, 150-152

criminal organisation 92, 133, 140

criminal subcultures 75-76, 100-112

criminalisation 92, 101, 110-115, 118, 143, 148

criminality 87, 90, 93, 105-111, 117-120, 124-125, 145

criminogenic capitalism 88

crisis of legitimacy 94

critical criminology 89-90, 94, 97, 99, 18, 151, 264

critical victimology 151-152

Crockett A 21, 30, 56

Crown Prosecution Service (CPS) 117

CUDOS norms 59-60

cults 18, 34, 44, 47-53, 56, 264

cultural amnesia 30, 41

cultural defence 25, 42, 44, 55, 264

cultural diversity 24, 240

cultural inclusion 100

cultural transition 25-26, 55, 264

cultural transmission 75

culture 32-33, 42-43, 54-55, 71-73, 125, 140, 200, 203, 235-240, 264

cybercrime 123, 128

dark figure of crime 80-82

Davie G 29-30, 39-41, 52-55

Davis K 72

Day A 30

Day D 135

De Haan W 82

Deepwater Horizon 135-137

degradation rituals 84

dehumanisation 139

deindustrialisation 140

de-labelling 92-93, 151

delinquency 75-76, 79-80, 107, 243, 246

demographic factors 116

denomination 7, 21-22, 47-52, 56 , 264

Denscombe M 109

deprivation 54-56, 99-102, 118-120, 125, 140, 164, 187-188

determinism 84, 90, 94, 211-214, 227, 228, 264

detraditionalisation 51

deviance 70-152, 265

deviance amplification 81-82, 84, 90, 126-128, 265

deviant career - see career

Dianetics 49

diaries 182-183

difference feminism 221

differential association 75, 93-94

differentiation 23-26, 204-205

disciplinary power 146-147, 152, 265

discourse 62, 152, 221-222, 238, 265

discrimination 73, 91, 102, 109, 115-120, 136, 162, 217-218, 246

disembedding 238

disenchantment 23, 32, 265

disengagement 24

disintegrative shaming 82

disorganised capitalism 236

dispersal of discipline 146

displacement 99, 143-144, 147

Ditton J 123, 148

diversity 21-26, 35-36, 40-44, 48, 71, 102, 206, 221-222, 236, 240

division of labour 54, 63, 71, 87, 139-140, 168, 209-210, 218-221

Dobash R and R 107

documents 157, 159, 174-175, 182-184, 189

domestic violence 99-102, 106-110, 145, 152, 219-222, 246

double standards 106

Douglas J 83, 190

Downes D 76, 81, 119, 144, 150, 180

Downes D and Rock P 81, 119

dramatisation 71, 124, 128

dramaturgical model 227-228, 265

Drane J 51

Drogus C 54

drugs 59, 81-82, 106-109, 112, 116, 123-126, 131-135, 140, 144-145, 150

dual systems feminism 220

Durkheim E 5-7, 33, 71-72, 187-190, 197-198, 203-204, 230-231

ecocentric view 135, 140

economic base 16, 88, 149, 152, 209, 213

economic determinism 211-214

economic exclusion 100, 118

El Saadawi N 10

elective affinity 13

empathy 175, 178

Engels F 16, 18

Enlightenment 33, 41, 51, 149, 157, 187, 197, 203, 217, 221-222, 235-240, 265

environmental crime prevention 144, 152, 265

environmental discrimination 136

Ericson R 123, 147

Erikson K 72

essentialism 221-222

established sects 51, 56

ethical deprivation 49, 54

ethics 165, 166, 172, 181, 183

ethnic differences 52, 55, 111, 115-119

ethnicity, crime and justice 114-120

ethnomethodology 225, 229-230, 232, 265

evangelical 10, 18, 25-35, 51

Evans Pritchard E 60

exaggeration and distortion 126

existential security theory 35-36, 265

expectancy effect 160

experimental effect 160

experimental group 145, 160-161

experimental method 160, 188

experiments 61, 157-162, 169, 172, 187-191, 230

exploitation 8-10, 138-139, 200, 206, 209-212, 220-221, 239, 245, 265

expressive roles 218

external validity 161

fallacy of induction 191

false consciousness 8-10, 13, 63, 89, 182, 191, 210, 214

falsificationism 59, 191-192, 194, 265

familism 220

Farrington D 106

Feeley M and Simon J 147

Felson M 98, 123, 143

feminism 62-64, 109, 151, 166-168, 171, 177, 190, 200, 217-222, 240, 245, 265

feminism and questionnaires 166

feminist research 177, 246

feminist theories 9, 90, 111-112, 156, 216-217, 222

Fenwick M and Hayward K 125

Ferguson C and Hussey D 52

feudal society 210

field experiments 159-162, 172

Finke R 35

Firestone S 218

FitzGerald M 119

flexible accumulation 240

Flood-Page C 105

focus groups 166

folk devils 71, 81-82, 123, 126-128, 265

forces of production 209-210

Ford J 191

Fordism 235, 240, 265

formal interviews see structured interviews

Foucault M 146-147, 150-152, 236, 238

free floating intelligentsia 64

free will 90, 98, 109, 161, 189-190, 206, 211, 213-214, 225-227

function 5-10, 13-14, 23-25, 60-63, 70-76, 88-89, 147-149, 150-151, 170-171, 203-206, 265

functional alternatives 7-8, 10, 205, 265

functional equivalents 7

functionalism 508, 10, 63, 70-76, 87, 107, 127, 149, 152, 202-206, 244, 265

fundamentalism 3, 38-41, 44, 53, 265

funding 34, 159, 199-200, 244-246

funerals 29

Garfinkel H 189, 229-230

Garland D 150

Geis G 93

Gellner E 63

Gelsthorpe L 110

gender deal 108-112, 170, 217-218

gender differences 52, 104-107, 217-218

gender roles 10, 16, 53-54, 106-109, 184, 218

General Household Survey 169

genocide 51, 74, 132, 136-140, 225

Giddens A 39-40, 231-232, 238-240

Gill A and Lundegaarde E 36

Gill M and Loveday M 147

Gill R 183

Gilliat Ray S 10

Gilroy P 118-119

Glaser B and Strauss A 176, 180, 189

Glendinning T 33

Glenny M 133

global criminal economy 131

global risk 132-134, 140

global warming 51, 59, 131, 134-135, 190, 239

globalisation 265

glocal 133, 140

goal attainment 204-205

Goffman E 84, 147, 199, 227-228, 232

going native 178-181, 184

Gordon D 88

Gouldner A 198-200, 211, 214

Graham H 168

Graham J and Bowling B 115-116

Gramsci A 18, 63, 212-214

Greeley A 53

green crime 69, 91, 130, 131, 133-135, 137, 140, 266

green criminology 134-136, 140

Green P and Ward T 136, 139

Greer C and Reiner R 125

Greer G 219

grounded theory 176, 180, 184, 189

group interviews 166

Gypsies 140

Hadaway K 25

Haggerty K and Ericson R 147

Hales J 106

Hall S 90, 118-119, 127

Hand T and Dodd L 110

Hare Krishna 35

harms 131-140

Hartmann H 220-221

Harvey D 237-240

Hawking S 191

Hawley J 39

Hawthorne effect 160-162, 179-181

Haynes J 40-42

Hayward K and Young J 125

hazardous waste 135

health and safety laws 88-91, 136

Heelas P 51-52, 56

Index

Heelas P and Woodhead L 32-33, 53

hegemony 18, 63, 212, 214, 266

Heidensohn F 105-109

Heidensohn F and Silvestri M 105

Helland C 31

Henry S and Milovanovic D 102

Herberg W 25, 55

Herrnstein R 97

Hervieu-Léger D 30-31, 40-41

high modernity 238

Hillyard P 138

Hindu, Hinduism 9, 13-14, 25, 40-44, 55, 64

Hirschi T 108

Hirst P 239

historical documents 182-183

historical materialism 197, 209

Hobbs D 133

holistic milieu 30-33, 36, 53

Holm J 9

Holocaust 139-140

homelessness 169

Hood R 117

Hoover S M 31

Hopi Indians 205

Hopkins Burke R 90

horoscope 33, 54

Horrie C and Chippindale P 42

Horton R 60

Hudson B and Bramhall G 117

Human Potential 48, 51

human rights 69, 130-131, 138-140

humanism 34, 213

humanistic Marxism 211-212

Hunter J 26

Huntington S 41-42

Husserl E 228-229

Hutus 137

hypothesis 161-170, 176, 179-180, 184, 188-191, 198

identity 30-31, 40-44, 50-55, 81-84, 126-128, 131, 140, 177, 228, 235-237, 240, 266

ideological state apparatuses 213-214

ideology 8-10, 16-17, 62-64, 100, 108, 138, 140, 171-172, 191, 206, 210-212, 266

imagined communities 24

immiseration 210

imperialism 42, 118, 138

impression management 227

incarceration 150-152

indexicality 230

individual sphere 53

individualism 24, 29, 30, 32, 51, 100, 235, 266

inductive reasoning 187, 190-191, 194

industrialisation 23-24, 63, 100, 112, 132-133, 140, 235

inequality 9-10, 13-17, 40-42, 99-100, 171-172, 210-211, 217-219

informal interviews see unstructured interviews

informed consent 159-160, 165-166, 172, 181, 183

Inglehart R and Norris P 42

innovation 73-76, 87, 93

institutional anomie theory 76

institutional racism 116, 120, 136

institutionalisation 84

instrumental roles 218

integration 5-10, 41, 100, 119, 188, 203-205, 236, 244

interactionism 68, 79, 90, 181, 212, 225-230, 266

internal validity 161

international law 134, 137-138, 140

International Monetary Fund (IMF) 132, 243

Internet 31, 39, 59, 123, 128, 131, 182, 235

interpretivism 159, 161, 165, 168, 170, 175, 180, 189,-190, 194, 266

interview schedule 167-170

interviewer 163, 166-168, 175-176, 180

interviewer bias 168

interviews 25, 83, 108, 157-162, 166-172, 174-177, 179-184, 189

Iran 25, 41-42

Iraq 92, 137-138

Islam 9-10, 21, 25, 40-42, 48-49, 118, 140

Islington Crime Survey 108

Jackson R 42

Jameson F

Jehovah's Witnesses 51

Jenabi F 89

Jesus Freaks 50

Jewkes Y 128

Jews 15, 39, 41, 140

Judaism 9-10, 40

Kautsky K 14

Kauzlarich D 138

Keat R and Urry J 160, 194,

Kelman H and Hamilton V 139

Kendal Project 30-33, 53, 56

key informant 178-180

King, Martin Luther 15

Kinsey R 101

Knorr-Cetina K 61

knowledge claim 59-62, 266

Koskela H 147

Kramer R 137

Kramer R and Michalowski R 91, 137

Kray brothers 133

Krishna Consciousness 48

Kuhn T 61, 64, 192-194

labelling 78-84, 87-90, 91-94, 97-99, 118-119, 227-228, 230, 266

labelling theory 72, 79, 82-84, 88-90, 93-94, 97-99, 138, 227-228, 232

laboratory experiments 159-162, 172, 187

ladettes 110

Laidler K and Hunt G 109

Lash S and Urry J 235-236

late modernity 29, 30, 100-101, 125, 127, 147, 234-239

latency 204-205

latent functions 72, 205-206

Lawrence Stephen 116, 120, 182

Lea J and Young J 99-101, 110, 118-119, 125

leading questions 168, 198

Lees S 108

left realism 99-102, 118, 266

legitimation 8-9, 245, 266

Lehmann D 17, 44

Lemert E 81-83, 227

Lenin 8

Lewis P 148

liberal feminism 217-218, 220

liberalism 39, 41

liberation theology 17, 18

liberation thesis 107, 109, 112

life chances 194, 200

life history 83

Lilly J 98

Livingstone S 124

Lombroso C and Ferrrero G 107

longitudinal study 145

looking glass self 227

Index

Löwy M 17
Lynd R and Lynd H 26
Lyon D 30-32, 148
Lyotard J 62, 237, 240

machismo 54
Macpherson Inquiry 182
macro-level 164, 182, 188, 203, 225, 266
Maduro O 17-18
mafia 76, 133, 135, 140
Maguire M
male gaze 147
Malinowski B 7
Mandel E 124
manifest function 182
Mann S 147
Mannheim K 64
Manson Family 48
manufactured risks 59, 134, 239
marginalisation 9, 82, 99-102, 118, 127
marginality 49, 56
Marks P 64
Marsh H 123
Marshall G 15
Martin B 54
Marx G T 148
Marx K 8-9, 13-14, 16-17, 63, 187, 197, 200, 208-214, 239-240
Marxism 16-18, 62-64, 88-90, 93-94, 149-151, 191-194, 208-214, 239-240, 266
Marxist feminism 219-221
Marxist theories of postmodernity 239-240
masculinity 105, 107, 111-112
mass incarceration 150, 152
master status 81, 84, 227
Mathiesen T 147
Mawby R and Walklate S 151
McCahill M 147
McLaughlin E 136
McMafia 133
McRobbie A and Thornton S 127
Mead GH 189, 226
means of production 8, 62, 88, 209-211, 235
mechanical solidarity 204
media representations 122-123, 184, 218
Melossi D and Pavarini M 149
mental illness 73, 83-84, 170-171, 227
meritocracy 7, 63, 100, 212, 214
Merton R 59-60, 72-76, 87, 93, 100, 185, 202, 205-206

Messerschmidt D 111-112
Messner S and Rosenfeld R 76
Mestrovic S 7
meta-narratives 32, 51, 62, 236-237, 240
Methodism, Methodists 21-22, 31, 47, 50
Michalowski R and Kramer R 136
micro-level 181, 232, 266
middle class 43-44, 49-50, 53-54, 73-76, 108-111, 211-212, 221-222
Miers D 151
military policing 101
millenarian movements 17-18, 49
Miller A and Hoffman J 52-53
Miller D 35
Miller W 76, 87
Mitchell J 220
mode of production 209
modern society 23-24, 29-30, 40-41, 100-102, 149, 187, 204, 232, 235, 237-240
modernism 235, 266
modernist theories 157, 217, 235-236
modernity 29-30, 39-41, 44, 50-52, 56, 63, 100-101, 125, 127, 139, 235-240, 266
Modood T 55
mods and rockers 81-82, 126-127
monotheism 10, 40
Moonies 48, 49
moral entrepreneurs 79, 81, 126
moral panic 81-82, 90, 110, 112, 119, 123, 126-128, 132, 266
Mormons 51
mortification of the self 84
Murray C 97-98, 246
Muslim, Muslims 10, 24-25, 42, 49, 55, 117-118, 148
My Lai Massacre 139
Myrdal G 199

Nanda M 43
nation state 7, 41, 133-135, 235-236, 240, 243
nationalism 41-44, 63-64
natural attitude 229
natural science 159-164, 167, 175, 186-194
Nazi Germany 8, 139
Nazism 191
Nelken D 93-94
neo-liberal 93, 132, 137

neo-Marxist 9, 17, 86, 89-90, 94, 99, 118-120, 182, 212
net widening 110-112
neutralisation techniques 140, 266
New Age spirituality 30-33, 40, 78, 266
New Christian Right 15-16, 18, 25, 40
New Labour 102, 149, 246
new religious movements 32, 48, 267
New Right 97, 100, 107, 246, 267
Newburn T and Rock P 152
news values 123,-124, 128, 267
Niebuhr R 47, 50-51, 56
non-participant observation 157, 177-179, 181, 184
non-representative sampling 164
non-utilitarian crime 88, 118
Noon M 162
normal science 61, 64, 192-193
norms 267
Norris C 147
Norris C and Armstrong G 148
Norris P and Inglehart R 35-36

Oakley A 168-9, 171, 177, 217
objectivity 165, 180, 197-200, 267
observation 59, 61, 157, 159, 165, 169, 174, 177-182, 184, 189-191
official documents 183
official statistics 78-121, 169-172, 188-190
official surveys 169-170
Ohmae K 236
online religion 31, 36
open belief systems 59, 267
open-ended questions 166, 176
opportunity sampling 164
organic analogy 203-204, 206
organic intellectuals 18, 63-64, 212
organised scepticism 60
organismic deprivation 49, 54
orientalism 42
overt observation 177-179, 181

Pagans 31
Palmer H 91
Panopticon 146-147
paradigm 61, 64, 192-194, 267
paranoia 83, 227
Park R and Burgess E 75
Parsons T 7, 23, 107, 203-206, 218, 229
participant observation 157, 159, 174-182

Index

Patel R 134

patriarchal control 107, 109, 112

patriarchy 9, 10, 13, 39, 106, 108, 1109, 151, 172, 198, 218-222, 246, 267

Pawson R 177

Pearce F 89, 91, 94

Pentecostal gender paradox 10, 54

Pentecostalism 4, 10, 17, 24, 38, 44, 48, 51, 53-55, 100

People's Temple 48

period or cohort effect 56

Perry Pre-school project 145

personal documents 159, 175, 182, 189

Pew Global Attitude Survey 43

phenomenology 198, 225, 228-229, 232, 267

Phillips C and Bowling B 116

Philo G and Miller D 237

piety movements 10

pilgrims 3, 30, 40

Piliavin I and Briar B 79

Platt A 79

plausibility structure 24

pluralism 8, 35, 267

plurality of life worlds 24

Polanyi M 61

polarisation 127, 210-211

policing 98, 101, 102, 116, 118-119, 123, 128, 144, 145, 152

political lesbianism 219

Pollak O 105

Pollert A 219, 221

Polsky N 72, 179

Popper K 59, 61, 64, 184, 190-194

positivism 157, 159, 163, 167, 170, 176-177, 180, 187-189, 244

positivist victimology 151-152

post-Confucian 44

post-Fordism 240

postmodern society 29, 30-32, 40, 51, 56, 112, 156, 206, 235-240

postmodernism 62, 190, 200, 206, 214, 236-239

poststructuralism 221-222, 238

poststructuralist feminism 221`-222

poverty 17, 36, 69, 88-89, 97-99, 108, 144-145, 237, 243-246

practical issues (methods) 159, 160, 163, 166, 1475, 178, 179

predestination 13, 14, 60

presentation of self 227

pre-set questions 168, 175, 179

priests 9, 10, 14, 17, 22, 47, 51, 64, 197

primary data 169

primary deviance 81, 83, 84

principle of hope 16

prison 84, 91 97, 98, 106, 108, 115, 117, 120

private sphere 10, 17, 22, 24, 41, 53, 124, 218

privatisation of religion 40, 267

problem makers 87, 199

problem takers 79, 87, 199

profane 6

profiling 148

project identity 40

proletariat 86, 88, 191, 197, 210-212, 214, 267

prosecution 89, 91-92, 106, 117, 145

prostitution 72, 98, 105, 108-109, 131

Protestant 10, 13-15, 18, 23,-24, 43,-44, 47, 50-51, 55, 59, 188, 211, 225, 232

Pryce K 55, 100

pseudo-patient 84

public documents 182-184

public sphere 10, 17, 41, 53, 218,

punishment 10, 18, 23, 68-69, 71, 94, 97-99, 105, 136, 142-143, 146, 148-150, 152, 267

Puritanism 59

Pynoos R 152

Quakers 10, 51

qualitative data 157, 159, 175-183, 190

qualitative research 36, 156, 157, 174, 15, 189

quantitative data 159, 161, 163, 167, 170, 175, 177, 181-184, 188, 190

quantitative research 156, 158, 159, 188

quasi-random sampling 164

questionnaires 157-159, 162-167

quota sampling 164

racism 41, 114, 116, 118-120, 136, 138, 140, 162, 221, 240

racist incidents 21, 170

radical feminism 218-220

Rainbow Warrior 135

rape 99, 106, 108, 123, 151-152, 168, 184, 219

Rastafarianism 55

rational action 225-226

rational choice theory 34, 98, 143, 268

rationalisation 23, 26, 32, 50, 53, 59, 267

rationality 23, 41, 98, 139, 199, 217-218, 225, 235, 238 -239

realism, science and technology 193, 268

realist theories of crime 96-102

rebellion 16, 73, 76, 90, 94

recipe knowledge 229

recreated memories 41

Redding G 44

re-enchantment 32

reflexivity 230, 238-239, 268

Reformation, the 13, 23-24, 47, 59, 225

registration data 170-171

rehabilitation 148-149

Reiman J and Leighton P 91

Reinharz S 168

reintegrative shaming 82, 168

relations of production 149, 209

relative autonomy 16, 213

relative deprivation 49, 56, 99-102

relativism 25, 26, 102, 200, 268

reliability 159, 161, 164, 268

religion as conservative force 13

religion as force for change 13

religion online 31

religiosity 3, 35-36, 43, 52-56

religious affiliation 21-22, 55

religious beliefs 5, 9-10, 13, 17, 21-22, 23-26, 29, 31-33, 47, 52, 64, 83, 200

religious consumerism 31

religious diversity 23-26, 36, 48

religious feminism 10

religious institutions 6, 22-24, 31-32

religious market theory 29, 34-36

religious movements 32, 48-50

religious organisations 3, 9, 15, 18, 24, 31, 34, 47-51, 56, 60

religious participation 25, 34-36, 52, 55, 56

repeat victimisation 152

representations, media 122-124, 184, 218

representative sample 164-5, 167, 170, 180-181, 184

representativeness 159, 161, 164, 165, 167, 170, 176, 180, 183, 268

repressive state apparatuses 213

reproduction 213, 231

research methods 156-199

reserve army of labour 220, 268

resistance identity 40

response rate 163, 165, 167

restitutive justice 149

retreatism 73, 76

retreatist subcultures 75

retribution 148

Reynolds L 228

Rich A 219

right realism 97-98, 268

Rinaldo R 10

risk management 147

risk society 134, 140, 190, 235, 239-240, 268

Risse T 139

ritualism 73, 76

role distance 228

role model 75, 81, 98, 107, 124, 217

Rosenhan D 84

Rosenthal R and Jacobson L 162

Rosoff S 136

Rothe D and Friedrichs D 132

Rothe D and Mullins C 138

ruling class 8-9, 18, 62-64, 88-89, 119, 171, 210, 212, 231, 237, 245

Runciman W 100

Rusche G and Kirchheimer O 149

Rustin M 239

Rwanda 132, 137, 139-140

sacred 6-7, 9, 24, 39-40, 43, 51, 59, 60

sacred canopy 24

sacred text 9, 39-40, 51

sample 160-161, 164-165, 167, 170, 172, 175-176, 180, 181, 184

sampling 164-165, 167, 170

Sampson C and Phillips A 120

sanctions 71, 150, 203

Savelsberg J 76

Schlesinger P and Tumber H 123, 125

Schofield M 165

Schramm W 124

Schutz A 225, 229-230

Schwendinger H and J 138-139

science 58-64, 140, 156-160, 163-164, 167-168, 174-175, 186-194, 197-198, 235, 244

scientific revolution 62, 192-191

Scientology 5, 48, 49, 192

Scott, John 183

secondary data 157, 162, 169

secondary deviance 81-83

secondary green crimes 135

secondary sources 172, 183, 184

secondary victimisation 152

sectarian cycle 51, 56

sects 24, 34, 47-54, 56, 268

secularisation 20-26, 28, 29, 32, 33, 34-36, 41, 43, 50-59, 268

Segal L 222

selective enforcement 88-89

self spirituality 32, 51

self sustaining beliefs 61

self-fulfilling prophecy 81, 83, 110, 126, 148, 150, 224, 227, 246

self-report studies 80, 105-106, 110, 115-116, 120, 268

semi-structured interviews 166

sentencing 106, 110, 117, 142

separatism 51, 219, 222, 246, 268

sex and gender 217-218

sex role theory 107, 112

sexism 138

sexual assault 102, 106, 110, 222

sexual politics 218

Sharia law 42

Sharp C and Budd T 116, 119

Sharpe G 106, 110

Sharpe G and Gelsthorpe L 110

Shaw C and McKay H 75

Sheilaism 33

Shi'a Islam 42

Shintoism 35

Shipman M 92, 166

Simmel G 110

Simon J 147, 150

simulacra 237

Situ Y and Emmons D 134

situational crime prevention 120, 143-144, 152

Sklair L 236

Smart C 106

Snider L 88

snowball sampling 164

social change 13-17, 21, 23, 49, 50, 52, 56, 64, 127, 183, 204, 211, 238

social class 47, 52, 69, 86-88, 122, 137, 158, 163, 170-172, 191, 194, 209, 268

social construction 5, 10, 62, 79-80, 97, 99, 101, 110, 118, 120, 123, 128, 138, 190, 268

social construction of crime statistics 80

social control 60, 69-72, 79-82, 99, 132, 143-144, 146-147, 203, 268

social democratic perspective 245

social deprivation 54

social exclusion 120, 125

social facts 83, 87, 157, 159, 170, 187-190, 204, 230-231

social integration 5-7, 41, 244, 268

social policy 156, 157, 242-246, 268

social problems 187, 197, 242-246

social protest 15

social solidarity 6-7, 13, 30, 63, 71, 149, 204, 206

social sorting 148, 152

social system , 72, 202-206, 230

socialisation 33, 52, 71, 87, 88, 97,-98, 107, 139, 192, 203, 217, 228

societal reaction 81-82, 84, 90, 127, 138

society as a system 203, 206

sociological problems 242-243

sociology and science 187-194

sociology and social policy 157, 242-246

sociology of scientific knowledge 61

sociology, subject matter of 189-190

Soka Gakkai 35, 48, 61

Solidarity (Poland) 42

Somerville J 219

South N 75, 135

sovereign power 146

Soviet Union 8, 42, 133, 190, 209, 211, 236, 237

Sparks R 110

Spiritual Health Service 29

spiritual revolution 32

spiritual shopping 30, 32, 36, 52, 268

spirituality 3, 30-33, 36, 40, 51, 56

standardised measuring instrument 164, 167, 170, 172, 176

Stark R and Bainbridge W 34-36, 48-51, 54, 56

state and law making 88

state apparatus 86, 149, 171, 213-214, 269

state crime 131, 136-140, 144, 269

state violence 135

state, the 36, 41, 47, 62, 79, 86, 88-89, 94, 98, 135-140

state-corporate crime 91-92, 130, 137

status 9, 49, 50, 53, 63, 81, 84, 91-92, 111-112, 123-124, 152, 168, 204, 211, 214, 227, 235, 269

status frustration 74-76, 87, 118

Index

status hierarchy 74-75, 87

status offence 79, 82

Steffensmeier D and Schwartz J 110

stereotype 9, 42, 80, 87, 91-92, 110, 116, 118, 151, 178, 184, 217-218, 220

stigma 71, 81-82, 127, 203

stop and search 101, 115-116, 126

strain theory 72-73, 76, 87, 93-94

Strand JR and Tuman JP 138

stratification 9

stratified random sampling 164

structural adjustment programmes 132, 243

structural differentiation 23, 26, 204-205

structural factors 72, 151-152, 184, 211, 214, 220, 225

structural theories 225, 226, 228, 231, 232

structuralist Marxism 211, 213-214

structuration theory 231-232

structure and action 231-232

structured interviews 83, 158-159, 166-169, 171, 172, 175, 176, 177, 179, 180, 184

structured nonparticipant observation 179, 181, 184

studying the past 160, 182

subcultural strain theories 74

subculture 71, 74-76, 81, 87, 90, 93, 99-100, 102, 112, 118, 224, 269

subjectivity 157, 196, 218, 269

Subud 48

suicide 49, 71, 78, 83-84, 126, 143-144, 162, 169, 171, 186, 188, 190, 197, 230

Sunni Islam 42

supernatural 5-6, 8, 18, 23, 25, 34, 36, 43, 48, 63

superstructure 8, 209, 211, 213

supply led religion 34-35

Surette R 124, 152

surveillance 147-148, 152

surveillant assemblages 147, 152

surveys 166-71, 179

Sutherland E 75, 91-93

Sykes G and Matza D 93, 140

symbolic interactionism see interactionism

symbolisation 126

system needs 203

target hardening 98-99, 143, 152

Tawney R 14

Taylor I 89-90, 132

technological worldview 23

technology 23, 39, 59, 62, 134, 140, 146-148, 235-236, 239-240

televangelism 16, 31, 34 ,39

terror 17, 39, 41, 92, 116, 118, 123, 126, 131-132, 135, 137, 140, 147-149

theodicy of disprivilege 49, 56, 100

theoretical issues 159, 161, 163, 167, 170, 175-176, 179, 182

Third World 40, 51, 131, 136

Thomas D and Loader B 128

Thomas W and Znaniecki F 183

Thomas WI 227

Thompson EP 149, 214

thought experiment 159, 162

Tombs S 91-92, 151

Tombs S and Whyte D 151

topic versus resource 80

torture 17, 74, 92, 136-140

total institution 84, 227

totemism 6

Townsend P 245

traditional action 225-226, 228

traditional criminology 134, 136

traditional societies 149, 204-205, 235

trafficking 131, 135, 140, 152

transcarceration 150

Transcendental Meditation 35, 48

transgressive criminology 134, 139

Triplett R 82

Trobriand Islanders 7, 226

Troeltsch E 47-49

truancy 72, 75, 79, 82, 169, 171

Tutsi 137

typifications 80, 148, 229-230, 232, 269

UFOs 49, 51

underclass 97-98, 101, 124, 246

unemployment 63, 100, 112, 118-20, 132, 144-5, 152, 169, 171, 205, 212, 225

Unification Church 48

Union Carbide 134

Unitarians 10

universalism 60

unstructured interviews 83, 159, 166, 169, 174, 175-177, 182, 184, 189

utilitarian crime 74-76, 87-88, 98, 118

utopian, utopia 16, 64, 219

validity 148, 159, 161, 165, 168, 171-172, 175-176, 180-184, 189, 246, 269

value consensus 6-8, 13, 71-71, 74, 76, 88, 102, 203-204, 206, 209, 244, 269

value freedom 157, 196-198, 269

values 7, 197-200, 269

values in sociology 197

vandalism 74-75, 88, 93, 98, 111, 144

Vàsquez M 36

Velikovsky I 61, 192-3

verificationism 187, 190-1, 194, 269

verstehen 178, 181, 189, 194, 226

vicarious religion 29, 36

victim surveys 80, 99, 102, 106, 110-111, 115-6, 120, 269

victimisation 110-111, 114, 120, 123, 128, 142, 143, 147, 150-2

victimology 143, 151-2, 269

victims of crime 84, 108, 120, `123, 142, 143, 151-152

Voas D 30, 52, 56

vocation 14, 64

voluntarism 90, 211, 269

von Hentig H 151

Walby S 111, 123, 184, 218, 221, 222

Walklate S 106, 107, 145, 151

Wall D 128

Wallis R 47-50, 56

Walters R 135

Walton P 89-90

war crimes 137-138

Watkins J 192

Weber M 5, 13-15, 18, 23, 32, 43-44, 49, 56, 100, 189, 197-200, 211, 225-226, 228, 232

weddings 21-22, 26, 29

welfare dependency 98

Westernisation 42-43

white collar crime 86, 88, 91-94, 108-109, 111, 115, 144, 211

White R 134-135

Whyte D 137, 145, 151

Whyte W 178-180

Williams P and Dickinson J 123

Willis P 111, 182, 212

Willmott P and Young M 166-167

Wilson B 21-22, 24-25, 50-51, 56

Wilson JQ 97-98, 144-145, 246

Wilson JQ and Kelling G 98, 144-145, 246

Winlow S 112, 133

witchcraft 3, 60-61, 64

Wolfgang M 151

women bishops 53
Women's Aid Federation 246
Woodhead L 10, 22, 32-33, 53
Woolgar S 61-62
working class 8, 13, 18, 50, 53, 62-64, 74-75, 80, 84, 87-94, 99, 108-9, 111-2, 118, 126-7, 164, 171, 210-4, 219-21, 236, 239-40, 245

World Bank 132
World Values Survey 42
Worsley P 6, 17-18, 243
Wrong D 206

Yinger M 5, 18
Young J 81, 89-90, 92, 98-102, 110, 118-9, 123, 125, 147

young offenders 82, 97, 148, 150, 244

zemiology 134, 138, 269
zero tolerance 97-99, 144, 152, 246, 269
Zionism 140